Interdisciplinarity

Interdisciplinarity

Essays From the Literature

WILLIAM H. NEWELL, *Editor*

With the support of the Association for Integrative Studies

COLLEGE ENTRANCE EXAMINATION BOARD
New York

Founded in 1900, the College Board is a not-for-profit educational association that supports academic preparation and transition to higher education for students around the world through the ongoing collaboration of its member schools, colleges, universities, educational systems and organizations.

In all of its activities, the Board promotes equity through universal access to high standards of teaching and learning and sufficient financial resources so that every student has the opportunity to succeed in college and work.

The College Board champions—by means of superior research; curricular development; assessment; guidance, placement, and admission information; professional development; forums; policy analysis; and public outreach—educational excellence for all students.

In all of its publishing activities, the College Board endeavors to present the work of authors who are well qualified to write with authority on the subject at hand and to present accurate and timely information. However, the opinions, interpretations, and conclusions of the authors are their own and do not necessarily represent those of the College Board; nothing contained herein should be assumed to represent the official position of the College Board. This volume has been produced from original material reprinted with permission from other sources and, as a result, the editorial style within is inconsistent.

Editorial inquiries should be addressed to Publications Services, The College Board, 45 Columbus Avenue, New York, NY 10023-6992.

Copies of this book may be ordered from College Board Publications, Box 886, New York, NY 10101-0886, (800) 323-7155. The price of this book is $24.95 for the paperback version and $29.95 for the hardcover.

Library of Congress Catalog Card Number: 98-71553

International Standard Book Number: 0-87447-600-3 (hardcover)
0-87447-608-9 (paperback)

Printed in the United States of America.

Contents

Contributors

Armstrong, Forrest H. Dean, Grand Valley State Colleges

Bal, Mieke. Director, ASCA, University of Amsterdam

Bechtel, William. Professor of Philosophy, Washington University

Benson, Thomas C. President, Green Mountain College

Carlisle, Barbara. Director of Theatre Arts and Women's Studies, Virginia Polytechnic Institute and State University

Cluck, Nancy Anne. Formerly Professor of Humanities, University of Texas at Dallas

Cornwell, Grant H. Associate Dean, St. Lawrence University

Fish, Stanley. Arts and Sciences Professor of English. Duke University

Fuller, Steve. Professor of Sociology and Social Policy, University of Durham (UK)

Gaff, Jerry G. Vice President, Association of American Colleges and Universities

Geertz, Clifford. Harold F. Linder Professor of Social Science, Institute for Advanced Study, Princeton

Green, William J. Professor of Interdisciplinary Studies, Miami University

Gunn, Giles. Professor of English and of Global and International Studies, University of California at Santa Barbara

Haas, Paul. Distinguished Teaching Professor of Economics. Bowling Green State University

Hershberg, Theodore. Professor of Public Policy and History, and Director, Center for Greater Philadelphia, University of Pennsylvania

Hübenthal, Ursula. Formerly a Philosophy doctoral student, University of Cologne

Hursh, Barbara. Formerly Assistant to the President, Northeastern Illinois University

Klein, Julie Thompson. Professor of Humanities, Wayne State University

Kockelmans, Joseph J. Emeritus Professor of Philosophy, The Pennsylvania State University

Lebow, Richard Ned. Director, Mershon Center, The Ohio State University

Moore, Michael. Director, Center for Aesthetic Development, Bowling Green State University

Newell, William H. Professor of Interdisciplinary Studies, Miami University

Peck, Jeffrey M. Professor of German, Georgetown University

Stember, Marilyn. Professor and Associate Dean, Health Sciences Center, University of Colorado

Stoddard, Eve W. Director of Studies Abroad, St. Lawrence University

Trow, Martin. Emeritus Professor of Public Policy, University of California at Berkeley

Turner, Bryan S. Dean of Arts, Deakin University (Australia)

Van Dusseldorp, Dirk. Emeritus Professor, Wageningen Agricultural University (Netherlands)

Wigboldus, Seerp. Student of the Tibetan language, Tibet University (Lhasa)

Foreword

The mentally active scholar will acknowledge, I think, that his mind roams far and wide. All is grist that comes to his mill, and he does not limit his supply of grain to any one fenced-off field.

—John Dewey

Just over a century ago, the American college found itself in deep difficulty. All around it, new knowledge was emerging at an unprecedented rate. Very little of this new learning, however, was reflected in the college curriculum. In fact, many leading educators argued against its inclusion, insisting that the task of the college was to transmit ancient truths rather than to inquire into the unknown. Voicing opposition, reformers replied that the college would recede into irrelevance if it did not follow wherever inquiry led. Change, they said, had become the hallmark of social reality; and therefore the college could no longer help students secure a viable future if it taught reliance on traditions handed down from the past.

Triumph for the reform camp came suddenly, though not as the result of design or planning. By 1900, the new knowledge had swept forcefully into the college curriculum before anyone was sure about how the dramatically increased number of "studies" could be organized into a coherent curriculum. The addition of many new "disciplines," in effect, had been gained at the expense of any understanding of the connections among the emerging fields. In a sudden transformative surge, the college curriculum had both expanded and fallen into many separate pieces.

The so-called "new education" progressed rapidly. By 1910, the typical college curriculum contained 20 or more new disciplines that had not existed in the 1880s.[1] Few educators, however, felt that the college had resolved its curricular difficulties. Even reformers continued to be uncomfortable with the situation. John Dewey, for example, had been a leading advocate of the new learning, but he now protested the confusion that resulted from the "segregation" of the disciplines from one another. This separation of one discipline from another, he argued, presented a defective image of the "actual advance of knowledge." In fact, Dewey said, experience showed that the rapid development of new knowledge across fields of study had "been attended by constant development of cross references, of interdependencies and interrelations." The pressing need was to make certain that student understanding of this "interrelation of subjects" was not lost amidst the new ever-expanding array of subject offerings. The curriculum, Dewey urged, must ensure that the outcome of each student's education should be a continuous "growing in intellectual integration."[2]

---

[1] This story is told succinctly in Douglas C. Bennett, "Innovation in the Liberal Arts and Sciences," included in Robert Orrill, editor, *Education and Democracy: Re-imagining Liberal Learning in America* (New York: The College Board, 1997).

[2] John Dewey, *The Way Out of Educational Confusion,* in Jo Ann Boydston, editor, *John Dewey: The Later Works,* Volume 6 (Carbondale: Southern Illinois University Press, 1989).

If anything, Dewey's concerns are more pressing today then when he expressed them. Knowledge grows now at an even faster rate. As a result, once seemingly intact and well-defined disciplines have divided into hundreds of subfields and specializations. Moreover, borrowing across disciplinary lines is done so frequently that boundaries blur and even dissolve. This requires almost unceasing attention to redrawing the knowledge map. At the close of the twentieth century, scholars have become cartographers of the ever-changing intellectual topography.

In such conditions, how can educators practice a pedagogy of integration? This problem is addressed by the essays collected in this volume. All were written within the last 20 years or so, and most assume that disciplines will continue to provide the organizing framework for the college curriculum. In this respect, they are for the most part more pragmatic than utopian. Moreover, each is regarded as something of a "classic" among practitioners of interdisciplinary teaching. Theory is present, but always in balance with pedagogical utility. Jerry Gaff accurately sums up the help that these essays offer when he says on the back cover that the volume "provides the best that has been written about the potential of interdisciplinary programs and about solutions to many practical problems encountered by interdisciplinary programs located in a university structured around disciplines."

This book is in all respects the work of William H. Newell, founding president of the Association of Integrative Studies (AIS). In preparing the essays for publication, he has been both judicious editor and resolute assembler of a literature of interdisciplinarity. It is not too much to say that he has created a professional literature through this collection where heretofore there have been only writings that were scattered and difficult to access. To him, and to AIS, we owe many thanks.

> Robert Orrill
> Office of Academic Affairs
> The College Board

Acknowledgments

The impetus for this anthology was the need to put together a reader for the Institute in Integrative Studies. A total of 125 participants read various versions of this anthology and provided invaluable feedback on the effectiveness of each reading. The anthology has been tempered in the forge of daily Institute seminars each summer for the last six years. Never before have guinea pigs provided such thorough, constructive criticism. Thanks to all of you.

The editorial committee of the Board of Directors of the Association for Integrative Studies (AIS) worked with me over two years to bring the anthology to its present form. It was they who insisted I compile the concluding chapter, "Professionalizing Interdisciplinarity" (not realizing that it would end up consuming an entire year of my life). Stan Bailis, the committee chair, deserves special thanks for his detailed feedback that saved me from numerous gaffes.

My largest debt of gratitude is to Julie Klein. Her initial compilation of the interdisciplinary studies literature in *Interdisciplinarity: History, Theory, and Practice* provided the basis for transforming an AIS preconference workshop reader into the first version of the anthology. Each year, she put together a pile of recent publications for me to read that might be mined for the next version of the anthology. Her exhaustive feedback on every paragraph of every draft of "Professionalizing Interdisciplinarity" makes it feel coauthored. Thanks for 15 years of professional collaboration and genuine friendship.

W.H.N.

Introduction

The genesis for this anthology of classic essays was a preconference workshop on "Interdisciplinary General Education Curriculum and Program Development" held at the 1989 annual meeting of the Association for Integrative Studies (AIS). The readings were drawn from the relatively few essays with which the leadership of AIS was then familiar. The following year, Julie Klein published *Interdisciplinarity: History, Theory, and Practice,* which included a one-hundred-page bibliography that expanded our awareness of the range of literatures providing insights into interdisciplinary study. Unfortunately, those insights are scattered across a wide range of specialized literatures.

When Fund for the Improvement of Postsecondary Education (FIPSE) funded the Institute in Integrative Studies in 1992 and I was faced with introducing interdisciplinary study to faculty who had little or no prior exposure to it, I updated the preconference workshop reader to include works identified in Julie's bibliography or published subsequently. The result was an unwieldy 543-page reader with a bright green cover that the first year's participants dubbed "the green monster." The reader for the next year's Institute (and for every year thereafter) was considerably more selective, reflecting evaluations of individual readings by the previous year's participants and supplemented by new essays typically brought to my attention by Julie Klein. Thus, the selections included in this anthology reflect the judgments of more than 125 Institute participants over a seven-year period.

While this volume contains many of the classic pieces in the field, a deliberate decision was made to exclude some important essays readily accessible elsewhere. Interested readers can find many of these in *Interdisciplinary Studies Today,* a collection of key essays on interdisciplinary resources, course development, administration, assessment, and networking edited by Julie Klein and William Doty and published by Jossey-Bass in 1994 as #58 in the New Directions for Teaching and Learning series. Those essays can be supplemented by the set of articles published in the *Journal of General Education* 45:2 (1996), most of which are the work of participants in the Institute in Integrative Studies. Any professional literature constantly evolves. To keep abreast of the latest developments in the field, readers should turn to the publications of the Association for Integrative Studies, its journal *Issues in Integrative Studies,* and its quarterly newsletter.

* * * * *

This volume is organized into sections, but the reader should be aware that the section titles represent only a rough guide to rather than a precise categorization of the focus and contents of the individual essays. Readers new to interdisciplinary studies may profitably start with the Overview section; those experienced in interdisciplinary teaching and/or research may choose to jump directly into later sections; those already well-versed in this literature may want to skip to the summary essay on "Professionalizing Interdisciplinarity" and then circle back to earlier essays in light of the issues raised there. Effective use of this volume is no more linear than the process of interdisciplinary study itself.

The Overview section starts with two synoptic essays. The most recent of the two is Klein and Newell's "Advancing Interdisciplinary Studies" (1996), which provides a comprehensive overview of interdisciplinary education from an administrative and curricular reform perspective. Readers who turn to Gaff and Ratcliff's *Handbook of the Undergraduate Curriculum,* from which this essay was reprinted, will find interdisciplinarity contextualized in the mainstream of current higher education reform. Newell and Green's "Defining and Teaching Interdisciplinary Studies," a 1982 essay, provides an accessible introduction to interdisciplinary course design, discussing most of the key issues explored in more depth elsewhere in this volume. Even experienced interdisciplinarians can profit from these essays, because they provide a breadth of perspective that often gets lost in the everyday details of teaching courses or carrying out research projects.

The remainder of the section includes three essays and a guide. "An Interdisciplinary Model to Implement General Education" by Hursh, Haas, and Moore presents a widely used model of the interdisciplinary process based on the educational theories of Dewey, Perry, and Piaget. This essay developed out of a 1979 conference on the teaching of interdisciplinary social science at which the Association for Integrative Studies was founded. Newell's "Interdisciplinary Curriculum Development" offers a survey of the nuts-and-bolts issues and addresses such topics as educational outcomes and the role of disciplines in interdisciplinary study. Kockelmans's "Why Interdisciplinarity?" is the oldest essay in the volume (1979) and perhaps has been the most influential. While the terminology is sometimes dated and the discussion is biased toward research concerns, the analysis is so penetrating and tightly reasoned that the essay repays close reading. Kockelmans outlines the classic rationales for interdisciplinarity and the traditional critiques of disciplines and presents the earliest arguments for using general systems theory, structuralism, and cybernetics to create a common ground for communication. He also offers the first vision of interdisciplinarians as specialized generalists. The Overview section concludes with a recently published "Guide to Interdisciplinary Syllabus Preparation" (1996) prepared jointly by the 1993–94 Institute in Integrative Studies and the Association for Integrative Studies. The guide draws upon the available literature to formulate a set of questions that provide pragmatic assistance in designing interdisciplinary courses.

The Philosophical Analysis section juxtaposes a debate between Benson and Newell, past presidents of the Association for Integrative Studies, with Fuller's dialectical analysis of interdisciplinary study. In "Five Arguments Against Interdisciplinary Studies," Benson takes on the role of devil's advocate by setting forth a strong critique of interdisciplinarity, focusing on alleged conceptual confusion and problems related to time, quality, and cost. Newell responds in

"The Case for Interdisciplinary Studies" with a conception of interdisciplinarity that holds the promise of answering Benson's critique. In contrast to these mainstream positions, Fuller's "Interdisciplinarity as Interpenetration" conceives of interdisciplinary study as a dialectical process that seeks to rearrange disciplinary boundaries as it "bootstraps" conceptual synthesis. Fuller advocates the imposition of zero-base budgeting on disciplines and opposes pluralism and triangulation in interdisciplinary study. The essays in this section speak to some of the philosophical issues related to interdisciplinary study. Thus far, no one has attempted to work out a thoroughgoing philosophy of interdisciplinarity.

The Administration section addresses the development of interdisciplinary curricula, faculty, programs, and public policy. Gaff's 1980 essay is still the classic on curriculum development. Based on a wealth of practical experience, it concerns academic innovation generally but is especially relevant to interdisciplinary general education. In another important 1980 essay, "Faculty Development Through Interdisciplinarity," Armstrong categorizes various approaches to designing interdisciplinary programs and identifies the characteristics of faculty they require. Trow's "Interdisciplinary Studies as a Counterculture" (1984–85) identifies attitudinal and structural factors that determine whether experimental interdisciplinary general education programs die out quickly, are destroyed by growth, or flourish. A dozen years later, undergraduate interdisciplinary programs have moved into the mainstream of liberal education reform, but the lessons Trow derives from early efforts still have much to tell us about the institutional politics of interdisciplinary administration. Hershberg's "The Fragmentation of Knowledge and Practice" extends interdisciplinary thinking from higher education to public policy. He calls into question the assertion that an interdisciplinary world lies outside the academy—interdisciplinarity is as difficult to initiate and administer and as rare in the public sector as in higher education. Taken as a whole, the essays in this section are replete with both constructive suggestions and caveats drawn from extensive pragmatic experience in administering interdisciplinary programs.

The Disciplinary Contexts section focuses on one of the most contentious issues facing the interdisciplinary practitioner—the appropriate relationship between disciplinary and interdisciplinary activity. An essay written for a European audience skeptical about the intellectual integrity of interdisciplinarity, Newell's "Academic Disciplines and Undergraduate Interdisciplinary Education" addresses some of the standard concerns of disciplinarians: the content and explicitness of disciplines offered in the interdisciplinary context, staff preparation, and the educational outcomes for disciplines of interdisciplinary courses. Geertz's oft-cited "Blurred Genres" identifies the shift in focus of the social sciences from an alliance with the natural sciences to the humanities and the transformative consequences of the resulting debate within the social sciences on the nature of knowledge. His essay concerns itself more with changes in the intellectual environment of disciplines than with interdisciplinarity itself. Fish's "Being Interdisciplinary Is So Very Hard to Do" offers an object lesson in why arguments for interdisciplinarity should not be grounded in any one ideology or academic fashion. He identifies interdisciplinarity with leftist cultural theory, claims in passing that right-wing arguments are hard to distinguish from those of the left (but ignores liberal or nonpoliticized arguments), proves (to his satisfaction) that the leftist analysis is ultimately hoisted on its own petard, and thus dismisses interdisciplinarity. Gunn's "Interdisciplinary Studies" provides a response to Fish by portraying interdisciplinarity as nonsystematic and pragmatic, hence essential to "refinement of debate" but not in itself a coherent field. In "Blurring, Cracking, and Crossing," Klein revisits Geertz as she examines the sources of disciplinary permeation. Arguing that the myth of disciplinary unity obscures the problems of crossing subdisciplinary boundaries and hence the location and nature of interdisciplinary study, she critiques the myth of disciplinary competence. The controversial issues raised by the Geertz and Fish selections make evident the disciplinary and ideological sensitivity of interdisciplinarity.

The Social Sciences section addresses interdisciplinary research, though it clearly has implications for interdisciplinary courses that are, after all, consumers of research findings. In "Interdisciplinary Research for Integrated Rural Development in Developing Countries," van Dusseldorp and Wigboldus focus on the potentials, constraints, and evaluation of "broad" interdisciplinary research when different disciplines come out of very different paradigms and hence bring very different perspectives to the research at hand. In "Advancing the Social Sciences Through the Interdisciplinary Enterprise," Stember offers general guidelines for interdisciplinary team research. This section concentrates on empirical research in interdisciplinary social science aimed at solving real-world problems; the essays do not consider the theoretical bombs described in the preceding section that are currently bursting overhead.

The Humanities and Fine Arts section brings forward a range of perspectives on interdisciplinarity that have emerged from the traditional humanities, postmodernism, and educational learning theory. Cluck's "Reflections on the Interdisciplinary Approaches to the Humanities" focuses on various disciplines' core contributions to the humanities. She provides excellent examples of areas/approaches within the humanities with interdisciplinary potential, such as the study of historical periods and the history of ideas and aesthetics. In her introduction to *Reading Rembrandt,* Bal employs postmodern rhetoric (couched in terms such as vision, narrative, and text) to suggest a rich variety of alternative strategies for integrating disciplinary insights. Carlisle's "Music and Life" starts with the disjunction between the multifaceted world we experience and our limited disciplinary attempts to engage it. She sees interdisciplinarity as a path to better understanding of the disciplines, seeing the world from new angles, and capturing what we learn in metaphor and artistic forms. This process leads to the discovery of new relationships and to rethinking what we know, ultimately enabling us to bridge the gap between education and life.

The Natural Sciences section introduces two philosophers of science, an established American and a German just completing her doctorate. The excerpt from Bechtel's "The Nature of Scientific Integration" deals with pragmatic research issues such as barriers to interdisciplinarity, disciplinary/interdisciplinary trade-offs, and motivations and institutional frameworks for crossing disciplinary boundaries. He examines the competing claims that the scientific disciplines are orthogonal and that work across the sciences is not truly interdisciplinary because those disciplines share a worldview. Bechtel further identifies the factors important in determining whether interdisciplinary research will spawn a new discipline. In "Interdisciplinary Thought" Hübenthal argues that interdisciplinarity should be seen as integrating partial explanations from different sciences not through global theory but through sensitivity to problems of language and the clarification of core questions. These two essays offer contrasting perspectives on the key issues of whether work within the natural sciences can be truly interdisciplinary and whether the goal is to produce interfield theories (Bechtel) or partial explanations (Hübenthal).

The next section, General Lessons From Specific Interdisciplinary Fields, examines how the ideas in the previous sections play out in particular interdisciplinary contexts and what special insights into interdisciplinarity they contribute. In brief essays on "Environment" and "Women," Klein challenges the uncritical presumption that so-called interdisciplinary fields will be studied in an interdisciplinary manner. In "Interdisciplinary Research and the Future of Peace and Security Studies," LeBow gives an excellent example of good interdisciplinary research, a sobering example of the danger of disciplinary research, and an example of the value of multidisciplinary research programs. He also provides a realistic assessment of the potential outcomes of interdisciplinary research. Peck, in "There's No Place Like Home," compares the scholarly impact of spatial and academic locations in an effort to reexamine disciplinarity. He offers German studies as a model for interdisciplinarity, an in-between space for what he calls "oppositional, counter-hegemonic discourse." In the context of medical education, Turner's "The Interdisciplinary Curriculum From Social Medicine to Post Modernization" takes a critical look at the societal forces promoting different kinds of interdisciplinary curriculum reform. Finally, Cornwell and Stoddard argue in "Things Fall Together" that multicultural education would be better served by what they call intercultural studies, an interdisciplinary approach that emphasizes the critical analysis of cultural interrelations rather than the mere celebration of cultural differences. Taken together, the essays in this section contribute to a nuanced analysis of interdisciplinarity by giving us a glimpse of efforts in specific interdisciplinary fields of study.

The concluding section features "Professionalizing Interdisciplinarity: Literature Review and Research Agenda," written for this volume. It treats the essays reprinted here as a corpus of professional literature in order to evaluate the current status of interdisciplinarity. Central issues are distilled and the extent of agreement and nature of disagreements assessed. Each section of the essay concludes with a set of research questions that need to be answered before the nature and potential of interdisciplinarity can be fully appreciated. If the reprinted essays in this anthology represent the best of interdisciplinarity, the concluding chapter represents its future.

Overview

Advancing Interdisciplinary Studies

Julie Thompson Klein and William H. Newell

When Levine's *Handbook on Undergraduate Curriculum* appeared in 1978, the era of innovation and reform that marked the late 1960s and early 1970s had passed. For interdisciplinary studies (IDS), it had been a watershed era. New interdisciplinary universities, cluster colleges, programs, and courses documented the growth and diversification of IDS. By 1978, the euphoria had passed, and retrenchments were cutting deeply into once-heralded experiments. Even as the death knell of IDS was being sounded, however, a rebirth was already under way in the form of new integrated approaches to general education, new interdisciplinary fields, and integrated problem solving. This chapter is a result of those developments. The 1978 *Handbook* contained only a few scattered references to IDS. Today, not only is there an entire chapter devoted to the subject, the rhetoric of interdisciplinarity pervades the entire book.

Conceptualizing Interdisciplinary Studies

Approaches vary and disputes over terminology continue. Broadly speaking, though, *interdisciplinary studies* may be defined as a process of answering a question, solving a problem, or addressing a topic that is too broad or complex to be dealt with adequately by a single discipline or profession. Whether the context is an integrated approach to general education, a women's studies program, or a science, technology, and society program, IDS draws on disciplinary perspectives and integrates their insights through construction of a more comprehensive perspective. In this manner, interdisciplinary study is not a simple supplement but is complementary to and corrective of the disciplines.

Origins and Motivations

IDS can no longer be defined by pointing to a few exemplary practices and program types. Levine's typology encompassed interdisciplinary, field, and joint majors. His leading examples of interdisciplinary majors were American studies, applied mathematics and psychology, modernization, urban studies, art and aesthetics, social psychology, and environmental studies. Since the 1970s, interdisciplinary studies have expanded in kind as well as in number. Diverse structures and practices emanate from diverse motivations and purposes. This diversity was already apparent in the late 1960s, when the Organization for

Klein, Julie Thompson and William H. Newell. Ch. 19 "Advancing Interdisciplinary Studies" in Jerry Gaff and James Ratcliff (eds.) Handbook of the Undergraduate Curriculum. *San Francisco: Jossey-Bass, 1996. Reprinted with permission.*

Economic Cooperation and Development (OECD) conducted the first international survey of interdisciplinary activities. The OECD found five major origins of interdisciplinary activity: the development of science (knowledge), student needs, the need for professional training, original needs of society, and problems of university functioning and administration (Center for Educational Research and Innovation, 1972, pp. 44–48).

When we ask the same questions today—the what and the why of interdisciplinary study—familiar motivations reappear alongside new ones:

- General and liberal education
- Professional training
- Social, economic, and technological problem solving
- Social, political, and epistemological critique
- Faculty development
- Financial exigency (downsizing)
- Production of new knowledge

Traditional IDS

In the first half of the century, the most prominent interdisciplinary presence was in general education. The most influential models were programs at Columbia, Chicago, and Wisconsin; the most influential thinkers were Hutchins, Meiklejohn, and, to a lesser extent, Dewey. Data continue to reveal that general and liberal education programs remain prominent sites of IDS, from Levine's 1976 study of college catalogues (Levine, 1978) to Klein and Gaff's 1979 survey of 272 colleges and universities (Klein and Gaff, 1982) to Newell's 1986 questionnaire results from 235 interdisciplinary programs. The most recent data, gathered by Newell for *Interdisciplinary Undergraduate Programs: A Directory* (1986), indicated that a renaissance of IDS was under way across geographical locations, institutional types, and curricular areas. The greatest increases were in general education, followed by honors and women's studies. The greatest growth in subject-matter areas of general education encourages interdisciplinary curricula in areas such as international studies, American multicultural and gender studies, and the inherently synoptic areas of historical consciousness and ethical understanding (Casey, 1994, p. 56).

IDS Today

Despite the continuing prominence of its role in general education, IDS today includes a great deal more. The fuller extent was noted in 1990, in the first authoritative national report on IDS. Emanating from the three-year study of the undergraduate major by the Association of American Colleges, the report of the Interdisciplinary Studies Task Force highlighted the evolution of new fields of knowledge in a history that spans the rise of American and area studies in the 1930s and 1940s; women's, urban, and environmental studies in the 1960s and 1970s; and the current expansion of cultural studies, cognitive science, and science, technology, and society. The task force found a wide range of interdisciplinary majors, including international and public policy studies, area studies, labor and legal studies, programs in human ecology and social ecology, neuroscience, biochemistry, and molecular biology, environmental sciences and marine biology, and cognitive and information sciences. They also found numerous individual courses in disciplinary departments, such as a physics course designed to familiarize students with cutting-edge research connecting theoretical physics and biology; as well as courses bridging business and law or history and political science (Association of American Colleges, 1990, 1991b).

The task force findings also confirm a widely held belief that knowledge has become increasingly interdisciplinary. The reasons include new developments in research and scholarship, the continuing evolution of new hybrid fields, the expanding influence of particular interdisciplinary methods and concepts, and the pressing need for integrated approaches to social, economic, and technological problems. The growing inclusion of new elements in professional courses and programs is another important indicator. Management studies are appearing in engineering, social analyses in medicine, and foreign language or computing applications in professions.

This development and the problems of interrelating constituent elements in these fields are usually discussed in terms of companion notions of integration and coordination, not interdisciplinarity per se. The problems at stake are largely pragmatic or organizational, not theoretical (Squires 1992, pp. 206–207). At the same time, interdisciplinarity is conceived in theoretical terms. The claims of theory differ, from general systems theory, holistic paradigms, and transdisciplinary schemes to critiques of knowledge and culture in Marxism, feminism, and post-structuralist practices that reformulate as they cross disciplinary boundaries. As we move into the twenty-first century, pragmatism, holism, and critique will all continue to be influential in conceptualization of interdisciplinary approaches. Marking this trend, multiple conceptualizations have been prominent in major reports on the undergraduate curriculum over the past decade.

The National Institute of Education report *Involvement in Learning* (1984) urged that liberal education requirements be expanded and reinvigorated to ensure that content is directly addressed not only to subject matter but also the capacities of analysis, problem solving, communication, and synthesis. Students and faculty alike should be able to integrate knowledge from different disciplines, both in the academic setting and in real-life situations. *Integrity in the College Curriculum* (Association of American Colleges, 1985) called, additionally, for curricula capable of enabling faculty to escape departmental confines, to attain contextual understanding, to assess multifaceted problems, to gain a sense of the complexities and interrelationships of society, and to examine the human, social, and political implications of research. In 1990, in *The Challenge of Connecting Learning*—a report framed by a widely noted blurring of disciplinary boundaries—the Association of American Colleges highlighted the need for curricular coherence while extolling promising practices that enable connection making and interdisciplinary skills of synthesis.

Clearly, the strong intellectual and educational value of IDS has been a major theme of modern educational reform. However, because the structure of higher education has been dominated over the course of the twentieth century by disciplines and departments, interdisciplinary study was often regarded as additive or separate from the main business of higher education. The increase in the sheer amount of interdisciplinary activity strains this concept. Financial belt tightening will continue to create pressures to return to basics, construed in terms of traditional disciplines and departments. What is new since the 1978 *Handbook* is the perception that interdisciplinary approaches have become essential, not peripheral, in thinking about institutional structure, about curriculum, and about faculty development.

Interdisciplinary Forms and Structures

The coexistence of older and newer interdisciplinary activities has created greater heterogeneity and complexity in higher education. These conditions are apparent in the variety of forms and locations where interdisciplinary study occurs today—in traditional, formal, and visible structures—and involves a wider, more heterogeneous, informal, and nontraditional set of activities.

From Simple to Complex Structure

General systems theory suggests a fruitful metaphor for conceptualizing what has happened and its implications. The structure of higher education is shifting from simple systems to complex ones. *Simple systems* may have multiple levels and connections arranged in a hierarchy, but they still operate according to a single set of rules. *Complex systems,* in contrast, are nonhierarchically structured. They obey multiple conflicting logics, employ both positive and negative feedback, reveal synergistic effects, and may have a chaotic element. To understand them, linear and reductionist thinking must be replaced by nonlinear thinking, pattern recognition, and analogy. Simple structures still exist, but the multiplicity of hybrid interdisciplinary forms has fueled a change in the way many faculty members think of knowledge and the academy.

Metaphors for describing knowledge have shifted from foundational and linear structures to networks, webs, and complex systems. Correspondingly, IDS is no longer a simple matter of adding a few formal interdisciplinary programs to the existing structure of the institution. (For a parallel view of science and research, see Gibbons and others, 1994.)

We describe the difference in terms of two categories. The first category comprises traditional and familiar bridging structures typical of simple systems:

- Free-standing institutions
- Autonomous and cluster colleges
- Centers and institutes

- Interdisciplinary departments
- Interdisciplinary majors, minors, and concentrations
- Mainstream and alternative general education programs
- Individual courses within disciplinary departments
- Tutorials
- Independent study and self-designed majors
- Travel-study, internships, and practicums

These structures have yielded exemplary models and practices that span hybrid specialization (the Social Ecology Program at the University of California, Irvine, and the Consciousness and Culture Program at the College of the Atlantic), interdisciplinary degree programs in the liberal arts tradition (Eugene Lang College at the New School for Social Research and the State University of New York (SUNY) College at Old Westbury), general education in the tradition of Great Books and great ideas (St. John's College and Shimer College), and the clustering of disciplinary courses around a common integrative seminar (the Federated Learning Communities at SUNY, Stony Brook, and the loop sequencing of traditional courses with a third bridging course at California Lutheran College). In addition to honors and general education programs, Newell's 1986 *Directory* called attention to long-standing American studies programs (the University of Minnesota and University of Texas at Austin), freestanding interdisciplinary institutions (Evergreen State College and Hampshire College), and cluster colleges surviving from the late 1960s and early 1970s (Watauga College at Appalachian State University, the Paracollege at St. Olaf College, and the Hutchins School of Liberal Studies at Sonoma State University), as well as science and society programs, women's studies programs, self-consciously interdisciplinary world studies programs, and environmental, ethnic, and urban studies.

From Visible to Invisible Forms

The second and growing category encompasses hybrid communities and interactions that are less visible, if not invisible, on organizational charts:

- Learning communities of students and of faculty
- Problem-focused research projects
- Shared facilities, databases, and instrumentation
- Interdisciplinary approaches and schools of thought
- Enhanced disciplinary curricula to accommodate new developments in scholarship and research
- Subdisciplinary boundary crossing
- Educational functions of centers and institutes
- Training in collaborative modes and teamwork
- Interinstitutional consortia and alliances

The Washington Center for Improving the Quality of Undergraduate Education epitomizes the second category. An interinstitutional consortium of over forty public and private colleges and universities in the state of Washington, the center was founded in 1985. The idea of a *coordinated studies program,* or learning community design, is at the core of the center's work. Learning communities are envisioned as a low-cost, holistic approach to curriculum restructuring and reform, faculty development, and assessment (see Chapter Twenty-Two). Faculty cite the revitalization afforded by the interdisciplinary environment, *team-teaching,* and interactions with students in learning communities. Maintaining a nonbureaucratic approach in its retreats, workshops, and conferences, the center has expanded to include a range of innovative pedagogies linked with collaborative learning, cultural pluralism, and respect for diversity.

The second category also includes the host of study groups, interest groups and networks that enable faculty to stay abreast of developments in research and in higher education. Most of these hybrid communities do not appear on organizational charts, but they are vital sources of faculty learning as well as new programs, centers, and reformulations of departmental curricula. Faculty are involved, additionally, in interinstitutional and community-based projects that cross the traditional boundaries separating the academy, government, industry, and the community. These structures indicate that curricular reform is not simply a matter of courses and programs for students. It also entails the continuing educator and development of faculty. As a result of the complexity and heterogeneity of both knowledge and faculty activities, interdisciplinary structures may be interconnected in a shifting matrix, replete with feedback loops and unpredictable synergistic relationships. The evidence is familiar.

The same faculty member may be involved in multiple activities: a scientist teaching in a new basic science course while conducting research in molecular biology, an engineer conducting problem-focused research in an industrial partnership program while working with members of the business school to restructure the business curriculum, a social scientist teaching a capstone course in the sociology department and holding a joint appointment in a center for urban studies, a member of the English department serving as a member of a planning group for a new cultural studies program, a member of the history department teaching in a women's studies program while collaborating with a colleague in the art department on representations of women in early American painting, a political scientist gathering support for a new environmental studies program while studying the history of environmental legislation, a faculty member teaching French while designing a minor in Canadian studies and team-teaching a section of a general education core curriculum, or a faculty member teaching Spanish while designing a new course on the U.S.-Mexico borderlands and conducting research on settlement patterns in the Southwest.

The lesson of complex structure has powerful implications for institutional change. Managing a complex system requires recognizing the coexistence of multiple activities and their essential heterogeneity. Whether the context is a large research university, a comprehensive institution, a small private liberal arts college, or a community college, there are often several roles, forms, and sites of interdisciplinary study.

Institutional Change

Two principles of institutional change apply in thinking about IDS. The first and most important principle is the importance of listening to the system to find out what is actually happening. Rather than imposing a single model or making a priori assumptions about what will work best, administrators and curriculum planning groups should identify what motivations exist and what changes are desired. Recent institutionwide efforts to make campus climates more conducive to interdisciplinary education and research reveal an added lesson of complex structure: there will be more interdisciplinary activity and interest than initially supposed.

The second principle is that interdisciplinarity will not be a matter of agreement, conceptually, practically, or politically. Interdisciplinarity is a complex concept. Attitudes are shaped by differences of disciplinary worldview, professional training, and educational philosophy. Given this diversity, a vital first step is to clarify what each group means by the concept and its related terminology. This step may be taken with the aid of an outside consultant or as part of the planning process through discussion of the literatures on IDS and pertinent fields of knowledge. The goal is twofold: to promote a general climate of innovation in which a variety of activities can coexist and to foster an agreement on a common language and conception of the outcomes envisioned from any given activity.

Conceptual and Organizational Variables

In taking the next steps in curriculum planning, participants need to realize that between motivations and structures, a number of intervening variables are at work in curriculum change:

- The nature of the institution (size, mission, financial base)
- The institutional culture (past experience with curricular reform, patterns of interaction among faculty and administration, the nature of the academic community, and assumptions about the learning styles of students)
- The level of the desired change (institution-wide, program, or course)
- The nature of the desired change (general education, interdisciplinary majors and concentrations, department and program enhancement, bridging research and the classroom, learning communities)
- The extent of faculty capabilities and interests
- The variety of academic cultures within disciplines, professional fields, and interdisciplinary areas

Institutional contexts vary greatly. Some—for example, the University of Chicago, Hobart and William Smith Colleges, and the University of California, Irvine—have strong traditions of interdisciplinary work. At others, the institutional mission may be highly compatible with a given initiative. The Human Development and Social Relations Program at Earlham College is a case in point. The program was founded in 1976 to provide interdisciplinary, values-oriented preparation for the helping professions, in addition to a focused *liberal education* that draws on the social sciences and philosophy. It combines team-developed and team-taught interdisciplinary courses with a base of disciplinary courses and a senior seminar that synthesizes theory and practice while providing a bridge to careers. The same type of program will also reflect local needs and philosophies. The University of Hartford's guidelines for interdisciplinary general education seek to place learning for students in a contextual framework that unites knowledge and human experience with such courses as "Living in a Social Context" and "Living in a Scientific and Technological World." Bradford College seeks to link liberal and professional education and the world of work (Casey, 1994, pp. 58–59).

Size is an added factor. In a large university, a new curriculum may take years to work its way through various planning and policy committees. In a smaller institution, change may come more quickly. Even in a large institution, however, comprehensive change may occur in a relatively short timescale. At Michigan State University (MSU), the necessity of shifting from a quarter system to a semester system provided an opportunity for recasting an older program of general education into a new set of college-level schools of Integrative Studies in the Social Sciences, Humanities, and Sciences. The schools are attached to MSU's colleges of Social Science, Arts and Letters, and Science.

The MSU example raises another important consideration. Change occurs at different levels and on differing timescales, even in the same institution. Regardless of institutional size and mission, regardless of the particular activity, a number of questions should be addressed early in the planning stages:

- Does the program or course require small, limited, localized, and incremental interventions or more global, comprehensive, or even radical actions?
- Does it entail a modification of existing structures or the creation of new ones?
- Are existing material resources and personnel adequate for the change, or are external consultation and financial support necessary?
- Who are the key administrative and faculty personnel for the initial development?
- What is the appropriate administrative structure?

Fostering Communication and Collaboration

To foster communication and collaboration, interdisciplinary curricula need clearly defined administrative responsibility. In small liberal arts colleges, responsibility might be assigned to an associate provost or a dean; in a large institution, a dean for undergraduate studies. A central office or coordinating structure has tremendous value. Names and formats vary: Office of Interdisciplinary Studies, Division of Interdisciplinary Programs, Interdisciplinary Activities Committee, or Chair of Interdisciplinary Studies. A central office facilitates coordination of resources, effective use of facilities and instrumentation, and provisions for annual reports and program evaluation. It also ensures greater visibility and protection for individual programs while illuminating the whole context of interdisciplinary activity on campus. One of the first functions of such a body should be an inventory of existing activities and interests, an initial step toward establishing an information clearinghouse. A central office can also sponsor an interdisciplinary forum series and coordinate visits to campus by outside scholars. Quite often, featured speakers in departmental lecture series and seminars represent cutting-edge research and new developments that are interdisciplinary in nature.

A central oversight office or body can aid in another important way, providing an adequate resource base for all interdisciplinary activities on campus. In conjunction with the main library, individual departments and programs, and a center for teaching and learning, a central office can build a library of publications and teaching materials, including a bank of syllabi and program models. The office can also aid in literature searches and publish a newsletter keeping the campus informed of local and national developments, including news of funding agencies that support participation in pertinent conferences, seminars, workshops, post-docs, and summer fellowships. The office can also manage an internal electronic bulletin board for interdisciplinary conversations and information.

Examining the existing structure for mechanisms that stimulate and support IDS is another important means of fostering communication and collaboration. Sabbatical and other professional leaves may be used for faculty development in interdisciplinary areas. Curriculum- and research-development programs are excellent sources of seed money that may lead to external funding. Release time from teaching one or more classes is the most common means of enabling faculty members to develop new competencies and possibly to prepare for collaborative teaching. Cross-listing of courses enables wider student participation, and joint appointments formally recognize faculty participation in a wider array of activities. The eternal problem of budget and teaching-load credit can be handled in several ways, by doubling, splitting, or rotating course credits. Not all support for interdisciplinary activity, moreover, requires large financial outlays. Budgeting a few hundred dollars for lunch or social gatherings goes a long way toward facilitating the dialogue that is crucial to interdisciplinary interaction. For more substantial stimulus, new seed grants, challenge grants, and curriculum-development funds may be established and, if possible, resident or visiting professorships may be established using endowment funds.

Visibility and Legitimacy

Visibility and legitimacy must be considered from the outset. On too many campuses, good interdisciplinary programs are minimally visible in catalogues and bulletins. Correspondingly, they are underrepresented in admissions and counseling. All internal documents should be examined for inclusion, with separate material developed for each program articulating its mission, structure, relation to the larger institution, and sources of further information. Interdisciplinary activities need to become part of the way the institution represents itself to students, faculty, and the community. Just as excellence in disciplinary and professional study is recognized, interdisciplinary study should be recognized by means of prizes, awards, and public celebration at graduation and convocations.

From a faculty standpoint, the bottom line is inclusion in the reward system. An institution gets what it rewards. Even the most valued and stimulating curriculum will dwindle or fail if faculty participation is not rewarded. This is an especially pressing issue in institutions that weigh research more heavily than teaching in making decisions about tenure, promotion, and salary. Participation in interdisciplinary activity needs to be spelled out explicitly and continuously—in the initial interview, in the letter of hire, and in formal guidelines for tenure, promotion, and salary. Matrix evaluation is an approach that specifies, explicitly, how much an activity counts and at which levels it is counted. Evaluative categories are determined interactively by the institution, the individual, and the program so as to recognize and thereby sanction the kinds of activities the faculty member engages in. These matters are of particular concern when junior faculty are borrowed from departments where they hold their primary appointments, though even senior faculty permanently assigned to interdisciplinary programs may find themselves subject to tensions between programs and academic departments. Lessons derived from general systems theory would suggest that complex structures are most likely to succeed when they stimulate interaction among disciplines and IDS units and reward faculty who engage in such activity. Because faculty are engaged increasingly in greater numbers and kinds of activities that are not adequately accounted for in traditional organization charts or evaluated by a single set of global criteria, institutions of higher education need to respond appropriately.

Teaching and Learning

The acid test of IDS is the extent to which integration is achieved in the learning experience of students (Squires, 1992, p. 206). Ever since the 1970 OECD seminar, the degree of interdisciplinary integration has been indicated by labels such as multidisciplinary and interdisciplinary. The difference is important.

Integration

In *multidisciplinary* courses, faculty present their individual perspectives one after another, leaving differences in underlying assumptions unexamined and integration up to the students. In *interdisciplinary* courses, whether taught by teams or individuals, faculty interact in designing a course, bringing to light and examining underlying assumptions and modifying their perspectives in the process. They also make a concerted effort to work with students in crafting an integrated *synthesis* of the separate parts that provides a larger, more holistic understanding of the question, problem, or issue at hand. Smith's iron law bears repeating: "Students shall not be expected to integrate anything the faculty can't or won't" (quoted in Gaff, 1980, pp. 54–55).

Armstrong's definition of four levels of integration and synthesis clarifies levels of curricular integration. At the first level, students take a selection of courses from different departments, counting them toward a specific major. This is the cheapest, least demanding, and usually the most easily achieved variant but, from an interdisciplinary standpoint, probably the least effective. At the second level, students have an institutionally provided opportunity to meet and to share insights from disciplinary courses, often in a capstone seminar. Responsibility for achieving integration, however, may be left largely to the students. At the third level, a significant change occurs as faculty join students in the process of synthesis. This level implies creation of courses focused on interdisciplinary topics and may require the participation of more than one faculty member. Even at this level, though, the degree of interaction varies. In many team-taught courses, individual faculty simply bring their disciplinary wares to the class. At the fourth and highest level a conscious effort is made to integrate material from various fields of knowledge into a "new, single, intellectually coherent entity." This step demands understanding the epistemologies and methodologies of other fields and, in a team effort, requires building common vocabulary and assumptions (Armstrong, 1980, pp. 53–54).

Integration is not a strictly linear process, either in education or in research. Most interdisciplinary programs use a combination of disciplinary courses, multidisciplinary formats, and interdisciplinary elements and approaches. A number of mechanisms facilitate integration:

- Courses and course segments clarifying the concept of interdisciplinarity
- Capstone seminars
- Capstone theses, essays, and projects
- Coordinated alignment of parallel disciplinary courses
- Clustering of disciplinary courses around a common integrative seminar or discussion groups
- Organizational structure based on a topic, theme, issue, problem, or question
- Specific integrative approaches, theories, or concepts (such as systems theory, feminism, Marxism, textualism)
- Course learning portfolios and academic career portfolios
- A specific learning model
- Common living arrangements, shared facilities, and equipment
- Field work, work experience, travel-study

These mechanisms have yielded exemplary practices in strikingly different contexts. The Interdisciplinary Studies Program (ISP) at Wayne State University begins with a seminar that introduces its student population of working adults to interdisciplinary study through sequenced orientation to the concepts of disciplinarity and interdisciplinarity. The ISP also clarifies what IDS means in its promotional material. The Department of Human Development at California State University, Hayward, uses sequences of videotaped disciplinary lectures, symposia, and modules for use at home or in a listening center. These elements are integrated through student- and instructor-led seminars, as well as team-teaching and group learning in separate IDS courses. In the context of travel-study, Cultural History Tours at Eastern Michigan University employ teams of faculty from history, art, literature, and political science who form mobile residential colleges with students. Interdisciplinary learning occurs in the dialogue that develops not only in formal meetings—often at the actual sites of museums, monuments, and ruins throughout Europe and Asia—but also in the sense of community that evolves through sharing meals and traveling together.

Hursh, Haas, and Moore's (1983) model of an interdisciplinary solution to a given problem in general education has the widest generic value in the curriculum. The model identifies two levels in interdisciplinary process: *identification and clarification* of salient concepts and skills to be used, then *resolution* of differences. A course on U.S. energy policy, for example, may draw on the geology of coal and oil formation, the chemistry of energy storage, the physics of energy release and transformation in a power plant, the chemistry of air pollution, the biology of low-level ionizing radiation, the economics of energy pricing, and the politics of big oil. The concept of efficiency, central to combining these disciplinary insights into policy, is defined differently in physics, economics, and political science. They all recognize efficiency as a measure of output per unit input, but vary in what they include as input and output. By contrasting the ambiguities and assumptions of individual definitions, one can construct a higher-order, comprehensive meaning, accommodating discrepancies and integrating around identified commonalities. Resolution does not mean a false consensus or unity, as differences are neither reduced nor blurred. Instead, resources are marshaled for the task at hand.

Course Design

In designing courses, planning groups and faculty need to consider a number of issues. Most interdisciplinary courses are organized around a particular topic, theme, problem, question, issue, idea, person or persons, cultural or historical period, or world area or national region. Once curricular purpose has been clearly established, the first task is to select the organizing principle of the course and determine how it will be defined. If the course is part of a program or a sequence of courses, its relationship to other components of the program needs to be clarified. The next task is to determine what knowledge and information—out of all that is possible—will be presented and what texts used. The final task is to define the sequence of the course and how the interdisciplinary process will be addressed. Interdisciplinary courses, like the interdisciplinary process itself, require achieving a working balance among breadth (to ensure a wide base of knowledge of information), depth (to ensure the quality of requisite knowledge and information for the task at hand), and synthesis (to ensure integration of knowledge) (Association of American Colleges, 1990, pp. 65–66).

Achieving synthesis requires proactive attention to process. That means examining how the elements to be synthesized are obtained and interrelated. The skills involved are familiar ones: differentiating, comparing, and contrasting different disciplinary and professional perspectives; identifying commonalties and clarifying how the differences relate to the task at hand; and devising a holistic understanding grounded in the commonalities but still responsive to the differences. The worldview and underlying assumptions of each discipline must be made explicit. By doing so, an interdisciplinary approach promotes "strong sense critical thinking," going beyond logical skills to become critically reflexive of discipline and self (Newell, 1992, p. 220). Students and faculty are able to structure a framework flexible enough to allow for shifting groupings of information and knowledge, to define adequate depth and specificity as well as breadth and general connection, to identify salient concepts and global questions, then to use them in an integrative manner to clarify and present results for mutual revision (Klein, 1996). An important part of course planning, therefore, is determining how and when comparative analysis of pertinent methods and tools takes place, and ensuring that the goals of both depth and breadth are explicitly defined and pursued (Association of American Colleges, 1991b, p. 74).

The tendency in designing interdisciplinary courses is to try to cover too much content, especially in general education curricula that place greater value on the breadth part of the breadth-depth-synthesis triad. An interdisciplinary course needs to be conceptualized as covering disciplinary perspectives the way a disciplinary course covers subject matter. A narrower topic leaves more time to apply diverse disciplinary perspectives and increases the likelihood that those perspectives confront the same issues instead of talking past one another. The narrower the topic, the more complex its examination can be and the more the various perspectives themselves can be probed. The choice of topic further requires balancing faculty expertise and student interest. Since the topic is often shaped for the disciplines it introduces and the skills and sensibilities it cultivates, as much as by faculty interest, it is important to distinguish between this subtext, which constitutes the real course for faculty, and the common-sense understanding of the course by students (Newell, 1994).

Pedagogy and Team-Teaching

One of the first questions faculty ask is what constitutes *interdisciplinary pedagogy*. There is no unique interdisciplinary pedagogy. IDS typically draws on innovative pedagogies that promote dialogue and community, problem-posing and problem-solving capacities, and an integrative habit of mind. Collaborative work is one way of achieving a sense of community, usually through exercises and small-group projects. Because collaborative inquiry alters the strict hierarchy of teacher and student, traditional roles are redefined in the process. Discovery- and praxis-based learning, as well as game and role-playing, also encourage making connections, while dialogic and process models of learning heighten awareness of the role of critical thinking. Learning portfolios encourage integration of subjects as well as personal synthesis of knowledge and experience. Lectures are used, especially in core curricula that combine large plenary sessions with small discussion workshops. In interdisciplinary settings, however, the lecture format may not be useful. A teaching team may engage in dialogue in the middle of a classroom discussion, interrupting each other for clarification and questioning their definitions and assumptions. Faculty in the American studies program at Tufts University have a self-imposed ten-minute rule that restricts lecturing to imparting necessary information. The Tufts team also uses *dyads,* exercises between two students focusing on course issues and tasks. In addition, many interdisciplinary courses also use free-writing exercises to stimulate thinking.

Team-teaching is frequently associated with interdisciplinary study, though more often courses are team planned but individually taught. A team may teach together for the initial offering of a course; then, as individuals become more comfortable with the perspectives and contributions of other disciplines, they may teach sections individually. Team-teaching is more expensive than individually taught sections of a team-designed course. For that reason, the University of Maine's program in general education brings six faculty members together for course development and lectures to promote dialogue and community within each course, but then splits them up into teams of two for separate seminar sections.

Generally speaking, even members of the same teaching team tend to lack consensus on a definition of interdisciplinarity and engage in little philosophical discussion. Through pragmatic faculty discussions in the classroom, different operational and implicit definitions evolve. Whether a course is team-taught or team-designed and individually taught, a regular meeting of the teaching faculty is vital for tending to day-to-day operations. Discussions tend to center on topics to cover, passages in assigned readings to emphasize, issues to raise, concepts and theories to master, sensibilities and skills to develop the next week, and effective pedagogy. Presemester and postsemester as well as summer workshops afford more time for evaluation, reflection, and bringing new faculty on board. Collaborative construction of course portfolios, with teaching versions of syllabi and readers, are excellent means of focusing on definitions and the evolving shape of courses. (See Davis, 1995, for a comprehensive guide to the subject shaped by organizational and group theory, practical wisdom, and program models.)

Interdisciplinary curriculum development and teaching are vital forms of faculty development. Individuals contribute their own expertise, but they grow intellectually through exposure to other viewpoints and the interrogative learning that ensues. Faculty seminars, workshops, and study groups are the primary mechanisms. Whether scheduled during the academic year or in summer, on a voluntary basis or in connection with an internal or external grant, whether self-directed through reading of common texts or in conjunction with seminars with visiting scholars, they are cost-effective investments in the intellectual life of an institution. The key to stimulating interaction is providing nonhierarchical structures that foster dialogue, self-criticism and risk taking, trust and mutual respect, and a sense of mutual ownership. This environment aids in the essential and sometimes thorny task of bridging disciplinary and professional worldviews, styles of working, and ways of dividing up subject matter.

Assessment and Evaluation

Criteria for assessment are the least understood aspect of IDS, partly because they have been least studied and partly because multiple motivations and tasks militate against any single standard. The recent appearance of a comprehensive discussion of the issues involved in assessment of interdisciplinary learning provides a much-needed clarification (Field, Lee, and Field, 1994).

Assessment of Learning

The traditional conceptual focus of assessment has been on acquisition of knowledge in established curricular areas, usually using nationally normed tests. By their very nature, though, interdisciplinary programs tend to be unique. No standard curriculum provides an index, and many veterans of interdisciplinary teaching find acquisition of knowledge alone a questionable goal. Lack of a standard curriculum is often held to be a major disadvantage. Yet, it may well be an advantage, because it requires a shift in focus from a fixed body of information to the students' cognitive development and integration. Field, Lee, and Field (1994) suggest that intellectual maturation and cognitive development may, in fact, be the most appropriate conceptual frameworks for assessment. (For more information on assessment, see Chapters Twenty-Eight and Twenty-Nine.)

Some standardized instruments are useful. The College Outcomes Measures Project (COMP), developed by the American College Testing Program as an evaluation of learning in general education, measures a wide range of intellectual skills instead of specific intellectual content. The School of Interdisciplinary Studies at Miami University has used COMP for pre- and postcourse testing of students. The General Intellectual Skills test, currently being developed by the Educational Testing Service (ETS), will measure critical thinking and communication skills, with grading by local faculty equipped with ETS protocols. The more discipline-oriented ETS instrument, the Academic Profile, measures college-level reading, writing, mathematics, and critical thinking in relation to the humanities, social sciences, and natural sciences. Either a long or a short form may be used. Field, Lee, and Field note additional measures such as the Test of Critical Thinking, the Reflective Judgment Interview, the Watson-Glaser Critical Thinking Appraisal Test, the College Student Experiences Questionnaire, the Measure of Intellectual Development, and ACT ASSET. Yet they caution that many of these instruments are not standardized and lack full validation. For interdisciplinary majors and concentrations, instruments or parts of instruments that test knowledge in pertinent subject areas will also be relevant. Still, the limits of standardized, quantitative instruments underscore the importance of local control.

A number of recommendations emerge from the 1990 report of the Interdisciplinary Studies Task Force and from Field, Lee, and Field (1994). The keys to appropriate assessment are taking a developmental perspective, applying multiple strategies, combining qualitative and quantitative measures, and devising locally designed measures tied to local goals. Using multiple, ongoing instruments and methodologies balances the weaknesses of any one instrument and addresses the full range of IDS goals. The locally designed measures in Field, Lee, and Field's exemplary models—the School of Interdisciplinary Studies at Miami University, the Evergreen State College, and the Interdisciplinary Studies Program at Wayne State University—include contextualized use of quantitative measures, portfolio analysis of student work in individual courses, comprehensive multiyear portfolios, written and oral performance in capstone seminars and theses, entry and exit interviews, courses focused proactively on the nature of interdisciplinary process, regularized faculty feedback on student capabilities, data on graduate- and professional-school placement, career placement, and retrospective evaluations by alumni. Faculty and administrators should also consider whether standard measures can be adapted to local needs or new qualitative measures must be designed. Regularly updated, accessible data are crucial to quantitative tracking of students, though plans should not be more ambitious than local resources allow or so complex they become ends in themselves. When an assessment plan is being formulated, goals should also be articulated early in the development process and feedback loops incorporated, leading back to improvement of both teaching and curriculum design.

Until recently, hard evidence on the outcomes of interdisciplinary education was rare in the published literature. Interdisciplinarity was almost never a factor included in major educational studies. In their massive compendium of research on higher education over the last twenty years, Pascarella and Terenzini (1991) do not even include interdisciplinary studies or integration in the index, though they report that "A second general conclusion is that change in a wide variety of areas is stimulated by academic experiences that purposefully provide for challenge and integration. . . . [A] curricular experience in which students are required to integrate learning from separate courses around a central theme appears to elicit greater growth in critical thinking than does the same curricular experience without the integrative requirement" (p. 619).

In *What Matters in College?* Astin (1992) related the number of interdisciplinary courses, the number of faculty teaching them, and student satisfaction with opportunities to take interdisciplinary courses. While in general he discovered that what is taught in college and how the curriculum is structured have much less impact on students than active learning pedagogies, student-orientation of faculty, and students' interaction with peers, the one major exception was interdisciplinary studies. Astin reported that "the true-core interdisciplinary approach to general education, in which all students are required to take precisely the same set of courses . . . does appear to have generally favorable effects on many of the twenty-two general education outcomes" (pp. 424–425).

In particular, he discovered that interdisciplinarity has widespread effects on cognitive and academic development, including knowledge of field as well as general knowledge, critical thinking, GPA, preparation for graduate and professional school, degree aspirations, intellectual self-concept, and performance on MCAT, LSAT, and NTE examinations. He also determined that IDS has extensive impact on affective development, including all self-reported growth measures except job skills and foreign language, and virtually all diversity outcomes. The next task for studies of higher education is to probe the precise mechanisms through which interdisciplinary study has such widespread effects.

Program Review

Evaluating the effectiveness of the curriculum should be an ongoing process tied to feedback loops from assessment measures. Carefully designed instruments can play an important role in testing claims about attainment of program goals. The St. Andrew's College general education program uses multiyear comparison both within and across individual courses of the program. Student evaluations include targeted questions about the effectiveness of particular texts, lectures, workshops, the syllabus, the reader, and teaching strategies. Aided by this data, discussions of program effectiveness combine quantitative measures with qualitative impressions, without undue balance of one over the other.

Every five years, a more formal review should be conducted and external evaluators involved. In addition to following the procedures stipulated by a local institution for program review, interdisciplinary program review should also address the following questions:

- How effective are the faculty? If faculty are borrowed from departments, are there problems of availability and rotation? Whether they are borrowed or resident in an IDS program, is their interdisciplinary teaching (and research) adequately evaluated and rewarded?
- Is there an adequate system of faculty development? Are there adequate resources available on campus for curriculum development and learning in pertinent fields?
- Do the organizational and budgetary procedures of the institution facilitate and enhance interdisciplinary programs and other forms of interaction and collaboration? Do programs have secure budgetary lines in hard money, thereby integrating them into the life of the campus? Is there sufficient flexibility to allow shifting groupings of faculty and courses as topics and projects change? Are there incentives to encourage this?
- Is the breadth-depth-synthesis triad fully and adequately addressed? Is there sufficient specificity as well as sufficient breadth? Is adequate attention paid to integrating elements to ensure adequate synthesis?
- How effective is the counseling and information system? Do students understand the goals and structure of the interdisciplinary program? Are they aided in articulating their interdisciplinary experience when they apply for graduate, professional, and career placement (Lynton, 1985, pp. 144–150)?

Additional Resources

The difference between 1978 and 1996 is striking in a final respect. In 1978, no comprehensive bibliographies on IDS existed. Since then, Klein (1990, 1994) has identified core literatures, and Klein and Doty (1994) have provided overviews of the literatures and strategies for locating resources, program administration, course design, assessment, and networking. The latter source is a good beginning point for administrators, curriculum committees, and faculty seeking information about all points of program life cycle, from planning and implementation to review and revitalization.

The ready availability of resources underscores the recommendation of the Interdisciplinary Studies Task Force that faculty be formally prepared for IDS. The quality of interdisciplinary program design and teaching is directly related to development of a shared body of knowledge and a shared sense of what is at stake, both conceptually and pragmatically. Echoing the importance of networking, relevant professional bodies—disciplinary, professional, and interdisciplinary—are also vital sources of information, contacts, guidelines, and intellectual community. For continuing developments, the Association for Integrative Studies (AIS), a national professional organization for interdisciplinarians, functions as a clearinghouse for information, pertinent professional groups, consultants and external evaluators.

To reiterate the importance of an adequate resource base, colleges and universities seeking to provide better support for interdisciplinary needs and interests can use the holdings in the King Library of Miami University as a defining touchstone for collection building. To gain access to the library's on-line catalogue via Internet, type Sherlock@lib.muohio.edu, then log in as "library." In case of technical difficulties, phone the reference desk at 513-519-4141, then ask for the current liaison to the School of Interdisciplinary Studies. Interdisciplinary material appears under many subject headings, but the most fruitful for searching in the King collection, in local collections, an in electronic databases are *interdisciplinary approach in education* and *interdisciplinary approach to knowledge*. In addition, the Institute in Integrative Studies, located at Miami University, houses an archive of syllabi generated by participants in the institute's seminars and workshops on interdisciplinary methodology, pedagogy, and curriculum design.

Conclusion

Making use of the abundance of resources available today is all the more imperative when the current financial strains on higher education are considered. As Eckhardt observed in 1978, "The intelligent management of change is never easy, and it becomes particularly difficult at a time when change no longer implies an overall growth in size" (pp. 2–3). Eckhardt's caveat rings even truer today as colleges and universities are expected do more with less, attempting to maintain existing offerings while devising new structures to accommodate a wider range of students. The cost-saving measure of downsizing raises an issue that will loom larger in the future. In cases where departments have been combined and modular approaches to the curriculum developed, IDS has been seen as a way to achieve greater efficiency in allocating faculty resources. This strategy can provide a partial solution for financially strapped institutions, but it is not a sufficient condition for interdisciplinarity. Simply combining disparate units is unlikely to produce integration in the curriculum. At the other end of the scale, collapsing interdisciplinary programs back into disciplinary departments with assurances their interests will be protected is a naive hope. Combining interdisciplinary programs into a unit of interdisciplinary studies is a better solution than collapsing them altogether.

As we move from the twentieth into the twenty-first century, IDS is no longer considered marginal to the curriculum, from K–12 through higher education. Interdisciplinary studies will continue to promote greater coherence, focus, and connectedness in order to mitigate the costs of fragmentation. Interdisciplinary approaches to research will continue to promote effective problem solving at the same time they stimulate the production of new knowledge and propel the critique of existing intellectual and institutional structures. The lessons of interdisciplinary history are clear and abundant. The challenge now is to use them widely.

References

Armstrong, F. "Faculty Development Through Interdisciplinarity." *Journal of General Education*, 1980, *32*(1), 52–63.

Association of American Colleges. *Integrity in the College Curriculum: A Report to the Academic Community.* Washington, D.C.: Association of American Colleges, 1985.

Association of American Colleges. *Liberal Learning and the Arts and Sciences Major.* Vol. 1: *The Challenge of Connecting Learning.* Washington, D.C.: Association of American Colleges, 1991a.

Association of American Colleges. "Interdisciplinary Studies." In *Reports from the Field.* Washington, D.C.: Association of American Colleges, 1991b. Excerpted version of the Report of the Interdisciplinary Studies Task Force. Complete version appears in "Interdisciplinary Resources," *Issues in Integrative Studies*, 1990, *8*, 9–33 (special issue).

Astin, A. W. *What Matters in College? Four Critical Years Revisited.* San Francisco: Jossey-Bass, 1992.

Casey, B. "The Administration and Governance of Interdisciplinary Programs." In J. T. Klein and W. Doty (eds.), *Interdisciplinary Studies Today.* New Directions for Teaching and Learning, no. 58. San Francisco: Jossey-Bass, 1994.

Center for Educational Research and Innovation (CERI). *Interdisciplinarity: Problems of Teaching and Research in Universities.* Paris: CERI/Organization for Economic Cooperation and Development, 1972.

Davis, J. *Interdisciplinary Courses and Team Teaching: New Arrangements for Learning.* American Council on Education. Phoenix, Ariz.: Oryx Press, 1995.

Eckhardt, C. D. *Interdisciplinary Programs and Administrative Structures: Problems and Prospects for the 1980s.* University Park, Pa.: Center for the Study of Higher Education, 1978.

Field, M., Lee, R., and Field, M. L. "Assessing Interdisciplinary Learning." In J. T. Klein and W. Doty (eds.), *Interdisciplinary Studies Today.* New Directions for Teaching and Learning, no. 58. San Francisco: Jossey-Bass, 1994.

Gaff, J. G. "Avoiding the Potholes: Strategies for Reforming General Education." *Educational Record*, 1980, *61*(4), 50–59.

Gibbons, M., and others. *The New Production of Knowledge: The Dynamics of Science and Research in Contemporary Societies.* Newbury Park, Calif.: Sage, 1994.

Hursh, B., Haas, P., and Moore, M. "An Interdisciplinary Model to Implement General Education." *Journal of Higher Education*, 1983, *53*, 42–59.

Klein, J. T. *Interdisciplinary: History, Theory, and Practice.* Detroit: Wayne State University Press, 1990.

Klein, J. T. "Finding Interdisciplinary Knowledge and Information." In J. T. Klein and W. Doty, eds.

Interdisciplinary Studies Today. New Directions for Teaching and Learning, no. 58. San Francisco: Jossey-Bass, 1994.

Klein, J. T. *Crossing Boundaries: Knowledges, Disciplinarities, and Interdisciplinarities.* Charlottesville: University Press of Virginia, 1996.

Klein, J. T., and Doty, W. (eds.). *Interdisciplinary Studies Today.* New Directions for Teaching and Learning, no. 58. San Francisco: Jossey-Bass, 1994.

Klein, J. T., and Gaff, J. *Reforming General Education: A Survey.* Washington, D.C.: Association of American Colleges, 1982.

Levine, A. *Handbook on Undergraduate Curriculum.* San Francisco: Jossey-Bass, 1978.

Lynton, E. "Interdisciplinarity: Rationales and Criteria of Assessment." In L. Levin and I. Lind (eds.), *Inter-Disciplinarity Revisited: Re-Assessing the Concept in the Light of Institutional Experience.* Stockholm: OECD, Swedish National Board of Universities and Colleges, 1985.

National Institute of Education. *Involvement in Learning: Realizing the Potential of American Higher Education.* Report of the Study Group on the Conditions of Excellence in American Higher Education. Washington, D.C.: U.S. Government Printing Office, 1984.

Newell, W. H. *Interdisciplinary Undergraduate Programs: A Directory.* Oxford. Ohio: Association for Integrative Studies, 1986.

Newell, W. "Academic Disciplines and Undergraduate Disciplinary Education: Lessons from the School of Interdisciplinary Studies at Miami University, Ohio." *European Journal of Education,* 1992, *27*(3), 211–221.

Newell, W. "Designing Interdisciplinary Courses." In J. T. Klein and W. Dory, eds. *Interdisciplinary Studies Today.* New Directions for Teaching and Learning, no. 58. San Francisco: Jossey-Bass, 1994.

Pascarella, E. T., and Terenzini, P. T. *How College Affects Students: Findings and Insights from Twenty Years of Research.* San Francisco: Jossey-Bass, 1991.

Squires, G. "Interdisciplinarity in Higher Education in the United Kingdom." *European Journal of Education,* 1992, *27*(3), 201–210.

Defining and Teaching Interdisciplinary Studies

William H. Newell and William J. Green

Recent articles on the nature and prospects of liberal learning in American higher education have increasingly called attention to the crucial role of interdisciplinary studies in any ideal vision of the Academy. This insistence on the need for understanding the relationships between and among disciplines seems to arise as much from practical considerations as from any traditional belief that knowledge is somehow all of a piece and deserves to be exhibited as such. Gresham Riley, for example, in his essay on the goals of a liberal education, claims that "never more than at the present time has there been a need for citizens to be able to focus the insights of various disciplines on the problems and issues which beset our collective existence."[1] Underlying such calls for an interdisciplinary component to liberal education is the recognition that interdisciplinary studies encourage breadth of vision and develop the skills of integration and synthesis so frequently demanded by the problems of a culture in the midst of a profound transition.

The apparent movement away from interdisciplinary studies and other so-called "frills" in the early 1970s has obscured the creation of new interdisciplinary departments and even colleges in the last decade. The newly formed Association for Integrative Studies has members from over 100 colleges and universities, and a 1977 directory of interdisciplinary studies in the humanities lists over 2300 programs in senior institutions.[2] Another listing shows over 5000 faculty who teach interdisciplinary courses in environmental studies alone.[3]

Despite these impressive numbers, it is an unusual institution of higher education where many of the faculty do not view the interdisciplinary program on their campus with skepticism, if not hostility. They typically suspect that the program has little substance, and that what substance it does have merely duplicates the offerings of disciplinary departments. While much of this discrepancy in perspective can safely be attributed to less than noble motives, such as protection of 'turf,' a residue of well-placed criticism remains. There are courses claiming to be interdisciplinary which are academic froth, or merely serial presentations of disciplinary material. But the lack of legitimacy accorded sound and genuine programs may stem from causes much more basic than these.

We see four fundamental issues which must be resolved before interdisciplin-

Newell, William H. and William J. Green. "Defining and Teaching Interdisciplinary Studies." Improving College and University Teaching *30:1 (Winter 1982), 23–30. Reprinted with permission of the Helen Dwight Reid Educational Foundation. Published by Heldref Publications, 1319 18th St. N.W., Washington, D.C. 20036-1802. Copyright 1982.*

ary studies acquire the status which their advocates contend they deserve. The most basic of these is definitional. The term "interdisciplinary studies" itself is so loosely and so inconsistently used that almost any course which does not fit neatly within disciplinary departments is apt to be labeled "interdisciplinary." Second, the liberal arts objectives of interdisciplinary studies are vague at best; even where practitioners can agree on what they mean by the term, it is unclear what they are trying to accomplish. Third, there are no widely accepted canons of interdisciplinary scholarship by which to judge excellence. Finally, it is not certain what the appropriate relationship is between interdisciplinary studies and the academic disciplines themselves. Should interdisciplinary studies try to overthrow the disciplines, or reform them, or stand alongside them? These are the questions we address here, with the hope that we can move the interdisciplinary studies profession toward some degree of consensus and possibly toward a wider acceptance within academia.

To illustrate the range of genuine interdisciplinary courses and to lend concreteness to our proposed definition, we draw freely upon courses offered in our own Western College Program. These examples are of more than parochial interest. "Western" is one of the new interdisciplinary programs founded in the 1970s; it is more ambitious than most, with a four-year sequence of team-taught interdisciplinary seminars in the humanities, social sciences, and natural sciences, taught by a faculty, representing eleven disciplines, which collaborates intensively on the development of new courses.

Definition

We define interdisciplinary studies as inquiries which critically draw upon two or more disciplines and which lead to an integration of disciplinary insights.[4] It may seem obvious that interdisciplinary studies would involve the integration of disciplinary materials or insights, but it has been our experience that considerable misunderstanding exists on this point among purported interdisciplinarians themselves—a fact which has resulted in the overuse and misuse of the term.[5]

Two groups who dismiss the importance of the disciplines themselves in integrative work might be termed "adisciplinists" and "transdisciplinists." The former hold that the disciplines are fundamentally misguided and should be abandoned. The problem with their approach, which is to begin an inquiry *de novo* without benefit of disciplinary knowledge, is that it ignores the reality that scholars do not work in an intellectual vacuum. Scholars have all been exposed to disciplines; their habits of thoughts, their choice of certain problems over others, and their methods of problem solving all owe something to this tutelage. We suspect that courses such as these lead to the charge that interdisciplinary studies are without substance.

Transdisciplinists, on the other hand, take as an article of faith the underlying unity of all knowledge. This assumption, that everything is related to everything else, makes the division of knowledge otiose from the outset and leads to the search for a superdiscipline, based, for example, on systems theory or structuralism. The validity of the premise which informs transdisciplinary work, however, can only be determined empirically after years of interdisciplinary studies. The transdisciplinary approach is not so much wrong as premature.

Two other groups recognize the salience of disciplines for interdisciplinary study, but fail to meet the other requirements of the definition. Multidisciplinarians ignore the condition that interdisciplinary studies involve an integration of disciplinary insights. They appear to believe that any time two or more disciplines impinge upon a particular subject matter or are brought together in a single context, the result must be interdisciplinary. Multidisciplinary courses arrange in serial fashion the separate contributions of selected disciplines to a problem or issue, without any attempt at synthesis. While these courses appear to be given the label "interdisciplinary" more out of ignorance than ideological conviction, this confusion tends to reinforce the criticism that interdisciplinary studies offer little more than a conjunctive arrangement of the disciplines.

Cross-disciplinary inquiries, such as the physics of music, might well be conducted in an interdisciplinary way, but in practice they seldom are. The problem here is that one of the disciplines involved usually exercises complete hegemony (a kind of disciplinary imperialism) over the other in such fashion that the second discipline (or, more properly, its *subject matter*) becomes a passive object of study rather than an active system of thought, so that the analysis draws critically on only one discipline. Courses on the physics of music apply the principles of physics to (the subject matter of) music, but the discipline of music—its aesthetic standards and so on—is rarely considered.

Much of the confusion over the definition of interdisciplinary studies can be traced to the ill-defined nature of the disciplines themselves. Disciplines have been variously characterized by their subject matter (e.g., the past), their method (e.g., participant-observer), their perspective (e.g., the economic man), or the questions they ask (e.g., philosophic). Some scholars despair of ever conceptually distinguishing their discipline from others, resorting to assertions of the type "Physics is what physicists do." Such assertions, however, do contain an important insight, namely that disciplines are not natural species amenable to systematic characterization through a taxonomy, but rather social organizations whose origins and continued existence are as much attributable to educational politics as to the needs of scholarly inquiry. A discipline is perhaps best characterized as a socio-political organization which concentrates on a historically linked set of problems. Toulmin has suggested that it is this peculiar "genealogy of problems" (e.g., the characteristic concerns of atomic physicists from Rutherford to Heisenberg) which gives a discipline its identity and which delineates it from others.[6] Disciplines are also distinguished from one another by the questions they ask about the world, by their perspective or world view, by the set of assumptions they employ, and by the methods which they use to build up a body of knowledge (facts, concepts, theories) around a certain subject matter.

What serves to demarcate two disciplines will vary depending on which pair is at issue. For example, physics and chemistry share something approximating a hypothetico-deductive method; they assume that the world is governed by deterministic or probabilistic laws which are in principle knowable, and they frequently ask questions about the same theoretical or empirical entity (e.g., the electron or liquid benzene). Yet the questions they ask about these entities are usually quite different. Both physics and chemistry texts deal with heat, for example, but once the formalism of thermodynamics has been developed, chemistry becomes concerned almost exclusively with the effects of heat and temperature in molecular processes and transformations, while physics tends to consider a broader range of phenomena, generally at the macroscopic level (e.g., heat transfer). To take another case, economics and sociology sometimes look at the same subject matter (urban problems), raise the same questions ("What are the causes of unemployment?"), and even use the same quantitative methodology, but unlike physics and chemistry, their perspectives may contrast sharply. ("Economics is all about how people make choices. Sociology is all about why they don't have choices to make."[7])

To complicate matters further, some disciplines are so fragmented into competing methods and schools of thought that what gives them a loose coherence at best is some minimal agreement on subject matter. For example, the discipline of English is split into phenomenology, structuralism, and other competing schools whose only common denominator is the study of literature written in the English language.[8]

Because the disciplines themselves are so inherently complex, it is necessary to try to be somewhat more precise in defining the nature of an interdisciplinary study. What we envision is a process that starts with a question of such scope that it lies outside the purview of a single area of knowledge (e.g., "What form should U.S. energy policy take in the 1980s?"). To such a question it is necessary to bring a variety of narrowly disciplinary insights, each of which grows out of a more specific question, appropriate to, and approachable by a single discipline. It is the set of answers to these latter questions—questions that can be addressed by disciplines using disciplinary methods—which is then reconciled and integrated. To take an example, chemistry, geology, and economics all provide answers to questions which are of fundamental significance in setting U.S. energy policy. (What is the sulfur content of Eastern and Western coals? What is the projected rate of U.S. petroleum recovery? What effect will dwindling Mid-East reserves have on gasoline prices?) Yet none of these disciplines alone can adequately address the larger issue.

Questions such as "What are the causes of unemployment?" may be assumed by members of a discipline to be adequately addressed by its concepts, theories, and methods, while reasonable persons outside that discipline may believe that the insights of another discipline can contribute to the answer. The test of whether a question is disciplinary or interdisciplinary ultimately resides in the contribution of each approach to answering the question. If an interdisciplinary study of unemployment, drawing on other social science disciplines as well as economics, contributes substantially more to answering the question than economics can alone, then the question is interdisciplinary. Our belief is that many, if not most, questions phrased in everyday language are properly interdisciplinary, while questions phrased in the technical language of a discipline are typically limited to treatment by a single discipline.

To complete our definition of interdisciplinary studies, it is worthwhile to look more closely at what is meant by integrating disciplinary insights. First, it is important to recognize that these insights may well prove independent in a given study; that is, one discipline may have little or nothing to offer another. If the disciplinary insights are in fact interdependent and mutually enriching, they may be integrated by reconciling them if they are inconsistent, or combining them into a larger whole if they are consistent. Either way, this process of synthesis requires an appreciation of the full complexity of the disciplines involved, especially an awareness of their often unconscious assumptions, in order to discern the underlying common ground or conflict between their insights. It is in these acts of conciliation and integration of disciplinary insights that the art of interdisciplinary inquiry is fully realized.

Curricular Examples

We turn now to a description of courses taught in the Western College Program at Miami University which we believe exemplify the notion of interdisciplinary studies developed above.

Energy: A Natural Sciences Approach

Our decreasing oil reserves and an increasing energy demand provide an opportunity for presenting theory from the natural sciences in a visible and controversial context—the energy crisis. This sophomore course was designed by a chemist and physicist to explore energy alternatives and to allow students to design an energy policy for the United States consistent with scientific principles. The approach was to examine in sequence the major energy sources—fossil fuels, nuclear power, and alternatives such as solar—from several disciplinary perspectives and then to combine the varied insights into a summary of the appropriate role of each energy source in U.S. energy policy.

The unit on fossil fuels illustrates the teaching strategy. Students were introduced to the geology of coal and oil formation, with emphasis on past environments suitable for the genesis of these biogenic deposits. This was followed by a moderately detailed study of the organic geochemistry of coal and oil. Once it was clear how energy could be stored in the bonds of organic structures and how it could be released on combustion, the laws of thermodynamics were introduced, by means of the Carnot engine, to point out the limitations which nature places on efficient energy use. The unit then moved to a consideration of such undesirable byproducts of fossil fuels as SO_2 production, acid rain, and CO_2 buildup in the atmosphere.

The emphasis throughout the unit was first on the derivation of disciplinary contributions from basic scientific principles, and then on the modifications of these contributions so that they could be integrated into a picture of the total energy system for coal and oil. At the end of the unit, each student was asked to evaluate this energy system in a policy statement about the appropriate future role of fossil fuels as energy sources. This same procedure was repeated for nuclear fuels and for the emerging alternatives. In the final two weeks, discussion centered on an appropriate balance of technologies to meet U.S. energy needs. During this period students had to make choices among resource abundance, technological feasibility, and environmental impact.

The course was interdisciplinary rather than multidisciplinary because of its emphasis on the modification of disciplinary contributions. For example, physicists *qua* physicists are led by their disciplinary perspective to evaluate a coal-fired power plant in terms of its thermodynamic efficiency. When the power plant is also seen from the ecological perspective of a biologist, thermodynamic efficiency must be viewed as only one element in a matrix of concerns which includes the loss of fish life from thermal pollution. As more disciplines were brought to bear and new sets of questions were answered, the nature of the energy problem shifted.

Modernization

This sophomore course examined the structural changes accompanying the transition from a traditional to a modern society. Interrelations among the industrial revolution, urbanization, demographic changes, and the modern political situation were examined for England, Europe, and the United States. The course ended with a case study of the post-World War II impact of these changes on a third world nation. The analysis used the concepts, theories, and perspectives of a number of disciplines, including economics, sociology, and political science.

Unlike the physical science course on energy, where the disciplines share assumptions about the world and differ primarily in their choice of problems or their level of analysis, "Modernization" attempted to integrate the insights of disciplines which are often characterized by contrasting and competing perspectives and assumptions. It soon became apparent to the faculty that one could not take at face value the conclusions from economic analysis, that changes in industrial organization were due largely to the response of individuals to sifting economic incentives. Nor could one take unquestioningly the claim of sociology that social change was more or less imposed upon individuals by forces outside their control. Rather, in this case, as in other interdisciplinary social science inquires, an explicit rendering and critique of disciplinary assumptions is needed before integration. It is this additional step which seems to distinguish the method of interdisciplinary social science from that of interdisciplinary natural science.

The Individual in Society

The need to focus on the assumptions of each of the social science disciplines is also apparent in a required freshman course on the rationality and autonomy of the individual. This course looks at the theory of consumer behavior from economics, where individuals are portrayed as both rational and autonomous; at social control theory from sociology and at operant conditioning from behavioral psychology, where the individual is so nonautonomous that the question of rationality is moot; at Freudian psychology and cognitive dissonance theory from social psychology, which portray people as irrational; and at the existential psychology of Rollo May and the humanistic sociology of Peter Berger, where the argument is advanced that people are both determined and free, rational and irrational. The central question of the course, "Is the individual free?" is then answered by reconciling these conflicting claims, once the working assumptions of each school of thought have been identified.

Southern Consciousness: Junior Methodology Seminar in Arts, Humanities, and Culture

At one level, this course is an interdisciplinary search for the special character of the American South in works of music, sociological analysis, historical narrative, literature (historical novel and biography), film, popular culture, and psycho-history. More fundamentally, however, it is a comparative examination of specific interdisciplinary approaches in the humanities. Each work asks a different set of questions (implicit or explicit), represents a different method of interpretation, and presents a different perspective on southern regional consciousness. For each work, students are asked to identify the questions it asks, its method and underlying assumptions, its interpretative processes, its creative and analytical techniques, and finally its relationship to other works. At the end of the semester, students are required to evaluate how their understanding of the definition of the problem, their insight, and their grasp of scholarly and artistic technique have changed.

As an interdisciplinary course in the humanities, this differs from the social science offerings described above in several respects: first, the underlying assumptions are not so much conflicting, as compatible but different; second, the assumptions are less closely tied to particular disciplines; and finally the differing perspectives affect interpretation or expression more than they do the underlying view of reality.

As a course exploring interdisciplinary interpretations of culture, "Southern Consciousness" emphasizes to students that interdisciplinary studies *are* a methodology. In this sense, any course which is self-consciously interdisciplinary becomes a course in interdisciplinary methodology. While we have tried to set out this methodology in the definitional section of this paper, we cannot specify how the process of integration must be carried out in particular cases. Indeed, integration involves an element of creativity which often makes it more of an art, or at least a craft, than a science. Yet only to this extent can we agree with authors who claim that there can be no clear-cut interdisciplinary methodology.[9] But here, interdisciplinarians are not that different from disciplinarians. Both have their concrete methods, e.g., regression analysis, but both require creativity and craft in applying their overall methodology.

Still, there are guidelines for integration which can be spelled out. The good interdisciplinarian must be well versed in how each discipline looks at the world, what questions it has asked or would ask in a given situation, and, at least in the social sciences and humanities, what assumptions underlie its world view. The interdisciplinarian must be aware that insights arising from different disciplines do not always carry the same meaning; for example, concepts such as "culture" or "efficiency" are often found to have different meanings. "Southern Consciousness" emphasizes that an impórtant element may be finding the right question and couching it in such terms that the disciplines can complement, not talk past, one another.

Energy: A Combined Physical and Social Science Approach

Despite the advantage of the interdisciplinary approach over more narrowly disciplinary ones, it was obvious that the first course on energy needed a social science component if it were truly to do justice to the issue of energy policy. Reorganization and restaffing ensued so that currently a physical chemist and a social scientist trained in economics offer a revised version which includes a major section on economic theory. The issue of extensive development of coal reserves is now explicitly linked to the economics and politics of foreign oil, and alternative energy sources are evaluated not only for their engineering efficiency and for their effects on environmental quality, but also for their economic efficiency, and political and social acceptability.

This course differs from the earlier version not only in its breadth and complexity, but also in the reevaluations necessary of the disciplinary contributions. The physical and biological sciences are largely concerned with the material inputs and outputs of each energy system, so concepts like efficiency merely need extending to a more comprehensive domain. When the social sciences are introduced, the system is also integrated with various social systems which operate by quite different rules. With economics, efficiency can no longer be measured only in units of energy input; but also with the input of capital and labor, and dollars become the appropriate unit of measurement. When political science enters the picture, the choice of an energy policy is no longer seen as the rational weighing of costs and benefits to society. Not only efficiency, but powerful interest groups, elections, bureaucratic organization, and even past energy policy become significant factors. It appears that these differences in disciplinary perspective require a more complex process of integration than the interdisciplinary approach of the earlier course.

Another effect of moving from an interdisciplinary course within the natural sciences to one between the natural and the social sciences is that students (and faculty) find it necessary to reexamine parts of their world-taken-for-granted. Natural scientists, for example, readily see the feedback mechanisms in the natural world, but they tend to treat human behavior (which is exogenous to their system) as given and unchanging. One of the insights afforded by the social sciences is the fact that human institutions have feedback mechanisms as well. One cannot project future energy demand at the same exponential rate of growth when energy becomes more scarce; the price mechanism signals growing scarcity, and people do (and have) cut back on energy consumption in response to increasing prices.

Interdisciplinary Pedagogy

The foregoing examples of courses at Western provide some insights into interdisciplinary curriculum development. First, unless a faculty member has a broad background in the disciplines engaged, team development of courses is essential. Even after faculty have developed the skills to teach an interdisciplinary course on their own, team curriculum development remains valuable because it helps sharpen and renew command of familiar disciplinary perspectives.

We have found that it is important that students be exposed to the basic concepts, methodologies, and theories of relevant disciplines, not just to their findings. Only by confronting the discipline itself, by looking at the world through its eyes, can the student appreciate how that discipline would approach another problem. In our four-semester lower division sequence of required courses in interdisciplinary social science, students learn the functional equivalent of a semester of introductory sociology, almost all of microeconomic principles, roughly one semester of political science, a quarter of the introductory psychology course, and a similar proportion of introductory anthropology as well as a smattering of geography. Students completing this interdisciplinary sequence are able to enroll directly in most upper division disciplinary courses in the social sciences, including intermediate theory courses, and the grades they earn in those courses are comparable to those of students who have taken the introductory course in the discipline.

The success of these lower division courses demonstrates that interdisciplinary studies need not be limited to upper division students who have extensive exposure to a discipline. In fact, upperclassmen with exclusively disciplinary training tend to find interdisciplinary studies harder than do entering freshmen. At another institution, a philosophy professor teaching an upper division course for majors in science or in art found that

> . . . they had already acquired the jargon of their instructors and committed themselves to an ideal of thought whose value seemed to them proportionate to its exclusivity . . . They made an existential leap and stayed where they landed.[10]

Faculty, as well as students, can learn the interdisciplinary approach without a Ph.D. in the field. All our faculty in the social and natural sciences were trained in disciplines, and only two had interdisciplinary teaching experience before coming to Western. All of our humanities faculty, on the other hand, hold interdisciplinary Ph.D.'s. While the science faculty have been most cautious about moving outside their areas of expertise, they have also developed some of the most innovative and successful interdisciplinary courses offered in the College. The critical factor in successful interdisciplinary teaching seems to be the willingness to engage other disciplines and to adopt temporarily their assumptions and world views. In spite of the jealousy with which disciplines guard their material, it turns out to be relatively simple for a liberally educated Ph.D. to learn enough about another discipline to teach at the freshman level, especially when the preparation is carried out under the tutelage of a colleague in that discipline, and as long as the tutee remains flexible. The interdisciplinary method itself is easily learned through alertness to differences between disciplines and through close examination of disciplinary assumptions, but foremost, it is learned through team teaching with colleagues experienced in interdisciplinary studies.

Educational Outcomes of Interdisciplinary Courses

Kavaloski identifies three standard objectives of interdisciplinary education: "integration of knowledge"—the awareness of the interconnectedness of the world, the ability to see the larger context; "freedom of inquiry"—the opportunity to follow an issue without regard to artificial disciplinary barriers; and "innovation"—the chance for unconventional thinking and original insights.[11] While these are all credible expectations for interdisciplinary courses, our approach suggests a number of other desirable outcomes as well.

Interdisciplinary studies should foster several intellectual skills. Deductive reasoning is required to identify the disciplinary assumptions underlying a theory, and reasoning by analogy is required to see the application of an idea from one discipline to the problem of another. More important, however, is the synthetic thinking demanded by the integrative process. Synthesis is one of the higher order skills in Bloom's taxonomy,[12] and we know that it is one of the few educational products which students retain after leaving college.[13] Best of all, synthesis enhances creativity; certainly there is a creative component to synthesis.

The importance of these intellectual skills is becoming increasingly recognized by educators. Dartmouth's John G. Kemeny, for example, recently commented on the society's need for individuals who are capable of integrating the knowledge of many disciplines in a single mind.[14] Kemeny's sense of the importance of this integrative facility corresponds with our belief that many of the urgent problems which we face today are solvable only if we have individuals who are practiced in interdisciplinary inquiry. We agree with Kemeny when he suggests that the sine qua non of a liberal education in our day is the ability to transcend disciplinary training and to think connectively.

More closely developed, and probably more long lasting, are several habits of mind instilled by interdisciplinary studies. The students in the Western Program tend to look at arguments more critically; they are less willing to take them at face value. They are more likely to search for bias (because they know how perspective or world view can influence an argument), and for ideology (because they are sensitive to the schools of thought within and across disciplines). They are more receptive to new ideas because they are accustomed to seeking out new perspectives and learning from them. Insofar as their studies have connected the humanities with the social or natural sciences, they are alert for the ethical dimension of research in the social and natural sciences, and attuned to value-judgments generally.

Most enduring and hardest to influence are personality traits, one of which we see associated with interdisciplinarians. Because students see the developmental and provisional nature of knowledge through their interdisciplinary work, and because they come to accept and become comfortable with the incompleteness of the integration process, they develop more tolerance for ambiguity, as measured on the Omnibus Personality Inventory.

The Role of Interdisciplinary Studies in the University

The skills, traits, and personality characteristics set out above suggest that interdisciplinary studies have a rightful place in academia, certainly in liberal arts institutions that pride themselves on just such educational outcomes. We are now left with specifying more precisely the appropriate relationship between the disciplines and interdisciplinary studies.

Our experience during the past six years at Western has shown that there are few limitations on the kinds of disciplinary materials that can be successfully introduced in an interdisciplinary course, provided the central question of the course is properly chosen. This means it is possible for students to meet core liberal learning requirements by taking a series of interdisciplinary offerings which introduce them to selected disciplines in the natural and social sciences and humanities as well as illustrating points of connection among them. Somewhat surprising, perhaps, is the ease with which the so-called "hard sciences" may be treated within interdisciplinary courses. In addition to the energy policy course described above, the Western faculty have offered seminars in American Environmental History, the World Food Problem, Cubism and Relativity, Darwinian Influences on Nineteenth- and Twentieth-Century Thought, and Creativity and Imagination in the Physical Sciences—all of which have required students to master technical subject matter in chemistry, physics, biology, and geology. For nonmajors, these courses provide a context for appreciating the relationship between science and their own area of interest. One of the distinct advantages of including interdisciplinary studies alongside the disciplines is that they help bridge the gap between C. P. Snow's two cultures.

Perhaps the ideal organization for undergraduate institutions would be a series of interdisciplinary courses which introduce students to the disciplines of the liberal arts by exhibiting their interdependence and interpenetrations. Disciplines would then take on the major task of training students in their respective specializations. Alongside the disciplines, at the upper division level, would be interdisciplinary courses in applied topics which overflow disciplinary bounds. An interdisciplinary social science course on the city, for example, might replace present courses in urban economics, urban politics, urban sociology, and urban geography. In a university structure where disciplines are entrenched in departments, interdisciplinarians might be well served by their own departments, and we believe they would serve the other departments of the university in turn.

Notes

1. Gresham Riley, "Goals of a Liberal Education: Making the Actual and the Ideal Meet," *Liberal Education* 4 (1979): 436–44.
2. Elizabeth Bayerl, *Interdisciplinary Studies in the Humanities: A Directory* (Metuchen, N.J.: Scarecrow Press, 1977).
3. *The Educational Directory,* 1 Park Ave., Suite No. 2, New York, N.Y. 10016.
4. For other notable attempts at defining interdisciplinary studies, see L. Richard Meeth, "Interdisciplinary Studies: A Matter of Definition," *Change Report on Teaching,* (August 1978): 10; William V. Mayville, "Interdisciplinary: The Mutable Paradigm" (Washington, D.C.: ERIC, 1978); Centre for Educational Research and Innovation, *Interdisciplinarity: Problems of Teaching and Research in Universities* (Paris: OECD, 1972); and Joseph J. Kockelmans (ed.), *Interdisciplinarity and Higher Education* (University Park, PA: Pennsylvania State University Press, 1979).
5. Michael W. Messmer, "The Vogue of the Interdisciplinary," *Centennial Review* 4 (1978): 467–78.
6. Stephen Toulmin, *Human Understanding. Vol. 1. The Collective Use and Evolution of Concepts* (Princeton: Princeton University Press, 1972): 148.
7. James Duesenberry, "Comment," in Universities-National Bureau of Economic Research, *Demography and Economic Change in Developed Countries* (Princeton: Princeton University Press, 1960): 233.
8. William Randel, "English as a Discipline," in Robert Merideth (ed.), *American Studies: Essays on Theory and Method* (Columbus, Ohio: Charles E. Merrill, 1968).
9. Jonathan Broida, "Interdisciplinarity: Reflections on Methodology," in Kockelmans, *Interdisciplinarity.*
10. Charles B. Fethe, "A Philosophical Model for Interdisciplinary Programs," *Liberal Education* 4 (1973): 490–97.
11. Vincent Kavaloski, "Interdisciplinary Education and Humanistic Aspiration: A Critical Reflection," in Kockelmans, *Interdisciplinarity.*
12. B. S. Bloom, ed., *Taxonomy of Educational Objectives, Handbook 1: Cognitive Domain* (New York: Longmans, Green, 1956).
13. Robert F. Biehler, "Teaching for Transfer," *Psychology Applied to Teaching* (Boston: Houghton Mifflin, 1978).
14. John G. Kemeny, "What is an Educated Person?" *The New York Times,* 18 May 1980, Education Section.

An Interdisciplinary Model to Implement General Education

Barbara Hursh, Paul Haas, and Michael Moore

While there is little opposition to the concept that general education should be a major component in the higher education curriculum, there is no general agreement on the means to achieve the aims of general education. Although general education should enable students to deal with issues and problems from a broad, integrative perspective, as well as to know major forms of inquiry, institutions continue to teach students how to think solely within the confines of disciplines. Each college or department often develops strong programs in its disciplines, recruits majors, and, by implication, worries little about general education and a concern for integration. By default, general education curricula become a series of loosely related, if not unrelated, courses that emphasize specific disciplinary content. Students are left on their own to see connections, recognize commonalities, and evaluate disparities in methods, assumptions, and values. Despite the mounting evidence that not all students accomplish this task, students must enroll in X number of courses in Area I, Y number of courses in Area II, and so on.

Curriculum designers are hard pressed to cite any theory of learning that advances certain disciplines as being necessary—in whatever proportions—to intellectual development. Most general education curricula appear to be formed more by political struggles among academic departments than by struggles among advocates of competing educational theories. This process may account for the relative sameness of the debates—and the curricula—year after year. The traditional discipline-based recipe continues as the dominant paradigm, even in the more recent of the so-called general education reforms.

The thrust of this article is to demonstrate the construction of a general education program with a different paradigm. We believe that general education should be more than a diverse knowledge base from which students leap forward to areas of specialization. In fact, we argue that the political approach to curriculum design ignores some very important aspects of cognitive development, one of which is the ability to integrate, or at least organize, the knowledge and skills of the different disciplines.

It is true that disciplinary specialization provides indispensable tools with

Hursh, Barbara, Paul Haas, and Michael Moore. "An Interdisciplinary Model to Implement General Education." Journal of Higher Education 54:1 (Jan/Feb 1983), 42–49. Reprinted with permission. Copyright 1983 by the Ohio State University Press. All rights reserved.

This paper was originally conceptualized at the initial meeting of the Association for Integrative Studies held at Miami University in April 1979. We wish to thank Mel Shelly and Carney Strange of Bowling Green State University for reading and commenting on earlier drafts. However, the authors accept full responsibility for what has been written.

which to assess relationships among highly selected variables within manageable sectors of knowledge. Without disciplines we would have trouble deciphering many of the causal links that provide us with important answers to specific problems in the humanities, sciences, and social sciences. However, specialized nomenclature becomes dysfunctional for comprehension of the interrelationships among the disciplines. This specialization threatens to erect a new Tower of Babel in which highly trained disciplinarians, using precise, newly coined definitions, may speak meaningfully only to those small groups who share their special language.

If we wish to pursue general education, we need to loosen, although not discard, the shackles of the disciplines. We must recognize that general education is intended to "liberate," that is, to develop a capacity for discovery and exploration of various modes of thinking, inquiring, and searching for patterns of meaning that are embedded in the disciplines. As problems are identified, we need to understand the limits of unidisciplinary thought and expand our horizons by a coordinated examination of alternative modes of description, conceptualization, and evaluation.

We believe that this need can be addressed by an integrative, interdisciplinary model of general education grounded in theories of learning associated with John Dewey, Jean Piaget, and William Perry. The model emphasizes what we call "generic skills," which include such cognitive functions as recognizing and defining problems; analyzing the structure of an argument; assessing the relationships of facts, assumptions, and conclusions; and performing hypothetico-deductive processes.[1] These capacities can be seen as generic rather than discipline-specific (or even departmentally induced); we hold, therefore, that they furnish an appropriate basis for a model of general education.[2]

Theoretical Background

The model that follows was constructed by a social/educational psychologist, an economist, and a humanist, each with experience in teaching both discipline-based and interdisciplinary courses. Quite independently of each other, we had concluded that the discipline-based recipe for general education could be improved upon and that one key for doing so was the introduction of multiple perspectives upon specific issues in order to exercise, among other things, skills of comparison, contrast, analysis, and above all, synthesis. Upon discovering one another, it became clear that our common beliefs about learning/teaching had theoretical foundation in the works of Dewey, Piaget, and Perry. These three scholars converge in a number of ways, two of which are of particular significance for a model of general education: (1) each has asserted the importance of the reciprocal relationships between knowledge (cognition) and experience, and (2) each emphasized the epistemological significance of multiple perspectives.

Dewey addresses perspective management in a variety of ways; a notable example is his treatment of means/ends relationships [2, pp. 100–10; 13, p. 43]. Piaget and Perry have articulated stage development theories in which the capacity to handle multiple perspectives is a factor differentiating stages of cognitive growth. Piaget has labeled this ability "cognitive decentering" [6, pp. 342–45; 15], while Perry refers to an analogous, although more abstract, ability as "relativistic thought," which includes the capacity to "think about thinking" [10, p. 205].[3]

To be specific, cognitive decentering is the intellectual capacity to move beyond a single center or focus (especially the innate tendencies toward egocentrism and ethnocentrism) and consider a variety of other perspectives in a coordinated way to perceive reality more accurately, process information more systematically, and solve problems more effectively. Piaget's classic beaker experiments [15] demonstrated the necessity of considering both the height and the width of beakers in order to estimate correctly the relative quantities of water each would hold. Each dimension is a "center" or focus of attention in the phenomenological field.

As problems become more complex or abstract than estimating quantities of water in beakers, the "centers" of attention may more reasonably be called perspectives, frames of reference, or even disciplines. The term decentering is still appropriate to denote the ability to shift deliberately among alternative perspectives or frames of reference and to bring them to bear upon each other or upon a problem at hand.[4] This construct may be seen as an analogue for the type of cognitive functioning that we assert as a major outcome of an appropriate liberal education. This type of functioning allows for the apprehension of connections between theories, disciplines, and schools of thought; between practical problems and accumulated knowledge; and between societal assumptions and cross-cultural variation. Above all, it enables individuals to better assess the utility of the various disciplines for specific purposes and to acquire the habit of bringing scientific, humanistic, and social scientific perspectives to bear on complex problems. The importance of this process is evident in everyday decision making, as well as in scientific pursuits. For example, the cognitive functioning described above is essential in the search for solutions to such problems as energy depletion, environmental pollution, health care delivery, and urban decay, or in considering aesthetic qualities of line, color, form, and texture from the standpoint of music, art, dance, or theater.

The relationship between the simple concept of decentering and the foregoing assertions is elucidated by the work of William Perry. While Piaget's work was based primarily on the study of young children, Perry applied some of the same methods to the study of cognitive functioning in college students. The result was an extension of Piaget's theory into a form useful for understanding adult intellectual functioning. Specifically, Perry asserts that a stage developmental process is observable during late adolescence. According to Perry, students in their early college years exhibit "dualism," a form of thinking that is authoritarian, relatively passive, and basically one-dimensional in that it organizes information according to bipolar dimensions such as true versus false, right versus wrong, or black versus white. A subsequent stage of development is labeled "multiplicity" to indicate the tendency to see multiple truths, shades of gray, and phenomenological variations. In terms of the Piagetian model, multiplistic thinkers can accommodate many centers or perspectives, but they lack the cognitive structures necessary to organize them, bring them to bear upon one another, or evaluate their relative validity or utility. Hence, this stage is vulnerable to indiscriminate judgments, a conscious advocacy of what amounts to solipsism, and a tendency to ignore conflicting evidence. Correction of such errors becomes possible with the attainment of the next stage, "relativism." In relativism, the individual has acquired the capacity to consider multiple perspectives relative to each other, and more importantly, relative to a set of higher order constructs—or what might be called "metaperspectives"— which can provide bases for organizing alternative perspectives or assessing their worth for specific purposes. We shall return to consideration of this stage after attending to the final stage in the Perry scheme.

The most advanced stage of development according to Perry is "commitment" (or "commitment in relativism"), the distinguishing feature of which is the willingness to act upon a belief. This stage entails a readiness to tolerate paradox, take risks, embrace irony, and identify oneself with chosen notions, even when perfectly plausible alternatives exist and are acknowledged. Perry implies that commitment is the only way to escape being "at sea in relativism" [11, p. 94]. Other scholars, especially those interested strictly in *cognitive* development, have suggested that Perry's description of relativism represents the highest stage in developmental transformations of cognition [7, pp. 12, 17, as interpreted in 11, p. 99; 8]. The implication is that commitment in relativism, rather than representing further cognitive development, actually represents a characterological phenomenon that is informed by relativistic thought but does not necessitate any further cognitive restructuring. Indeed, commitment in and of itself is not uncharacteristic of dualists, solipsists, and even fanatics, suggesting that commitment may be independent of a stage of cognitive development. What is crucial is whether or not choices among multiple perspectives can be articulated and justified relative to metaperspectives, which clarify both the empirical and the value-based rationales for acting in a given way. It is at least arguably true that the stage Perry labels as relativism incorporates all of the cognitive machinery that is necessary for making such choices.[5] Therefore, the model that follows focuses on cognitive development, takes relativism as the desirable end, and does not attempt to explain how students move into commitment.

Returning therefore to relativism, an elementary graphic representation of this stage would place multiple perspectives along a horizontal axis and organizing structures along a vertical axis, and in grid-like fashion submit the perspectives to analysis in accordance with selected metaperspectives. Both horizontal and vertical dimensions, therefore, are taken into consideration relative to each other in complex thought. This calls for cognitive functioning analogous to Piaget's decentering, although at a much more complex level because it not only includes multiple perspectives, but also multiple organizing constructs.

The nature of the vertical organizing constructs, or metaperspectives, is difficult to specify in concrete terms because they can take a great variety of forms at a great many levels of abstraction. They include conceptions of relationships;

frameworks that allow for categorizing on qualitative as well as quantitative dimensions; criteria against which to assess the significance of objects or ideas; and constructs that create new unities out of disparate parts. The concept of metaperspectives can be illustrated through a simple analogy. If four pieces of fruit—an apple, an orange, a pear, and a peach—are placed on a table, specialists in each of those varieties may readily describe their differences. Their very existence as separate entities invites that discrimination, given the predilections of western thought toward specialization and analysis. If, however, those four entities are collected into a basket, our specialists must shift their perspectives to recognize that a new entity is created: a fruit basket. This is a higher order construction, synthesizing into one construct the common attributes of the four entities. The sheer existence of the basket creates order—or unity—out of four disparate yet related items. The fruit basket represents generalization and synthesis, processes that can and should be developed through general education.

While much work needs to be done to document the character and function of organizing constructs in complex adult thought, it is nonetheless possible to use the Dewey, Piaget, and Perry formulations in a model for general education. Accordingly, traditional academic disciplines may be seen as individual "perspectives" on a horizontal axis, each with its own base of knowledge and methodology. Along the vertical axis would be, among others, the metaperspectives by which principles, assumptions, or organizing structures in those disciplines can be extrapolated, reclassified, compared, and contrasted with each other. Thus, one "metaperspective" might serve to organize the types of methodologies used by the various disciplines; a second might classify the preferred level of analysis; a third might be the quantitative-qualitative gradation; and others might serve to organize any number of other transdisciplinary variables (see Fig. 1).

A general education model using this scheme would be concept based (or problem based) rather than discipline based. It would specify certain concepts or problems to be examined from multiple perspectives. The model is inherently interdisciplinary in that the assumptions and tools of various relevant disciplines will be utilized as different perspectives on the same concept or problem. The model is interactive, that is, it does not just call for a one-way flow of information into the minds of students; rather it insists that students act upon that information and construct ways of organizing it. This is essential in order to stimulate cognitive development.

This approach parallels Piaget [6, pp. 342–45], Perry [10], and Kitchener and King [8] who recognize that movement from one developmental stage into a more advanced stage is not simply a function of additional information. Rather, such movement involves new ways of organizing and processing information. As mentioned earlier, the mastery of relativistic thought, in Perry's terms, implies the use of metaperspectives—that is, the application of organizing schemes to existing or attainable information. The use of metaperspectives cannot be taught by delivering them as information. Rather, students must be encouraged to construct them. The leading method for enabling students to do

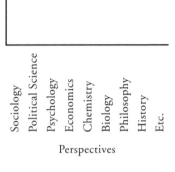

1. Major Disciplinary Assumptions
2. Major Units (Levels) of Analysis
3. Preferred Form of Experimentation
4. Preferred Methods of Data Collection
5. Preferred Methods of Data Analysis
6. Rules of Evidence for Asserting Fact
7. Relevance to Specific Problem
8. Definition of Relevant Concepts

Metaperspectives*

Perspectives

Sociology / Political Science / Psychology / Economics / Chemistry / Biology / Philosophy / History / Etc.

*These are suggested, not exhaustive.

FIGURE 1. Sample of Relativistic Analysis Pertinent to Understanding the Disciplines

so is to confront them with disparate or even incompatible elements of information; this causes the students to address the discrepancy. This process induces disequilibrium, an uncomfortable psychological condition that stimulates efforts to regain equilibrium. As often as not, and in accordance with Piaget's observations about disequilibrium, the most effective resolution is to invent a higher order construction, as in the fruit basket analogy. Acquiring the habit of responding in this way is a central characteristic of movement from one developmental stage to the next.

A considerable amount of attention has been given to the concept of sequentiality in stage development theories, not only by their proponents but also by their critics. The assumption most widely held by proponents is that development from one stage to the next can be stimulated only by causing individuals to engage in cognitive operations that are characteristic of the next most immediate stage of development. A rival hypothesis is that disequilibrium *of any sort* will prompt stage development. It is at least arguably true that Piaget held this latter view. If this latter view is correct, then the model described herein will be of utility regardless of the level of cognitive development brought by students to the course. The introduction of multiple perspectives is easily as instrumental in moving students from dualism to multiplicity as it is in moving students from multiplicity to relativism. Although the ultimate goal of the model is to aid the student's cognitive development toward reasoned action grounded in relativistic thought, movement from any stage to the next is certainly acceptable progress.

In what follows, we attempt to illustrate the application of this set of principles by expliciting a model that emphasizes the process of education and that can be used with various types of content or subject matter. For purposes of specificity, we have chosen social scientific material to illustrate the model;

however, its applicability in the sciences and humanities is equally viable [9], and its true promise resides in its use in bridging the three major divisions of knowledge.

Interdisciplinary Model of General Education

This interdisciplinary model has several distinctive attributes: (1) it reflects a skills-oriented approach to teaching; (2) it may be applied to a wide range of topics; (3) it familiarizes students with methodologies from the social sciences and the humanities; and (4) it provides a mechanism that (a) permits students to reflect upon the material and their approaches to it and (b) underscores the fact that conclusions in the field of serious scholarship must be regarded as provisional, even though subsequent behavior may be influenced and directed by those conclusions.

The skills component of the model emphasizes generic skills, that is, those skills that support all forms of critical thinking, such as identifying the structure of arguments and identifying and utilizing assumptions that are critical to the reasoning process of posing and solving problems. These skills are emphasized because they transcend disciplinary boundaries. For instance, if we wish to examine the political process of electing a president, several disciplines including political science, history, sociology, psychology, and economics would be relevant. Since each of these disciplines utilizes specific tools, common analysis and interpretation may not be readily apparent. If, however, we question ambiguity and search for alternative assumptions, we may discover, for example, that some economic forces and certain psychological motivations may actually be closely analogous and may figure similarly in influencing voter behavior.

In any given course the generic skills to be emphasized must be predetermined by the instructors according to their program and educational objectives.[6] The identification of a specific set of skills permits both students and faculty to focus on the importance of, and the methods of, integrating content from different disciplines. More specifically, the emphasis on generic skills requires the learners to question the solutions achieved by particular disciplinary approaches.

The emphasis on skills serves several functions: (1) development of problem-posing and problem-solving capacity; (2) acquisition of a sense of confidence that conclusions can be achieved or, at least, that intelligent questions can be raised; (3) mastery of the ability to apply and evaluate specific disciplinary methodologies; (4) development of a capacity to identify and evaluate different value patterns that influence the reasoning process; and (5) encouragement of learners to abstract and generalize from specific findings to a higher order of knowledge (conceptualization), perhaps even to the level of being able to organize several orders of concepts. The skills should also lead the learners to develop a habit of mind that is capable of dispassionate analysis.

At this point we believe a short digression is necessary to explain why we emphasize skill development so vigorously. Certainly we agree that knowledge acquisition is an essential component of cognitive development, but simply identifying the importance of knowledge begs the question about "what" knowledge is essential. The very movement toward greater specialization clearly indicates that few of us have the capability to comprehend the depth and breadth of even one discipline without considering whether we can comprehend the intricacies of multiple disciplines. This fact makes all of us very dependent upon "experts." Yet, if we permit ourselves and the "experts" to develop myopia as a result of increasing specialization, the "expert" conclusions may become increasingly one-dimensional and, therefore, increasingly divorced from reality. To protect against this potential, the general education thrust should be designed to equip learners with the ability to probe into the domain of the "experts" and identify fundamental assumptions and processes. The probing capability is enabled by the acquisition of generic skills. Consequently, it is the learning of skills and gaining of confidence in their utilization that will address the aims of general education and in the process foster greater cognitive development. It is highly likely that with this model students will acquire a better appreciation of the changing nature of knowledge and the dynamics of observer interactivity with that which is observed.

To return to the specifics of the model, the content or knowledge component of this design provides the subject matter upon which the skills will be developed and practiced. This component should be inherently worth knowing and of relevance to at least two disciplines. In addition, the content should be chosen to permit the instructor and learners not only to understand the nature of the problem, but also to appreciate how concepts from different disciplines can interact in the pursuit of problem resolution.

The content component differs from the skill component in that the content can be altered to fit the needs of the instructors, students, or institution, whereas once the program has identified the generic skills it wishes to address in general education, the development of these skills can be addressed with whatever content is actually chosen. The content, although inherently important, is primarily the vehicle with which the skills are taught.

Accordingly, the instructor must identify some concepts that are (1) salient in understanding the problem and (2) of interest to more than one discipline. Once defined, these "salient concepts" become the ideas around which the course content and skill development processes are organized. For instance, if we choose health care delivery systems as our content, we can identify "power" as one of our "salient concepts" and can examine such aspects as the economists' concern about the control of resources, the psychologists' interest in the effects of power on human behavior, the sociologists' interest in class-related power structures, and the political scientists' concern about government power.

Studying these "salient concepts" from multiple perspectives is an integral part of the process through which general education is accomplished. The mechanics of the integration will be achieved by explicitly defining each "salient concept" from the perspective of each discipline involved in the course. Through these definitions the instructors and students must come to grips with the disequilibrium that follows from the discrepancies between the disciplines. This coping process should flesh out the different value perspectives and concerns of the different disciplines and force the learning process into another stage of integration. For example, from an economics perspective the conflicting desires to maximize sellers' profits and minimize consumers' prices will force the providers of health care to make what economists consider to be proper allocative decisions. A sociologist may observe, however, that class distinctions prohibit some people from acquiring a fair share of health care. This sociological view may suggest that we consider altering our health care delivery system from dominant private interests into some form of public or social medicine.

Admittedly the example is superficial, yet it suggests that by identifying some interdisciplinary "salient concepts" one is forced to deal with the assumptions and modes of reasoning present in the different disciplines. In some cases the approach of one discipline will support that of another, but in others the approaches may conflict or bear an orthogonal relationship to each other. In any case, however, delving into the different approaches to the "salient concepts" can only enrich one's understanding of a problem. Furthermore, instances of conflict between the implications of disparate perspectives may be exceedingly useful in promoting the construction of metaperspectives (see Fig. 2). It is precisely this conflict that will induce the disequilibrium necessary to prompt cognitive development, a notion explicit in Piaget, implicit in the Perry scheme, and born out by research conducted by Petr [12], Althoff [1], Fuller [5], and others.

In this interdisciplinary model, the process by which the integration is achieved necessitates a two-level approach. The first level focuses upon the development and understanding of both the "salient concepts" and the skills that are to be utilized in evaluating these concepts. These tasks can be accomplished by exercising the generic skills in examining the "salient concepts." This allows the student to see the importance of both as tools for interacting with the problem. For example, although "power" is a concept relevant to virtually all the social sciences, each discipline has its own definitions. By contrasting the ambiguities and assumptions of those definitions, students can understand and practice the skill of clarification and build higher order constructions that accommodate the discrepancies. In other words, through this examination process the student will gather a list of definitions of "power" according to each discipline and can construct a composite understanding of "power" that is consistent with the disciplines under consideration. Care should be exercised to remember that these definitions are provisional and professors teaching at this level should focus primarily upon problem posing rather than certainty and conclusiveness. This recognition will accommodate students functioning at a lower stage of cognitive development.

The second level centers on a more thorough integration of the different perspectives identified by the definitions of the "salient concepts" as seen by the different disciplines involved. Since the first level has introduced the realization that the disciplines approach specific content from different perspectives, this level can attack statements, essays, and so on, written on the content (e.g., health care delivery) from each of the disciplines under study. Students will be

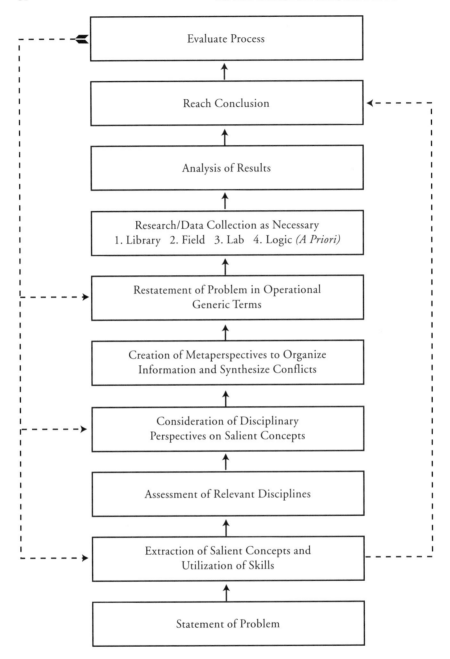

FIGURE 2. Process for Interdisciplinary Study of a Given Problem

confronted with some apparent contradictions and disagreements, which they must then attempt to resolve with the use of the skills developed in the first level. For instance, an economist may argue that private payment of health care will ensure quality because personal motivations to be "best" will result in more patients and profits for both doctors and hospitals. History, however, informs us that medicine has experienced significant degrees of governmental influence and regulation. Can we examine these two positions to determine whether legitimate reasons exist for the influence and regulation by government? Furthermore, can we integrate the disciplines by examining health care systems with the "salient concepts" as seen through the perspective of one discipline while holding the definitions from the other disciplines constant? For example, if we assume that low income groups simply cannot afford adequate medical care or that medical research and development may produce some significant negative side effects, then some forms of regulation of medical care may be considered desirable. In both of these cases there is the question of whether the competitive mechanism of demand and supply is the best process by which to allocate medical care. In short, we may discover that medical care is a social good that is not properly allocated in a private, competitive market. If so, then maintaining medical care delivery in private hands may deny some people access to medical care and eventually influence the distribution of power within the society. Confronting this prospect should, at the very least, stimulate a search for more creative solutions to the problem of equitable health care delivery. The process of searching, more than the process of finding, is exceedingly important in stimulating cognitive development in Piaget's observations about disequilibrium and in Dewey's conception of knowledge as a process.

By combining inputs from more than one discipline, students can challenge conclusions and eventually work toward a more comprehensive understanding of the problem at hand. If students achieve this level of sophistication, they have moved into the stage of relativism as described by Perry. Further, through manipulation of the different definitions and assumptions, students should eventually be able to reach a conclusion that moves them from blind acceptance of one particular point of view to a position of reasoned judgment that Perry associates with the stage he labels "commitment" [10, pp. 153–76]. At this stage of the model we expect the students to articulate reasoned judgments that they, at least presently, are willing to defend against questions and concerns raised from the perspectives of at least one other discipline.

Throughout the model, the "process" of challenging must occur. As implied in the discussion of the model, the emphasis upon skills necessitates that students respond actively to the content under examination. Students should be required to subject every inference to examination with the generic skills and the rules of evidence espoused by the different disciplines. Once students show an inclination to make reasoned judgments, however, another level of challenge is essential to achieve the full integrative effect of the model; that is, when a conclusion is reached, it must be accepted as tentative. Upon acceptance of the tentative nature of one's conclusion, the instructor and students are ready to act upon, or at least willing to consider, systematic reexamination of the conclusion, thus achieving the full meaning of reflective thought. More specifically, the reexamination process, depicted by the broken lines in Figure 2, raises the following questions.

1. Were the "salient concepts" the most important factors upon which to focus attention given the content (health care delivery) that was chosen?
2. Could our understanding of the issue be improved by changing or by adding concepts?
3. Have the most fundamental and salient assumptions been examined, that is, can we more clearly understand differences by ferreting out other value conflicts inherent in the issue?
4. Could the skills have been applied in a different manner, thereby influencing the nature of the original conclusion?

Through this reexamination process students are alerted to the importance of remaining open to new ideas and avenues of approach that are essential to understanding and appreciating inferences. Although the model thus far is aimed at helping students arrive at solid conclusions, the reexamination mechanism provides the warning device that can either identify some critical elements that were ignored in reaching the original conclusion or discover new information that forces reexamination of that conclusion. In essence the model describes a learning process that never completely achieves closure. Rather, the model emphasizes the importance and methods of searching for good, substantial conclusions, but admits that in a world that possesses a myriad of goals, any one conclusion is subject to change as new information is developed or as perspectives shift.

Clearly, one reason why legitimate alternative conclusions may exist is the existence of different value systems—different assumptions about what is important. Herein lies another aspect of the utility of this model for the humanities. Through reexamination, students must identify conflicting value systems and subject them to evaluation. By scrutinizing the potential positive and negative consequences of each set of assumptions, students may start to appreciate why reasonable people disagree. This process of scrutinizing should aid students' understanding that differing conclusions have varying kinds of consequences, and that we must reckon with these consequences prior to accepting or advocating a conclusion.

The resemblance of this model to the work of Dewey should now be evident. In his *Experience and Education* Dewey wrote:

> Anything which can be called a study, whether arithmetic, history, geography, or one of the natural sciences, must be derived from materials which at the outset fall within the scope of ordinary life-experience. . . . Finding material for learning is only the first step. The next step is the progressive development of what is already experienced into a fuller and richer and more organized form, a form that gradually approximates that in which subject-matter is

presented to the skilled, mature person. . . . It thus becomes the office of the educator to select those things within the range of existing experience that have the promise and potentiality of presenting new problems which by stimulating new ways of observation and judgment will expand the area of further experience. [4, pp. 73–75]

Implementation of the Model

The interdisciplinary general education model could be implemented at the freshman-sophomore level prior to any serious pursuit of specialization by the students or it could be taught at a junior-senior level as a capstone type of course wherein the differences in the definitions of specific concepts will be readily apparent. The primary intent of the authors is to establish the utility of the first option for two reasons: (1) the generic skills are applicable throughout a college experience and thereafter, and (2) a solid interdisciplinary foundation hopefully will provide students not only with an understanding of how and why disciplines enhance subsequent study, but also with a defense mechanism against the myopia that may insinuate as a result of specialization.

If we wish to be heroic in our expectations, we advocate the use of the model in the freshman year because through experiencing a program designed around the model, students will be encouraged and trained to be better students. Through the emphasis upon skills and active learning, students will be equipped to ask their instructors more probing questions. In like manner, as the students probe for more complete insights into a problem, instructors may be motivated to rethink their approach to teaching. Instead of focusing primarily upon knowledge transfer, instructors may turn their attention to the higher levels of cognitive activity: analysis, synthesis, and evaluation. Of course, this prediction assumes that a substantial percentage of freshmen experience the interdisciplinary general education program.

Although we believe this model could be applied to a course that focused on one particular content area, such as health care delivery, the full implementation of the model to achieve the aims of general education and the highest levels of cognitive development implies a continuing commitment of at least one course per term for two or more years. Our reasons for advocating this time commitment can be easily summarized by indicating that the model includes discussion of at least two disciplines and an examination of issues from those disciplines with generic skills. Furthermore, the skills themselves must be learned sufficiently well so that they can become essential tools in evaluating the substantive arguments presented in defense of different positions. Finally as Perry observes [11, p. 89], transitions between stages may take more than a year.

Realistically, we expect that the implementation of one course per term is politically much easier than a major change in curriculum. Thus, if freshmen and sophomores were taught a course suggested by our model once per term, advancement to the higher cognitive levels could be continued by inserting elements of reinforcement into other courses in the curriculum.

Finally, we want to emphasize that the model will be a success only if students are required to engage in active participation. Students must constantly be required to think, challenge, infer, and synthesize disparate elements of information. The classroom should contain a healthy blend of Socratic techniques and explications. If the students are permitted to remain passive, they are likely to gain an awareness of the significance of the interdisciplinary model, but they will not gain the competence necessary to integrate the skills and the concepts. Piaget's concept of disequilibrium is indispensable, whether or not it runs contrary to an educator's genuine interest in making subject matter easily digestible.

This program is not one that assumes that learning is easy. The structure of this program will demand serious commitment from both faculty and students. The faculty must pursue faculty development whereby they learn about other disciplines and, more importantly, work with other faculty to articulate their respective disciplines. The "habit of mind" advocated throughout this discussion would influence not only the structure of a general education program, but also the approach that a faculty member may use in teaching a typical course in a discipline. Specifically, faculty must agree on content areas and "salient concepts." The faculty must also develop and agree upon the definitions of these "salient concepts" and how these definitions interact to suggest a conclusion that differs from one suggested by any one discipline. The students, meanwhile, must read, think, and write. Especially if we teach the program at the freshman level, the students must read to gain familiarity with the content area; they must think to challenge the contrasting views they read; and finally, they must write to clarify their ideas and subject them to examination by the faculty.

In essence, we have proposed a model of interdisciplinary general education that we believe will enrich the faculty, students, and university. It is applicable in greater or lesser measure to all disciplines, but it moves the debate away from disciplinary sampling that results from departmental political struggles and toward a curriculum based upon how students learn. It need not preclude disciplinary sampling, nor argue against disciplinary majors. Rather, it may be incorporated as an augmentation of the general education program, and as such, approach in a new and promising way some of the goals traditionally presumed to inhere in the concept of a liberal arts education.

Endnotes

1. In actuality, these generic skills are the scientific skills utilized by the disciplines, but stripped of their discipline-specific identity. For example, in assessing the relationships of facts, assumptions, and conclusions, we must understand how ambiguous language, alternative assumptions, fallacious reasoning, questionable use of data, and neglected perspectives may significantly alter the conclusion in a problem-solving effort.

2. We would also hold that what follows might be of significant value in the delivery of courses that are expressly "disciplinary," given that most disciplines embrace differing schools of thought, permitting a fertile framework for the exercising of generic skills.

3. The Perry conception is not strictly equivalent in meaning nor origin with Piaget's concept of "decentering," in that Perry's concept is rooted in Polanyi's notion of "personal knowledge," a concept more philosophical than empirical. Despite the difference in derivation, however, the two concepts bear a strong conceptual resemblance to each other, and many of their implications for instruction are the same.

4. This concept is similarly illustrated by Simmel's well-known analogy of the study of a painting. Different vantage points allow for different perceptions and different types of analysis, but it is essential to integrate them in order to achieve an elaborated understanding of the art work.

5. It is not clear that Perry would disagree with this assertion, since his interest in human development clearly involves questions that go beyond cognition itself.

6. Our experience suggests that it is not realistic to emphasize more than two or three generic skills in any one course. They may be selected from among those mentioned in this report or other pedagogical works, or identified through a priori logic.

References

1. Althoff, J. "Cognitive Developmental Outcomes from Field Experience Instruction: A Theoretical Model and Recent Research." Paper presented at the annual meeting of the Society for Field Experience Education, Los Angeles, California, 1976.
2. Dewey, J. *Democracy and Education.* New York: Macmillan, 1916.
3. ———. *How We Think.* New York: D. C. Heath, 1933.
4. ———. *Experience and Education.* New York: Macmillan, 1938.
5. Fuller, R. "Coherence for a Core." Paper presented at the annual meeting of the Association for Integrative Studies, Grand Rapids, Michigan, 1981.
6. Inhelder, B., and J. Piaget. *The Growth of Logical Thinking from Childhood to Adolescence.* New York: Basic Books, 1958.
7. King, P. M. "Taking a Stand With Yourself: Making Commitments in a Relativistic World." Unpublished manuscript, University of Minnesota, 1977.
8. Kitchener, K. S., and P. M. King. "Reflective Judgement: Concepts of Justification and Their Relationship to Age and Education." *Journal of Applied Developmental Psychology.* 2 (Summer 1981), 89–116.
9. Magada, V., and M. Moore. "The Humanities Cluster College at Bowling Green: Its Middle Years." *Liberal Education,* 62 (March 1976), 100–12.
10. Perry, W. *Forms of Intellectual and Ethical Development in the College Years.* New York: Holt, Rinehart, and Winston, 1968.
11. ———. "Cognitive and Ethical Growth: The Making of Meaning." In *The Modern American College,* edited by A. Chickering, pp. 76–116. San Francisco: Jossey-Bass, 1981.
12. Petr, J. "Social Science Education from a Developmental Perspective." Paper presented at the annual meeting of the Association for Integrative Studies, Washington, D. C., 1980.
13. Phenix, P. H. "Dewey's War on Dualism—Its Bearing on Today's Education Problems." In *Dewey on Education,* edited by R. D. Archambault, pp. 39–51. New York: Random House, 1966.
14. Piaget, J., and B. Inhelder. *The Psychology of the Child.* New York: Basic Books, 1969.
15. Piaget, J., and A Szeminska. *The Child's Conception of Number.* New York: Humanities Press, 1962.

Interdisciplinary Curriculum Development

William H. Newell

The Promise of Interdisciplinarity

I had the opportunity last year to sit down with alumni of the interdisciplinary University Studies / Weekend College Program at Wayne State University and ask them what they had gotten out of their education. Many of their responses seemed to reflect the **quality** of their education, not its interdisciplinary nature. They spoke of analytical thinking, critical thinking, how to write and do research and organize their thoughts, and how to communicate with others. They agreed that they had developed a deeper understanding of the world around them, an understanding that came from repeatedly asking "why?" instead of regurgitating memorized answers. In short, they gave some of the same responses we would look for from students who had received a high-quality discipline-based liberal arts education. Students in other interdisciplinary programs may emphasize clarity and precision in reading, thinking, and writing, or on how their assumptions about themselves and their world have been challenged, but the general conclusion is the same—interdisciplinary courses provide an effective vehicle for promoting traditional liberal arts skills.

The students at Wayne State also mentioned the spirit of mutual respect that developed between faculty and students in the program, and even between students of widely divergent backgrounds. Several revealed that life-long friendships had grown out of the seminars. These outcomes seem to reflect primarily the **ambiance** of the program, though interdisciplinary courses that stress the complementary role of diverse disciplinary perspectives certainly set a tone of respect for diversity which promotes that ambiance. While interdisciplinary courses can be taught in a formal, traditional manner, they lend themselves nicely to more student-centered, interactive teaching styles associated with progressive education and its outcomes.[1]

Some of the outcomes they mentioned, however, seem to flow directly from the **interdisciplinary** nature of the program. They reported being able to "see all sides of the story," to appreciate another's perspective of the same situation. They felt able to evaluate the testimony of experts, knowing that "they don't have the final word." And they had confidence in their ability to write on a wide range of subjects. These outcomes are grounded in the lesson from interdisciplinary courses that each discipline has a valuable but limited insight into the issue at hand, as are the demystification of experts and the feeling of empowerment to examine issues in their full complexity.

Results from longitudinal comparisons of students in the interdisciplinary

Newell, William H. "Interdisciplinary Curriculum Development." Issues in Integrative Studies 8 (1990), 69–86. *Reprinted with permission.*

Paracollege with their counterparts in traditional majors at St. Olaf College show that students in that interdisciplinary program showed more tolerance of ambiguity or paradox—in fact, they seem to seek out ambiguity.[2] These findings are confirmed by students in other interdisciplinary programs who show more receptivity to new ideas or who move beyond tolerance to a celebration of diversity.

Beyond these outcomes, the questionnaires completed by directors of interdisciplinary programs for *Interdisciplinary Undergraduate Programs: A Directory*[3] provided anecdotal evidence that their students show:

More sensitivity to ethical issues (stemming, no doubt, from the humanities perspective included in courses traditionally limited to the social or natural sciences)

Ability to synthesize or integrate (from the distinguishing feature of interdisciplinary courses, that they pull together limited disciplinary insights into a more holistic understanding)

Enlarged perspectives or horizons, reduced privatism, and greater awareness of communal or public issues (from the topical, issue-oriented focus of most interdisciplinary courses)

More creative, original, or unconventional thinking (perhaps from the difficult task of integration)

More humility or listening skills (as students become conscious of the partial validity of *any* perspective including their own and how it can be enriched by learning from other perspectives)

Sensitivity to bias, whether it be disciplinary, political, or religious (probably from probing the assumptions underlying disciplinary perspectives)

Interdisciplinary courses have advantages for institutions beyond these educational outcomes for students:

The topical or issue-oriented approach of most interdisciplinary courses is inherently **more interesting** to students than survey courses or introductions to disciplines. For students who are often resentful of required general education courses, the motivation of an interdisciplinary approach may be invaluable.

Interdisciplinary courses can be designed to provide an efficient **introduction to the disciplines** themselves by showing how each discipline arrives at its distinctive perspective on the issue.

Interdisciplinary programs can provide an opportunity for administrators faced with tenured faculty in underutilized departments to **reallocate faculty resources** to where there is more student demand.

Interdisciplinary teaching offers an exciting form of **faculty development** since it necessarily stretches faculty, demanding that they come to grips with new perspectives that challenge long-held assumptions from their own disciplinary training.[4]

These desired outcomes must be kept clearly in mind as interdisciplinary courses and programs are developed. Different strategies for organizing and teaching interdisciplinary courses have different educational outcomes. While it may only be of semantic interest whether a particular course design is "truly" interdisciplinary by any one definition, its educational outcomes are what ultimately determine the value of the course. The recommendations that follow for developing interdisciplinary courses and programs are designed to produce courses which fulfill the promises held out above.

Interdisciplinary Courses

Definition of Interdisciplinarity

What I have in mind are courses that "critically draw upon two or more disciplines and . . . lead to an integration of disciplinary insights."[5] While the discussion that follows assumes that interdisciplinary courses are organized around a topic, the suggestions apply with equal force to courses organized around a theme, problem, issue, region, cultural or historical period, institution, figure, or idea.[6]

Breadth of Topic

An integrative course "covers" reductionist perspectives (typically disciplines or schools of thought) the way a disciplinary course covers subject matter. Topics need to be quite focused in order to allow sufficient time for each perspective in a 10–15 week course. For example, an integrative social science course might focus on "U.S. Unemployment," drawing on the disciplines of economics, history, political science, psychology, and sociology to examine the causes of unemployment and its "solutions." Such a course might start with a week on some provocative pieces (e.g., articles, films, short stories) on unemployment that "hook" the students' interest. It might then spend one to two weeks per discipline on the insights afforded by each perspective, and then conclude with a week devoted to synthesizing them into a more holistic perspective. Similarly, an interdisciplinary humanities might examine "abortion" from the perspectives of philosophy, religion, history, and literature, and an interdisciplinary natural science course might focus on "the energy crisis" from the perspectives of chemistry, physics, geology, and biology. (See the distinctions among multidisciplinary, pluridisciplinary, crossdisciplinary, and interdisciplinary in the section of this article on *Indicators of Levels of Integration*.)

There is a temptation in designing interdisciplinary general education courses to cover too much subject matter. One might prefer the topic of "U.S. Urban Problems," for example, to the seemingly narrower course on unemployment. However, if the course is to cover even the most major of urban problems—housing, race, education, government, crime, renewal, as well as unemployment—there will be no time left in the semester to explore more than one perspective on each topic. What appeared at first to be the narrower course on unemployment turns out to be much broader in terms of perspectives presented. Similarly, an interdisciplinary humanities course on "contemporary moral issues" (instead of "abortion") or an interdisciplinary natural science course on "energy" (instead of "the energy crisis") might appear preferable, but each would find itself over-extended as well. As long as an interdisciplinary course focuses on a topic of inherent interest to students and faculty, it is unlikely that the topic will be too narrow.

Instead of attempting to present the most important concepts and theories of each discipline in an interdisciplinary introduction to the social sciences, humanities, or natural sciences, it is preferable to give students a "feel" for each discipline by learning how it attacks a single problem. That way, students come away with some comparative sense of the disciplines. Since it is impossible anyway to include **all** major concepts and theories (even in a disciplinary course), the topical approach provides a rationale for selection that is apparent to students as well as faculty. Coverage is complete because every discipline's perspective is presented.

Interdisciplinary courses tend to appear fragmented and incoherent to students as the term progresses because they shift from one disciplinary perspective to another. Teachers have a special obligation in interdisciplinary courses to keep the logic of the course organization in front of the students. The narrower and more tightly defined the topic, the easier it is for students and teacher alike to keep track of where the course is heading.

The Role of Disciplines in an Interdisciplinary Course

It is important for interdisciplinarians to keep in mind the value of the disciplines. It is easy to dismiss them as arbitrary or artificial ways of dividing up reality, ignoring the extent to which they offer alternative ways of viewing reality, each grounded in a worldview that has demonstrated its fruitfulness over time for a range of topics studied by an on-going group of scholars. The disciplines can provide valuable insight into the complexity of an issue as a whole, not just into different pieces of that whole. To ignore the disciplines as adisciplinary courses attempt is to ignore the accumulated wisdom of different approaches to understanding as well as the specific insights they afford.

Disciplines and not substantive facts are the raw materials of an interdisciplinary course. Students need to understand not only what each discipline has to say about the topic but *why* it says it. In the course above on "U.S. Unemployment," for example, students need to confront not only the arguments of a Milton Friedman but the supply and demand curves lying behind them, and they need to probe those supply and demand curves to see the assumptions in which they are grounded. Similarly, students in the course on "abortion" need to understand *why* different religions take the positions they do on abortion; in the course on "the energy crisis," they need to understand *why* power plants are inherently inefficient. Instead of simply initiating students into a single disciplinary craft or guild, teaching them to accept the "truth" of that discipline's perspective, we need to help students appreciate the powerful contributions of the disciplines at the same time that they come to recognize their inherent limitations and biases. There is a remoteness and detachment from the disciplinary activity when we merely read about it, and an incomparable feel for that activity when we experience it. Students come to understand the scientific perspective, for example, much better when they put on scientific lenses than when they read the pronouncements of scientists.

Integration

I used to think of integration as analogous to completing a jigsaw puzzle (when disciplinary insights are complementary, as they often are in the natural sciences) or as a problem in identifying and choosing among assumptions underlying disciplinary insights (when they conflict, as they often do in the social sciences). In the course on "the energy crisis," the jigsaw analogy might fit, in which geology explains the location and extent of fossil fuels, physics explains how their energy is released in a power plant, and chemistry and biology explain the environmental consequences of the pollutants given off in the process. In the course on "abortion," one might argue that the integrative task is to choose among competing ethical or moral assumptions. Over the years I have come to realize, however, that the external reality scholars confront is often complex, variegated, and contradictory, so that mutually incompatible assumptions can all be "correct." Human beings, for example—the building block of the social sciences and the focus of much of the humanities—are rife with internal contradictions; consequently assumptions of freedom and determinism, for example, may both be correct at the same time for a particular individual in a particular situation. I now see integration in interdisciplinary study as essentially holistic thinking, in which the different facets of a complex reality exposed through different disciplinary lenses are combined into a new whole that is larger than its constituent parts, that cannot be reduced to the separate disciplinary insights from which it emerged. Whether we call it integration, synthesis, or synergy, this process is more organic than mechanical, involving coordination as well as cooperation among disciplinary perspectives. It requires an act of creative imagination, a leap from the simplified perspectives that give the disciplines their power to a more holistic perspective of a richer, more complex whole. That leap is motivated by a dissatisfaction with the partial insights available through individual disciplines.

Models of integration such as systems theory, structuralism, and marxism are examples of the standard repertoire available to the interdisciplinarian. Neophyte interdisciplinarians may be well advised to study these models for their heuristic value. Yet there is some advantage to moving beyond well-established strategies for integration, since they tend to lose their responsiveness to disciplinary insights as they develop into a new school of thought with an orthodoxy of its own. While there are no firm guidelines for developing one's own integrative strategy, since it is an essentially creative act, there are a number of books that suggest techniques for promoting creativity that may prove beneficial to interdisciplinarians.

Indicators of Levels of Integration

Ever since *Interdisciplinarity: Problems of Teaching and Research in Universities* was published by the OECD in 1972, the extent of integration in a course has been indicated by the labels "multidisciplinary" (the serial presentation of disciplines with no integration attempted), "pluridisciplinary" (disciplinary insights into the topic are compared or contrasted but still not integrated), "cross-disciplinary" (one discipline is applied to the characteristic subject matter of another, yielding new insights but not an integration of the insights of both disciplines, and providing a new but not a larger perspective) and "interdisciplinary" (the insights of the disciplines are integrated into a larger, more holistic perspective). For a more complete discussion of the various uses of these terms since 1972, see Julie Klein's *Interdisciplinarity: History, Theory, and Practice.*[7] Less apparent from the literature is that there are characteristic patterns of course development and design indicative of each of these levels, even when faculty from different disciplines collaborate.[8]

In multidisciplinary courses, faculty tend to work separately on "their" part of the course. They tend to see the topic only from the perspective of their discipline, and that perspective is unaltered by the course development process. Indeed, the course topic itself may be grounded in the perspective of a single discipline (perhaps that of the faculty member who proposed the topic). There is no section at the end of the course reserved for integration, and any integration is undertaken by the students without faculty assistance. The methodologies and epistemologies underlying the disciplines are unexamined, perhaps even unstated.

In pluridisciplinary courses, a section at the end of the course becomes "ours," where faculty involved in the course can talk to each other even though no explicit integration takes place. Faculty members begin to understand each other's perspective, though their own remains unaltered. There is still no explicit examination of epistemology or methodology, though it may become implicit in the discussion at the end of the course.

In cross-disciplinary courses, faculty interactions follow a dominant/subordinate pattern and one faculty member prevails. There is a conclusion to the course resulting from the new insights, but still no integration because only one perspective is evident.

In an interdisciplinary course, faculty tend to work together as much as alone, interacting instead of merely working jointly. The topic may well have shifted as the course evolved, and faculty perspectives on it have been altered. In the integration section at the end of the course, faculty work with students in forging a new synthesis, which results in a larger, more holistic perspective. In order to bring about that synthesis, the worldview and some of its underlying assumptions of each discipline are brought to light and made explicit.

Implicit in these indicators are some strategies for faculty participating in team-course design. In addition to some modest expertise in their discipline if not in the topic, faculty must come into the course development process with an openness to hearing what other faculty say about the topic from the perspective of their discipline, and with enough humility to recognize that much of what they thought they knew (and their colleagues back in the department are still sure they know) is at best partial truth if not misleading, distorted, or just plain wrong. Faculty should be representatives of their disciplines in the sense of a senator or congressperson who embodies the value and local wisdom of her or his constituency but who listens to the debate, studies the issues, and votes according to his or her own judgment. They should not emulate the member of the House or Senate who takes polls back home on each issue and then votes in Washington the way folks back home want even though they cannot see beyond the horizons of their county. Faculty need to work together on the course, representing their discipline by virtue of having been trained in it but not fighting on its behalf.

Once individual faculty members have had sufficient experience designing and team-teaching interdisciplinary courses, they should be ready to "go it alone." Beyond the obvious requirement of commitment to holistic thinking and the interdisciplinary process, two tests of readiness stand out. One is their command of the perspectives and underlying assumptions of disciplines other than the one(s) in which they received graduate training. Can they present those perspectives not just accurately, but sympathetically, persuasively, and comfortably to their students? Second, are they prepared to guide their students through the integrative process?

Disciplines do not need protection, nor do their pet theories, concepts, and methods. The problem the faculty member faces is not getting enough economics, say, into the course, but figuring out what economics can best contribute to the topic, and how that contribution relates to the contributions of the other disciplines. If there is insufficient time to include the entire theory of pure competition, for instance, in the course, no harm is done. If economics is well represented in the course, so that students come away with a respect for what economists have to say on the topic and some sense of how the economist's insights differ from those of other disciplines[9], those students who find that way of looking at the world congenial will be more inclined to sign up for economics courses (and more likely to pass them) than students who have a mistaken impression of what economics is about. Interdisciplinary courses are the discipline's chance to "strut its stuff"; to learn the discipline, students will have to take a course in that department.

Enforcing Interdisciplinarity

Even the best team-developed interdisciplinary course can degenerate into a disciplinary course when it is taught by one faculty member from one disciplinary perspective. This problem occurs most frequently when a faculty member is "drafted" to teach a section of a required interdisciplinary general education course (though it can appear in any individually-taught interdisciplinary course). In the interests of economic feasibility, these courses are often team-developed but each section is individually taught and the faculty recruited to teach these sections were often not involved in developing the course. While faculty development (discussed below) is essential in preparing these faculty members, it can be supplemented by several structural features:

The different sections should share a common syllabus and readings. Even where a team has designed a "model" course when the requirement was adopted, the faculty actually teaching the course need a specific topic with which they feel comfortable. The process of tailoring the course to their interests ensures that they get some exposure to other perspectives on the topic *and* that their discipline's perspective is represented.

It is also useful to have all sections meet once a week for a common lecture (given by the faculty member with the most expertise on that week's material). Students get some exposure to each discipline's perspective from an adherent of that discipline. The lecture also provides a regular point of contact among sections, giving students and faculty alike the sense that they are part of a larger, cohesive course.

A weekly faculty seminar is invaluable. Faculty teaching different sections of the same course should meet weekly to go over what will go on in section the next week—issues to raise and their order, key questions, educational objectives; faculty take turns leading the seminar, depending on who has the most expertise in that week's material.

Finally, paper topics and examinations should be common to all sections, with grading standards worked out or at least ratified in faculty seminar. The first time around, one faculty member might grade several papers from her or his section, selecting out examples of A, B, C, D, and F papers and circulating them among the other faculty teaching in the course. They would be discussed in faculty seminar before others started grading.

Interdisciplinary Curricula

Factors Promoting Interdisciplinarity

The long-term prospects for an interdisciplinary curriculum are best if it fits logically into the educational mission of the institution. As long as proponents can demonstrate its centrality to the mission, they can defend it in time of budget shortages or periodic curricular restructuring. Otherwise, scarce faculty or financial resources are likely to be reallocated to other programs more attuned to the institution's guiding vision.

Distinct interdisciplinary programs stand a better chance of long-term survival if their faculty have full-time appointments in the program. Faculty whose professional rewards of tenure, salary increases, and promotion emanate from the interdisciplinary program are taking much less of a professional risk to devote the considerable time required to learn other disciplinary perspectives and develop interdisciplinary research agendas. In fact, the interdisciplinary program is well advised to use those professional incentives to promote the interdisciplinary professional development of its faculty; otherwise, they may choose to redefine its interdisciplinary mission at some later date when institutional problems with enrollment or budget create pressure for retrenchment.

Institution-wide interdisciplinary curricula such as a required core of interdisciplinary liberal education courses must borrow faculty from disciplinary departments, so a different long-term strategy is required. Central administrators with responsibility for liberal education must provide sufficient faculty development opportunities over a period of years to create a critical mass of tenured faculty who are experienced in interdisciplinary curriculum development and pedagogy and committed to interdisciplinary education. Some of these faculty need to be widely recognized within the institutions as excellent teachers and scholars to dispel any claim that interdisciplinary courses are of inherently low quality. Others need to be leaders in the institution's governance procedure who can come to the defense of the interdisciplinary curriculum if it is threatened politically.

Administrators need to foster a spirit of innovation in order for interdisciplinary education to thrive. Faculty need to experiment, to take risks; they need to be able to fail with impunity. It takes time to learn how to organize and teach an interdisciplinary course in the context of a particular institution for a particular student body. It is threatening for faculty new to interdisciplinary study to teach outside their area of expertise, to seek help from their colleagues, and to admit to their students that they are co-learners to some extent. It is unsettling for faculty to discover that long-cherished assumptions of their discipline are sometimes misleading if not wrong, and it is harder still to admit it to their colleagues.

Finally, faculty should be encouraged to come to some consensus about the nature of interdisciplinary study (perhaps through the faculty seminars discussed above). Without at least some boundary conditions on what is and is not good interdisciplinary study, it is very difficulty to elicit high quality proposals for interdisciplinary courses and to improve existing interdisciplinary courses. The problem is especially serious for faculty who were not involved in the process of setting up the curriculum and designing the initial courses.

Sequencing

Interdisciplinary courses represent a significant departure from the course structure and style of teaching and learning to which students are typically exposed in high school. They are most likely to accept the unfamiliar roles of faculty and students and the structure of an interdisciplinary course, and embrace its active, critically questioning style of learning, if they are exposed to it in the first semester of their first year in college, when studies indicate that the significant changes normally take place in college students. It is true that the relativistic thinking required in an interdisciplinary course may clash with the concrete thinking of some entering students[10], but interdisciplinary courses are an effective vehicle for moving students through Perry's stages (because they demonstrate the inadequacy of concrete thinking and the necessity of relativistic thinking and commitment), and the first semester of the first year is the time in college when they are most open to new thinking styles. Thus there are important advantages in introducing students to an interdisciplinary curriculum their first semester in college.

Since interdisciplinary study builds directly on the disciplines while offering a holistic counterbalance to the reductionist perspectives they afford, a curriculum that intersperses disciplinary and interdisciplinary courses allows each to build on the strengths of the other. For example, after taking intermediate theory courses in economics, sociology, and political science, students might take interdisciplinary topical courses drawing on those analytical tools; e.g., an interdisciplinary course on modernization (replacing currently offered courses on political modernization, economic development, and the sociology of modernization). With the assistance of interdisciplinary courses, students can place in perspective the disciplinary tools they are acquiring, keeping sight of their limitations as well as their strengths, and assessing their relative contributions to complex issues. Through disciplinary courses, students can extend and refine their command of the analytical tools they bring to an interdisciplinary course, yielding more sophisticated insights into its complex topic.[11] And the slow process of moving students through Perry's scale can be continued, to the benefit of disciplinary as well as interdisciplinary courses.

After students have taken the bulk of their upper-division coursework in a single discipline, steeping themselves in its specialized way of looking at the world, it is important to conclude their undergraduate education with an interdisciplinary course that humanizes their new-found expertise by placing it in a larger context. One effective strategy is to conclude with a senior capstone seminar where students from a variety of disciplinary or professional majors gather to discuss a complex interdisciplinary issue. Topics in the general area of science, technology, values, and society are particularly effective in eliciting insights from the full range of disciplines and professions. Since the students themselves bring the requisite disciplinary expertise to the course, it can be staffed by a single faculty member broadly interested in the topic. Different capstone seminars can be offered by individual faculty members, each on a different topic.

In general, upper-division interdisciplinary courses can gain in sophistication and depth of analysis if they build on any required general education core or if they have disciplinary prerequisites that allow the discussion to move beyond introductory concepts and theories. Disciplinary prerequisites also simplify the task of making explicit the disciplinary worldview and its underlying assumptions. Students are then able, in an upper-division interdisciplinary course, to focus more attention on the challenging process of integration.

Resource Requirements

Interdisciplinary programs, especially institution-wide general education programs of interdisciplinary core courses, necessitate extra initial resources and special administrative structures not required by their disciplinary counterparts. This is *not,* however, because they are more expensive to teach in the long run, but because they require more faculty time to design the courses and prepare to teach them. As discussed above under *Indicators of Levels of Integration,* once faculty have gained the requisite command of other disciplines, they can teach an interdisciplinary course (or their own section of it) by themselves. The ongoing major expense of team-teaching (with more than one faculty member teaching in the same room at the same time) is not required for high quality interdisciplinary courses. On the other hand, special administrative structures *must* be on-going to solicit and evaluate proposals for future courses and to ensure that they are adequately staffed.

Even after faculty committees have invested considerable time in designing an interdisciplinary curriculum and sketching out sample interdisciplinary syllabi in preparation for a faculty vote on a new interdisciplinary program, the demand for extra institutional resources has just begun. The faculty who will be teaching a given interdisciplinary course need to be the ones to select its substantive topic if they are to be expected to put the requisite effort into preparing themselves to teach it. Consequently, syllabi developed during the program approval process must be viewed as purely illustrative models only, and new syllabi will have to be developed by the actual teaching teams. It takes a lot of time to develop a good interdisciplinary course even when working from well-thought-out models. It takes time to negotiate with colleagues from other disciplines over which sub-topics to include under the agreed-upon topic, and which disciplinary concepts and theories are most needed to explore those sub-topics. It takes time to find the appropriate readings, films, exercises, and so forth when working outside the area of one's expertise. The institution needs to provide either released time or summer stipends to faculty preparing these courses, both to free up the requisite faculty time and to send the message to faculty that the administration recognises and values the time it takes to prepare interdisciplinary courses.

Once a teaching team has been assembled and a common syllabus prepared, a major faculty development task remains to prepare faculty to actually teach the course they have developed. Since each faculty member must be prepared to present to her or his own students *all* the disciplinary perspectives in the course (and not just that of his or her own discipline), faculty need both assistance and extra time to develop the requisite grounding in the other disciplines. The most effective way I know to prepare first time interdisciplinarians to teach their own sections of a multisectioned interdisciplinary course is to have them meet weekly in a faculty seminar where they can take turns training each other in their respective disciplines. Such a seminar represents a major intellectual undertaking by faculty and a considerable expenditure of time. To ensure that they can put adequate time and effort into the seminar, it is desirable that it count in their teaching load. (If stipends are offered in lieu of course-load reductions, it must be accompanied by dramatic reduction in committee assignments to free up enough time for faculty to prepare adequately for the seminars.) Two times through an interdisciplinary course is usually sufficient to prepare them to handle discussions without the assistance of the faculty seminar, though at least one veteran would need to continue to work with any new additions to the staff of the course.

The cost to the institution of providing inadequate resources for course and faculty development are predictable and serious. Inadequate preparation time for designing and teaching interdisciplinary courses will result in weak, ineffectually taught courses. In a few years, the faculty as a whole will grow disaffected with what they will have come to see quite rightly as intellectually irresponsible core courses, and the program will be voted out of existence. Not only that, interdisciplinarity itself will probably come to have a bad name on campus ("We tried the interdisciplinary approach already and it didn't work.") and opportunities for future innovations will be lost as well. Faculty frustration with interdisciplinary courses can also be avoided by exposing them to the interdisciplinary literature, which is replete with warnings about strategies that have failed at other institutions as well as tips on ideas that have worked. With the publication of Julie Klein's comprehensive bibliography[12], the scattered and fragmented nature of the literature on interdisciplinary education need no longer force faculty to reinvent interdisciplinary wheels.

Since an interdisciplinary course of necessity falls outside normal administrative structures, interdisciplinary programs require their own coordinator. That person needs access to support staff and enough power to ensure that courses are staffed with appropriate faculty even when department chairs balk at releasing them from departmental teaching duties. That person should also have some input into the promotion and tenure process at the institution-wide level to help balance out departmental assessments that may not take participation in interdisciplinary programs as seriously as departmental teaching or research; otherwise, faculty may feel that the extra expenditure of time and psychic energy required for participation in an interdisciplinary program will not be rewarded (and may even be penalized). For institutional-wide general education programs, that person has to have the stature of a dean or vice-provost, and for large institutions it is a full-time job. It takes someone with considerable stature within the institution to serve as an effective advocate for interdisciplinary programs, protecting them from the inevitable attacks at some point in the future by faculty whose vision of education values a more narrow professionalism. That tension between different visions of education will always be with us. Institutions need to find structural mechanisms to ensure an on-going balance between reductionist and holistic perspectives within the curriculum, much as do individual interdisciplinary courses.

Community

Interdisciplinary courses, with their holistic perspective on complex topics, lend themselves well to the development of living-learning communities, which take a holistic view of students (and faculty) as complex individuals who live as well as learn. Both perspectives emphasize the importance of moving beyond relativistic understanding to commitment. Both stress praxis, the application of classroom theories to real world issues we face in our lives. A program of required interdisciplinary core courses has the potential of contributing to the development of a coherent intellectual community. Students not only have a common vocabulary and set of intellectual skills, but they (and many of the faculty) have confronted a common set of issues within those courses and each has had to develop a personal position that takes the different disciplinary perspectives into account. But the formal curriculum alone cannot create a community. If the ideas, ways of thinking, and sensibilities students (and many faculty) share from these courses are to become connected to the rest of their lives, they must be placed in an environment that facilitates those connections. The institution can do much to promote such a sense of community by focusing its lecture and concert series, residence halls programming, exhibits, and so forth on themes raised in the required core courses. The coordination of these efforts would need to come from the office of the person administering the interdisciplinary program.

Individualized Interdisciplinary Programs

Many so-called interdisciplinary programs are more accurately individualized or self-designed majors that students put together from disciplinary offerings, though they may be used by students to explore an interdisciplinary topic. I conclude with some criteria for evaluating these programs. These criteria overlap with those for other kinds of interdisciplinary programs discussed above, but they are reiterated here for convenience's sake:

Explicit focus. Each student's proposal should have a brief title that captures the essential integrating thread that ties the courses together.

Coherence. Students should provide a well-thought-out rationale that explains why a particular set of courses was selected.

Depth. There should either be a set number of credit hours in upper-division courses required, or they should meet more generic criteria for depth, such as acquisition of higher-order thinking skills, appreciation of the complexity of a discipline, and awareness of its epistemology.

Breadth. Students should be asked to demonstrate that their major is not so narrowly technical that it is inappropriate for a bachelor's degree. They should be encouraged to take courses that offer significantly different perspectives; e.g., English and business, not speech and theater.

Capstone experience. Students should take an interdisciplinary seminar or write an interdisciplinary senior project that gets them to pull together their major.

Interdisciplinary method. Students need an introductory interdisciplinary course that is explicitly designed to prepare them to integrate the courses they take in different departments. It should prepare them to draw effectively and critically on the disciplinary courses in their concentration and to place them in a holistic framework.

Appropriate program title. Truth-in-packaging considerations demand that an institution decide whether it is truly offering a flexible interdisciplinary major or merely an individualized major, and then label it accordingly. Students have enough trouble explaining these majors to prospective graduate schools and employers without being further burdened with an inappropriate label.

Publicity. Even if the institution wishes to keep the program small (or low-visibility for fear of losing the program through departmental turf protection), it is still important to make sure that students, especially nontraditional ones most likely to benefit from the program, are made aware of its existence. On campuses where the program is of particularly high quality, it may be important in terms of campus politics to publicize its successes even though the program may not be able to grow in size.

Student ownership of their education. Students in these programs have a special need to clearly articulate their educational goals for their program and explain how each course within their concentration contributes to those goals.

Administrative location. These programs are most likely to thrive when they are housed administratively in divisions or schools with a commitment to innovation and student-centered education, and that support broad-gauged (if not interdisciplinary) approaches.

Explicit guidelines. Since program directors come and go, written guidelines for preparing proposals (aimed at students) and for evaluating them (aimed at faculty or administrators) provide a valuable institutional memory of the criteria currently in use.

Faculty. Since the perceived caliber of individualized programs rests in the eyes of the faculty at large with the reputation of the faculty sponsoring them, it is important to attract faculty to the program with some stature within the institution. If such faculty are not interested in participating, it would be useful to ask them how the program might be changed to make them interested. Then the program's structure should either be reexamined in the light of their comments, or faculty misperceptions about the program need to be corrected.

Faculty advisory committee. These programs are normally well served by a formal advisory committee that provides oversight as well as review.

Faculty rewards. In most programs, the rewards for faculty are only intrinsic. This is fine as long as the primary institutional emphasis is on teaching and advising over research and publication. Problems arise when institutions shift this emphasis while leaving the reward structure unaltered.

Testing the waters. Individualized programs are a useful institutional tool for identifying potential future programs or majors, since any groundswell in student demand should be felt there first. Institutions need to monitor these programs and probe the sources of any unusual increase in the numbers of students putting together concentrations on any one topic.

Endnotes

1. William H. Newell and Allen J. Davis, "Education for Citizenship: The Role of Progressive Education and Interdisciplinary Studies," *Innovative Higher Education* 13:1 (Fall/Winter, 1988), pp. 27–37.
2. Allen J. Davis and William H. Newell, "Those Experimental Colleges of the 1960's: Where Are They, Now that We Need Them?" *The Chronicle of Higher Education* (November 18, 1981), p. 64. Reprinted in Stephen H. Barnes (ed.), *Points of View on American Higher Education,* Volume 2 Institutions and Issues (Lewiston, NY: Edwin Mellen Press, 1990), pp. 38–43.
3. William H. Newell, *Interdisciplinary Undergraduate Programs: A Directory* (Oxford, OH: Association for Integrative Studies, 1986).
4. Forrest H. Armstrong, "Faculty Development Through Interdisciplinarity," *The Journal of General Education* 32:1 (Spring, 1980), pp. 52–63.
5. For an extended examination of this definition, see William H. Newell and William J. Green, "Defining and Teaching Interdisciplinary Studies," *Improving College and University Teaching* 30:1 (Winter, 1982), pp. 24–25.

6. The interdisciplinary process underlying this definition is set up in some detail in Barbara Hursh, Paul Haas, and Michael Moore, "An Interdisciplinary Model to Implement General Education," *Journal of Higher Education* 54 (1983), pp. 42–59.

7. Julie Thompson Klein, *Interdisciplinarity: History, Theory, and Practice* (Detroit: Wayne State University Press, 1990).

8. See Forrest Armstrong, "Faculty Development Through Interdisciplinarity," *The Journal of General Education* 32:1 (Spring, 1980), pp. 52–63.

9. Again, see Hursh, et al., *op. cit.*

10. William Perry, *Forms of Intellectual and Ethical Development in the College Years: A Scheme* (New York: Holt, Rinehart, and Winston, 1970).

11. William H. Newell, "The Role of Interdisciplinary Studies in the Liberal Education of the 1980s," *Liberal Education* 69:3, pp. 245–255.

12. Julie Thompson Klein, *op. cit.*

Why Interdisciplinarity?

Joseph J. Kockelmans

The literature on interdisciplinary issues is often confusing. One reason is that the authors who concern themselves with interdisciplinarity do not use a uniform terminology. People who have come to the conclusion that in many instances research projects can no longer be defined strictly within the boundaries of one of the "classical" disciplines and for that reason would like to follow a research project wherever it may lead, rather than redefine the project so as to make it fit the requirements stipulated by a given discipline, will often argue in favor of interdisciplinarity. Authors who firmly believe that in an educational setting it is incorrect to expose students to a one-dimensional contact with Western civilization, because this may produce well-trained specialists but certainly not well-educated people, will often argue in favor of interdisciplinarity. And people working in the social sciences who have concluded that one cannot fully understand any social phenomenon if one tries to approach it exclusively from the perspective of one social science alone, and thus are looking for a broader framework in which social phenomena can be more adequately described and explained, will sometimes also favor an interdisciplinary approach.

In order to avoid unnecessary confusion we suggest that one should choose a much more carefully defined terminology, so that a special label can be reserved for each of these legitimate concerns: In so doing it will be easier to examine each one of the proposals made on its own merits. Then if the debate about interdisciplinarity were to end up negatively in one particular area, it would no longer be legitimate to generalize and to declare all forms of interdisciplinarity impossible or meaningless.

For those who are seriously concerned with interdisciplinarity, it is particularly frustrating to have to defend their legitimate concern against the claim that all forms of interdisciplinarity are attempts to solve problems that do not really exist, and that one thus should be glad that this "fad" finally is on the way out. A mistake often made in this connection is the assumption that interdisciplinarity is an attempt to create various kinds of generalists. Once this assumption is made and then interpreted in its most negative form, it is relatively easy to explain that one cannot improve a situation in which there are people who know everything about nothing (Chesterton's definition of the specialist), by urging that we must now move to a situation in which we will have people who know nothing about everything.

Yet one obviously should not make the opposite mistake either. Let us assume that one could make a legitimate point for one particular type of interdisciplinarity; it does not follow from this that everything suggested under the general label of interdisciplinarity will be justified by this fact alone. Yet there continue to be a number of people who, without further specification, defend the view that the solutions for most problems that plague our society and our universities can be found by means of interdisciplinarity. These people have done much damage to all legitimate claims that can be made about interdisciplinary issues.

Thus it is important to make clear distinctions and to examine carefully for each particular form of interdisciplinarity why one should engage in it. This is what I plan to do in this chapter. To that end I shall first make some remarks about the debate on terminology, then I shall discuss the importance of concerning oneself with interdisciplinarity in the limited sense of the term, with crossdisciplinarity, and finally with transdisciplinary efforts. Some critical reflections will conclude this chapter.

Various Forms of Interdisciplinarity; Suggestions for a Uniform Terminology

Need for a Uniform Terminology; Criteria to Be Applied

In the literature the term *interdisciplinarity* is used in both broad and narrow senses. When the term is used in the narrow sense, it refers to efforts geared towards the constitution of a new discipline whose field of study lies between two other disciplines already in existence. A number of these interdisciplines have already been developed over the past decades: social psychology, biophysics, psycholinguistics, etc. In these cases interdisciplinarity is often distinguished from other nondisciplinary approaches to research and education through the use of such expressions as *multidisciplinarity, pluridisciplinarity, crossdisciplinarity, transdisciplinarity,* etc. If the term is used in the broad sense it indicates all nondisciplinary endeavors in research, education, or administration.

There is no unanimity in the literature concerning the terminology itself and particularly concerning the question of how the meanings of the different expressions are to be defined. The differences in the labels and their definitions as proposed by the various authors flow from a number of sources: difference in overall philosophical outlook, difference of opinion concerning what constitutes a discipline, difference of opinion about the sociopolitical function of science and of our entire educational system, about the basic aim to be achieved by nondisciplinary efforts, about whether the debate on interdisciplinary issues is concerned in each case primarily with a research, an educational, or an administrative body of problems, and other questions.

If the debate on interdisciplinarity is to serve a practical purpose, it is important to eliminate unnecessary confusion, while avoiding the mistake of believing that all the relevant issues can be settled by fiat and in a manner which will

satisfy everyone. Clarification of the terminology to be employed seems to be a
first step in that direction. I will here attempt to define the terminology carefully and to justify the decisions made in such a way that the choices appear to
be reasonable but not dogmatic. Yet this principle of tolerance obviously cannot
be applied so rigorously that philosophical and scientific discourse and argumentation become impossible. Thus I will attempt to justify the choices without using insights or terminology that will be either incomprehensible or
unacceptable to most people. It seems to me that such an effort will succeed to
the degree that it relies more on ideas immediately connected with the goal to
be achieved than on specific philosophical a prioris.

In selecting and defining the terms to be used here I have been guided by
the following principles:

1. The list of terms should not contain anything not immediately relevant to
   the debate on interdisciplinary issues.
2. The list should be complete in the sense that the labels selected are adequate
   to characterize the various nondisciplinary efforts in teaching, research, and
   administration.
3. The terminology should be defined as clearly as possible.
4. Neither the terminology itself nor the definitions given should contain an
   explicit reference to scientific, methodological, sociopolitical, or philosophical issues about which there is no common agreement.

I am not the first to argue in favor of a clear and universally acceptable
terminology. Many authors have already attempted to achieve this goal. Some
of these efforts can be found in a book published by the Centre for Educational
Research and Innovation,[1] whereas others have been discussed systematically in
an unpublished dissertation by Jack L. Mahan, entitled "Toward Transdisciplinary Inquiry in the Humane Sciences."[2] Without the work done by these
authors I would not have been able to make the suggestions listed below. However, I wish first to explain my reasons for not fully affiliating myself with any
one of the terminological suggestions made by previous authors. These reasons
are all connected with the principles just formulated.[3]

Heckhausen's attempt to develop the necessary terminological distinctions
has, all of its positive aspects notwithstanding, two weaknesses.[4] First of all the
author tries to found his distinctions among six different forms of interdisciplinarity on the assumption that seven criterion levels for defining disciplines
should be distinguished. Now in view of the fact that these criterion levels are
not universally accepted by scientists and philosophers without modification, it
seems very unlikely that those concerned with interdisciplinarity will adopt the
terminology that Heckhausen suggests. Furthermore the labels used to distinguish the six forms of interdisciplinarity are developed by the author specifically
for this purpose and are notably different from the terms used by most authors.

The reason I prefer not to follow the suggestions made by Piaget, Jantsch,
and others is that these authors presuppose either a certain conception of structuralism and genetic epistemology, or a general systems theory on the basis of

which they try to clarify and justify the necessary distinctions.[5] Since both structuralism and general systems theory have a limited applicability only, and the philosophical assumptions underlying these positions are not universally accepted, it seems again unlikely that all interdisciplinarians will be comfortable with the suggestions made by these authors.

The proposal by Boisot, which is much more formal in character than those mentioned thus far, is in my opinion a very promising one.[6] I share his position, but prefer to select a slightly different terminology in light of the fact that the one proposed below has already been adopted by many authors working in the field. What Boisot calls "linear interdisciplinarity" is usually labeled by the term *pluridisciplinarity*; for structural interdisciplinarity the term *interdisciplinarity* in the strict and limited sense is commonly used, whereas restrictive interdisciplinarity is known under the label *crossdisciplinarity*.

The suggestions made by Michaud and Abt overlap to a very great extent the terminological suggestions made by Mahan on the basis of the latter's study of the available American literature.[7] The terminology I am proposing is derived from both of these efforts and is the result of combining some ideas suggested by the two European authors and some others made in the American literature as discussed by Mahan. But I find it necessary to change some of the suggestions made by these authors, because the list suggested by Michaud and Abt is incomplete and in addition employs for the description of the term *transdisciplinarity* a formulation that is both too formal and too restrictive. On the other hand, the terminology used by many American authors does not always make clear distinctions about the realms to which the various labels immediately apply.

Suggested Terminology

Discipline

A branch of learning or a field of study characterized by a body of intersubjectively acceptable knowledge, pertaining to a well-defined realm of entities, systematically established on the basis of generally accepted principles with the help of methodical rules or procedures; e.g., mathematics, chemistry, history.

Disciplinary Work

In an educational context we speak of disciplinary work as referring to scientific work (research, teaching, or both) done by one or more scientists within the boundaries of one discipline; e.g., work of a mathematician or a group of mathematicians within the realm of the discipline "mathematics."

Multidisciplinary Education

Education sought by a person who wishes to acquaint himself with more than one discipline, although there may be no connection at all between the disciplines involved; it is often assumed that teaching and research in this instance is done by educators who in each case act as disciplinarians, under whom a person for instance may study simultaneously or successively Greek, French, and mathematics.

Pluridisciplinary Work

Scientific work (teaching, research, learning) done by one or more scientists that implies such juxtaposition or subordination of different disciplines that the competence in one discipline presupposes a rather thorough knowledge of other disciplines, e.g., a biologist who in addition to biology devotes himself to physics, chemistry, and mathematics.

Interdisciplinary Work

Scientific work done by one or more scientists who try to solve a set of problems whose solution can be achieved only by integrating parts of existing disciplines into a new discipline, e.g., psycholinguistics, biophysics. This work does not imply that the original disciplines themselves become totally integrated, although this is not excluded either. The term predominantly refers to research and only secondarily to education.

Crossdisciplinary Work

Scientific work done by one or more scientists who try to solve a problem or a set of problems that no discipline in isolation can adequately deal with, by employing insights and methods or techniques of some related disciplines, without, however, any attempts being made to integrate the disciplines themselves or even parts thereof into a new discipline. It is obviously mandatory to integrate the scientific knowledge that immediately pertains to the problems at hand; however, it is not assumed that the integration achieved in this way and the experience so gained can be used as a paradigm for the solution of other analogous problems, without major modification. The scientists involved in such a project must have some common ground; the work proceeds from such a common ground but does not aim at developing this ground; e.g., economists, social scientists, physicians, and architects trying to find a better solution for the housing problem in a large city. This term is used predominantly to refer to large research projects.

Transdisciplinary Work

Scientific work done by a *group* of scientists, each trained in one or more different disciplines, with the intention of systematically pursuing the problem of how the negative side effects of specialization can be overcome so as to make education (and research) more socially relevant. In transdisciplinary work the discussion between the members of a carefully selected group may also focus on the concrete problems with which society confronts the members of a society or an academic community. The difference between crossdisciplinarity and transdisciplinarity consists in the fact that crossdisciplinary work is primarily concerned with finding a reasonable solution for the problems that are so investigated, whereas transdisciplinary work is concerned primarily with the development of an overarching framework from which the selected problems and other similar problems should be approached. For some authors transdisciplinary investigations should focus primarily on the unification of all sciences concerned with man; in their opinion the aim of transdisciplinary work consists in the development of an all-encompassing theoretical framework that is to be taken as the basis for all empirical research in the behavioral and social sciences. For other authors transdisciplinary efforts are concerned primarily with the unity of our world view; in their view transdisciplinary work presupposes that those who participate in it first try to establish a common ground that implies a conception of our culture, the function of science and education in it, and the basic elements of the entire process of acculturation.

Some Additional Observations

To prevent misunderstanding and to clarify the definitions that have been proposed here, the following observations may be helpful. First of all, today it has become questionable just how the concept of "discipline" should be defined vis-à-vis possible nondisciplinary endeavors. For many classical disciplines of the past have developed to a point where division and subdivision of the realm of study has become mandatory. One could now ask whether or not physics, biology, or psychology can still be called disciplines in the traditional sense of the term, or whether it would not be better to refer to these classical disciplines with expressions such as *superdisciplines* or *federated disciplines,* reserving the term *discipline* for some of the subdisciplines of the classical disciplines of the past. This development has clouded the interdisciplinarity issue to a great extent, because one could wonder whether the relationship between some particular subdiscipline of chemistry and some particular subdiscipline of physics or biology is not much closer than the relationship of the same subdiscipline of chemistry to another subdiscipline of chemistry. If this is the case, then it seems clear that the concept of discipline has to be redefined, so that in turn the term *interdisciplinarity* will receive a totally new meaning.

The distinction between science and discipline can help us to unravel this problem. The term *science* predominantly refers to a complex of related research projects, whereas the term *discipline* has a more educational meaning: one "does" science, but one "studies" a discipline. Once this distinction is made, one can then say that although physics taken as a science may have many subdivisions, educationally it is still possible to select a certain portion of the available knowledge in this realm of investigation that forms a harmonious educational unit, and with which anyone who is educationally introduced to physics ought to become familiar. When we speak of the discipline "physics" we mean that part of the science "physics" which, from an educational point of view, should be taken as its basic unit. This obviously will change over time. Time and again since the beginning of the twentieth century new sciences have developed between two or more existing sciences. Although this phenomenon is closely related to the one just dealt with, it originated from a different intention. In the case of the *division* and *subdivision* of existing sciences the development had its origin in a number of factors, all of which were inherent in the science in question. Division and subdivision of existing sciences became necessary either because the realm of phenomena to be dealt with became too large to be treated effectively without some division into smaller fields of research, or because certain phenomena appeared to require special principles and laws, or because it appeared possible to apply principles, laws, and structures developed for one realm of phenomena to other realms of phenomena. In the case of *the development of new sciences* between existing sciences, new sciences were developed, because it appeared that effective treatment of certain phenomena would be impossible without combining and integrating insights originally developed in two or more existing sciences. Examples of this type of development are biochemistry, social psychology, psycholinguistics, etc. According to Donald Campbell, underlying this development was the conviction that one must develop a fish-scale model of omni-science that gradually must take the place of the classical sciences.[8] This phenomenon is now generally referred to by the label *interdisciplinarity,* which in this instance is to be taken in a narrow and limited sense.

The question of whether or not scientists working in the area between two existing sciences should develop a new interscience, and how they should go about materializing such a project, should be answered by these scientists themselves—for they alone are competent in the relevant area—and not by philosophers or educators. Yet once such a new interscience has been developed, there are two new problems: a) is this new interscience of such a nature that as an interdiscipline it should become part of a university's regular curriculum? and b) should there be an administrative unit in the university functioning as a department or institute and being responsible for making available staff, facilities, curricula for students, etc.? It is this partly educational and partly administrative phenomenon which constitutes the subject of the contemporary debate about interdisciplinarity in the narrow and strict sense of the term, and to that debate philosophers, educators, and administrators can, in principle at least, make a positive contribution.

There never has been a time that someone's education was strictly disciplinary. Today too education is in principle never strictly disciplinary, if one looks at it from the perspective of the person who is being educated. In high school, on the undergraduate level, and even on the graduate level, all students are constantly being exposed to more than one discipline at a time, although the doctoral research projects may very well be strictly disciplinary in character. When we talk about interdisciplinarity we usually do not mean to refer to this educational phenomenon, because in the Western world all education is inherently multidisciplinary. It is clear also that as an educational term *multidis-*

ciplinarity should not be used as an expression to be meaningfully applied to possible research projects.

Since the beginning of the universities in the Middle Ages someone who wished to study a certain discipline had first to study certain other auxiliary or propaedeutic disciplines. This is still true today. A physicist must study mathematics before he can turn to mechanics; someone concerned with Old French must study Latin first; a theologian must study philosophy before he can devote himself to theology. When we talk about interdisciplinarity nowadays, we do not mean to refer to this phenomenon either, although it is not exclusively an educational one. In both education and research the subordination and integration of two related disciplines is often essential for the success of the enterprise. We reserve the term *pluridisciplinarity* for this particular phenomenon. The main reason this phenomenon is not treated in the contemporary debate on interdisciplinarity is twofold: first of all, it is not a new phenomenon; pluridisciplinarity is an essential element of our Western idea of science and education; the problems one encounters in this realm have been studied for centuries, and in most cases we know how to handle them. Second, the scholars working in the different sciences will have to decide for themselves if, when, and how combination, subordination, and integration should take place in any given case in both research and education.

In this discussion, therefore, little will be said about multidisciplinarity and pluridisciplinarity. Our focus instead will be on one of the following issues:

1. The question of why the creation of new sciences "between" other existing sciences in necessary or desirable, and of the attitude one should adopt from an educational as well as an administrative point of view in regard to interdisciplinarity in the narrow and strict senses of the term. In other words, the basic question here is, is it correct to continue to develop ever-new educational and administrative units for the ever-increasing number of new sciences developed at the borderlines of the classical sciences? Formulated in another way, is the classical division of the sciences still adequate for the purpose of defining meaningful educational and administrative units (interdisciplinarity in the strict sense)?
2. What to say about research projects and educational efforts which imply a thorough introduction into different, not closely related disciplines for the purpose of coming to grips with certain socially relevant problems, without the explicit intention, however, of creating new disciplines? One particular problem that is connected with the first and seems of great practical importance is whether these efforts too should eventually lead to the introduction of new educational and administrative units (crossdisciplinarity).
3. How to evaluate the efforts of people who are trying to establish a new type of discourse that would facilitate the exchange of ideas between people trained in different disciplines or interdisciplines? Should one search for several conceptual frameworks valid only from realms of phenomena, or should one look for an all-encompassing framework? Many people argue

that such an exchange of ideas is necessary in order to guarantee the unity of our conception of world (transdisciplinarity).

Why Interdisciplinarity in the Limited Sense of the Term?

In this section I shall present a brief summary of the most important arguments that have been proposed to justify involvement in strictly interdisciplinary research projects, as well as the question of to what kinds of innovations such efforts should lead from an educational and administrative point of view. My primary aim is to provide the reader with information about some of the ideas that various authors have suggested in the past. Where it appears to be meaningful, some critical observations will be added.

All those who have concerned themselves with interdisciplinarity in the strict and limited senses of the term agree that it is necessary in research and teaching to sometimes engage in investigations concerning problems or problem areas that cannot be defined from the viewpoint of the existing classical disciplines but are to be found somewhere between the borderlines of these disciplines. Yet there is little agreement about why one should engage in such investigations or about the practical implications of such efforts. Furthermore there are many reasons that suggest this issue cannot be handled for the natural sciences in exactly the same way as for the behavioral and social sciences. Because two chapters of this book will be concerned with limited interdisciplinarity in the realm of the natural and the social sciences, I shall keep my reflections general here. First I shall describe three different attempts to formulate reasons for engaging in strictly interdisciplinary endeavors; then I shall compare these ideas and add some critical reflections.

A first group of authors share with Donald Campbell the conviction that no individual can achieve genuine competence in one discipline, and thus that multidisciplinary competence is completely impossible for individuals; this is the case in both the natural and the social sciences. What is to be brought about therefore is a comprehensive and integrated multiscience.

Many interdisciplinary programs have tried to combine comprehensiveness with depth. Institutions have tried to train individual, multidisciplinary scholars who have mastered more than one discipline. One should realize, however, that in our modern world there is no longer room for such a Leonardesque aspiration. Where an attempt has been made to institutionalize this aspiration, a system producing shallowness and a lowest-common-denominator breadth has developed. What we need today is not a number of Leonardos, but rather groups of *genuine* interdisciplinarians. Until now people have believed that scientific knowledge and competence can find their locus in single individuals. Now it becomes clear that the locus of scientific knowledge is shifting from individuals to groups. Scientific knowledge has become a collective product that is only very imperfectly represented in isolated individuals. Given this fact, it seems more reasonable to train younger scientists in such a way that they do not have a comprehensive knowledge of one of the institutionalized disciplines, but so that they know whatever they need to know to solve important problems and deal with urgent issues in cooperation with other similarly trained specialists.

Thus one must not think of the multiscience mentioned previously as something that an individual alone could ever master; only the community of scholars can in time bring this ideal closer. Such a collective comprehensiveness of all realms of knowledge should be brought about by means of overlapping patterns resulting from efforts of a unique and deliberate narrowness. Each narrow specialty can be compared to a fish scale on a fish. For every systematically knowable subject matter there should be an adequate scientific approach that leads to a discipline concerning that subject matter or problem area.

The development of this ideal is impeded by the ethnocentrism of the existing disciplines, i.e., by the in-group partisanship in the internal and external relations between academic disciplines, university departments, and scientific organizations and institutions. Most interdisciplinary programs too have impeded the development of this ideal rather than promoting it, in that they tend equally to lead to the organization of ever-new specialties into new departments for decision-making and communication. This ethnocentrism of the institutionalized disciplines and interdisciplines leads to a redundant piling up of highly similar specialties, while leaving great interdisciplinary gaps. Rather than trying to fill these gaps by training scholars who have mastered two or more existing disciplines, one should be making those socioorganizational innovations that will encourage narrow specialization in the areas between these disciplines. One should realize also that the present institutionalized disciplines are just arbitrary composites, and that the present organization by departments is in large part just the product of an historical accident. If the scientists wish to engage in relevant research, they will have to go beyond the existing institutions and work in the direction of a comprehensive, collective multiscience.

A second group of authors shares with the first the conviction that it is indeed impossible for a single person to know the vast accumulation of findings, research techniques, and the different formulations of basic problems across the sciences.[9] Division of labor, specialization, and some form of cooperation are necessary. Given these facts, each scientist and specialist finds himself confronted with the problem of learning where, what, and how to borrow from other disciplines. Such borrowing can be done intelligently only if two major requirements are met. 1) The scientist specialized in one discipline must know what developments in other disciplines have been accumulated in problem areas that relate to his own research interests, so that he will know where to turn when he needs to borrow methods and information. This, the authors argue, can be facilitated by joint seminars, conferences, and readily available literature. 2) The specialist in one science will very seldom find a completely satisfactory solution to his own problem in another discipline, because the units of analysis as well as the levels at which they take place are mostly quite different. In other words the findings made available in one discipline are to be adapted and then incorporated into those of another discipline. These authors feel that if these conditions are met, the methods and findings of two or more disciplines working on related problem areas can serve as a check on the validity of their generalizations to the advantage of each discipline involved.

The authors admit that the results of interdisciplinary endeavors have been rather disappointing until now, for various understandable reasons: many scientists appear to have misunderstood the meaning of interdisciplinary projects; they have often underestimated the difficulties involved in such efforts; administrators are reluctant to change existing institutions; experts in one field can talk to each other relatively easily, whereas the discourse between people who have specialized in different areas seldom leads to a meaningful dialogue. However, the authors argue, much of the discontent and many practical difficulties have arisen through failure to deal adequately with the central and substantive issue, namely, the core problem of why interdisciplinary efforts came into existence at all, and why they are necessary for the development of each of the sciences and not just a matter of individual preference. An examination of this substantive issue, which is at the core of all interdisciplinary relationships, will reveal that each discipline needs the others in a fundamental and basic sense, because each discipline needs the findings of the others as a check on the validity of its own generalizations and theories. When this substantive issue is examined more carefully, many current problems associated with interdisciplinary trends turn out to be minor issues. They merely seem large and even insurmountable as long as the substantive question has not been examined with care. Administrative problems in particular can be solved relatively easily once the basic problem has been clarified.

These authors are thus convinced that the basic considerations that brought problems of interdisciplinary relations to the foreground in an irreversible way will ultimately force the development of continuing interdisciplinary efforts, regardless of the ups and downs to be suffered from the imperialism and self-contained ethnocentrism of the various disciplines or from the blind spots in administrative arrangements.

It is particularly in the realm of the social sciences that one discovers that man does not divide and arrange his individual and social problems neatly along lines laid down by academic disciplines. If the social sciences wish to engage in investigations of genuine human problems, they will have to concern themselves with the real problems human begins actually experience. There is nothing basically wrong with a division of labor in this realm and thus with specialization, as long as one realizes that there is a great deal of overlap in the subject matters or topics considered by the various social disciplines. Which among the social sciences would care to abdicate altogether any reference to human motives, language, the family, the different groups, religious institutions, political and economic life? Thus the different disciplines are actually studying and theorizing about the same problems or closely related problems of the human condition. And if this is so, then no social science can solve its relevant problems in isolation. For those disciplines concerned with man, one of the inherent dangers in working in isolation is the sacrifice of the validity of their generalizations and theories. The best means available for checking the validity of findings and generalizations in social science today, before any application is attempted, is to measure them against the findings and generalizations established on the same or related problems by another social science.

In both the natural and social sciences the core problem of interdisciplinary relationships for a particular discipline is to determine the findings and concepts it must borrow, and to decide in which matters it has to be in transaction with other disciplines in order to stand firmly on its own feet, with all of the supporting evidence it needs to insure the validity of its formulations. Assessment of what a science needs from other disciplines and with whom it needs to transact will provide the ingredients for weaving its own fabric.

As for practical problems connected with interdisciplinary efforts, the authors do not suggest engaging in activities that would ultimately lead to abolishing the distinction between the existing sciences; neither do they advocate a total reorganization of the structure of the university. What is needed in most cases is a careful selection of a small number of people of different backgrounds who are concerned with related problems and are willing to engage in interdisciplinary efforts, and arrangements that permit sufficient time and opportunity for joint efforts without making supreme the physical aspects of the program. For the great problem in interdisciplinary ventures is still the development of coordination and cooperation among people who can pull together, instead of being pulled asunder by disciplines, schools, and organizational pressures.

There is a third group of authors who, although convinced that the authors whose views were briefly described in the preceding pages have made an important contribution to the debate on interdisciplinarity, nonetheless believe that the real issue and its solution is to be sought for elsewhere.[10] They point out that sometimes we find ourselves in a position in which we have to admit that we do not know, or do not yet know, enough about the relevant phenomena. Sometimes we can legitimately say that we have discovered a number of insights concerning a given realm of phenomena, but that it gradually becomes questionable what the precise meaning and value of our insights really is, due to the fact that conflicting claims are being made in other related fields. In addition, we often find ourselves in a situation in which we begin to realize that all of our findings are questionable in the final analysis, as long as no one is able to indicate how the divergent aspects of the relevant phenomena (which from the viewpoint of the different disciplines appear to be isolated, uncoordinated, and incomparable) constitute some kind of harmonious unity. In the first case we are confronted with a lack of knowledge that the different *disciplines* attempted to overcome; in the second we experience a lack of knowledge that can be overcome through interdisciplinary efforts; the lack of knowledge that confronts us in the third case cannot be conquered by either disciplinary or interdisciplinary efforts, but requires efforts of a *transdisciplinary* nature.

These authors agree with those of the first and the second groups that one should not hold that there is something basically wrong with specialization. In many disciplines specialization has proven to be the road to a solution of a great number of real problems. It may be true that particularly in the realm of social phenomena, specialization is confronted with many and unexpected difficulties not encountered in some branches of the natural sciences; yet it seems unfounded to defend the thesis that specialization has no place in the social sciences. What is needed is not the abolishing of specialization but the development of inter- and transdisciplinary approaches that can deal meaningfully with the negative side effects of one-sided specialization.

For it is indeed true that specialization, institutionalization, and compartmentalization through departmental regulations tend to fragment our knowledge more and more. To obtain a unifying picture of these vast areas of fragmented knowledge, comprehensive analyses seem necessary. Those who engage in these kinds of analyses must go beyond the traditional approaches to scientific inquiry and its techniques of investigation. One such supplementary alternative is the interdisciplinary approach. Yet, although this approach is needed in addition to the disciplinary ones, it appears to be necessary to go even beyond this form of interdisciplinarity. We must develop methods of inquiry that transcend the traditional boundaries and provide integrating and synthesizing frameworks for disciplinary and interdisciplinary investigations. This is to be done by means of transdisciplinary research projects. The weakness of the views presented by the first two groups of authors is that they did not realize that in most cases their suggestions will not work without a transdisciplinary framework.

A careful comparison of these views shows that for the last group of authors it is important to distinguish between interdisciplinary and transdisciplinary efforts and projects and that, as far as limited interdisciplinarity is concerned, the view proposed by the second group of authors appears preferable to that suggested by the first.

As for the first view, no doubt everyone will agree with these authors that the time of Leonardos has past. More and more in our modern world research projects begin to imply groups instead of isolated specialists. Both government and industry often look for teams of well-chosen specialists who can work meaningfully together on large research projects. It seems reasonable to conclude from this that the university should prepare its students for this type of research. Yet it seems that this first group of authors underestimates the complexity of the issues at hand. The basic problem they leave unanswered concerns how narrowly trained specialists can meaningfully communicate with one another and how groups of specialists can successfully cooperate. The authors must presuppose that there is already some general framework, some common ground that all specialists and groups of specialists share and to which they may return when they try to cooperate and communicate.

The second basic problem with this view is that it is difficult to understand how someone could call himself a well-educated person if he were to be ignorant in all fields of learning except in that of his own specialty. Without a rather extensive training in the humanities, mathematics, the sciences, and the arts he would often be totally incapable of correctly perceiving the relevant problems and certainly incapable of adequately dealing with them. This is true particularly for all research projects that directly or indirectly affect society and our environment. The suggestions made by these authors may still be important, but they seem to be relevant only for older graduate students and postdoctoral fellows who can devote themselves to specialization on the basis of a broad education.

Within certain limits I tend to agree with the first group of authors that the ethnocentrism of disciplines, professional organizations, journals, and departments should be criticized. Yet it may very well be that all of these institutions still have an important function, not for the preparation of someone who wishes to engage in meaningful research projects with colleagues trained in other disciplines, but for the balanced education of specialists and teachers.

As for the second and third groups of authors, generally speaking I tend to agree with their ideas and suggestions. The views proposed by the second group of authors does not imply the creation of an encompassing framework. The research projects with which they are predominantly concerned merely presuppose that those engaging in strict interdisciplinary work must have a rather thorough knowledge of the fields and subfields from which they borrow ideas, methods, or results. Yet even these authors admit that in certain areas important interdisciplinary work cannot be done except by groups, the members of which come from different disciplines. In this case too some form of cooperation between specialists with different training is necessary, and the latter again presupposes that some common framework of meaning be developed to make cooperation effective.

These authors could say that the third group of authors is mistaken in searching for such a common ground in advance. Yet I must admit that I cannot envisage a meaningful dialogue or discourse between the representatives of different disciplines except on the basis of a (perhaps limited) realm of meaning that they share or at least are willing to agree upon, and which they do not wish to question, at least for as long as they engage in this kind of dialogue. This in my opinion is a necessary condition for any meaningful exchange of ideas; the question is what this limited frame of reference should be in each case. A second question pertains to the manner in which such a frame of reference can be either discovered or developed. It will not do simply to refer to the life world they all share or to appeal to our ordinary language, because the latter frames of reference are much too unarticulated and thus incapable of directly incorporating any of the specialized frames of reference and languages of the different disciplines involved in each case.

Discovering or developing relevant overall frameworks of meaning seems to be the primary concern of those who write about transdisciplinarity. For this reason I should like to return to this issue in one of the sections to follow.

Strictly interdisciplinary endeavors have led to a number of new interdisciplines. In some instances these interdisciplines developed into regular disciplines with their own departments, professional journals, societies, national and international meetings. In other instances the new interdisciplines became subdisciplines of one of the original disciplines involved. In the literature with which I am familiar I have been unable to find a clear answer to the following three questions: a) Is it in principle correct to continue to develop ever-new disciplines for all the fields of research that are continuously being discovered? b) What conditions must be fulfilled to warrant the development of new educational units, be these departments, institutes, or even colleges? c) In light of the limited resources, what attitude should administrators adopt with respect to this development, and by what standard should they let themselves be guided when choices are to be made?

Prima facie one would be inclined to defend two seemingly contradictory theses: obviously research must go on wherever it is meaningful and feasible; yet on the other hand, it seems unreasonable to argue that new disciplines and new educational and administrative units are to be developed for each new field of research. As far as the latter is concerned, the actual development has perhaps already gone much too far. What ought to happen if the latter were to be correct is not at all clear, in that any reasonable proposal one could make would encounter economic difficulties of astronomical proportions. Some aspects of the problems hinted at here will be discussed in chapters to come.

Why Crossdisciplinarity?[11]

Crossdisciplinarians are people who attempt to tackle problems and issues that cannot be properly defined and solved within the boundaries of any given discipline. These problems and issues may be found in the realm of the natural sciences or the social sciences; many of them, however, seem to involve both the natural and social sciences. People concerned with this type of research usually have no intention of developing a new discipline or interdiscipline; neither do they envisage new educational and administrative units in the university. Most of them will make the claim, though, that our contemporary universities do not live up to all of their obligations, in that they usually do not prepare students for crossdisciplinary work. Yet, so they say, most students who are preparing themselves for a career outside the university (perhaps more than 90 percent of our students) will in their chosen professions, vocations, or careers have to deal continually with problems and issues that no discipline taken in isolation can properly formulate or effectively deal with. Thus these authors argue that every university should prepare its students for crossdisciplinary research.

Although in some instances one individual could engage in crossdisciplinary work, the work can most often be done effectively only by teams. This is due mainly to the complexity of the issues involved and the rather severe limitations placed on the scientific knowledge that one individual can normally master. In those cases in which crossdisciplinary work can be done by one isolated individual, the concern of the crossdisciplinarian runs parallel to that of the interdisciplinarian. One should realize here that crossdisciplinarity and interdisciplinarity overlap to a great extent. The difference between the two consists primarily in the goal the researchers attempt to achieve. Interdisciplinarians attempt to develop new research fields that eventually will lead to new disciplines. Crossdisciplinarians wish to solve important and urgent problems that cannot be defined and solved from the perspective of any one of the existing disciplines. Yet this difference in aim notwithstanding, the actual work in which both types of scientists engage will be very similar. This is the reason that some of the arguments given in favor of interdisciplinarity in the limited sense also apply to crossdisciplinarity.

Many authors who have written on crossdisciplinarity often use the labels inter- or transdisciplinarity to identify this form of nondisciplinary research. Yet in view of the fact that crossdisciplinarians usually have no intention of developing a new discipline, I prefer not to use the term *interdisciplinarity* in this connection. Furthermore, since the primary goal of crossdisciplinarity consists in finding solutions for important and urgent problems, I prefer to avoid the term *transdisciplinarity* here also, although it is true that both cross- and transdisciplinarians have in common their concern with the development of encompassing frames of reference, as will be shown shortly.

Those who are in favor of developing crossdisciplinary research projects share the view that the search for a common ground is the fundamental element of all crossdisciplinary investigation. Without such a common ground there would be no overarching conceptual framework, and thus genuine communication between those who participate in the discussion would be impossible. It is very difficult to discover or establish such a common ground, in that everyone who participates in the discussion brings with him his own discipline's conceptual framework and sensitivity for methods and techniques. Furthermore, when at first agreement sometimes seems to exist among the members of a crossdisciplinary group, often it later becomes clear that the agreement was merely verbal.

Several authors have explicitly addressed the question of how one could facilitate the discovery or development of a common ground necessary for crossdisciplinary discourse. The general consensus is that there cannot be one approach to this problem that would be correct for all types of crossdisciplinary research projects: the solution to the problem depends to a great extent on the kind of investigation that is attempted (Luszki et al.). Those who are familiar with general systems theory, structuralism, or cybernetics have suggested that these approaches, which originally were not developed for crossdisciplinary research projects, might very well contain the core of the answer to the question of how to develop a common ground. Careful reflection, however, shows that each one of these approaches will be valuable only in some but not in all areas of crossdisciplinary research. Furthermore, taken by themselves these approaches provide us only with the formal skeleton of a conceptual framework; to the question of how in each case this formal framework is to be concretized, no universally valid answer is to be expected.[12]

Yet the goal of all crossdisciplinary inquiry is the discovery of overarching conceptual frameworks that will facilitate the unification of the sciences and eventually the solution of important problems with which the existing disciplines acting in isolation are incapable of dealing effectively. Crossdisciplinarians who work exclusively in the realm of the natural sciences usually have no great difficulty in discovering a common framework. In most cases it will consist in the basic principles and methods of physics, chemistry, or biology. On the other hand, crossdisciplinary research projects in the social sciences, and particularly those involving both the natural and the social sciences, confront us with great theoretical and methodological problems. Research projects involve both the natural and social sciences when, in addition to sociopolitical and economic issues, there are technological problems that presuppose a rather sophisticated knowledge of the natural sciences.

Some authors have suggested that the basic problem facing scholars engaged in these types of research projects cannot be solved except by creating specialized generalists, i.e., people competently trained in one discipline who in addition have received a rather thorough training in a number of other disciplines. Most authors feel that this suggestion will usually not work. In their view the members of a given team must in each case discover or develop their own crossdisciplinary frame of reference with its typical theoretical framework and its characteristic methodology, without which it is virtually impossible to integrate the relevant insights already gained in the individual branches of learning represented by the members of the team.

Social scientists who have written about crossdisciplinary research stress that it is not their intention to promote a new school of thought in the realm of the social sciences, a new philosophy or a new ideology. Their efforts flow rather from a sensitivity to problems of human relevance. Their interest thus is in a kind of inquiry that is concerned with social phenomena without compartmentalizing human experiences and depersonalizing man's life because of a too-narrow scope, and without distorting his experiences through the use of scientific frames of reference that are reductionist and reifying. Crossdisciplinary inquiry attempts to examine man and society from a perspective that transcends disciplinary interests and institutional loyalties. It presupposes and takes its point of departure in the insights gained in the various disciplines and interdisciplines; it tries to integrate these insights with the help of a conceptual framework that transcends each one of them and remains much closer to the social phenomena as they are experienced by living human beings in actual societies.

Gordon DiRenzo describes the characteristics typical of crossdisciplinary work as follows. The first is the development of an awareness of what is going on in the different but related disciplines. The second is the development of a sensitivity to convergence; one must learn to recognize where the several disciplines do, and must, come together theoretically and facilitate such a unification; the necessary condition for this is a close focus on the arbitrariness of disciplinary boundaries as well as on their interpenetration. The third is the standardization of scientific concepts and the development of a common scientific language for all behavioral sciences.[13]

Many crossdisciplinary efforts have been disappointing. This has been the result of a number of problems whose force is often too easily underestimated. First of all there is the problem of ethnocentrism: those who play a leading role in the social sciences, either because of their publication record or because of their position in the profession, often explicitly argue that there is no need for crossdisciplinary efforts; all attempts to develop such a crossdisciplinary approach have failed; the work of those who engage in this kind of work is of inferior quality; and most importantly, there never have been generalists and there should not be any now either. Second, it appears to be enormously difficult to engage in crossdisciplinary research in universities where the structure is usually strictly disciplinary. Some people have claimed that this kind of research cannot get off the ground as long as these sciences remain located within specialized departments, because this situation conflicts with the development of the potential of these sciences as contributors to the solution of large-scale problems. Some even wondered whether the traditional relationships between scholars, teachers, and students does not work against large-scale crossdisciplinary research.[14]

Third, crossdisciplinary work is done most effectively by groups of scientists trained in different disciplines. Now it appears that crossdisciplinary collaboration has a number of difficulties of its own that, as was to be expected, are connected with personal idiosyncrasies, difference in philosophical orientation, and differences of opinion concerning the desirability of conceptual frameworks, methods, and techniques; the latter problems have their origin mainly in the affiliation of the various scientists with their "home" disciplines. Luszki has devoted a monograph to these problems: *Interdisciplinary Team Research: Methods and Problems* and has made a number of important suggestions that can facilitate crossdisciplinary team research efforts.[15] However, in view of the fact that team work in this area is relatively new, there are still a number of fundamental problems for which no one as yet has found a reasonable solution.

Yet all of these and other difficulties notwithstanding, the authors maintain that crossdisciplinary research efforts are necessary if research is to be relevant to the real needs of our complex society. Furthermore, they feel, one should not forget that the problems connected with one-sided compartmentalization are even more serious. As for the claim of opponents that it is not desirable and is even wrong to create generalists who know almost nothing about everything, the proponents of crossdisciplinary research projects argue first that there is a great difference between a superficial generalist and a specialist generalist in the sense of a true crossdisciplinarian; for the latter is supposed to have specialized knowledge of at least one of the relevant disciplines and to be willing to engage in efforts geared toward overcoming the limitations of too narrowly defined specialties. Furthermore they agree with those who promote interdisciplinarity in the limited sense, when they defend the view that in our complex society there is need for generalists in the common sense. It may be true that these people should not seek employment at a university; yet the university should prepare some generalists who as "science brokers" can mediate between the specialists and the public at large.

I believe that the authors concerned with the promotion of crossdisciplinary research projects are engaged in an important enterprise. Our complex societies confront us with problems that the sciences in isolation cannot adequately treat. A genuine understanding of these problems and an attempt to suggest solutions presupposes cooperation between those who have specialized knowledge of their relevant aspects. This cooperation in turn presupposes that all of those involved in the discussion try to discover a common ground. This ground need not always be so encompassing that it could serve as a basis to deal meaningfully with all large-scale problems. It seems reasonable to assume that a limited common ground will be effective, provided it be broad enough to encompass the dimensions that are essential to the problems at hand.

In fact both in government and in industry a number of these crossdisciplinary projects have been and are being developed. It seems to me that the university should prepare younger scientists for crossdisciplinary research. In view of the fact that this type of education conflicts with the departmental structure of the actual university, I share the opinion of the Social Science Research Council that in the larger universities the necessary structure should be developed in which during the last years of their training graduate students could be introduced to crossdisciplinary research projects.[16]

Why Transdisciplinarity?

Those who defend the need for transdisciplinary projects attempt to bring about an all-encompassing framework of meaning, valid either for all sciences or at least for all sciences concerned with man. In their view a transdisciplinary framework is a necessary condition for making integration of insights gained in isolated disciplines and interdisciplines possible, and for restoring a uniform conception of world. Our world has become splintered and fragmented by the fact that each individual discipline and interdiscipline has developed its own general conceptual framework, its own set of theories and methods, all of which in the final analysis rest on implicit philosophical assumptions and ultimately lead to different conceptions of world.

Those who engage in transdisciplinary work are not primarily concerned with improvement of the empirical disciplines in their research aspect; the primary focus of all transdisciplinary work is to be found rather in the educational and philosophical dimensions of the sciences. This is the reason why those who write on transdisciplinary issues are very often educators, philosophers-scientists, and philosophers, and why they place such stress on the idea that transdisciplinary work is absolutely necessary to guarantee that all learning in the university *at all levels* is not just training but also genuine education. Many authors are convinced that genuine transdisciplinary work is impossible without a philosophical reflection on man and society.

There is little unanimity among the authors who have written on transdisciplinarity. Next I shall describe four different views proposed in the literature and conclude this section with some critical reflections of my own.

According to a *first view,* interdisciplinarity has become a fashion; in some cases the interdisciplinary movement has deteriorated into snobbism.[17] Often one does not realize that interdisciplinarity is not progress but rather a symptom of the pathological situation in which man's theoretical knowledge finds itself today. For more than two hundred years specialization has been the predominant trend in research and education; this has led to the dangerous fragmentation of our entire epistemological domain. Our theoretical knowledge has disintegrated, and the human personality has been affected by this lack of integration. Alienation through science is one of the causes of the crisis of our contemporary Western civilization.

A diagnosis of the actual situation does not necessarily give us a solution for the basic problem that confronts us here. Interdisciplinarity, which many people have suggested as the solution for this problem, is counterproductive in that it does not touch on the heart of the matter. The main issue is not one of how to reorganize higher education but one that concerns the meaning of a man's life in a scientific era. The disintegration of the unity of our theoretical knowledge and the corresponding disintegration of our entire intellectual framework has taken place gradually since the time of the Renaissance. It was particularly in the nineteenth century that our knowledge became fragmented due to ever-increasing specialization. The closer our sciences came to a mature state, the more disintegration of the unity of our theoretical knowledge appeared to be an inevitable consequence of the desire to know more and more about minute details. Not only did new disciplines and interdisciplines develop, but in each discipline specialization became necessary. Although much accurate and important knowledge concerning these details has been acquired in this way, the development as a whole has much in common with a cancerous process. This development had particularly ruinous consequences for the university, which is not longer a cultural community. Our universities have become prisons with hermetically sealed cells for inmates with the same record.

People who believe they can counteract this development through interdisciplinary efforts have underestimated the enormous difficulties which prevent genuine *inter*disciplinarity. First of all there are the *epistemological* obstacles: specialization seems to be a necessity; accurate knowledge about details that we need can, as far as we know, not be achieved otherwise; yet specialization makes integration virtually impossible. Then there are *institutional* obstacles: specialization in the disciplines logically led to the departmentalization of the university; it is not easy to see how one could reasonably change this development. Third, there are *psychosociological* obstacles: people educated in our universities are incapable of conceiving of the situation other than it actually has become; neither as individual persons nor as groups can they maintain themselves without this form of institutionalization, professionalization, and bureaucratization. And there are the *cultural* obstacles: development in our epistemological domain is connected with the general conception of our Western culture that one must be able to compete, excel, dominate, and control, and specialization is more conducive to these activities.

In light of these obstacles it is evident that a few conferences or colloquia, some new books and anthologies, or even the development of new interdisciplinary universities will not really contribute much to the solution of the basic problem.

Our theoretical knowledge was originally developed as a function of the humanization of man and nature. Modern science, on the other hand, contributes much to the dehumanization of both man and his environment. Since our specialized disciplines have become disciplines-without-wisdom, they are without direction and without any possibility of human evaluation. This is the reason why a merely formal unification of the sciences is unable to have a positive function in regard to the main problem at hand.

If interdisciplinary efforts are going to bring us to a solution for the problems caused by one-sided specialization and reduction, they must concern themselves first with the origin. Unification that comes after the facts by means of addition is meaningless. Specialization itself must flow from genuine concern for the whole. Thus transdisciplinary efforts that focus on the whole are necessary. Transdisciplinarity can never consist in retroactive measures, whether they be by addition or by formalization. The transdisciplinary concern for the unity of our world must be there first, and from it specialization should flow. It is true that specialization is unavoidable and necessary if we are to survive. Yet specialization without guidance and without concern for the unity of our world is self-destructive. As far as the university is concerned, this suggestion does not mean that the departments and institutes are to be abolished, but that one should stress first that they are the places from which a dialogue concerned with the humanness of man and his world must begin.

In a *second view* transdisciplinary efforts are recommended on the basis of a similar concern for the unity of our theoretical knowledge, with the feeling that the preceding view is much too pessimistic.[18] In this view, instead of acting as a doomsday prophet, one should more carefully reflect on *how* transdisciplinarity could contribute to an effective restoration of the unity of our conception of world. Because the quest for the unity of our scientific knowledge has a history almost as old as the idea of theoretical reason itself, it seems reasonable to suggest that one turn once more to this history in order to see whether a hint can be found there concerning how to deal with the basic problem. In this long history the claim has been made repeatedly that philosophical reflection, which inherently has an integrating function, should play an important part in a search for the unity of our theoretical knowledge. This, however, should not be understood in an imperialist manner, as if only that which philosophy can integrate into an overall perspective can be accepted from all the insights the sciences have to offer us. Just the opposite is to happen: by reflecting critically upon the foundation from which all theoretical efforts flow, philosophy can make a positive contribution to the transdisciplinary unification of the sciences. Philosophy, precisely because it is concerned with beginnings and foundations, should not try to play a role in the integration of the data provided by the sciences; rather philosophical reflection should contribute to the unification of all theoretical knowledge by reflecting on what all sciences presuppose and from which they ultimately flow: the universe, man, and man's world. One should not interpret these statements to imply that the concern for unity is the concern of professional philosophers only. A philosophical dimension is present in all theoretical efforts, and thus the concern for the unity through transdisciplinary efforts is an aspect of all the sciences. It may be true that the scientists often forget that (among many other things) they should be concerned with the whole, precisely because they are so deeply engaged in research concerning details. Yet it cannot be denied that the tendency toward unity is an integral element of all theoretical efforts. It seems that today this concern for unity is served better by cooperation than by efforts of individuals.

A *third group of authors* tries to defend transdisciplinary efforts by an appeal to the social relevance of higher education.[19] As they see it, the basic cause of crisis in the university is its increasing maladjustment to a rapidly changing society. Transdisciplinarity's first objective is to reestablish contact between university and society. The most important problems confronting our society cannot be dealt with meaningfully by any given traditional discipline taken in isolation. What is needed is a set of new interdisciplines and an effective integration of the existing sciences. The traditional disciplines, including the human sciences, developed as the result of a long process of specialization. All specialization in theoretical knowledge implies reduction. The consequence of this process is that the problems that the different disciplines are able to handle are no longer problems that the members of a society really experience at any given moment in time, but merely reduced and idealized aspects of these problems. If one is to come to grips with the basic problems of our modern world, a reorganization of our theoretical knowledge along transdisciplinary lines is mandatory.

The question of why the university should engage in transdisciplinary research projects and teaching programs has often been explained with the help of the distinction between training and teaching.[20] There are authors who think that over the past fifty years many universities have produced specialists highly trained in some fragment of knowledge; yet these universities have educated relatively few people. Transdisciplinarity is thus often offered as a vehement protest against bits of knowledge that are as alienating culturally as bits of work are in the production process. Transdisciplinarity should be understood as an attempt to restore the goals of teaching that were gradually diverted from their declared purposes.

According to these authors neither the sciences nor the various inter- and crossdisciplinary efforts can help us in this regard. The reason for this is that disciplinarians are primarily committed to the careful study of a limited field of phenomena. In so being they apply methods, follow standards, and try to discover ever-new results. In all of these efforts they identify with their social position as scholars who belong to a certain profession and search for recognition from their peers. Most interdisciplinary and crossdisciplinary efforts are not very helpful in this connection, in that these efforts often lead to new disciplines, aim at addition of new knowledge rather than integration, and sometimes lead to subordination of disciplines, which does not always do justice to the insights presented by all the disciplines involved. Transdisciplinary efforts should therefore be oriented towards the humanities, which are primarily concerned with man and his environment. History and literature, together with some kind of philosophical reflection, constitute the framework in which transdisciplinary work will flourish.[21]

The *fourth view* on transdisciplinarity is in my view the most intriguing of them all. In attempting to explain this view systematically, I shall use some ideas suggested by Schwartz.[22] According to this view it is very important to realize that in our contemporary Western world the sciences have become the actual basis for the lives we are living. Our contemporary way of living was formed by the sciences and has adapted itself to the scientific way of thinking, particularly to that found in the natural sciences and employed in modern technology. The sciences have become an integral part of the destiny of contemporary man. For many centuries people have identified science with progress. In classical antiquity scientific speculation was a goal and value in itself. In the Middle Ages it was thought that the sciences retraced the thoughts of the Creator. In the era of humanism and enlightenment it was believed that the sciences enhanced the humanity of man (humanism). In the nineteenth century people believed that the sciences helped us to conquer and control the earth. Today there are people who believe that the sciences teach us the "real" truth about things, a task formerly attributed to either religion or philosophy; for others the sciences are the most powerful instrument we have to change the world including the structure of our society.

Most people today believe that as long as people had their religious or philosophical convictions, shared by the greater part of Western society, the thesis that science can be identified with progress could indeed be justified. However, now that people no longer universally share either a religious view or a philosophical conception of man and world, the question concerning the real meaning and function of science has become problematic. Science appears as a human creation, which, although neutral in itself, can be used both positively and negatively. The sciences can help us control our environment; yet they also contain the possibility of total self-destruction for man. Although the sciences have helped to shape our self-conception, yet they also contain elements that prevent man from realizing his genuine self.

Those who are concerned with transdisciplinarity basically agree with this view and suggest that the correct conception of science for our world can be discovered only through investigations that transcend the boundaries of the individual disciplines. The goal of these investigations precisely is to ensure that through the sciences man can provide for himself a position within the cosmos that is at the same time rational, critical, and humane.

Transdisciplinarians strongly stress the point that there cannot be any science that does not make some presuppositions and that does not imply some kind of preunderstanding and some form of evaluation. No science can be called a genuine science if it objects to these presuppositions being critically examined. The idea of a critique of scientific reason is obviously not new. We are familiar with Kant's *Critique of Pure Reason,* Dilthey's critique of historical reason; and much of our contemporary philosophy of science can be viewed from this perspective, particularly now that logical and methodological reflections on the sciences are complemented by insights from the history of science and sociology of knowledge. Transdisciplinarians have high esteem for these investigations in the realm of philosophy of science and urge the leading scientists to engage in the debate in order to make certain that the perspectives of *all* the sciences are properly represented. It cannot be denied that many people concerned with philosophy of science exclusively or at least predominantly focus on the natural sciences; some others are mainly concerned with the behavioral, social, and humanist disciplines. What is needed, particularly from an educational point of view, is an all-encompassing philosophy of science that concerns itself with all essential aspects of all the sciences and disciplines.

Transdisciplinarians conceive of specialization as a necessity. Until the beginning of the nineteenth century specialization did not lead to grave problems because the unity of the world view as well as the unity of the sciences was then guaranteed either by an all-encompassing religious view, a universally accepted philosophy, or a common ideology. In those days one could speculate about precisely what each individual science was contributing to the conception of the whole. Today we have a great number of highly specialized sciences to which an equally great number of conceptions of world correspond. The question of precisely what each science contributes to our conception of world has become a meaningless question, if it is understood to imply that, independent of the sciences, there is already a uniform conception of world available to all. The unity of the world may no longer be presupposed; it is something to be brought about, and the sciences will have to play some part in the realization of this task.

Yet if one looks at the actual situation it is difficult to understand how the individual sciences could ever make a meaningful contribution to the constitution of the world's unity. For specialization went historically hand in hand with professionalization and compartmentalization. True, some authors have pointed out that specialization need not lead to professionalization and fragmentation. Each science, provided it is learned correctly, is and remains a legitimate perspective on the whole; if conducted properly scientific research leads to a transgression of the borderlines that each science had stipulated for itself originally; if studied in depth every science leads to a center where all sciences converge.

Transdisciplinarians do not deny this, and they admit that one-sided fragmentation is not a necessary consequence of specialization. Yet the real point is still overlooked in these reflections. One continues to presuppose that contemporary man may appeal to a world that already constitutes a harmonious unity in advance. If one looks at the actual facts he will see that each science has tried to develop its own conception of world and then tried to impose that conception on all other sciences. That is why the question of the unity of the sciences must be examined more systematically.

In classical antiquity and throughout the entire Middle Ages it was thought that everything that can be known scientifically constitutes a harmonious unity (*kosmos, creatura*). The sciences were to discover this unity and make it explicit in systematic fashion. The rationality inherent in the unity of the sciences was to reflect the rationality present in the cosmos (order of things = order of ideas). The same conception, but now defended on different grounds, can be found in Descartes's *Système du monde,* Spinoza's *Ethics,* and Leibniz's *Monadology.*

After Kant this conception was given up. For even if God created the cosmos as a rational unity, still we must maintain 1) that we do not know anything about the order of things, except insofar as this order is accessible to us through the scientific study of the way in which the things appear to us (phenomena), and 2) that the realm of phenomena now studied by the sciences is much broader and much more complex than the classical *kosmos*.

Thus, if today the unity of our entire theoretical framework remains to be explained, it must be done on grounds that do not imply any advance knowledge of the order inherent in things. Some people have therefore tried to justify the unity of our theoretical knowledge by appealing to the function of the knowing *ego*; later an attempt was made to explain this unity by positing it as the consequence of man's explicit intention to bring about this unity, or by showing that in his theoretical activities, man is bound by a moral imperative. In our own time most people try to account for the unity of the sciences through reflections of a more formal nature and by appealing to standards dictated by logic and methodology. Others believe that the development of an appropriate metalanguage is a necessary and sufficient condition for the mediation between the different sciences. Some of them are of the opinion that this metalanguage should be derived from our ordinary language in which all transdisciplinary problems are already articulated as life-world issues.

When it became clear that none of these attempts was completely satisfactory, some people thought that perhaps general systems theory, structuralism, or cybernetics could help us account for the unity of the sciences; others have suggested that perhaps the idea that all sciences ultimately flow from the life world could provide us with a clue as to how the basic problem is to be solved. Transdisciplinarians feel that there may be a core of truth in most of these suggestions, but still maintain that we shall not come to an acceptable solution of the basic problem if we cannot find a perspective from which all of these suggestions can be fitted together. In their opinion such an all-encompassing perspective can only be found through philosophical reflection, the latter understood as the critical reflection on man's experiences from the perspective of the *totality of meaning of which we at this moment in time can conceive.*

Be this as it may, all authors agree on one basic point, namely that the unity of the sciences will not follow automatically from the conviction that the order of ideas has to adapt itself to a pregiven order of things. Instead this unity is continually to be brought about and accounted for by those who actually engage in scientific research. These efforts will remain fruitless if we cannot first come to some agreement about the totality of meaning in which, in light of our Western tradition, we would like to live, and about the position that the sciences will have in that totality of meaning in addition to religion, morality, the arts, and our sociopolitical praxis. And this agreement cannot be brought about except by philosophical reflection.

Many scientists will reject these ideas, not realizing that the expression *philosophy* is not used here to refer to the work in which philosophers "of profession" engage but to that dimension in every man's life that critically mediates between what is and what is to come. This suggests that the *entire* community of scholars should continuously reflect critically upon the past in order to prepare the totality of meaning or world in which all of us would like to live.

If the question concerning the unity of the sciences is understood as a philosophical problem in this sense, namely, as a problem intrinsic to man's continuous tending toward meaning, then integration becomes the principle of genuine research, and the questions that lie at the borderlines of each discipline will then appear to be the most fundamental ones. Transdisciplinarity will then be understood as a specific attitude in regard to the sciences, an attitude oriented toward comprehending the contributions of each discipline from the perspective of man's search for meaning, which itself is suprascientific because inherently human.

The individual sciences taken in isolation cannot provide us with such a perspective, except when they become ideologies. There was a time when people believed that the world described by physics could be one in which people can live meaningfully, humanly, and humanely. Today the social sciences often appear as the ideology for our time. Genuine transdisciplinarity implies that one is willing to transcend the limited perspective of one's own discipline, and this implies that transdisciplinarity is possible only in the form of a critical, philosophical reflection in the sense indicated.

Many scientists will object that our transdisciplinarians are being carried away here. They will argue either that all this talk about meaning is nonsense, because it is totally incomprehensible; or they will say that there is no genuine meaning except that for which the sciences themselves can account; or they will perhaps argue that the concern for meaning is the task of philosophy of science. Yet problems of meaning and humane relevance are alien to the sciences, if the term *science* is taken in the strict sense. When the sciences speak about man, they speak about man as an object; some form of abstraction, reduction, and idealization is the price we have to pay in order for them to achieve the greatest possible clarity and certainty. Thus it is understandable why scientists, strictly speaking as scientists, at first have difficulty in seeing the real point transdisciplinarians try to make. Maybe they will begin to see the concern of the transdisciplinarian, when they reflect on those cases in which scientific data were and are being used to promote obviously inhumane causes.

Thus transdisciplinarians suggest that it is important to distinguish between two kinds of reflections scientists may engage in; the first is concerned with the establishment and explanation of the facts and the real state of affairs; the second focuses on the clarification of the meaning of the first in regard to the life we have to live in our world. To these different forms of reflection there correspond two different ways of conceiving of the world and of man himself. When C.P. Snow spoke of two different cultures in Western civilization, he identified the first with the world of the natural and behavioral sciences, and the second with that of the humanities. Perhaps it would have been more important for him to refer here to the two basic ways in which scientific man can and must conceive of the world and of himself. For the real issue to which Snow's distinction points is not one that separates scientists from humanists but one with which *every* scientist has to cope when he realizes that to be scientific and to be human and humane do not necessarily coincide. The question becomes one of how we can make certain that these two indeed will go hand in hand.

The crisis in which modern man finds himself today is connected with the fact that he has lost the unquestionable foundations of the past: religion, a universally accepted morality on the basis of religion, and a universally accepted philosophical world view, in which always a certain ideal conception concerning the humanity of man was implied. Whether religion and a certain conception of morality are inherent dimensions of a man's life or whether they are not, the fact is that both have become powerless in our scientific era as a base upon which all of us can stand. Furthermore it is clear by now that an appeal to traditional forms of humanism cannot save us from nihilism and total alienation. According to transdisciplinarians, neither science nor technology, neither scientism nor technocracy, neither humanism nor nihilist skepticism can lead us away from the crisis in which we find ourselves today, because none of them is capable of transcending the antinomy between a purely scientific conception of world and a human conception of it. If we are to overcome the grave dangers of our era, we shall have to turn to the second form of reflection mentioned above.

No one is saying here that science and technology do not have their positive sides; the point merely is that we shall be confronted with very serious problems if we do not try to mediate the tension between science and life, between a scientific and a livable world. In this process of mediation, both history and literature play an important role along with philosophical reflection.

It will be obvious that the ideas suggested by transdisciplinarians have important implications for the political responsibility of all scientists as well as the educational task of those who teach the sciences at the universities. Over the past 150 years many scientists have based their scientific activities on the following assumptions: 1) science is the only access to the truth; 2) taken as theoretical enterprise science is inherently value free; 3) those who contribute to the advancement of science bear no responsibility for the way the results of scientific research can or are being used; 4) when scientific ideas are to be applied, only scientific and pragmatic criteria are to be taken into consideration. These assumptions create a sphere in which politicians have used or abused scientific findings to further their political ideologies. Obviously on many occasions scientists have objected to their scientific insights being abused; yet even in these cases the ethical principles employed were principles that were determined merely scientifically. Transdisciplinarians are fully aware that transdisciplinary research and reflection are incapable of creating or inventing values and moral standards and of forcing politicians to abide by moral principles. Yet they believe that transdisciplinary reflections could bring about an important change if they were to become an essential part of everyone's education, scientists and politicians alike.

Summary and Conclusion

From the preceding pages it will be clear that the answer to the question of why one should engage in transdisciplinary reflections contains elements that can be set forth in favor of all nondisciplinary efforts in research and education. Of all of these efforts one can say that they have their origin in a dissatisfaction with the compartmentalization of our disciplines and interdisciplines, both as research and educational enterprises. According to many, the administrative structure of our universities has promoted this compartmentalization and thus makes nondisciplinary efforts both necessary and difficult. What is asked for in all of these nondisciplinary efforts is cooperation between the representatives of disciplines and interdisciplines in order to come to a solution for important problems that go beyond the borderlines and the range of competence of our traditional disciplines.

I agree with the authors concerned with interdisciplinarity in the limited sense, that if there are important problems to be found in areas lying between the domains of existing disciplines, which neither of the respective disciplines is capable of adequately formulating and treating, then new research areas are to be opened up and new interdisciplines to be developed. Yet I have been unable to find in the literature a *satisfactory* solution for the problems to which this development leads from an educational and administrative point of view.

As for crossdisciplinary efforts, our complex world confronts us with important and urgent problems that the existing disciplines cannot adequately treat, although in many instances a concern with these problems does not imply the necessity of developing a new discipline or interdiscipline. In these cases an adequate and genuine understanding of these problems and any attempt to find a reasonable solution for them presupposes cooperation between those who have specialized knowledge of the relevant aspects of these complex problems. In the literature I have not found a convincing answer to the question of what steps crossdisciplinarians should take in order to make certain that they have a firm common ground from which they can come to a meaningful exchange of ideas concerning a given problem.

Many authors feel that nondisciplinary efforts are only partly justified by reference to complex problems that the isolated disciplines and interdisciplines are incapable of solving. It seems to be the transdisciplinary efforts in particular that refer to a basic tension between science and society. Specialization in the sciences can regain its value for a man's life only through transdisciplinary efforts, because these contribute immediately to the unification of our overall conception of world. Thus it is not the formal unification of the sciences as promoted by the Vienna Circle that is searched for under the label of transdisciplinarity but rather a uniform framework that is capable of reducing the tension between the world in which we would like to live and the fragmented worlds depicted by the different sciences.

I agree with Gusdorf that transdisciplinary efforts should be concerned primarily with the unity of our entire intellectual framework as well as with the unity of our conception of world, and that all measures to reconstruct this unity out of the fragmented worlds depicted by the sciences are ineffectual. Luyten appears to be correct when he suggests that philosophy and history must play an important part in these efforts. What these authors actually propose seems to imply that all specialization should flow form a very broad education involving both the sciences and the humanities. And this suggestion is in harmony with the idea proposed by other authors to the effect that our universities should not limit their efforts to *training* students, but in addition should focus on an all-around *education* for everyone who enters the university. Schwartz has synthesized these ideas somewhat more harmoniously by asserting that the unity of our conception of world is not to be found or discovered, but that time and again it is *to be brought about,* and that our theoretical justification for such a unity will have to take the form of a transdisciplinary effort.

In order to prevent misunderstanding I would like to make two observations. First, it is generally accepted that far-reaching specialization makes an effective dialogue between scientists of different background very difficult. These difficulties are much greater in the discourse between scientists and social leaders, politicians, and citizens. To facilitate these necessary forms of discourse the university will have to train people who are capable of translating scientific ideas into insights that can be understood by the educated members of the community at large, so that the most important findings of the sciences can be applied to the good for society. Some people believe that transdisciplinary efforts are primarily concerned with the popularization of scientific knowledge. This is obviously not the case, although it is true that our society is in need of such popularization through "science brokers."

Second, people who argue in favor of transdisciplinarity do not suggest that one could educate people to become nothing but transdisciplinarians. Most authors think that the university should educate students to be disciplinarians with a transdisciplinary concern. At any rate, these authors do not intend to suggest that all students should be exposed systematically to all disciplines.

It seems to me that transdisciplinarians tend to get carried away once in a while. Some of them have formulated their basic concern from a conceptual framework and in a language not universally shared by all philosophers, scientists, and educators. Yet I find the basic point stressed by the transdisciplinarians to be a correct one, and a very important one: the tension between the worlds which our sciences describe and the world in which we would actually like to live must be overcome. This cannot be accomplished on the basis of scientific rationality alone; scientific rationality is to be complemented by a form of critical reflection that is of a typically philosophical nature. This reflection will have to become an integral part of all forms of research and education. In other words, the basic thesis of the transdisciplinarians has important implications, which are both educational and political in character. What these implications may be in detail is at this point less important than the willingness to discuss them where they arise. Finally our university students will be prepared for such a discussion to the degree that their specialization has flowed naturally from a broad education in which both the humanities and the sciences have been integral parts.

Notes

1. *Interdisciplinarity: Problems of Teaching and Research in Universities* (Paris: OECD, 1972).
2. Ms., United States International University, San Diego, 1970.
3. To prevent misunderstanding I wish to stress here that it is not my intention to "freeze" a develop-

ment that is still in progress. My aim thus is not to try to settle the discussion on terminology once and for all, but rather to make a positive contribution to this discussion.

4. Heinz Heckhausen, "Discipline and Interdisciplinarity," in *Interdisciplinarity*, pp. 83–89.
5. Jean Piaget, "The Epistemology of Interdisciplinary Relationships," in *Interdisciplinarity*, pp. 127–39, and *Main Trends in Inter-Disciplinary Research* (New York: Harper and Row, 1973); Erich Jantsch, "Towards Interdisciplinarity and Transdisciplinarity in Education and Innovation," in *Interdisciplinarity*, pp. 97–121; cf. Russell L. Achoff, "Systems, Organizations, and Interdisciplinary Research," *General Systems* 5 (1960): 1–8.
6. M. Boisot, "Discipline and Interdisciplinarity," in *Interdisciplinarity*, pp. 89–97.
7. Cf. *Interdisciplinarity*, pp. 25–26.
8. Donald D. Campbell, "Ethnocentrism of Disciplines and the Fish-Scale Model of Omniscience," in *Interdisciplinary Relationships in the Social Sciences*, ed. Muzafer Sherif and Carolyn W. Sherif (Chicago: Aldine, 1969), pp. 328–48.
9. Muzafer Sherif and Carolyn W. Sherif, "Interdisciplinary Coordination as a Validity Check," in *Interdisciplinary Relationships in the Social Sciences*, pp. 3–20; cf. pp. vii–xii.
10. Mahan, chapters 4–6; Asa Briggs and Guy Michaud, "Problems and Solution," in *Interdisciplinarity*, pp. 185–252; J.R. Gass, "Preface," ibid., pp. 9–10; Guy Michaud, "General Conclusions," ibid., pp. 281–88; H. Holzhey, "Interdisziplinarität (Nachwort)," in H. Holzhey, ed., *Interdisziplinär* (Basel: Schwabe, 1974), pp. 105–29; Reimut Jochemsen, "Zur gesellschaftspolitischen Relevanz interdisziplinärer Zusammenarbeit," ibid., pp. 9–35.
11. Cf. Mahan, pp. 119–96.
12. Cf. Piaget, *Main Trends in Inter-Disciplinary Research*; Anthony J. Wilden, *System and Structure: Essays in Communication and Exchange* (London: Tavistock, 1972); L. von Bertalanffy, *General System Theory: Foundations, Development, Applications* (New York: George Braziller, 1968); E. Laszlo, *Introduction to System Philosophy* (New York: Gordon and Breach, 1972); Mahan, chapter 5. For further bibliography, see the works by Wilden, Laszlo, and Mahan.
13. Gordon J. DiRenzo, "Toward Explanation in the Behavioral Sciences," in Gordon J. DiRenzo, ed., *Concepts, Theory, and Explanation in the Behavioral Sciences* (New York: Random House, 1966), p. 238.
14. Guy Berger, "The Interdisciplinary Archipelago," in *Interdisciplinarity*, pp. 35–74; Briggs and Michaud, "Problems and Solutions," ibid., pp. 185–252; Mahan, chapter 5.
15. Washington, D.C.: National Laboratories, 1958.
16. *The Behavioral and Social Sciences: Outlook and Needs* (Englewood Cliffs, N.J.: Prentice-Hall, 1969), pp. 202 ff.
17. Georges Gusdorf, "Interdisciplinaire (Connaissance)," in *Encyclopedia Universalis*, vol. 8 (Paris: 1970), pp. 1086–90. Cf. Gusdorf, *Les sciences humaines et la pensée occidentale*, 6 vols. (Paris: Payot, 1966–73); *Introduction aux sciences humaines* (Paris: Belles Lettres, 1960).
18. Norbert A. Luyten, "Interdisziplinarität und Einheit der Wissenschaft," *Int. J. Interdis. Forschung*. 1 (1974): 132–53.
19. Cf. Briggs and Michaud, "Problems and Solution"; Reimut Jochimsen, "Zur gesellschaftspolitischen"; Helmut Holzhey, "Interdisziplinarität."
20. Cf. Guy Berger, "Opinions and Facts," in *Interdisciplinarity*, pp. 21–74.
21. George W. Morgan, "Disciplinary and Interdisciplinary Research and Human Studies," *Int. J. Interdis. Forschung*. 1 (1974): 263–81.
22. "Interdisziplinarität der Wissenschaften als Problem und Aufgabe heute," *Int. J. Interdis. Forschung*. 1 (1974): 1–131 and the literature quoted there, particularly the publications of W. Dilthey, E. Spranger, E. Cassirer, E. Husserl, M. Heidegger, K. Jaspers, A. Dempf, P. Lorenzen, J. Habermas, W. Pannenberg, H. Albert, K. Popper, H. Schelsky, Fr.-J. von Rintelen, R. Guardini, H.J. Meyer, K.-O. Appel, J. Ritter, H. von Hentig, W. Stegmüller, H.-G. Gadamer, O. Bolnow, E. Fink, etc. Cf. also: E. Becker, *The Structure of Evil: An Essay on the Unification of the Sciences of Man* (New York: George Braziller, 1968); William K. Kapp, *Toward a Science of Man in Society: A Positive Approach to the Integration of Social Knowledge* (The Hague: Nijhoff, 1961); L. Leary, *The Unity of Knowledge* (New York: Doubleday, 1955); Margaret Baron Luszki, *Interdisciplinary Team Research: Methods and Problems* (Washington, D.C.: The National Training Laboratories, 1958); C.F.A. Pantin, *The Relations Between the Sciences* (New York: Cambridge University Press, 1968).

Guide to Interdisciplinary Syllabus Preparation

Association for Integrative Studies and Institute in Integrative Studies

A. Relation to the Disciplines

1. Is the course issue-based (e.g., societal problem, historical moment, text, geographical region, or a key concept)? What question about the issue is the course designed to explore? What makes that question appropriate to interdisciplinary inquiry?
2. Is the issue focused enough? Are there few enough sub-issues, for instance, for students to develop an understanding of the various perspectives on the issue (and facility with the concepts, theories, and methods introduced)?
3. Are the perspectives of disciplines or schools of thought explicit? Are their respective contributions to the issue explicit?
4. How dominant is one discipline? Do the less-dominant disciplines provide more than subject matter?

B. Course Structure

5. Is there a "hook" or "grabber" at the beginning that draws students into the issue, motivating them to learn about it, and that serves as touchstone for the course (e.g., movie, newspaper article)?
6. Is the structure of the course clear? Does the syllabus serve as a map of, or orientation to, the course? Do the tools, readings, and subtext for each week reinforce each other and advance the understanding of the issue? (Note: Starting with a conceptual map or flowchart may help in thinking about the structure and facilitate connections.)
7. Does the instructor have an explicit subtext (the "real" educational agenda—e.g., exposure to disciplines, development of skills/values/sensitivities—of which the substantive topic is a particular embodiment)?
8. Is integration on-going, or does it appear only at the end of the course (following serial presentation of disciplinary perspectives, insight, or methods)?
9. Is the level of the course (introductory, more advanced, senior) consistent with the depth in which disciplinary perspectives are presented, the explicitness with which their assumptions are probed, the sophistication of the

"Guide to Interdisciplinary Syllabus Preparation." Journal of General Education 45:2 (1996). Reprinted with permission.

disciplinary tools and their use by students, the explicitness about interdisciplinary method, and the overall balance between breadth and depth?

10. Does more than one discipline contribute to the depth in the course?

11. If the course is multi-sectioned, is there a common syllabus and readings? Do faculty consult weekly to determine what should be discussed in sections? Are there common paper assignments and exams and explicit agreement on a common set of grading standards?

12. Have connections been explored to complementary pedagogies or concerns reflecting other institutional objectives such as collaborative learning, critical thinking, learning styles and stages, or multiculturalism?

C. Level of Integration Attempted

Multidisciplinary?

- Do contributing faculty tend to work on their separate parts of the course?
- Do they tend to see the topic only from the perspective of their discipline?
- Has their disciplinary perspective remained unaltered while developing the course?
- Is the contact among disciplines limited to sharing data?
- Is there not even a section at the end of the course reserved for integration?
- Are students expected to undertake any integration without faculty assistance?
- Are disciplinary methodologies and epistemologies unexamined or unstated?

Pluridisciplinary?

- Is there a section of the course that is "ours" instead of "mine" or "yours," where faculty can talk to each other even if no integration occurs?
- Do faculty begin to understand each other's perspective, though their own remains unaltered?
- Does the contact among disciplines include recognizing similarities and differences in their interpretations of data, methodologies, or assumptions?
- Is methodology or epistemology implicit in discussion at the end of the course?

Cross-disciplinary?

- Is there a dominant-subordinate pattern to faculty interactions, where one faculty member tends to prevail?
- Does the practice of one discipline become the subject matter of the another discipline?
- Is there a conclusion resulting from new insights but no integration because only one disciplinary perspective is evident?

Interdisciplinary?

- Do faculty tend to work together as much as alone?
- Do they interact instead of merely working jointly?
- Did the issue of the course shift as the course evolved?
- Have faculty perspectives on that issue been altered in the process?
- Is there collaboration between students and faculty in forging a synthesis/integration?
- Does the synthesis result in a larger, more holistic understanding of the issue? Has a new metaphor been created?
- Have the perspective of each discipline and some of its key underlying assumptions been brought to light and made explicit?
- Does the contact among disciplines include: reasoning by analogy from the data, theory, methods, or models of another discipline? revising hypotheses or principles in light of evidence uncovered by another discipline? redefining or extending definitions of key concepts from each discipline to form a common ground on which to integrate their insights? replacing conflicting assumptions with new variables (e.g., assumptions that people are free or determined are replaced by looking at the extent of influence)?

Philosophical Analysis

Five Arguments Against Interdisciplinary Studies

Thomas C. Benson

In our enthusiasm and occasional defensiveness concerning interdisciplinary studies, we sometimes fail to listen carefully to the arguments of its numerous opponents. Instead of attending to the diverse charges and criticisms, it is tempting to concentrate on the strengths and merits of interdisciplinary studies—presumably on the assumption that well-articulated pluses will cancel the alleged minuses. After all, there is no defense like a good offense. This inattentiveness to the substance of the criticisms of interdisciplinary studies is not without its consequences. Not only do we squander opportunities to respond effectively to arguments that rest upon correctable misperceptions of interdisciplinary studies, but we also neglect potentially valuable instruction concerning our weaknesses.

In this brief paper, I shall identify five of the most popular arguments against a substantial role for interdisciplinary studies in the undergraduate curriculum. Each argument will be sketched in broad terms, with no attempt made to defend interdisciplinary studies from the respective charges. Call this, if you will, a bit of enlightened devil's advocacy. The temptation to respond to the diverse arguments has been checked, not for want of inspiration, but in keeping with the stated purpose of the paper: to focus attention on the nature of the arguments against interdisciplinary studies. It is clear that there are some important arguments against interdisciplinary studies neglected in my brief inventory. Those that I have included, however, strike me as being at or near the top of the list in popularity and forcefulness.

The first argument against interdisciplinary studies is that it rests upon *serious conceptual confusion*. Quite simply, the practitioners of interdisciplinary studies lack a coherent, defensible sense of their purposes. Interdisciplinary studies purports to be concerned with examining and developing significant lines of connection between two or more disciplines. It is not at all clear, however, just what it means to connect the disciplines nor what the value of such activity might be. Most of the discussion of interdisciplinary or integrative studies assumes clarity in these matters and moves on to other concerns. Part of the difficulty here might be thought to derive from the notorious uncertainties surrounding the nature of the disciplines themselves. Seen in the worst light, integrative studies is a fool's project, propounding equations where *all* the terms are unknown. Things are not quite this bad, however, and although the arbi-

Benson, Thomas C. *"Five Arguments Against Interdisciplinary Studies."* Issues in Integrative Studies *1 (1982), 38–48. Reprinted with permission.*

trary hands of chance and politics have played important roles in the definition of the disciplines,[1] their latter-day contours and boundaries turn out, on the whole, to make surprisingly good sense. Each of the disciplines offers us some general criteria for locating questions inside or outside of its boundaries. For the most part, the boundary lines among the disciplines are drawn by means of appeal either to a distinctive subject matter or to a distinctive method of inquiry. There is, of course, nothing perfectly neat or grayless in such boundary demarcations; but most of the problems are confined to marginal cases and relatively minor "turf" disputes. The lack of clarity associated with integrative studies cannot be excused, then, as derivative from the underlying vagueness of the concept of the disciplines.

If the connection among the disciplines contemplated by integrative studies is nothing more than a matter of borrowing insights or methods from one or more disciplines to illuminate problems in another, it seems fair to ask why such extra-curricular borrowing is called "integration." The concept of integration suggests a more substantial and enduring bond than that involved in the paradigms of integrative studies. Indeed, the proponents of integrative studies seem unwilling to regard the envisioned connections among the disciplines as forming a permanent bond. The disciplines are not dissolved in the transactions of integrative studies. Moreover, the kind of borrowing suggested in the proposed account of integrative studies already occurs routinely within the framework of most disciplinary activity. The physicist is lost without the tools of mathematics; the political scientist borrows insights from sociology, history and economics; the literary studies scholar makes use of the methods of linguistics and analytic philosophy. There is nothing special about this import/export business across disciplinary lines; and it hasn't occurred to anyone to call the process integrative or interdisciplinary. Clearly, the proponent of integrative studies owes us a better account of the nature of the integration he contemplates, one that is, at once, coherent and non-trivial.

In addition to demystifying the nature of the disciplinary connections he seeks, the proponent of integrative studies should be prepared to articulate more fully the principle or principles that determine when these connections are to be sought. The disciplines, as we have noted, are guided by broad, internal standards of relevance, whether that of distinctive subject matter or of method. But what principles guide the integrative studies practitioner in choosing to make these connections rather than those? Is he responding to some larger teleological sense of the natural connectedness of things or is his motivation essentially pragmatic, stimulated by what he sees as theoretical or practical impasses within specific disciplines? There appears to be no agreement among integrative studies advocates in this matter. Some talk about a grand holistic scheme and the unity of knowledge, while others speak more modestly about the practical value of interdisciplinary projects in the solving of specific problems. Still others see the applications of integrative studies as primarily centered in instruction rather than research. However sharp the contrasts here, the diverse options tend to be discussed with a characteristic air of romance and all too little rigor and specificity. For all of their worried criticism concerning the dominance of the disciplinary model in higher education and their curative ambitions, the proponents of integrative studies have given surprisingly little attention to the important work of defining their goals and their methods clearly. The consequences of this neglect can be seen both in the lack of reliable traditions and literature concerning interdisciplinary studies teaching and in the widespread doubts about the intellectual foundations and value of integrative studies.

A second argument against interdisciplinary studies holds that it is a *pedagogically doubtful business to spend time in interdisciplinary learning projects when the student lacks a mature base in any of the contributing disciplines.* Sound educational development requires proper background and critical participation on the part of the student. Having no firm hold on any of the associated disciplinary traditions, the student in an interdisciplinary studies course or curriculum can be little more than a spectator to the marshalling of arguments, methods, and insights from the diverse contributing disciplines, with their voluminous literature and often highly technical research traditions. However exhilarating the discussion, the interdisciplinary studies course promises little in the way of long-term benefits for the student. If integrative studies are to be pursued properly and have lasting value, the student must first acquire a strong foundation in at least one of the contributing disciplines. This suggests that substantial involvement in integrative studies should be deferred to a point relatively late in the undergraduate career. And, even at this point, given the demands associated with the acquisition of disciplinary competence, it is likely to be of doubtful value.

Undergraduate programs in interdisciplinary studies appear fated to wander between two unattractive poles—either they assume disciplinary sophistication in the students, in which case most, if not all, of the students are left in the dark, unable to manipulate the central issues at stake or—and this is much more frequently the case—they assume little, and the program of study is diluted and homogenized to the point where it is almost totally devoid of a critical base. Under the guise of an invitation to wrestle with what are frequently fascinating and important issues, the student is cheated of a precious opportunity to develop the skills and background required for mounting a proper attack on the issues. As Robert Paul Wolff has noted in *The Ideal of the University,* undergraduate courses in theoretical economics and logic may well do more to prepare students for grappling with the socio-political crises of their time than interdisciplinary seminars on poverty and the philosophy of war.[2]

We are facing a growing crisis in the planning and politics of the undergraduate curriculum. The explosion of knowledge in the disciplines is leaving less and less time for study outside the student's major disciplinary program. On many campuses, the requirements for major programs in mathematics and the natural sciences constitute as much as 2/3's of the student's academic program. Although a backlash in favor of stronger liberal arts distribution requirements has appeared on some campuses, it is difficult to see how the tide of early and intensive specialization in a disciplinary area can be resisted. Adequate preparation for graduate and professional study and for careers in the disciplinary area requires increasing amounts of course work in the major program.

On this account, a third argument against interdisciplinary studies has acquired heightened importance. It is argued that *a substantial commitment to integrative studies in the undergraduate program will impede the student's development of an essential disciplinary competence.*

However attractive the ideal may be in the abstract, there simply is not enough time within the traditional four year, 120 credit framework of undergraduate education to do all of the things that our educational ideals suggest. We are being forced with increasing urgency to cut corners, to choose the lesser from among a number of curricular evils. Whatever sacrifices we make, it seems clear that we cannot forfeit the development of sound, critically based disciplinary competence. Such competence is best fostered in the rigorous and orderly pursuit of a well-designed sequence of disciplinary courses. The idea that disciplinary competence can be acquired in the midst of a substantial commitment to a program of integrative studies is so much wishful thinking—given the time, energy, and learning abilities of most undergraduate students. Of course, a proper regard for the liberal arts ideal requires some learning experiences beyond the disciplinary concentration. Here it seems preferable to introduce the undergraduate to the foundations, the essential concepts, methods and traditions of a range of disciplines through undiluted, introductory level courses. Rather than teasing a student with fragmentary exposure to philosophy and literary studies in an interdisciplinary course in philosophy and literature, let him take a rigorous course in the classics of Western literature and/or a challenging introductory course in philosophy.

The primary responsibility of the university, given the premium on time and study opportunities, is to equip the student with adequate foundations for future growth and development. Although a course here and there along the way in interdisciplinary studies may make sense for some students, such activity should be kept to a minimum and pushed to the margins of the college agenda. Interdisciplinary studies opportunities on a more substantial scale are best left to extracurricular agencies, e.g., community forums, topical conferences and institutes, and continuing education programs.

The cultivation of competence in a particular discipline is not just a matter of educational ideals, it is also, increasingly, a matter of practical importance. Students seeking admission to graduate school and entry to highly competitive career areas are faced with requirements and expectations that stress close identification with and substantial development in a particular disciplinary tradition. However arbitrary and unfair such standards may be, they are part of the post-graduate world to which the student must adapt. Students must be advised of these expectations and assisted in finding a sensible pattern of response. It is unconscionable for interdisciplinary studies faculty to use students as unwitting flag bearers for their dreams of educational reform. To be sure, there are student aspirations and career plans that can be adequately served by undergraduate programs concentrating in integrative studies. For most students, however, the price of concentration in integrative studies, with the attending neglect of a disciplinary base, will be the risk of disqualification from coveted graduate school and job opportunities.

Among the more popular arguments directed against interdisciplinary studies programs none is as widely subscribed as the charge that *integrative studies courses are characteristically shallow, trading intellectual rigor for topical excitement.*[3] This fourth argument has special currency among academic traditionalists who are instinctively suspicious of any course that sounds remotely "relevant" or of popular interest, and among rivals in the disciplinary departments who are sensitive to what they see as naked marketing ploys in the escalating competition for student registration. Some of it, however, issues from a genuine concern for academic integrity and what might be called truth-in-teaching standards. Student enrollment response to an appealing seminar theme and even favorable student course evaluations are not necessarily the best measures of the worth of a course. The emphasis in contemporary mass media on "big picture" treatment of broad themes has stimulated a demand in the academic market for comparably wide-angled course offerings. Some integrative studies faculty play to this vogue with results that can only re-inforce the hostile stereotypes of the interdisciplinary studies course. Although there are, to be sure, many demanding and intellectually rich programs and courses focusing on attractive topical issues, there are simply too many interdisciplinary studies faculty driving curricular ice cream trucks down the academic alleys.

Not only are many of the "big picture" integrative seminars ill-conceived, but there is also a disturbing tendency for such courses to be taught in a sloppy, chat-in-the-round fashion that does little to cultivate either critical skills or a systematic grasp of the issues under review. The pedagogical deficiencies in these courses are frequently compounded by a heavy reliance on splashy special events: guest speakers, films, video-cassettes, and other classroom equivalents of easy-listening radio. Instead of a carefully planned, intellectually demanding mix of lectures, sharply focused discussions, exams, and papers, the student is exposed to a semester long variety show, doubtless interesting, but of very little long term educational value. Moreover, even where there are adequate measures of order, method, and rigor in the integrative studies seminar, the theme often fails to "pan out." The anticipated synthesis fails to materialize. In such cases, some may wish to write the seminar off as a noble experiment that failed. Such failures are so common, however, as to raise serious questions about the judgment and, still worse, the integrity of many interdisciplinary studies teachers. It is irresponsible to use students as semester-long guinea pigs in the testing of what are frequently half-baked notions of curricular value. As the popular television spots for the Black colleges insist: "A mind is a terrible thing to waste."

A fifth argument against interdisciplinary studies programs focuses on the *relatively high cost of the typical integrative studies course.* In a time of embattled budgets and overburdened academic resources, it is argued that the interdisciplinary studies programs, with their heavy reliance on team-teaching methods, special events, independent study, and relatively low faculty-student ratios, are extravagant and cost ineffective. It is assumed that the interdisciplinary studies programs cannot accomplish their goals without substantial resort to such expensive practices. The integrative studies programs are not charged with profligacy, but rather with a lack of redeeming educational value, sufficient to offset their hefty price tags. Proponents of this argument also note that many interdisciplinary studies programs place further burdens on severely limited academic budgets by either borrowing adjunct teachers from the disciplinary departments, creating thereby a need for part-time replacements, or by hiring their own psychologist or sociologist or historian, etc., and thus duplicating—albeit with dubious quality control—the faculty resources already available in the department.

There are additional complaints about interdisciplinary studies worth examining; e.g., there is the claim that integrative studies faculty are, for the most part, second-class scholars, exiles and refugees from the disciplinary departments, where they either failed to measure-up or found themselves incapable of sustaining the kind of rigor and focus required for success in disciplinary scholarship. However painful the project, it would be a useful service to integrative studies to identify these additional arguments. It would also be helpful to examine the criticisms of interdisciplinary studies in an historical light and with a view toward the discover of both patterns of frequency and the correlations between particular arguments and the disciplinary base of their proponents.

Beyond the extension of the list of significant criticisms of interdisciplinary studies and the varieties of analysis suggested above lies the important and difficult work of responding to the arguments, both intellectually and politically. In meeting this challenge, it will not suffice simply to impart what we already know. Clearly, we need to know more. We need to think more fully and critically about the logical foundations of integrative studies. We need to develop more compelling justifications for including substantial integrative studies work in the ever more crowded undergraduate curriculum. We need to articulate more fully the connections between disciplinary work and interdisciplinary studies in the realization of the liberal arts ideal. We must cultivate and give increased attention to post-graduate study and career opportunities for students concentrating in integrative studies. We must place a greater emphasis on rigor and learning that lasts in the design and teaching of interdisciplinary studies courses; and, finally, we must give more urgent attention to program economies that will allow integrative studies work to continue, while not sacrificing the unique values and traditions that have distinguished our work.

Notes

1. Cf. Frederick Rudolph, *The American College and University* (New York, 1962), pp. 399–400.
2. Robert Paul Wolff, *The Ideal of the University* (Boston, 1969), pp. 78–79.
3. Cf. Christopher Jencks and David Riesman, *The Academic Revolution* (New York, 1968), p. 498.

The Case for Interdisciplinary Studies

Response to Professor Benson's Five Arguments

William H. Newell

The objective of this paper is to respond serially to Professor Benson's five arguments by setting forth a conception of interdisciplinary study, not necessarily as it is practiced but as it should be, which largely meets his criticisms.[1] The final section of the paper offers suggestions for steps that the interdisciplinary studies profession should take to respond fully and effectively to its critics.

A. Responses to the Five Arguments

1. Interdisciplinary Studies Rest on Serious Conceptual Confusion.

While single interdisciplinary courses may have a clear sense of purpose and method, it is undeniable that the practitioners of interdisciplinary or integrative studies share no such clear sense. This is apparent in the very analysis used by Professor Benson. While he assumes that interdisciplinary studies are concerned with "connections . . . between disciplines,"[2] he recognizes that some interdisciplinarians are more concerned with connections in the real world ("the natural connectedness of things"[3]), others with connections in ("the unity of") our knowledge of that real world, while still others emphasize the "practical value of interdisciplinary projects in the solving of specific problems"[4] where it is unclear that any of the above connections are of direct concern. In my view this last problem-solving conception of interdisciplinary studies is the most fruitful. It has the greatest capability of meeting the five arguments against interdisciplinary studies, and the connections that it requires are different from any of the above.

Interdisciplinary study should be understood to start with the confrontation of the interdisciplinarian with the world, be it a problem, an event, or even a painting. Out of that phenomenological confrontation comes a question, one which is too broad to be answered by any single discipline. The strategy of the interdisciplinarian is to bring the relevant disciplines (or schools of thought) to bear upon the question, one at a time, letting each illuminate that aspect of the question which is amenable to treatment by the characteristic concepts, theories, and methods of the respective disciplines. Out of the resulting disciplinary insights, the interdisciplinarian fashions a response to the question that would ideally be a complete answer but which at the least leads to a greater apprecia-

Newell, William H. "*The Case for Interdisciplinary Studies: Response to Professor Benson's Five Arguments.*" Issues in Integrative Studies 2 (1983), 1–19. *Reprinted with permission.*

tion of the nature and complexity of the question. What distinguishes interdisciplinary study from simple eclecticism is that disciplines provide much more than pieces of a jigsaw puzzle that the interdisciplinarian need merely arrange in proper order. Disciplinary insights are often conflicting, and when the disciplines are chosen from more than one area, such as the natural sciences and the humanities, their insights are typically of a qualitatively different nature as well. As Professor Miller stresses,[5] disciplines each have their distinctive world view or way of looking at the world, and it is these world views with their often contradictory underlying assumptions and diverse value judgments that lead to conflicting or incommensurate insights. The interdisciplinarian, then, may not simply combine disciplinary insights; rather, each world view and its assumptions underlying those insights must be illuminated and then evaluated in the context of the question at hand, before any interdisciplinary answer can be attempted. Out of this process comes a richness of insight not available to the adherent of any one disciplinary orthodoxy, as the interdisciplinarian comes to appreciate the value and legitimacy of alternative perspectives.

Professor Benson asks that we construct a "coherent, defensible sense of (our) purposes," that we be clear on "what it means to connect the disciplines" and on "what the value of such activity might be,"[6] and that we refrain from excusing our lack of clarity on the purported vagueness of the disciplines themselves. He is correct in his contention that none of the notions of "connecting disciplines" which he presents meets these requirements, but I submit that the conception set out above does meet them. The disciplines can give only partial answers to questions that go beyond their bounds, and when seen from the perspective of certain other disciplines their answers seem flawed as well as incomplete.

The purpose of interdisciplinary study is to address questions that transcend disciplinary boundaries. Only the interdisciplinarian, who is familiar with and receptive to those contrasting world views, can deal adequately with such questions. Further, interdisciplinary study does not directly involve the connection of disciplines, which would constitute a colossal intellectual task and a politically hopeless one in times of turf protection. Instead the interdisciplinarian connects disciplinary insights. This task is formidable but limited to the one question at hand, and it admits of the possibility for specialization, so that, for example, an interdisciplinarian might specialize in questions related to the modernization process. Professor Weaver has argued quite convincingly, I believe, that interdisciplinarians can only achieve intellectual respectability when they specialize.[7] Further, the value of interdisciplinary study lies in the fact that many important questions transcend the disciplines.[8] Finally, this conception of interdisciplinary studies in no way depends on well-defined boundaries between disciplines, only on clarity in their insights and in the world view underlying those insights.

Professor Benson goes on to criticize interdisciplinary studies which are nothing more than "a matter of borrowing insights or methods from one or more disciplines to illuminate problems in another." He also insists that we "should be prepared to articulate more fully the principle or principles that determine when these connections are to be sought." He asks, "What principles guide the integrative studies practitioner in choosing to make these connections rather than those?"[9] Finally, he requests that we define our methods more clearly. The conception of interdisciplinary study presented in this paper involves questions transcending any one discipline, thus avoiding the first criticism. The second one is not so easily addressed. Certainly it can be argued that the interdisciplinarian chooses disciplines that purport to address at least some aspect of the question, and the interdisciplinary specialist may only ask questions which require a certain set of disciplines for an answer. But it is not so clear what principles guide the interdisciplinarian in constructing a coherent response to the question out of mutually incoherent disciplinary insights. How does the interdisciplinarian, for example, connect the ethical insights of the philosopher, the technical insights of the natural scientist and the behavioral insights of the economist and political scientist into a coherent proposal for U.S. energy policy? Developing sensitivity to the world views and underlying assumptions of each discipline points out the direction, at least, which the interdisciplinarian must take to look for connections, but we are still far from meeting the last requirement that we spell out our method with some precision.

2. Interdisciplinary Study Requires a Mature Base in the Disciplines.

Professor Benson presents the argument that until a student has a "firm hold" on "at least one of the contributing disciplines," that student can be "little more than a spectator" in interdisciplinary studies because of the "voluminous literature and often highly technical research traditions" of the disciplines. He goes on to note that if students are assumed to have little disciplinary sophistication, the course will be "almost totally void of a critical base."[10]

The appropriate relationship between the disciplines and interdisciplinary study is a divisive issue among interdisciplinarians too. Even those who accept the notion of interdisciplinary study presented in this paper might well argue that it takes time to learn the world view and assumptions of various disciplines, to say nothing of their characteristic concepts, theories, and methods. If interdisciplinary study builds on all these, then perhaps graduate school is the earliest we can expect students to be prepared to undertake serious interdisciplinary study.

I believe, however, that there is an essential complementarity between the disciplines and interdisciplinary study that makes it desirable for students to learn them together, from first semester freshman year on if not in high school. An academic discipline is a challenging intellectual game at best, and a sterile and meaningless exercise at worst, when it is taken out of the context of human experience, which is always too broad and complex to be captured fully by any one discipline. The disciplines need interdisciplinary studies to come alive to the students, to connect meaningfully to their lives, fully as much as interdisciplinary study needs the disciplines. Moreover, when students are thoroughly grounded in a discipline before becoming exposed to interdisciplinary studies, they tend to become indoctrinated into its world view, uncritically accepting its often implicit assumptions.[11] This indoctrination makes even more difficult the task of developing in students the openness to alternative ways of looking at the world which lies at the heart of the interdisciplinary method.

Interdisciplinary studies should, and can, be taught alongside the disciplines. A typical freshman takes four or five courses at a time, each in a different discipline. An early and continuing task in each of these introductory courses is to get the student to think like an economist, a physicist, or whatever, to imbue her or him with the world view of that discipline. Moreover, students are usually given problem sets or writing assignments in each course, in which they are asked to apply what they are learning. No one expects the freshman to bring the sophistication of the graduate student to these tasks, to address the assignments in their full complexity, or to select from the full range of concepts and theories in the technical literature of the disciplines. Why should we think any differently about the freshman student undertaking an interdisciplinary analysis?

A freshman could reasonably take a load of three or four disciplinary courses and an interdisciplinary one that builds on those disciplines. As the student learns the world views of each discipline, she or he can learn to contrast them and scrutinize their assumptions in the interdisciplinary course. The assignments in the interdisciplinary course can start out as simple as those in the disciplinary course, leading the student to draw rudimentary connections between the insights of those disciplines. In fact, the problem can be chosen so that the student need draw only on those disciplinary insights taught so far in the disciplinary courses. Were we to construct such a freshman year, our students would not only learn solid disciplinary material, but they would also learn an interdisciplinary appreciation for those disciplines as limited but useful tools in their own lives.

When the curricular relationship between the disciplines and interdisciplinary studies is viewed in this light, it becomes possible to appreciate the educational merit of a well-conceived interdisciplinary program for freshmen. Instead of the administratively cumbersome freshman year sketched out above, why not set up a program where students are taught the relevant disciplinary materials in the same course where they learn to think about problems from an interdisciplinary perspective? Interdisciplinarians can select and teach the relevant disciplinary materials in the context of analyzing an interdisciplinary question. Disciplinary world views can be contrasted as they are learned and their strengths and limitations revealed as they are applied to an interdisciplinary question that grows out of the experience of the students. For example, I teach a first semester freshman social science course that examines what kind of control the students have over their own lives. They learn a portion of each social science discipline dealing with individual freedom, which means they learn everything from the theory of consumer behavior in economics, to operant conditioning in psychology, to the socialization process in sociology. The theories are treated in their full academic rigor, right down to problem sets with graphs; and their underlying assumptions are examined and explicitly compared. In the concluding section of the course entitled "Freedom within Social

Controls," we pull together these disciplinary insights into a discussion of how much freedom students have and how that freedom can be expanded. Students come away from the course with a critical appreciation of a representative portion or two of each discipline, an appreciation for its analytical power and for its limited but genuine applicability to the world of their experience, and the beginnings of an awareness of the interdisciplinary process. Over a series of such courses, students become familiar with a considerable body of disciplinary material as they develop increasing sophistication in the interdisciplinary method.

While I believe that students can and should learn interdisciplinary studies alongside the disciplines, the difficulty of teaching the interdisciplinary approach should not be underestimated. The kinds of thinking involved in interdisciplinary study are more difficult and require more intellectual maturity than do the disciplines. Scholars studying the process of intellectual development of college students, from Bloom to Piaget to Perry to Kohlberg,[12] have argued that there is a hierarchy of intellectual skills or a series of stages of intellectual development through which students must pass on their way to full intellectual maturity. The integrative thinking required in interdisciplinary study which involves pulling together and synthesizing disparate disciplinary insights into a coherent whole is at the top of the hierarchy. The ability to embrace tentatively the use of one disciplinary world view and then switch to using another, possibly opposing, world view, and take that equally seriously requires some of the most advanced stages of intellectual development. Most freshmen I have taught find these skills difficult to develop, and a few never do; but the majority have risen to the occasion. In spite of the intellectual challenge of interdisciplinary studies, I conclude that they can and should be taught in conjunction with the disciplines instead of waiting for students to develop disciplinary competence first.

3. Interdisciplinary Study Impedes Essential Disciplinary Competence.

The substance of Professor Benson's third argument is that time is scarce in the undergraduate curriculum, time that is required to provide adequate training in the more important disciplines rather than in possibly desirable but clearly less important interdisciplinary study. Disciplines are not only more rigorous and their study an orderly progression into more sophisticated thinking, but they are also practical preparation for graduate schools and competitive careers that expect and require disciplinary training. Time spent outside a disciplinary major in general education, so the argument goes, is best spent in disciplinary introductory courses because they are "rigorous" and "challenging" (not "fragmentary" like interdisciplinary courses) introductions to the "concepts, methods, and traditions" which form the foundations of the disciplines.[13]

The first part of this argument strikes me as having the most force. Certainly some students should major in disciplines, specializing in one intellectual tradition in preparation for a career as a specialist. After all, division of labor based on specialization is essential to an industrialized society. But many, if not a majority, of the jobs in our society bear scant correspondence to any one liberal arts discipline: retail salesmen and administrators are more common than industrial chemists. For such positions, the abilities to understand and critically evaluate the work of experts and to make decisions based on that evaluation seem more important than a specialized knowledge of any one discipline. Furthermore, increasing numbers of careers require specialized backgrounds that are interdisciplinary. Dealing with environmental problems, urban problems, energy problems, and many others requires training in synthetic thinking, in weighing arguments from diverse narrow disciplinary perspectives, and in placing them in the larger context. The narrow vision and piecemeal approaches of disciplinary specialists have only exacerbated these problems.

While the expectations of employers are that college graduates applying for jobs will have a disciplinary major, most employers have no particular loyalty to the academic disciplines, especially when they are hiring for jobs that do not build directly on disciplinary competence. Employers are particularly attracted to interdisciplinary majors because of the abilities of the students "to think conceptually, to identify and solve problems, to understand other value systems, to evaluate alternatives and decide on a course of action, and to change one's opinion in the light of facts."[14] Employers also cite traditional liberal arts skills of effective written and oral communication when they explain why they hired graduates of interdisciplinary programs, as well as affective skills like effective group participation, ethical sensitivity, and constructive response to criticism which reflect the experimental college setting of many interdisciplinary programs. According to available data, placement rates of graduates from interdisciplinary programs are quite high.[15]

The charge that the disciplines are more rigorous and ordered than interdisciplinary studies has some limited validity as well. Because the disciplines have been around longer than formal interdisciplinary study, they have evolved further, become more codified and articulated, and have developed more systematic methods. But if one accepts the conception of interdisciplinary study as based on the disciplines, then serious interdisciplinary studying involves these disciplines in their full intellectual rigor. In addition, it is not at all clear that interdisciplinary study is inherently less rigorous than a discipline at the same point in its evolution. After all, rather rigorous and technical fields like biochemistry can be argued to have grown out of interdisciplinary efforts. Few scholars today would wish to claim that oceanography, for example is nonrigorous. Surely the intellectual skill of synthesis is as challenging as any required by the disciplines. There is an element of art in the interdisciplinary process of synthesis or integration which may never prove amenable to systematization, but many disciplines in the humanities contain similar room for creativity in their method without charges of nonrigor, and there is no basis in principle why interdisciplinary study should face that charge as well.

The argument for a general education composed of introductory disciplinary courses is curious indeed. What can be more fragmented than a series of disciplinary courses that are completely insulated from one another? What can be less fragmented than a well-constructed interdisciplinary course? Nor is it clear that rigor in general education is best served by more of the same disciplinary training. After all, the real claim to rigor by the disciplines is based on their highly developed literatures and technical methods which are inaccessible to students in the introductory course. It may be that the charge here is fundamentally one of poor quality, not fragmentation or lack of rigor. In part, however, I suspect the basis for the charge lies in the implicit premise that the disciplines are sufficient as well as necessary to the world of the intellect, and consequently that introductory courses should have as their primary goal the introduction of a discipline, and only secondarily the introduction of knowledge or intellectual skills. This logic clearly relegates interdisciplinary study to secondary importance at best, but it also begs the question.

On the other hand, if one believes that most use of the disciplines by non-specialists requires the judicious weighing of the contributions of several disciplines to the analysis of a problem and the eventual formulation of a means of dealing with the problem that goes beyond any of the disciplines while being informed by them, then interdisciplinary study forms a necessary component of general education alongside the disciplines. Certainly the trend in higher education over the last few years has been to increase substantially the role of interdisciplinary study in general education. Klein and Gaff found that 69% of the colleges they surveyed include an interdisciplinary component in their new general education programs; 55% require a core of interdisciplinary courses.[16] The motivation for including interdisciplinary study in general education appears similar, at least, to the argument presented here: 53% cite the ability to synthesize as a major objective of their new general education programs.[17]

4. Interdisciplinary Courses Are Shallow.

Professor Benson's fourth argument against including interdisciplinary courses in an undergraduate liberal arts education is that they trade "intellectual rigor for topical excitement."[18] Three criticisms are leveled under this heading. First, too many interdisciplinary courses are big-picture counterparts of the trendy, relevant and superficial treatments of important issues by the mass media: "There are simply too many interdisciplinary faculty driving curricular ice cream trucks down the academic alleys."[19] Second, such courses are "taught in a sloppy, chat-in-the-round fashion that does little to cultivate either critical skills or a systematic grasp of the issues. . . . compounded by a heavy reliance on splashy special events . . ." such as films and guest speakers.[20] Third, too often "the anticipated synthesis fails to materialize," leaving students as guinea pigs for irresponsible faculty who have not thought out the course with sufficient care.[21] Each of these charges is serious, in my opinion, because each contains a substantial element of truth, and my discussion of each is aimed at understanding why, inasmuch as it is defending interdisciplinary studies.

One can reasonably point out, in response to the first point, that interdisciplinary study is ideally suited to address the relevant issues of the day crying out for analysis, that there is educational merit in enhancing student motivation to learn through the use of interesting examples, and that disciplinary criticism comes from sour grapes tasted by faculty whose fields have less innate interest and less direct applicability to the world we all live in than does interdisciplinary study. Nonetheless, I saw many so-called interdisciplinary courses taught in the late 60s and early 70s that were little more than academic froth, and I still run into such courses today on occasion. These courses lack substance, in my opinion, because they ignore the disciplines, preaching instead an ideology or simplistic solution—say the 'soft-path' approach to energy—which draws selectively upon disciplinary findings without giving students any feel for how each discipline arrives at those findings or how each has a different perspective on the issue that might contribute to a richer analysis. I call this approach 'adisciplinary' because it tries to operate in an intellectual vacuum, drawing facts from the disciplines while pretending that their extensive intellectual traditions and well-developed perspectives are nonexistent or worthless.[22] In some cases this approach stems from the faculty member's adherence to any of several partisan ideologies, but in others it simply reflects a lack of clear notion of the nature of interdisciplinary study.

It is not surprising that faculty who are curricularly innovative will be pedagogically innovative as well. Indeed it must take a moss-backed traditionalist to argue that films and guest lectures lead to lack of rigor. But too often self-styled interdisciplinary courses are little more than a sequence of "splashy special events" which replace critical student thinking more than they excite it. Too often discussion groups in interdisciplinary courses slide from recognizing the limited validity of alternative disciplinary perspectives into accepting each participant's perspective as equally valid, without examining either the limitations or interrelationships of those perspectives, and certainly without attempting to synthesize them into a more comprehensive approach to the issue under discussion.

One consequence of innovation is that well-established norms are left behind. Faculty attempting to put together and teach interdisciplinary courses can draw upon no clear curricular and pedagogical guidelines, any more than interdisciplinary researchers can be guided by the canons of interdisciplinary scholarship. Until the interdisciplinary studies profession reaches some agreement on what it means to put together and teach an interdisciplinary course, and do it well, we will continue to find nonrigorous and uncritical interdisciplinary courses designed in good faith by faculty in pursuit of the elusive goal of interdisciplinarity.

The third point especially hits home to me, since most interdisciplinary courses I have taught failed to result in a clear-cut synthesis. My observation is that most other interdisciplinary faculty encounter similar difficulties even though there is widespread agreement that a synthesis at the end of the course is desirable. In some cases, synthesis is attempted by assigning a paper at the end of the course in which the student is asked to integrate the course material into a coherent position or policy or personal statement. I have used this device myself on several occasions. When a paper assignment replaces an integrative unit in the course, however, faculty are simply asking the students to do what they themselves cannot or will not. Synthesis is a skill that requires training and practice and feedback like any other skill: assigning the task of synthesis and grading the result does little to foster the development of this skill. Especially with a higher order skill like synthesis, students need exposure to several alternative attempts at synthesis which are analyzed and critically evaluated before attempting their own. They need guidelines, or helpful hints at least, to get them started, and they need standards by which to judge their own progress. Unfortunately guidelines and standards are hard to come by in our profession. The process of integration or synthesis is poorly understood and little studied by professional interdisciplinarians. It is no wonder that we achieve synthesis so seldom in our courses.

There is a sense, however, in which it is unnecessary as well as unreasonable to expect that each interdisciplinary course should end with a synthesis. Perhaps interdisciplinary courses, like disciplinary ones, should not be expected to present definitive answers to the important questions they raise. Perhaps synthesis should be an ideal, not a goal. It seems more realistic to ask that interdisciplinary study illuminate the question, pointing up the limitations and strengths of competing disciplinary approaches, exploring the full scope and implications of the question, clarifying the nature of the question, and devising standards which an answer must meet, rather than insisting that the question be answered. After all, the pedagogical value comes from getting the students to see the richness of the question and what would be involved in answering it, more than from learning the answer itself.

5. Interdisciplinary Courses Are Relatively Expensive.

The final argument that Professor Benson raises against interdisciplinary studies is that their heavy reliance on "team-teaching methods, special events, independent study, and relatively low student-faculty ratios" makes them too "cost-ineffective," at least during the era of fiscal austerity faced by higher education during the next decade. In addition, he points out, many interdisciplinary programs compound this waste by "borrowing adjunct faculty from the disciplinary departments, creating thereby a need for part-time replacements, or by hiring their own psychologist . . . etc., and thus duplicating . . . the faculty resources already available in the departments."[23] Even if one grants the validity of the responses in this paper to the other four criticisms of interdisciplinary studies, one might still oppose them on the basis of this argument alone—such is the power of economic arguments today in educational decision-making.

Two of the four examples on which this argument is based are simply inappropriate. Special events and independent study can enrich any course, interdisciplinary or disciplinary, but they play no inherent part in interdisciplinary study as it is conceived in this paper. Innovative faculty can be expected to include them in their courses, and if such innovators are found in disproportionately large numbers in interdisciplinary programs, then it is easy to see why faculty unacquainted with the nature of interdisciplinary study might leap to the conclusion that such features are necessary to it.

The example of low student-faculty ratios is equally inappropriate, but for different reasons. High student-faculty ratios are achieved largely through lectures, which have come to gain acceptance in most disciplines, but which seem to me to serve the same limited functions in the disciplines as in interdisciplinary study, namely to summarize large bodies of literature by placing the issue in its intellectual context, to impart facts, or to explain a technical process. While such background information is necessary to any intellectual process, the heart of that process begins later as we critically evaluate, proffer alternative hypotheses or interpretations, and move towards an appreciation of the issue and towards our own position. This process can be done on one's own, with sufficient feedback from the instructor, or it can be done rather more expeditiously in a well-conducted seminar or discussion section where the group as a whole explores the issue and feedback is more frequent; but it cannot be done in a lecture, where the student is passive recipient not active learner. It is unclear to me that disciplinary inquiry needs active student participation and interaction any less than does interdisciplinary study, or that discussion groups need be smaller in interdisciplinary courses. The problem of student-faculty ratios is not that interdisciplinary courses require lower ones, but that the disciplines have come—perhaps through previous encounters with financial exigency—to accept uncritically a predominantly lecture format for their lower division high-enrollment courses. Because the interdisciplinary programs are the "new kids on the block," and their faculty more idealistic perhaps, they may understandably insist on lower student-faculty ratios; but as they and their faculty grow more worldly in the face of economic pressures, there is no reason inherent in the nature of the interdisciplinary process why they cannot come to tolerate ratios fully as high as those of disciplinary departments.

The example of team-teaching, on the other hand, points up a serious economic problem facing interdisciplinary studies. Team-teaching, meaning two or more faculty in the same classroom at once and hence greater expense, has become a common feature of interdisciplinary programs because it is the simplest way to ensure that different disciplinary perspectives are accurately and convincingly presented to the students, and that any synthesis take full account of each discipline involved. Advocates of team-teaching for interdisciplinary courses argue that a faculty member alone in the classroom is likely to present the strongest case for the discipline of her or his graduate training because it is most familiar, and more likely to accept its implicit presumptions uncritically. Since most faculty in interdisciplinary programs do not have interdisciplinary graduate degrees (and those that do seldom have the kind of grounding in several disciplines needed for interdisciplinary study as conceived in this paper), this argument appears to have considerable force.

Where interdisciplinary courses can attract sufficient enrollment to justify multiple sections, however, team-teaching can profitably be replaced by team-curriculum development. In the Western College Program at Miami University, for example, we rely on team-curriculum development in all our lower division core courses: faculty teach separate sections of a multisection course but they plan the course together and, most importantly, they cover the same material in their respective sections and evaluate their students with the same examinations and paper topics.[24] In my experience, this approach has educational as well as economic advantages over team-teaching. Because faculty must confront the students alone when they lead discussions that prepare students for common course examinations, the faculty are motivated to take seriously the disciplines outside their expertise and to learn them carefully. Faculty colleagues become important educational resources, and weekly staff meetings of the course become cooperative learning experiences as well as an opportunity to debate conflicting disciplinary perspectives. While this approach loses the spontaneous fireworks in the classroom from untrammeled debate between team-teachers, through which the relative merits of each disciplinary perspective are sorted out in front of the students, I believe it more than compensates by forcing the faculty to appreciate the strengths of opposing perspectives before they come into the classroom. Students become more active in the process of exploring the relative merits and weaknesses of competing disciplinary perspectives when they are not observing faculty argue among themselves, and faculty can better guide them through the process because the faculty have been through it themselves and need not concentrate on defending their discipline. Team-curriculum development is no more expensive than traditional teaching since only one faculty member is in the classroom at a time. Its staff meetings may appear to cost more faculty time, but the difference lies more in the manner of course preparation, where individual contemplation of a text is partly replaced by group discussion.

In courses where multiple sections are simply not feasible, the additional expense of team-teaching is more difficult to get around. Most interdisciplinary programs I have visited hold regular faculty seminars that are designed to break down the disciplinary parochialism of faculty. Sometimes these seminars are tied to courses where faculty teach their own sections as they wish; other times, they are unrelated to any course, moving from topic to topic of mutual interest to the participants. Stockton State College, New Jersey, has developed a peer curriculum review process which provides an alternative other than team-teaching to ensure that individually taught courses are in fact interdisciplinary. Their general education curriculum committees review course proposals and talk with the faculty submitting them while the courses are still in the planning stage. They offer suggestions for readings and topics and for ways to make the course more interdisciplinary, much as faculty do in our program during the early stages of team-teaching curriculum development. The proposals are reviewed again before they can appear in the catalog. These examples point up the feasibility of alternative means to team-teaching for promoting the full interdisciplinarity of courses that wish to be interdisciplinary. In my view they are not as effective as team-teaching, but they are possible compromises. Much more effective is to train faculty in interdisciplinary studies through team-curriculum development or team-teaching, and then wean them to individually taught interdisciplinary courses after they have demonstrated sufficient command of and sensitivity to the other relevant disciplines and sufficient familiarity with the interdisciplinary method. This last approach is effective, as I can testify from personal experience, and while it is expensive at first, it holds the promise of future costs more in line with disciplinary teaching.

The final charge under Professor Benson's fifth argument is that interdisciplinary programs are expensive because they borrow or duplicate faculty in disciplinary departments. The preceding discussion has already shown that many interdisciplinary courses can be staffed at a full cost quite comparable to that of disciplinary ones. In these cases, faculty may be borrowed to expand the disciplinary perspectives available in the interdisciplinary program or to make professional development opportunities available to faculty in disciplinary departments, but the program would be well served politically to compensate departments fully for borrowed faculty in order to make it clear that it is not hiding excessive costs in the process.

The duplication argument, on the other hand, reflects a confusion caused by the lack of Ph.D. programs in interdisciplinary studies. When a interdisciplinary program hires a new faculty member with a Ph.D. in psychology and a specialty in social psychology, the department of psychology sees that person duplicating the social psychologist in their department, while the interdisciplinary program believes it has hired someone with interest in and commitment to interdisciplinary studies who will bring the perspective of psychology to the program. What appears by virtue of formal training to be an overlapping specialty in social psychology is by virtue of interest a nonoverlapping specialty in interdisciplinary studies. This confusion would be reduced, but not eliminated, by establishing Ph.D. programs for those wishing formal credentials in interdisciplinary studies. Some disciplinary faculty will still be attracted to interdisciplinary study, however, as part of the process of normal intellectual growth after graduate school. Neither the borrowing nor the apparent duplication of faculty, however, constitutes support for the criticism that interdisciplinary programs are too expensive. Such criticism need only be well-grounded when interdisciplinary programs cannot attract the enrollment to justify multiple section courses and when they are also too young to have trained their faculty on-the-job in interdisciplinary teaching. Even then, the root cause of the expense is the lack of graduate training in interdisciplinary study and not its nature.

B. Where Do We Go From Here?

The model set out above of what interdisciplinary studies should be seems to meet all five criticisms identified by Professor Benson. If our profession were to agree on a conception of interdisciplinary studies similar to it, we would be in a position to argue that, in principle at least, interdisciplinary studies can answer its critics. Until such agreement is reached, however, we are quite vulnerable to attack at the very time in American higher education when weak or ill-defined programs are being cut back or eliminated. The traditional means for reaching such accord is debate at professional conferences and in professional journals. The annual meetings of the Association for Integrative Studies provide such a forum, and with the advent of this publication we now have the other one in embryonic form at least. I hope that this exchange between Professor

Benson and myself turns out to be the opening of a debate that will move our profession towards consensus on the nature of interdisciplinary study.

Even if that consensus is achieved, we then face the further challenge of bringing our practice in line with our rhetoric before our courses can meet the arguments against interdisciplinary studies. The preceding analysis of these arguments identifies two major tasks essential to meeting that challenge. We need to set standards of excellence in the conduct of interdisciplinary study, and we need to train faculty who teach interdisciplinary study in its method.

We need to agree, in particular, on what it means to teach interdisciplinary studies well. We need to exchange information on individual interdisciplinary courses from a variety of institutions in order to identify models of the most effective ways of introducing students to the interdisciplinary approach or to essential interdisciplinary skills. We need to examine sequences of interdisciplinary courses at various interdisciplinary programs to explore the most fruitful ways of developing interdisciplinary competence in our students; the sequence for introducing disciplinary concepts, theories, and methods; the timing of the introduction of models for bridging disciplines such as a structuralism, general systems, etc. And we need to examine the process of teaching itself, not just of curriculum development. Are there special pedagogical or classroom techniques which are particularly appropriate to teaching interdisciplinary studies?

Finally, we need to train faculty in interdisciplinary study. In part, this means training them in the interdisciplinary method, but probably more importantly it means developing in them an appreciation for the world views of the disciplines in which they have not been trained but which are relevant to the kinds of interdisciplinary problems they address. Of course, that appreciation comes only with command of the concepts and theories of at least one portion of the discipline, making the task of training rather substantial. We need to retrain faculty already teaching in interdisciplinary programs as well as training those about to enter the profession. For the latter, we will eventually require a solid graduate program in generic interdisciplinary studies, or at least core courses of such strategies in graduate programs in interdisciplinary topics like urban or women's studies. Retraining of existing faculty, both to sharpen their interdisciplinary competence and to provide them with the formal interdisciplinary credentials most lack, can be accomplished in a variety of ways—faculty seminars on individual campuses leading to summer workshops,[25] national summer institutes, summer courses offered by new interdisciplinary graduate programs, leading perhaps to formal certification. The tasks are formidable, as is that of securing consensus, but I am confident that we will accomplish them, and that we will be able to meet the arguments of our critics, both in principle and in practice. I hope that Professor Benson's article plays a key role towards the achievement of that goal.

Footnotes

1. This conception is presented in my article with William Green, "Defining and Teaching Interdisciplinary Studies," *Improving College and University Teaching* 30:1 (Winter 1982), pp. 23–30.

2. Thomas C. Benson, "Five Arguments Against Interdisciplinary Studies," *Issues in Integrative Studies* 1 (1982), pp. 39.

3. Benson, p. 40.

4. Benson, p. 41.

5. Raymond C. Miller, "Varieties of Interdisciplinary Approaches in the Social Sciences," *Issues in Integrative Studies* 1 (1982), pp. 4–8.

6. Benson, p. 39.

7. Frederick S. Weaver, "A Study of Interdisciplinary Learning and Teaching at Hampshire College" (Amherst, MA: Hampshire College, 1981).

8. Ralph Ross, "The Nature of the Transdisciplinary: An Elementary Statement," in Alvin White (ed.) *Interdisciplinary Teaching* (San Francisco: JosseyBass, 1981), p. 23.

9. Benson, p. 40.

10. Benson, pp. 41–42.

11. Charles B. Fethe, "A Philosophical Model for Interdisciplinary Programs," *Liberal Education* 4 (1973), pp. 490–497.

12. B. S. Bloom (ed.), *Taxonomy of Educational Objectives, Handbook I: Cognitive Domain* (New York: Longmans, Green, 1965).
    Jean Piaget, "Intellectual Evolution from Adolescence to Adulthood," *Human Development* 15 (1972), pp. 1–12.
    Willaim Perry, *Forms of Intellectual and Ethical Development in the College Years: A Scheme* (New York: Holt, Rinehart & Winston, 1970).
    Lawrence Kohlberg and E. Turiel, *Recent Research in Moral Development* (New York: Holt, Rinehart & Winston, 1973).

13. Benson, pp. 43–44.

14. William H. Newell, "Interdisciplinary Studies Are Alive and Well," *AIS Newsletter* 10:1 (March, 1988), pp. 1, 6–8; reprinted in *AAHE Bulletin* 40:8 (1988), pp. 10–12; also reprinted in *The National Honors Report* 9:2 (Summer, 1988), pp. 5–6.

15. Newell, "Interdisciplinary Studies," p. 2.

16. Thomas Klein and Jerry Gaff, "Reforming Higher Education: A Survey" (Washington, D.C.: Association of American Colleges, 1982), p. 4.

17. Klein and Gaff, p. 6.

18. Benson, p. 45.

19. Benson, p. 45.

20. Benson, p. 45.

21. Benson, p. 46.

22. Newell and Green, p. 24.

23. Benson, pp. 46–47.

24. William H. Newell, "Interdisciplinary Curriculum Development in the 1970s: The Paracollege at St. Olaf and the Western College Program at Miami University," in Richard Jones and Barbara Smith (eds.), *Alternative Higher Education* (Cambridge, MA: Schenkman, 1984, 127–147).

25. Alvin M. White, "Developing and Challenging Faculty Through Interdisciplinary Teaching-Learning," in William C. Nelson and Michael E. Siegel (eds.), *Effective Approaches to Faculty Development* (Washington, D.C.: Association of American Colleges, 1980), pp. 71–76.

The Position

Interdisciplinarity as Interpenetration

Steve Fuller

The Terms of the Argument

Interdisciplinarity can be understood as either a fact or an ideology (cf. Klein 1990). I endorse both. The fact is simply that certain sorts of problems—increasingly those of general public interest—are not adequately addressed by the resources of particular disciplines, but rather require that practitioners of several such disciplines organize themselves in novel settings and adopt new ways of regarding their work and co-workers. As a simple fact, interdisciplinarity responds to the failure of expertise to live up to its own hype. Assessing the overall significance of this fact, however, can easily acquire an ideological character. I am an ideologue of interdisciplinarity because I believe that, left to their own devices, academic disciplines follow trajectories that isolate them increasingly from one another and from the most interesting intellectual and social issues of our time. The problem is only masked by dignifying such a trajectory with the label "progress." Thus, I want to move away from the common idea that interdisciplinary pursuits draw their strength from building on the methods and findings of established fields. Instead, my goal is to present models of interdisciplinary research that call into question the differences between the disciplines involved, and thereby serve as forums for the renegotiation of disciplinary boundaries. This is perhaps the most vital epistemological function for rhetoric to perform in the academy, the need for which has become clear only with the emergence of STS.

An interesting, and probably unintended, consequence of the increasing disciplinization of knowledge is that the problem of interdisciplinarity is drawn closer to the general problem of *knowledge policy,* that is, the role of knowledge production in a democratic society. In the first place, as disciplines become more specialized, each disciplinary practitioner, or "expert," is reduced to lay status on an expanding range of issues. Yet, specialization serves to heighten the incommensurability among the ends that the different disciplines set for themselves, which, in turn, decreases the likelihood that the experts will amongst themselves be able to coordinate their activities in ways that benefit more than just their respective disciplinary constituencies. The increasingly strategic roles that deans, provosts, and other trans-departmental university administrators play in shaping the future of departments testify to this general

Fuller, Steve. Ch. 2 *"The Position: Interdisciplinarity as Interpenetration."* Philosophy, Rhetoric, and the End of Knowledge: The Coming of Science and Technology Studies. *University of Wisconsin Press, 1993, 33–65. Reprinted with permission.*

tendency to assimilate the problem of interdisciplinary negotiation to the general problem of knowledge policy (e.g., Bok 1982). A complementary trend is the erosion of the distinction between academic and nonacademic contexts of research. Nowadays, corporations not only subsidize academic research but also often pay for the university buildings in which the research takes place. Be it through government initiatives, venture capitalism, or the lure of the mass media, the nonacademic public is potentially capable of diverting any narrowly focused disciplinary trajectories. Social epistemology's contribution to these tendencies, one might say, is to make such initiatives intellectually respectable. The key is to cultivate *the rhetoric of interpenetrability*. Although the technofeminist Donna Haraway (especially 1989) has recently revived the idea behind "interpenetration" (to produce "cyborgs," techno-organisms that interpenetrate the nature/culture distinction), the term probably still carries enough of the old Marxist baggage to merit unpacking.

"The interpenetration of opposites," also known as "the unity and conflict of opposites," is one of the three laws of dialectics identified by Friedrich Engels in his 1880 work on the philosophy of science, *The Dialectics of Nature*, which has since become a staple of orthodox Marxism. To put it metaphysically, the idea is that stability of form—the property that philosophers have traditionally associated with a thing's identity—really inheres in parts whose tendencies to move in opposing directions have been temporarily suppressed. Perhaps the most familiar application of this idea appears in Marx's concept of *structural contradiction,* which purports to explain the lack of class conflict between the workers and the bourgeoisie by saying that the workers unwittingly buy into capitalist ideology and hence fail to identify themselves as a class with interests opposed to those of the bourgeoisie. The Italian humanist Marxist Antonio Gramsci popularized the term "hegemony" to capture the resulting ideological harmony, which leads workers to blame themselves for their lowly status (cf. Bocock 1986). However, armed with the Marxist critique of political economy, the workers can raise this latent contradiction to the level of explicit class warfare, for once they identify exclusively with each other, they are in a position to destroy the stability of the capitalist system. Now consider a rhetorical example that makes the same point. Whereas philosophers since Plato have supposed that communication involves speaker and audience partaking of a common form of thought having its own natural integrity, rhetoricians have taken the more interpenetrative view that any apparent meeting of minds is really an instance of strategically suppressed disagreement that enables an audience to move temporarily in a common direction.

One of the least likely places for this last point to apply, yet where it applies with a vengeance, is in the *history of tolerance,* a concept worthy of the rhetorician's conquest by division. First, there is what might be called *passive tolerance,* the ultimate target of sophisticated forms of censorship, yet still unrecognized by philosophers as a legitimate epistemological phenomenon. In the 1950s Carl Hovland and his Yale associates captured it experimentally as "the sleeper effect." It is the tendency for subjects to become better disposed to a message after repeated exposure over time, even if they were originally ill disposed because of the source of the message (Hovland et al. 1965). Thus, even conservatives may start to express sympathy for a social program originally proposed by a liberal, once they get used to hearing it and forget that a liberal first proposed it. At least, the burden of proof starts to shift in their minds, so that now they might want to hear arguments for why the program should *not* be funded. Managing this form of tolerance, especially in a democracy whose mass media are dedicated to the equal-time doctrine, is a rhetorical and epistemological challenge of the first order, especially as the proliferation of messages serves only to increase the amount of passive tolerance in society. The trick then is to "activate" tolerance without thwarting it.

Thus, there is *active tolerance,* the sort for which one openly campaigns. In theory, it aims to empower groups by channeling their attention toward one another. In practice, it often turns out to be a version of "my enemy's enemy is my friend," whereby otherwise squabbling factions agree to cease hostilities to fend off a still greater and mutual foe. In the case of John Locke's *Letter on Toleration,* which was influential in the establishment of religious tolerance in the American colonies, the common enemy was an ominously defined band of "atheists" who had no place in a Christian commonwealth. The logic of interpenetration can work in this environment, if the threat posed by the foe forces the factions beyond mere peaceful coexistence to active cooperation in combating the foe (cf. Serres 1982, on the strategy of removing a "parasite"). For once the foe has been removed and all the actions are able to go their own way, they will have been substantially transformed as a result of their previous collaboration.

The rhetoric of interpenetrability aims to recast disciplinary boundaries as artificial barriers to the transaction of knowledge claims. Such boundaries are necessary evils that become more evil the more they are perceived as necessary. The rhetoric that I urge works by showing that one discipline already takes for granted a position that contradicts, challenges, or in some way overlaps a position taken by another discipline. As a dialectical device, interpenetrability goes against the grain of the current academic division of labor, which typically gives the impression that issues resolved in one discipline leave untouched the fate of cognate issues in other disciplines. For example, it is routine to think that whatever psychological findings are reached in laboratory settings have no necessary bearing on the psychological makeup of the sort of ordinary "situated" reasoners that historians and other humanists study. That is to say, no mutual challenge is posed by the juxtaposition of laboratory cognizers and historical cognizers, and hence any interaction between the two types will be purely a matter of the inquirer's discretion. It is in this context that advocates of interdisciplinarity, especially the cultural anthropologist Clifford Geertz (1983), have traditionally spoken of social scientific theories as "interpretive frameworks" that can be applied and discarded as the inquirer sees fit—but never strictly tested.

In stressing applicability over testability, Geertz and other interdisciplinarians are, in part, reacting—perhaps overreacting—to positivist academic rhetoric, which culminated in Popper's falsificationist methodology, with its explicit aim of *eliminating* false hypotheses. The finality of such eliminationist rhetoric made one close follower of Popper, Imre Lakatos, squirm over the possibility of preemptively squashing fledgling research programs, and ultimately drove another of Popper's famous students, Paul Feyerabend, to espouse the anarchistic doctrine of letting a thousand flowers bloom. Moreover, even as a simple fact about the history of science, eliminationism is hard to justify. For better or worse, once articulated, theories tend to linger and periodically reemerge in ways that make "half-life" an apt unit of analysis.

Unfortunately, the explicitly nonconfrontational strategy of Geertz and his cohort plays in the worst way to the exigencies of our cognitive condition. There is little need to belabor the point that, for any field, more theories are generated than can ever be given a proper hearing. How, then, does one decide on which theories to attend to, and which to ignore? Testability conditions of the sort Popper offered under the rubric of falsifiability constitute one possible strategy. For example, a theory may challenge enough of the current orthodoxy that the orthodoxy would be significantly overturned if the theory were corroborated. This is the sort of theory that Popper would test. However, if inquirers are allowed complete discretion on how they import theories into their research, then it is likely that they will capitalize on their initial conceptions as much as possible and ignore—not test—the theories that implicitly challenge those conceptions. Thus, in the long term, the nonconfrontational approach would probably lead to the withering away of subversive theories that could be accommodated into standing research programs only with great difficulty. My point here is not that inquirers will converge on dogma if they are not required to confront each other critically; rather, unless otherwise prevented, inquirers will diverge in ways, mostly involving the elaboration of incommensurable technical discourses, that will make critical engagement increasingly difficult.

I believe that much of the sting of Popper's rhetoric could be avoided if testing were seen more in the spirit of a Hegelian *Aufhebung,* that is, the incorporation and elimination of opposites in a more inclusive formulation. Concretely, I am suggesting that when disciplines (or their proper parts, such as theories or methods) interpenetrate, the "test" is a mutual one that transforms all parties concerned. It is not simply a matter of one discipline being tested against the standards of its epistemic superior, or even of both disciplines being evaluated in terms of some neutral repository of cognitive criteria (as might be provided by a philosopher of science). Rather, *the two disciplines are evaluated by criteria that are themselves brought into being only in the act of interpenetration.* And while these criteria will undoubtedly draw on the settlements reached in earlier interdisciplinary disputes, the exact precedent that they set will depend on the analogies that the current disputants negotiate between these prior exchange and their own.

Consider, once again, historians and psychologists confronting each other's explanations of scientific behavior. To put the difference in starkest terms, whereas humanistic historians think that scientists strive to emulate the geniuses in their fields, cognitive social psychologists are more inclined to believe that scientists are motivated to take each other down in order to make room for themselves. In both cases, the scientist is portrayed as "rational," albeit on the basis of divergent conceptions of rationality, which presuppose a strong difference of opinion on whether intelligence is intrinsic to the individual or emergent from the group. Now suppose that after protracted discussion historians came to abolish the term "genius" from their lexicons to reflect a revision in their estimates of intellectual merit in light of the psychological evidence, yet the psychologists remained unmoved by anything in the historians' original explanatory strategy. Although the psychologists would have thereby gained the upper hand in dialogue with the historians, that would not be the end of the story. In particular, onlookers in other disciplines also have a stake in whether the knowledge system as a whole has benefited from this capitulation of history to psychology. Their opinions will count significantly with regard to the long-term viability and generalizability of the psychologists' victory. However, if there were sustained discourse between history and psychology, then both disciplines would probably be transformed in somewhat different ways that together help enable them to see each other as engaged in a common enterprise. This would be especially true if practitioners of the two disciplines considered how their respective methodologies functioned as means toward a common end, say, an understanding of the scientific mind. In this regard, the historian might be able to show the psychologist that the sort of laboratory findings that she would normally attribute to inherent properties of the subject are in fact emergent features of the social situation co-produced in the lab by experimenter and subject (cf. Billig 1987: chap. 4; Danziger 1990). In that case, the roles of experimenter authority and subject compliance are highlighted in a way that renders "laboratory life" more political, and hence more reformable, without necessarily invalidating the experimental method as such. It is this prospect that calls for the resources of the epistemically interested rhetorician.

The Perils of Pluralism

While the three presumptions that social epistemology takes from STS—dialectical, conventionality, democratic—make me a natural enemy of "traditionalists" in the academy (e.g., Bloom 1987), my comments in the last section are meant to throw down the gauntlet to many of the so-called *pluralists* (e.g., Booth 1979) who normally oppose the traditionalists. In spite of their vocal support of interdisciplinary research, pluralists nevertheless tend to assume that, left to their own devices and absent any overarching institutional constraint, the practitioners of different disciplines will spontaneously criticize one another in the course of borrowing facts and ideas for their own purposes. If Popper's Open Society were indeed a by-product of such a pluralistic academic environment, the social epistemologist would not need to cultivate interventionist impulses. However, I believe that, like any activity which is clearly beneficial if everyone does it but is potentially dangerous if only a few do so, criticism requires special external incentives. Otherwise, each discipline will tend to politely till its own fields, every now and then quietly pilfering a fruit from its neighbor's garden but never suggesting that the tree should be replanted in a more mutually convenient location. My view here rests on the observation that criticism flourishes in the academy—insofar as it does—only within the confines of disciplinary boundaries (say, in journal referee reports) and erupts into symbolic violence when it spans such boundaries. Given this state of affairs, the "tolerance" that is much revered by pluralists turns out to be the consolation prize for those who are unwilling to face their differences.

In terms of the idea of active tolerance raised initially in this discussion, there are two directions in which a tolerant community may go at this point. On the one hand, it may take advantage of the opportunity provided by realizing that "my enemy's enemy" is really "my friend" and foster an interpenetrative intellectual environment. On the other hand, it may foster just the reverse, perhaps out of fear that voiced disagreements would allow the enemy to reappear. As the "tolerant" Christian commonwealth would have it, interdenominational strife is Satan's calling card. In a more secular vein, it has been quite common in the history of academic politics for rival schools of thought to cease fire whenever it seemed that a more powerful "third party," usually a government agency, was in a position to use the disagreement to gain advantage over the feuding parties, often by discrediting the knowledge produced in such a fractious setting. For example, Proctor (1991: chap. 8) has argued that sociologists in early-twentieth-century Germany became preoccupied with appearing as "value-neutral" inquirers, just at the point it became clear that, from within their ranks, an assortment of conflicting normative programs were being advanced on the basis of scholarly research. By suppressing these deep disagreements, the sociologists believed (with mixed results) that they could counter government suspicions that the classroom had become the breeding ground for alternative ideologies, and thereby salvage the "autonomy" of their inquiries. (Furner 1975 offers the American analogue to this story.) From the standpoint of social epistemology, a better strategy would have been for the sociologists to argue openly about what they really cared about—the normative programs that they wanted their research to legitimate—and to enroll various government agencies as allies in the ensuing debate, thereby dissipating whatever leverage the state could exercise in its official capacity as "external," "neutral," and, most important, *united.*

We see, then, that tolerance works homeopathically: in small doses, it provides the initial opportunity for airing differences of opinion, which will hopefully lead to an engagement of those differences; however, in large doses, tolerance replaces engagement with provincialism, thereby producing Robert Frost's policy of "good fences make good neighbors," and the veiled sense of mutual contempt that it implies. The unconditional protection of individual expression not only fails to contribute to the kind of collaborative inquiry that sustains the growth of knowledge (cf. Elgin 1988, on a related contrast between the pursuits of "intelligence" and "knowledge"), but also fails to foster healthy social relations among inquirers. In particular, individual expression instills an ethic of *learning for oneself* at the expense of *learning from others.* This accounts for the tendency of interdisciplinarians to become "disciplines unto themselves," increasingly fragmented sects that unwittingly proliferate old insights in new jargons that are often more alienating than those of the disciplines from which they escaped.

My complaint here is not that interdisciplinary discourses tend to mutate into autonomous fields, but rather that they mutate *without replacing some already existing fields*. Thus, they merely amplify, not resolve, the level of babble in the academy. Given the exigencies of our epistemic situation, pluralists hardly help matters by magnanimously asserting that anyone can enter the epistemic arena who is willing to abide by a few procedural rules of argument that enable rival perspectives to remain intact and mutually respectful at the end of the day. (After all, isn't the security of this outcome what separates the interdisciplinary environment of the academy from the rough-and-tumble world of politics?) In practice, this gesture amounts to one of the following equally unsavory possibilities:

1. Everybody gets a little less attention paid to her own claims in order to make room for the newcomer.
2. The newcomer starts to adopt the disciplinary perspective of the dominant discussants, and consequently is seen as not adding to the level of academic babble.
3. Given that the newcomer starts late in the discussion, her claims never really make it to the center of attention.

Newcomers, of course, fear that (3) is the inevitable outcome, though the path of cooptation presented in (2) does not inspire confidence, either. As a result, newcomers have been known to force themselves on the discussion by attempting to "deconstruct" the dominant discussants, which is to say, to call into question the extent to which the discussants are really so different from one another, especially in a world where there are still many other voices yet to be heard. Aren't they all *men?* Aren't they all *white?* Aren't they all *bourgeois?* Aren't they all *normal scientists?* The suggestion here is that if the discussants are "really" all the same, then they can easily make room for the genuine difference in perspective offered by the newcomers. Clearly, the deconstructive newcomers are trying to totalize or subsume all who have come before them, which gives their discourse a decidedly *theoretical* cast. Critics of untrammeled tolerance and pluralism have observed that pluralists become extremely uncomfortable in the face of this theoretical cast of mind, regardless of whether the source of the theory is Marxism (Wolff et al. 1969), feminism (Rooney 1991)—or positivism, for that matter. (Kindred suspicions have surrounded "synthetic" works in history, which, while not especially theoretical, nevertheless juxtapose pieces of scholarship in ways other than what their authors originally intended; cf. Proctor 1991: chap. 6). After all, the deconstructors have turned the pluralist's procedural rules into topics in their own right. No longer neutral givens, the rules themselves now become the bone of contention, as they appear to foster a spurious sense of diversity that, in fact, excludes the most challenging alternatives. I will return to this topic under the rubric of "knowledge politics" in Chapter 8.

People aside, the basic problem with pluralist forms of interdisciplinarity is that they reinforce the differences between disciplines by altering the *products* of research, while leaving intact research *procedures*. A good piece of interdisciplinary research is supposed to abide by the local standards of all the disciplines drawn upon—this, despite the fact that most disciplines are born of methodological innovations that, in turn, reflect deep philosophical dissatisfaction with existing methods. Given such a historical backdrop, it is hard to imagine that research simply combining the methods of several disciplines—say, a study of attitude change that wedded historical narrative to phenomenological reports to factor analysis—would constitute an improvement on the rigorous deployment of just one of the methods. To think that such a combination would automatically constitute an improvement is to commit the *fallacy of eclecticism,* the belief that many partial methods add up to a complete picture of the phenomenon studied (rather than simply to a microcosm of cross-disciplinary struggles to colonize the phenomenon). The fallacy is often undetected in practice because interdisciplinarians deftly contain the reach of any one method so as to harmonize it with other methods that together "triangulate" around the author's preferred account of the phenomenon. Readers, of course, are free to infer that one method was brought in to compensate for the inadequacies of another, but the nature and potential scope of the inadequacies are passed over by the author in tactful silence.

In this regard, it is worth considering the favorable light in which triangulation is regarded in the social science methods literature (e.g., Denzin 1970; Webb et al. 1981). Here triangulation appears as a means to ensure that the inherently partial and reductive nature of a given research tool does not obscure the underlying complex reality that the researcher is trying to capture. Not surprisingly, then, discussions of triangulation tend to focus on the need for multiple methods in order to achieve a balanced picture of reality—not on the more basic fact that the biases introduced by divergent methods persistently reemerge across virtually all research contexts. Thus, triangulation simply defers an airing of these differences to another day—or perhaps another forum, philosophy of social science, where the results of deliberations are less likely to be felt by research practitioners. (It is for this reason that ethnomethodologists have been especially insistent on letting these metascientific concerns interrupt and shape their research practices; cf. Button 1991: especially chaps. 5–6).

Consider, by way of illustration, the oft-cited exemplar of triangulation in the sociological literature, James Coleman's *The Adolescent Society* (1961), which revealed the existence of a high school subculture in the United States, whose value structure is oriented more toward athletics and extracurriculars than toward academics. Coleman studied students, parents, and school personnel, using data collected from questionnaires, interviews, and school records. Although Coleman says that all the methods were administered to all three groups, in fact *Adolescent Society* reports most of its findings about students from questionnaires and most of its findings about the adults from interviews. Coleman (1961: vii) even remarks on this asymmetry, but makes little of it. From a narrative standpoint, the combination of student questionnaires and adult interviews biases the reader toward Coleman's view that the world of adolescents is so detached from that of adults that interpersonally based methods may provide unreliable access to the adolescent mind. No doubt, too, it was easier to administer questionnaires to students captive in the classroom, for whom the discipline of exam taking is part of their everyday lives, than to parents and school personnel, who are allowed the luxury of circumventing the exercise for more convenient means of expressing their views. These features of the social backdrop against which the triangulation occurred served only to reinforce Coleman's expressed (and influential) desire to demonstrate uniformity among adolescents across a wide range of schools, so as to embolden adults to design educational policy for keeping students within striking distance of the normative mainstream.

Another sort of triangulation is prominent among humanists who attempt to "blur genres," in Clifford Geertz's (1980) memorable phrase. Geertz (especially 1973) himself is among the most masterful of these eclectics. A discussion ostensibly devoted to understanding the practices of some non-Western culture will draw upon a variety of Western interpretive frameworks that sit well together just as long as they do not sit for too long. For example, an allusion to the plot of a Shakespearean tragedy may be juxtaposed with Max Weber's concept of rationalization to make sense of something that happens routinely in Southeast Asia. The juxtaposition is vivid in the way a classical rhetorician would have it, namely, as a novel combination of familiar tropes. In fact, the brilliance of the novelty may cause the reader to forget that it is meant to illuminate how a non-Western culture actually is, rather than how a Western culture might possibly be. But most important, Geertz's eclecticism caters, perhaps unwittingly, to what the structural Marxist Louis Althusser (1989) astutely called the *spontaneous philosophy of the scientists*. By this Althusser meant the tendency for an inquirer to understand her own practice in terms of her discipline's standing with respect to other disciplines, which is usually as part of a sensitive and closely monitored balance of power. Goldenberg's (1989) survey of scientists' attitudes toward science—to be discussed at the end of this chapter—illustrates nicely the way in which the philosophical self-images of the various sciences reinforce one another. Of special interest here is the fact that this reinforcement takes place, *regardless* of whether the sciences in question respect or loathe one another. In both cases, interdisciplinary differences are merely affirmed without being resolved, which, to follow Althusser, disarms the critical impulse that has traditionally enabled the discipline of philosophy—and now social epistemology—to force the sciences to see the deep problems that arise, in part, from the fact that they treat each other as "separate but equal."

It is understandable why an eclectic author would want to make it seem as though the mere juxtaposition of methods establishes common epistemological ground. The impulse is a strategic one that also caters to readers' interests. After all, if you accept the validity of any of the methods used in an eclectic study, you can incorporate the study into your own research. Such a study is thus very "user-friendly" to the normal scientist. By contrast, revolutionary theorists have refused to ignore the problematic status of common epistemological ground.

Their answers have typically involved an interpenetration that leaves the constitutive methods or disciplines permanently transformed. New presumptions are instituted for the threshold of epistemic adequacy, which, in practice, means that new people with new training are needed for the evaluation of knowledge claims. Consider these uncontroversial cases of successful revolutionary theorizing. After Newton's *Principia Mathematica,* astronomy could no longer just yield accurate predictions, but also had to be physically realizable. After Darwin's *Origin of Species,* no account of life could dispense with either the "nature" or the "nurture" side of the issue. After Marx's *Capitol,* no study of the material forces of production would be complete without a study of the social relations of production—a point that was rhetorically conceded even by Marx's opponents, who then started designating their asocial (i.e., "neoclassical") economics a "formal" science. After Freud's *Interpretation of Dreams,* any psychology based primarily on conscious introspection would be dismissed as at least naive (and at most spurious, à la behaviorism's response to cognitivism).

Interpenetration's Interlopers

Equipped with her rhetorical skills, the social epistemologist can facilitate revolutionary theorizing and its attendant mutations in our epistemic institutions. Whereas classical epistemologists and philosophers of science normally evaluate revolutionary theories in terms of their adequacy to the phenomena they purport to explain, the social epistemologist wants to unearth the implicit principles by which the revolutionary theorist managed to translate the concerns of several fields into an overarching program of research. In the days of logical positivism, this project would have been seen as involving the design of the "metalanguage" that enables the revolutionary theory to subsume disparate data domains. However, the social epistemologist regards translation as very much a bottom-up affair, one in which the concerns of different disciplines are first brought to bear on a particular case—be it historical, experimental, hypothetical, or anecdotal—and then bootstrapped up to higher levels of conceptual synthesis. In that case, the relevant linguistic model is borrowed, not from metamathematics, set theory, and symbolic logic, but from the evolution of a trade language, or pidgin, into a community's first language, or creole, which over time may become a full-fledged, grammatically independent language. The positivists erred, not in thinking that there could be global principles of knowledge production, but in thinking that those principles could be legislated a priori from the top down rather than inferred inductively as inquirers pool their epistemic resources in order to reconstitute their world.

At this point, let me distance what I have in mind from a related idea that has become popular in rhetorical studies of physics and economics, namely, the *trading zone,* an idea most closely associated with the historian of twentieth-century physics Peter Galison (1992), and economist Donald McCloskey (1991). McCloskey offers the most succinct formulation of the idea, one that goes back to Adam Smith's *Wealth of Nations.* As a society becomes larger and more complex, people realize that they cannot produce everything they need.

Consequently, each person specializes in producing a particular good that will attract a large number of customers, who will, in exchange, offer goods that the person needs. Thus, one specializes in order to trade. McCloskey believes that this principle applies just as much to the knowledge enterprise as it does to any other market-based activity. Galison's version of the trading zone draws more directly from the emergence of pidgins mentioned in the previous paragraph. His account has the virtue of being grounded in a highly informed analysis of the terms in which collaborative research has been done in Big Science-style physics. For example, determining the viability of the early nuclear bombs required a way of pooling the expertise of pure and applied mathematicians, physicists, industrial chemists, fluid dynamicists, and meteorologists. The pidgin that evolved from this joint effort was the Monte Carlo, a special random number generator designed to simulate stochastic processes too complex to calculate, such as the processes involved in estimating the decay rate of various subatomic particles. Nowadays, the Monte Carlo is a body of research in its own right, to which practitioners of many disciplines contribute, now long detached from its early nuclear origins (cf. Galison 1992: chap. 7). There are two questions to ask about the models that McCloskey and Galison propose:

1. Are they really the same? In other words, is Galison's history of the Monte Carlo trade language properly seen as a zone for "trading" in McCloskey's strict economic sense?
2. To what extent does the trading-zone idea capture what is or ought to be the case about the way the knowledge enterprise works?

The short answer to (1) is no. McCloskey is talking about an activity in which the goods do not change their identities as they change hands. The anticipated outcome of McCloskey's trading zone is that each person ends up with a greater number and variety of goods than when she began. The process is essentially one of redistribution, not transformation. In this way, Galison's trading zone is closer to the idea of interpenetration. The Monte Carlo simulation is an emergent property of a network of interdisciplinary transactions. It is not just that, say, the applied mathematicians learn something about industrial chemistry that they did not know before, but rather that the interaction itself produces a knowledge product to which neither had access previously. By contrast, then, McCloskey's idea perhaps captures the eclecticism of the human sciences in the postmodern era, which, to answer (2), calls its desirability into question. Interestingly, another economist, Kenneth Boulding (1968: 145–47), has already offered some considerations that explain why "Specialize in order to trade!" is not likely to become a norm of today's knowledge enterprises—though it perhaps should be. Boulding points out that in order to enforce Smith's imperative in the sciences, one would need two institutions, one that was functionally equivalent to a common currency (e.g., a methodological standard that enabled the practitioner of any discipline to judge the validity, reliability, and scope of a given knowledge claim) and one to an advertising agency (e.g., brokers whose job it would be to persuade the practitioners of different disciplines of the mutual relevance of each other's work). Short of these two institutions, the value of knowledge products would continue to accrue by producers' hoarding them (i.e., exerting tight control over their appropriate use) and making it difficult for new producers to enter their markets.

However, Galison's trading zone has its own problems from the standpoint of interpenetration to be promoted here. It does a fine job of showing how a concrete project in a specific place and time can generate a domain of inquiry whose abstractness enables it to be pursued subsequently in a wide variety of disciplinary contexts. In this way, he partly overcomes a limitation in Mc-Closkey's trading zone; namely, he shows that the trade can have conse-quences—that is, costs and benefits—that go beyond the producers directly involved in a transaction. But Galison does not consider the *long-term* conse-quences of pursuing a particular trade language. Not only does a pidgin tend to evolve into an independent language, as in Galison's own Monte Carlo ex-ample, but it also tends to do so at the expense of at least one of the languages from which it is composed. Either that, or one of the source languages reab-sorbs the developed pidgin in a process of "decreolization." In any case, there is just no practical way of arresting language change, short of segregating entire populations (cf. Aitchison 1981: especially pt. 4).

This empirical point about the evolution of pidgins may carry some norma-tive payoff, insofar as the mere invention of new languages does not clarify the knowledge enterprise, if old ones are not at the same time being displaced. Since we are ultimately talking about scientists whose energies are distributed over a finite amount of space and time, cartographic metaphors for knowledge prove appropriate. You cannot carve out a new duchy without taking land away from neighboring realms—even if the populations of these realms are steadily growing. The strategy of interpenetrability that I support is, ultimately, a pro-gram for rearranging disciplinary boundaries. It presumes that the knowledge enterprise is most creative *not* when there are either rigid boundaries or no boundaries whatsoever; nor is creativity necessarily linked with the simple addi-tion or elimination of boundaries; rather, creativity results from moving bound-aries around as a result of constructive border engagements.

The social epistemologist thus imagines the texts of, say, Marx or Freud as such border engagements, the conduct of cross-disciplinary communication by proxy. They implicitly represent the costs and benefits that members of the respective disciplines would incur from the revolutionary interpenetration pro-posed by the theorist. For example, in the case of *Capital,* the social epistemolo-gist asks what would an economist have to gain by seeing commodity exchange as the means by which money is pursued rather than vice versa, as the classical political economists maintained. Under what circumstances would it be worth the cost? Such questions are answered by examining how the acceptance of Marx's viewpoint would enhance or restrict the economist's jurisdiction vis-à-vis other professional knowledge producers and the lay public. More specifi-cally, we would have to look at the audiences that took the judgment of econo-mists seriously (for whatever reason) at the outset, Marx's potential for affecting those audiences (i.e., his access to the relevant means of communication), and the probable consequences of audiences' acting on Marx's proposal. And while this configuration of *Capital*'s audience would undoubtedly do much to facilitate understanding the reception and evolution of Marxism, the social epistemologist is aiming at a larger goal, namely, the generalizability of the judgments that Marx made about translating distinct bodies of knowledge into a common framework: What was his strategy for removing interdisciplinary barriers? How did he decide when a key concept in political economy was really bad metaphysics in disguise, and hence replaceable by some suitably Hegelized variant? How did he decide when a Hegelian abstraction failed to touch base with the conception of material reality put forth in classical political economy? Is there anything we can learn from Marx's decisions for future interdisciplinary interpenetrations? So often we marvel at the panoramic sweep of revolutionary thought, when in fact we would learn more about revolutionary thinking by examining what was left on the cutting-room floor.

The practice of the social epistemologist would thus differ from that of mainstream hermeneuticians and literary critics in emphasizing the *transferability* of Marx's implicit principles to other potentially revolutionary interdisciplinary settings. However, none of these possibilities can be realized without experimental intervention, specifically, the writing of new texts that will, in turn, forge new audiences, whose members will establish the new terms for negotiation that will convert current differences into strategies for productive collaboration. The three presumptions that social epistemology derives from STS are meant to render explicit what revolutionary theorists have tacitly supposed about the nature of the knowledge enterprise.

The Pressure Points for Interpenetration

In terms of the original three STS presumptions, the kind of pressure point I want is the unit that best epitomizes the Conventionality Presumption. As it turns out, a survey of the various sociological units in which the knowledge enterprise can be analyzed reveals that the most conventional are disciplines, which correspond more exactly to technical languages and university departments than to sets of skills or even distinct subject matters (Fisher 1990). For example, some skills are common to several disciplines, and other skills may be combined across disciplines with potentially fruitful results. However, the institutional character of disciplinary differences encourages inquirers to forgo these points of contact and to concentrate, instead, on meeting local standards of evaluation. This, in turn, perpetuates the misapprehension that disciplines carve up a primary reality, a domain of objects (cf. Shapere 1984), whereas interdisciplinary research carves up something more derivative. Indeed, sometimes in the effort to shore up their autonomy, disciplines will retreat to their signature topics, which are highly stylized (or idealized) versions of the phenomena they purport to study. Thus, when political science wants to demonstrate that it is a science, its practitioners will retreat from its programmatic aspirations of wanting to explain life in the *polis,* and instead point to the track record of empirical studies on voting behavior, as if the full complexity of political life could be constructed from a concatenation of such studies (J. Nelson 1987). If special steps are not taken to stem this tide of gaining more control over less reality, it is by no means clear that the situation will remedy itself (cf. Campbell 1969; Schaefer 1984; Fuller 1988a: chap. 12). On this basis, we can specify two sets of tensions—conveniently labeled *spatial* and *temporal*—that make disciplines especially good pressure points for interpenetration.

In terms of the spatial tension, disciplines are defined by two forces—*the university* and *the profession*—that are largely at odds with one another, although much of the conflict remains at the implicit level of structural contradiction. A university occupies a set of buildings and grounds in (more or less) one place, and each discipline a department in that place. The limits of university expansion are dictated by a budget, from which each department draws and to which each contributes. The idea of "budget" should be understood here liberally, to include not only operating funds, but also course assignments and space allocation (cf. Stinchcombe 1990; chap. 9). Of course, universities expand, but the interests of particular departments are always subserved to that of the whole. The brutest way of making this point is to recall the overhead costs that researchers receiving government grants must turn over to their universities for general operating purposes. But, in more subtle ways, the particularity of departments comes out in how curricular responsibilities are distributed among disciplines in different universities. The intellectual rigor or epistemic merit of a discipline may count for little in determining the corresponding department's fate in the realm of university politics.

In moving from the university department to the professional association, we see that the latter has indefinite horizons that stretch across the globe and determine the networks within which practitioners do and share their work. Such an association is more readily identified with technical languages and their ever-expanding publication outlets than with fixed ratios of money, courses, or space. Indeed, much of the information explosion that makes the access to pertinent knowledge increasingly difficult may be traced to the fact that most professional associations view the relentless promotion of their activities to be an unmitigated good (cf. Abbott 1988: chap. 6). The spatial tension between universities and professions is recognizable in many sociodynamic guises. Sociologists, following Alvin Gouldner (1957), see university versus profession as a case of "local" versus "cosmopolitan" allegiances. Political theorists interested in designing a "Republic of Science" may see a couple of familiar options for representing the disciplined character of knowledge: the subordination of professional to university interests, on the one hand, and the subordination of university to professional interests, on the other. The former is analogous to representation by geographical region, whereby the republic is conceptualized as a self-contained whole divided into departments; the latter resembles representation by classes, whereby a given republic is simply one site for managing the interplay of universally conflicting class interests. One might expect the teaching-oriented faculty to prefer regional representation, while research-oriented ones prefer the more corporatist model. But perhaps the most suggestive way of presenting the structural contradiction in disciplined knowledge is in terms of Immanuel Wallerstein's (e.g., 1991) world-system model, which attempts to explain the course of modern history as temporary resolutions of the ongoing tension between the proliferation of capitalist markets across the world (most recently in the guise of transnational corporations) and the attempts by nation-states to maintain and consolidate their power base (most recently in terms of high-tech military systems).

But how close is the analogy between, on the one hand, capital and professional expansion or, on the other, national and university consolidation? To consider just the first analogy, the sociologist Irving Louis Horowitz (1986) has argued that transnational publishing houses have been decisive in the proliferation of professional specialties by making it easier to start journals than to publish books, as the latter tend to attract a larger and more interdisciplinary audience but in a one-shot fashion that generates much smaller revenues. (This has to do with the traditionally transient character of most interdisciplinary endeavors: once the specific interdisciplinary project is complete, the parties return to their home disciplines.) Beyond this rather literal case of professionalization as a form of capital expansion, a fruitful site for investigation is intellectual property law. Here the explicit treatment of knowledge as a material, specifically economic, good forces professional bodies to think of themselves as companies and universities to think of themselves as states. As the economic consequences of embodied forms of knowledge become more apparent (especially as the difference between "basic" and "applied" science vanishes), universities are claiming proprietary rights to knowledge products and processes that would otherwise be more naturally identified with the professional skills of its creator. Will there come a point in which a widely distributed technology is more closely associated with the name of a university than of its creator's profession? How literally should we take the nickname of the first patented genetically engineered animal, "The Harvard Mouse"?

In presenting the spatial tension surrounding a discipline, I may have given the impression that, on balance, professional interests are more "progressive" than university-based ones. I happen to think that this is generally true, if by "progress" is meant the tendency to make the academy more permeable to the public. (I say this in the full knowledge that professionalism has much the same self-serving motive as capitalism's own reduction of indigenous social barriers— namely, to increase mobility of the labor force and the number of paying customers.) Yet, at the same time, professionalism left to its own devices will reify itself into perpetuity, a tendency that this book is largely designed to combat— that is, the tendency of professional associations to cast themselves as having special access to distinct realms of being. Here the university functions as an effective foil, as budgetary constraints naturally curb ontological pretensions. It is a mistake to think that knowledge is best served by maximizing the pool of funds available. At most, an ample budget will enable all to continue on their current trajectories as they see fit. However, it is an open question whether the undisturbed course of "normal science" will likely lead to genuine epistemic growth, since there would then be little incentive to engage in interdisciplinary interpenetration. Tight budgets, by contrast, provide an incentive for interpenetration by forcing a discipline to distinguish essential from nonessential aspects of its research program, and to recognize situations where some of those aspects may be more efficiently done in collaboration with, if not turned over to, researchers in other disciplines. Nevertheless, the emancipatory character of budgetary constraints is often obscured because of the bad rhetoric that accompanies talk of "eliminating programs," which forces departments to think that some of them will benefit only at the expense of others.

Fatalism is superimposed on this image of fatalities by a version of the fallacy of division that I will dub *The Dean's Razor,* namely, the inference that because interdisciplinary programs consist of people trained in regular disciplines, it follows that nothing essential to the knowledge production process will be lost by eliminating the programs (and keeping the original disciplines) when times are tough. Instead of a razor, a better instrument for the Dean to wield would be what economists call "zero-based budgeting," whereby each discipline would have to make its case for resources from scratch each year. I would go further: In the university's accounting procedure, while members of the faculty would continue to be treated as university employees, they would no longer be considered the exclusive properties or representatives of particular departments. Their specific departmental affiliations would therefore have to be negotiated with each academic year. Departments would take on the character of political parties pushing particular (research) programs, probably at the behest of professional associations, but allowing also for some locally generated interdisciplinary alliances, to which faculty will need to be recruited from the available pool each year. While, in practice, few faculty members would probably want to shift departmental affiliation very often, such a set-up would nevertheless loosen the grip that professional associations often have on the constitution of departments, as departments would have to come up with ways to attract particular personnel who might also be desired by competing departments within the university. There are more epistemic consequences to budgetary practices, specifically at a national level. I will turn to these after discussing the temporal tension that defines a discipline.

A discipline's temporal tension can be analyzed in terms of two countervailing forces: the *prospective* judgment required to legitimate the pursuit of a research program and the *retrospective* judgment that figures in explaining the research program's accomplishments. Our earlier example of the fate of political science makes the point nicely. The original promise of the discipline, repeatedly stressed by its most innovative theorists, was to explain the totality of political life by mechanisms of power, ideology, and the like, whose ontological purchase would cut across existing disciplinary divisions in the social sciences. However, when forced to speak to the field's empirical successes, political scientists fall back on, say, the many studies of voting behavior, which display the virtuoso use of such discipline-specific techniques as cross-national questionnaires (cf. Almond and Verba 1963) but which make little direct contribution to the larger interdisciplinary project.

Reflected in this tension are the two sorts of strategies that philosophers have used to account for the "success" of science. *Realists* put the emphasis on the prospective judgments, which are often expressed as quests for a desired set of mechanisms or laws able to bring disparate phenomena under a single theory. Realists see the scientific enterprise as continuing indefinitely, anticipate many corrections and even radical reversals of the current knowledge base, and typically regard the current division of disciplinary labor, at best, as a necessary evil and, sometimes, as a diversion from the path to unity. By contrast, *instrumentalists* stress retrospective judgments of scientific success, which turn on identifying specific empirical regularities that have remained robust in repeated testings under a variety of conditions. These regularities continue to hold up long after theories explaining them have come and gone (cf. Hacking 1983: pt. 2). Indeed, any new theory is born bearing the burden of "saving" these phenomena. Quite unlike the realist, the instrumentalist welcomes the increased division of disciplinary labor as issuing in a finer grained level of empirical analysis and control.

Symptomatic of the atemporal way in which philosophers think about this matter is their failure to see that the relative plausibility of realism and instrumentalism depends on the historical perspective on science that one adopts. From the standpoint of the present, the realist is someone who projects an ideal future in which the original promise of her research program is fully realized, whereas the instrumentalist is someone who reconstructs an ideal past in which the actual products of her research turn out to be what she had really wanted all along. Both perspectives are combined in the history of science that Philosophers—both realists and instrumentalists—have typically told since the advent of positivism: The Greeks started by asking about the nature of the cosmic order, and today we have answers that, in part, complain about the ill-formedness of their original questions and, in part, specify empirical regularities by which we can elicit more "order" (properly redefined) than the Greeks could have ever imagined. It is quite common for philosophers in this context to claim that, insofar as the early Greeks were "seriously" inquiring into the nature of things, they would recognize our accomplishments as substantial steps in that direction. The difference here between the Greeks looking forward to us and our looking backward at them reflects an underlying psychodynamic tension. Generally speaking, the history of disciplines presents a spectacle of research programs whose actual products are much more modest than what their original promise would suggest—if not actually tangential to that promise; yet, those products would probably not have been generated had inquirers not been motivated by a more comprehensive project. Thus, one doubts that any of the special sciences would have inspired much initial enthusiasm if its proponents promised merely to produce a set of empirical correlations, the reliability of which could be guaranteed only for highly controlled settings. Such prescience on the proponents' part would have doomed their project at the outset!

The psychodynamics between the realist and instrumentalist orientations may provide a neat explanation for what Hegel and Marx called "the cunning of reason" in history. But from the standpoint of social epistemology, this psychodynamics has more immediately pressing implications. Consider the

most recent comprehensive statement by the US government on research funding and evaluation: *Federally Funded Research: Decisions for a Decade* (Chubin
1991). This report, prepared for Congress by the Office of Technology Assessment, drew attention to the fact that research funding increasingly goes to
glamorous and expensive "megaprojects," such as the Human Genome Project,
the Orbiting Space Station, and the Superconducting Supercollider. These
megaprojects promise major breakthroughs across several disciplines and many
spinoffs for society at large. However, a megaproject is rarely evaluated by its
original lofty goals. Rather, its continued support typically depends on a series
of solid empirical findings, the significance of which, however, is probably too
limited to justify (in retrospect) the amount of money that was spent to obtain
them. Nevertheless, these findings are typically couched as "just the start"
toward delivering on the original promises. If the history of science policy is a
good inductive guide, however, the odds that this is an accurate prognosis of
the project's research trajectory are low. But that does not stop policymakers
from being suckered into supporting projects that can only be counted on to
deliver diminishing returns on continued investment. As suggested above, the
interactive effects of the policymaker's prospective and retrospective judgments
on research make any solution to this problem complicated. On the one hand,
it might be reasonably argued that even findings of limited scope would not
have been made had scientists not aspired to more. On the other hand, such a
judgment itself becomes clearer as it seems less feasible to divert funding from
that line of research. This should give us pause.

The political theorist Jon Elster (1979, 1983) has a striking way of characterizing our quandary. The realist vision of a megaproject is necessary to "precom-
mit" policymakers to a funding pattern that they would otherwise find very
risky. In that sense, realism girds the policymaker against a weakness of the
fiscal will. But evaluating the products of a megaproject by the instrumentalist
criteria of particular disciplines makes the policymaker prone to develop a version of "sour grapes" called "sweet lemons," an exaggerated sense of the project's accomplishments that results from deflating "what can now be seen" as
the project's original pretensions, which no one could have been expected to
meet. But does sour grapes do anything more than pervert precommitment? In
whose moral psychology is self-deception an adequate solution to weakness of
the will?

My point here is not to dump the idea of megaprojects, largely because I do
not (yet) have a substitute for the motivational role that the realist vision has
played in scientific research throughout the ages. However, if delusions of gran-
deur are unavoidable at the planning stage of a megaproject, it does not follow
they must also dominate the evaluation stage. In particular, policymakers
should be able to separate out their interest in sustaining the vision that informs
the megaproject from whatever interest they might have in supporting the specific research team that first proposed it. Sour grapes may be seen to result from
too closely associating the project's potential with the actual research results,
which ends up leading policymakers to indefinitely support the team behind
the results, regardless of whether that team is *now* in the best position to take

the next step toward realizing the project's full potential. Thus, one way to address this problem is to carefully distinguish the processes of *rewarding* and *reinforcing* scientists for their work. To prevent the scientists who first staked out a megaproject from indefinitely capitalizing on their original research investment, they should be rewarded for their pioneering work but not expected to continue in their original trajectory. Incentives may be set in place—say, in terms of the grant sizes made available—to encourage the research team to break up and recombine with members of other teams in other projects, with the megaproject's own future being placed in the hands of another team (or at least a significantly altered version of the original one).

The Task Ahead (and the Enemy Within)

Whether one approves or disapproves of the current state of knowledge production, there is a tendency to see "science" as a unitary system, a *universitas* in the original medieval sense, which emphasizes the departmental over the professional character of disciplines. This suggests that the disciplines see themselves as part of the same team, engaged in relations of mutual respect, if not outright cooperation. In that case, criticisms of the knowledge enterprise should appear as rather generic attacks on academic practices, not as cross-disciplinary skirmishes. Indeed, this is a fair characterization of the scope of science evaluation, ranging from science policy advisors to popular critics of science. Not since C. P. Snow's famous 1959 Rede Lecture on "two cultures" has anyone systematically raised the social epistemological consequences of disciplines' refusal to engage issues of common and public concern because they suspect *one another's* methods and motives (Snow 1964; cf. Sorell 1991: chap. 5). The rhetoric of interpenetration is meant to address this most open of secrets in the academy. The Canadian sociologist Sheldon Goldenberg (1989) has recently performed an invaluable service by surveying both social and natural scientists about their attitudes toward the knowledge enterprise: What books influenced how they think about the pursuit of knowledge? Can work in other disciplines be evaluated by the same standards used to evaluate work in their own? If not, is the difference to be explained by the character of the discipline or of its practitioners? Before proceeding to my own specific interdisciplinary incursions, it might be useful to get a sense of the dimensions of the task ahead for the social epistemologist interested in having disciplines deal with each other in good faith. For Goldenberg enables us to map *the structure of academic contempt.*

Telescoping Goldenberg's data somewhat, we can discern three general attitudes to the knowledge enterprise that are in sharp tension with one another. These attitudes are associated with *natural scientists, social scientists,* and *philosophers of science.* Natural scientists tend to think that something called "the scientific method" can be applied across the board, but that social scientists typically fail to do so because they let incompetence, politics, or sloth get in the way. In this portrayal, social scientists suffer from weakness of the will, while natural scientists persevere toward the truth. Not surprisingly, social scientists see the matter much differently. They portray themselves as reflective, self-critical inquirers, who are not so easily fooled by the ideas of a unitary scientific method bringing us closer to the truth. Natural scientists appear, in this picture, to be naive and self-deceived, mistaking big grants and political attention for epistemic virtues. Philosophers of science occupy a curious position in all this. On the one hand, social scientists are more likely to read the philosophical literature than natural scientists, but, on the other hand, they are also more likely to disagree with it, insofar as philosophers tend to believe that science does, indeed, work if applied diligently. Thus, social scientists often regard philosophers as dangerous ideologues who encourage natural scientists in their worst tendencies, whereas philosophers regard the natural scientists as spontaneously vindicating philosophical theses in their daily practices. As the philosopher sees it, her job is to raise the efficacious aspects of scientific practice to self-consciousness, as scientists themselves tend not to have the broad historical and theoretical sweep needed to distinguish what is essential from what is nonessential to the growth of knowledge. In that sense, philosophers and social scientists are in agreement that natural scientists are typically ignorant of the principles that govern their practice—the difference between the two camps being that philosophers also tend to believe that science works *in spite of* that ignorance, as if it were governed by an invisible (philosophical) hand.

The rhetoric needed to perform social epistemology in this environment consists of a two-phase "argumentation practice" (Keith 1992). This practice may be illustrated by the following exchange between "you" and "me." Before I am likely to be receptive to the idea that I must change my current practices, I must be convinced that you have my best interests at heart. Here the persuasive skills of the Sophist come into play as you try to establish "common ground" with me. The extent of this ground can vary significantly. At one extreme, you may simply need to point out that we are materially interlocked in a common fate, however else our beliefs and values may differ. At the other, you may claim to be giving clearer expression to views that I already hold. In either case, once common ground has been established, I am ready for the second, more Socratic side of the process. I am now mentally (and socially) prepared to have my views criticized without feeling that my status as an equal party to the dialogue is being undermined. Ideally, this two-step strategy works a Hegelian miracle, the mutual cancellation of the Sophist's manipulative tendencies and Socrates' intellectually coercive ones. For persuasion arises in preparation of an open encounter (and so no spurious agreement results), while criticism arises only after the way has been paved for it to be taken seriously (and so no fruitless resistance is generated).

The argumentation practice of classical epistemology is distinguished from that of social epistemology by its elimination of the first phase. Instead of establishing common ground between "you" and "me," the classical epistemologist simply takes common ground for granted. As a result, any failure on my part to respond adequately to the second phase, criticism, is diagnosed as a deep conceptual problem, not as the consequence of a bad rhetorical habit, namely, your failure to gauge the assumptions I bring to our exchange prior to your beginning to address me. This diagnosis of classical epistemology is supported by the following rhetorical construction of how the problem of knowledge is currently posed by analytic philosophers.

In order to understand this "modern problem of knowledge," we must first realize that it is a technical problem of definition, most of which has already been solved. This explains the narrowness of the debate over the "missing term." All parties to the debate seem to follow (more or less) Plato, Descartes, and Brentano in granting that knowledge is *at least* "justified true belief." The putative advance that has been made since World War II (according to a standard textbook, Chisholm 1977) is to realize that there is a little bit more to the story—but what? A major breakthrough was staged in a three page article by Edmund Gettier (1963), who independently restated a point that was neglected when Bertrand Russell first raised it, fifty years earlier. The breakthrough consisted of some thought experiments designed to isolate the missing term. In brief, the "Gettier Problem" is the possibility that we could have a justified true belief which ends up being mistaken for knowledge, because the belief is grounded on a false assumption that is never made explicit. For example, outside my house are parked two cars, about which I have a justified true belief that one belongs to John and the other to Mary. Thus, when asked for the whereabouts of one of the vehicles, I rightly say, "John's car is outside." Unfortunately, John and Mary traded cars with each other earlier that morning, and so the car that I thought was John's now turns out to be Mary's. And, if my interlocutor does not ask which car is John's, my ignorance will remain undetected as a false assumption. There is a tendency for people outside of epistemology to dismiss the Gettier Problem as simply more of the idle scholasticism for which they have come to fear and loathe philosophers. However, the unprecedented extent to which Gettier has focused the efforts of epistemologists over the last thirty years testifies to the rhetorical appeal of the problem bearing his name (cf. Shope 1983). A brief look at the social dynamics presupposed in the problem should, therefore, reveal something telling about the susceptibility of philosophers to persuasion.

Let us start by taking the Gettier Problem as a purely linguistic transaction, or speech act. I am asked two questions by you, my didactic interlocutor. In response to the first, I correctly say that John's car is outside; in response to the second, I incorrectly say that Mary's car is John's. You frame this sequence of questions as occurring in a context that changes sufficiently little to allow you to claim that our second exchange is an attempt at deepening the inquiry begun in the first exchange. As a piece of social dynamics, this "deepening" is none other than your ability to persuade me that your evaluation of my second response should be used as a standard against which to judge my first response, which, prior to your asking the second question, seemed to be unproblematic. But why should I assent to this shifting of the evaluative ground? The reason seems to be that I accept the idea that my second response had already been implicit in the first response when I made it, and in that sense constitutes the deep structure of the first response. As the "essence" of the first response, the second response existed *in potentia* all along. If nothing else, this linguistic transaction defines the social conditions for attributing the possession of a concept to someone: to wit, I have a concept, if you can get me to follow up an initial response with an exchange that you deem appropriate to the situation.

Now, this ontologically loaded view of language as replete with hidden essences and deep structures—concepts, to say the least—recalls the Socratic rhetoric of *anamnesis,* the recovery of lost memories. However, as against all this, it may be said in a more constructivist vein that reality normally transpires at a coarser grain of analysis than our language is capable of giving it, which implies that if all talk has some purchase on reality, then it is only because talk can bring into being situations and practices that did not exist prior to their appearance in discourse. In terms of the Gettier Problem, why should we suppose that, under normal circumstances, I would have something definite to say about which car is John's prior to your actual request? Moreover, why should we suppose that the answer I give to your request has some retroactive purchase on my answer to your previous query, instead of simply being a new answer to a new question posed in a new context? The constructivist view that I make up new levels of analysis as my interlocutor demands them of me, and then back-substitute those levels for earlier ones, puts a new spin on the verificationist motto that all conceptual (or linguistic) distinctions should make an empirical (or "real-world") difference. The Gettier Problem shows that instead of eliminating conceptual distinctions that make no empirical difference, the epistemologist, in her role as my interlocutor, can produce empirical differences in my response based on the conceptual distinctions raised in her questions. To follow a line of reasoning initiated by social psychologist Michael Billig (1987: chap. 8), here the epistemologist proves herself a master dialectician, as she manufactures a world which I am willing to adopt as my own, even at the (unwitting) expense of relinquishing my old one.

If the reader detects perversity in the epistemologist's strategy of manufacturing occasions that enable her talk to acquire a significance that it would not have otherwise, then you have just demonstrated some rhetorical scruples. Joseph Wenzel (1989) has observed that a good way of telling the "rhetoricians" from the "dialecticians" (or philosophers) among the Sophists was that the former engaged arguments only as part of a general plan to motivate action, whereas the latter argued so as to reach agreement on a proposition. What philosophers have traditionally derided as "mere persuasion" is simply the idea that talk only goes so far toward getting people to act appropriately. But the truly heretical thesis implied in this simple idea is that from the standpoint of appropriate action, it may make no difference whether everyone agrees on a given proposition or whether they instead diverge significantly, perhaps even misunderstanding each other's point of view, Contrary to what many philosophers continue to believe, rhetoricians realize that consensus is not a prerequisite for collaboration—in fact, consensus may often prove an obstacle, if, say, a classical epistemologist has convinced the practitioners of different disciplines that they must agree on all the fundamentals of their inquiry before proceeding on a joint venture. In that case, the convinced parties would have simply allowed the epistemologist to insert her project ahead of their own without increasing the likelihood that theirs will ever be carried out. The *social* epistemologist promises not to make that mistake!

While the social epistemologist cannot be expected to resolve incongruous, contempt-breeding cross-disciplinary perspectives immediately, she may begin by identifying modes of interpenetration appropriate to situations where several disciplines already have common concerns but no effective rhetoric to articulate those concerns as common. Four such modes are examined in the first part of this book. They vary along two dimensions. The first dimension concerns the difference between *persuasion* (P) and *dialectic* (D): rhetoric that on the one hand aims to minimize the differences between two disciplines, and on the other aims to highlight those differences. In terms of a pervasive stereotype, persuasion is the Sophist's art, dialectic the Socratic one. The former seeks common ground, the latter opposes spurious consensus. The second dimension concerns the direction of cognitive transference, so to speak. Does a discipline engage in persuasion or dialectic in order to import ideas from another discipline (I) or to export ideas to that discipline (E)? This distinction corresponds to the two principal functions of metaphor (Greek for "transference") in science: respectively, to test ideas in one domain against those in another ("negative" analogy), and to apply ideas from one domain to another ("positive" analogy). Together the two dimensions present the following four interpenetrative possibilities. Each possibility is epitomized by a current interdisciplinary exchange in which I have been a participant. In the elaborations that follow in the next four chapters, I do not pretend that these exchange represent "pure" types. However, for analytical purposes, we may identify four distinct processes:

(P + I) *Incorporation*

Naturalized epistemologists claim that epistemology can itself be no better grounded than the most successful sciences. Classical epistemologists counter that naturalists presuppose a standard for successful knowledge practices that is logically prior to, and hence must be grounded independently of, the particular sciences deemed successful. There is much at stake here, as captured by the following questions: Is philosophy autonomous from the sciences? Is philosophy's role to support or to criticize the sciences? Have the sciences epistemologically outgrown philosophy? Not surprisingly, the impasse that results between the two positions in this debate is often diagnosed in terms of the radically different assumptions that they make about the nature of knowledge. However, I see the problem here as being quite the opposite, namely, that the two sides have yet to fully disentangle themselves from one another. I show this to be especially true of the naturalist, who often shortsells her position by unwittingly reverting to classicist argument strategies. But after the naturalist has disentangled her position from the classicist's, she needs to address specific classicist objections in naturalistic terms. In that sense, the naturalist needs to "incorporate" the classicist. Otherwise, a rhetorical impasse *will* result.

(D + E) *Reflexion*

Disciplinary histories of science tend to suppress the fact that knowledge is *in* the same world that it is *about*. No representation without intervention; no discovery without invention. Yet knowledge is supposed to pertain to the world prior to any "artificial" transformation it may undergo during the process of knowing. The natural sciences can suppress the transformative character of knowledge production more effectively than the social sciences. The discourses of the natural sciences are relatively autonomous from ordinary talk, and their techniques—"laboratories," in the broadest sense—for generating and analyzing phenomena are relatively insulated from the normal course of events. By contrast, because societies have placed some fairly specific practical demands on the social sciences, they have not enjoyed the same autonomy and insulation. The seams of social intervention in their attempts at representation are easily seen, especially when a social science tries to explain its own existence in its own terms. The results typically turn out to reveal the discipline's blind spots, highlighting the artifice with which disciplinary identity is maintained. For example, economics has appeared most authoritative in periods of economic turbulence, during which economists are hired to dictate policy to a market supposedly governed by an "invisible hand." However, the point of revealing such paradoxicality by historical "reflexion" (a process both *reflexive* and *reflective*) is to undermine not social science per se, but only its division into discrete disciplines. For together the social sciences have the investigative apparatus needed for showing that the natural sciences, too, are world-transformative enterprises.

(P + E) *Sublimation*

Practitioners of the Sociology of Scientific Knowledge (SSK) and artificial intelligence (AI) should be natural collaborators, bringing complementary modes of analysis to their common interest in the cognitive capacities of the computer. However, most of the exchanges to date have been hostile, often based on mutually stereotyped views that reverberate of earlier debates, especially "mechanism versus humanism" or "positivism versus holism" (Slezak 1990), often filtered through the coarse-grained representations of the mass media. As science gets a longer history and becomes more permeable to public concerns, this tendency is likely to spread. The solution explored here is for each side to export ideas that are essential to the other's project. Thus, differences are "sublimated" by showing them to be natural extensions of one another's position. The AI researcher needs to see that competence is a social attribution, in order to test empirically the cognitive capacities of a particular computer. Conversely, the SSK researcher should realize that the possible success of AI would testify to the constructed character of cognition, such that not even the possession of a human body is deemed necessary for thought. Given the tendency of debates of this sort to amplify into a Manichaean struggle, the presence of the computer as a "boundary object" of significance for both sides turns out to be crucial in facilitating the sublimation process by forcing each side to map its cosmic concerns onto the same finite piece of matter (Star and Griesemer 1989; cf. McGee 1980, on "ideographs," as pieces of language that perform much the same function).

(D + I) *Excavation*

After the initial promise of studying science historically, both in the nineteenth century and especially in the work of Thomas Kuhn, the history and philosophy of science (HPS) appears to be at a conceptual standstill, not quite prepared to make the leap beyond the disciplinary boundaries of history and philosophy to the new field of STS. I diagnose this reluctance in terms of a failure, especially on the part of historians, to explicitly discuss the assumptions they make about theory and method, which are often at odds with what the social sciences have to say about these matters. Especially suspect are the assumptions about the human cognitive condition that inform historical narratives, even narratives that avowedly draw from cognitive psychology. To "excavate" these assumptions is to articulate long suppressed differences between humanistic and social scientific approaches to inquiry. While it is perhaps too much to expect historians to become social scientists overnight, nevertheless a willingness on the part of humanists to hold their research accountable to the standards of social science would tend to break down the remaining disciplinary barriers that inhibits HPS's passage to STS. It would also enable the historian to use the social scientists' own methods to keep them scrupulous to historical detail. I end by suggesting that some of the normative issues that have made philosophers impatient with historians could be better addressed by experimental social psychology, and perhaps even the "case-study" methodology traditionally championed in law and business schools.

Rhetorical Aim / Trade Strategy	PERSUASION (Difference Minimizing)	DIALECTIC (Difference Amplifying)
IMPORT (Negative Analogy)	INCORPORATION	EXCAVATION
EXPORT (Positive Analogy)	SUBLIMATION	REFLEXION

FIGURE. The Modes of Interdisciplinary Interpenetration

Here I Stand

Since the reader is about to embark upon a dialectical journey from which few have returned unconfused, let me state briefly where I position myself in each interpenetration. In the case of Incorporation, I am a staunch naturalist who believes that the letter of classical epistemology has compromised the naturalist's spirit. In the case of Reflexion, I am a staunch advocate of social science who believes that its fragmentation into disciplines has undermined the social scientist's capacity for critiquing and reconstructing the knowledge system. In the case of Sublimation, I am a staunch supporter of the sociology of scientific knowledge who agrees that yet again philosophers have injected false consciousness into another community of unsuspecting scientists, namely, researchers in artificial intelligence, but I also believe that the sociologists are being duplicitous when they make a priori arguments against the inclusion of computers as members of our epistemic communities. Finally, in the case of Excavation, I am a staunch ally of those who want to facilitate the transition from HPS to STS, but I also believe that it is naive to think that this transition can succeed if both parties simply adopt new theories and look at new data—a new social formation is also needed.

References

Abbott, Andrew. 1988. *The System of Professions.* University of Chicago: Chicago.
Aitchison, Jean. 1981. *Language Change: Progress or Decay?* Universe Books: New York.
Almond, Gabriel, and Verba, Sidney. 1963. *The Civic Culture.* Princeton University Press: Princeton.
Althusser, Louis. 1989. *Philosophy and the Spontaneous Philosophy of the Scientist Scientists.* Verso: London.
Billig, Michael. 1987. *Arguing and Thinking.* Cambridge University Press: Cambridge.
Bloom, Allan. 1987. *The Closing of the American Mind.* Simon and Schuster: New York.
Bocock, Robert. 1986. *Hegemony.* Tavistock: London.
Bok, Derek. 1982. *Beyond the Ivory Tower.* Harvard University Press: Cambridge.
Booth, Wayne. 1979. *Critical Understanding.* University of Chicago Press: Chicago.
Boulding, Kenneth. 1968. *Beyond Economics.* University of Michigan Press: Ann Arbor.
Button, Graham, ed. 1991. *Ethnomethodology and the Human Sciences.* Cambridge University Press: Cambridge.
Campbell, Donald. 1969. "Ethnocentrism of Disciplines and the Fishscale Model of Omniscience." In Muzarif Sherif, ed., *Interdisciplinary Relationships in the Social Sciences.* Aldine Press: Chicago.
Chisholm, Roderick. 1977. *Theory of Knowledge.* Prentice-Hall: Englewood Cliffs NJ.
Chubin, Daryl, project director. 1991. *Federally Funded Research: Decisions for a Decade.* Office of Technology Assessment: Washington DC.
Coleman, James. 1961. *The Adolescent Society.* Free Press: New York.
Danziger, Kurt. 1990. *Constructing the Subject.* Cambridge University Press: Cambridge.
Elgin, Catherine. 1988. "The Epistemic Efficacy of Stupidity." *Synthese* 74: 297–311.
Elster, Jon. 1979. *Ulysses and the Sirens.* Cambridge University Press: Cambridge.
———. 1983. *Sour Grapes.* Cambridge University Press: Cambridge.
Engels, Friedrich. 1934. *The Dialectics of Nature.* Progress Publishers: New York.
Fisher, David. 1990. "Boundary Work and Science." In Cozzens and Gieryn 1990.
Fuller, Steve. 1988. *Social Epistemology.* Indiana University Press: Bloomington.
Furner, Mary. 1975. *Advocacy and Objectivity.* University of Kentucky Press: Lexington.
Galison, Peter. 1992. "Image and Logic." Manuscript.
Geertz, Clifford. 1973. *Interpreting Cultures.* Harper and Row: New York.
———. 1980. "Blurred Genres." *American Scholar* 49: 165–79.
———. 1983. *Local Knowledge.* Basic Books: New York.
Gettier, Edmund. 1963. "Is Justified True Belief Knowledge?" *Analysis* 23: 121–23.
Goldenberg, Sheldon. 1989. "What Scientists Think of Science." *Social Science Information* 28: 467–81.

Gouldner, Alvin. 1957. "Cosmopolitans and Locals." *Administrative Science Quarterly* 2: 281–306, 444–80.

Horowitz, Irving Louis. 1986. *The Communication of Ideas.* Oxford University Press: Oxford.

Keith, William. "Argument Practices." Forthcoming in *Argumentation.*

Klein, Julie. 1990. *Interdisciplinarity.* Wayne State University Press: Detroit.

McCloskey, Donald. 1991. *If You're So Smart . . .* University of Chicago Press: Chicago.

McGee, Michael Calvin. 1980. "The 'Ideograph': A Link between Rhetoric and Ideology." *Quarterly Journal of Speech* 66: 1–16.

Proctor, Robert. 1991. *Value-Free Science?* Harvard University Press: Cambridge.

Rooney, Ellen. 1991. *Seductive Reasoning.* Cornell University Press: Ithaca.

Schaefer, Wolf, ed. 1984. *Finalization in Science.* Kluwer: Dordrecht.

Serres, Michel. 1982. *Parasite.* Johns Hopkins University Press: Baltimore.

Shapere, Dudley. 1984. *Reason and the Search for Knowledge.* D. Reidel: Dordrecht.

Shope, Robert. 1983. *The Analysis of Knowing.* Princeton University Press: Princeton.

Slezak, Peter. 1990. "Man Not a Subject for Science?" *Social Epistemology* 4: 327–42.

Snow, C. P. 1964. *The Two Cultures and a Second Look.* Cambridge University Press: Cambridge.

Sorell, Tom. 1991. *Scientism.* Routledge: London.

Star, Leigh, and Griesemer, James. 1989. "Institutional Ecology, Translations, Boundary Objects." *Social Studies of Science* 19: 387–420.

Stinchcombe, Arthur. 1990. *Information and Organizations.* University of California Press: Berkeley.

Wallerstein, Immanuel. 1991. *Unthinking Social Science.* Blackwell: Oxford.

Webb, E. J.; Campbell, D. T.; Schwartz, R. D.; Sechrest, L. B.; and Grove, J. B. 1987. *Non-reactive Measures in the Social Sciences.* Houghton Mifflin: Boston.

Wenzel, Joseph. 1989. "Relevance—and Other Norms of Argument: A Rhetorical Exploration." In Maier 1989.

Wolff, Robert Paul; Moore, Barrington; and Marcuse, Herbert. 1969. *A Critique of Pure Tolerance.* Beacon Press: Boston.

Administration

Avoiding the Potholes

Strategies for Reforming General Education

Jerry G. Gaff

General education is undergoing a revival of interest today: hundreds of colleges and universities have assembled committees and task forces to review their general education programs. Members of such committees and task forces usually bring much talent and enthusiasm to the task of reforming general education, but few have experience in providing leadership for institutional change.

Faculty members tend to be attracted to substantive issues—the nature of general education, the qualities of an educated person, problems with the current program, facets of an ideal general education—and much less interested in the strategies and procedures to be used by the group. Furthermore, committees and task forces tend to adopt common-sense approaches to fashion a report. Unfortunately, some common-sense approaches turn out to be naïve, and proposals—even good ones—hit potholes along the way. Such potholes can slow down the progress of curriculum reform and, in some cases, lead to a breakdown altogether. Although common-sense approaches sometimes prove to be best, they are more likely to work if they are consciously chosen in the light of alternatives rather than regarded simplistically as the only way to proceed.

The biggest pothole to avoid, then, is the notion that strategies are unimportant and that they enter the picture only after a proposed program is approved and about to be implemented. Rather, strategies are critical; they are as important as the substantive issues and they need to be considered from the outset.

The information presented here is based on a three-year Project on General Education Models (GEM), sponsored by the Society for Values in Higher Education. Initiated in 1978, Project GEM consists of twelve diverse institutions, including state colleges and universities, private colleges and universities, community colleges, and a technical institute. Each institution has designated a task force consisting of administrators, faculty members, and students that provides leadership for strengthening the general education program. The Project has a small staff and an advisory board that assist the work of campus task forces by holding workshops, assembling resource material, providing consultation, conducting studies, publishing a newsletter, and awarding modest activity funds. The Project is supported by grants from the Exxon Education Foundation and the Fund for the Improvement of Postsecondary Education. Much

Gaff, Jerry G. "Avoiding the Potholes: Strategies for Reforming General Education." Educational Record *61:4 (Fall 1980), 50–59. Reprinted with permission of the American Council on Education.*

has been learned in this effort about the process of curricular change in different campus settings.

Some committees have learned the hard way that the strategies for curricular change are as important as the substance, and their experiences may help fellow travelers on the road to general education reform. Forty-three common strategies for change—potholes, if you will—have been culled from the work of general education reform committees. For each pothole an alternative strategy is suggested.

Misconceptions About the Task

1. Find a Program to Import

During the first workshop of the Project on General Education Models (GEM), many participants—task force members from GEM institutions—came with the idea that they would be presented with an array of model programs. They expected to look over this menu, make their selections, and take a proposed program back to their schools for debate and speedy approval. Instead, the staff urged the task force members to develop their own homegrown program with the advice and support of the workshop and Project staff. Some participants thought the staff members were incompetent because the staff *couldn't* offer them a "quick fix" for their institution's general education needs; other participants were angry because they thought the staff *wouldn't* provide ready-made solutions. In contrast, within a year some of the same participants were on a panel at a professional meeting and were asked by members of the audience for program models to take back to campus. Every GEM task force presenter on the panel replied that a program for reforming general education should be designed around each institution's character, the strengths and interests of its faculty, and the needs of its students.

2. Expect a Holistic Change

Some committee members approach a curricular reform assignment expecting to fashion a comprehensive curricular program that is to be introduced all at once to produce revolutionary change. Radical departures from established traditions are, in fact, rare in the history of American higher education. They have occurred but usually because of the creation of a new institution, such as Empire State College and Evergreen State College in the 1960s. In addition, crises have sometimes forced major change, for instance, when Antioch College's curriculum was radically restructured in 1919; charismatic individuals, such as Robert M. Hutchins of the University of Chicago, have sometimes fashioned distinctive programs. But most changes are evolutionary and introduced in a piecemeal fashion or phased in over time.[1] Furthermore, the holistic approach is a high-risk strategy. A comprehensive proposal takes a long time to fashion, yet a faculty can turn it down in a single meeting, thereby aborting the entire effort. A proposal designed to effect change through evolutionary, piecemeal action has a greater chance of having at least a portion of it accepted. A footnote in the Carnegie Foundation report, *Missions of the College Curriculum,* declared, "Curricular reform of significance requires (1) overall thought but (2) piecemeal action."[2] Several committees that have seen their proposals rejected can attest to the practical wisdom of this strategy.

3. Reinstate Distribution Requirements

Amid the current debate about general education, two approaches have emerged. One approach seeks to reinstate conventional distribution requirements, which largely consist of introductory courses in traditional liberal arts disciplines usually taught by standard lecture or seminar methods. This approach may indeed improve the general education of students at some institutions, but it has three major limitations. First, although most institutions have had extensive experience with a distribution requirements system (approximately 85 percent of all colleges and universities have one), distribution requirements have spawned the very problems that current reform efforts are seeking to overcome.[3] These problems include fragmentation of the curriculum; erosion of an accepted education rationale; lack of commitment on the part of the faculty; loss of interest by students; and absence of any central administration or supervision of the general education program. Second, most people think of breadth of knowledge as only one component of general education. But the Carnegie Foundation report, for example, cited learning skills— such as communication, mathematics, statistics, and possibly a foreign language—as a second component and various forms of integrative learning across the various disciplines as a third component.[4] Neither of these other two components is well served by distribution requirements. Finally, distribution requirements represent a return to earlier forms of general education that may not be suitable today. However useful they may have been, distribution requirements may be inappropriate for a student clientele that consists of more adult, underprepared, minority, women, and other nontraditional students. Furthermore, general education has traditionally stressed western civilization, and no matter how important this one tradition has been, it is necessary today to incorporate more nonwestern perspectives and knowledge. Lockwood has expressed skepticism about the distribution requirements approach:

> The current trend at colleges of reviving distribution requirements does not convince me that we are improving the quality of education. Giving the curriculum more structure doesn't necessarily give it coherence. I am skeptical that meaningful educational reform can occur if it is not based on a new philosophy of education and shared assumptions by faculty members of what education should be in the last quarter of the twentieth century.[5]

Therefore, rather than merely reviving distribution requirements, Project GEM has taken another approach, where different member institutions are helped to develop new philosophies for building contemporary programs of general education. Such philosophies seem to provide a sound long-term basis for specific reforms.

Erroneous Task Force Procedures

4. Working Through the Curriculum Committee

That curriculum review or reform should be conducted by the standing curriculum committee seems reasonable. However, forming a special task force might be a better route to take. Although a standing committee has its regular business to accomplish, which can consume large amounts of time, a task force can devote all its energy to a single purpose. In addition, unlike a special task force, a standing committee has provisions for regularly changing membership, and more than one group has found that new members can sidetrack its work by reintroducing issues and arguments that had been settled earlier. Furthermore, curriculum committees traditionally react to proposals from faculty members of departments and operate with a veto-power mentality. Efforts to reform general education require a group to develop a proposal and actively gather campus support for their ideas.

5. Assembling the Best Thinkers

A common-sense approach is that the best thinkers on the faculty should be assembled to prepare the best possible proposal. In practice, however, this approach may generate heady debate about high principles but little action. Robert Chambers, dean of the College of Arts and Sciences at Bucknell University, lamented, "I'm afraid we will spend three years talking about change rather than doing it." A good task force needs various kinds of talent—thinkers and doers, idealists and pragmatists, educational innovators and conservatives, and campus politicians and persons knowledgeable about national trends and resources. Failure to include a mix of talent may result in more progress reports like the one issued by Richard Clinton of Oregon State University: "When all is said and done, more is said than done." Furthermore, Project GEM task forces are required to include other persons in addition to faculty members. Guidelines specify that each task force should have from five to seven faculty members to provide faculty leadership, an administrator to provide institutional support, and from three to five students to remind all that *they* are the ultimate beneficiaries of the curriculum. Each of these constituencies has a legitimate interest in the quality of general education, and each should be represented in the reform process.

6. Working Without Any Special Support

An amazing number of committees try to effect massive curriculum reform without adequate support. This situation frequently occurs when the task is given to a standing committee, because such committees seldom receive any special budget or other assistance. Project GEM institutions were required to provide three kinds of support to their task forces. First, reduced teaching assignments were deemed essential if faculty members were to have the time and energy to provide leadership for the curriculum revision. In some cases, a half-time reduction in teaching assignments was provided for the chairperson; in others, a similar reduction, and sometimes a greater one, was distributed among several task force members. Schools were urged to either pay students with work-study funds or structure the task force's work so that students could earn academic credit for it. Second, schools were expected to pay travel expenses to send their GEM task force members to projectwide meetings. Third, each task force needed a modest fund to purchase materials, hold retreats, invite consultants, reproduce papers for campus distribution, and the like. Some funds were provided by the project, but usually these were supplemented by the institutions. Unless adequate support is given, a task force or committee cannot be expected to provide creative and effective leadership for curriculum reform.

7. Planning for a Short-Term Project

Many committee members assume that their work will span only a few months and then become frustrated and disappointed when the work takes much longer. Harvard University provides an example of how the curriculum reform process can take many years. In 1974 a group was first assembled to address the question of the quality of undergraduate education at Harvard. A report of the Task Force on the Core Curriculum was issued in 1977, when the faculty approved it in principle. In 1978 a more detailed proposal was presented and approved. Subsequently, a standing committee to oversee this part of the curriculum was established, and specific course proposals were solicited from the faculty and negotiated. In 1982 the program will be fully operational—eight years after the process began. General education reform committees would do well to keep in mind the dieter's dictum: Fat that took years to put on cannot be removed in a few days. The difficulties surrounding general education are so severe and deep-seated they cannot be resolved overnight, and more time than is usually anticipated is needed to rectify them.

8. Having the Committee Work by Itself to Develop a Proposal

The rationale for committees is that a small group can probe a subject in depth, issue a report, and have the larger group make an informed decision without investing all of the time of the larger group. This rationale has led some committees to work in isolation, survey the state of the art around the country, examine alternative forms of general education, and issue a report to the faculty at large. The faculty frequently perceives such reports as coming out of the blue and accuses the committee of holding secret discussions; the faculty feels that its prerogative to be actively involved in curriculum policy making has been ignored. This procedure was followed by a summer planning group of faculty at Eckerd College, and the rest of the faculty killed the report without its ever being submitted to a formal vote. A reconstituted committee, which spent a great deal of time at the outset outlining a procedure for involving the entire Eckerd faculty, is now engaged in a number of institutionwide activities, such as a monthly colloquium on general education, to prepare a proposal that has a better chance of winning widespread support.

9. Issuing a Single Final Report

When writing scholarly papers, academics typically wait until their ideas are fully developed and well expressed before submitting papers for publication or critical scrutiny by their colleagues. Applying this common-sense approach to the preparation of a curriculum proposal can be catastrophic. One institution had a committee working laboriously for two years to develop an elegant and comprehensive proposal. The document, although lengthy, was impressive in its philosophy of education, analysis of the institution, and number of recommendations. Unfortunately, it contained something for everyone to dislike and was defeated by a coalition of opposition. Other groups are finding they are more successful when they issue a series of reports, hold discussions of each report along the way, and seek approval of portions as the enterprise unfolds. Several schools have used this procedure to obtain consensus on some learning goals for students. For example, at Valparaiso University, a set of assumptions about general education was developed and debated before a specific program was developed. And at the Community College of Denver, a framework for the curriculum was presented for discussion and approval before specific courses and other details were fleshed out. Such a procedure has the advantage of involving the faculty as the committee progresses with its task.

10. Analyzing the Big Issues

One way task forces are sidetracked is debate over large and enduring issues, such as the plight of undergraduate education, faculty lack of interest in teaching, or the absence of professional incentives for teaching general education courses. These are important and legitimate issues, and they deserve a portion of any group's time. But a committee is often stymied for an inordinate time by hand wringing about matters over which it has little control. In contrast, productive groups tend to take a practical stance and focus on "what we can do here using our own resources." The large-scale changes toward competency-based curricula at Alverno College and Mars Hill College were effected because leaders of the reform efforts kept a practical focus on their agendas.

Mistaken Concepts of General Education

11. There Is Only One True Meaning of General Education

Each committee member tends to vest his or her own definition with unmerited authority. Naturally, different concepts, strongly held, can lead to disagreements and even conflicts. After hearing members articulate their views over and over again, some members lament that the group cannot even agree on the meaning of general education, let alone ways to strengthen it. Eventually the committee may realize that general education is fraught with meaning, that it has several definitions, and that each person has a legitimate claim to his or her view. The committee may then adopt a provisional definition, attempt to explore and elaborate its meaning as work progresses, and seek to understand the assumptions and values that underlie the various concepts of general education. Typically, the committee will have a richer sense of the meaning of the term at the conclusion of their efforts than at the outset.

12. General Education Deals Only with Breadth of Knowledge

This common presupposition tends to be associated with the notion that students should be introduced to an array of academic disciplines. Few would dispute the contention that breadth of knowledge is *part* of general education. However, in addition to breadth of knowledge, the Carnegie typology included learning skills and integration of knowledge as important components of general education. As soon as a committee learns to substitute *a* definition for *the* definition of general education, it is free to consider various ways to enhance this part of the curriculum. Indeed, some thinkers argue that a core curriculum that is based on common needs, concerns, and themes and that takes the form of interdisciplinary courses is more productive than distribution requirements.[6]

13. General Education Is Only Cognitive in Character

The starting place for many faculty members is asking the perfectly reasonable question, What knowledge should a generally educated person have? They are then led into a consideration of which disciplines are the most basic or important, which naturally leads directly to legendary battles over "turf." Some committees have found that they can avoid these difficulties by seeking to identify the qualities, not only the knowledge, that mark the generally educated person. Northeastern Illinois University, for example, developed a list of desirable qualities of a generally educated student that included effective communication skills, critical thinking abilities, problem definition and solving skills, human relations competencies, and commitment to ideals such as truth and social justice. Thus, many affective qualities, attitudes, values, and skills can be goals of general education, and purely cognitive knowledge, however important, represents only some of the attributes of an educated person.

14. A Program of General Education Is Only Curricular

Again, the question of what *knowledge* a student should possess leads to a question that is essentially curricular: how many courses in this subject area and how many in that? However, when the question is expanded to what the *qualities* of an educated person are, then the question of how best to teach these traits arises. Although much can be taught directly through the curriculum, attitudes toward knowledge, relationships with others, and awareness of one's values may be better taught through the college community, dormitory life, informal relationships with faculty and students outside class, and off-campus experiences.

15. Liberal Arts Faculties Constitute the Rank-and-File Defenders of General Education

A common myth is that liberal arts faculties are the beleaguered defenders of culture and general education against the infidels in the professional and practical arts. To the contrary, the faculty director of undergraduate programs in the Department of Business Administration at Pennsylvania State University reported that enrollments in his school are mushrooming not only because of the increase in majors, but also because more students in the arts and sciences want to take courses in business. His school is called upon to provide "service" courses to the College of Liberal Arts, reversing the former relationship. Furthermore, he worries that the students are taking narrowly specialized courses designed for management majors and that these electives do not form a coherent program. He would, therefore, like to design a few minors around the special needs and interests of students who have majors in the liberal arts. At Valparaiso University, the general education task force encountered some initial opposition to its proposals in the professional schools. On closer inspection the task force found that, at least in some departments, the concern did not stem from narrow specialization. The nursing department, for instance, requires relatively few nursing courses but does require several cognate courses, for example, courses in biology and chemistry. Furthermore, the national accrediting association specifies general education requirements so that baccalaureate nursing students get a general education. A nursing student, therefore, is required to take several liberal arts courses. This combination of major, cognate, and general education requirements packs a nursing student's program. The nursing department's opposition to the task force's program was thus not based on a rejection of general education per se. Committees at other institutions have sometimes discovered that they enjoy more support for general education proposals from professional schools than from the supposedly amenable liberal arts departments.

16. The Humanists Are the True Defenders of General Education

A variation of the above myth identifies scientists as opponents of genuine culture. The General Education Committee at the State University of New York at Buffalo conducted a study that led to different conclusions.

> Overspecialization is a fault usually associated with the rigorous re-
> quirements of vocational or preprofessional majors, and the decline
> of general education is presumed to relate to the increasing propor-

tions of students seeking such majors. Yet it appears from statistics recently generated by the General Education Committee at SUNYAB that students majoring in other areas, particularly the humanities, are as likely to avoid certain major knowledge areas and thus leave the quality of their general education open to question. In the fall of 1977, English majors at SUNYAB took only 3.5 percent of their courses in natural sciences, mathematics, health sciences, or engineering. This matches, almost exactly, the proportion of engineering students taking courses in arts and letters and is significantly less than the comparable figures for students in health science and management majors.[7]

Rather than polarizing the faculty by pointing at "good guys" and "bad guys," many committees have found it productive to assume that general education is a problem in all fields of study and for all types of students, which allows them to consider how faculty from all fields can improve course offerings.

17. Integration Is the Responsibility of Students

Nearly everyone agrees that students should not merely master discrete bits of knowledge but integrate them as well. However, some faculty members are content to leave the full responsibility to students. Jonathan Smith, dean of the college at the University of Chicago, has declared an "iron law": "Students shall not be expected to integrate anything the faculty can't or won't." The rationale for this principle is that the integration is not likely to occur unless it is consciously planned and structured as a regular part of the academic program. When such a principle is rigorously applied, faculty members from different academic disciplines must engage in dialogue over substantive issues and build an academic community to sustain their general education program. Lockwood has expressed it well:

> For several decades—from the 1930s until the mid-50s—the general education movement represented much of what was best in undergraduate education. The late Lionel Trilling has recalled that, for most of that period, he and his colleagues, at Columbia and elsewhere, 'inhabited an academic community which was informed by a sense not merely of scholarly but of educational purpose and which was devoted to making ever more cogent its conception of what a liberal and humane education consists in.' Does a similar sense of purpose, some shared conviction, characterize most current curricular reforms? I tend to doubt it.[8]

Misunderstood Notions About Program Planning

18. Change by Addition

In recent decades academic change has been accomplished largely by adding new programs, securing larger budgets, recruiting more students, and hiring more instructors. Today this avenue is closed off at most institutions. Now programs are being introduced by shifting priorities, reallocating resources, re-assigning faculty members, and developing the professional competence of ex-isting personnel. Although a much more complicated route to reform than change by addition, it is the only road available to most schools.

19. Keep the Debate Internal to the Campus

Many committees begin their deliberations by having the members share their best thinking and offer their ideas for improving general education. This ap-proach is guaranteed to pool a great deal of ignorance and half-truths, and it frequently results in premature polarization of the group. Other task forces have embarked on an exploration of the topic and have consciously cultivated a spirit of inquiry so that each person learns to expand, refine, and alter his or her initial ideas. These task forces read the literature, secure a consultant or two, attend a conference or workshop, or visit other institutions. For example, the University of Tennessee committee is launching an extensive educational campaign by creating a series of faculty study groups and providing participants with a few key volumes to read and discuss; specific proposals will not be pursued until the faculty develops sophistication on the topic of general educa-tion. Project GEM has prepared a guidebook about ideas, programs, and litera-ture to help GEM task force members in this area.[9]

20. Proposals Are Autobiographical

Innovators frequently lament that faculty members, because they are relatively isolated, offer ideas that are largely autobiographical. Although proposals may be motivated by personal experience, the danger is that faculty members will prescribe for today's students what was done for (or to) them in their own general education. Groups that encourage members to transcend personal expe-riences have a better chance of designing programs that are responsive to the interests of today's students and to contemporary realities.

21. Assume that the Committee Knows the Experiences and Views of Relevant Constituencies

Because members of a committee are from the campus, they are often presumed to be aware of faculty and student perspectives. Some committees have found it instructive to conduct studies to test their preconceived ideas, and sometimes reach surprising conclusions, as in the SUNY-Buffalo example mentioned in 16. As another example, the Rochester Institute of Technology has surveyed its students, faculty members, alumni, and members of the local community as an aid to planning. To assess the two key constituencies of students and faculty, Project GEM has used a survey of students and developed a faculty interview.

22. Plan Rationally

Virtually all rational planning models call for planners to specify goals, assess needs, determine alternatives, design and implement a program, and evaluate outcomes. Although such models are useful, effective programs are actually fashioned in many different ways. For example, the Community College of Denver was faced with the requirements of a new state law, and it hastily devised a promising program with little help from any rational planning model. Columbia University is creating a series of "teaching companies," upper-division interdisciplinary study groups, by having faculty members identify common interests that transcend their disciplines and by offering courses on such topics. The university is building this part of the program around faculty rather than the usual practice of recruiting faculty to staff the program.

23. Use "Either-Or" Thinking

Because some people regard alternative ideas as anathema, preliminary conversations often pit one pet idea against another. However, general education is so complex that several steps must be taken to strengthen it at most institutions. Some committees have discovered that "both-and" thinking allows many additional features to be incorporated and avoids the political fallout of rejecting polar alternatives. For example, the Community College of Denver adopted a program that calls for all degree students to take four skills courses—communication, critical thinking, computation skills, and interpersonal skills—and for students seeking an Associate of Arts degree to take in addition three disciplinary courses and three interdisciplinary courses. This scheme not only follows the Carnegie Foundation's creative thinking on the topic but also incorporates the desires of those faculty members who demand attention to basic skills, those who favor surveys of academic disciplines, and those who prefer some interdisciplinary mode of integration. Thus, by using the "both-and" thought process, a committee can develop a sophisticated program with greater political support.

24. Search for the "One Best" Program

In *Growing Up in America,* Fred and Grace Hechinger concluded that educators have a penchant for standardized answers to all problems.[10] The American educator's search for the "one best way" is largely responsible for education fads that range from one extreme to the other. Many general education committees search for the one best program without realizing that because of the human diversity, any single program is likely to be a Procrustean bed. Some schools are seeking to avoid such rigidities by providing a good measure of freedom of choice for students. Some, like Harvard, provide a limited array of courses for each required area of study. Others, such as Spelman College, are developing a series of interdisciplinary and thematic courses of study, and students select from these structured alternatives. Even more radical approaches include the creation of an alternative, tightly integrated core curriculum at Pacific Lutheran University, a series of federated learning communities with thematic topics at SUNY-Stony Brook, and an alternative college at St. Olaf College. Each approach is based on a respect for common standards as well as an aversion to standardized solutions.

25. Keep the Committee Out of Politics

The committee at Southern Illinois University, seeking to avoid partisanship within its ranks, was guided for many months by the rules of "objective scholarship," under which members were expected to keep their personal biases out of the discussions. The hope was that this technique would help prevent partisan political issues from arising within the committee and spreading throughout the campus. Other committees take the opposite tack and strive to uncover the biases of various groups so that those views can be explicitly incorporated into their proposals. This strategy involves consciously building coalitions and showing how the self-interest of various departments and other campus groups is served by a proposal.

26. Couch Proposals in the Language of Innovation

Because committee members think of themselves as being engaged in innovation or reform, they naturally use such language in their reports and written materials. Because this rhetoric may create resistance to change, some groups have chosen to heed the lesson cited by A. Lawrence Lowell in his 1938 book, *What a University President Has Learned:* "If he desires to innovate he will be greatly helped by having the reputation of being conservative, because the radicals who want a change are little offended by the fact of change, while the conservatives will be likely to follow him because they look on him as sharing their temperament and point of view."[11] Proposals that seem to advocate a return to fundamental purposes and procedures rather than a radical departure from present practices may draw support from both liberal and conservative campus groups.

27. Assume that the Plan Is the End of the Process

The process of planning a program is so demanding and time-consuming that a committee is only too eager to complete the planning so that it can turn the responsibility for approving and implementing the program over to somebody else. The preparation of a plan that merits the support of the committee is seen as the end of a long haul. One institution dropped out of Project GEM in part because once the committee had prepared its report on the general education program and submitted it to the faculty, its work was seen as completed. But as James Q. Wilson, who chaired Harvard's task force, said after the faculty approved the new core curriculum, "To paraphrase Churchill, we are not at the end, or at the beginning of the end, but at the end of the beginning."[12] A responsible committee must secure approval of its proposals and help implement them.

Faulty Methods for Securing Approval of Proposals

28. Have the Committee Play a Passive Role in the Debate and Approval Process

Some committees adopt the scholarly model of publishing their best thinking and waiting for the reviews and reactions from their professional colleagues to come in. The faculty must have a full and fair debate on the issues, of course, but several task forces have learned that they must take an active part in the debate and orchestrate the approval process if their proposals are to have any chance of passing. The role of the committee may shift from that of a study and recommending body to that of an advocate for the proposals. After all, if the committee members will not speak for their own recommendations, who will? The faculty has only a few months to process all the issues, problems, recommendations, and rationales that the committee grappled with for perhaps years. Committee members can greatly aid the approval process by initiating conversations with key people such as committee chairpersons, department chairpersons, faculty leaders, and deans.

29. Present the Proposal in an Open Hearing

GEM task force members at Northeastern Illinois University held a productive two-day retreat during which they developed a set of goals, brainstormed some possible model curricula, and planned strategy. Toward the end of the retreat, one person suggested that the task force members hold an open hearing on campus for interested faculty members and present the task force's best thinking to their colleagues for a critique. Another person remarked that the task force's ideas had grown out of the constructive and enjoyable atmosphere of the retreat and expressed the fear that an open hearing would provide a negative atmosphere in which faculty members would criticize the task force's best efforts. The decision was to try to recapture the spirit of the retreat by having several small group meetings before attempting an open hearing. Although time-consuming, this technique succeeded in engaging more people in thinking about how to enhance the quality of general education, and it laid the groundwork for subsequent efforts.

30. Seek Approval of a Comprehensive Proposal

Although a comprehensive proposal can generate a coalition of opposition, at least some of its recommendations may be accepted if it has several features that can be debated and acted upon separately. For example, at the College of Brockport in the SUNY system, the first collegewide Committee on General Education was created before the nature of the general education program was voted on. This procedure helped resolve some of the political ambiguities before the program itself was discussed. Other schools break down a comprehensive proposal into preliminary portions that are brought before the faculty.

31. Assume that the Political Task Is to Get Others to Accept the Committee's Proposal

Most committees eventually ask the question, How can we get *them* to approve *our* recommendations? When the question is posed that way, it is very difficult to answer, because faculty members will not vote for something that they perceive to be undesirable or not in their best interest. The most reliable strategy is to make sure the proposal contains portions that represent the ideas and values of those who must approve it. Fostering a sense of ownership among the faculty for portions of the proposal is the key to gaining speedy and convincing support for the proposal as a whole.

32. Avoid and Isolate Opponents

Because avoiding persons who disagree with one is human nature, critics are often isolated and ignored. Ignoring them does not make them go away; indeed, they may become more persistent and vocal. Some committees have deputized members or small delegations to meet quietly with these critics, hear their concerns, and either incorporate features that respond to their concerns or explain why that cannot be done. This procedure may improve the proposal as well as silence some of the opposition.

33. Assume that Any Opposition Is Irrational

Some committee members have difficulty acknowledging that a person may have good reasons for opposing new policies to strengthen general education. However, many potential supporters may have legitimate concerns and, therefore, some groups go out of their way to reassure faculty members that the group's proposals to strengthen undergraduate general education are not, for example, antithetical to specialization, a threat to graduate education, contrary to the interests of departments, or a way to rid the institution of some faculty members. Some committee reports make it clear that not all faculty members would be involved in teaching new courses, and other reports insist that resources be available to assist faculty members in adjusting to new courses and the new program.

34. Assume that Faculty Members Understand the Proposals

Distributing a written report and holding discussions are essential to educate faculty members about a proposed program. Yet, rare is the vote that takes place without at least some people misunderstanding portions of the report. Some opposition comes from simple misinformation about the current situation, the proposed improvement, the implications for other parts of the institution, and the like. One committee decided to do everything in its power to ensure that nobody would vote on the basis of misinformation. This decision requires having someone talk with known opponents to make sure that they are genuinely in disagreement rather than merely misinformed.

35. Use Regular Voting Procedures

Some task forces never question the business-as-usual approach for voting on a major curriculum proposal. But the University of Tennessee adopted its current curriculum by a mailed secret ballot to minimize the oratorical influence of opponents in open faculty meetings and the undue influence that some persons might wield over others in a public vote. Because any curriculum should ideally have widespread faculty support, some institutions require a majority that is greater than the usual 51 percent for passage of a curriculum reform proposal. At the University of the Pacific, the voting procedure for a curriculum proposal was determined by a group other than the committee preparing the proposal. Because this group ruled that a nonvote would be treated as a no vote, not only did the committee members have to persuade the faculty of the merits of their proposal, but also, as in any political campaign, they had to get out the vote.

36. Schedule a Vote After a Reasonable Time for Discussion

This method seems to be sensible; however, after a task force has spent years working on a proposal and holding extended discussions with the faculty, scheduling a definitive vote would be suicidal if the outcome is in doubt. Further discussion and negotiation can keep the proposal alive and perhaps win a few more advocates. The Machiavellian answer to the question of when to put the proposal to a vote is, "When the votes are assured."

37. Assume a Negative Vote Is Final

The road to curriculum reform is strewn with abandoned vehicles that have fallen into the trap of interpreting a negative vote as the end of the road. The University of the Pacific committee found that its proposal was narrowly defeated in the college of liberal arts, where it was first acted upon. Instead of abandoning the proposal, the committee immediately activated a contingency plan that had three steps. First, the dean asked every department to state in writing specific problems with the document and specific ways it could be modified to meet their objections. Second, committee members were added from the professional schools where there was strong support for the committee's recommendations. Third, another vote was planned to occur after additional work would have been done. Because the group had met and worked on their plan for nearly three years, they were not about to abort the effort when they were so near the end of the journey.

Illusions About Program Implementation

38. *The Task Force Should Issue a Report for Others to Implement*

Typically, when a faculty committee issues a report and its recommendations are accepted, an administrator is given responsibility for carrying out the new policies. With curriculum revisions, however, there must be some continuity between the planners and the implementers and, therefore, at least some members of the planning group often play central roles in implementing the program. For example, Eva Wanton, the chairperson of the GEM task force at Florida A&M University, was asked to serve as director of the new general education program that her group had developed. Furthermore, committee members frequently end up teaching courses in the new program and helping to secure colleagues to teach with them. Committee members often find that the program operates best when they take an active part in the actual implementation.

39. *Faculty Members Are Willing to Teach in the Program*

Just because the faculty approves a new program does not necessarily mean that faculty members are willing to teach in it. The SUNY College at Brockport program called for a freshman course, Dimensions of Liberal Education, to be offered to all entering freshmen. Nearly seventy sections were planned, so that each section would be small enough for personal interaction and discussion. A major concern was to attract enough faculty members to teach this course, which is only one part of the college's overall general education program. In general, some rewards are necessary to attract and retain faculty. Often the opportunity to learn a new subject, to teach in a new context, or to work with stimulating new colleagues is seen as a stimulus to growth and renewal and will suffice to lure faculty members. But sometimes material rewards or, at the very least, assurances that this kind of teaching will not be held against faculty members in decisions about salary, retention, and promotion are necessary.

40. *Anybody Can Teach General Education Courses*

Courses that stress skills rather than content, that range beyond disciplinary boundaries, or that deal with value implications of knowledge pose challenges for any teacher, and such courses are especially difficult for teachers who are cut out of a traditional mold. Several institutions have found it necessary to provide for the professional development of faculty members who teach these courses. For example, Pacific Lutheran University held intensive workshops for the faculty members teaching in the Integrated Studies Program, which is an alternative to the standard core curriculum. In addition, team-teaching and periodic faculty meetings throughout the term helped professors integrate course material to provide more coherence for students.

41. The Entire Program Should Be Implemented at Once

Some committees expect that once the program is approved, it can be implemented in one fell swoop. On the contrary, Ohio University is phasing in its new program with positive results. According to Dean William Dorrill, phasing in the new program makes securing the necessary personnel easier, is less disruptive to the rest of the instructional program, and helps identify problems that can be more easily dealt with on a small scale before the entire program is in place. Other schools, such as Bucknell University, are attempting to run a pilot program involving a few faculty members and students before a course or an entire program is fully implemented.

42. The Program Will Work Well the First Time

After investing so much time and energy in developing a new curriculum, committee members naturally have high expectations, but often the expectations are too high. A committee member does not have to accept Murphy's Law—"If something can go wrong, it will"—in order to realize that any new program will encounter some difficulties. Personnel problems, misunderstandings, personality conflicts, logistics, and other difficulties cannot all be avoided, even with the best advanced planning. The first time that courses, programs, or services are offered, even on a permanent basis, program implementers might aid their mental health by conceiving of the offerings as a trial run with the goal of improving the operation on succeeding trials.

43. Evaluation Is Unnecessary

By the time a committee travels this far it will look for any excuse to stop its work. The committee may regard evaluation as a dispensable burden, the esoteric exercise of an arcane specialty, or the reduction of grand purposes and aspirations to mere numbers. Furthermore, committee members often feel that an unspecified "we" will know whether the program is working. But a careful study of the program, the reaction of students, faculty teaching effectiveness, and the like—particularly if the study is focused on identifying problem areas that can be corrected during subsequent rounds—can significantly aid program implementation. Evaluation is one means of providing continual monitoring of the general education of students. What is more, there are political points to be gained. As one person put it, "If *we* conduct an evaluation of our program, *they* won't be able to get us on that one."

In traveling the road to general education reform, committee members should keep six basic ideas in mind. First, potholes should be expected because the task of reconstructing the general education program of a college or university is difficult and complicated. Second, no one piloting a curriculum proposal down the road toward approval can expect to miss all the holes in the road; even the best driver is jarred occasionally. Third, hitting a hole or two can slow the pace, but it will seldom knock the vehicle off course. Fourth, falling into too many potholes can make people take another road altogether (or, if care is not taken, abandon the entire journey). Fifth, alternative routes can be bumpy, too, so the best route may be the original one rather than the suggested alternative. Finally, avoiding potholes is an art; it involves some luck, but one's skill can be improved.

Endnotes

1. J. B. L. Hefferlin, *Dynamics of Academic Reform* (San Francisco: Jossey-Bass, 1969), pp. 22–32.
2. Carnegie Foundation for the Advancement of Teaching, *Missions of the College Curriculum* (San Francisco: Jossey-Bass, 1977), p. 16.
3. A. Levine, *Handbook on Undergraduate Curriculum* (San Francisco: Jossey-Bass, 1978), p. 11.
4. Carnegie Foundation, *Missions of the College Curriculum,* pp. 167–69.
5. T. O. Lockwood, "A Skeptical Look at the General Education Movement," *Forum for Liberal Education* (Washington: Association of American Colleges, November 1978), p. 1.
6. E. L. Boyer and M. Kaplan, *Educating for Survival* (New Rochelle, N.Y.: Change Magazine Press, 1977).
7. General Education Committee, State University of New York at Buffalo. Application to the Project on General Education Models, 1978.
8. Lockwood, "A Skeptical Look at the General Education Movement," pp. 1–2.
9. Project on General Education Models, *General Education: Issues and Resources* (Washington: Association of American Colleges, 1980).
10. F. M. Hechinger and G. Hechinger, *Growing Up in America* (New York: McGraw-Hill, 1975).
11. A. L. Lowell, *What a University President Has Learned* (New York: Macmillan, 1938).
12. J. Q. Wilson, cited in "The Core Curriculum: What It Means for Undergraduate Education," *Harvard Gazette,* June 8, 1978, p. 7.

Faculty Development Through Interdisciplinarity

Forrest H. Armstrong

One of the trends of the past decade has been the gradual expansion of interest in interdisciplinarity. In a few cases—Evergreen, Wisconsin at Green Bay—whole institutions have been organized in interdisciplinary rather than disciplinary modes, with a significant amount of attendant publicity within higher education. Less visible, but far more pervasive, have been the attempts of a significant number of faculty, students, and administrators at institutions of every conceivable type to blend knowledge from diverse disciplines so that we may come to know and understand things which are beyond our reach while we observe traditional disciplinary boundaries.

The impetus for such efforts has often come from students who, not having been sufficiently socialized into the norms of a given discipline, are confused and possibly angered when told "That's not relevant; that is sociology, and we are in an economics class." Or, variously, students may have come to their education with a desire to grapple with some pressing societal problem, only to find that to do so effectively requires a more wholistic approach than any discipline, strictly construed, would allow. Whatever the reasons, interdisciplinary undertakings in contemporary higher education are both numerous and diverse. In addition to the advances in knowledge that may result from such efforts, this paper poses the thesis that interdisciplinary ventures may benefit individual faculty members and their institutions by being an especially effective mode of faculty development, and then offers some suggestions for persons seeking to foster such developments.

It is clear that interdisciplinarity embraces a fairly broad range of variants upon a common theme. Intellectually, they seek in one way or another to organize knowledge in such a fashion that traditional disciplinary boundaries no longer serve as barriers to knowledge. The success of interdisciplinary undertakings will be greatly affected by three key elements: the models adopted for organizing and transmitting knowledge at the course and program levels, the status of the program within the institution, and the staffing of the program. Particularly in the latter instance, there may be some counter-intuitive aspects to the analysis which bear close attention.

Though there can be many variants on a common theme, when I speak of interdisciplinary faculty development efforts I am thinking of some arrange-

Armstrong, Forrest H. "Faculty Development Through Interdisciplinarity." The Journal of General Education *32:1 (Spring 1980), 52–63. Copyright 1980 by The Pennsylvania State University. Reproduced by permission of The Pennsylvania State University Press.*

ment that brings a team of faculty members (two or more), typically from
different disciplines, together around a common intellectual task such as the
development of a course or sequence of courses. Thus the project has both
individual and institutional benefits, developing both the curriculum and the
faculty members who teach it. One could also have interdisciplinary projects
focussed on research rather than curriculum development, but for a variety of
reasons research projects seem to be a more difficult sort of undertaking. Especially for persons new to interdisciplinary work, I think it best to begin with a
teaching focus and allow research projects to emerge as a second phase of successful collaboration.

Inspection reveals at least four different approaches to, or levels of, the intellectual integration and synthesis of knowledge. In the first case, the student
may be allowed to take a selection of the normal disciplinary offerings from
more than one department and count them all toward a distinctive major.
Here, the interdisciplinary synthesis of ideas is left entirely to the student, with
no specific faculty involvement. This is, of course, the cheapest, least demanding, and perhaps most easily achieved of all the interdisciplinary variants, but
one wonders if it might not also be the least effective.

The second level of integration occurs with the institutionally provided opportunity for students within the same interdisciplinary area to meet and share
insights gained from their various disciplinary courses. One common approach
to this end is a capstone seminar, run by a faculty member from one of the
disciplines, wherein students in the same program may meet each other, some
for the first time. Recognizing the purpose behind such a course, the conscien-
tious faculty member teaching it will probably choose to make it "a-disciplin-
ary" rather than imposing the approach of any single discipline upon it. Here
again, the responsibility for achieving the interdisciplinary integration of
knowledge is left largely upon the shoulders of the student, though he does
have peers in the program who are pursuing a similar synthesis and with whom
he can share his thoughts.

At the third level of integration a significant change occurs: faculty members
as well as students become participants in the process of synthesizing knowledge. This implies the attempt to create courses through which the student can
address interdisciplinary topics directly and requires the participation of more
than one faculty member. But faculty members can be involved to a greater or
lesser degree in this process; the third level of integration is marked by courses
that feature a parade of faculty from different specialties, each of whom brings
what he knows to the student within the framework of a given course. This
process might best be termed "serial teaching" rather than team teaching, since
individual faculty participants are not required to make an interdisciplinary
contribution of their own; instead, they simply bring their disciplinary wares
to be displayed in a different context. The significant step here is that some
faculty member or group has had to conceptualize a whole: to decide which
colleagues to invite, what their presentations should address, and how all the
material fits together intellectually. For that faculty member, at least, the process of personal involvement in interdisciplinary inquiry has begun.

The fourth and highest level of interdisciplinarity is marked by the attempt fully to integrate material from various fields of knowledge into a new, single, intellectually coherent entity. To do this requires that the persons involved develop the capacity to meet various fields of knowledge on their own terms, especially by understanding and respecting the epistemologies and methodologies which underlie those fields with which they will work, and to build a vocabulary that can be precisely understood across the fields of knowledge. (The matter of vocabulary is perhaps most acute in those fields, like the social sciences, in which the language of scientific discourse is also the language of ordinary discourse. The esoteric language of natural science sub-specialties may make it difficult for persons in one branch of a discipline to communicate with others in his own discipline, much less with members of the lay public, but at least it removes the possibility of confusion from intrusion of conventional uses of terms which are part of ordinary discourse. Regardless of which problem must be overcome—the learning of a new, specialized vocabulary or the clarification of precise scientific meanings for ordinary terms—the communication barrier is the first that the would-be interdisciplinarian must clear.) This fourth and most difficult level of interdisciplinarity generally requires the involvement of more than one faculty member from the inception of the project, including the conceptualization of the course, building of the syllabus, and actual classroom presentations (what I shall call "true" team teaching), though over time the need to team teach should be eliminated as the faculty members involved improve their mastery of the new material. Because of the extensive involvement by the faculty members themselves in the difficult process of integrating knowledge, this sort of teaching should normally be the most helpful to students. However, individual and institutional considerations may make it the most difficult to achieve. Though my suggestions can be applied to other situations, it is to this fourth level of interdisciplinary undertaking that I refer in this paper.

Faculty Considerations

The organization of American higher education into disciplines may be its most salient intellectual dimension at present. Virtually all of us were originally trained in a discipline, even if some of us have branched out a bit in later life. The disciplinary orientation among academics may rival even our socialization into identifying with one of the two major political parties in terms of its pervasiveness and impact. The effort to mount interdisciplinary education, no less than to mount a third-party challenge in national politics, has significant obstacles to overcome.

A major drawback for faculty members who are considering interdisciplinary work is simply the opportunity cost it entails. One might assume that any good faculty member will continue to invest time after receiving the terminal degree in learning new things; the pursuit of knowledge, after all, is something we all have had in common. But it is almost certain that the time he must invest to develop a sophisticated grasp of interdisciplinary material will result in a lower

yield, at least in the short run, than an equal amount of time invested in furthering his disciplinary knowledge; this is due, in part, to the necessary investment of time in developing the introductory or background material from
other fields which he has already achieved in his discipline. Moreover, because
so many areas of interdisciplinary interest have been left basically untouched by
researchers, faculty members may find themselves working in the interstices of
knowledge, doing research for which there are no models and for which no
previously established body of theory is sufficient or wholly appropriate. In
such cases, which are not at all unusual, the task of interdisciplinary work may
be much more difficult than, say, the application of a well-tested disciplinary
technique to a new body of data.

Unfortunately, there are also opportunity costs associated with the "marketing" of interdisciplinary expertise and accomplishments. Compared to the
number of disciplinary programs, the incidence of interdisciplinary ones,
though growing, is still small. As a result, the person who develops strong
interdisciplinary credentials may find his professional mobility but little improved. Furthermore, he may find that the opportunity for publication of interdisciplinary work is limited: the number of interdisciplinary journals is small
compared to disciplinary ones, and the number of interdisciplinary books or
texts required is restricted because the courses in which they might be adopted
have not become standardized and nationally pervasive.

Another cost which may be associated with interdisciplinary work is simply
the anxiety it can produce. I know of no body of hard data to support or deny
the hypothesis, but in conversations with colleagues around the country who
are deeply involved with building interdisciplinary programs, there seems to be
some consensus, on the impressionistic level, that personality variables may be
of real importance in determining whether a faculty member will (or will not)
succeed as a member of an interdisciplinary undertaking. Through the first
three levels of interdisciplinary work, as we have noted, the need for faculty
to do anything different from their normal disciplinary endeavors is relatively
minimal; at the fourth level, though, the situation is markedly different. At this
point, the faculty member is a full participant with the student, fully involved
in learning and intellectual synthesis. No longer is it sufficient to be a circuit
rider, dropping off the day's or week's load of disciplinary knowledge without
seeking to integrate it with other such inputs. At the fourth level, the faculty
member must be prepared to venture into perhaps uncharted waters, where he
is essentially a neophyte, a learner as well as a teacher. In the process of stepping
outside of his discipline he must be prepared to learn new concepts, new vocabulary, and new uses of the concepts he may once have seen as the province of
his discipline alone. Perhaps his most psychologically demanding task is to step
out from under that comforting, protective blanket of theory whose gaps he
has learned to accept and, often, ignore through years of socialization into his
discipline. Instead, he must be willing to begin the difficult process of saying,
to himself and his public, "I do not know all the answers or all that I need to
know in this area; but I will expose my ignorance to you in the hope that

together we may begin to discover things that each of us separately could never know."

Any interdisciplinary program that has been in operation more than a short time is likely to have experienced the fact that some outstanding disciplinary faculty members simply could not make the necessary transition. A particularly graphic illustration of the problem occurred several years ago, at a distinguished Middle Atlantic university which began a new interdisciplinary graduate program. Mindful of the advantages that would come from a fully-integrated course of our fourth type, three of its most distinguished professors, a political scientist, an economist, and a sociologist, were assigned to the course, given released time for course development, and allowed to count the team-taught course as a full portion of their normal instructional load. Yet, in spite of the fact that the institutional arrangements had been correct (as we shall see below), the course was an obvious failure: the faculty members involved were never able openly to share both the strengths and weaknesses of their disciplines with their colleagues or their students. Instead, the three of them withdrew from the intended integration of ideas by enveloping themselves in the protection afforded by their respective disciplines; as if to underscore their retreat from intellectual interchange, they chose to ensconce themselves in three of the four corners of the room, physically separated from their colleagues as far as possible.

Why did the course fail? Certainly it was not due to their lack of scholarly credentials, for each was a respected scholar in his discipline. Nor were they hamstrung by the institutional arrangements. Instead, the answer may be that both of those considerations are necessary but not sufficient to the task if the faculty members involved are not psychologically prepared to engage in it. It has been my experience that broadly educated individuals with a high degree of ego strength, a tolerance for ambiguity, above-average initiative and assertiveness, and a fairly well-developed understanding of what is involved in interdisciplinary work before undertaking it are persons ideally prepared to succeed. Their motivation will likely come, in part, from feeling constrained from some intellectual pursuit by the confines of their discipline. And, as there is often a team effort required, at least in the formative stages of interdisciplinary education, faculty members with openness and particularly well-developed interpersonal skills will be more effective than those who work best alone.

Faculty Development

There may be as many reasons for faculty development programs as there are organizations undertaking them. A global sort of rationale for such programs, though, might be that they exist to help faculty members lead professional lives which are as effective, productive, and rewarding as possible. Because to us at Green Bay it was clear from the beginning that our graduate work had not prepared us adequately to do the sort of interdisciplinary work the institution required of us (a statement that is as true for me, a graduate of an interdisciplinary program, as for persons with straight disciplinary degrees), we all knew from the onset that we would be participating in such development efforts as a matter of course, and most of us looked forward to the opportunity to do so. Thus, at Green Bay such programs never developed the image of "remedial" programs. Just as a structural situation—the institution's unique academic plan—gave rise to our collective need for faculty development, so also have structural changes heightened the importance of faculty development opportunities for a wide variety of faculties, both individually and as members of some domains of knowledge, in institutions across the country.

In addition to structural changes of the sort undertaken at Green Bay, consider the impact of just two developments in modern higher education: the trend toward quantification and the boom period of the 1960's. As the application of mathematical, statistical, and high-speed data-handling techniques has spread across the full range of disciplines, significant numbers of faculty members have been left unable to cope with a major determinant of knowledge in their field. This development is as true in natural sciences, where mathematically oriented biologists model the dynamics of populations alongside persons trained in classical taxonomy, as it is in the social sciences and humanities, where institutionalists are being challenged by experimentalists and behaviorists, and where even persons dealing in language are counting, quantifying, and computerizing. As the dominant thrust of professional journals moves toward aping the mathematical elegance attributed to the natural sciences, more and more faculty members who lack the training necessary to employ such tools can come to feel that they have been left behind, discarded and undervalued by their disciplinary colleagues. And, to the extent that their lack of such skills precludes them from publishing their scholarly work, they may well be tempted to give up scholarship.

Similarly, the mini-boom for higher education during the 1960's, combined with the subsequent structural changes in the nation's population profile, has helped to create a situation in which many, many faculty members find themselves facing at least one more generation of labor in a professional environment that does not meet the expectations with which they entered it. Not only has the enrollment decline foreclosed most of the opportunities for faculty mobility that were a highly attractive feature of a higher-education career in the 1960's; that decline also threatens faculty members in traditional liberal arts fields (especially the humanities) with the loss of their jobs. Pressured by declining enrollments, perceiving that his contributions are undervalued by his colleagues in more prosperous departments as well as by the public at large, and perhaps unhappy in his present location, the faculty member may still feel that the protection afforded by tenure, or the lifestyle to which he has become accustomed, is too comfortable to be given up for an altogether uncertain future. All too frequently he feels trapped, unable to move within his profession, lacking confidence, perhaps, in his profession and in even himself. This is not the profile of the sort of person who is most likely to be effective at his job: thus, faculty development.

The dispirited faculty member who is lacking in self-confidence and feeling trapped in his profession is a far different sort of person from the one whom I profiled earlier as being an ideal candidate for interdisciplinary work. Yet, I propose that interdisciplinarity is an ideal approach to faculty development. Any faculty development program can be operated in such a fashion as to affirm the institution's faith in the participants' capability to make a valued contribution. Faith is perhaps the most important message that can be communicated, and an interdisciplinary approach does not necessarily convey it any better than any other. Neither is interdisciplinarity unique in seeking to build upon that love of learning which probably stimulated almost all of us to become faculty members, though the freshness of the ideas to be addressed may have some greater attractiveness than a retraining effort in a closely related field. This approach does, however, offer significant advantages in at least two respects: it emphasizes close peer support through the team approach, and it provides a context in which all participants are simultaneously expected to be teachers and learners. The close peer support is important because it emphasizes to the participant that he is not alone in his labors, that others are engaged in the same process, suffering the same frustrations and same joys; thus there are persons who can share experiences in an empathetic way and be mutually supportive. Such a context also provides the opportunity for modeling to take place, since persons new to interdisciplinary work can be included in teams with more experienced colleagues. Even more important, interdisciplinarity provides a context in which it is clear that no one's previous education has adequately prepared him for the task. The stigma of having somehow failed at that education is removed; everyone must necessarily continue to learn, because the focus of attention is not one that is dealt with in standard disciplinary programs. Thus every participant is going to be a co-learner with his peers; in this context the participant becomes not so much a person who knows less than his peers, as one who knows different things than they do. And, for the effective pursuit of the team's interdisciplinary goals, it will become clear that every member has to become an active contributor of what he knows, as well as a processor of what others know. The participant in such an interdisciplinary enterprise must necessarily be both teacher and learner simultaneously, a situation that can enhance the sense of self-worth of the participants and encourage their wholehearted support of the project. These dimensions of interdisciplinary efforts—close peer support, a focus for which anyone's previous education is presumed to have been inadequate, and the necessity to be both teacher and learner simultaneously—are ones that simple retraining in a closely allied field cannot offer, and that compel us to consider interdisciplinarity a viable alternative model for faculty development.

An interesting dimension to any interdisciplinary enterprise is that it provides a modicum of what I have chosen to call "internal mobility" for the faculty participating in it. Regardless of the size of the institution, it is likely that an individual typically works with and gets to know well the other persons in his department (his work group) before, and perhaps instead of, others. Interdisciplinary undertakings offer the opportunity to expand one's work group and to become closely associated with persons, ideas, and perhaps even locations on campus which were previously unexplored. Often this change of scenery, even though it is only within the institution, can serve to rekindle creativity and enthusiasm in someone who has grown tired of his previous surroundings. Such a change also provides the opportunity for something of a new start, the chance to remake one's image with new acquaintances in a new setting around a new venture, rather than having to overcome old stereotypes among persons who have been close associates over the years. Though not a full substitute for the opportunity to change institutions, this sort of internal mobility provides many of the ingredients essential to a new beginning for the individual who wishes to try to make one, and allows significant change to be made gradually. Since such an opportunity is unlikely to obtain in faculty development efforts within the person's discipline and department, it is a contribution which interdisciplinary undertakings uniquely can provide.

Institutional Considerations

Though our focus is on faculty development per se, I want to refer briefly to some institutional considerations that can enhance the likelihood both that people will be willing to engage in faculty development programs, and that those programs will benefit both the participants and the institution over time. Two simple suggestions can go a long way toward making faculty development projects work and keep working: (1) give participants in such projects the time necessary to do the job they are being asked to do, by making appropriate adjustments in the load they are asked to carry, and (2) make appropriate adjustments in the reward system, by taking into account what the institution is asking them to do. I have already suggested that team teaching can be an almost ideal way to help engender interdisciplinarity. It would be best if all the team members could have some released time during the term they were preparing the course; but the least the institution could responsibly do, in my judgment, is to consider team teaching (not serial teaching) to count as a full course for each of the participants. Team teaching is a good investment, and one could justify using it as a faculty development device on economic grounds alone. But true team teaching is also more *work* than teaching a course alone; the availability of more than one person to present the material is far outweighed by the time necessary for coordination, for melding divergent views (on everything from the meaning of the readings to grading standards), and for developing a language through which to communicate clearly. Thus, faculty development through interdisciplinary team teaching is going to require the participants to invest additional time during the course-planning process and during at least the first team-taught offering of the course. The learning curve, of course, varies widely across individuals, but in my experience team teaching an interdisciplinary course twice is probably enough to make it possible for any of the participants to teach it alone thereafter. Thus, not only will the cost of teaching the course revert to normal after a year or two, but the institution will then have the flexibility which comes from having more than one person (and probably from different departments) who can teach the course. This sort of institutional flexibility is an especially important by-product of interdisciplinary faculty development projects, because it can enable adjustments in individual teaching schedules through which to accommodate changing student demands without requiring draconian measures such as faculty layoffs.

Consider also the opportunity cost of investing in an interdisciplinary faculty development project through team teaching. Investment of fixed-cost resources (such as salaries of tenured faculty) in some sense costs less than other sorts of investment; rather than determining whether the expenditure in such a salary is reasonable (a previously-made decision which cannot be changed in the short run), one is seeking to maximize the return on that investment. Hence increasing the long-term yield on a fixed-cost investment is often an economically sound decision. Moreover, if the short-term yield on that investment is likely to be low, as it might be for marginal courses in an "overstaffed" department, the cost of investing some released time in a faculty development effort of this sort can be low indeed. (This points out another institutional advantage to the sort of interdisciplinary faculty development effort I am suggesting: because both teachers and learners can be funded through released time, a redeployment of a fixed-cost resource, the out-of-pocket expense to the institution is minimized.)

The final suggestion I would make is that the reward system be attuned to recognize the contributions made to the institution by persons participating in interdisciplinary faculty development projects. Perhaps this might mean that personnel committees would study course syllabi, position papers delivered to the faculty development group, and the like as being products that can reflect the person's creative use of his intellectual resources, just as can articles in refereed journals; in many ways, the fact that the person has been making effective use of those intellectual resources, that they have been expanding and improving his teaching, is of more importance than the forum in which they appear. Openness to such an approach can do wonders to enhance the effectiveness of such projects.

Similarly, the institution should be prepared to attune the reward system to compensate in the area of teaching evaluation. The courses developed and taught as part of interdisciplinary faculty development projects are quite likely to be more difficult for anyone to teach, the first few times, than even a new disciplinary course: there are few models for such courses, often few textbooks or precisely focussed readings, a greater opportunity for at least an apparent lack of organization compared to standard courses, and perhaps a lack of an appropriate frame of reference on the part of persons, students and faculty alike, who evaluate the course. For at least the first time or two the course is offered, the institution should make certain that the persons willing to undertake it are not unduly penalized for doing so. Perhaps this means acceptance by the institution of the idea that these are developmental efforts in a variety of ways, and that the freedom to succeed will be maximized if it is accompanied (at least in the short run) by the freedom to fail. To do otherwise, I think, is likely to doom most such ventures to failure before they even begin.

Summary

In this paper I have suggested that we consider the advantages of faculty development through interdisciplinarity. The model I have proposed calls for an interdisciplinary team to be given released time to address a common intellectual goal that cannot be met through a single discipline alone; typically, this team's effort will result in the planning and mounting of courses, a result which yields curriculum development simultaneously with faculty development, and at no added cost. The model of interdisciplinarity proposed is a fully integrated one, in which all faculty participants seek to effect the same intellectual synthesis they expect of students, including the need to meet each field on its own terms; it further means that the faculty members offering the course must be full team teachers, rather than serially appearing to offer their unsynthesized disciplinary knowledge.

The ideal participant in such an interdisciplinary endeavor may well be a person with a high degree of ego strength, a tolerance for ambiguity, and considerable initiative and assertiveness; someone who is broadly educated (preferably in more than one field), yet dissatisfied with the constraints placed upon his quest for knowledge by the bounds of his intellectual field. Yet I have also suggested that the interdisciplinary model may also be quite effective with faculty who are unlike that profile, because of three ways in which it differs from the usual sort of development undertaking: it is a group endeavor (thus providing close and empathetic peer support) around a task which is clearly outside the preparation normally to be expected of faculty and in a situation in which every participant must be learner and teacher simultaneously. Combined with important institutional accommodations, such as attuning the teaching load and the reward system to take into account the nature of the difficult interdisciplinary task the faculty member has been asked to undertake, these distinctive features of the interdisciplinary model can encourage faculty members to be open to development activities that they otherwise would shun, and can thereby enhance the likelihood for such efforts to be successful.

References

L. Apostel, et al., *Interdisciplinarity: Problems of Teaching and Research in Universities* (Paris: Centre for Educational Research and Innovation, Organisation for Economic Cooperation and Development, 1972).

B. Hill, "Multi-disciplinary Courses—Mush or Muscle?" *Australian University,* 14 (May 1976), 48–57.

L. Humphreys, "Interdisciplinarity," paper presented to the Association for Innovation in Higher Education, Chicago, Illinois, March, 1978.

E. Jantsch, "Inter- and Transdisciplinary University: A Systems Approach to Education and Innovation," *Higher Education,* 1 (February 1972), 7–37.

J. Kockelmans, *Interdisciplinarity and Higher Education* (University Park, Pa.: The Pennsylvania State University Press, 1979).

M. Levensky, "Trying Hard: Interdisciplinary Programs at the Evergreen State College," *Alternative Higher Education,* 2 (Fall 1977), 41–6.

W. Mayville, *Interdisciplinarity: The Mutable Paradigm* (Washington, D.C.: American Association for Higher Education/ERIC Clearinghouse on Higher Education, the George Washington University, 1978).

M. Sherif and C. Sherif, eds., *Interdisciplinary Relationships in the Social Sciences* (Chicago: Aldine, 1969).

G. Squires, et al., *Interdisciplinarity* (London: Group for Research and Innovation in Higher Education, Nuffield Foundation, 1975).

E. Weidner, "Interdisciplinarity and Higher Education," *International Journal of Environmental Studies,* 5 (1973), 205–214.

Interdisciplinary Studies as a Counterculture

Problems of Birth, Growth and Survival

Martin Trow

Introduction

In this essay I want to raise at least these questions:

1. Why do some innovative interdisciplinary programs succeed, while others fail?
2. What are the effects of the legacy of the 60's, when so many innovative programs had their start? How much of a burden is that legacy in the 80's? Is it necessary "to change with the times" and can that be done while maintaining the integrity of interdisciplinary programs?
3. What are the special difficulties encountered during the start-up years of interdisciplinary programs?
4. How can we reconcile the reformist commitments of innovative programs with the necessity for these programs to establish good and warm relations with other more traditional parts of their host institutions?

I take it as self-evident that interdisciplinary studies at their best are among the most powerful and effective perspectives for teaching undergraduate students. Note that I said "among," and that is indeed the heart of my message. Interdisciplinary studies "embody programs of teaching and research that transcend the methods and subject matter of single scholarly disciplines or academic departments," and "seek to use perspectives of seemingly disparate disciplines simultaneously and interactively to define common problems, issues and ideas, and to pose solutions based on genuine dialogue."[1] When that is done, when interdisciplinary studies succeed, they are a joy to behold, and even more to take part in. I use the word "joy" because of the sheer pleasure in the intellectual play that they afford to students and teachers alike, the pleasures of roaming across disciplinary boundaries, and of finding connections and links, illuminations and insights in the ideas and discoveries of disparate disciplines.

Trow, Martin. "Interdisciplinary Studies as a Counterculture: Problems of Birth, Growth and Survival." Issues in Integrative Studies 4 (1984–85), 1–15. Reprinted with permission.

This chapter is a paper read as the keynote address at the Conference on the Future of Interdisciplinary Studies, sponsored by the Association for Integrative Studies, and the Western College Program of Miami University, Oxford, Ohio, February 1984. This essay can be seen as an extended footnote to Gerald Grant and David Riesman, The Perpetual Dream: Reform and Experiment in the American College, *Chicago, Illinois: University of Chicago Press, 1978.*

Having said that, I must also say that I have seen powerful and effective teaching and learning in quite different forms and contexts. For example, the Undergraduate Research Opportunity Program at MIT, and its counterparts elsewhere, give to undergraduate students an opportunity to join ongoing faculty research projects, and bring them very quickly to the frontiers of a discipline, though often on a very narrow front. I recognize that undergraduate research done within departmental structures may well push against the boundaries of those disciplines, and resemble closely the kinds of research that are done within interdisciplinary programs, such as those at Western College, Miami of Ohio, or Worcester Poly. (And the blurring of distinctions between what is done in interdisciplinary programs and in departments may be the kind of imitation that is the sincerest form of flattery.) More important than where it is done, the rewards of actually helping to create knowledge through specialized research can affect a student's motivation across the board, and give to him or her a totally different sense of the provisional, the unfinished nature of science, of academic work, and indeed of intellectual life. And even the more routine forms of disciplinary study, the ordinary departmental major, if it is well-organized, can give a student the beginnings of a real familiarity with a body of knowledge organized as a discipline or a sub-discipline. It is true that this can become more pedantry, or a premature introduction to specialized graduate study in an academic discipline. But the value for some undergraduates of studies in depth of a single discipline ought not to be dismissed too quickly. It may be that students, at least some students, need to gain familiarity with the methods and subject matter of a single scholarly discipline before they can transcend them.

I mention this not because traditional disciplinary studies need any further defense, and if they did this would hardly be the place for it. I mention it because I am interested in why some interdisciplinary programs and institutions succeed while others fail. And I have come to believe that the success or failure of these programs is only in part related to their quality or to the demand for them locally. To a great extent, I think, the success and failure of interdisciplinary programs are a function of their relation to the rest of higher education, in their own institutions and elsewhere. My reading of the history of innovative programs in higher education over the past two decades—and interdisciplinary programs especially at the undergraduate level have appeared most of the time as innovative programs—is that the fate of any given program has depended heavily on whether its founders saw American higher education as a failure which they would try to repair or redeem, or as a system of great richness and diversity to which they would add additional richness and diversity, seeking for their own ecological niche in the jungle of American colleges and universities. If their founders were sure that the rest of higher education, and that includes the rest of their own university, was incompetent or venal, then their innovative programs were created to stand in witness to that failure, and to their own calling to provide alternative models. And if I speak here of sin and redemption, of bearing witness and having a calling, the religious overtones are not accidental.

On the whole, programs that have abused their hosts while claiming unique and almost ethereal virtues, have failed. Those that have claimed a place in the spectrum of higher education to serve that segment of the student population which wants and can profit from what interdisciplinary programs and colleges can offer, have on the whole survived and flourished.

But while most of the people in this field may be chiefly interested in this latter group (among which I number Miami's Western College), that is to say, interested in what successful programs look like and how they work, I hope I can interest you for a few minutes in a consideration of why so many innovative and interdisciplinary programs of the sixties and seventies failed. I think that if we look at them closely we will learn something about the nature of educational reform in this country, and perhaps about American higher education more broadly, and about the environment in which innovations in higher education seek for legitimacy and resources. In this effort I have to start by locating the innovations that I will be talking about in the broader spectrum of academic reform in the United States since World War II.

Types of Academic Innovation

It may be useful to distinguish three different kinds of recent innovation or reform in American higher education. The first was the general loosening of the curriculum that took place in very many small colleges and universities during the decade 1965–1975, largely as a response or reaction to the heightened meritocratic pressures of the late 50's and 60's. The rapid growth of college and university enrollments in the 1960's—involving more than a doubling in the number of students—led to a very sharp competition for admissions to the elite colleges and greatly increased academic pressures on undergraduates who were competing for admission to graduate school. Students sought relief, and found a sympathetic ear among many faculty members who resented the dominance of the graduate schools over the liberal arts colleges both within and outside universities. The "reforms" which were adopted very widely gave students more freedom of choice in the curriculum and more freedom in the sequencing of their courses. Three of the commonest reforms were: 1) a sharp reduction or the abolition of required courses; 2) a free choice of curriculum, that is to say, a reduction in the sequencing of courses; and 3) student-designed majors outside of departmental boundaries.[2] These "popular" reforms were very widespread although rarely advertised, but they modified the means of education within the bounds of the existing goals of a research oriented university, and of the colleges that fed them.

Another type of academic innovation took the form of educational inventions designed to achieve learning in ways other than through traditional lectures and seminars. These reforms were less focused on the curriculum than on the modes of instruction, affecting the relationship of teacher and student and a body of knowledge or skills. The Undergraduate Research Opportunity Program at MIT is an example here, as are self-paced courses, the use of videotapes, and the significant reforms of engineering education pioneered in the Worcester

Polytechnic Institute Plan. These are indeed academic innovations, but still lying within the assumptions of discipline-oriented colleges and universities.

A third type of academic innovations comprise what David Riesman and Gerald Grant call "telic" or purposive reforms.[3] These center on a significantly different conception of the *goals* of undergraduate education. Such ambitious aims require not just the reform of a curriculum or the invention of an instructional technology, but the creation of new educational institutions which embody these new goals. In a sense these institutions can be seen as a criticism of the central values of the research oriented multiversity, of the pre-eminence of the academic discipline and the academic career. These values—of "competitive excellence" in the service of specialized research and scholarship, based on individual achievement, and a cognitive style that subordinates "feeling" to "knowing," "being" to "becoming"—had in the decade of growth after World War II come also to dominate a wider circle of satellite four-year colleges, and through their power as models, a much larger number of more modest colleges and universities.

While the enormous expansion of higher education (and of federally supported research) after World War II greatly strengthened the disciplines as well as the reaction against them, it is important to emphasize that colleges designed in opposition to the dominant models began to emerge as long ago as the thirties. Among the older "telic" institutions were St. John's, Antioch, Bennington, Black Mountain, Goddard and Sarah Lawrence. But much larger numbers of such institutions emerged after World War II; among these were Old Westbury (both I and II), Franconia, Hampshire, Evergreen, Green Bay, the College of Human Services in New York, New College in Sarasota, and Stockton State and Ramapo Colleges in the New Jersey state system. They also included institutions embedded within larger and more conventional universities: examples here were Bensalem in Fordham, both Tussman College and Strawberry Creek College in Berkeley, Kresge College in Santa Cruz, Western College in Miami of Ohio, and Livingston College in Rutgers.

David Riesman and Gerald Grant in their book *The Perpetual Dream* develop an interesting typology of these institutions they call "telic," or purposeful. They distinguish four types of such colleges by reference to their basic conceptions of education, their students' motivations for choosing the college, the institution's own valued ends, their social models, core values, educational styles, historical roots, and the nature of the authority that each invokes and accepts. The types they identify are the "neo-classicals," among them St. John's and the Tussman College at Berkeley; the "aesthetic-expressives," for example, Bennington and Sarah Lawrence as well as Black Mountain; the "communal-expressives," including both Kresge and Bensalem; and the "activist radicals," including Antioch College, Old Westbury in its first phase, and the College for Human Services in New York.

But while there is much to be said about these different types of "telic" institutions and the differences among them, they all shared certain characteristics in common. First, each had a sense of *mission*. They aspired above all to be distinctive, and the distinctiveness lay both in the set of positive characteristics which they embodied and also in their assertion that they were not like the "ordinary" college or university. The claim to "distinctiveness" is made by faculty and students in these institutions who are on the whole dissatisfied with the competitive life of the university, and yearn for a sense of identity; they want to be part of an institution that can evoke from them deep loyalties, and in which their own sense of themselves as persons is ratified and justified. For both teachers and students, to join such a place is not just to get a job, or to go to college: it is to make a *commitment,* a commitment that for the faculty may involve sacrifices in their academic career. For faculty especially, but for students also joining such an institution may mean that bridges have been burned and that costly career choices have been made that reflect their deep personal and social ideals.

There is in all of these purposive institutions also an intensity in the student-teacher relationship that is rare in "ordinary" colleges and universities, an intensity partly reflecting their common recoil against research and publication norms. It also reflects the value held in all of these experimental forms of innovation that teachers and students are to be seen as "co-learners." They are not necessarily egalitarian—for example, they surely are not at St. John's—nor does it necessarily require the dominance of charismatic leaders. What they do share is the commitment to a community and the ceremonies of a community. In such institutions, as Riesman and Grant observed, "the important judgements are common judgements about whether students measure up to the ideals of the college, not whether they are excellent students in the traditional sense, as in the judgements of a departmentally organized faculty."[4]

The historian, Lawrence Veysey, captures the spirit of these telic institutions in a review of Martin Duberman's *Black Mountain:*

> Many of us yearn in some part of our minds for a college setting utterly free from bureaucratic harrassment, a place where nothing distracts from mutual learning and creation. The dream merges with that of community—an educational environment to be sure but one where life and classroom merge into each other, and where status dissolves in genuine human relationships.[5]

The primary values of these institutions are *anti-institutional.* What is valued is the enduring personal relationship, rather than the tangential and fleeting encounters of persons and roles that are so common in large traditional institutions. They are hostile therefore to the university model, the large, formal organizations of specialized roles and statuses, and are committed to small size, informal structures, and less specialized academic roles which blur the distinction between disciplines, between academic ranks, and between teacher and student. The curriculum places great value on interdisciplinary studies which drastically subordinate the disciplines (and their administrative arms, the departments) to the "natural articulations of knowledge" as in the neoclassical institutions, or to "creativity," as in the aesthetic-expressive institutions, or to the "human community" as in the communal-expressive institutions, or to "social change and the activist professional" in the activist radical institutions.

Institution Building

I have been describing a broad movement in American higher education that includes programs and institutions that have succeeded and survived as well as others that failed and disappeared. I want now to look even more closely at some of the characteristics of those innovative institutions which put them at risk, and have led some to fail. I want to do that by looking at the early years of newly-created, purposefully innovative, "telic" institutions, to consider the peculiar problems and tensions that arose, and perhaps still arise, as they move from birth, through infancy, toward adult status and full maturity. It is the perspective of the institutional life-cycle.

Let me start by considering what are, or more accurately what were, some of the peculiar characteristics and advantages of the start-up years—the years of "institution building"—in these innovative programs and colleges.

1. The earliest years of a new and innovative program are marked by a highly selective recruitment of staff and students. Typically, the new institution attracted faculty for whom the college offered not a job but a calling, no 9–5 day but an opportunity and challenge. Founding faculty were quite often enthusiasts, true believers, for whom the institution and its philosophy was not just another education option but a kind of secular religion.

Similarly, the students of this first generation were often brought there by advance publicity about the institution or program, in some cases by energetic efforts to bring to the institution the kind of student whom the founders believed would help give it its unique character. They were, on the whole, enthusiastic and dedicated to the ideals of the college. Moreover, many saw themselves as pioneers solving problems, and quickly gained the high sense of efficacy associated with the experience of a pioneer generation faced with a great variety of problems for which there are no institutional answers or precedents, or specialized problem-solvers already in place. The first few classes in such institutions were also often (but not always) better students: more imaginative, independent, and self-directed, more adventurous and more highly motivated. They often were a very hard class to follow.

2. The resources available to the institution in the first few years were often unusually abundant. There were commonly special start-up resources, one-time subventions from "special" funds for just such innovative ventures. In addition, the newly recruited staff was often given a planning year, or were recruited faster than the students so that there was an early favorable staff-student ratio. Very often, the first year or two in the institutions saw a staff-student ratio of about one to five or six. Three or four years later, it was one to twenty or twenty-five. The experience of that change alone was a shock that the young program had difficulty surviving.

3. The new college was, for obvious reasons, almost always very small. Small size allows the emergence of a "handicraft culture" and obscures the implica-

tions of the absence of procedures. Small size allows communal and often consensual decision-making. This may also be ideologically required, and in the beginning it was just barely possible, given the small size and the recruitment of staff and students around common values. Small size allowed each problem that arose to be defined as unique, to be solved in a communal atmosphere of sentiment, feeling, and comradeship, working together as substitutes for precedents and procedure.

4. Both the ideology of many telic institutions and the lack of precedent in all very new ones made for a readiness to treat each student, each problem, as if it were the first and wholly unique. "Every student is a unique exception,"—with respect to grades, to course requirements, and to everything else. (This principle, incidentally, exposed the teacher in these colleges to enormous pressures from solipsistic and exploitative operators among the students.) The lack of precedent and institutional procedures, the weakness of boundaries and routines also required that each case be the object of willful decision, one that squared with principle and ideal. Moreover, each such decision had to be made with great care and deliberation, both for its own sake and also because it would become a precedent. The experience of making a world and not merely serving it was for many of the participants both exhilarating and exhausting. Characteristically, over time, it became increasingly exhausting and decreasingly exhilarating.

5. The new college, if it was embedded in a larger, more conventional institution, was at this very early stage not yet seen as a threat to other parts of the larger institution. Its demand on resources was not yet large, and even its opponents felt the necessity to "give it a chance" after the decision had been made to set it up. This was an important if temporary advantage of the new institution.

Partly as a result of all these special (if temporary) advantages, the first few years of life of a new telic institution were often marked by the euphoria of creation, and of high morale arising out of a steady flow of problems and the pleasures and rewards of "solving them" and building an institution.

Problems Arising From the Transition to Steady State

But for every Eden there is a world, and for young innovative institutions the agents of the world come not in the form of a serpent and an apple, but of growth. And with growth came the inevitable emergence of secondary relationships among people, in place of the primary relationships of whole persons that characterized the early years. This development was especially hard on the "communal-expressive" type of telic institution. (We see the consequence of growth in such institutions in the evocative picture that Riesman and Grant sketch of Kresge College at Santa Cruz, and the split that occurred within that college after its first few years.)

Students after the initial years start coming to an established institution. They are expecting to find a program in place, rather than to be helping to create one. This reflected and accelerated changes in the character of student recruitment; a different kind of student comes to an established program than to a brand new one in the making.

Moreover, there was a measure of faculty turnover during the first few years as some of the early founders left, disaffected by their experience in an institution which did not, and could not, remain permanently malleable and uninstitutionalized.

One result of a high level of faculty turnover (and the academic market was much stronger before 1975) was to weaken further the new program's already weak capacity to develop formal procedures and organizational routines. It increased the instability of the students' experience, and it also changed in the aggregate the character and values of the staff. With faculty as with students, the second generation of recruits is never like the first and founding generation. The difference between them was that in the faculty, the first, second and third generations of recruits were intermingled; and differences among them in the passion and purity of their commitment made for dissension and conflict.

After a year or two, typically the faculty and staff began to search for ways of managing overload. The overload arose essentially out of the fact that increasing numbers of students began to come to an institution whose ways of working and teaching were highly personalistic, and ill adapted to the conditions of mass education for which many of these telic institutions were destined. The initial response of such institutions was always to try to expand the personalistic response developed in the first year or two to the larger numbers coming in the third and fourth years. When this was experienced as impossible overload, there was a search for procedures to manage the relationship between faculty and these larger numbers of students. And ironically, another source of overload was the growth of demands on the faculty arising from the necessity of their developing the very procedures needed for managing large numbers. The third and fourth year of such institutions was often experienced as the worst of both worlds: a large number of students without the routines and impersonal procedures which allow large numbers to be taught and managed in more traditional programs and institutions.

On top of all this, there was characteristically the loss of the early extra resources. Governing agencies started to require the new entity to function at cost levels of comparable traditional programs or institutions, or of traditional units in the host institution. This was partly due to pressures from older units. There are enormous leveling pressures in multi-unit institutions: legitimacy requires equity, and in many such institutions marked differences in *per capita* support among departments are defined as inequalities, and inequalities as inequities. These norms did not usually operate during the very first start-up years, and that is in part why the Golden Age of such telic institutions usually lies in the institution-building years. (That, of course, was not the only reason.) But when these norms were applied, they had drastic effects on the budgets of these innovative programs, and on the sometimes costly practices that they had developed.

Sooner or later during the innovative institution's transitional years it experienced the emergence of conflict, latent but obscured during the early communal phase by the consensus of a small, relatively self-recruited faculty and student body around a common ideology. (In some institutions—e.g. Old Westbury I—fierce conflict was present from the very beginning, as if by design.) Conflict always emerges around conflicting interests, as for example, between the tenured and the non-tenured faculty, the publishers and non-publishers, the faculty and the administration. It arises also around ideology, as between people on the "left" and those on the "right." It also arises from differences between those who prefer spontaneity and those who prefer predictability and order, between those who place greater value on personal qualities and those who would reward achievement. These differences come to be more or less organized, structured and contained within most colleges and universities—where they don't, the department or institution suffers. But telic institutions usually have few procedures for adjudicating conflict—conflict tends to be seen not as part of the ordinary life of the institution, but as evidence of the loss of Eden, as a failure of the communal ideal. The emergence of conflict is especially painful in a communal setting where people interact as persons rather than in roles; in such circumstances, conflict tends to be personalized. Moreover, where decisions are meant to emerge from consensus, conflict often results in decision paralysis: the "Polish parliament" phenomenon.

Another aspect of the transition to a steady state after the first few years in the life of these innovative programs was the growing evidence of faculty fatigue arising out of a continuing overload. This overload was due in part to the highly individualized modes of instruction, associated both with educational ideology and the favorable staff-student ratios of the first few years, and in part the constant meetings associated with participatory decision-making without procedures or precedent.

This overload and fatigue in turn led to a pattern of withdrawal and privatization on the part of at least some of the faculty members. As they stopped going to meetings, that in turn delegitimized the decisions made at those meetings. (Non-participation delegitimizes decisions more quickly where there is a reliance on participatory democracy and the politics of consensus.) Also, it further overburdened the continuing participants, and drove more of them to reduce some of their exhausting involvement in the never ending process of making decisions about every event as if it were absolutely new and unique.

Privatization—the reduction or withdrawal of their involvement in the political life of the institution—by at least some of the faculty does not have necessarily destructive consequences in traditional institutions, nor is it severely condemned there by the other participants. In the early days of a telic institution, by contrast, it is seen as a "betrayal" and evidence of the failure of the communal ideals. The expectation in such institutions was that each faculty member had to continue to give evidence of a deep and abiding commitment to the college's ideals, and that participation was in response to an inner calling. Such institutions demanded not just a fair day's work but "a full measure of devotion." Any qualification of that devotion, as, for example, a genuine but *limited* commitment to innovative forms of undergraduate teaching, is quite unacceptable in the telic institutions.

As time went on, routinization, conflict, privatization all in one way or another were growing evidence to the participants that the institution was not able to maintain the requisite levels of spontaneity, creativity, community, commitment and involvement of all of its participants. This growing recognition, feeding back on the institution, was reflected in declining morale, animosities among colleagues and growing evidence that *ad hoc* procedures do not work very well. All of these developments, the institutional as well as the psychological, contributed to a widespread sense of failure among faculty members. In these institutions, the judgement of failure was made not by any reasonable comparison with other institutions of higher education, but rather against the utopian criteria that the founders had in mind when they created the institution. But against utopian criteria, only failure is possible.

There are other reasons for the difficulties that some of these innovative colleges and programs experienced, difficulties that were more a consequence of the nature of their host institutions than of the innovations themselves. For one thing, the very fact that innovative colleges were so passionately devoted to teaching made them suspect to a large part of the faculty of the research-oriented university. And in the big research universities, where the academic career is so closely linked to research motivations and achievements, it was difficult for these innovative "teaching" colleges to attract and retain many regular faculty.[6] They too often lived on the energies of their senior founders and a small band of temporary non-tenured and non-tenurable assistants, and died when those energies were exhausted.

Moreover, these programs often were funded as "experimental" units, without a permanent "line" in the operating budget of the university. The resources they drew on were designed for academic innovations, and were easily withdrawn when university budgets were cut, or were shifted to other newer claimants for experimental funds. After all, when a college program had been in existence for five years or more, it could hardly be considered "experimental" any longer. It was then often told that it had to find a place on the ordinary operating budget of the university, but could not. So a major difficulty for some of these programs was that they were never fully institutionalized, either with respect to staff recruitment or budget.

To sum up, the difficulties faced by innovative programs during their early start-up years are broadly of two kinds: those inherent in the transition from an experimental or pilot program to the status of a regular and institutionalized school or program, and those that result from the romantic, evangelical and utopian ideologies of some of the founders of innovative programs.

The two kinds of difficulties, when found together, are nearly always fatal—they tend to enhance or exacerbate each other. The former set of problems are still with us, or rather with new programs. The latter, I suspect, are less so—but they are not wholly absent, nor are they likely to be wherever passions and commitments to innovations in undergraduate teaching are strong.

Successful Transition to the Steady State

The successful transition of an innovative program from its initial phase to a stable steady state is highly dependent on its success in developing academic and administrative routines. "Routines" and "routinization" have a bad name in academic life. They are thought to be the enemies of creativity, spontaneity, and of the lively interaction of people and ideas that makes for the best learning and teaching. A great deal of academic innovation is designed precisely to break routines, and enable institutions to find new ways of pursuing familiar ends.

Routines are viewed with special hostility in innovative institutions during their formative years. But the evidence suggests that for such institutions there are two possible paths. One involves a search for stability; the other is marked by a steady slide toward collapse. Bensalem at Fordham, and Old Westbury I were illustrations of what failed telic institutions looked like before they were mercifully terminated. By contrast, those institutions that survived were marked by a search for academic routines and institutional procedures that would be compatible with their basic purposes. And those routines that were not at odds with an institution's goals were likely to be routines that an institution chose to create rather than those it fell into.

What are some of the functions of routine? Some routines can be seen as "solved problems" thereby conserving the time and energy of participants. Another name for routines is regular procedures. Until it develops procedures, a new academic unit is likely to spend a very considerable amount of time and energy in discussion and debate about each case or problem, as well as about all the principles associated with it.

But academic routines are not necessarily the enemy of creativity and spontaneity; on the contrary, they make it possible to respond to some occasions, persons and issues in wholly unroutine ways. Institutions which resist developing any routines demonstrate how oppressive (and uncreative) an educational environment can be in which all people and problems are defined as absolutely unique and as having an equally urgent claim on the faculty's time and energy.

Routines are also the basis of institutional predictability. They allow people to act with some idea of how others are going to act and react in specific circumstances. An example here is the establishment of faculty office hours. Office hours are especially interesting precisely because many innovative programs and institutions resisted just such "routinization" of the student-teacher relationship. They argued that teachers should be available for spontaneous interactions, and that the very idea of office hours is at odds with the kind of close personal relationship between student and teacher that the institution is designed to foster. But being always potentially available was one of the sources of strain and overload on teachers in these institutions, which in turn led them to find other ways of rationing access to them by the growing numbers of students. And those other ways—especially privatization and "hiding"—have other consequences for the life of the institution which are more deleterious than is the "routinization" associated with establishing office hours.

We can look at the functions of routines in yet another way—by considering the outcomes of their performing these several functions. Routines are "solved problems" and introduce a certain economy, both of energy and money, into the institution. The problems that are dealt with by routines and procedures do not have constantly to be solved. The routine as a basis for predictability means that the institution is able to plan and coordinate action without constant consultation among its members. The main business of the institution can then be teaching and learning, and not meeting and decision-making. Predictability also provides a measure of psychological security to its members.

The provision of legitimacy by routines is illustrated by those routines which become procedures—accepted ways of doing things. Procedures, equitable and predictable ways of reaching decisions and adjudicating disputes, are the very opposite of arbitrary rulings and *ad hoc* decisions in problem situations. The hostility in the early years of many innovative institutions to all procedures had as an unintended consequence the denial to the institution of one of the most powerful forces for gaining and *holding* the willing participation of its members, that is, the shared sense that the institution is operating in fair and equitable ways, ways that are embodied in its broadly accepted procedures.

One crucial question in relation to routines for any institution, and not least for those in transition from institution building to steady state, is: what aspects of the life of the institution should be subject to routine and "administration," what left to spontaneous response, and what left to group decision-making, i.e. the political process? Institutions have only this limited number of ways of reaching decisions on academic issues and the determination of what kinds of decisions are or should be made by which of these different processes tells a lot about the dominant character and values of the institution.

The tension between spontaneity and routines is inherent in education. It is a question of what is given and what is problematic. If everything is problematic, then the world is as William James saw it to be for the newborn infant, "a bloomin', buzzing confusion." On the other hand, if nothing is problematic, then the institution has in fact ritualized its operation, that is to say, transformed its means into ends; it is wholly in the service of its own continued operation. A danger for every institution, and perhaps most sharply for colleges and universities, is the tendency to resolve the tension between spontaneity and routine either by resisting the emergence of any routines, as in the failed programs of the 60's, or by routinizing everything possible, as in the dreariest departments we know.

Lessons for Interdisciplinary Studies

Why raise these questions now, when most of these innovative institutions are either dead or safely institutionalized? My motive, I hope, is not to give support to the principle which, it is alleged, governed the University of Oxford for so many years—i.e. that "nothing should ever be done for the first time." I think there are other and better reasons for looking at innovative institutions, and at their difficulties during their early years. One of these is to learn about the relations of individuals and institutions under the conditions of high stress, in which institutional mechanisms for adaptation to stress and the resolution of conflict—that is to say, the mechanisms which permit institutional survival and the achievement, or at least the pursuit, of intellectual goals—are highly visible by virtue of their very weakness or absence. The extreme case is a useful comparative case, throwing into bold relief what otherwise one takes for granted in ordinarily successful functioning institutions where the observer is lulled by familiarity and routine, and where the mechanisms for survival are obscured by their interpenetration with each other in a web of patterns and activities which we cannot easily disentangle.

So one motive for studying innovative institutions is the identification of institutional mechanisms for coping with stress and change, and a clarification of their functions in higher education.

Another motive for our interest in "telic" institutions lies in the light they can shed on the potentialities for purposeful social action in higher education, and a better awareness of its limitations. It is one thing to create institutions with broad and largely traditional social functions—for example, a college—and then allow it to find its functions through its institutional forms and processes. It is rather different to create a program or institution that means to achieve new ends through specific intended means—where what is being specified in and by the institution has a close link between means and end. Anyone interested in educational policy may find in telic institutions some of the possibilities, problems and limitations of purposeful innovation in higher education, as contrasted to the responsive adaptations that are our more common springs of action.

Finally, it may appear that I have been talking more of the past than of the future. But as we have been warned, if we forget or ignore the lessons of the past, we are condemned to repeat them.

What are those lessons? As I read our recent history, here are some lessons for interdisciplinary studies.

1. First, programs of interdisciplinary studies can be critics of other more conventional discipline-centered studies; but they ought not to be their enemy. For one thing, the disciplines are simply too strong, too institutionalized in the academic departments. Departments are the forms that the disciplines take in our colleges and universities; they link the organized bodies of knowledge, and their research and scholarly activities, to the administrative units of universities—the units that appoint and promote faculty and manage the academic career, organize most of the undergraduate curriculum, and all of graduate studies. We cannot fight the disciplines; they manage the creation and extension of knowledge across national boundaries, and almost everywhere control the reward structures of both teachers and students. We *can* point out and demonstrate that discipline-based departments are not always the best units in which to organize instruction; and that there is a difference between the creation and transmission of knowledge, and the deepening of understanding, and that the latter is uniquely served by interdisciplinary studies.

I think there is a broad sympathy for and acceptance of that perspective even among specialized and self-limiting disciplinarians. But that sympathy is likely to disappear if the interdisciplinary studies movement claims not only that it adds something important and unique to the diversity of forms of higher education, but that it is the *only* way or the best way to organize higher education.

2. Second, I have said that many interdisciplinary studies programs have a

certain evangelical element to them, and that is only a short step from fanaticism. Almost a century ago, Peter Finley Dunn, the wry commentator on American life and customs, observed that "A fanatic is a person who is sure that God would be on his side if He only knew the facts of the case." There is something of that spirit among partisans of any movement; the trick is to find a way to reconcile partisanship and commitment with tolerance and civility. Can we be passionate partisans without abusing our neighbors, especially when resources are at issue?

3. And finally, and here I would anticipate spirited disagreement within the community, it may be that interdisciplinary studies are not for everybody; that they are, so to speak, a curriculum for students (and teachers) who have an unusual love of learning, who are self-motivated, and who are curious beyond the average about the world they live in, and who welcome chances to see that world, its history, social structure, politics, economy, art, literature, and its social and environmental problems, in a perspective that transcends the disciplines. We can, of course, try to engender and encourage that curiosity and motivation, but when those qualities are absent, and stubbornly absent, interdisciplinary studies may not be the best way to reach students who fear and resist the play of mind, the unfamiliar connection, the disturbing insight. And it may be that interdisciplinary studies, having made peace with its institutional environments, needs to find and acknowledge the limits of its relevance to American higher education, at the same time as it extends and fulfills its own intellectual potential as a unique way of learning and teaching.

Notes

1. *Newsletter,* Association for Integrative Studies, #13, 1983.
2. On the sources of these pressures on students and some of their reactions see Christopher Jencks and David Riesman, *The Academic Revolution,* (Garden City, N.Y.: Doubleday) 1968, see Chapter 1. See also Martin Trow, "Bell, Book, and Berkeley," *American Behavioral Scientist* (May–June 1968).
3. Gerald Grant and David Riesman, *The Perpetual Dream,* (Chicago: University of Chicago Press) 1978.
4. *Ibid.*
5. Quoted by Grant and Riesman, *Ibid.,* p. 33.
6. See Grant and Riesman, *op. cit.,* pp. 370–373.

The Fragmentation of Knowledge and Practice

University, Private Sector, and Public Sector Perspectives

Theodore Hershberg

Abstract

The fragmentation of knowledge and practice abounds—an un-desired and unanticipated consequence of disciplinary specialization and a symptom of our current inability to understand and manage complex systems. This problem, which confounds our ability to comprehend social change and deal effectively with perplexing issues of public policy, is examined from personal experience in the university, private sector, and public sector. Each illustration is described and analyzed in its immediate context, but underlying all of them is a common problem—the absence of systems theory and method. Although many obstacles must be overcome and much time will be required, the future will bring widespread adoption of systems approaches from which fundamental improvement will spring.

Introduction

An after-dinner speaker carries the burden of obligatory humor. For this gathering of academics, I consulted the Proceedings of the Third International Conference on Humor. One of the more amusing sessions dealt with oxymorons.

An *oxymoron,* you will recall, joins two seemingly contradictory words in a single phrase. The dictionary gives us *sweet sorrow.* Among my favorites are *military intelligence, athletic scholarship, jumbo shrimp,* and *postal service.* Academics take special delight in *faculty salaries.*

And what of *integrated knowledge?* Not long ago that phrase would have qualified as an oxymoron. Indeed, the more cynical among us would insist little has changed.

In any event, I'm delighted to be with you. I'm thrilled to find kindred spirits. People whom I've never met, but who read my book and understood what I meant about the quest for multi- and interdisciplinary knowledge. People who think that disciplinary lines are inappropriate boundaries for the intellect. People who know that our great universities are poorly organized to

Hershberg, Theodore. *"The Fragmentation of Knowledge and Practice: University, Private Sector, and Public Sector Perspectives."* Issues in Integrative Studies *6 (1988), 1–20. Reprinted with permission.*

This chapter was the Association for Integrative Studies keynote address at Pennsylvania State University on November 7, 1987.

conduct cross-disciplinary research. People who realize the greatest challenge ahead is the integration of knowledge, not its continued pursuit in fragmented specialties alone. People who appreciate that, without major changes in how knowledge is produced, our efforts to solve seemingly intractable social problems are doomed to failure. People who understand that the *sociology of knowledge* is not the sole dominion of the philosopher or the historian of science, but a common realm that must be traversed by all of us. If we work hard enough, and if we work together, we can change in fundamental ways the reward structures and research paradigms that dominate our universities.

It is really good to be with you tonight.

I want to talk with you about fragmentation—about the undesired and unanticipated consequences of disciplinary specialization and the symptoms of our current inability to understand and manage multiple interrelationships in complex systems. I want to share with you what these problems look like from three vantage points: the university, the private sector, and the public sector. In each setting, the fragmentation of knowledge, ideas, people, issues, and services abounds, and it confounds our ability to comprehend social change and deal effectively with perplexing issues of public policy.

In largest part, my remarks are devoted to a description of how in each setting knowledge and practice are fragmented. For each illustration I provide an analysis of immediate causes, but I also want to suggest that underlying all of them is a common problem—the absence of systems theory and method. While this absence is a major source of contemporary fragmentation, the widespread adoption of systems approaches in the future will be the source from which fundamental improvement will spring. Since the illustrations are derived from personal career experiences, what follows is autobiographical, necessarily limited to the experience of the practitioner. The three experiences were:

- *The Philadelphia Social History Project,* which I founded in 1969 and actively directed to 1981. This segment of my career took me from lecturer to full professor and from the Department of History to the School of Public and Urban Policy at the University of Pennsylvania.
- *Philadelphia: Past, Present and Future,* a private and public sector planning effort, the public policy component of the tricentennial celebration of Philadelphia's founding, which I conceived and directed from 1980 to 1983 and which served as the bridge over which I traveled from the academy to the public sector.
- *Assistant to the Mayor for Strategic Planning and Policy Development,* a position I held in the administration of W. Wilson Goode, Philadelphia's first black Mayor, during an eighteen-month leave of absence from the University of Pennsylvania (January, 1984 to June, 1985).

The Philadelphia Social History Project

The PSHP was a computer-based, collaborative, cross-disciplinary research effort.[1] It brought together historians, sociologists, demographers, economists, geographers, and epidemiologists to focus on the industrial development of Philadelphia and the experience of its diverse ethnic groups. At the project's official close in 1985, upwards of thirty researchers had written over one hundred scholarly papers, most published in refereed journals, several books, and fourteen doctoral dissertations in five disciplines.[2]

The foundation of these collaborative, cross-disciplinary efforts was an extraordinarily comprehensive machine-readable data base.[3] The entire 130 square miles of Philadelphia's geographic plain was divided into a grid network consisting of thousands of areal units, each one by one and one-quarter blocks. Depending on the question, these were aggregated into larger spatial sets. To make comparisons between the nineteenth and twentieth centuries, these areal units were converted to contemporary U.S. Census tracts. Every variable—individual persons, families, business firms, factories, transportation routes, sewer lines, voluntary organizations and death records—shared a location within a specific "x/y" coordinate in urban space.

This *integrated* data base was indispensable—not in the ordinary sense that without it systematic quantitative research into the process of urban-industrial development would have been impossible, but—in the special sense that it facilitated the cross-disciplinary research by attracting scholars from different disciplines. The data base, with its broad range of variables, provided the information researchers wanted to analyze and the machine-readable form in which they could apply their distinct methodological and analytic tools.

PSHP researchers won funding in eleven national competitions from 1969 to 1981 from the National Institute of Mental Health, the National Science Foundation, the National Endowment for the Humanities, and the National Institute for Child Health and Human Development. Over two million dollars were committed to the project to build the data base, buy time on a large mainframe computer, and pay the salaries of researchers and support staff.

The PSHP enjoyed a highly successful first phase in which it developed appropriate methodologies and constructed its data base. Its second phase was *multi-disciplinary,* characterized by research in which the concerns and variables of different disciplines were integrated in specific analyses. For example:

- a labor historian's interest in how an immigrant work force was disciplined, coupled with an economist's concern with changing productivity as the shop floor mechanized;
- the collaboration of medical historians, epidemiologists and demographers to explain the sharp decline in mortality and morbidity at the turn of the twentieth century;
- a sociologist's interest in family structure, a demographer's concern with marriage rates and labor force entry, and an historian's desire to learn how the organization of the life course differed in 1880 and 1970.

Like observers of a many-sided, ecologically-differentiated mountain, who shared information about their respective vistas, PSHP researchers collaborated in producing far more integrated knowledge about the industrial development of a great American metropolis than could have been achieved if the model of the disciplinary scholar alone had been pursued.

Yet the project's final interdisciplinary research phase never materialized. Although many individual essays met tests of interdisciplinarity—because variables central to different disciplines were integrated—the *overall* effort does not merit the label *interdisciplinary.*

I wish I could say that interdisciplinarity eluded us despite our best efforts, that our failure was a straightforward consequence of the complexity of our goal. But in fact there was no such "best effort." Participating researchers, despite the stated objective, never quite came to work as a *team.* They did not engage in a *shared* effort to define and write an interdisciplinary history of the city. This goal was never genuinely pursued.

There are many reasons for this failure beyond the personal limitations of the project's director. Consider the most significant. First, the inability to grant tenure (universities do not give such authority to institutes, centers or projects) means that PSHP researchers were constrained by their disciplinary concerns. When research designs were executed, disciplinary interests consistently triumphed over interdisciplinary ones. Given the career consequences, it was hard to fault individuals for their choices. When the chickens come home to roost, they do so in disciplinary hen houses.

When, for example, the School of Public and Urban Policy at the University of Pennsylvania closed in 1983, many of my colleagues did not appreciate the loss. They reasoned that since all the programs were being continued elsewhere in the University, the same graduate education would be possible. But, by then, my PSHP experience had taught me that something terribly important had been lost—the ability to protect and promote interdisciplinary knowledge through the essential act of hiring and tenuring scholars committed to interdisciplinary research.

Second, the inability to involve faculty at Penn, particularly tenured faculty, meant that when the external funding came to an end in 1985, there was no group of committed faculty who could lobby for the use of limited University resources to maintain the project at a minimal level (i.e., space and computer programming assistance for the data base users).

In more generic terms, the inability to involve faculty from the university where the research is based can be understood in terms of a *match-up* argument. What is the fit between the research interests of the faculty and the subject matter of the research project? If the fit is good—if faculty see research opportunities in the project which match-up with their existing interests—they are far more likely to participate in or at least be supportive of the larger research effort. On the other hand, if the fit is poor, the reverse will be true. Unfortunately for the PSHP, Penn in the 1970's, as today, was not a place where empirical, quantitative research in the social sciences—especially in economics, demography and sociology, let alone such research with an *historical* emphasis—found many practitioners.

In striking contrast was the *match-up* experience of Eliot Stellar. Leaving The Johns Hopkins University as an assistant professor in 1951 because it did *not* provide an hospitable environment for the kind of interdisciplinary research he wanted to undertake at the juncture of physiology, anatomy and psychology, Stellar was drawn to the University of Pennsylvania precisely because it did. At Penn he found a critical mass of researchers who shared these interests. Thirty-five years later, there is much evidence of Stellar's successes at Penn.[4] His efforts led to the creation of a new interdisciplinary department and a major research institute with well over one hundred affiliated faculty, and he also served as a distinguished provost of the University.

The inability to grant tenure and to involve Penn faculty in the PSHP research led to the predictable outcome: when federal funding ended, the project closed.[5] Ultimately, however, the failure of the PSHP to realize its interdisciplinary potential lies in the *disciplinary* nature of the research models and reward structures which dominate the social sciences and humanities.

The *culture of individualism* which characterizes our nation's educational systems is not at fault. If it were, what would explain the success of real teamwork throughout society, particularly in the corporate world? If such a culture truly influenced normative behavior, then all reward structures and research models in our universities would reflect a disciplinary and highly individual approach to scholarship. Yet one has only to look at the hard and applied sciences to see they are governed by a reward structure quite different from those in the humanities and social sciences. In these sections of our universities there is no problem bestowing awards on those who participate in collaborative, cross-disciplinary research. Indeed, such behavior defines the norm.

To understand why this striking difference exists within our universities, one must come to grips with two basic questions: For whom is the research intended? What are the consequences of the answer for how the research is organized? In the hard and applied sciences, to simplify, the *client* represents a constituency for whom the research must have applicability—that is, it must work. The distinction here is not a simple-minded one between applied and pure research because there is a great deal of cross-disciplinary collaboration by scholars doing pure research in the hard sciences. Nonetheless, in these disciplines there is an awareness that cross-disciplinary collaboration is indispensable for successful applied research, and appropriate reward structures and research models have necessarily evolved to support these efforts.

In the humanities and social sciences, by contrast, the client is much more frequently other colleagues. Success is defined as a positive response to one's scholarship, rather than efficacy in a real world application. The goal is not the creation of something that *works* in application, but the publication of something that is considered brilliant or pioneering by one's peers. Even when the client is outside the university, scholars are still influenced by reward structures and research models which favor non-collaborative, disciplinary approaches. Unlike the tradition and culture of research in the hard sciences, which stresses building on the efforts of those who have gone before, in the humanities and social sciences graduate students and junior faculty are encouraged to strike out on their own and to stress originality and creativity over theoretical continuity.

Until and unless fundamental changes are made in the research models which dominate the humanities and social sciences and in the reward structures which protect and sustain them, little progress will be made in these fields to promote interdisciplinary or cross-disciplinary research.

Philadelphia: Past, Present and Future

The second career experience took me outside the University and beyond the academic boundaries within which I had always worked. My work with the PSHP prepared me well for this effort. I knew a great deal about how Philadelphia had come to its present condition—a city shedding its industrial skin in a kind of economic molting process and emerging as a diversified services center—and I was accustomed to thinking about the city in holistic terms. Most importantly, however, I was sensitive to the need to find ways to facilitate the integration of people and knowledge.

"Philadelphia: Past, Present and Future" was a broad-based exercise in public policy and strategic planning undertaken on the eve of the 300th anniversary of Philadelphia's founding. It was designed to analyze the major problems and opportunities facing the city and to develop specific policies and projects to respond to them. Surrounded by civic celebration, P:PPF was the vehicle through which the city's future would be seriously addressed.

Roughly 1,000 Philadelphians participated in this two and one-half year effort, which began in 1980. They were neither ordinary citizens nor the city's power elite. They were characteristically senior members of the city's many *policy communities*. They included, for example, presidents and executive directors of community groups and civic agencies, corporate vice-presidents and public affairs officers, deputies and senior staff from government departments and agencies, and academic experts. CBS, Inc.'s initial grant of $250,000 launched the project, and an additional half million dollars, raised from local foundations and corporations, sustained it.

The project had three phases concerned, respectively, with *analysis, integration* and *action.*

Phase I, "The Task Force Effort," began with the launching of a dozen task forces. These covered the basic public policy areas of economic development, transportation, taxes, education, housing, infrastructure, culture and recreation, and so on. Their common mandate was to prepare written reports which identified the critical issues and the strategies to address them. With focus on discrete policy areas, *fragmentation* was present from the beginning, but it was purposeful. An integrative approach was eschewed at the outset, albeit reluctantly, in favor of providing participants easy access—that is, familiar doorways into the project.

The design of the individual task forces, however, was sensitive to the need for integration. Each was composed of 20–25 members, all with expertise in the subject matter and selected from each of six basic constituencies: business, labor, government, neighborhood groups, civic associations, and universities or colleges. The project's integration of persons from diverse personal backgrounds and policy communities was striking. "Who are these people?" was the undertone of conversation among the 700 invited guests who attended the opening conference.

The Phase I task force meetings were plagued by parochialism. Since my Center coordinated all meeting schedules, I was able to attend over eighty separate two-hour seminars. A characteristic illustration of this parochialism was provided by the Housing Task Force. After heated debate over solutions for the housing crisis of the poor and homeless, the task force concluded that the city's 22,000 abandoned houses should be rehabilitated and turned over to the needy. Normally, I remained silent in these meetings, absorbing all that I could and answering, when they arose, questions about the project as a whole. On this occasion, I suggested (ignoring for the moment the fact that resources were unavailable to bring these abandoned dwellings into compliance with city building codes) that, since the housing problems of the poor resulted from inadequate income, any strategies proposed by the Housing Task Force to help these groups should be coordinated with the Economic Development and Poverty and Unemployment task forces. Task force members responded with a memorable example of the narrow, "blinders-on" thinking that limits our problem-solving capacity. "Our responsibility is to provide adequate housing," they replied. "The provision of jobs and job training is someone else's problem."

Phase II was titled "Integration." The introductory pamphlet, which described the project as a whole and was distributed at the opening conference, included this quotation from Oxford philosopher, Stuart Hampshire (1977), writing about "The Future of Knowledge":

> We may not know what we know, in the sense that we may not realize what is known, and if we don't know what we know, then our first order of knowledge is apt to be unused, almost as if it did not exist.

Phase II was the "Humpty-Dumpty" phase—that is, it was concerned with putting the fragmented pieces back together again. The rationale for this phase was described in the project pamphlet. The full passage is reproduced below to document the extent to which the project took this concern seriously and how it communicated this concern to participants.

> The second stage of the project is devoted to the integration of people and ideas. In order to devise effective programs and establish new coalitions that are capable of implementing the action agendas which will be developed later in the project, it will be necessary to overcome the fragmentation of knowledge, experience, and expertise which currently limits us.
>
> The integration stage will expose all participants to the full range of problems and their proposed solutions in order to learn how each is related to the others. Each element in this stage is designed to facilitate the integration process. The "real world" is not com-

partmentalized by policy area. Changes in the province of each topical task force affect all the others. Moreover, all are tied to each
other through the common denominator of budget dollars.

Task force membership, especially as a core participant, already
implies considerable expertise in given policy areas. During the integration stage of the project we will introduce people who have
been largely concerned with a single issue to the city's many other
problems and the limited resources available with which to deal
with them. Solutions in the 1980's will have to maximize efficient
use of scarce resources. A standard with which to evaluate policy
might be to ask whether the proposed policy permits "the simultaneous realization of multiple program goals." For all of these reasons, it is clear that the effective solutions are more likely to emerge
after we have carefully considered the full range of the issues that
confront us.

Phase II had several features designed to facilitate integration. Five will be described here. *First,* the task force reports were supposed to be circulated project-
wide. Although the cost and logistics for this mailing would have been considerable (twelve reports for each of 1,000 participants), the reason it was not
done was absence of demand among project participants. People simply were
not interested in reading the reports from other task forces.

Second, eight committees were launched to consider integrative themes
which cut across all twelve task force reports. Among these were technology,
venture capital, communications, governance, and urban design and land use.
The written committee reports were circulated widely (and skeptically, given
the lack of project-wide interest in the task force reports).

Third, ten public conferences were held at which each task force report was
reviewed by two national experts to ensure that the reports were informed by
exogenous trends, strategies, and federal legislation—which is to say: let's not
waste time reinventing the wheel, and let's not miss the forest for the trees.

Fourth, immediately following the public portion of each conference, at
which the national consultants shared their reactions with the audience as a
whole, a private luncheon seminar was held. While only task force members
whose report was under consideration that morning could attend, the leaders
of *all* other task forces were invited. It was thought essential that all task force
leaders be present at each of these ten seminars so that they would expand their
horizons and improve their ability to revise their respective task force reports.
Complete integration would have been achieved, in quantitative terms, if all
thirty-five task force leaders attended all ten Conferences, a total of 350 appearances. The results were dismal and surprising, even for the cynical. On only *ten*
occasions did a task force leader attend a luncheon seminar other than his or
her own. As the task force leaders explained their absences to me, it became
clear that the commitment of time the project required was well beyond what
they were prepared to contribute, but more to the point, they were either unin-

terested in the work of the other task forces or failed to appreciate the value of their involvement in these integrative activities.

Fifth, an integrative seminar series was scheduled. This was an effort to bring together project participants who had the talent to serve as *generalists*. As a condition of participation they were to read all the task force reports. Over a seven-week period, a group of twenty-five generalists met at our Center every Wednesday evening for dinner and roughly three hours of discussion.

The experience of the integrative seminar is one of those "bad news, good news" stories. The bad news was that on the level of *analytic integration* the seminar was a total failure. Integration on the level of systems understandings—for example, if energy prices continue to increase at current levels, what are the implications for economic development and transportation policies?—was either too difficult, too abstract or too boring. Whatever the reason, this more analytic approach got us nowhere. The good news was that on the level of *operational integration* the seminar was extremely successful. A kind of "Rubic's Cube" approach was developed consisting of three axes for *specific* project proposals. First came *Goals:* what do we want to accomplish? Second came *Actors:* who needs to be involved? Third came *Action:* what steps need to be taken to achieve desired ends?

In *Phase III,* "Action," the operational integration approach led to the publication of the *Philadelphia Investment Portfolio,* which contained fifty-six specific proposals recommended by the project for adoption by civic agencies and city government.

To describe in detail the many ways in which P:PPF affected Philadelphia would take more space than is available here and move us away from our central topic. Assigning a summary verdict to the project as a whole is difficult because it involves value judgments and many different measures. First, the project affected the public policy debate in the city. Its close coincided with the mayoral primary and general election in 1983, which meant that the task force reports and related publications were circulated widely. Many of the specific projects and policies P:PPF proposed were incorporated in the platforms of the mayoral candidates.

Second, the verdict of the local media in editorials and news stories judged P:PPF a major success. Third, of the fifty-six projects recommended for adoption in the *Philadelphia Investment Portfolio,* just about half, in one form or another, have been or are now being implemented. Fourth, in quantitatively calculated cost-benefit terms, the project paid for itself several times over considering only the energy conservation savings to the local economy (dollars not exported to energy suppliers) which resulted from the adoption by the local gas utility of the project's *Residential Energy Weatherization Program.* Finally, the project's *Literacy Commission* concept was implemented with enormous success: it is part of the Mayor's Office, has hundreds of centers across the city staffed by thousands of volunteer tutors, and has received over one million dollars from foundations to support its efforts.

As an exercise in overcoming the fragmentation of knowledge or in introducing systems approaches to local problems, the project made only limited progress. Its greatest success was in promoting a broad definition of *economic development.* Since only this phase could capture the attention of the city's movers and shakers, it was argued that economic development could not succeed if the schools did not work, mass transit did not function, illiteracy was not addressed, and the city failed to afford a sufficiently high level of amenities so that the people with a choice chose to remain or settle in Philadelphia. By tying culture and recreation to successful economic development, for example, support was won for many important initiatives which otherwise would have failed.

Assistant to the Mayor

By the end of P:PPF, I had absorbed so much information, become so familiar with the broad range of issues which faced Philadelphia, and had met so many people in the city's different policy communities that Mayor-elect W. Wilson Goode asked me to take an eighteen-month leave of absence from the University of Pennsylvania to serve as his Assistant for Strategic Planning and Policy Development. Although the experience was even more frustrating than I expected it to be—the reasons for which are the subject of a different essay—it was a remarkable opportunity for a student of public policy to see from the inside how the nation's fourth largest city was governed.

I was a senior member of the administration and participated in meetings of the Mayor's Cabinet. My portfolio of responsibilities was threefold: first, to deal with specific projects of importance to the Mayor; second, to serve as the executive director of the Mayor's Commission on the 21st Century; and third, to work on city-suburban relations, which have become the focus of my efforts since my return to Penn.

Working as Assistant to the Mayor was also an opportunity to continue my observations on the sociology of knowledge and how fragmentation manifested itself in a very different setting. As I began my work, I recalled an eye-opening exchange I had with George Peterson of the Urban Institute, one of the P:PPF's national consultants. I had remarked that I envied his working with upwards of seventy Ph.D.'s in a truly interdisciplinary approach to urban problems. He chuckled and proceeded to disabuse me of this illusion. Requests from public sector agencies, he explained, rarely required interdisciplinary responses. The contracts into which they entered were usually narrowly focused, reflecting the client's desire for compartmentalized solutions.

Peterson was correct. I found the public sector to be even more fragmented than the university environment I had left (for at least there the hard sciences make good use of interdisciplinary approaches). Despite the fact that the social world is more complicated than the physical world—it deals with people and their irrationality, not the predictable behavior of atoms—the public sector is even more ill-organized for its demanding tasks than universities are to promote interdisciplinary research.

Where the university's building blocks are the separate disciplines (history, physics, economics), city government's are the units of basic service delivery (policy, fire, sanitation). When well managed, these operating departments can usually get their jobs done (arrest criminals, put out fires, pick up the garbage). But when major issues such as homelessness, neighborhood revitalization and drug addiction arise, requiring for solution an integrated response from many different city departments (housing, welfare, job training), city officials find this organizational structure severely limiting.

The symptoms of this fragmentation abound. Some are easily recognizable and maddeningly humorous, as when streets are torn up, worked on, and then paved by one unit of government or utility only to have the same stretch of pavement torn up, worked on and repaved by another group the following week. Others are just inefficient, for example, the reading of residential utility meters. Although virtually every household in the city has electric, gas and water meters, they are read by three different persons rather than one.

Less obvious, but especially frustrating to anyone trying to obtain useful integrated information about a particular section of the city, is the absence of common geographic-based data. In Philadelphia, there are at least two dozen different areal units used by government departments (police precincts, mental health catchment areas, fire districts), which make it exceedingly difficult to collect information across what should be compatible geographic boundaries.

This public sector fragmentation exists for many reasons. Some are histori- cal. As cities grew, so did the demand for services. As new operating depart- ments emerged, each developed separate hierarchies and distinct modes of service delivery. Like all bureaucratic structures, each zealously protects its turf and responsibilities—that is, each fights to maintain control over its budgetary and staffing levels.

Other city departments developed in response to social problems. These can be described as *pathology focused* operating agencies. Such units, by definition, are organizationally fragmented because the problems they deal with are them- selves symptoms of problems occurring within larger systems. Health and Human Services is an excellent example of such a *non-system* and dysfunctional approach. Rather than a life-cycle organization (in which people's needs are addressed as they pass through the life course from the cradle-to-the-grave), where the focus is on prevention and the individual is at the center, the field currently organizes its services by compartmentalized topical areas (health, mental health and social welfare), where the focus is on the symptomatic pa- thology and the professional is at the center.

Meanwhile, the need to overcome this widespread fragmentation in the op- eration of local government has never been greater. During the 1980's, new federal policies dramatically reduced the level of funding received by the na- tion's cities. Philadelphia lost over $200 million annually as some programs were eliminated and others sharply reduced (e.g., general revenue sharing and job training).[6] This loss of federal aid coincided with the decline of local tax revenue, as jobs and people left central cities for the suburbs and exurbs. More- over, the legacy of the Reagan era is a staggering national debt. Its sheer size and the politics which surround it (neither political party will reduce the mid- dle-class entitlement programs which comprise more than half the federal budget) effectively guarantee the absence of substantial funding for new urban aid programs.

Unfortunately, the wrong debate is now underway in most cities. The choice is framed as between higher taxes *or* reduced city services—a no-win situation. The challenge at the local level is to improve services while maintaining current tax levels. This can be accomplished only through the introduction of *systems* approaches. Without this fundamental reorganization in the delivery of city services, it will not be possible to achieve the necessary operating efficiencies.

Many obstacles stand in the way of this reorganization. Most important is the political philosophy that runs City Hall: local government is seen as an *employer* rather than a *provider* of efficient city services. The paramount consideration of elected officials is to stay in office and, given the state of voter apathy, they find patronage to be a more effective means of doing so than the provision of good public service.

Then, too, reorganizing city government would mean direct conflict with the forces of the status quo. In this respect, the councilmen, commissioners, and deputies behave very much like the chairmen, deans and directors in universities. Consider, for example, the difficulties of implementing a radically redesigned health and human services system where the key professionals (e.g., physicians and social workers) would be required to treat each other as peers. Bringing them together, with their differential status, access to funding, salary levels, educational backgrounds and therapeutic approaches, would give new meaning to the word problematic.

In discussions with city officials about fundamental organizational change, it is inescapably clear that their concerns go beyond those noted above. Almost no one has been trained to think in system terms about the provision of city services. Few people have the innate ability to grasp complicated systemic relationships. The integrated data bases, which could organize vast quantities of information and facilitate the understanding of these relationships, do not exist. Nor are funds available to create such data bases and train the managers to use them, or to pay for the education of managers to think in system terms. Finally, faced by the daily demands of managing a large city with limited staff and resources, and of responding to the frequent crises that paralyze normal governmental functioning, to say nothing of fear of major opposition from public sector labor unions whose contracts contain no lay-off clauses, few public officials are prepared even to consider new and threatening organizational strategies.

Before concluding, let me note here that the work I undertook since returning to the University of Pennsylvania embodies my respect for system approaches. Philadelphia is embedded in a great many systems from the neighborhood to the globe, and the *regional system* was one I thought I could do something about. Thus I designed and now facilitate a process—the *Southeastern Pennsylvania State Legislators' Conference*—which brings together corporate leaders and state Senators and Representatives from the city and the suburbs to address common problems and opportunities in the five-county region (including roughly one-third of the state's population). This effort builds on my understanding of the growing importance of regional cooperation in a new era marked by a global economy and the emergence of state government as a major player in the domestic policy arena, and it provides me an opportunity to operationalize my concepts about systems approaches by creating new institutional and inter-personal networks on a region-wide basis.

Closing Observations

University, private sector, and public sector environments are not likely to change much in the near future. The traditions and norms which govern current thinking and behavior are strong. The fragmentation of knowledge, ideas, people, issues, and services I've described will be with us for a long time. Yet, significant change will come. I sense a certain inexorability about the future in this regard—and given some of the obstacles described in the preceding pages, this optimism must appear akin to science fiction—but I minimize neither the attendant difficulties nor the time which will be required for these changes to come about.

When change comes it will be driven by necessity and opportunity. Universities will face a growing demand to direct more of their resources toward pressing issues of public policy, and they will find it necessary to embrace models of interdisciplinary research and alter their reward structures so that scholars will be encouraged to undertake new forms of collaborative inquiry.[7] Governments, under increasing fiscal pressures and public demand to provide more services with fewer dollars, will slowly and reluctantly make the necessary organizational changes in their operations to accommodate systems approaches. The private sector, driven by uncertainties in an environment characterized by rapid economic, technological and political change, has already begun to adopt systems thinking, particularly in the corporate world and in the scientific and planning communities, but this is an observation of relative rather than absolute accomplishment. Although the private sector effort has begun to develop systems approaches, much remains to be done.

The desire to make changes in all these environments will be facilitated by major advances in systems theory and method, and by widely available new technologies—largely inexpensive computer hardware with enormous data-handling capacity and software with easy-to-use programs (with an almost plain language command structure) for modeling multiple and complicated interrelationships.[8]

It is not surprising that our present grasp of these interrelationships is limited. Philadelphia, for example, is an enormous arena of people, institutions, businesses, cultural networks, political alliances and economic transactions. The boundaries and participants of its spatial, technical and environmental structures shift with each separate event and issue. This complexity has led us to simplify. The response, as we have seen, has been to think about and administer the city through its component parts. Until we adopt systems approaches, we will continue to suffer from the unexpected and inadequate results of our actions.

This should not be surprising, because although a system can be divided structurally, it is functionally indivisible. "Even if each part of the system . . . is made to operate as efficiently as possible," Russell Ackoff reminds us, "the system as a whole will not operate as efficiently as possible (1974)." The performance of a system depends more on how its parts interact than on how they act independently of each other.

We are now only at the dawn of the *Systems Age,* and much effort will be required before the implications of this new way of comprehending and acting is widely understood. Much time will pass before the necessary education, training and technologies become widely accessible. Given the deplorable state of math education in the United States, this transition will be especially difficult, but I am convinced that the need will be sufficiently compelling and the new technologies sufficiently attractive to carry the day.

In the meantime, before we overcome the fragmentation of knowledge, learn how to model the consequences of simultaneity and complex feedback loops, understand how actions taken in one sphere of human endeavor affect others, and move fully into the Systems Age, we will just have to make the best of it as reluctant students in the only educational institution these days with an expanding enrollment: *The School of Unintended Consequences.*

Notes

1. In the discussion which follows, a distinction will be made between multi disciplinary and inter disciplinary research. Cross-disciplinary refers here to both.
2. For an anthology of PSHP essays, see Theodore Hershberg, ed., *PHILADELPHIA: Work, Space, Family and Group Experience in the Nineteenth Century* (Oxford University Press, 1981). A copy of the 1985 bibliography is available from the Center for Greater Philadelphia at the University of Pennsylvania.
3. Reference here is to the internal characteristics of the research. Without adequate external funding, of course, the data base could not have been built.
4. Stellar identified many factors essential for success. Included among these were: control over a department and the allocation of the rewards at its disposal; a critical mass of personnel required to form the working nucleus to which others would be attracted; an adequate level of funding; an institution undergoing expansion, as Penn was in the 1950's; available tenure-track positions; the support of key institutional leaders (deans, provost and president); programs for training in two or more disciplines which attracted the most able graduate students.
5. What remains is not satisfactory from the vantage point of cross-disciplinary research. The data base exists in two parts. The first consists of hard copy; that is, everything but the machine-readable data; it is housed as a locked archival collection in the University's main library and is stored on 350 linear feet of shelf space. The second consists of the machine-readable tapes, over 300 in number, containing thousands of data sets, with rather good documentation, housed at the University's Population Studies Center. Although each collection has an archivist, in neither instance is anyone present with first-hand knowledge of the PSHP. To be sure, it could have been worse—the data could have been destroyed or left in the basement of my home—but the current situation leaves a great deal to be desired.
6. The cut-backs in federal job training programs (CETA and JTPA) meant there were 3,000 fewer jobs in city government (a decline of 15%) when Mayor Goode took office in 1984 than there were when the programs were at their height in 1980.
7. I have written elsewhere that the federal government could initiate new programs (when at some future date funds are again available) to promote interdisciplinary research in the humanities and social sciences. The ground rules for university receipt of the substantial funding made available for the new research would be conditioned on the commitment of universities to make significant changes in their reward structures. (Hershberg, 1981; 1987:8:17)
8. I am thinking here of the breakthrough Steven Jobs has apparently made with the NEXT computer

work stations. This generation of computers begins to provide the public with extraordinarily powerful computing and modeling capacities heretofore available only to those with highly specialized education and considerable financial resources.

Bibliography

Ackoff, Russell (1974), *Redesigning the Future: A Systems Approach to Societal Problems,* Wiley-Interscience.

Hampshire, Stuart (1977), "The Future of Knowledge," *New York Review of Books,* November.

Hershberg, T. ed. (1981), *"Philadelphia: Work, Space, Family and Group Experience in the Nineteenth Century,"* Oxford University Press. 'Epilogue: Sustaining Interdisciplinary Research,' Reprinted in *INTERSTUDY,* Vol. 8, no. 17 (December 1987).

Hershberg, T. (1981), "Philadelphia: Past, Present, Future—Conference Pamphlet" Center for Philadelphia Studies, University of Pennsylvania (March).

Hershberg, T. & Rubin, M. (1982), *Philadelphia Investment Portfolio,* Center for Philadelphia Studies, University of Pennsylvania.

Hershberg, T. (1985), "Philadelphia Social History Project: Bibliography," Center for Greater Philadelphia, University of Pennsylvania.

Disciplinary Contexts

Academic Disciplines and Undergraduate Interdisciplinary Education

Lessons From the School of Interdisciplinary Studies at Miami University, Ohio

William H. Newell

How much disciplinary background do students need before they are ready to take interdisciplinary courses? How much background in relevant disciplines do academic staff need to develop and teach an interdisciplinary course? How visible should disciplines be and what role should they play in interdisciplinary courses? Can students learn intellectual skills often associated with disciplinary education, such as rigorous or critical thinking, through interdisciplinary courses? Can interdisciplinary courses adequately prepare students for more advanced work in disciplines or for careers that draw upon a disciplinary base?

These questions about the relationship between disciplines and interdisciplinary education, posed by its advocates as well as its critics, are typically addressed deductively, at a philosophical rather than empirical level. Given the measurement problems involved in assessing interdisciplinary education (see the article by Michael Field & Russell Lee in this issue), it is understandable that such questions are not normally answered through quantitative data and statistical methods. The strategy employed in this article is to explore how these issues are resolved in practice within the context of an exemplary interdisciplinary programme—the School of Interdisciplinary Studies at Miami University in Oxford, Ohio.

Overview of the School of Interdisciplinary Studies

Miami University's School of Interdisciplinary Studies is widely recognised as one of the premier undergraduate interdisciplinary programmes in the United States. This four-year degree-granting school of 300 students and 14 full-time academic staff offers a core curriculum of exclusively interdisciplinary courses in the humanities and arts, social sciences, and natural sciences and technology, as well as a residential learning programme, a writing-across-the-curriculum programme (with parallel programmes emerging in quantitative reasoning and discovery science) and interdisciplinary contract-based majors culminating in a

Newell, William H. "Academic Disciplines and Undergraduate Interdisciplinary Education: Lessons from the School of Interdisciplinary Studies at Miami University, Ohio." European Journal of Education 27:3 (1992), 211–221. Reprinted with permission of Carfax Publishing Limited, PO Box 25, Abingdon, Oxfordshire OX14 3UE, United Kingdom.

year-long senior project. Team-developed, individually taught courses during the freshman year explore interdisciplinary topics within each of the three core areas of humanities, social sciences and natural sciences, asking 'Is freedom possible?' for example, in the social science course or examining historic revolutions in each of the physical sciences. Second-year courses bring together core areas, e.g. the social and physical sciences in an examination of US energy policy. Third-year seminars, developed and taught by individual members of staff, focus on more specialised topics to exemplify interdisciplinary methodology in each core area. A year-long fourth-year workshop co-ordinates and facilitates the development of individual senior projects that explore an interdisciplinary topic in depth within the focus of each student's major. The emphasis throughout is on challenging students' unexamined assumptions about themselves and their world, on the limitations as well as the strengths of each discipline, and on developing a holistic understanding informed by materials from various disciplines. Since its founding in 1974, the School has been one of seven separate divisions of Miami University, with its own Dean and administrative staff; its academic staff are appointed full-time to the school and promoted and tenured within it.

This programme has received five major grants in the last six years attesting to its academic excellence: two Academic Challenge grants and two Program Excellence Awards from the Ohio Board of Regents, and a three-year Fund for the Improvement of Post-secondary Education (FIPSE) grant. The FIPSE grant has made it possible to document the educational outcomes of the programme with detail that is quite uncommon in US higher education. The programme's senior project conference was cited by Ernest Boyer in *College* as a model for assessing capstone achievement of seniors, and its learning community was praised in George Kuh's *Involving Colleges*.

Disciplinary Preparation for Interdisciplinary Courses

Since interdisciplinary study is grounded by definition in disciplines, it seems reasonable to ask how much background in the concepts, theories, methods and factual base of each discipline is required before students are adequately prepared for interdisciplinary courses. Should undergraduate interdisciplinary courses stipulate a prerequisite of at least the introductory course in each discipline on which they draw? Should interdisciplinary education perhaps even be deferred to postgraduate level? Alternatively, is it possible to offer introductory-level interdisciplinary general education courses that presume no prior background in the disciplines? If so, one might wonder in what sense such courses are inter-'disciplinary' and be understandably sceptical about their intellectual rigour. Yet it is precisely this last approach to interdisciplinary education—general education courses without disciplinary prerequisites—that more and more colleges and universities in the United States are adopting. In fact, the renaissance in interdisciplinary higher education over the last decade has been dominated by institution-wide general education reform (Newell, 1988), and, almost without exception, these new interdisciplinary courses have no disciplinary prerequisites.

The courses in the School of Interdisciplinary Studies are no exception to the national trend. Save for a couple of third-year seminars in the natural sciences, none of the courses over its 18-year history has had disciplinary prerequisites, though its second-year courses have often built on those of the first year. Like their national counterparts these interdisciplinary courses solve the problem by providing their own disciplinary base. Each interdisciplinary course teaches students what they need to know about the various disciplines on which it draws.

The requisite disciplinary knowledge depends not only on the substantive topic of a given course, but on the particular definition of interdisciplinary studies held by the staff member teaching it. Surprisingly, perhaps, for a group of professional interdisciplinarians teaching in a self-consciously interdisciplinary programme, there is no formal consensus within the School about the definition of interdisciplinary studies; indeed, there has been little philosophical discussion about it. Instead, different operational (and usually implicit) definitions have evolved out of pragmatic discussions among different combinations of staff about what topics to cover, what books to read, what issues to raise, and what sensibilities to develop within students in a particular course. As a result, some courses draw basic concepts from disciplines (e.g. discourse communities from literature, marginal utility from economics, or old field succession from biology), while others draw theories (e.g. dependency theory from political science or plate tectonics from geology), facts (Avogadro's number from chemistry or the differential life chances of the lower and middle classes from sociology), or methods (ethnography from anthropology or laboratory experiments from the physical sciences). Explicitly or implicitly, however, every course draws on the perspectives or world views of more than one discipline.

The lens through which a discipline views the world is its most distinctive feature, as the incorporation or integration of disciplinary perspectives into a larger, more holistic perspective is the chief distinguishing characteristic of interdisciplinary studies. In the long-standing first-year course in the social sciences, for example, the possibility of individual freedom is examined from the contrasting perspectives of economics (that individuals make rational choices which maximise their material self-interest by balancing out external constraints and internal preferences), sociology (that individual behaviour is greatly circumscribed if not determined outright by society, operating through external social pressure and an internalised socialisation process), behavioural psychology (that an individual's apparent choices are nothing more than responses to environmental stimuli), and so on. As the course proceeds, each perspective is contrasted to the previous ones, and their key distinguishing assumptions are ferreted out. At the end of the semester, students read several authors who attempt to reconcile these perspectives (e.g. Rollo May, who argues that we oscillate back and forth between treating ourselves as object and experiencing ourselves as subject; Peter Berger, who points out the inability of science to discover freedom and the mechanisms of transformation, manipulation, and detachment by which individuals can exercise freedom within social controls; and Dorothy Lee, who argues that social structures can facilitate as well as threaten individual freedom). Having seen how others have confronted the question of individual freedom, students are then asked to forge their own synthesis, one that is sensitive to each perspective in the course. Most courses in the School are not so explicit about their underlying interdisciplinary methodology, but they all draw upon different perspectives, each affording a context within which the other perspectives should be understood.

Much of the apprehension about providing a disciplinary base for interdisciplinary courses stems from a misconception of their intent. While interdisciplinary courses indeed make use of concepts, theories, methods and factual knowledge from various disciplines, the interdisciplinary understanding they develop is grounded primarily in the perspectives from which those concepts, theories, methods and facts emerge. It takes many years to learn a discipline; it takes only a few readings to begin to develop a feel for how that discipline characteristically looks at the world, its angle of vision, its perspective. An interdisciplinary course can easily provide illustrative readings, each written from the point of view of a different discipline, that offer contrasting perspectives on the same topic. In short, when it is recognised what interdisciplinary courses draw from the disciplines, it is much easier to understand how they can be taken without disciplinary prerequisites.

Staff Preparation for Interdisciplinary Curriculum Development

It is one thing to accept that students can learn within an interdisciplinary course what they need of the disciplines on which it draws. It is quite another to see how staff can develop sufficient insight into enough disciplines to put together and teach an interdisciplinary course. If the task is difficult for courses that cut across one area, say the social sciences, is it not impossible for courses that cross two (let alone three) areas? Must one be another Leonardo da Vinci to teach with intellectual integrity broad-ranging interdisciplinary general education courses? Should one be expected to have amassed this Renaissance knowledge as a postgraduate, or can one hope to acquire it on the job—during the process of developing and teaching an interdisciplinary course?

Again, the national consensus may seem surprisingly counter-intuitive. Most institutions expect staff with wide-ranging interests but prefer traditional postgraduate training (i.e. focused primarily if not exclusively on a single discipline) to develop and teach interdisciplinary courses jointly with similarly trained colleagues from other disciplines. Their staff and administrators are apprehensive about this situation, but not because they believe teaching interdisciplinary general education courses requires graduate training in many different disciplines. In most cases, what they seek is advice on how to conceptualise and design an interdisciplinary course and on how to set up sufficient opportunities for staff to learn about the other disciplinary perspectives from their colleagues. To facilitate this process, the Association for Integrative Studies (AIS—the national professional association of interdisciplinary staff and administrators) has provided consultants over the last half-dozen years for many colleges and universities starting or modifying such courses. A few years ago, AIS also offered a pre-conference workshop on designing and teaching interdisciplinary general education courses. If the expected funding materialises, an Institute in Integrative Studies will be established next year at Miami University that will provide key staff members from dozens of other colleges and universities planning interdisciplinary liberal education courses with exposure to the School of Interdisciplinary Studies and with a summer workshop providing training in interdisciplinary curriculum development and pedagogy so that they can create and teach their own interdisciplinary courses and then assist their colleagues in designing and teaching interdisciplinary courses.

Interdisciplinary general education courses are normally team-developed (and occasionally team-taught) by staff from different disciplines. Initial exposure to the perspectives of other disciplines on the topic of the course comes through the committee meetings in which the course is designed, both orally and from perusal of readings for the course proposed by other team members. Typically, however, agreement on the readings and the precise content of the course reflects faith in the expertise of one's colleagues as much as or more than it does a full appreciation of the perspective of their discipline. Many institutions provide release time during the school year or summer stipends for staff preparing new interdisciplinary courses to read outside their discipline and discuss these readings with one another. Even so, much of the command of other disciplinary perspectives ends up being developed as the course is taught. The single most common structural device for promoting staff insight into other disciplines is the weekly staff seminar. Here staff meet to discuss common readings for their individual sections of the same course or for their separate courses designed to meet the same general education requirement. Depending on which disciplinary perspective is reflected in that week's reading, different staff members will lead the discussion. It is in these seminars that staff confront the perspectives of other disciplines in rigorous detail and come to develop a respect for their strengths as well as a sense of their shortcomings.[1]

Primarily through these procedures, disciplinary staff now develop the requisite insights into the perspectives of one another's disciplines to teach interdisciplinary general education courses. More thorough grounding, such as the Institute in Integrative Studies will afford, is clearly desirable, but disciplinary staff who are veterans of two or three interdisciplinary courses typically develop a sympathetic feel and respect for the perspectives of other disciplines with which they have worked. Most have learned to work competently at the introductory level with a few concepts and perhaps a theory or two from that discipline, but they would quickly disclaim any expertise in those disciplines. The point is that interdisciplinary general education requires an informed appreciation of the perspective of other disciplines, not expertise in their full range of concepts, theories and methods.

Because it has the luxury of hiring staff to teach full time in interdisciplinary studies, the School of Interdisciplinary Studies can select staff with advanced training in more than one discipline or with previous interdisciplinary teaching experience. In fact, we have discovered that the key to successful interdisciplinary teaching is neither broad graduate training nor prior experience (though they are helpful indicators), but willingness, and preferably eagerness, to learn other perspectives. Pragmatically, even the broadest postgraduate training could not cover the range of disciplines staff end up utilising in their teaching in this programme, so they have to learn new disciplinary perspectives in any case. In fact, the depth and rigour of their postgraduate education is more important than its breadth. We want staff who have a sophisticated understanding of a discipline at the same time as they chafe under its limitations, so that when they turn to the task of learning about other disciplines, they will not content themselves with a superficial understanding of the aspects of the discipline they utilise in their courses.

Staff in the School of Interdisciplinary Studies have a number of resources at their disposal for learning about other disciplines. Foremost among these, perhaps, are the other staff at Miami University. Recently, Chris Wolfe and I developed a new interdisciplinary social science course for second-years on Social Movements and Strategies for Change, which included a section on Third World development. Even though I have been teaching interdisciplinary social science courses for over 20 years and am consequently quite familiar with the perspectives of each of the social sciences, I went around to each department in the social sciences at Miami University to talk with the staff member with the most expertise in development. I asked what topics the current professional literature examines under the general heading of Third World development, and what standard concepts and theories the discipline now uses to explore them. I spent hours with some disciplinary staff poring over texts and reading books. When I encountered an unfamiliar theory, I asked them to identify some key articles in the professional literature where I could learn more about it.

Disciplinary staff at Miami have also been most gracious about giving guest lectures in the School of Interdisciplinary Studies. Our courses typically meet for one lecture a week and then split up into separate discussion sections two or three times a week. Lectures can provide students with a historical, cultural or intellectual context within which to place the readings for the week, or they can present a relevant theory from a particular discipline. Staff as well as students in the programme learn from these guest lecturers about how their discipline approaches the topic.

Interdisciplinary courses that are offered a number of times in the School can also be enriched by the participation of staff with different disciplinary expertise. Each time a different staff member is brought into the team, the course is modified to take advantage of their insights. The 'Is Freedom Possible?' course described earlier has over the last 18 years had 10 different staff teaching it, with backgrounds as varied as American studies, anthropology, economics, history, sociology, political science and psychology (social, cognitive and phenomenological). Each left her or his mark on the course in the form of readings utilising concepts or theories that reflect a different perspective on individuality, rationality or autonomy.

The Visibility and Roles of Disciplines in Interdisciplinary Courses

Even if we accept that the interdisciplinary approach builds primarily on the perspectives of contributing disciplines, it is still unclear what else disciplines ought to contribute to interdisciplinary courses and how explicit that contribution should be. Is it necessary to present each discipline's concepts, theories and methods pertinent to the topic, or should it suffice to read what representatives of the various disciplines have to say on the topic? In other words, can a responsible interdisciplinary course focus on the conclusions from disciplinary analyses, or is it important to study how each discipline arrived at those conclusions?

While definitions of interdisciplinary studies differ from one staff member to another, more and more colleges and universities are opting for interdisciplinary courses that present disciplinary analyses of the topic instead of settling for an examination of their conclusions. How technical, rigorous or theoretical the analyses are appears to be more a function of the academic sophistication of the students than of any principled position on the nature of interdisciplinarity.

There is a principled argument to be made, however, for the explicit use of disciplinary analyses. If students are to develop a feel for a discipline's perspective, they must learn to think like a practitioner of that discipline. Members of a discipline are not so much characterised by the conclusions they arrive at, but by the way they approach the topic—the questions they ask, the concepts that come to mind and the theories behind them. Without some sense of these, we offer our students dogma rather than empowerment, training rather than education. A discipline's perspective provides the means by which it arrives at an answer, it is not the answer itself.

As mentioned earlier, practice varies widely within the School of Interdisciplinary Studies on the depth of disciplinary analyses in its interdisciplinary courses, though all of them explicitly present several disciplinary perspectives. Courses in the natural sciences make extensive use of technical concepts and theories in the development of disciplinary perspectives. Since they differ primarily in the scale of analysis, not in their underlying assumptions, these perspectives are seen as complementary, affording mutual context. The course on energy policy, for example, examines the geology of coal and oil formation, the physics of the Carnot engine, the chemistry of air pollution and the biological effects of low-level ionising radiation using the same concepts at the same level of technical detail and rigour as in introductory courses in those disciplines. In fact, some readings are drawn from standard introductory college-level texts in those disciplines.

Social science courses in the School make explicit use of disciplinary concepts and theories as well, though the emphasis seems to be on clear thinking more than technical rigour. Reflecting the nature of the social science disciplines themselves, these courses tend to present the various disciplinary perspectives as conflicting alternatives. Whether explicitly or implicitly, the social science courses consequently probe these perspectives for their underlying assumptions, in search of the source of the conflict and a basis on which to attempt their integration. The 'Is Freedom Possible?' course, to continue an earlier example, presents the theory of consumer behaviour from microeconomics and the principles of operant conditioning from behavioural psychology with the same rigour found in the natural science courses. More commonly, however, when concepts like socialisation and internalisation from sociology or emic and etic perspectives from anthropology are presented, the pedagogical emphasis is on their accurate usage more than their position in a theoretical structure. This difference in emphasis between the social and natural sciences again presumably reflects differences between the disciplines in these areas.

The humanities courses typically eschew jargon as they draw on 'ideas' (more than 'concepts') developed in the various disciplinary literatures. Their emphasis is more on clarity and creativity of expression than on precision and rigour. Still, they draw from time to time on identifiable concepts (e.g. 'thick description' from Geertz), theories (from women's studies, for example), or systems of thought (such as liberation theology).

In general, the number of concepts and theories drawn from disciplines and the rigour and technical precision with which they are developed seem to be a function of the nature of the disciplines involved and the academic strength of the students taught, more than of the particular definition of interdisciplinary studies. The presumed relationship between disciplinary perspectives (i.e. conflicting or complementary) also seems to reflect mostly the disciplines involved. In any case, there is an emerging consensus that students (no matter what their academic ability) must learn something of a discipline (whether in the natural or social sciences or the humanities) to develop a genuine appreciation of its perspective.

Disciplinary Outcomes of Interdisciplinary Courses

Even with agreement that interdisciplinary courses are grounded in disciplinary perspectives and should draw explicitly on the concepts, theories, methods and facts of the disciplines, that still leaves the question of just what students learn from these courses. Is anything of value learned in an interdisciplinary course beyond its disciplinary content? Are there any advantages to learning about disciplines within an interdisciplinary course? Do students gain any of the more general liberal arts skills claimed for disciplinary education, such as precise, critical thinking? Claims abound for interdisciplinary education, but they are seldom supported by more than anecdotes, impressions and *a priori* reasoning. While 'evidence' of this sort should not be dismissed out of hand—it may be of some use in deciding what to try or change in an ongoing interdisciplinary course—it is of no value in convincing sceptics and of modest value at best for staff deciding whether or not to offer interdisciplinary courses. The assessment of interdisciplinary education is treated at length in the article by Field & Lee in this issue, so the focus here is primarily on the kinds of evidence developed in the School of Interdisciplinary Studies.

One way to evaluate the disciplinary content of interdisciplinary courses is through pragmatic judgments by disciplinary departments. After reviewing syllabuses with staff from the School of Interdisciplinary Studies, the departments of sociology and political science at Miami University approved the first-year interdisciplinary social science courses as alternatives to their introductory courses: Interdisciplinary Studies majors may take any upper-division courses in those departments after their first year. The psychology department allows IS majors to take social psychology courses after the first year, and the economics department permits them to take intermediate microeconomic theory after the second year, each waiving the normally invariate disciplinary prerequisite. The zoology department accepts one of the first-year natural science courses as an alternative to one of its principles courses. The English department recognises the writing-across-the-curriculum programme as the only alternative to English 111, 112; in fact, members have said they would prefer all students at the university to learn English composition through such a programme. The School of Education accepts many of the interdisciplinary core courses in lieu of disciplinary requirements for teacher certification. In sort, staff protecting disciplinary standards in their departments have repeatedly been impressed by the disciplinary content of the interdisciplinary courses in the School of Interdisciplinary Studies.

Disciplinary departments also make judgments about the disciplinary competence of IS staff. Many staff in the School of Interdisciplinary Studies have received appointments as Affiliates from other departments, both so they can be eligible to teach courses and direct theses in the department, and so the department can take some credit for their publications. Several have been sought out to conduct joint research or develop joint performances with staff in these departments. When staff have been recommended by the School of Interdisciplinary Studies for promotion or tenure, they have (almost without exception) received approval as well by the all-university committee, which is accustomed to judging staff by traditional disciplinary standards. Generally speaking, disciplinary staff at Miami University have been favourably impressed by the disciplinary competence of the interdisciplinary staff.

Other strategies can be employed to determine how well an interdisciplinary education prepares students for disciplinary courses. For example, one can determine how well IS majors do in upper-division disciplinary courses. The only study of the performance of students from the School of Interdisciplinary Studies in disciplinary courses at Miami University found that approximately half the IS seniors had higher grade point averages in their disciplinary courses than in the interdisciplinary courses they took within the programme; the other half had lower averages outside the programme. Another approach is to examine the success of graduates of the School of Interdisciplinary Studies in gaining admission to disciplinary postgraduate schools. The proportion of IS majors who go on to work towards a PhD is higher than the national average: 22% for female alumni (compared to a national norm of 8% cited by American College Testing) and 14% for male alumni (compared to 12% nationally). All but 3% of the graduates of the programme have taken at least one postgraduate course and 75% report having earned more than 20 graduate credit hours. The average percentile ranking on the Law School Admission Test for IS majors applying to law schools was 85.7%. The average percentile ranking on the Graduate Record Examination for IS majors applying to graduate school was 79.3% (verbal) and 69.2% (quantitative). None of these measures constitutes proof of the effectiveness of interdisciplinary courses in preparing students for disciplinary education, but taken together they call into question the claim that interdisciplinary education disadvantages students in disciplinary settings.

The School of Interdisciplinary Studies has also undertaken several studies that assess the effectiveness of its interdisciplinary programme at providing skills traditionally associated with disciplinary education. The most comprehensive set of assessment instruments employed was the ACT College Outcomes Measurement Program (COMP/Assessment of Reasoning and Communication Test—Total, Speaking, Writing and Reasoning), which was administered to matched samples of freshmen and seniors from the School of Interdisciplinary Studies and from the rest of Miami University. IS seniors scored higher on every test instrument than either group of first-year students; in fact, they scored significantly (.05 level) higher on the ACT COMP Total than their freshman counterparts even though they started college with scores more than two points below them. In general, performance on standardised tests tends to show that students gain in traditional intellectual skills through an interdisciplinary education.

Instead of trying to measure disciplinary skills, one can look instead at student behaviour. One instrument that focuses on what students report that they do instead of what they know is the College Student Experiences Questionnaire, a nationally normed instrument which was again administered to students in the School of Interdisciplinary Studies as well as to a sample (n = 428) of students from the rest of Miami University. While there are 142 questions in the questionnaire and 87 where the responses of IS majors were significantly different from those of other Miami students or from the norm of highly selective liberal arts colleges, a few will quickly give a feel for the nature of those differences. (Responses are given for majors in the School of Interdisciplinary Studies, with those for the Miami sample and the selective liberal arts colleges norm respectively, in parentheses thereafter.) Often/very often 'worked with staff on a research project': 20% (4%, 10%). Very often 'thought about practical applications [of ideas from the classroom]': 63% (32%, 35%). Very often 'revised a paper twice or more': 24% (18%, 19%). Often/very often engaged in discussion outside class in which they 'referred to knowledge from [course] reading': 88% (50%, 70%). Often/very often 'changed opinion after discussion': 40% (25%, 23%). Read more than 20 assigned books in the last year: 49% (12%, 40%). More than 10 nonassigned books read: 24% (33%, 29%). These responses do not measure the quality of these traditional academic behaviour patterns, but they do demonstrate that an interdisciplinary programme can promote the kinds of behaviour that typically lead to the development of intellectual skills, attitudes and values prized by traditional disciplinary education.

Finally, the School of Interdisciplinary Studies has assessed its impact through retrospective evaluations of their education by its graduates. In a 1983 study with an unusually high response rate (75% of all graduates), 83% rated preparation for career in the highest two categories, and 91% rated satisfaction with the academic programme similarly. A 1986/87 longitudinal study of alumni (with a response rate judged 'extremely high' in professional reports on the ACT instrument used) found that 84% compared the School favourably to other colleges (compared to a national norm of 36%); 76% said it helped them define and solve problems (vs. a norm of 44%). In general, skills acquisition was rated very highly: writing 85% (vs. a norm of 40%), speaking 51% (vs. a norm 35%) and working independently 78% (vs. norm 54%).

Having reviewed some pragmatic evidence which suggests that the School of Interdisciplinary Studies does indeed provide solid grounding in the disciplines and the skills it promotes, it may be useful to step back and ask why one might reasonably expect that interdisciplinary courses would develop in students the skills of rigorous and critical thinking that have long been associated with traditional disciplinary education. From what has been said earlier in this article about the role of disciplines in interdisciplinary courses, it should be quite evident why interdisciplinary courses promote intellectual rigour: concepts, theories and methods from various disciplines are presented with exactly the same rigour as in traditional disciplinary courses. Students undergo the same intellectual challenges as they confront the indifference curves and budget constraints of the theory of consumer behaviour whether they learn it in 'Principles of Microeconomics' or in 'Is Freedom Possible?' Since interdisciplinary courses are constructed from pieces of disciplines, it should not be surprising that they yield many of the same educational outcomes, and if students have been exposed to enough pieces of a discipline through their interdisciplinary courses, that they are adequately prepared for many advanced disciplinary courses.

But interdisciplinary courses are more than the pieces of disciplines from which they are constructed. They extract the world view or perspective embedded in each of those pieces, comparing them and ferreting out their underlying assumptions when they conflict, and then integrating or synthesising them into a broader, more holistic perspective.

This interdisciplinary process is ideally suited for the promotion of what Richard Paul (1987) calls 'strong sense critical thinking,' while disciplinary courses are often more likely to promote 'weak sense critical thinking.' The latter includes a number of valuable informal logic skills such as distinguishing evidence from conclusions, relevant from irrelevant facts, and facts from ideals; assessing the validity of assumptions and arguments; and recognising internal contradictions, implicit value judgments, unstated implications of arguments, and the power and appropriateness of rhetorical devices. Stated most broadly, strong sense critical thinking involves turning that critical eye inward upon oneself, becoming critically self-reflective. Through the identification of the assumptions and values of competing perspectives, including those they find most appealing, students are encouraged to recognise and formulate a critique of their own irrationally held beliefs and biases. Through the process of deriving insights into a topic from diverse disciplinary perspectives, students learn what

Paul terms 'multilogical' thinking—'the ability to think accurately and fair-mindedly within opposing points of view and contradictory frames of reference'—as well as 'the ability to enter sympathetically into and reconstruct the strongest arguments for points of view fundamentally opposed' to their own.

Interdisciplinary courses are as well suited to the development of these skills as disciplinary courses are for the former ones. Since both weak and strong sense critical thinking are important to what most of us expect of a liberal arts education, it appears that students would be best served by a balanced curriculum of disciplinary and interdisciplinary courses. And since interdisciplinary courses depend on the disciplines for their perspectives as much as disciplinary courses depend on interdisciplinary ones to provide context and restraint, it may be that such a balanced curriculum would make both disciplinary and interdisciplinary courses stronger.

Note

1. Interestingly enough, it is through discussion of the readings from their own discipline with colleagues from other disciplines that staff come to see, often for the first time, the limitations as well as the comparative strengths of their own discipline's perspective. This unexpected side-effect of interdisciplinary teaching, a revised understanding of one's own discipline, can have powerful effects on how staff subsequently design and teach disciplinary courses in their own departments.

References

Newell, W.H. (1988) Interdisciplinary studies are alive and well, *The National Honors Report*, 9(2), pp. 5–6.
Paul, R.W. (1987) Critical thinking and the critical person, in: D. Perkins, J. Lochhead & J. Bishop (Eds) *Thinking: the second international conference* (Hillsdale, NJ, Lawrence Erlbaum Associates), pp. 373–403.

Blurred Genres

The Refiguration of Social Thought

Clifford Geertz

I

Certain truths about the social sciences today seem self-evident. One is that in recent years there has been an enormous amount of genre mixing in social science, as in intellectual life generally, and such blurring of kinds is continuing apace. Another is that many social scientists have turned away from a laws-and-instances ideal of explanation toward a cases-and-interpretations one, looking less for the sort of thing that connects planets and pendulums and more for the sort that connects chrysanthemums and swords. Yet another truth is that analogies drawn from the humanities are coming to play the kind of role in sociological understanding that analogies drawn from the crafts and technology have long played in physical understanding. I not only think these things are true, I think they are true together; and the culture shift that makes them so is the subject of this essay: the refiguration of social thought.

This genre blurring is more than just a matter of Harry Houdini or Richard Nixon turning up as characters in novels or of midwestern murder sprees described as though a gothic romancer had imagined them. It is philosophical inquiries looking like literary criticism (think of Stanley Cavell on Beckett or Thoreau, Sartre on Flaubert), scientific discussions looking like belles lettres *morceaux* (Lewis Thomas, Loren Eiseley), baroque fantasies presented as dead-pan empirical observations (Borges, Barthelme), histories that consist of equations and tables or law court testimony (Fogel and Engerman, Le Roi Ladurie), documentaries that read like true confessions (Mailer), parables posing as ethnographies (Castenada), theoretical treatises set out as travelogues (Lévi-Strauss), ideological arguments cast as historiographical inquiries (Edward Said), epistemological studies constructed like political tracts (Paul Feyerabend), methodological polemics got up as personal memoirs (James Watson). Nabokov's *Pale Fire,* that impossible object made of poetry and fiction, footnotes and images from the clinic, seems very much of the time; one waits only for quantum theory in verse or biography in algebra.

Of course, to a certain extent this sort of thing has always gone on—Lucretius, Mandeville, and Erasmus Darwin all made their theories rhyme. But the present jumbling of varieties of discourse has grown to the point where it is becoming difficult either to label authors (What *is* Foucault—historian,

Geertz, Clifford. *"Blurred Genres: The Refiguration of Social Thought."* The American Scholar *49:2 (Spring 1980), 165–79. Copyright © 1980 by the author. Reprinted by permission of the publisher.*

philosopher, political theorist? What Thomas Kuhn—historian, philosopher, sociologist of knowledge?) or to classify works (What is George Steiner's *After Babel*—linguistics, criticism, culture history? What William Gass's *On Being Blue*—treatise, causerie, apologetic?). And thus it is more than a matter of odd sports and occasional curiosities, or of the admitted fact that the innovative is, by definition, hard to categorize. It is a phenomenon general enough and distinctive enough to suggest that what we are seeing is not just another redrawing of the cultural map—the moving of a few disputed borders, the marking of some more picturesque mountain lakes—but an alteration of the principles of mapping. Something is happening to the way we think about the way we think.

We need not accept hermetic views of *écriture* as so many signs signing signs, or give ourselves so wholly to the pleasure of the text that its meaning disappears into our responses, to see that there has come into our view of what we read and what we write a distinctly democratical temper. The properties connecting texts with one another, that put them, ontologically anyway, on the same level, are coming to seem as important in characterizing them as those dividing them; and rather than face an array of natural kinds, fixed types divided by sharp qualitative differences, we more and more see ourselves surrounded by a vast, almost continuous field of variously intended and diversely constructed works we can order only practically, relationally, and as our purposes prompt us. It is not that we no longer have conventions of interpretation; we have more than ever, built—often enough jerry-built—to accommodate a situation at once fluid, plural, uncentered, and ineradicably untidy.

So far as the social sciences are concerned, all this means that their oft-lamented lack of character no longer sets them apart. It is even more difficult than it always has been to regard them as underdeveloped natural sciences, awaiting only time and aid from more advanced quarters to harden them, or as ignorant and pretentious usurpers of the mission of the humanities, promising certainties where none can be, or as comprising a clearly distinctive enterprise, a third culture between Snow's canonical two. But that is all to the good: freed from having to become taxonomically upstanding, because nobody else is, individuals thinking of themselves as social (or behavioral or human or cultural) scientists have become free to shape their work in terms of its necessities rather than received ideas as to what they ought or ought not to be doing. What Clyde Kluckhohn once said about anthropology—that it's an intellectual poaching license—not only seems more true now than when he said it, but true of a lot more than anthropology. Born omniform, the social sciences prosper as the condition I have been describing becomes general.

It has thus dawned on social scientists that they did not need to be mimic physicists or closet humanists or to invent some new realm of being to serve as the object of their investigations. Instead they could proceed with their vocation, trying to discover order in collective life, and decide how what they were doing was connected to related enterprises when they managed to get some of it done; and many of them have taken an essentially hermeneutic—or, if that word frightens, conjuring up images of biblical zealots, literary humbugs, and Teutonic professors, an "interpretive"—approach to their task. Given the new genre dispersion, many have taken other approaches: structuralism, neo-positivism, neo-Marxism, micro-micro descriptivism, macro-macro system building, and that curious combination of common sense and common nonsense, sociobiology. But the move toward conceiving of social life as organized in terms of symbols (signs, representations, *signifiants, Darstellungen* . . . the terminology varies), whose meaning (sense, import, *signification, Bedeutung* . . .) we must grasp if we are to understand that organization and formulate its principles, has grown by now to formidable proportions. The woods are full of eager interpreters.

Interpretive explanation—and it is a form of explanation, not just exalted glossography—trains its attention on what institutions, actions, images, utterances, events, customs, all the usual objects of social-scientific interest, mean to those whose institutions, actions, customs, and so on they are. As a result, it issues not in laws like Boyle's, or forces like Volta's, or mechanisms like Darwin's, but in constructions like Burckhardt's, Weber's, or Freud's: systematic unpackings of the conceptual world in which *condottiere,* Calvinists, or paranoids live.

The manner of these constructions itself varies: Burckhardt portrays, Weber models, Freud diagnoses. But they all represent attempts to formulate how this people or that, this period or that, this person or that, makes sense to itself and, understanding that, what we understand about social order, historical change, or psychic functioning in general. Inquiry is directed toward cases or sets of cases, and toward the particular features that mark them off; but its aims are as far-reaching as those of mechanics or physiology: to distinguish the materials of human experience.

With such aims and such a manner of pursuing them come as well some novelties in analytical rhetoric, the tropes and imageries of explanation. As theory, scientific or otherwise, moves mainly by analogy, a "seeing-as" comprehension of the less intelligible by the more (the earth is a magnet, the heart is a pump, light is a wave, the brain is a computer, and space is a balloon), when its course shifts, the conceits in which it expresses itself shift with it. In the earlier stages of the natural sciences, before the analogies became so heavily intramural—and in those (cybernetics, neurology) in which they still have not—it has been the world of the crafts and, later, of industry that has for the most part provided the well-understood realities (well-understood because, *certum quod factum,* as Vico said, man had made them) with which the ill-understood ones (ill-understood because he had not) could be brought into the circle of the known. Science owes more to the steam engine than the steam engine owes to science; without the dyer's art there would be no chemistry; metallurgy is mining theorized. In the social sciences, or at least in those that have abandoned a reductionist conception of what they are about, the analogies are coming more and more from the contrivances of cultural performance than from those of physical manipulation—from theater, painting, grammar, literature, law, play. What the lever did for physics, the chess move promises to do for sociology.

Promises are not always kept, of course, and when they are, they often turn out to have been threats; but the casting of social theory in terms more familiar to gamesters and aestheticians than to plumbers and engineers is clearly well under way. The recourse to the humanities for explanatory analogies in the social sciences is at once evidence of the destabilization of genres and of the rise of "the interpretive turn," and their most visible outcome is a revised style of discourse in social studies. The instruments of reasoning are changing and society is less and less represented as an elaborate machine or a quasi-organism than as a serious game, a sidewalk drama, or a behavioral text.

II

All this fiddling around with the proprieties of composition, inquiry, and explanation represents, of course, a radical alteration in the sociological imagination, propelling it in directions both difficult and unfamiliar. And like all such changes in fashions of the mind, it is about as likely to lead to obscurity and illusion as it is to precision and truth. If the result is not to be elaborate chatter or the higher nonsense, a critical consciousness will have to be developed; and as so much more of the imagery, method, theory, and style is to be drawn from the humanities than previously, it will mostly have to come from humanists and their apologists rather than from natural scientists and theirs. That humanists, after years of regarding social scientists as technologists or interlopers, are ill equipped to do this is something of an understatement.

Social scientists, having just freed themselves, and then only partially, from dreams of social physics—covering laws, unified science, operationalism, and all that—are hardly any better equipped. For them, the general muddling of vocational identities could not have come at a better time. If they are going to develop systems of analysis in which such conceptions as following a rule, constructing a representation, expressing an attitude, or forming an intention are going to play central roles—rather than such conceptions as isolating a cause, determining a variable, measuring a force, or defining a function—they are going to need all the help they can get from people who are more at home among such notions than they are. It is not interdisciplinary brotherhood that is needed, nor even less highbrow eclecticism. It is recognition on all sides that the lines grouping scholars together into intellectual communities, or (what is the same thing) sorting them out into different ones, are these days running at some highly eccentric angles.

The point at which the reflections of humanists on the practices of social scientists seems most urgent is with respect to the deployment in social analysis of models drawn from humanist domains—that "wary reasoning from analogy," as Locke called it, that "leads us often into the discovery of truths and useful productions, which would otherwise lie concealed." (Locke was talking about rubbing two sticks together to produce fire and the atomic-friction theory of heat, though business partnership and the social contract would have served him as well.) Keeping the reasoning wary, thus useful, thus true, is, as we say, the name of the game.

The game analogy is both increasingly popular in contemporary social theory and increasingly in need of critical examination. The impetus for seeing one or another sort of social behavior as one or another sort of game has come from a number of sources (not excluding, perhaps, the prominence of spectator sports in mass society). But the most important are Wittgenstein's conception of forms of life as language games, Huizinga's ludic view of culture, and the new strategies of von Neumann's and Morgenstern's *Theory of Games and Economic Behavior*. From Wittgenstein has come the notion of intentional action as "following a rule"; from Huizinga, of play as the paradigm form of collective life; from von Neumann and Morgenstern, of social behavior as a reciprocative maneuvering toward distributive payoffs. Taken together they conduce to a nervous and nervous-making style of interpretation in the social sciences that mixes a strong sense of the formal orderliness of things with an equally strong sense of the radical arbitrariness of that order: chessboard inevitability that could as well have worked out otherwise.

The writings of Erving Goffman—perhaps the most celebrated American sociologist right now, and certainly the most ingenious—rest, for example, almost entirely on the game analogy. (Goffman also employs the language of the stage quite extensively, but as his view of the theater is that it is an oddly mannered kind of interaction game—Ping-Pong in masks—his work is not, at base, really dramaturgical.) Goffman applies game imagery to just about everything he can lay his hands on, which, as he is no respecter of property rights, is a very great deal. The to-and-fro of lies, meta-lies, unbelievable truths, threats, tortures, bribes, and blackmail that comprises the world of espionage is construed as an "expression game"; a carnival of deceptions rather like life in general, because, in a phrase that could have come from Conrad or Le Carré, "agents [are] a little like us all and all of us [are] a little like agents." Etiquette, diplomacy, crime, finance, advertising, law, seduction, and the everyday "realm of bantering decorum" are seen as "information games"—mazy structures of players, teams, moves, positions, signals, information states, gambles, and outcomes, in which only the "gameworthy"—those willing and able "to dissemble about anything"—prosper.

What goes on in a psychiatric hospital, or any hospital or prison or even a boarding school in Goffman's work is a "ritual game of having a self," where the staff holds most of the face cards and all of the trumps. A tête-à-tête, a jury deliberation, "a task jointly pursued by persons physically close to one another," a couple dancing, lovemaking, or boxing—indeed all face-to-face encounters—are games in which, "as every psychotic and comic ought to know, any accurately improper move can poke through the thin sleeve of immediate reality." Social conflict, deviance, entrepreneurship, sex roles, religious rites, status ranking, and the simple need for human acceptance get the same treatment. Life is just a bowl of strategies.

Or, perhaps better, as Damon Runyon once remarked, it is three-to-two against. For the image of society that emerges from Goffman's work, and from that of the swarm of scholars who in one way or another follow or depend on him, is of an unbroken stream of gambits, ploys, artifices, bluffs, disguises, conspiracies, and outright impostures as individuals and coalitions of individuals struggle—sometimes cleverly, more often comically—to play enigmatical games whose structure is clear but whose point is not. Goffman's is a radically unromantic vision of things, acrid and bleakly knowing, and one which sits rather poorly with traditional humanistic pieties. But it is no less powerful for that. Nor, with its uncomplaining play-it-as-it-lays ethic, is it all that inhumane.

However that may be, not all gamelike conceptions of social life are quite so grim, and some are positively frolicsome. What connects them all is the view that human beings are less driven by forces than submissive to rules, that the rules are such as to suggest strategies, the strategies are such as to inspire actions, and the actions are such as to be self-rewarding—*pour le sport*. As literal games—baseball or poker or Parcheesi—create little universes of meaning, in which some things can be done and some cannot (you can't castle in dominoes), so too do the analogical ones of worship, government, or sexual courtship (you can't mutiny in a bank). Seeing society as a collection of games means seeing it as a grand plurality of accepted conventions and appropriate procedures—tight, airless worlds of move and countermove, life *en règle,* "I wonder," Prince Metternich is supposed to have said when an aide whispered into his ear at a royal ball that the czar of all the Russians was dead, "I wonder what his motive could have been."

The game analogy is not a view of things that is likely to commend itself to humanists, who like to think of people not as obeying the rules and angling for advantage but as acting freely and realizing their finer capacities. But that it seems to explain a great deal about a great many aspects of modern life, and in many ways to catch its tone, is hardly deniable. ("If you can't stand the Machiavellianism," as a recent *New Yorker* cartoon said, "get out of the cabal.") Thus if it is to be countered it cannot be by mere disdain, refusing to look through the telescope, or by passioned restatements of hallowed truths, quoting scripture against the sun. It is necessary to get down to the details of the matter, to examine the studies and to critique the interpretations—whether Goffman's of crime as character gambling, Harold Garfinkel's of sex change as identity play, Gregory Bateson's of schizophrenia as rule confusion, or my own of the complicated goings-on in a mideastern bazaar as an information contest. As social theory turns from propulsive metaphors (the language of pistons) toward ludic ones (the language of pastimes), the humanities are connected to its arguments not in the fashion of skeptical bystanders but, as the source of its imagery, chargeable accomplices.

III

The drama analogy for social life has of course been around in a casual sort of way—all the world's a stage and we but poor players who strut and so on—for a very long time. And terms from the stage, most notably "role," have been staples of sociological discourse since at least the 1930s. What is relatively new—new, not unprecedented—are two things. First, the full weight of the analogy is coming to be applied extensively and systematically, rather than being deployed piecemeal fashion—a few allusions here, a few tropes there. And second, it is coming to be applied less in the depreciatory "mere show," masks and mummery mode that has tended to characterize its general use, and more in a constructional, genuinely dramaturgical one—making, not faking, as the anthropologist Victor Turner has put it.

The two developments are linked, of course. A constructionalist view of what theater is—that is, poiesis—implies that a dramatistic perspective in the social sciences needs to involve more than pointing out that we all have our entrances and exits, we all play parts, miss cues, and love pretense. It may or may not be a Barnum and Bailey world and we may or may not be walking shadows, but to take the drama analogy seriously is to probe behind such familiar ironies to the expressive devices that make collective life seem anything at all. The trouble with analogies—it is also their glory—is that they connect what they compare in both directions. Having trifled with theater's idiom, some social scientists find themselves drawn into the rather tangled coils of its aesthetic.

Such a more thoroughgoing exploitation of the drama analogy in social theory—as an analogy, not an incidental metaphor—has grown out of sources in the humanities not altogether commensurable. On the one hand, there has been the so-called ritual theory of drama associated with such diverse figures as Jane Harrison, Francis Fergusson, T. S. Eliot, and Antonin Artaud. On the other, there is the symbolic action—"dramatism," as he calls it—of the American literary theorist and philosopher Kenneth Burke, whose influence is, in the United States anyway, at once enormous and—because almost no one actually uses his baroque vocabulary, with its reductions, ratios, and so on—elusive. The trouble is, these approaches pull in rather opposite directions: the ritual theory toward the affinities of theater and religion—drama as communion, the temple as stage; the symbolic action theory toward those of theater and rhetoric—drama as persuasion, the platform as stage. And this leaves the basis of the analogy—just what in the theatron is like what in the agora—hard to focus. That liturgy and ideology are histrionic is obvious enough, as it is that etiquette and advertising are. But just what that means is a good deal less so.

Probably the foremost proponent of the ritual theory approach in the social sciences right now is Victor Turner. A British formed, American re-formed anthropologist, Turner, in a remarkable series of works trained on the ceremonial life of a Central African tribe, has developed a conception of "social drama" as a regenerative process that, rather like Goffman's of "social gaming" as strategic interaction, has drawn to it such a large number of able researchers as to produce a distinct and powerful interpretive school.

For Turner, social dramas occur "on all levels of social organization from state to family." They arise out of conflict situations—a village falls into factions, a husband beats a wife, a region rises against the state—and proceed to their denouements through publicly performed conventionalized behavior. As the conflict swells to crisis and the excited fluidity of heightened emotion, where people feel at once more enclosed in a common mood and loosened from their social moorings, ritualized forms of authority—litigation, feud, sacrifice, prayer—are invoked to contain it and render it orderly. If they succeed, the breach is healed and the status quo, or something resembling it, is restored; if they do not, it is accepted as incapable of remedy and things fall apart into various sorts of unhappy endings: migrations, divorces, or murders in the cathedral. With differing degrees of strictness and detail, Turner and his followers have applied this schema to tribal passage rites, curing ceremonies, and judicial processes; to Mexican insurrections, Icelandic sagas, and Thomas Becket's difficulties with Henry II; to picaresque narrative, millenarian movements, Caribbean carnivals, and Indian peyote hunts; and to the political upheaval of the sixties. A form for all seasons.

This hospitableness in the face of cases is at once the major strength of the ritual theory version of the drama analogy and its most prominent weakness. It can expose some of the profoundest features of social process, but at the expense of making vividly disparate matters look drably homogeneous.

Rooted as it is in the repetitive performance dimensions of social action—the reenactment and thus the reexperiencing of known form—the ritual theory not only brings out the temporal and collective dimensions of such action and its inherently public nature with particular sharpness; it brings out also its power to transmute not just opinions, but, as the British critic Charles Morgan has said with respect to drama proper, the people who hold them. "The great impact [of the theater]," Morgan writes, "is neither a persuasion of the intellect nor a beguiling of the senses. . . . It is the enveloping movement of the whole drama on the soul of man. We surrender and are changed." Or at least we are when the magic works. What Morgan, in another fine phrase, calls "the suspense of form . . . the incompleteness of a known completion," is the source of the power of this "enveloping movement," a power, as the ritual theorists have shown, that is hardly less forceful (and hardly less likely to be seen as otherworldly) when the movement appears in a female initiation rite, a peasant revolution, a national epic, or a star chamber.

Yet these formally similar processes have different content. They say, as we might put it, rather different things, and thus have rather different implications for social life. And though ritual theorists are hardly incognizant of that fact, they are, precisely because they are so concerned with the general movement of things, ill-equipped to deal with it. The great dramatic rhythms, the commanding forms of theater, are perceived in social processes of all sorts, shapes, and significances (though ritual theorists in fact do much better with the cyclical, restorative periodicities of comedy than the linear, consuming progressions of tragedy, whose ends tend to be seen as misfires rather than fulfillments). Yet the individuating details, the sort of thing that makes *A Winter's Tale* different from *Measure for Measure*, *Macbeth* from *Hamlet*, are left to encyclopedic empiricism: massive documentation of a single proposition—*plus ça change, plus c'est le même changement*. If dramas are, to adapt a phrase of Susanne Langer's, poems in the mode of action, something is being missed: what exactly, socially, the poems say.

This unpacking of performed meaning is what the symbolic action approaches are designed to accomplish. Here there is no single name to cite, just a growing catalogue of particular studies, some dependent on Kenneth Burke, some on Ernst Cassirer, Northrop Frye, Michel Foucault, or Emile Durkheim, concerned to say what some bit of acted saying—a coronation, a sermon, a riot, an execution—says. If ritual theorists, their eye on experience, tend to be hedgehogs, symbolic action theorists, their eye on expression, tend to be foxes.

Given the dialectical nature of things, we all need our opponents, and both sorts of approach are essential. What we are most in want of right now is some way of synthesizing them. In my own about-to-be-published analysis of the traditional Indic polity in Bali as a "theater state"—cited here not because it is exemplary, but because it is mine—I have tried to address this problem. In this analysis I am concerned, on the one hand (the Burkean one), to show how everything from kin group organization, trade, customary law, and water control, to mythology, architecture, iconography, and cremation combines to a dramatized statement of a distinct form of political theory, a particular conception of what status, power, authority, and government are and should be: namely, a replication of the world of the gods that is at the same time a template for that of men. The state enacts an image of order that—a model for its beholders, in and of itself—orders society. On the other hand (the Turner one), as the populace at large does not merely view the state's expressions as so many gaping spectators but is caught up bodily in them, and especially in the great, mass ceremonies—political operas of Burgundian dimensions—which form their heart, the sort of "we surrender and are changed" power of drama to shape experience is the strong force that holds the polity together. Reiterated form, staged and acted by its own audience, makes (to a degree, for no theater ever wholly works) theory fact.

But my point is that some of those fit to judge work of this kind ought to be humanists who reputedly know something about what theater and mimesis and rhetoric are, and not just with respect to my work but to that of the whole steadily broadening stream of social analyses in which the drama analogy is, in one form or another, governing. At a time when social scientists are chattering about actors, scenes, plots, performances, and personae, and humanists are mumbling about motives, authority, persuasion, exchange, and hierarchy, the line between the two, however comforting to the puritan on the one side and the cavalier on the other, seems uncertain indeed.

IV

The text analogy now taken up by social scientists is, in some ways, the broadest of the recent refigurations of social theory, the most venturesome, and the least well developed. Even more than "game" or "drama," "text" is a dangerously unfocused term, and its application to social action, to people's behavior toward other people, involves a thoroughgoing conceptual wrench, a particularly outlandish bit of "seeing-as." Describing human conduct in the analogy of player and counterplayer, or of actor and audience, seems, whatever the pitfalls, rather more natural than describing it in that of writer and reader. Prima facie, the suggestion that the activities of spies, lovers, witch doctors, kings, or mental patients are moves or performances is surely a good deal more plausible than the notion that they are sentences.

But prima facie is a dubious guide when it comes to analogizing; were it not, we should still be thinking of the heart as a furnace and the lungs as bellows. The text analogy has some unapparent advantages still insufficiently exploited, and the surface dissimilarity of the here-we-are-and-there-we-are of social interaction to the solid composure of lines on a page is what gives it—or can when the disaccordance is rightly aligned—its interpretive force.

The key to the transition from text to text analogue, from writing as discourse to action as discourse, is, as Paul Ricoeur has pointed out, the concept of "inscription": the fixation of meaning. When we speak, our utterances fly by as events like any other behavior; unless what we say is inscribed in writing (or some other established recording process), it is as evanescent as what we do. If it is so inscribed, it of course passes, like Dorian Gray's youth, anyway; but at least its meaning—the *said,* not the *saying*—to a degree and for a while remains. This too is not different for action in general: its meaning can persist in a way its actuality cannot.

The great virtue of the extension of the notion of text beyond things written on paper or carved into stone is that it trains attention on precisely this phenomenon: on how the inscription of action is brought about, what its vehicles are and how they work, and on what the fixation of meaning from the flow of events—history from what happened, thought from thinking, culture from behavior—implies for sociological interpretation. To see social institutions, social customs, social changes as in some sense "readable" is to alter our whole sense of what such interpretation is toward modes of thought rather more familiar to the translator, the exegete, or the iconographer than to the test giver, the factor analyst, or the pollster.

All this comes out with exemplary vividness in the work of Alton Becker, a comparative linguist, on Javanese shadow puppetry, or the *wayang* as it is called. Wayang-ing (there is no other suitable verb) is, Becker says, a mode of text building, a way of putting symbols together to construct an expression. To construe it, to understand not just what it means but how it does so, one needs, he says, a new philology.

Philology, the text-centered study of language, as contrasted to linguistics, which is speech centered, has of course traditionally been concerned with making ancient or foreign or esoteric documents accessible to those for whom they are ancient or foreign or esoteric. Terms are glossed, notes appended, commentaries written, and, where necessary, transcriptions made and translations effected—all toward the end of producing an annotated edition as readable as the philologist can make it. Meaning is fixed at a meta-level; essentially what a philologist, a kind of secondary author, does is re-inscribe: interpret a text with a text.

Left at this, matters are straightforward enough, however difficult they may turn out to be in practice. But when philological concern goes beyond routinized craft procedures (authentication, reconstruction, annotation) to address itself to conceptual questions concerning the nature of texts as such—that is, to questions about their principles of construction—simplicity flees. The result, Becker notes, has been the shattering of philology, itself by now a near obsolescent term, into disjunct and rivalrous specialties, and most particularly the growth of a division between those who study individual texts (historians, editors, critics—who like to call themselves humanists), and those who study the activity of creating texts in general (linguists, psychologists, ethnographers—who like to call themselves scientists). The study of inscriptions is severed from the study of inscribing, the study of fixed meaning is severed from the study of the social processes that fix it. The result is a double narrowness. Not only is the extension of text analysis to non-written materials blocked, but so is the application of sociological analysis to written ones.

The repair of this split and the integration of the study of how texts are built, how the said is rescued from its saying, into the study of social phenomena—Apache jokes, English meals, African cult sermons, American high schools, Indian caste, or Balinese widow burning, to mention some recent attempts aside from Becker's—is what the "new philology," or whatever else it eventually comes to be called, is all about. "In a multicultured world," Becker writes, "a world of multiple epistemologies, there is need for a new philologist—a specialist in contextual relations—in all areas of knowledge in which text-building . . . is a central activity: literature, history, law, music, politics, psychology, trade, even war and peace."

Becker sees four main orders of semiotic connection in a social text for his new philologist to investigate: the relation of its parts to one another; the relation of it to others culturally or historically associated with it; the relation of it to those who in some sense construct it; and the relation of it to realities conceived as lying outside of it. Certainly there are others—its relation to its *materia,* for one; and, more certainly yet, even these raise profound methodological issues so far only hesitantly addressed. "Coherence," "inter-textuality," "intention," and "reference"—which are what Becker's four relations more or less come down to—all become most elusive notions when one leaves the paragraph or page for the act or institution. Indeed, as Nelson Goodman has shown, they are not all that well-defined for the paragraph or page, to say nothing of the picture, the melody, the statue, or the dance. Insofar as the theory of meaning implied by this multiple contextualization of cultural phenomena (some sort of symbolic constructivism) exists at all, it does so as a catalogue of wavering intimations and half-joined ideas.

How far this sort of analysis can go beyond such specifically expressive matters as puppetry, and what adjustments it will have to make in doing so, is, of course, quite unclear. As "life is a game" proponents tend to gravitate toward face-to-face interaction, courtship and cocktail parties, as the most fertile ground for their sort of analysis, and "life is a stage" proponents are attracted toward collective intensities, carnivals and insurrections, for the same reason, so "life is a text" proponents incline toward the examination of imaginative forms: jokes, proverbs, popular arts. There is nothing either surprising or reprehensible in this; one naturally tries one's analogies out where they seem most likely to work. But their long-run fates surely rest on their capacity to move beyond their easier initial successes to harder and less predictable ones—of the game idea to make sense of worship, the drama idea to explicate humor, or the text idea to clarify war. Most of these triumphs, if they are to occur at all, are, in the text case even more than the others, still to come. For the moment, all the apologist can do is what I have done here: offer up some instances of application, some symptoms of trouble, and some pleas for help.

V

So much, anyway, for examples. Not only do these particular three analogies obviously spill over into one another as individual writers tack back and forth between ludic, dramatistic, and textualist idioms, but there are other humanistic analogies on the social science scene at least as prominent as they: speech act analyses following Austin and Searle; discourse models as different as those of Habermas's "communicative competence" and Foucault's "archaeology of knowledge"; representationalist approaches taking their lead from the cognitive aesthetics of Cassirer, Langer, Gombrich, or Goodman; and of course Lévi-Strauss's higher cryptology. Nor are they as yet internally settled and homogeneous: the divisions between the play-minded and the strategy-minded to which I alluded in connection with the game approach, and between the ritualists and the rhetoricians in connection with the drama approach, are more than matched in the text approach by the collisions between the against-interpretation mandarins of deconstructionalism and the symbolic-domination tribunes of neo-Marxism. Matters are neither stable nor consensual, and they are not likely soon to become so. The interesting question is not how all this muddle is going to come magnificently together, but what does all this ferment mean.

One thing it means is that, however raggedly, a challenge is being mounted to some of the central assumptions of mainstream social science. The strict separation of theory and data, the "brute fact" idea; the effort to create a formal vocabulary of analysis purged of all subjective reference, the "ideal language" idea; and the claim to moral neutrality and the Olympian view, the "God's truth" idea—none of these can prosper when explanation comes to be regarded as a matter of connecting action to its sense rather than behavior to its determinants. The refiguration of social theory represents, or will if it continues, a sea change in our notion not so much of what knowledge is, but of what it is we want to know. Social events do have causes and social institutions effects; but it just may be that the road to discovering what we assert in asserting this lies less through postulating forces and measuring them than through noting expressions and inspecting them.

The turn taken by an important segment of social scientists, from physical process analogies to symbolic form ones, has introduced a fundamental debate into the social science community concerning not just its methods but its aims. It is a debate that grows daily in intensity. The golden age (or perhaps it was only the brass) of the social sciences when, whatever the differences in theoretical positions and empirical claims, the basic goal of the enterprise was universally agreed upon—to find out the dynamics of collective life and alter them in desired directions—has clearly passed. There are too many social scientists at work today for whom the anatomization of thought is wanted, not the manipulation of behavior.

But it is not only for the social sciences that this alteration in how we think about how we think has disequilibrating implications. The rising interest of sociologists, anthropologists, psychologists, political scientists, and even now and then a rogue economist in the analysis of symbol systems poses—implicitly anyway, explicitly sometimes—the question of the relationship of such systems to what goes on in the world; and it does so in a way both rather different from what humanists are used to and rather less evadable—with homilies about spiritual values and the examined life—than many of them, so it seems, would at all like.

If the social technologist notion of what a social scientist is is brought into question by all this concern with sense and signification, even more so is the cultural watchdog notion of what a humanist is. The specialist without spirit dispensing policy nostrums goes, but the lectern sage dispensing approved judgments does as well. The relation between thought and action in social life can no more be conceived of in terms of wisdom than it can in terms of expertise. How it is to be conceived, how the games, dramas, or texts which we do not just invent or witness but live, have the consequence they do remains very far from clear. It will take the wariest of wary reasonings, on all sides of all divides, to get it clearer.

Being Interdisciplinary Is So Very Hard to Do

Stanley Fish

I

Interdisciplinary has long been a familiar word in discussions of education and pedagogy, but recently it has acquired a new force and urgency, in part because as an agenda interdisciplinarity seems to flow naturally from the imperatives of left culturalist theory, that is, from deconstruction, Marxism, feminism, the radical version of neopragmatism, and the new historicism. Each of these movements, of course, should be distinguished from the others in many respects, but it is fair to say that they are alike all hostile to the current arrangement of things as represented by (1) the social structures by means of which the lines of political authority are maintained and (2) the institutional structures by means of which the various academic disciplines establish and extend their territorial claims. Often this hostility takes the form of antiprofessionalism, an indictment of the narrowly special interests that stake out a field of inquiry and then colonize it with a view toward nothing more than serving their own selfish ends.

In the antiprofessional diatribe, specialization stands for everything that is wrong with a practice that has lost its way, everything that is disappointing about an educational system that seems out of touch with the values it supposedly promotes. Of course the antiprofessionalist attack on specialization is by no means the exclusive property of the left: it has long been a stable of conservative jeremiads against the decline of culture in a world where all coherence is gone and the center has not held. Indeed, at times it is difficult to distinguish the two ends of the political spectrum on this question. When Russell Jacoby reports that intellectuals have moved out of the coffeehouses and into the faculty lounge and complains that by doing so they have abandoned their responsibility to the public—"as professional life thrives, public culture grows poorer and older" (8)—we might well be hearing the voice of Lynne Cheney contrasting the vigorous cultural life of the American mainstream to the increasingly narrow and jargon-ridden practices of the academy.

Yet, if both the left and the right can lay claim to an anti-professionalism that regards with suspicion activities tied narrowly to disciplinary pressures, there is nevertheless a difference in the ways in which the antiprofessional stance is assumed. The difference is one of sophistication and complexity in the presentation: whereas the right tends to issue its call for a general, nonspecial-

Fish, Stanley. "Being Interdisciplinary Is So Very Hard to Do." [reprinted from Profession 89 (1989), 15–22 in Issues in Integrative Studies 9 (1991), 97–125.] Reprinted by permission of the Modern Language Association of America.

ized pedagogy in the same flag-waving mode that characterizes its celebration of the American family, the left urges its pedagogy in the context of a full-fledged epistemological argument, complete with a theory of the self, an analysis of the emergence and ontology of institutions, and a taxonomy of the various forms of pedagogical practice, from the frankly oppressive to the self-consciously liberating.

At the heart of that argument is the assumption that the lines currently demarcating one field of study from another are not natural but constructed by interested parties who have a stake in preserving the boundaries that sustain their claims to authority. The structure of the university and the curriculum is a political achievement that is always in the business of denying its origins in a repressive agenda. Knowledge is frozen in a form supportive of the status quo, and this ideological hardening of the arteries is abetted by a cognitive map in which disciplines are represented as distinct, autonomous, and Platonic. Once knowledge has been compartmentalized, the complaint continues, the energy of intellectuals is spent within the spaces provided by a superstructure that is never critically examined. Disciplinary ghettos contain the force of our actions and render them ineffectual on the world's larger stage. In Michael Ryan's words, the present disciplinary "divisions conceal the relationality" of supposedly independent enterprises and prevent us from seeing "that they are nothing 'in themselves' and that they constitute each other as mutually interdependent determinations or differentiations of a complex system of heterogeneous forces" (53–54). One who uncritically accepts the autonomy of his or her "home enterprise" and remains unaware of the system of forces that supports and is supported by that enterprise will never be able to address those forces and thereby take part in the alteration of that system.

This analysis of our situation implicitly includes an agenda for remedying it. One must first (and here Bruce Robbins is speaking) "affirm . . . that no institution is an island" and that while "exercising our profession, we simultaneously occupy overlapping and conflicting institutions" (3). We must, that is, become sensitive to what Vincent Leitch calls "the 'made up' quality of knowledge" as our present institutional categories deliver it to us (53); and then, as S. P. Mohanty urges, "we must seek to suspend the process of this continuity, to question the self-evidence of meanings by invoking the radical—but determining—alternatives that disrupt our . . . discourses of knowledge" (155). That is to say, and Jim Merod says it, we must learn "to situate texts in the field of institutional forces in which they are historically conceived" rather than rest content with regarding them as the special isolated objects of an autonomous practice (92). Once we do this, the smooth coherences and seamless narratives that form the basis of our present knowledge will be disrupted; artificially constructed unities will fall apart; the totalizing discourse in which discrete and independent entities are put into their supposedly natural places by a supposedly neutral discursive logic will be replaced by discontinuity, disorientation, decentering, transformation, fluidity, relation, process. Moreover, as the bonds of discourse are loosened, the mind will be freed from the constraints those bonds imposed, and the person thus freed will move toward "the full development of all human faculties" (Ryan 49), leaving behind the narrowness of vision that befalls those who remain tied to the confining perspectives of the ideologically frozen divisions of intellectual labor.

Of course the program requires some mechanism of implementation, and it is here that we arrive at interdisciplinary study by a route Jeffrey Sammons charts for us. Sammons points out that American education derives from a German model whose goal is "the cultural formation of the self so that it might teach the fullness of its potentialities" (14). In the context of that model it is the task of particular disciplines to contribute to that fullness and avoid the temptation to become ends in themselves, to become nothing more than training schools for entrance into a trade or profession. It always happens, however, that as soon as disciplines are fully established they come quickly to believe in the priority of their own concerns and turn from their larger mission to the training of professionals for whom those concerns are not only prior but exclusive. In short, the structure of the curriculum, or rather the very fact that it has a structure, works against its supposed end, and therefore something must be built into that structure to counter the tendency to produce nonresponsive spheres of self-contained complacency. By definition interdisciplinary studies do exactly that—refuse to respect the boundaries that disciplines want always to draw—and thus encourage a widening of perspectives that will make possible the fullness education is supposed to confer.

Although Sammons and Ryan share the word *full* as a component in their briefs for interdisciplinary thinking, they mean different things by it. Sammons's fullness is the fullness of the imagination. He writes, however critically, in the tradition of High Humanism, and that is why he can locate the potential for destabilizing activity in the humanities or, as he calls them, "the disciplines of the imagination," of a Coleridgean faculty that sees similarities and differences as constructed. Such a faculty, he claims, is inherently "subversive," and therefore the humanities are inherently subversive because they introduce "people to the inexhaustible alternative options of the imagination" (10). Persons so introduced would be "full" in the sense that their intelligences would not be captured by any one point of view but would, rather, be engaged in exploring points of view other than those authorized by current orthodoxies.

To someone like Ryan (or Robbins or Merod) all this would seem suspiciously familiar, especially when Sammons approvingly quotes Robert Scholes's assertion that "poetic texts are designed to discomfort us" (Scholes 43). Left ears will hear this as just another version of a hoary and suspect *disciplinary* claim, which, instead of decentering the curriculum or exposing its affiliations with political and economic forces from which it thinks itself separate, gives it an even firmer center in the humanities and then has the nerve to call that center "subversive." Insofar as such an agenda envisions a fullness, it is merely a fullness of the reflective intellect, an intellect detached perhaps from any of the particular interests that vie for territory in the academy but an intellect nevertheless confined in its operations—however full—to that same academy. What Ryan, Merod, and Robbins want is a fullness of *engagement,* a mind and person that refuses to segregate its activities, to think, for example, that literary study is one thing, participation in the national political process quite another. They would say that the point is not to determine which of the presently situated fields of study is the truly subversive one but to call into question the entrenched articulations within which the divisions between fields (and knowledge) emerge, and *thereby* (or so the claim goes) to subvert the larger social articulation within which the articulations of the academy are rendered intelligible and seemingly inevitable. In short, for these more radical voices, interdisciplinary study is more than a device for prodding students to cross boundaries they would otherwise timidly respect: it is an assault on those boundaries and on the entire edifice of hierarchy and power they reflect and sustain. If you begin by transgressing the boundaries, say, between literature and economics as academic fields of study, you are halfway to transgressing the boundaries between the academy and its supposed "outside," and you are thus brought to the realization that the outside/inside distinction is itself a constructed one whose effect is to confine academic labor to a neutral zone of intellectual/professional play—a realization that then sends you back to operate in that zone in a way that is subversive not only of its autonomy but of the forces that have established that autonomy for their own unacknowledged purposes. In this vision, interdisciplinary study leads not simply to a revolution in the structure of the curriculum but to *revolution tout court.* In the classical liberal paradigm, interdisciplinary studies seek only to transform the academy while maintaining the wall between it and the larger field of social actions; and thus, as Ryan points out, "the radical position of pedagogic activism for the sake of an alternative social construction seem[s] a deviation" (49), an intrusion of the political into precincts it is forbidden to enter. Radical interdisciplinarity begins with the assumption that the political is always and already inside those precincts and that the line separating them from the arena of social agitation is itself politically drawn and must be erased if action within the academy is to be continuous with the larger struggle against exploitation and oppression.

II

It is a stirring vision, but it is finally at odds with the epistemology that often accompanies it. That epistemology is either deconstructive or psychoanalytic or a combination of the two, and in any of its forms its thesis is that "meanings do not exist as such [that is, as freestanding and "natural" entities] but are produced" (Mohanty 15). What they are produced *by* is a system of articulation from which we as either speakers or hearers cannot distance ourselves, because we are situated within it. Since that system (call it *différance* or the unconscious) is the unarticulated ground within which specification occurs, "it" cannot be specified and always exceeds—remains after, escapes—the specifications it enables. What this means, as Shoshana Felman observes, is that knowledge is "a knowledge which does not know what it knows, and is thus *not in possession of itself*" (40). That is, as knowledge it cannot grasp, or name the grounds of, its possibility, and whenever it thinks to have done so, those grounds are elsewhere than they seem to be; they are once again under the would-be knower's feet. It is to this point that Felman quotes Lacan—"the elements do not answer in the place where they are interrogated, or more exactly, as soon as they are interrogated somewhere, it is impossible to grasp them in their totality" (Felman 29)—and she might just as well have invoked Derrida as he explains why *différance,* although it makes presentation possible, can never itself be presented: "Reserving itself, not exposing itself, . . . it exceeds the order of truth . . . , but without dissimulating itself as something, as a mysterious being. . . . In every exposition it would be exposed to disappearing as disappearance. It would risk appearing: disappearing" (122). Or again, "the trace is never as it is in the presentation of itself. It erases itself in presenting itself, muffles itself in resonating . . ." (Derrida 133). That is to say, the truth one would know has always receded behind the formulations it makes possible, and therefore those formulations are always ignorant of themselves and incomplete. Indeed, ignorance, the forgetting of the enabling conditions of knowledge (conditions that cannot themselves be known), is constitutive of knowledge itself. Thus, Felman declares, "human knowledge is by definition that which is untotalizable, that which rules out any possibility of totalizing what it knows or of eradicating its own ignorance" (29). It follows then that if ignorance is the necessary content of knowledge as presented at any particular moment, knowledge is not something that should be preserved or allowed to settle, since in whatever form it appears it will always be excluding more than it reveals; and indeed it is only by virtue of the exclusions it cannot acknowledge that it acquires a (suspect) shape.

Not surprisingly, the pedagogy demanded by this insight is a pedagogy of antiknowledge, of the refusal of knowledge in favor of that which it occludes. There must be a new way of teaching, one that "does not just reflect itself, but turns back on itself so as to *subvert itself* and truly *teaches* only insofar as it subverts itself" (Felman 39), a pedagogic style that in Lacan's words is "the ironic style of calling into question the very foundations of the discipline" (qtd. in Felman 39). Lacan is referring to the discipline of psychoanalysis but, vigorously pursued, the strategy calls into question the foundations of all disciplines, since those foundations will in every case be made of ignorance and therefore must be first exposed and then removed. The way to do this is to work against the apparent coherences that support and are supported by ignorance and to engage in a kind of guerilla warfare in which the decorums disciplines ask us observe are systematically violated, so that we proceed, "not through linear progression, but through breakthroughs, leaps, discontinuities" (qtd. in Felman 27). Rather than teach meanings, we must undo the meanings offered to us by hidden ideological agendas, poking holes in the discursive fabric those agendas weave, replacing the narcotic satisfactions of easy intelligibility with the disruptive disease of relentless critique. The call to battle is sounded in summary but representative form by Vincent Leitch in the name of Roland Barthes:

> . . . uproot the frozen text; break down stereotypes and opinions; suspend or baffle the violence and authority of language; pacify or

lighten oppressive paternal powers; disorient the Law; let classroom
discourse float, fragment, digress. (51)

And then what? Does the pedagogy of anti-knowledge hold out the hope of
anything beyond its repeated unsettling of whatever claims us in the name of
established knowledge? It is in the answer to this question that the tension
between the political and the epistemological arguments for interdisciplinary
studies comes to the surface. In the political argument, which sees us currently
inhibited in our actions by lines of demarcation we did not draw, the demonstration that those lines and the distinctions they subtend are not natural but
historical will remove their power and free us from their constraints. "The
classroom," says Jeffrey Peck,

> then becomes a productive rather than a reproductive environment.
> . . . In the spirit of critical reflection meanings and values of tradi-
> tional pedagogy can be scrutinized. . . . The intersubjectivity of
> meaning can be exposed, and education institutions, the classroom,
> the discipline, and the university can be seen to construct and con-
> dition knowledge. In this way literary study, as the study of textual-
> ity, . . . reveals the epistemological structures that organize how we
> know, how our knowledge gets transmitted and accepted, and why
> and how students receive it. (51)

To this heady prospect, which will end, Peck predicts, with students becoming
better readers "of their own lives, as well as of texts" (53), the epistemological
argument poses a dampening question—from what vantage point will the
"structures that organize how we know" be revealed?—and the answer can only
be, from the vantage point of a structure that is at the moment *un*revealed
because it occupies the position formerly occupied by the structures it now
enables us to analyze. The strategy of "making visible what was hidden" can
only be pursued within forms of thought that are themselves hidden; the bringing to light of what Edward Said calls "the network of agencies that limit,
select, shape, and maintain" meaning requires the dark background of a network that cannot be seen because it is within it that seeing occurs (34–35).
Partiality and parochialism are not eliminated or even diminished by the exposure of their operation, merely relocated. The blurring of existing authoritative
disciplinary lines and boundaries will only create new lines and new authorities;
the interdisciplinary impulse finally does not liberate us from the narrow confines of academic ghettos to something more capacious; it merely redomiciles
us in enclosures that do not advertise themselves as such.

   In short, if we take seriously the epistemological argument in the context of
which the gospel of interdisciplinary study is so often preached, we will come
to the conclusion that being interdisciplinary—breaking out of the prison
houses of our various specialties to the open range first of a general human
knowledge and then of the employment of that knowledge in the great struggles of social and political life—is not a possible human achievement. Being

interdisciplinary is more than hard to do; it is impossible to do. The epistemological argument deprives the political argument of any possible force, because it leaves no room for a revolutionary project. Or, rather, it leaves us with projects that look disconcertingly like the disciplinary projects we are trying to escape. Either (as some contributors to a recent piece in the *Chronicle of Higher Education* complain) the announcement of an interdisciplinary program inaugurates the effort of some discipline to annex the territory of another, or "interdisciplinary thought" is the name (whether acknowledged or not) of a new discipline, that is, of a branch of academic study that takes as its subject the history and constitution of disciplines. Either the vaunted "blurring of genres" (Clifford Geertz's now famous phrase) means no more than that property lines have been redrawn—so that, for example, Freud and Nietzsche have migrated respectively from psychology and philosophy to English and comparative literature—or the genres have been blurred only in the sense of having been reconfigured by the addition of a new one, of an emerging field populated by still another kind of mandarin, the "specialist in contextual relations" (Alton Becker; qtd. in Geertz 521).

III

Needless to say, this is a conclusion many are loath to reach, but in order to avoid it, the proponents of radical pedagogy must negotiate an impasse produced by one of their own first principles, the unavailability of a perspective that is not culturally determined. Since a perspective from which the determinations of culture can be surveyed is a requirement of the radical project, one must ask how that project can even get started. In general, two answers have been given to this question. The first is to move from Robbins's observation quoted above, that "while exercising our profession, we simultaneously occupy overlapping and conflicting institutions," to the critical practice of allowing the claims made on us by one institution to stand in a relation of challenge to the claims made on us by another. As Samuel Weber puts it, "in interpreting a literary text, an interpreter will not necessarily be limited to confronting those interpretations previously certified as inhabiting the discipline of literary studies"; rather, "he may also invoke interpretations emanating from other regions (philosophy, psychoanalysis, etc.) and these in turn may well challenge the unifying assumptions of the discipline of literary studies in America" (38). That is to say, one's practice within a discipline can be characterized by invocations of and frequent references to the achievements, dicta, emphases, and requirement of other disciplines.

This is certainly true (my own practice, like yours, has often been answerable to such a description), but the question is, does the practice of importing into one's practice the machinery of other practices operate to relax the constraints of one's practice? And the answer I would give is no, because the imported product will always have the form of its appropriation rather than the form it exhibits "at home"; therefore at the very moment of its introduction, it will already be marked by the discourse it supposedly "opens." When something is brought into a practice, it is brought in in terms the practice recognizes; the practice cannot "say" the Other but can only say itself, even when it is in the act of modifying itself by incorporating material hitherto alien to it. As Peter Stearns says of history (and it could be said of any discipline), "What has happened is that social historians have borrowed topics, concepts and vocabulary . . . but they have then cast them in an essentially historical frame," and he adds, "This is something . . . more modest than a 'blurring of genres' " (qtd. in Winkler 14). Just so, and it is hard to see how it could be otherwise: terms and distinctions could arrive intact in the passage from one discipline to another only if they had some form independent of the discipline in whose practices they first became visible; but, in our brave new textualist-historicist world, terms and distinctions are no less socially constructed than anything else, and therefore the shape they appear in will always be relative to the socially constructed activity that has received them and made them its own.

Moreover, if materials, concepts, and vocabularies take on the coloring of the enterprise that houses them, so do practitioners, and that is why the second strategy by which pedagogy will supposedly transcend the disciplinary site of its activities fails. That strategy is a strategy of self-consciousness, and it requires us, while performing within a discipline, to keep at least one eye on the larger conditions that make the performance possible. (This is the implication of Robbins's subtitle: "Toward Productively Divided Loyalties.") While some agents confine themselves to the horizons of a particular profession, others situate themselves in the wider horizons of a general cultural space and therefore manage to be at once committed and not committed to the labors they perform. It is the latter group that keeps faith with a higher vision by not forgetting "the forces and factors" that underlie and give point to local urgencies (Weber 37). They remain aware of "the reader's and writer's immersion in a network of social forces that both grant and limit the possibility of intellectual authority" (Merod 93); and unlike their less enlightened brethren they resist the tendency of any "regime of truth" to deny its "constitutive dependence on what it excludes, dethrones, and replaces" (Weber 38). That is, they contrive to practice a particular craft without buying into the claims of that craft to be self-justifying and autonomous and without allowing the perspective of that craft to eclipse the other perspectives that would come into view were the craft's demands sufficiently relaxed.

The question is, as it was before, is this a possible mode of action? Again the answer is no, and for reasons that will become clear if we rephrase the question: can you simultaneously operate within a practice and be self-consciously in touch with the conditions that enable it? The answer could be yes only if you could achieve a reflective distance from those conditions while still engaging in that practice; but once the conditions enabling a practice become the object of analytic attention (against the background of still other conditions that are themselves unavailable to conscious inspection), you are engaging in another practice (the practice of reflecting on the conditions of a practice you are not now practicing), and the practice you began to examine has been left behind, at least as something you are doing as opposed to something you are studying.

Once you turn, for example, from actually performing literary criticism to examining the "network of forces and factors" that underlie the performance, literary criticism is no longer what you are performing.

The point of course is tautological, and it would seem unnecessary to make it, except that in recent years it has been obscured by an illegitimate inference that has been drawn from a legitimate thesis. The thesis is the one we began with: disciplines are not natural kinds; they emerge in the wake of a political construction of the field of knowledge. The illegitimate inference is that since disciplinary boundaries are constructed and revisable, they are not real. But of course they are as real as anything else in a world in which *everything* is constructed (the world posited by those who make this argument); even though the lines demarcating one discipline from another can in time blur and become rearranged, until that happens the arrangements now in force will produce differences felt strongly by all those who live within them. Although it is true that disciplines have no essential core (another way of saying that they are not natural kinds), the identity conferred on them by a relational structure—a structure in which everything is known by what it is not—constitutes (however temporarily) a core that does all the work an essentialist might desire, including the work of telling community members what is and is not an instance of the practice it centers. Someone who says, as I have done in the previous paragraph, "that's not literary criticism" has said something that has a basis in fact, even if that fact itself—the fact of the present shape of a diacritically constituted discipline—is one undergoing continual modification and transformation. Again the lesson is only apparently paradoxical: because the core of the discipline is a historical achievement, it is capable of alteration, but as an achievement it exerts, if only for a time, a force that cannot be ignored or wished away.

This does not mean that a worker in a discipline knows its core in the sense of being able to hold its differential (nonpositive) identity in mind. Indeed, in order to function in the discipline (as opposed to being a student of its formation), the fragility of that identity is something the worker cannot know or at least must always forget when entering its precincts.[1] The mark of that forgetting is the unintelligibility to practitioners of questions one might put from the outside, questions like (for teaching)"why is it that you want your students to learn?" or (for criminal law) "why should we be interested in the issue of responsibility at all?" or (for history) "why would anyone want to know what happened in the past?" You can't be seriously asking these questions and still be a member of those communities, because to conceive of yourself (a phrase literally intended) as a member is to have forgotten that those are questions you can seriously ask. This is the forgetting that Weber, Robbins, Merod, and other excoriate, but it is also the forgetting that is necessary if action of a particular kind is ever to occur. Denying and forgetting are not reformable errors but the very grounds of cognition and assertion. If one were to remember everything and deny nothing, assertion, directed movement, politics itself would have no possible shape.

Some of those who find magic in the word *interdisciplinary* come very close to making this point but shy away from it at the last moment. Richard Terdiman observes, correctly I think, that while "we attend to the content of our instruction, we are fundamentally, but imperceptibly, molded by its form"— that is, by the disciplinary structures within which the instruction occurs—and that therefore "the ideological representation of the world is involuntarily naturalized even through critique of its specific detail" (221). "Are our ways of teaching students to ask *some* questions," asks Barbara Johnson, "always correlative with our ways of teaching them *not to ask*—indeed to be unconscious of—others?" ("Teaching" 173). The answer is yes, and because the answer is yes our pedagogical imperative, no matter how radical its stance, will always turn out, as Terdiman observes, "to have sources and serve interests other than those we thought" (222). In the act of producing this insight, Terdiman terms it "unhappy." But why? All it means is that we will never achieve the full self-consciousness that would allow us at once to inhabit and survey reflectively our categories of thought, but that incapacity only affects our ability to be gods; and were we indeed to become gods, no longer tethered to the local places within which crises and troubles emerge, we would not feel the urgencies that impel us forward. The fact that we do feel these urgencies and are moved by that feeling to act depends on the very limitations and blindnesses Terdiman and company deplore. It is only because we cannot achieve an "authentic critique" (Terdiman 223)—a critique free of any political or conceptual entanglements—that the critiques we do achieve have force, even if it is the nature of things for the force of those critiques to be as vulnerable and transient as the conditions that give them form.

The impossibility of authentic critique is the impossibility of the interdisciplinary project, at least insofar as that project holds out the hope of releasing cognition from the fetters of thought and enlarging the minds of those who engage in it. The obvious response to this conclusion is to point out that interdisciplinary studies are all around us. What is it that all these people are doing? The answer has already been given; either they are engaging in straightforwardly disciplinary tasks that require for their completion information and techniques on loan from other disciplines, or they are working within a particular discipline at a moment when it is expanding into territories hitherto marked as belonging to someone else—participating, that is, in the annexation by English departments of philosophy, psychoanalysis, anthropology, social history, and now, legal theory; or they are in the process of establishing a new discipline, one that takes as its task the analysis of disciplines, the charting of their history and of their ambitions. Typically the members of this new discipline will represent themselves as antidisciplinary, that is, as interdisciplinary, but in fact, as Daniel Schön points out, they will constitute a "new breed" of "counter-professionals/experts" (340). Nor is there anything necessarily reprehensible about these activities. Depending on one's own interests and sense of what the situation requires, the imperial ambitions of a particular discipline may be just what the doctors ordered; and it may equally well be the case that, from a certain point of view, the traditional disciplines have played themselves out and it is time to fashion a new one. For my own part I subscribe to both these views, and therefore I find the imperialistic success of literary studies heartening and the emergence of cultural studies as a field of its own exhilarating. It is just that my pleasure at these developments has nothing to do with the larger claims— claims of liberation, freedom, openness—often made for them. The American mind, like any other, will always be closed, and the only question is whether we find the form of closure it currently assumes answerable to our present urgencies.

Note

1. Stephen Booth tells me that this formulation may be too strong, and he reminds me of an experience many of us will be able to recall, knowing while watching a horror movie that certain devices are being used to frighten us and yet being frightened nevertheless despite our knowledge. In experiences like this an analytical understanding of what is happening exists side by side with what is happening but does not affect or neutralize it. It would be too much to say, then, that when engaging in a practice (and watching horror movies is a practice) one must forget the analytical perspective one might have on the practice at another time. It would be more accurate to say that an analytical perspective on a practice does not insulate one from experiencing the practice in all its fullness, that is, in the same way one would experience it were the analytical perspective unavailable.

Works Cited

Adams, Hazard, and Leroy Searle, eds. *Critical Theory since 1965.* Tallahassee: Florida State UP, 1986.
Cheney, Lynne V. *Humanities in America: A Report to the President, the Congress, and the American People.* Washington: NEH, 1988.
Derrida, Jacques. "Differance." Adams and Searle 120–36.
Felman, Shoshana. "Psychoanalysis and Education: Teaching Terminable and Interminable." Johnson, *Pedagogical Imperative* 21–44.
Geertz, Clifford. "Blurred Genres: The Refiguration of Social Thought." Adams and Searle 514–23.
Jacoby, Russell. *The Last Intellectuals.* New York: Basic, 1987.
Johnson, Barbara, ed. *The Pedagogical Imperative. Yale French Studies* 63 (1982): 1–252.
———. "Teaching Ignorance: *L'Ecole des Femmes.*" Johnson, *Pedagogical Imperative* 165–82.
Leitch, Vincent. *"Deconstruction and Pedagogy."* Nelson 45–56.
Merod, Jim. *The Political Responsibility of the Critics.* Ithaca: Cornell UP, 1987.
Mohanty, S.P. "Radical Teaching, Radical Theory: The Ambiguous Politics of Meaning." Nelson 149–76.
Peck, Jeffrey M. "Advanced Literary Study as Cultural Study: A Redefinition of the Discipline." *Profession 85.* New York: MLA, 1985. 49–54.
Robbins, Bruce. "Professionalism and Politics: Toward Productively Divided Loyalties." *Profession 85.* New York: MLA, 1985. 1–9.
Ryan, Michael. "Deconstruction and Radical Teaching." Johnson, *Pedagogical Imperative* 45–58.
Said, Edward. Interview. *Diacritics* 6 (1976): 30–47.
Sammons, Jeffrey L. "Squaring the Circle: Observations on Core Curriculum and the Plight of the Humanities." *Profession 86.* New York: MLA, 1986. 14–21.
Scholes, Robert. *Semiotics and Interpretation.* New Haven: Yale UP, 1982.
Schön, Daniel. *The Reflective Practitioner.* New York: Basic, 1983.
Terdiman, Richard. "Structures of Initiation: On Semiotic Education and Its Contradictions in Balzac." Johnson, *Pedagogical Imperative* 198–226.
Weber, Samuel. *Institution and Interpretation.* Minneapolis: U of Minnesota P, 1987.
Winkler, Karen J. "Interdisciplinary Research: How Big a Challenge to Traditional Fields?" *Chronicle of Higher Education* 7 Oct. 1987: 1+.

Interdisciplinary Studies

Giles Gunn

In the strict sense of the term, *interdisciplinary studies* is not a "field." Even if many scholars and critics think of themselves as participating in interdisciplinary studies, they do not, by virtue of this understanding, share anything like a set of interests, methods, or problems. What they share, instead—for want of a better term—is a predisposition to pursue their questions into areas of critical inquiry that cannot be mapped at all by the cartographic practices of contemporary disciplines or that can be mapped only when one redraws the critical coordinates supplied by those disciplines. Either way, students of interdisciplinary studies are marked by their willingness not simply to challenge, but also to cross, traditional disciplinary boundaries. Their hope, or at any rate their assumption, is that important dimensions of human experience and understanding lie unexplored in the spaces between those boundaries or the places where they cross, overlap, divide, or dissolve.

These practices involve risks of several kinds. The first relate to the disciplinary structure of the university system itself, at least in the United States, and the possibility that attempts to question its territorial boundaries and experiment with changing them may look like subversive activities. These risks are particularly high for junior scholars who lack the protection of tenure but possess the creative impatience necessary to the continuing development not only of the university but also of any particular field. Youthfulness—or, rather, inexperience—often entails a second kind of liability for interdisciplinary study. To bring two or more disciplines into significant interaction with one another requires considerable mastery of the subtleties and particularities of each, together with sufficient imagination and tact, ingenuity and persuasiveness, to convince others of the utility of their linkage. Such mastery, and the finesse that must accompany it, is not often acquired quickly or without extensive research and reflection. In rapidly changing fields such as the natural and physical sciences, where the bulk of graduate education is devoted to the state of the art of a particular discipline or subdiscipline, interdisciplinary reconfigurations of methods and subject areas can—and often must—occur quite swiftly, but in the humanities, where one can scarcely learn the state of the art of any discipline without acquiring considerable knowledge of its history, they occur more slowly. It would be a mistake, however, to suppose that boundary-crossing is either an infrequent practice in humanistic studies or a recent one.

The humanistic practice of interdisciplinary excursions into foreign territor-

Gunn, Giles. "Interdisciplinary Studies." Joseph Gibaldi (ed.) Introduction to Scholarship in Modern Language & Literature. *New York: Modern Language Association, 1992, 239–261. Reprinted by permission of the Modern Language Association of America.*

ies goes all the way back in the West to classical antiquity, when Greek historians and dramatists drew on medical and philosophical knowledge, respectively,
for clues to the reconception of their own material. It has continued down to
our own time, where much social thinking has been "refigured," to use the
coinage of the cultural anthropologist Clifford Geertz, by encouraging social
thinkers from a variety of disciplines to explore analogies between their own
material and such aesthetic activities as play, ritual, drama, symbolic action,
narrative, speech acts, games, and writing ("Blurred Genres"). In the Middle
Ages, literary study put itself in the debt of systematic theology for its theories
of interpretation and language. In the Renaissance, or early modern period
as it is now called, the theologians, philosophers, and scholars known as the
"humanists" differentiated themselves as a semiprofessional class by adopting,
over against the medieval schoolmen, the theories and practices of the classical
Greek and Roman philosophers. The movement known as the Enlightenment,
in the eighteenth century, could easily be described as a raid by the philosophes
on the conceptions and methods of the physical sciences, and what we call
nineteenth-century Romanticism is only another term for what might be
thought of as the intellectual appropriation, by fields such as theology, philosophy, literature, and the fine arts, of biologic and organic metaphors drawn from
the natural sciences.

But if there is nothing unusual about humanists conducting sorties into
alien "disciplinary" territory (students of comparative literature have made a
virtue of such necessities), there is nonetheless something distinctive and exciting about the modern interest in such cross-field and cross-disciplinary peregri-
nations. This has to do with the reasons why, and the ways in which,
contemporary literary scholars and critics have permitted such sallies to redefine
both their subject matter and the kinds of questions they put to it. That is to
say, the interdisciplinary move to explore the alien terrain of nonliterary genres
and fields has amounted to considerably more than an attempt to draw different disciplines into conversation with one another, or to broaden the horizons
of one discipline by borrowing some of the insights and techniques of another.
Even where the interdisciplinary impulse has been prompted by motives no
more suspect than the desire to improve communication across territorial
boundaries or to expand the parameters that define them, it rarely ends there.
What may have begun as the simple promotion of a kind of good neighbor
policy, or as an innocent exploration of the exotic material of some foreign
field, often results in something less benign than boundary-crossing and more
unsettling than boundary-changing. What is at stake, to return to Geertz, is not
just another redrawing of the disciplinary map but the principles of mapping as
such. In this more contemporary sense, then, interdisciplinarity is not achieved
through simple confrontations between specialized fields of knowledge—
literature with history, chemistry with engineering, art history with the history
of ideas—or through the placement of the insights and techniques of one discipline on loan to another—textual study borrowing the methods of computer
science, history utilizing the techniques of demographers. The effect, if not the

purpose, of interdisciplinarity is often nothing less than to alter the way we think about thinking ("Blurred Genres" 165–66).

Contemporary Interdisciplinary Practice

The process of interdisciplinary revisionism usually begins with a period of courtship between two distinct and often diverse disciplines that suddenly discover spheres of mutual interest and complementary resources, then proceeds to a kind of marriage based on the belief that there are significant areas of compatibility between their respective methods and intellectual focus, and culminates in the production of offspring who share the parental genes and some of their dispositional features but possess a character all their own. Hence interdisciplinary exchanges depend on something more than ratcheting up the level of sophistication with which one explores the relations between literature and another endeavor—myth, psychology, religion, film, the visual arts—by utilizing methods appropriate to the study of each in a close, perhaps even symbiotic, cooperation. Interdisciplinarity requires, instead, an alteration of the constitutive question that generates such inquiry in the first place. Thus where relational studies proceed from the question of what literature (in its traditions, its formal conventions, and its thematic concerns) has to do with some other material (like music or social behavior) or some other field (such as history, political science, or sociolinguistics), interdisciplinary inquiries proceed from the double-sided question about how the insights or methods of some other field or structure can remodel our understanding of the nature of literature and the "literary" and, conversely, about how literary conceptions and approaches can remodel our conception of the allied field and its subject material.

An excellent example can be found in the emerging field of ethical criticism, first explored by moral philosophers like Iris Murdoch, Mikel Dufrenne, Bernard Williams, and Hilary Putnam, and now being developed by, among others, Wayne Booth and Martha Nussbaum. An outgrowth of an ancient interest in the relations between literature and philosophy that has been maintained for moderns by writers such as Friedrich Schiller, Samuel Taylor Coleridge, Friedrich Nietzsche, Martin Heidegger, John Dewey, Stuart Hampshire, Isaiah Berlin, Stanley Cavell, and Nelson Goodman, the interdisciplinary challenge of ethical criticism is conceived to be the transcendence of two related views. The first is that literature possesses moral dimensions even though it is not a form of moral experience. The second is that philosophical conceptions of morality can be illustrated by literary forms despite the fact that such forms are incapable of reflecting systematically on moral questions.

In *The Fragility of Goodness* and *Love's Knowledge,* Nussbaum in particular is concerned to revise both nostrums by arguing, first, against most academic moral philosophers, that certain conceptions of the good life, both individual and social, are not fully or adequately represented in forms of writing as abstract and affectless as traditional philosophical disputation; and, second, against many literary critics and theorists, that the conventional aesthetic prejudice against the ethically heuristic value of forms of writing like prose narrative or lyric poetry derives in part from a false assumption (widely shared by most moral and other philosophers as well) that the emotions lack cognitive content even where they convey felt quality.

Nussbaum's argument against both fallacies turns on their traditional resistance to the view that aesthetic forms play an educative as well as illustrative role in practical reflection on ethical issues, and it expresses itself in the assertion that while works of art often represent and express emotional effects, their deeper significance stems from the fact that their forms "are themselves the sources of emotional structure, the paradigms of what, for us, feeling is" ("Narrative Emotions" 236). Nussbaum is therefore interested in developing a new structure of interdisciplinary inquiry that will demonstrate, at the same time, the extent to which certain kinds of moral reflection and insight are dependent on narrative and other aesthetic structures and the extent to which practical ethical reasoning is in many instances a concomitant result of literary interpretation.

However, it must be added immediately that ethical criticism is by no means confined to Nussbaum's adroit and compelling practice of it. The term—which has been the source of opprobrium by critics as various as Northrop Frye and Fredric Jameson, and of praise by the likes of F. R. Leavis, Lionel Trilling, and David Bromwich—can be applied more widely to various kinds of interdisciplinary study that go by different names—feminist criticism, African American criticism, postcolonial criticism, ideological criticism, cultural studies—that also seek to submit literary forms to moral scrutiny or to challenge ethical reflection with metaphoric restructuring (see the essays by Schor, Allen, Gates, and Bathrick in this volume).

The interdisciplinary field of American studies provides another example of how such inquiry reconfigures the constituent disciplines that compose it. Beginning in the 1930s as an attempt to link literary and historical studies— when literature was viewed by historians as little more than a set of illustrations of themes, ideas, and events from beyond the world of literature, and history was seen by critics as merely the background of literature—American studies quickly turned into a more complicated attempt to examine the interactions between forms of collective mentality such as myths and archetypes, products of individual consciousness such as works of art and intellect, and social structures such as institutions and practices. In this interdisciplinary reformulation, accomplished by the "myth and symbol" school, as it is now called, a loose grouping of critics that included Henry Nash Smith, John William Ward, and Leo Marx, literature was reconceived both as a repository of historical value and as an example of historical practice; history, as a perceptual as well as material field significantly defined by large imaginative constructs such as myths and other metanarratives that can fuse concept and emotion in an image. In more recent years, with the help of conceptual and methodological insights borrowed from Marxist criticism, social history, feminist criticism, and other areas, the notions of literature and history operative in American studies have been revised even further as studies like Myra Jehlen's *American Incarnation* and Alan Trachtenberg's *Reading American Photographs* have shown how figurative representations become a historical force in their own right and operate like any other material factor in the public world.

It has lately been claimed that the American studies movement failed because it never led to the creation of separate departments of American literature, but this claim amounts to measuring the success of an interdisciplinary field of inquiry in terms of whether it achieves full institutional recognition by various fields it succeeds in at least partially redefining (Culler 8; Graff 211). The success of the American studies movement derives, rather, from the number of separate undergraduate programs and majors it has generated throughout the United States and the world, the kinds and quality of graduate programs it has produced, the new areas of research it has opened up, the professional associations it has sponsored, and, most important, the creativity, integrity, and resilience of the scholarship produced in its name. Judging by these standards, American studies has been as effacious an interdisciplinary initiative as any undertaken in American higher education in the postwar period.

But this only indicates how difficult it is to demarcate precisely where, and how, to draw the boundaries not only *between* different kinds of interdisciplinary study but also *within* them. For example, feminist criticism, like cultural critique or African American or postcolonial criticism, is more of a composite methodological site where other interdisciplinary modes cross and recross— reader-response criticism, semiotic analysis, psychoanalytic inquiry, ethnic studies, cultural anthropology, gender studies—than a unitary mode of interdisciplinary study all its own. Furthermore, there are sharp and sometimes seemingly incommensurable differences between and among, say, feminist critics over whether to organize their research around biological, psychological, cultural, or linguistic models. What this suggests, to repeat, is that interdisciplinary studies may not refer to anything as specific or unified as a "field" in itself so much as to a predisposition to view all fields as potentially vulnerable to re-creation in the partial image of some other or others. This, in turn, renders the fields in question what Roland Barthes calls "transversals," whose reconfiguration seeks to produce or recover meanings that their formerly configured relations tended to blur, camouflage, or efface ("From Work to Text" 75).

The Theory of Interdisciplinary Studies

As numerous students of interdisciplinarity in all fields can attest, the process of converting disciplines into transversals can be not only discomfiting but also potentially violent. When the parameters of traditional fields grow permeable or suspect under the pressure of questions that, as presently constituted, they cannot address, such fields grow ripe for infiltration, subversion, or outright assault. Such military metaphors may seem excessive, but they are apt. When the academic field now called anthropology first attempted to carve out a space for itself between history and sociology, it was described by one of its proponents, and not altogether inaccurately, as "a disciplinary poaching license." Thus images of encroachment, trespass, offense are inescapable; interdisciplinary studies risk disciplinary transgression in the name of interdisciplinary independence, disciplinary revisionism in the name of interdisciplinary emancipation and creativity (Fish, "Being Interdisciplinary" 15–21).

But the ideology of interdisciplinary freedom captures only those aspects of interdisciplinary activity that are potentially invasive and disruptive. There is another side to interdisciplinary practice that, according to some, is by contrast peremptory, juridical, prescriptive, and imperialistic. This threat derives from the fact that the redescriptive impulses of interdisciplinary studies almost of necessity place one discipline in a position of subordination to another. As a result, the subordinated discipline is not only destabilized but threatened with subsumption in an anomalous, substitutionary structure that on the pretext of situating itself, as the prefix *inter* implies, between the two more traditionally constituted matrices, actually manages to incorporate them both in some larger hegemonic framework. Whether one construes the new interdisciplinary formation as merely a product of the merger of the other two, or as itself a metadiscipline beyond them, seemingly matters scarcely at all. A new field has been produced, the imperiousness of whose procedures often runs counter to the redemptive heuristics used to justify it. Thus if interdisciplinarity is most often legitimated in the name of greater intellectual autonomy and openness, the transdisciplinary exploration it sanctions possesses the capability of masking another form of metadisciplinary despotism. Barthes writes:

> Interdisciplinary work is not a peaceful operation: it begins *effectively* when the solidarity of the old discipline breaks down—a process made more violent, perhaps, by the jolts of fashion—to the benefit of a new object and a new language, neither of which is in the domain of those branches of knowledge that one calmly sought to confront. . . . [T]here now arises a need for a new object, one attained by the displacement or overturning of previous categories.
>
> ("From Work to Text" 73–74)

Barthes defines this new mutational object as the *text,* arguing that it displaces or overturns the old "Newtonian" concept of the "work." By "text" Barthes means to refer less to a specifiable entity than to a site or intersection of productive activity—that is, to processes of signification rather than to forms of the signified. But whether the metadiscipline Barthes invokes is described as textual studies, or intertextuality, or—as certain contemporary critics now argue—cultural studies, his view that interdisciplinarity always supplants one set of structures with another, still more encompassing and dominant is by no means shared by all scholars. What looks to Barthes like a monolithic metadiscipline rising from the imperialistic subversion and partial fusion of two others appears to another group of scholars and critics rather more like the integration of strategies, methods, and queries that acquire their particular sense of authority from what the two disciplines on which heretofore they have traditionally drawn have customarily dismissed, repressed, or occluded. I cite but two examples. Feminist studies, as the chapter by Naomi Schor in this volume suggests, arose initially as a protest against the stereotypes created about women in the literature written by men and sought to recuperate the very different representations that women had furnished of their experience in their own writing. In like fashion, the successive stages of African American criticism—from its inception in the Black Arts movement of the 1960s to its attempt, in the late 1980s and early 1990s, to retheorize social and textual boundaries in all American cultural contexts and thus turn black studies into a critique of American studies generally—demonstrate, as the essay by Henry Louis Gates, Jr., in this book reveals, that African American criticism arose in part out of discoveries of what more conventional inquiries had typically omitted.

Mapping the Interdisciplinary Terrain

For purposes of this discussion, it is perhaps enough to say, then, that there is a loose historical connection between the various associations that literature has for some time, and in some instances for many centuries, enjoyed with other fields or structured forms—forms like painting, film, sculpture, architecture, discursive argument, dogmatic and speculative theology, social thought, music, and, now, photography and the law; fields like jurisprudence, linguistics, anthropology, sociology, musicology, philosophy, religion, science, history, and politics—and the development of at least some interdisciplinary approaches to such relations. But this assertion needs to be qualified to the bone. These developments have not followed an orderly pattern; they are by no means fully descriptive of all the fields with which literature has possessed important conceptual and methodological filiations; and they are related closely, as might be expected, to developments in literary and critical theory as well as to the emergence of new notions of textuality and intertextuality, particularly as they apply to the concept of culture itself. More exactly, genuinely interdisciplinary modes of study have usually developed through the crossing, displacement, or alteration of the boundaries between forms of relational study, or have otherwise constituted themselves in the spaces between those forms as attempts to understand the asymmetric relations between the protocols and perspective that divide them.

As a case in point, deconstruction arose as a joining of the philosophical interest in the critique of Western metaphysics and the new science of linguistics that in Ferdinand de Saussure's version stressed that language is composed of signs that can be differentiated as to function: the material means of transmission or acoustic image of any sign is known as the signifier, the conceptual image or intellectual referent of any sign as the signified. The relation between signifier and signified is what becomes problematic for the deconstructionist by virtue of his or her perception of the irreducible *differance*—as in the words *differing* and *deferring*—between them, and the inevitable suppression, repression, and dissemination of meaning to which it leads. Often misdescribed as a method or critical theory, its chief aim, according to its founder and most famous exponent, Jacques Derrida, is to deconstruct all the classical oppositions on which literary criticism (like theology and philosophy) is based—between word and referent, language and being, structure and process, text and context—in order to see what such oppositions have traditionally veiled or disguised. By contrast, the new historicism, discussed in detail by Annabel Patterson in this book, has taken up methodological residence somewhere between deconstruction's preoccupation with the conflicting, if not self-canceling, forces of signification in any text and the neo-Marxist fascination with how processes of textualization not only reflect material circumstances and institutional patterns but frequently, and often simultaneously, generate them.

But if interdisciplinary studies is sometimes formed by traversing inherited disciplinary boundaries, sometimes by transfiguring them, and sometimes by exploring the spaces between them, how is one to go about mapping the studies' own permutations and forms? The simplest answer is probably to be found by reverting to the set of critical coordinates that have conventionally been employed to model literary texts—the author, the reader, the material or linguistic components of the text itself, and the world to which the text refers. This model, first delineated by M. H. Abrams in *The Mirror and the Lamp,* has been vastly complicated in recent years as our sense of each one of its coordinates has been extended, but its use can nonetheless be instructive (Hernadi). Such a model helps clarify immediately, for example, that much of the activity in interdisciplinary studies in recent years has been selectively focused. Because of suspicions about the status of the author in contemporary criticism and the whole question of authorial intention, and the no less grave theoretical misgivings about the mimetic properties of art and the role of representation generally, interdisciplinary work has placed far less emphasis on the first and last coordinates of this literary model, the author and the world, than on the middle two, the reader and the work.

This selectivity is apparent everywhere. It is as visible in all the contemporary variants of psychological criticism, which tend to be preoccupied with the mental and emotional states of individuals, even when such states are taken to represent real-life psychological processes in the world, as it is in social and political criticism that is typically concerned with the way the material environment serves either as a source of literary production, as an object of literary representation, or as a determinant of literary reception and influence. Thus Freudian criticism has for some time been less interested in the psyches of individual authors, or the capacity of literary texts to mirror the psychological processes of persons and groups, than in the way psychological structures, such as the unconscious, can be viewed as analogues to literary structures like language, or in the way strategies of literary typification and signification, such as metonymy, synecdoche, and irony, can be read psychoanalytically both as representing and as enabling processes of repression, displacement, transference, and countertransference. Similarly, much of the most influential interdisciplinary criticism promoted by the newer Marxist theories has abandoned careful examination of the class background of writers, or the sociopolitical verisimilitude of the world they create, in favor of exploring the manner in which works of literature and other art forms not only reflect discursive traces of the class struggle and resolve social conflicts symbolically but also inscribe stylistically the modes of production by which they were first legitimated.

The map of interdisciplinary studies would look rather different, however, if only one of these critical coordinates were used as the cartographic axis. Take, for example, the focus in recent criticism on the reader, which links the phenomenological criticism that Wolfgang Iser practices in *The Implied Reader* and *The Act of Reading* with the *Receptionsästhetik* of Hans Robert Jauss that examines, in studies like *Toward an Aesthetic of Reception* and *Aesthetic Experience and Literary Hermeneutics,* the changing responses of entire peoples or communities over time. Nevertheless, under the same heading one could make room for the parallel, and much more empirical, emphasis of critics like Nina Baym, in *Novels, Readers, and Reviewers,* and Cathy N. Davidson, in *Revolution and the Word,* who seek to rehistoricize the reading experience itself by examining the recorded responses of the readers of any text or the history of the use of particular books, and align such criticism with the stress that Frank Kermode, in *The Classic,* and Stanley Fish, in *Is There a Text in This Class?,* have placed on the roles, respectively, of interpretive institutions and interpretive communities. Such a map would reveal that much recent interdisciplinary criticism focusing on the experience of the reader has been propelled by a grammar of feminist, ethnic, or class-oriented ideological motives, but it would also disclose that some of this criticism—Norman Holland's *Dynamics of Literary Response,* Barthes's *Pleasure of the Text,* Gilles Deleuze and Félix Guattari's *Anti-Oedipus,* Julia Kristeva's *Powers of Horror,* Peter Brooks's *Reading for the Plot,* Robert Scholes's *Textual Power,* and Mary Jacobus's *Reading Women*—has reflected interests that were psychoanalytic, structuralist, feminist, deconstructionist, semiotic, or a combination of all five.

Were one to redraw the map of contemporary interdisciplinary studies in relation to the critical coordinate of the text itself, however, one could similarly highlight, as well as link, a variety of still other kinds of interdisciplinary studies. One point of departure for such a cartographic exercise might be the extraordinary developments that followed on the emergence of modern linguistics, a field that grew out of the convergence of work by Russian formalists, like Viktor Shklovsky and Yuri Tynyanov, and Czech linguists associated with Jan Mukarovsky and the Prague school, with, again, the language theory of Saussure and the semiotics theory of Charles Sanders Peirce, all of which conspired to produce methods that applied linguistic insights to the study of culture conceived as a system of signs. A key figure in these developments was Roman Jakobson, who, in emigrating first from Moscow to Prague and then from Prague to the United States, helped bridge the gap between linguistics and semiotics and thus encouraged interdisciplinary activities as widely varied as the stylistics criticism of Michael Riffaterre, the poetics analysis of Juri Lotman, and the narratological studies of scholars like A. J. Greimas, Tzvetan Todorov, Gérard Genette, Claude Bremond, and, now, Paul Ricoeur (see also the essay by Finegan in this volume).

But the emergent field of linguistics also promoted interdisciplinary work in areas quite distant from the study of the structure and properties of language.

In one direction, it influenced the structuralist orientation that Claude Lévi-Strauss, and later Edmund Leach, brought to ethnographic studies and the development of social anthropology in general (see the essay by Baron in this volume). In another, it helped shape formalistic and generic interests that run from the conservative, archetypal criticism represented by Northrop Frye's *Anatomy of Criticism* to the radical dialogic criticism associated with Mikhail Bakhtin's *Rabelais and His World* and *The Dialogic Imagination.*

But the field of linguistics and its many affiliations (indeed, far more than can be enumerated here) is only one of the interdisciplinary modes of study promoted by (even as it promoted) the study of the literary coordinate known as the text. To draw out the lines of interdisciplinary relation that emanate from the textual coordinate, one would have to take into account everything from the development of hermeneutics (or interpretation theory), starting with the work of Wilhelm Dilthey and Martin Heidegger and continuing through that of Hans-Georg Gadamer and Paul Ricoeur, to the new criticism of what Fredric Jameson calls "the political unconscious." The latter has its roots in the work of Walter Benjamin and other members of the Frankfurt school (Max Horkheimer and Theodor Adorno), as well as in the writings of Antonio Gramsci, and its expression in the writings of critics as various as Lucien Goldmann, Louis Althusser, Raymond Williams, Pierre Macherey, and Robert Weimann (see also the essay by Marshall in this volume).

Still another way to map the varieties of interdisciplinary study would be to start with some of the new subjects it has helped make available for critical analysis—the history of the book; the materialism of body; the psychoanalysis of the reader and the reading process; the sociology of conventions; the semiotics of signification; the historization of representation; the ideology of gender, race, and class; intertextuality; power; otherness; and undecidability—but it would be necessary to add that each of these topics, as currently, though variously, construed, has also served both to attract and to project still further lines of interdisciplinary investigation. Studies like *The Body in Pain* by Elaine Scarry, for example, have woven psychoanalytic, cultural, materialistic, neo-Marxist, and new-historicist strands of disciplinary interrogation; studies of representation such as Stephen J. Greenblatt's *Shakespearean Negotiations* have drawn into new combinations historicist, reader-response, cultural materialist, hermeneutic, semiotic, and often deconstructionist inter- and cross-disciplinary modes. But in much of the newer interdisciplinary scholarship, studies of the body become studies of representation. Thus the threading of disciplinary principles and procedures is frequently doubled, tripled, and quadrupled, in ways that are not only mixed but, from a conventional disciplinary perspective, somewhat off center.

So described, the overlapping, underlayered, interlaced, crosshatched affiliations, coalitions, and alliances toward which these cartographic operations lead can become truly baffling. Furthermore, insofar as they imply that disciplinary traditions of descent or influence always flow in one direction and in continuously visible and hence traceable channels, such mapmaking exercises can also become misleading, since the inevitable result of much interdisciplinary study, if not its ostensible purpose, is to dispute and disorder conventional under-standings of the relations between such things as origin and terminus, center and periphery, focus and margin, inside and outside.

These observations raise an obvious question about whether the simplest, or at least the most coherent, way to conceptualize the kinds of interdisciplinary studies that have emerged from relational or interrelational studies might not be to focus directly on the associations that literature, or rather literary study, have developed with other recognized, institutionalized fields of academic in-quiry. On this basis one could simply describe the interdisciplinary endeavors that have grown out of the study of, say, literature and philosophy (phenome-nological criticism, hermeneutics, deconstruction, neopragmatism, ethical criti-cism, the new rhetorical criticism), literature and anthropology (structuralism, ethnography, or "thick description," folklore and folklife studies, myth criti-cism), literature and psychology (psychoanalytic criticism, reader-response criti-cism, anxiety-of-influence criticism, cultural psychology), literature and politics (sociological criticism, cultural studies, ideological criticism, materialist stud-ies), literature and religion (theological apologetics, recuperative hermeneutics, generic and historical criticism, rhetoric studies), and literature and linguistics (Russian formalism, stylistics, narratology, semiotics). However, what has to be borne in mind is that these correlate fields (anthropology, philosophy, religious studies, psychology, etc.) have themselves changed—and sometimes dramati-cally—during the last quarter century, and among a variety of factors generat-ing that instability and revisionary ferment has been the success of the particular interdisciplinary initiatives they have either stimulated or helped sus-tain. It is also worth noting that fewer than half the academic fields with which literature has historically enjoyed or established important ties are even men-tioned here (some of the others cited in specific chapters of Barricelli and Gibal-di's *Interrelations of Literature* include myth, folklore, sociology, law, science, music, the visual arts, and film). Among those omitted, several, like law and science, are tethered to literature's earliest beginnings, and at least one—film studies—is intimately connected to literature's future fortunes.

But if relational and interrelational studies have precipitated and promoted the creation of certain kinds of interdisciplinary studies, they have clearly dis-couraged the development of others. Consider, for example, the relations be-tween literature and music. Study of the relations between literature and music goes back to the prehistory of literature itself, when verbal forms were first emancipated from their sedimentation in sound and song. This interest has taken a variety of forms over the ages, from the study of such musical elements as rhythm, rhyme, alliteration, tone, voice, variation, balance, repetition, con-trast, and counterpoint, to the vast and complex historical ties between particu-lar musical types, like the rondeau or the symphony, and the verse forms of Alfred de Mussert and Algernon Swinburne or Thomas Mann's *Doctor Faustus* and Herman Broch's *Sleepwalkers*. The musicality of literature and the literari-ness of music are synonymous with works like Giuseppe Verdi's *Macbeth* and *Otello*, Alban Berg's *Wozzeck*, Benjamin Britten's *Billy Budd*, Franz Liszt's *Dante* and *Faust* symphonies, Richard Strauss's *Don Juan*, Claude Debussy's

Prélude à l'après-midi d'un faune. Writers such as Jean-Jacques Rousseau, Denis Diderot, Novalis, Heinrich Heine, E. T. A. Hoffmann, Giuseppe Mazzini, Friedrich Nietzsche, André Gide, Bertholt Brecht, Aldous Huxley, James Joyce, and T. S. Eliot have all sought to translate musical technique into literary practice. Yet despite the eloquent arguments of critics like George Steiner that the quintessential form of art in literature is its music, or the testimony of distinguished musicologists like Leonard B. Meyers that music can never rid itself completely of the element of story, the venerable association of music with literature and literature with music—so intelligently interpreted in texts like T. S. Eliot's *Music of Poetry,* Calvin S. Brown's *Music and Literature,* Carl Dahlhaus's *Musikästhetik,* Steven Paul Scher's *Literatur und Musik,* John Hollander's *Untuning of the Sky,* or even the chapter "Literature and the Other Arts" in *Theory of Literature,* edited by René Wellek and Austin Warren—has rarely led to the programmatic development of interdisciplinary approaches to the study of either the musicality of literary forms and meanings or of the literary dimensions of music. In musical studies itself, however, the case is different, as the interdisciplinary fields of opera studies, ethnomusicology, and even the aesthetics of music amply attest.

Similarly, despite countless distinguished examples, the long record of informed study of the relations between the visual and the verbal arts has only rarely resulted in the creation of interdisciplinary, as opposed to cross- or transdisciplinary, modes of study, in which disciplinary boundaries, instead of merely being bridged, are actually redrawn. While there have been numerous disciplinary exchanges between the literary and the plastic arts, there has been surprisingly little reconception of each in the image of the other. This is the more to be marveled at both because of the existence of academic programs organized to examine this relationship and because of the brilliant interdisciplinary research in which it has issued in the work of Rudolf Arnheim, E. H. Gombrich, Erwin Panofsky, Meyer Schapiro, Richard Wollheim, Ronald Paulson, Arthur C. Danto, Barbara Novak, and Michael Fried. There are countless literary texts that treat works of visual art or the things they delineate, that employ visual techniques, that are linked to historical movements and manifestos associated with the visual arts, that call on interpretive skills they have helped develop, or that otherwise inscribe visual modes of conception and assessment; but none has proved capable of overcoming either one of two kinds of resistance—the first to interpretation itself on the part of many art historians, the second to the intellectual power and percipience of the visual on the part of many literary scholars and critics. If art historians routinely eschew criticism for cataloging, evaluation for description, literary historians and critics have typically treated all the fine arts as mere complements, adjuncts, illustrations of the verbal arts.

Striking evidence of this latter phenomenon can be found in Thomas Bender's *New York Intellect,* a study of the intellectual life of New York City from the middle of the eighteenth century to the middle of the twentieth. By the end of this period, the culture of the city was recognized throughout the world for its eminence in at least three of the fine arts—painting, dance, and music.

By mid-century it had also nurtured an extraordinary group of critics, known as the New York intellectuals, who were associated with the *Partisan Review* and other magazines. Yet despite the cosmopolitanism of figures like Lionel Trilling, Philip Rahv, Alfred Kazin, Irving Howe, and Sidney Hook, virtually none of the New York intellectuals, with the occasional exception of a Harold Rosenberg and a Clement Greenberg, paid any attention to the artistic areas in which New York culture had achieved international recognition.

This is not to suggest, then, that there have been no interfield or transfield studies of literature and art or literature and music, much less that these initiatives have failed to produce work of enormous and lasting value. Nor is it to claim that in the future such initiatives may not generate still more systematic and more institutionalized modes of interdisciplinary inquiry that reconstitute the materials and methods that currently compose those modes. It is merely to assert that a new confederation of practices, however salutary, is not a new configuration of methods, however experimental; and until a new configuration of methods produces a refiguration of material, one does not have what can be called a genuinely interdisciplinary form of study. Interdisciplinarity involves a rethinking not just of conceptual frames but of their perceptual ground, as Alan Liu has argued in an as yet unpublished paper entitled "Indiscipline, Interdiscipline, and Liberty: The Revolutionary Paradigm." What gets reconceived, as Liu notes, are not only the paradigms by which one discipline makes sense of itself to itself with the help of another but the way such processes of reconception provide both disciplines with new ways of representing their own knowledge to themselves.

Factors Contributing to Interdisciplinarity

Where did this new interest in interdisciplinarity come from? Was it the result of factors confined to the institutional culture of academic literary studies or the product of wider educational and social forces? Did it emerge all at once or in successive historical stages? What forms of resistance has the development of interdisciplinarity met? How is one to assess its benefits, and what sorts of problems is interdisciplinary study likely to confront in the future?

These difficult and important questions are being vigorously contested. In addition to admitting of different and frequently conflicting answers, they are questions whose very form can be challenged as prejudicial. What they presume is that interdisciplinarity can be treated as a unified or coherent movement whose progress has typically been forward and uninterrupted, when its development seems more often to have described a course of successive, tentative, often uncoordinated forays and retreats whose progress was more crabwise than linear. Another way to put this would be to say that just as intelligent theory always holds out the possibility of unintelligent practice, as Gilbert Ryle once observed, so it is equally possible that intelligent practice can sometimes be performed in the name of unintelligent, or at least unconscious or only half-conscious, theory. If this notion tells us anything, it should confirm the fact that forms of interdisciplinary study often emerge by accident. When not driven simply by the vagaries of fashion or the metaphysics of theory, they are usually occasioned by critical conundrums and simply offer themselves as workable solutions to practical problems. In other words, interdisciplinarity is the pragmatist's response to the dilemma of disciplinary essentialism.

Yet this is not to say that interdisciplinary study can flourish in an unfavorable environment. After World War II, for example, when the pedagogy known in the United States as the New Criticism was in full sway, interdisciplinary literary studies were in a state of noticeable arrest and, where not arrested, were seriously eclipsed by other, more formalistic and inward-looking methodologies. But the ideology of interpretive refinement then epitomized by the New Criticism, or rather epitomized by its pedagogic practitioners in the schools— among its various proponents, like John Crowe Ransom, Allen Tate, R. P. Blackmur, Kenneth Burke, Cleanth Brooks, and Robert Penn Warren, there were sharp and sometimes irreconcilable differences in poetics and procedure— had a much more deleterious effect (and still does) in England than in the United States; and even where similar prejudices were at work on the Continent, Europeans have always been more responsive to interdisciplinary initiatives than either the British or the Americans. Part of this difference stems, no doubt, from the looser departmental structure of the European university system, and part, as well, from the role that philosophical discourse and ideas generally have traditionally played in European intellectual culture.

But generalizations like this are notoriously porous. The American university in the twentieth century has been surprisingly hospitable to a variety of interdisciplinary experiments without altering the way it organizes the structure of knowledge. With respect to literary study, this paradox has been explained by Gerald Graff as the result of the "field-coverage principle" (6–9). According to Graff, the principle enables departments of English to retain their power and organization by welcoming new fields and methods to the fold without permitting them to challenge their established hierarchies concerning the nature and teaching of literature.

The trouble with this explanation is that it may concede too much to the leftist view that identifies the American university with other institutions of the corporate state and postulates that its expansion, like that of capitalism generally, derives from its ability to absorb the elements of conflict it produces. While academic institutions certainly exhibit something of the "repressive tolerance," as Herbert Marcuse called it, of late capitalism, it would be more accurate to say that the movement toward interdisciplinary studies has no doubt resulted from many factors, both institutional and conceptual. If the field-coverage principle has proved influential in determining the way the field's intentions and achievements have been perceived and assimilated, the seismic theoretical shift that Roland Barthes first noticed from *work* to *text* has influenced the way interdisciplinary studies has, insofar as it can be said to possess an integrated vision at all, construed itself.

The discovery of the new world of textuality and intertextuality has served to question a number of interpretive shibboleths that controlled literary study for many decades. Among them are the following: that there is one "definitive" meaning of any text that is to be associated with the intentions of some transcendent Author; that there is any such thing as an Author, transcendent or otherwise, who is alone, or even chiefly, responsible for what a text means; that texts must be read independent of their relations, anxious or imperialistic, to other texts; that reading can be viewed only as a process of reception and absorption but not of production and intervention; and that when reading, interpretation, criticism are seen as creative and not merely reflective activities, their operations must still be restricted to individual works and cannot be expanded to apply "literary" modes of analysis to the entire spectrum of cultural phenomena (Macksey).

Recent exploration of the new world of the text and the intertext has brought with it a new diversification of our sense of the relations not only between one text and another but also between any text and its putative "context." Not only has the notion of "context" been broadened to encompass things that had never been construed as "literary" before—the experiences of women, of people of color, of members of so-called underclasses like the poor, the illiterate, and the homeless, of ethnic minorities, of regions like the South, the West, or the Northeast, and of marginalized groups like gays, the aged, and, now, thanks to the hospice movement and the awareness of AIDS, the terminally ill—it has also been reconstrued as a concept no less "artificial," "constructed," or "fictive" than that of "text" itself.

In modern literary study, the notion of "context" has been most closely associated with the notion of "culture," but in recent years "culture" has itself been radically historicized. As the concept of culture has been viewed against the background of its appearance in the eighteenth century and its transformation in the nineteenth century in response to such complex social and political developments as the rise of nationalism, the emergence of the middle class, the industrialization and urbanization of commerce, the democratization of social life, and the professionalization of the arts, it has become clear that cultures function in different ways in different historic communities, and even in various ways at different times in the same community. Like canons, cultures are always in the process of revision as their constituent elements are challenged, refashioned, and replaced. This same process of historicization has also raised important questions about whether the culture concept has not outlived its usefulness. As the anthropologist James Clifford has proposed (21–54), cultures are not only unstable, selective, contingent, strategic, and incompletely integrated; in actual historical experience, they tend to function less as enduring forms than as, in Wallace Stevens's phrase, "Supreme Fictions": ways of creating collective identity in the face of forces that threaten it.

The problematization of the concept of culture has in turn contributed to skepticism about the idea of the "West." This skepticism has naturally been aroused by discoveries by social and cultural anthropologists, but it has also been generated by the results of postcolonial criticism (in the work of, to name only a few, Octavio Paz, Nadine Gordimer, Homi Bhabha, Edward Said, Stuart Hall, and Carlos Fuentes) and the new interest now beginning to be displayed by departments of English and comparative literature in writers from

Central and South America, the Caribbean world, Africa, Asia, the Middle East, the Indian subcontinent, and Eastern Europe. Causing further erosion of the boundaries between cultures and contexts, these interdisciplinary undertakings have revealed how, when used comparatively, the idea of the "West" has been employed repeatedly to the disadvantage of its discursive opposites (the "Orient," the "Third World," "newly liberated peoples"), and how, when used normatively, as a broadly monocentric cultural entity, it has served to cloak many of the tensions, confusions, conflicts, and divisions that characterize it.

Taken together, these factors have created a more pluralistic and, in some ways, more adversarial, or at least more disputatious, climate in criticism, a climate that has opened the way for what Paul Ricoeur once called "the conflict of interpretations." Aside from the fact that some critics take this conflict of interpretations to be a cacophony, what really has occurred is not an increase in the level of discord so much as a realization that dialogue, contestation, diversity of opinion may be all that interpretation shall ever finally attain. But if the achievement of interpretive consensus, or agreement, or uniformity has come to be recognized as quite possibly an illusory ideal in the human sciences—just as, earlier, Thomas Jefferson perceived it to be an illusory ideal in political affairs—then one can begin to appreciate how essential, how really crucial, interdisciplinary studies are to that "refinement of debate," in Clifford Geertz's phrasing, that can be achieved in its place (*Interpretation* 29).

The Prospects of Interdisciplinary Studies

Interdisciplinarity will remain integral to this deepening of the debate in the human sciences only so long as it remains suspicious of its own grounds, only so long as it refuses to hypostatize or totalize its methodological fascination with discrepancies, divergences, disjunctions, and difference. The threat of hypostatization or totalization in interdisciplinary studies comes from one of two temptations. The first is disciplinary reductionism, or the temptation to think that the methods of one field are sufficient to interpret the materials of many. The second is the appetite for metaphorical transfer, or the temptation to treat the materials of one field as mere epiphenomena of the subjects of another. The future of interdisciplinary studies depends, of course, on avoiding such temptations. But it also depends on a number of other, more institutional and material factors, such as the availability of funds to support the development of graduate programs, centers for study, summer institutes, visiting and permanent professorships, outlets for publication, interdepartmental colloquia, and scholarships.

Chief among these more objective elements is the ongoing controversy within the humanities (and beyond them) about whether universities are to be defined as institutions devoted principally to the reproduction and transmission of culture or, rather, to the critique and re-creation of culture (Culler 33–36). While this is not a distinction anyone would have thought of making, at least in American higher education, twenty or thirty years ago, it now shapes much of the debate about the reorganization of knowledge and the politics of the academy. Within the humanities the debate centers on the nature and effect of cultural representations, and within interdisciplinary studies (if not also outside) the division takes place between those who see the study of cultural representations as a political struggle over the sources and symptomatics of power and those who view that study, instead, as a hermeneutic struggle over the hierarchies and heuristics of value. In studying cultural texts, what are we trying to do: determine how and by whom the world should be governed, or decide which values should organize our experience of it?

While these purposes are by no means unrelated, neither are they the same. The long-term challenge for interdisciplinary studies is to remain undaunted by the tension between them without being seduced into thinking that this tension can be easily reduced or overcome. What is most productive intellectually in the current practice of interdisciplinary studies is neither the utopian hope that the tension can ultimately be erased nor the complacent belief that it finally doesn't matter; what has been most productive is the inescapable fact of the tension itself and the deepened, pragmatic appreciation to which it has given rise: of how knowledge is always open to further interpretation and criticism, of how understanding is always susceptible to further correction and realization.

Suggestions for Further Reading

It is well to remember that reflection on interdisciplinary studies possesses a long and illustrious genealogy. In the West it begins with such texts as Plato's *Republic* and Aristotle's *Nichomachean Ethics* and proceeds through Francis Bacon's *Novum Organum* and Giambattista Vico's *New Science* to Georg Wilhelm Friedrich Hegel's *Phenomenology of Spirit*, Charles Sanders Peirce's pioneering essays on the theory of signs, and Wilhelm Dilthey's *Gesammelte Schriften*. As we move closer to the present and confine ourselves to works that have developed general models for the reorganization of disciplinary inquiry with particular bearing on literary studies, we must make special mention of Northrop Frye's compendium of myth and archetypal criticism, *Anatomy of Criticism;* Hans-Georg Gadamer's magisterial study of the theory of interpretation, *Truth and Method;* Michel Foucault's highly influential attempt to create an archaeology of the human sciences, *The Order of Things;* Umberto Eco's elaboration of a theory of signs, *A Theory of Semiotics;* Jacques Derrida's development of the theory of deconstruction, *Of Grammatology;* and Pierre Bourdieu's attempt to reground the social sciences in a theory of symbolic capital and authority, *Outline of a Theory of Practice.*

In American literary study, interdisciplinary thinking in a number of fields has been broadly influenced by a variety of important late-twentieth-century texts. Among the most important are Roland Barthes's *Writing Degree Zero,* Raymond Williams's *Culture and Society, 1780–1950,* Claude Lévi-Strauss's *Structural Anthropology,* E. D. Hirsch's *Validity in Interpretation,* Georg Lukács's *Realism in Our Time,* Clifford Geertz's *Interpretation of Cultures,* Hayden White's *Metahistory,* Walter Benjamin's *Illuminations,* Harold Bloom's *Anxiety of Influence,* Jacques Lacan's *Ecrits,* Sandra M. Gilbert and Susan Gubar's *Madwoman in the Attic,* John Searle's *Speech Acts,* Mikhail Bakhtin's *Rabelais and His World* and *Dialogic Imagination,* Paul Ricoeur's *Freud and Philosophy,* Edward Said's *Orientalism,* Stephen J. Greenblatt's *Renaissance Self-Fashioning,* and Roger Chartier's *Cultural History.*

The most readable history of interdisciplinary initiatives, and the resistances they have encountered, in the formation of American literary study is Gerald Graff's *Professing Literature.* The most accessible summary of the ideology of interdisciplinarity in contemporary literary studies appears in Stanley Fish's "Being Interdisciplinary Is So Very Hard to Do." But the most impressive demonstrations of the efficacy of interdisciplinary inquiry are still to be found in the way it has helped redefine and extend research in every period of literary study, from the Age of Pericles to postmodernism, and in every methodological orientation, from philology to phenomenology and from history to hermeneutics.

Works Cited and Recommended

Abrams, M. H. *The Mirror and the Lamp: Romantic Theory and the Critical Tradition.* New York: Oxford UP, 1953.

Althusser, Louis. *For Marx.* Trans. Ben Brewster. New York: Pantheon, 1969.

Aristotle. *Nichomachean Ethics.* Trans. L. H. G. Greenwood. Cambridge: Cambridge UP, 1909.

Bacon, Francis. *Bacon's Novum Organum.* Ed. Thomas Fowler. Oxford: Clarendon P, 1878.

Bakhtin, Mikhail. *The Dialogic Imagination.* Ed. Michael Holquist. Trans. Caryl Emerson and Michael Holquist. Austin: U of Texas P, 1981.

———. *Rabelais and His World.* Trans. Helene Iswolsky. Cambridge: MIT P, 1968.

Barricelli, Jean-Paul, and Joseph Gibaldi, eds. *Interrelations of Literature.* New York: MLA, 1982.

Barthes, Roland. "From Work to Text." *Textual Strategies: Perspectives in Post-structuralist Criticism.* Ed. Josue V. Harari. Ithaca: Cornell UP, 1979. 73–81.

———. *The Pleasure of the Text.* Trans. Richard Miller. New York: Hill, 1975.

———. *Writing Degree Zero.* Trans. Annette Lavers and Colin Smith. New York: Hill, 1967.

Baym, Nina. *Novels, Readers, and Reviewers: Responses to Fiction in Antebellum America.* Ithaca: Cornell UP, 1984.

Bender, Thomas. *New York Intellect: A History of Intellectual Life in New York City from 1750 to the Beginnings of Our Time.* New York: Knopf, 1987.

Benjamin, Walter. *Illuminations: Essays and Reflections.* Ed. Hannah Arendt. Trans. Harry Zohn. New York: Schocken, 1968.

———. *The Origin of German Tragic Drama.* Trans. John Osborne. London: New Left, 1977.

Bhabha, Homi, ed. *Nation and Narration.* New York: Routledge, 1989.

Bloom, Harold. *The Anxiety of Influence: A Theory of Poetry.* New York: Oxford UP, 1975.

Booth, Wayne C. *The Company We Keep: An Ethics of Fiction.* Berkeley: U of California P, 1988.

Bourdieu, Pierre. *Outline of a Theory of Practice.* Trans. Richard Nice. Cambridge: Cambridge UP, 1977.

Bremond, Claude. *Logique du recit.* Paris: Seuil, 1973.

Bromwich, David. *A Choice of Inheritance: Self and Community from Edmund Burke to Robert Frost.* Cambridge: Harvard UP, 1989.

Brooks, Peter. *Reading for the Plot.* New York: Knopf, 1984.

Brown, Calvin S. *Music and Literature: A Comparison of the Arts.* Athens: U of Georgia P, 1948.

Cavell, Stanley. *The Senses of Walden.* New York: Viking, 1972.

Chartier, Roger. *Cultural History: Between Practices and Representations.* Trans. Lydia G. Cochrane. Ithaca: Cornell UP, 1988.

Chodorow, Nancy. *The Reproduction of Mothering: Psychoanalysis and the Sociology of Gender.* Berkeley: U of California P, 1978.

Clifford, James. *The Predicament of Culture: Twentieth-Century Ethnography.* Cambridge: Harvard UP, 1988.

Coleridge, Samuel Taylor. *Biographia Literaria.* Oxford: Clarendon, 1907.

Culler, Jonathan. *Framing the Sign: Criticism and Its Institutions.* New York: Blackwell, 1988.

Dahlhaus, Carl. *Musikästhetik.* Köln: Gerig, 1967.

Danto, Arthur C. *The Philosophical Disenfranchisement of Art.* New York: Columbia UP, 1986.

Davidson, Cathy N. *Revolution and the Word: The Rise of the Novel in America.* New York: Oxford UP, 1986.

Deleuze, Gilles, and Félix Guattari. *Anti-Oedipus: Capitalism and Schizophrenia.* Trans. Robert Hurley et al. New York: Viking, 1977.

Derrida, Jacques. *Of Grammatology.* Trans. Gayatri C. Spivak. Baltimore: Johns Hopkins UP, 1976.

Dewey, John. *Art as Experience.* New York: Capricorn, 1959.

Dilthey, Wilhelm. *Gesammelte Schriften.* 14 vols. Leipzig: Tuebner, 1921–90.

Dufrenne, Mikel. *The Phenomenology of Aesthetic Experience.* Trans. Edward S. Casey and Albert Anderson. Evanston: Northwestern UP, 1973.

Eco, Umberto. *A Theory of Semiotics.* Bloomington: Indiana UP, 1976.

Eliot, T. S. *The Music of Poetry.* Glasgow: Glasgow UP, 1942.

Fish, Stanley. "Being Interdisciplinary Is So Very Hard to Do." *Profession 89.* New York: MLA, 1989. 15–22.

———. *Is There a Text in This Class? The Authority of Interpretive Communities.* Cambridge: Harvard UP, 1980.

Foucault, Michel. *The Order of Things: An Archaeology of the Human Sciences.* Trans. Allan Sheridan. New York: Vintage-Random, 1973.

Fried, Michael. *Realism, Writing, Disfiguration: On Thomas Eakin and Stephen Crane.* Chicago: U of Chicago P, 1987.

Frye, Northrop. *Anatomy of Criticism: Four Essays.* Princeton: Princeton UP, 1957.

Fuentes, Carlos. *Myself with Others: Selected Essays.* New York: Farrar, 1988.

Gadamer, Hans-Georg. *Truth and Method.* Trans. Garrett Barden and John Cumming. New York: Seabury, 1975.

Geertz, Clifford. "Blurred Genres: The Refiguration of Social Thought." *The American Scholar* 49.2 (1980): 165–79.

———. *The Interpretation of Cultures.* New York: Basic, 1973.

Genette, Gérard. *Narrative Discourse: An Essay in Method.* Trans. Jane E. Lewin. Ithaca: Cornell UP, 1980.

Gilbert, Sandra M., and Susan Gubar. *The Madwoman in the Attic: The Woman Writer and the Nineteenth-Century Literary Imagination.* New Haven: Yale UP, 1979.

Goldmann, Lucien. *The Hidden God: A Study of Tragic Vision in the* Pensées *of Pascal and the Tragedies of Racine.* Trans. Philip Thody. London: Routledge, 1964.

Gombrich, E. H. *Art and Illusion: A Study in the Psychology of Pictorial Representation.* New York: Pantheon, 1960.

Goodman, Nelson. *Languages of Art: An Approach to a Theory of Symbols.* Indianapolis: Bobbs, 1968.

Gordimer, Nadine. *The Essential Gesture: Writing, Politics, and Places.* Ed. Stephen Clingman. London: Cape, 1988.

Graff, Gerald. *Professing Literature: An Institutional History.* Chicago: U of Chicago P, 1987.

Gramsci, Antonio. *Letters from Prison.* Trans. Lynne Lawner. New York: Farrar, 1989.

Greenberg, Clement. *Art and Culture: Critical Essays.* Boston: Beacon, 1961.

Greenblatt, Stephen J. *Renaissance Self-Fashioning: From More to Shakespeare.* Chicago: U of Chicago P, 1980.

———. *Shakespearean Negotiations: The Circulation of Social Energy in Renaissance England.* Berkeley: U of California P, 1988.

Greimas, A. J. *Structural Semantics: An Attempt at a Method.* Trans. Daniele McDowell, Ronald Schleifer, and Alan Velie. Lincoln: U of Nebraska P, 1983.

Hall, Stuart, et al., eds. *Culture, Media, Language.* London: Hutchinson, 1983.

Hegel, Georg Wilhelm Friedrich. *The Phenomenology of Spirit.* Trans. A. V. Miller. Oxford: Clarendon—Oxford UP, 1977.

Heidegger, Martin. *The End of Philosophy.* Trans. Joan Stambaugh. New York: Harper, 1973.

———. *Poetry, Language, and Thought.* Trans. Albert Hofstadter. New York: Harper, 1971.

Hernadi, Paul. "Literary Theory: A Compass." *Critical Inquiry* 3 (1976): 369–86.

Hirsch, E. D., Jr. *Validity in Interpretation.* New Haven: Yale UP, 1967.

Holland, Norman. *The Dynamics of Literary Response.* New York: Oxford UP, 1968.

Hollander, John. *The Untuning of the Sky: Ideas of Music in English Poetry, 1500–1700.* Princeton: Princeton UP, 1961.

Horkheimer, Max, and Theodor Adorno. *Dialectic of Enlightenment.* Trans. John Cumming. New York: Seabury, 1972.

Iser, Wolfgang. *The Act of Reading: A Theory of Aesthetic Response.* Baltimore: Johns Hopkins UP, 1978.
———. *The Implied Reader.* Baltimore: Johns Hopkins UP, 1974.
Jacobus, Mary. *Reading Women: Essays in Feminist Criticism.* New York: Columbia UP, 1986.
Jakobson, Roman. *Selected Writings.* 2nd ed. The Hague: Mouton, 1972–85.
Jameson, Fredric. *The Political Unconscious: Narrative as a Socially Symbolic Act.* Ithaca: Cornell UP, 1981.
Jauss, Hans Robert. *Aesthetic Experience and Literary Hermeneutics.* Trans. Michael Shaw. Minneapolis: U of Minnesota P, 1982.
———. *Toward an Aesthetic of Reception.* Trans. Timothy Bahti. Minneapolis: U of Minnesota P, 1982.
Jehlen, Myra. *American Incarnation.* Cambridge: Harvard UP, 1986.
Kermode, Frank. *The Classic: Literary Images of Permanence and Change.* New York: Viking, 1975.
Kristeva, Julia. *Powers of Horror: An Essay on Abjection.* Trans. Leon Roudiez. New York: Columbia UP, 1982.
Lacan, Jacques. *Ecrits: A Selection.* Trans. Alan Sheridan. New York: Norton, 1977.
Leach, Edmund. *Genesis as Myth and Other Essays.* London: Cape, 1969.
Leavis, F. R. *The Great Tradition.* Garden City: Anchor-Doubleday, 1954.
Lévi-Strauss, Claude. *Structural Anthropology.* Vol. 1. Trans. C. Jacobson and B. G. Shoepf. London: Allen, 1968.
———. *Tristes Tropique.* Trans. John Weightman and Doreen Weightman. New York: Pocket, 1977.
Lotman, Juri. *Analysis of the Poetic Text.* Trans. D. Barton Johnson. Ann Arbor: Ardis, 1976.
Lukács, Georg. *Realism in Our Time: Literature and the Class Struggle.* Trans. John Mander and Necke Mander. New York: Harper, 1964.
Macherey, Pierre. *A Theory of Literary Production.* Trans. Geoffrey Wall. London: Routledge, 1978.
Macksey, Richard. "A New Text of the World." *Genre* 16 (1983): 307–16.
Macksey, Richard, and Eugenio Donato, eds. *The Structuralist Controversy: The Languages of Criticism and the Sciences of Man.* Baltimore: Johns Hopkins UP, 1970.
Marcuse, Herbert. *Eros and Civilization: A Philosophical Inquiry into Freud.* Boston: Beacon, 1974.
Mukarovsky, Jan. *Aesthetic Function: Norm and Value as Social Facts.* Trans. Mark E. Suino. Ann Arbor: U of Michigan P, 1970.
Nietzsche, Friedrich. *The Will to Power.* Trans. Walter Kaufmann. New York: Vintage, 1968.
Novak, Barbara. *Nature and Culture: American Landscape and Painting, 1825–1875.* New York: Oxford UP, 1980.
Nussbaum, Martha C. *The Fragility of Goodness: Luck and Ethics in Greek Tragedy and Philosophy.* New York: Cambridge UP, 1986.
———. *Love's Knowledge.* New York: Oxford UP, 1990.
———. "Narrative Emotions: Beckett's Genealogy of Love." *Ethics* 98 (1988): 225–54.
Panofsky, Erwin. *Studies in Iconology: Humanistic Themes in the Art of the Renaissance.* New York: Harper, 1972.
Paulson, Ronald. *Emblem and Expression: Meaning in English Art of the Eighteenth Century.* Cambridge: Harvard UP, 1975.
Paz, Octavio. *The Labyrinth of Solitude.* Trans. Lysander Kemp. New York: Grove, 1962.
Peirce, Charles Sanders. *Collected Papers.* Ed. Charles Hartshorne and Paul Weiss. 6 vols. Cambridge: Harvard UP, 1931–35.
Plato. *Republic.* Trans. Paul Shorey. Cambridge: Harvard UP, 1935.
Ricoeur, Paul. *The Conflict of Interpretations: Essays on Hermeneutics.* Ed. Don Ihde. Evanston: Northwestern UP, 1969.
———. *Freud and Philosophy: An Essay on Interpretation.* Trans. Denis Savage. New Haven: Yale UP, 1970.
———. *Time and Narrative.* Trans. Kathleen McLaughlin and David Pellauer. 3 vols. Chicago: U of Chicago P, 1984–88.
Riffaterre, Michael. *Text Production.* Trans. Therese Lyons. New York: Columbia UP, 1983.
Rosenberg, Harold. *The Tradition of the New.* New York: Horizon, 1959.
Said, Edward. *Orientalism.* New York: Pantheon, 1978.
Saussure, Ferdinand de. *Course in General Linguistics.* Trans. Wade Baskin. New York: McGraw, 1966.
Scarry, Elaine. *The Body in Pain: The Making and Unmaking of the World.* New York: Oxford UP, 1986.
Schapiro, Meyer. *Modern Art, Nineteenth and Twentieth Centuries: Selected Papers.* New York: Braziller, 1979.
Scher, Steven Paul, ed. *Literatur und Musik: Ein Handbuch zur Theorie und Praxis eines komparatistischen Grenzgebietes.* Berlin: Schmidt, 1982.
Scholes, Robert. *Textual Power: Literary Theory and the Teaching of English.* New Haven: Yale UP, 1985.
Searle, John. *Speech Acts: An Essay in the Philosophy of Language.* Cambridge: Cambridge UP, 1969.

Shklovsky, Viktor. *Works.* Moscow: Khudozh' Lit'ra, 1973–74.

Todorov, Tzvetan. *The Poetics of Prose.* Trans. Richard Howard. Ithaca: Cornell UP, 1977.

Trachtenberg, Alan. *Reading American Photographs: Images as History from Matthew Brady to Walker Evans.* New York: Hill, 1989.

Trilling, Lionel. *The Liberal Imagination: Essays on Literature and Society.* Garden City: Anchor-Double-day, 1950.

Tynyanov, Yuri. *The Problem of Verse Language.* Trans. Michael Susa and Brent Harvey. Ann Arbor: Ardis, 1981.

Vico, Giambattista. The New Science of *Giambattista Vico.* Rev. trans. of 3rd ed. (1774) by Thomas Bergin and Max Fisch. Ithaca: Cornell UP, 1968.

Weimann, Robert. *Structure and Society in Literary History: Studies in the History and Theory of Historical Studies.* Rev. ed. Baltimore: Johns Hopkins UP, 1984.

Wellek, René, and Austin Warren. "Literature and the Other Arts." *Theory of Literature.* New York: Harcourt, 1949. 124–35.

White, Hayden. *Metahistory: The Historical Imagination in Nineteenth-Century Europe.* Baltimore: Johns Hopkins UP, 1974.

Williams, Raymond. *Culture and Society, 1780–1950.* New York: Harper, 1966.

———. *Marxism and Literature.* London: Oxford UP, 1977.

Wollheim, Richard. *Painting as an Art.* Princeton: Princeton UP, 1987.

Blurring, Cracking, and Crossing

Permeation and the Fracturing of Discipline

Julie Thompson Klein

> Certain disciplinary categories will doubtless be supplanted by others of which little or nothing is heard today, and which result either from an awareness of new points of view, or from the conjunction of sectors of research belonging at present to separate disciplines.
>
> —de Bie, "Multidisciplinary Research"

Although disciplinarity is a relatively recent concept in human history, it has attained enormous influence over the organization and production of knowledge. So powerful is disciplinarity that it constitutes a "first principle." Knowledge specialities are the "fundaments on which all else is constructed" (Clark, *Higher Education System* 35). As a result one of the prominent themes in studies of disciplinarity is boundary-work, the set of differentiating activities that attribute selected characteristics to particular branches of knowledge on the basis of differing methods, values, stocks of knowledge, and styles of organization. Boundary-work is most likely to occur, Thomas Gieryn tells us, when ideologists of a profession or occupation pursue three goals:

1. *expansion* of professional authority or expertise into domains already claimed by other professions or occupations, thereby heightening the contrast between rivals
2. *monopolization* of professional authority and resources, thereby excluding rivals from within by defining them as outsiders who are "pseudo," "deviant," or "amateur"
3. *protection* of autonomy over professional activities, thereby exempting members from responsibility for consequences of their work by putting the blame on scapegoats from outside ("Boundary-Work" 782, 792)

The majority of studies concentrate on how boundary work divides and differentiates through construction and maintenance of boundaries. However, as Gieryn's list begins to suggest, boundary work also involves the crossing, deconstructing, and reconstructing of boundaries. Permeation occurs across the

Klein, Julie Thompson. "Blurring, Cracking, and Crossing: Permeation and the Fracturing of Discipline." Ellen Messer-Davidow, David R. Shumway, David J. Sylvan (eds.) Knowledges: Historical and Critical Studies in Disciplinarity. *Charlottesville: University of Virginia Press, 1993, 185–211. Reprinted with permission of the University Press of Virginia.*

boundaries that separate one discipline from another (physics from chemistry, history from anthropology), disciplinary groupings (the sciences, technology, social sciences, and humanities), taxonomic categories (hard versus soft, pure versus applied), and larger institutional constructs (the university, industry, government, and society). Because *discipline* has been the dominant category in studies of knowledge, permeation is usually undervalued or even dismissed as a peripheral or extra-disciplinary event. However, the permeation of boundaries is a major aspect of knowledge production with significant implications for the writing of disciplinary histories and the status of discipline as a category of knowledge.

Blurring, Cracking, and Crossing

If there is an undisputed truth about disciplinarity, it is that disciplines change. Even as they debate the proper business of discipline, even as they measure and value change differently, all disciplinarians acknowledge the phenomenon of change. A powerful paradigm or school of thought may dominate a discipline at one particular time, but disciplines have not been static because they do not live in isolation. They are constantly influenced by points of view and methods of related disciplines (Easton, "Knowledge" 13). Moreover, there are numerous gaps and overlaps in their coverage of knowledge domains (Becher, *Academic Tribes* 42). As a result lines between disciplines are sometimes poorly demarcated, making boundaries, as Gieryn said of science, "ambiguous, flexible, historically changing, contextually variable, internally inconsistent, and sometimes disputed" ("Boundary-Work" 792). Boundaries are not simply lines on a map. Rather, Tony Becher explains, "they denote territorial possessions that can be encroached upon, colonized and reallocated. Some are so strongly defended as to be virtually impenetrable; others are weakly guarded and open to incoming and outgoing traffic" (*Academic Tribes* 38).

The idea that boundaries blur is not new. Recognition of shared subject matter and the pull of general theory have been recurring themes in the construction of knowledge taxonomies since Plato. Widespread awareness of blurred boundaries, though, dates from the escalating presence of cross-disciplinary activities since the mid-twentieth century, and, if any single influential text can be isolated, the 1980 publication of Clifford Geertz's seminal essay "Blurred Genres." Geertz called attention to the way analogies from the humanities—game, drama, text, speech-act analysis, discourse, and representationalist approaches related to cognitive aesthetics—were playing an increasingly visible role in sociological and anthropological explanation. Subtitling his essay "The Refiguration of Social Thought," Geertz emphasized the shift occurring among an important segment of social scientists, from physical-process analogies to symbolic-form analogies. This shift provoked widespread debate on the methods and fundamental aims of social science. It occurred, furthermore, at a time when a series of "turns"—rhetorical, literary, and interpretative—were signaling widespread dissatisfaction with positivist models of knowledge and naive theories of representation, further stimulating communication across the disciplines of the social sciences and humanities and provoking debate on the validity of boundaries that divide the anthropological from the literary, the intellectual from the political, the empirical from the interpretative, and the pure from the applied. In the wake of these debates "blurred genres" became a metaphor of the times, a ready signifier of the growing number of cross-disciplinary borrowings, projects, and new categories of knowledge that document increased permeation of disciplinary boundaries.

There are many reasons why permeation occurs. Daryl Chubin suggests it is the cracks in institutionalized science that give scientific research, in particular, a "blurred and dynamic aura" (*Sociology of Sciences* 38). The blurring of disciplinary boundaries is typically associated with research at the innovative frontier of discipline, the rhetorical foil of the established cooling core. As a result of cracks the leading edge of a boundary that divides two disciplines is often fuzzy, and talk of blurring is quickly accompanied by talk of interdisciplinarity. Dogan and Pahre even suggest that one can survey most important new work in a field "simply by walking along its boundaries" (*Creative Marginality* 1). Yet the rhetoric of the disciplinary frontier, which abounds in reports on the current state of knowledge, does not account fully or adequately for the extent of permeation. Permeation occurs across the distance of discipline, from frontier to core. There are six major and sometimes overlapping explanations for permeation:

1. the epistemological structure of a particular discipline
2. relations with neighboring disciplines
3. the pull of powerful or fashionable new tools, methods, concepts, and theories
4. the pull of problem-solving over strictly disciplinary focus
5. the complexifying of disciplinary research
6. redefinitions of what is considered intrinsic and extrinsic to discipline

To begin with, the epistemological structure of a discipline plays a major role in promoting or retarding permeation. At the broadest and most general level of disciplinary description, the value-laden categories of hardness, tightness, restrictiveness, neatness, narrowness, compactness, and maturity are distinguished from their own rhetorical foils: softness, breadth, permeability, preparadigmatic development (Becher, *Academic Tribes* 13). Impermeable boundaries are generally associated with tightly knit, convergent communities, indicating both stability and coherence of intellectual fields. The physical sciences are the classic example, economics a leading example from the social sciences. In contrast, permeable boundaries are associated with loosely knit, divergent academic groups, signaling a more fragmented, less stable, and comparatively open-ended epistemological structure. Cognitive border zones with other subject fields are more liable to be ragged and ill-defined, thus not so easy to defend. The humanities are the classic example, sociology a leading example from the social sciences. Yet, Becher cautions, the correlation is not perfect.

Hard and *soft, pure* and *applied* do not apply exclusively to one discipline or another, despite a common tendency to distinguish the "hard" physical sciences from the "soft" humanities and the dual-leaning social sciences. What is regarded as a predominantly pure discipline, Becher explains, may have clearly applied elements—such as the development of optics within academic physics—or the reverse—such as jurisprudence as a specialty in law. A field regarded universally as hard and quantitative may contain soft, qualitative elements—for instance, the study of political economics in economics; at the same time soft, qualitative areas may host hard, quantitative components—for instance, aspects of philology or linguistics in literary studies. Certain disciplines also contain a multiplicity of subunits with contrasting properties, pure and applied, hard and soft. The synoptic disciplines of history, anthropology, literary studies, and geography are cases in point. Geography, for example, has a harder physical geography on the one side and a softer human geography on the other, a more pure historical geography on the one side and a more applied climatology on the other. Psychology, too, spans a broad range, from behaviorism and psychometric research to psychoanalysis, if industrial, social, and developmental psychology are considered (Becher, "Counter-Culture" 334).

A major question then arises. What counts as discipline? Close scrutiny of epistemological structures reveals that most modern disciplines embrace a wide range of subspecialties with different features. Unidisciplinary competence is a myth, because the degree of specialization and the volume of information that fall within the boundaries of a named academic discipline are larger than any single individual can master (Campbell, "Omniscience"). Consequently meetings of such massive professional organizations as the Modern Language Association, the American Anthropological Association, and the American Historical Association are actually congeries of specialties, some isolated from each other, others closely related. As disciplines have differentiated into increasing numbers of autonomous subunits that train practitioners and provide specialist identities, goals, and techniques, only a few departments now claim to represent fully the range of specialties categorized under a single disciplinary label. R. Whitley describes the implications for science: "Increasingly, universities specialize in which part of physics or chemistry they will try to excel even if the hierarchy of specialisms ensures that the top ones will be represented in most departments. The discipline as a set of research activities has outgrown the departmental basis of employment and careers. Consequently the identification of intellectual disciplines with university undergraduate departments is no longer a social reality in many sciences. Indeed, it is not at all clear what the discipline is in these fields in terms of research activities and results" ("Rise and Decline of Disciplines" 18).

Shifting the focus in discussions of disciplinarity from disciplinary to subdisciplinary units of analysis, Becher suggests, highlights certain aspects of academic knowledge otherwise likely to be overlooked, especially overlapping interests between specialist groups within neighboring disciplinary fields. Such overlaps may be apparent in several forms of boundary-work: conflicting interpretation of the same phenomena (manifested in boundary disputes), tacit or overt division of intellectual labor (boundary maintenance), or a closer sense of identification with the inhabitants of neighboring disciplinary territory (boundary blurring). Particular segments, subspecialties, schools of thought, and sects within a discipline may also "press against" the overall culture of the discipline ("Counter-Culture" 333–35), potentially undermining the authority of a dominant approach or school of thought.

The implications are apparent in proliferating gaps between cognitive and categorical identities. An embryologist and a geneticist, for instance, may be more alike in knowledge, techniques, and interests than two chemists. Yet is it proper to call collaboration between the embryologist and the geneticist interdisciplinary while classifying as disciplinary research the joint work of two chemists who must labor to understand each other (Wolfle, "Interdisciplinary Research" 5)? Nor does having certain researchers describe their research projects necessarily give adequate clues about what discipline they were trained in. Is it proper, Wolfram Swoboda asks, to classify the scientist investigating certain molecular structures of DNA a molecular biologist, a geneticist, a biochemist, or a quantum mechanic? Is the recipient of a Ph.D. in Arctic biology from the University of Alaska really practicing the same discipline as the holder of a degree in mathematical biology from the University of Chicago or the holder of a degree in radiation biology from the University of Rochester ("Disciplines and Interdisciplinarity" 53)?

Gaps in one discipline and overlaps with subfields in another are hardly confined to the sciences. Their significance varies greatly and lack of adequate cross-disciplinary forums often results in limited exchanges. Individuals interested in cross-disciplinary problems and questions often find it easier to communicate with individuals in other disciplines or disciplinary subgroupings, even though they retain disciplinary labels reflecting their original graduate training. Sociologist Trevor Pinch, for instance, often introduces himself as a sociologist, though his research on the rhetoric of science has much more in common with linguists working at other universities than with a departmental colleague working on sociological theory. Likewise, two other university colleagues, both computer scientists, have no common research interests or contacts. One works on neural nets, the other on formal methods of software testing (Pinch, "Disciplinary Rhetoric" 300). Another sociologist, specializing in urbanization, would have less in common with a sociologist studying social stratification than a geographer doing research on the distribution of cities. The second sociologist, in turn, would have more in common with someone in economics who is analyzing income distribution. Such examples, Dogan and Pahre suggest, are not anomalies. They indicate a general process. When older fields advance they split up and disciplinary fragments confront the fragments of other fields, thereby losing contact with siblings in their parent disciplines. As a result psychologists studying child development are more likely to use developmental physiology or the linguistic literature on language acquisition than clinical psychology. Similarly, three scholars working on French politics may speak different disciplinary languages and use different approaches: the first, working with game theory, may talk to other game theorists in economics or applied game theorists in international relations. The second, using sophisticated statistical methods, is likely to communicate with statisticians and social psychologists. The third, relying on empirical analysis expressed in the vernacular, is more likely to communicate with historians and sociologists (Dogan & Pahre, *Creative Marginality* 54, 65–66).

Because most research work tends to occur within identifiable areas that are subsidiary to an entire discipline, broad disciplinary labels confer a false unity on discipline. The notion of disciplinary unity is triply false: minimizing or denying differences that exist across the plurality of specialties grouped loosely under a single disciplinary label, undervaluing connections across specialities of separate disciplines, and discounting the frequency and impact of cross-disciplinary influences. When all three aspects of knowledge production are figured into the calculation of disciplinary work, discipline is revealed to be an interacting system in which research tasks and specialities are created, abolished, and reshaped by internal and external forces. Adjustments and redefinitions occur within disciplinary life cycles: growing, splitting, joining, adapting, and dying; achieving and losing consensus, affirming and challenging dominant practices (after Abbott, *System of Professions* xii, 33). Adopting ecology as a metaphor for the production and organization of knowledge opens the study of disciplinarity up to not only the hardening of categories typically associated with disciplinarity but also the loosening, crossing, and reformulating of categories. This expanded perspective does not deny the "inertial strength of institutionalized disciplinary formulation" (Stocking & Leary, "Social Scientific Inquiry" 57), or the dominant process of fracturing and refracturing of disciplines, or the professionalization of scholars and bureaucratization of scholarship (Scott, *Crisis of the University* 6). It does, though, illuminate the full range of forces in knowledge growth.

At the broadest and most general level, that range includes both *centripetal forces,* which propel discipline inwards toward more internally construed traditional ideology and conceptual predisposition, and *centrifugal forces,* which propel discipline outwards toward relations with other disciplines. In the latter, disciplines are experiencing both the *push of prolific fields* on other areas of knowledge and the *pull of strong new concepts and paradigms* that act as forces coordinating activities in various knowledge fields (Jantsch, "Interdisciplinarity" 306). The application of knowledge to solve social and technological problems exerts a further social pull on disciplines, indicating the two orthogonal directions in which advanced research can go. Steve Fuller explains:

> On the one hand, research may aim for increased systematicity, or *intensify,* by exploring domains that fall between already existing disciplines (the obvious cases include "sociobiology" and "biochemistry") or are at the extremes of our capabilities for inquiry (such as particle physics or cosmology) in order to, literally, "fill in the gaps" in the system of knowledge that the existing disciplines have been collectively (and often implicitly) articulating. On the other hand, research may aim for increased retrievability, or *extensify,* by drawing together existing disciplines to model phe-

nomena—such as most concrete economic and public health problems—that are more complex than the phenomena that these disciplines normally study on their own. Intensification and
extensification correspond roughly to the ways in which basic and
applied research draw on existing knowledge to produce more
knowledge. (*Social Epistemology* 285)

Cross-Disciplinary Outcomes

In their recent study of innovations at the intersections of the social sciences
(*Creative Marginality*), Dogan and Pahre claim that a specialization-fragmenta-
tion-hybridization process is characteristic of knowledge growth today. The
fracturing or fissioning of disciplines into new specialties has been the dominant pattern of knowledge growth in the twentieth century. Yet there have been
more breakups and recombinations throughout the sciences over the past three
decades than in the previous millennium. Moreover, innovative scholars increasingly cross the borders of formal disciplines, confirming a commonly expressed belief that "pathbreaking ideas within any specialty usually come from
cross-referencing ideas from other specialties or disciplines rather than from
research that is narrowly focused within the specialty" (Ralph Turner, "Many
Faces of Sociology" 70). *Hybridization,* as Dogan and Pahre use the term, corresponds to generic uses of *interdisciplinarity,* a term they associate narrowly
with an all-encompassing, naively utopian knowledge of two or more entire
disciplines that, realistically, never occurs. There are two basic types of hybrids:
an *institutionalized form,* which becomes a recognized subfield or permanent
cross-disciplinary committee or program, and *informal hybrids,* disciplinary exchanges that remain at the level of topics and cross-disciplinary contacts (*Creative Marginality* 63). The list of institutionalized hybrid fields is long,
incorporating a range of formal and looser examples such as child development,
Indo-European studies, criminology, artificial intelligence, folklore studies, cognitive science, and women's studies, as well as the newer field of biopolitics
(70). Beyond these institutionalized fields there is a remarkable diversity of
disciplinary exchanges in the form of analogies, methods, theories, topics, concepts, discoveries, and perspectives (121–60).

The consequences of permeation vary greatly, from isolated borrowings to
the emergence of new categories, movements, and fields to the highest level
of institutionalization, formation of a new hybrid discipline. The majority of
permeations occur at the level of instrumental borrowing rather than comprehensive conceptual revision. The emergence of new categories is a significant
interim point between borrowing and full-scale institutionalization, indicating
pressures for alternative strategies, modes of analysis, techniques, frames of reference, and concepts. In the history of the social sciences, Landau et al. explain,
a number of cross-disciplinary categories of analysis have cut directly across
the "vertical pillars" of disciplinary categories, resulting in a striking degree of
theoretical convergence: the use of *role, reference groups, mobility, status, self,*
and *area,* in addition to applications of *game theory, decision making, action,*

information, and *communication.* When such categories begin to characterize several disciplines or parts of them, a process of transmutation occurs. Theoretically speaking, transmutation of existing disciplinary categories fixes a new "field of focus" that implies different conditions for the production and organization of knowledge, making it difficult to distinguish designated disciplinary constructs such as the "political" from the "psychological." Original categories as effective divisions of labor are weakened, gaps between them emerge in starker outline, and cross-fertilization occurs. There is, in addition, an inevitable critical component to transmutation. Whereas older disciplines define themselves ostensively, by pointing to presentation of what the discipline has historically studied and what it studies now, transmutation of categories renders the definition of a field a theoretical problem, not a matter of conventional agreements in the discipline and recognized treaty agreements among subdisciplinary groups and other disciplines ("Interdisciplinary Approach" 14–17). The same process is apparent today with such categories as "structure," "system," "culture," "text," "representation," "gender," "environment," and "organism," the last a concept that has cut across traditional boundaries distinguishing the physical from the biological sciences.

There is a considerable gap, however, between abstract theory and the institutional conditions of cross-disciplinary work. The theory of transmutation suggests that when the same frame or concept begins to characterize several disciplines or parts of them, "it is then a short march to the effort to restructure fields in theoretic terms, to transcend institutionalism by providing a theoretical coherence, to produce a new system for the division of labor and the distribution of resources based upon a set of explicit ordering principles." Landau et al. cite the example of a political scientist who explicitly adopts decision making as a frame of reference, changing the field of focus so substantially that the charge of not studying politics but sociology or psychology arises (15–17). While this charge is to be expected, the problem of conventional boundaries is by no means irrelevant. The short march turns out to be a rather long, slow, and sometimes uncompleted walk. The presence of cross-disciplinary categories extends widely and has reorganized the research work of many individuals, groups, and sometimes large networks. Yet researchers who identify themselves professionally with cross-disciplinary categories face the entire panoply of gatekeeping mechanisms, which by and large favor existing disciplinary categories. They also face the underlying phenomenon of a discipline disciplining itself, which creates a drive toward fixing an agenda through professionalization of intellectual workers and bureaucratization of research.

Feminism is a case in point. As feminists began entering the academy in the early 1970s, the knowledge they produced was largely additive, evident in the mainstreaming of knowledge about women into the curriculum. Over time a transmutation occurred both in and to feminist studies (Minnich, *Transforming Knowledge* 12). Yet, as Ellen Messer-Davidow points out, in constituting a series of objects and redefining itself successively around each one, feminism has altered the disciplines but not transformed them because by and large they retain their traditional structures. Feminism has also encountered the added dilemma of becoming professionalized and thereby depoliticized through institutionalization. Thus feminism is in the paradoxical situation of building an academic apparatus that both enables and constrains feminist inquiry, of "existing both in the disciplines and in opposition to them" ("Know-How" 281–82). When cross-disciplinary categories attain the level of institutional visibility that feminism, American Studies, area studies, social psychology, and molecular biology have attained, there is a common tendency to dismiss them as "just another discipline." This dismissal is both warranted and mistaken. The institutionalization of a new field does create a further fragmentation of knowledge in the form of new and separate structures. Yet the dismissal ignores the plurality of practices and patterns of disciplinary dominance within hybrid fields, subsequent realignments within parent disciplines, and, ultimately, differing outcomes. Social psychology, one of the most frequently cited examples of a hybrid discipline, provides a telling example.

Represented initially by the work of Allport, Sherif, Chapman, Volkmann, and others, social psychology deals with problematics lying between sociology and psychology. A visible separation from its parent disciplines was apparent in 1908 when two textbooks with "Social Psychology" in their titles were published by the psychologist William McDougall and the sociologist E. A. Ross. This origin myth properly identifies the shared and interstitial character of the new hybrid discipline but also minimizes the complex pattern of its embeddedness in philosophy, *Volkerpsychologie,* social history, and psychiatry. In an analysis of "The Faces of Social Psychology," James House describes the twenty-five-year period including and following World War II as the Golden Age of social psychology, characterized by a great wave of enthusiasm for an interdisciplinary social psychology and the establishment of significant training programs and research centers in several major universities in the United States. By the mid-1960s, however, the Golden Age had vanished. By the 1970s social psychology was characterized by three separate and largely isolated divisions of social psychology: *"Psychological social psychology,* focused on individual psychological processes as related to social stimuli and emphasizing the use of laboratory experimental methods; *symbolic interactionism,* concentrated on face-to-face social interaction processes and using participant observation and informal interviewing in natural settings; *psychological sociology,* centered on the reciprocal relationship between social structure and individual social psychological behavior and relying mainly on survey methods (also labeled 'social structure and personality')." These three factions, which grew out of the institutional and intellectual contexts in which social psychology originally developed, have grown farther apart over the last two decades. As a result of this fracturing process a good deal of what is regarded as the "best social psychological research," Ralph Turner points out, is being done by sociologists who identify themselves with specialties such as sociology of education, sociology of the family, medical sociology, sociology of the life course, sociology of gender roles, and a sociology of the emotions, not social psychology per se. Consequently, sociologists working on similar problems are in many cases unaware of each other's research and using different names to describe the same phenomena ("Many Faces of American Sociology" 70).

In another recent analysis of the Golden Age of social psychology, William Sewell ("Reflections") indicated that the reasons social psychology failed to achieve its initial promise are linked to a complex set of conditions: the traditional institutional structure of American universities, the place of the social sciences in that structure, the systems for funding science that have become institutionalized in the United States, and internal conditions of social psychological theory and method. New interdisciplinary programs, Sewell reminds us, represent a threat to existing departments, though the better-funded sciences are more able to absorb new programs. As the trappings of an interstitial discipline emerged—with programs and departments established at major universities, new research centers, graduate student interest in the area, and training grants—the prospects for institutionalizing social psychology seemed strong. During its Golden Age social psychology even had access to funds from the National Institute of Mental Health (NIMH). Yet social psychology received far less than other branches of psychology and some other subfields of sociology. Funds needed to be justified on the basis of mental health relevance and were more readily available for research and training in medical sociology, social problems, urban problems, juvenile delinquency, substance abuse and aging. Those fields did involve social psychological research, but they were also competing with identified social psychology research and training programs. Furthermore, national survey research centers at Michigan and Chicago were underused as sources of training in social psychology and, despite some advances in theory, a unified body of social psychological theory did not emerge. (Rich & Warren note similar difficulties in urban affairs, Lynton Caldwell in environmental studies.) There was a great burst of research activity on a large number of social psychology topics, but more often with a view toward shedding light on problems of social behavior than on theory construction. As a result the explanatory influence of social psychology theories and models remained relatively modest, providing small though statistically significant results and making important use of computer technology and methods in multivariate cross-tabular analysis based on large samples and large-scale longitudinal and panel surveys.

In contrast, interdisciplinary programs in the natural sciences fared much better. Molecular biology, another frequently cited example of a hybrid discipline, was spurred by significant theoretical breakthroughs stemming from discovery of the structure of DNA, powerful new instruments, and complex research problems solved by bringing together the skills and knowledge of physicists, chemists, geneticists, bacteriologists, zoologists, and botanists. In the early years of molecular biology, Sewell explains, most of the scientists involved maintained departmental connections, performing their research in molecular biology teams. Although the level of cooperation between parent departments and new programs of molecular biology was not uniformly high in the early years, there was no great departmental resistance because adequate funding was available for researchers and graduate students, as well as the vital infrastructure of research, new buildings, laboratories, and equipment. In some cases molecular biology was even able to attain full departmental status. Today molecular biology is sufficiently dominant that it has displaced older, competing schools of biology. It is not, though, "just another discipline" whose story ends at the point of achieving disciplinary status. That is a naive view of both the complexity of modern disciplines and the nature of permeation. The work being done today in molecular biology has played a significant role in realignments of disciplinary relations based on new experimental and analytical tools. The development of biochemical and biophysical techniques of macromolecules, to cite a significant example, is reinforced by cybernetic and genetic theory, leading to overlapping of the languages of chemistry, physics, and biology (Habib, *Behavioral and Medical Sciences* 9).

It should come as no surprise, therefore, that the permeation of boundaries is having an impact on the writing of disciplinary histories.

The Writing of Disciplinary Histories

Disciplinary histories serve a number of representative functions, including indoctrinating new entrants into a field, legitimating the field to outsiders, and controlling, promoting, or opposing change. Steve Fuller raises an important question about disciplinary histories when he ponders the extent to which differences between earlier and later historical accounts reflect a difference between the relative openness and closure of disciplinary boundaries. Fuller predicts that later accounts will present a more continuous narrative, present disciplines are more "internally driven" (with fewer references to events in other disciplines or society in general), and attribute contemporary concepts and theories to disciplinary founders ("Disciplinary Boundaries"). Fuller's prediction properly identifies a tendency at work in disciplinary histories, to adopt the tropes of unity and progress. Yet the increasing fragmentation of knowledge born of multiplying specialties combined with proliferating forms of permeation has put pressure on disciplinary histories. This pressure is evident in widespread debates on the complexity of modern disciplines and the plurality of disciplinary practices, as well as mounting critiques of rigid boundaries. The debates constitute an important form of boundary work that reflects, to borrow Donald Preziosi's apt description, important "test trenches beneath the rhetorical surfaces of disciplinary practice" (*Rethinking Art History* xiii).

The pressure on disciplinary histories is further apparent in the labels being used to describe disciplines today. Physics, for example, has been called a "federation" of disciplines, a "superdiscipline" encompassing a broad range of identifiable, and in some cases autonomous, specialties. Geography is often deemed an "inherently interdisciplinary" field, a broad discipline encompassing a multiplying number of hybrid subfields from human geography to climatology. Each subfield, in turn, relates directly to specialties outside the parent discipline of geography (Dogan & Pahre, *Creative Marginality* 93–95). Economics has been described as an "agonistic and shifting field of fundamentally different and often conflicting discourse" (Amariglio et al., this volume), and history dubbed

"a federation of overlapping disciplines" (Tilly, "Historians" 87). Literary studies have been called a "contemporary battle of the books" (Said, "Recent American 'Left' Literary Criticism" 11), an "exploding" discipline (Bergonzi,
(*Exploding English*), and a "crowded terrain" occupied by still-powerful methods of New Criticism, archetypal criticism, positivistic literary history, and a
"criticism of consciousness" fueled by semiotic, poststructuralist, psychoanalytic, feminist, and Marxist approaches, in addition to social theories of literary
production and reception and a recent recuperation of the historical (Miller,
"Rhetorical Study" 92–93). Anthropology, likewise, is characterized by a variety of projects that compete for, as they question, the premise of authority
in discipline, including the interpretative and linguistic turns, polemics about
"culture and practical reason" and "cultural materialism," structuralism old
and new, phenomenology, Marxism, the study of world systems, political economy, sociobiology, and symbolism. Anthropologists, Bernard Cohn once remarked, argue about whether culture is "on the ground," "in the heads of the
natives," or made up of codes, metaphors, and texts ("Anthropology and History" 245). Similarly, medicine is not a singular construct by "loose amalgam-
ations of segments pursuing different objectives in different manners and more
or less delicately held together under a common name at a particular period in
history" (Bucher & Strauss, "Professions").

Pressure is especially apparent in the dispersed rhetoric of disciplinary "crisis" that appears in state-of-the-discipline books and special issues of journals,
revisions of and addenda to official histories, alternative histories, cross-disciplinary histories, special forums at professional meetings, and a fragmentary
critique located in editorial introductions and authors' introductory and concluding paragraphs. The definition of crisis varies greatly from discipline to
discipline and practitioner to practitioner, though it is usually linked with
wanting to move past exhausted modes of inquiry and limited methodology,
attempting to rekindle older ties with neighboring disciplines, expressing alarm
over the continuing fragmentation of knowledge, venting frustration over the
university's inability to accommodate cross-disciplinary work, and responding
to poststructuralist critiques of traditional strategies of representation, including
how disciplines represent their subjects. Crisis in discipline inevitably involves
introspection on the nature of disciplinary inquiry, though it does not necessarily supplant a dominant method or theoretical framework. The postbehavioral
stage in political science, for instance, has not led to abandoning scientific
method but has resulted in substantial modification of political scientists' understanding of the nature of science, a move echoed across the disciplines of
the human and natural sciences as questions about the social construction of
knowledge and the social responsibility of researchers are raised (Easton, "Political Science" 45).

Because permeation has been such a strong aspect of the growth of knowledge in the latter half of the twentieth century, the perception of crisis in discipline is also linked increasingly with debates on what is intrinsic and extrinsic
to discipline. In the humanities the debate has focused primarily on the issue of
inherent meaning in a work of art, with demands for a contextualized painting,

composition, or text creating pressure on formalist methodologies and their claim to scholarly objectivity. In the Winter 1982 issue of *Art Journal,* which was devoted to the topic "Crisis in the Discipline," members of the art history profession responded to expanded views of what constitutes artistic form and art-historical scholarship, informed by ethnic and cross-cultural awareness, semiotics, and other approaches. For some, these challenges are sufficiently strong to constitute a new orthodoxy in the discipline, but they remain matters of dispute. Other art historians, Thomas Crow reports, judge the structuralist, Marxist, and psychoanalytic pushes for construction of the social subject in art history as doing "maximum violence" to the integrity of the art object, thereby threatening the rigor of disciplinary method and validity of professional culture through preoccupation with social issues, ideology, and a revisionist agenda ("Codes of Silence" 2–3). In art history, as in other disciplines, it is not unusual to find defenders of traditional methodology claiming that recent critical ferment comes from outside the discipline.

In literary studies there is a similar debate occurring between supporters of intrinsic, formalist approaches and poststructuralist challengers of orthodoxy. The question of what is intrinsic and extrinsic to literature has even been the subject of two semiofficial treatises published by the organizational voice of the profession, the Modern Language Association: Thorpe's 1967 anthology of essays *Relations of Literary Study* and Barricelli and Gibaldi's 1982 collection of essay *Interrelations of Literature.* However, despite their pioneering role in putting the question of permeation before the profession, and despite some authors' implications to the contrary, these two books ultimately reflect a more centripetal than centrifugal picture of literature, since literature remains the dominant "logical locus" for integration of knowledge. This orientation is not surprising, since the assertion of disciplinary primacy is a common feature of cross-disciplinary genealogy in most disciplines. Extradisciplinary influences are integrated into, rather than alter, the calculus of discipline. (On art history, especially, see Preziosi 113–14.)

The themes of "crisis" and "intrinsic versus extrinsic" influences are further connected with growing awareness of how social and technological problems exert a cross-disciplinary pull away from strictly formal definitions of discipline. The literatures on design, planning, and policymaking reveal an important example discussed openly in the language of professional crisis. The crisis in planning is signaled by mounting challenges to the traditional paradigm of technical rationality, a theory of decision making based in positivist epistemology, and a repertoire of problem-solving and evaluative methods common to a group of disciplines spanning urban planning, policy analysis, operations research, and systems analysis (Alexander, "Paradigm Breakdown" 63). The formation of modern planning theory took place when the special model of rational behavior adopted by neoclassical economics developed into a general theory of rational decision making. Despite its more general scope and applicability, planning theory was basically framed by the definition of economic rationality. Yet the problems that planning professionals face are neither predictable nor simple. They are unique and complex. Arising from environments characterized by turbulence and uncertainty, complex problems are typically value-laden, open-ended, multidimensional, ambiguous, and unstable. Labeled "wicked" and "messy" (Mason & Mitroff, *Strategic Planning;* Rittle & Webber, "Theory of Planning"), they resist being tamed, bounded, or managed by classical problem-solving approaches. Complex problems are not in the book but out there, in the "indeterminate zones of practice" and the "swamp of important problems and nonrigorous inquiry" (Schön, *Educating the Reflective Practitioner* 3–6).

Challenges to the dominant paradigm have emerged in a variety of alternative practices and schools of thought, including logical incrementalism, buffered rationality, and a variety of practice models rooted in critical theory, ecological concepts, systems theory, existentialism, phenomenology, and social learning, as well as contingency models that advocate contextually determined decision making based on the unique demands of a particular situation. As a result of these challenges the rhetoric of "authority," "utility," "efficiency," "expertise," "logic," "scientific objectivity," "ends-means hierarchy," and "rational coordination" is being challenged by the rhetoric of "dialogue" and "dialectic," social and political "process," "communicative action," "participative management," "advocacy," and the "integrative," "interdisciplinary" approach. Lacking consensus on a comprehensive general theory, the planning profession is now in a state of "professional pluralism" (Schön, *Educating the Reflective Practitioner* 17), likened by some members to a "very broad and sometimes leaky umbrella" (Burchell & Hughes, "Planning Theory" xvii).

Despite their different status in the university, their different subject areas, and the local character of their debates, art history, literary studies, planning, and other modern disciplines are all confronted with common questions of where and why boundaries are drawn. Two additional extended examples, those of physics and history, illustrate in greater detail the pressure permeation is putting on disciplinary identity.

Physics

Physics is the "hardest" case. A strict reading of the hard-soft dichotomy implies that physics has the most impenetrable boundaries. A careful reading of disciplinary history, however, indicates that is not the case. The discipline of physics studies a set of problems concerning the structure and behavior of the physical world, seeking relations between different phenomena in that world (Verhagen, "Interdisciplinary Activities" 95). Before the mid-nineteenth century there was no physics community. None of the British specialist societies formed in the early 1800s was devoted specifically to physics, nor did many people think of themselves as physicists or their subject as physics. In the early 1900s the small groups of researchers engaged in what is now called physics were trained mainly as chemists. Even holders of degrees in physics were not even officially registered as physicists until 1917. Thus the disciplining of physics occurred primarily in the twentieth century (Vlachy, "Interdisciplinary Physics" 1314, 1316).

In the early 1900s physics was based in quantum physics of solids and atomic theory. Between 1930 and 1960 the discipline was reordered around the poles of a physics of solids and a physics of the atomic nucleus, at the same time theoretical physics was developing into a major field. In the United States a previous cross-disciplinary specialty of applied mathematics and a new astrophysics closely allied to theoretical physics was also developing, in addition to the older cross-disciplinary specialty of physical chemistry. Solid state physics, which only began assuming an intellectual and institutional identity as a research field in 1945, grew out of initially disconnected areas (Hoddeson, "Point-Contact Transistor" 42). British solid state physics was at most a loose federation of research groups until at least the 1950s, when academic posts and courses of study were finally developed for this broad subfield. Solid state physics developed significantly at the juncture of physics with chemistry, crystallography, and metallurgy. By 1960, because of its applications to solid state electronics and materials engineering, solid state physics had become both quantitatively and technologically the most important subfield of physics (Hoch, "New Scientific Ideas" 210, 235). By this point physics was also no longer considered a single discipline but a federation of disciplines, a "superdiscipline" (Verhagen, "Interdisciplinary Activities" 95) incorporating subdisciplines ranging from optics and astronomy to nuclear physics and solid state physics. Nuclear and solid state physics, though, have more in common with chemistry and engineering than traditional physics.

Since the 1960s permeations of the boundaries dividing the subfields of physics and other disciplines have displaced the notion of physics as a single, isolated discipline. By 1972 the Physics Survey Committee of the National Research Council (NRC) concluded there was "no definable boundary" between physics and other disciplines (*Physics in Perspective*). In 1986 the NRC issued a follow-up, eight-volume series "Physics through the 1990s," compiled by prominent academic and industrial leaders. The *Overview* and especially the final volume, *Scientific Interfaces and Technological Applications,* depict a physics characterized by cross-disciplinary permeations in the arenas of both fundamental and applied science, though permeations are rendering that distinction more problematic. In the realm of fundamental science there are five prominent indicators: biophysics, materials science, the chemistry-physics interface, geophysics, and mathematical and computational physics. In the realm of technical applications of physics, which are pivotal to large-scale industrial technology and thus to the international competitiveness of the United States, boundary blurring is occurring in six major areas: microelectronics, optical technology, new instrumentation for science and society, the fields of energy and environment, national security, and medicinal applications.

The picture of physics that emerges from the 1986 reports is a heterogeneous field of interactions in which the intellectual boundary between engineering and physics is vanishing in many areas of advanced technology, speeding technology transfer and innovation while pulling engineers and scientists "inexorably" into a cross-disciplinary continuum and away from disciplinary boundaries. The interface between physics and chemistry has been crossed "so often in both directions that its exact location is obscure; its passage is signaled more by gradual changes in language and approach than by any sharp demarcation in content" (*Scientific Interfaces* 53). Across the sciences of molecules and atoms, surfaces and interfaces, fluids and solids, disciplinary cultures are merging in the integrated study of complex problems and materials. In the areas of polymers and complex fluids, condensed-matter physicists have become increasingly concerned with problems involving macromolecular systems, to the point that traditional boundaries separating chemistry, physics, and to some extent biology, have become blurred. Where, then, is the "real" physics? In a 1977 issue of *Physics Bulletin,* P. H. Bligh lamented that what was once understood as "straight physics" has become an integral part of other professions: "All the immediately relevant physics is disappearing into other disciplines until finally we are left with a few remote areas such as particle physics—for which few can see any practical use—that we can call entirely our own" ("Territorial Physics" 73).

Scientific Interfaces is a significant barometer of the extent of permeation in contemporary science. Yet at the same time it provides telling evidence of what Stocking and Leary called the "inertial strength" of disciplinary formation. Even though chemical physics is a well-established component of most chemistry departments, synergistic interactions between chemists and physicists far from the traditional interface have usually occurred "in spite of department structures rather than because of them." Even as the cultures of chemists and physicists are merging at major synchrotron facilities; even as the boundaries between chemistry, physics, and to an extent biology have blurred in macromolecular research; even as advances in spectroscopy have linked chemistry and physics; even as university-affiliated centers for biophysics are revolutionizing research in materials science and in some areas of biology, academic reward systems continue to favor institutionalized disciplinary categories. Moreover, the new research patterns derived from modern advances in theoretical and experimental physics are not readily accommodated by the established support system. Thus much of what is reported in *Scientific Interfaces* bespeaks influence and interaction more than integration, additive permeation more than transmutation. The familiar barriers obtain: disciplinary language and orientation, narrow training programs, lack of joint Ph.D. programs, and organizational structures that impede collaborative work, plus the unique barriers erected by unfavorable tax policies, antitrust regulations, and inadequate policies for industrial and institutional collaborative research.

History

History is one of the traditional synoptic disciplines, so named because of their breadth. Called "one of the busiest areas of cross-disciplinary combinations" (Dogan & Pahre, *Creative Marginality* 87), history provides an important example of how a range of soft and hard approaches belies the premise of disciplinary unity. History as a discipline was rooted traditionally in narrative practice. Many reactions to new historical methods, in fact, are punctuated by calls for a return to what history is "supposed to do," tell stories. The distances of disciplinary space are apparent in recent internal histories that promote different views of the discipline based on how a variety of new methodological tools born of permeation are weighed and how their authors position the discipline in regard to its sociopolitical uses.

Conceding their value but arguing that they are not so novel as practitioners think, nor is the old history as archaic as its critics assume, Gertrude Himmelfarb responded to new practices in her 1987 book *The New History and the Old.* Even before the advent of "new history," Himmelfarb observes, the discipline was never so homogeneous or simplistic as stereotype has it. What concerns her, though, is the way *new history* has become an accepted shorthand term for a variety of modes of history that represent, singly and collectively, a serious challenge to traditional history, which is not without its own excesses. This is not, moreover, the first time a new history has swept history, though the current new history tends to be more analytic than narrative, more thematic than chronological. It relies, Himmelfarb explains, more on statistical tables, oral interviews, sociological models, and psychoanalytic theories than on constitutions, treaties, parliamentary debates, political writings, or party manifestos. It is also more interested in classes and ethnic groups, social problems and institutions, cities and communities, work and play, family and sex, birth and death, childhood and old age, crime and insanity than it is interested in regimes and administrations, legislation and politics, diplomacy and foreign policy, wars and revolutions. Thus the old "history from above" is now confronted by a "history from below." Yet the dominant thrust toward social history, she cautions, results in neglect of the historian's traditional concern, political history. This creates, in turn, new pressures toward "retooling" in order to avoid obsolescence and, in her view, loss of moral imagination in favor of variety, openness, and pluralism.

Theodore Rabb and Charles Tilly assess the status and implications of new practices quite differently. In a 1983 collection of essays *The New History: The 1980s and Beyond,* Rabb responded to fears that disciplinary coherence is vanishing and synthesis is no longer possible. Methodologically, historical research has never been a genuinely unified endeavor, although the subject of political history has been a recurring source of unity. That unity began disintegrating in the late nineteenth century with growing interest in economic history, various kinds of social history, new forms of cultural history, and, into the twentieth century, demands for reform, new methods, and new subjects. As the community and synthetic capacity of late nineteenth-century scholarship eroded, multitudinous voices rendered problematic the notion that a powerful group, however dominant at a particular time, could control the entire territory of history. This pluralistic view of discipline does not rule out defining common assumptions across divided parts of the profession, but it does resist totalizing definition by a single dominant part. What is lamented as a fragmentation of the historical discipline, Rabb suggests, may also be seen as the price to be paid for elaborating more powerful analytical tools. In a 1988 state-of-the-discipline piece written for an external audience, the Chinese Academy of Social Sciences,

Charles Tilly ("Historians") views history as a "federation of overlapping disciplines," noting the significant part it plays in analyses by geographers, economists, anthropologists, philosophers, and other observers of human affairs.
Different historical practices, Tilly contends, reflect divisions within Western
historical thinking dependent on philosophical choices about key alternatives:
large social processes versus individual experiences, systematic observation of
human action versus interpretation of motives and meanings, history and the
social sciences as the same enterprise versus distinct enterprises, and stresses in
historical writing on explanation versus narrative. Tilly positions these four
alternatives in a two-dimensional representation of variations in historical approaches that indicates poles of continua along which historians align themselves: small-scale—large-scale and social scientific—humanistic conceptions of
history. While not absolute positions on a chart, these are nonetheless very
"real and pressing" choices of disciplinary practice.

A significant part of the debate in history, as in most disciplines, turns on the
question of relations with neighboring disciplines. The history-anthropology
relation, to take one example, has been described as both "undertapped" and
as a "co-discipline." In a recent "Dialogue" published in the journal *Historical
Methods,* David Kertzer reports that "interdisciplinary forays" between history
and anthropology have ramified in a variety of directions over the past decade,
stirring considerable debate. The premise of a relationship is not so much disputed as the manner in which it is conducted. Individual historians align themselves differently, some identifying with an anthropology of social organization
and social structure, others with symbolism and the construction of reality.
Differing alignments reflect divisions about the discipline's drift toward social
science. Reacting to "Clio's Dalliances," Darrett Rutman questions the quick
succession of "wild but not very deep relationships with a number of the 'social
sciences,'" questioning the one-directional interest of historians in anthropology based on borrowing and simple crossings rather than a genuine melding or
collapsing of disciplinary boundaries. Sydel Silverman, in turn, suggests that
differences hinge on whether historians ought to move beyond current collaborations to the creation of a new discipline, whether it be an anthropological
history, historical anthropology, or another designation giving the two components equal status. While acknowledging that disciplinary contributions are
successfully merged in the work of individual scholars and that pressures for
eradicating disciplinary boundaries are quite real, Silverman considers the
breakdown of boundaries between the two disciplines neither possible nor desirable at present. The ultimate objective, he contends, is to make "better anthropology and better history, not a hybrid creature." Assuming final voice
in the dialogue, Andrejs Plakans emphasizes that forms of cooperation and
collaboration, borrowing and lending, have been many and varied. Some have
even attained legitimacy in the form of key prizes, though interactions extend
well beyond "the most public arena of interdisciplinary labors." Though a dis-
cipline-wide backlash in both fields may decrease interactions in the future,
prospects for continuing interaction are strong, judging by the age distribution
of scholars, interest among graduate students, support from granting agencies,

availability of conference and publication outlets, and the emergence of identifiable cross-disciplinary subfields such as family history and discourse analysis
as a practice in historical interpretation.

The Utility of *Discipline* as a Category of Knowledge

The evidence, then, indicates that discipline is neither simple nor undisputed.
"Surveying the development of any modern academic discipline," Donald Preziosi suggests, "is not unlike trying to read a heavily palimpsested manuscript
full of emendations, erasures, and marginalia, with innumerable graffiti added
by different hands over time" (xi). Rereading the history of physics, history, art
history, literary studies, planning, and other disciplines is not easy because their
development is not simple, progressive, or cumulative. The ramifications of
disciplinary practices, as Preziosi says of art history, are often contradictory and
complex rather than coherent, the contending visions of theory and practice
disparate rather than merging into the unity implied by the tropes of linearity
and directionality (*Rethinking Art History*). This complexity, though, does not
obviate the workings of the disciplinary core. Taking economics as an example,
Amariglio et al. (this volume) argue that perception of unity and disciplinarity
arises in some, though not all, of the different schools of economic thought,
positing the existence of a center or core of propositions, procedures, and conclusions, or at least a shared historical object of theory and practice. Portraying
economics as a discipline with distinct boundaries is often a discursive strategy
used by one school of economics to hegemonize the field of economic discourse, a political move with consequences throughout the entire system of
gatekeeping mechanisms. "The 'convention of unity,' " Mieke Bal adds from
the discipline of art history, "is a powerful ideological weapon because of the
pressure it exerts on the reader to choose one interpretation over another rather
than to read through the conflict of interpretations" ("De-disciplining the Eye"
507), or, as Gerald Graff has said of literary studies on so many occasions, to
"teach the conflicts." What, then, given the magnitude of contending practices,
the continued fracturing of discipline through specialization, and the plurality
of cross-disciplinary exchanges, is the current state of knowledge?

Knowledge is growing increasingly convergent and specific at the same time
its global scope expands and permeations multiply. This paradoxical development is beginning to have considerable impact on the structures and conduct
of research, education, and training (Roederer, "Disciplinary Barriers" 659).
The disciplining of knowledge continues to create smaller and smaller segments
at the same time cross-disciplinary exchanges are proliferating. The resulting
pressure has reached a critical point, evident in a widespread insistence that
gerrymandering, bridge building, and spot repairs are inadequate responses.
"The problem," George Allan contends, "is with the undergirding, with the
cultural joists and intellectual footings upon which everything else depends.
For that kind of problem, far more serious repairs are required" ("Canon in
Crisis" 89).

Not unexpectedly the nature of the repair work is also a matter of considerable dispute. What one disciplinarian would repair another would scrap in favor of a new building. The split is apparent in three separate explanations current in disciplinary and cross-disciplinary histories, explanations that embody a complex set of interested positions on the implications of fragmentation and significance of permeation. The "normal" explanation holds that crossing boundaries is a usual characteristic of knowledge growth, evident in extensive tool borrowing and the migration of intellectual workers across disciplinary borders to solve problems. In the logic of the normal explanation, permeations are part of, and thus brought back into, the disciplinary order, even if they have an initial counterdisciplinary thrust. The "exceptional" explanation holds that disciplinary boundaries are substantial obstacles to cross-disciplinary inquiry, spawning an adhocracy of mechanisms such as cross-departmental programs, research teams, centers, and hybrid fields. Yet even in the logic of the exceptional explanation the disciplinary center still holds and permeations end up being either normalized or marginalized. The "oppositional" explanation goes beyond assertions that disciplinary boundaries are arbitrary, frequently heard in both the normal and exceptional explanations, to contest the very premise of disciplinary organization and argue instead for permanent cross-disciplinary structures, problem-focused intellectual work, and political intervention. All three explanations have their blind spots. Radical reports on the end of disciplinarity and advent of the postdisciplinary age are naive, ignoring as they do the power of the prevailing "first principle." Yet normalizing explanations, exceptional accommodations, and outright dismissals of cross-disciplinary work are equally short-sighted, discounting as they do the changed landscape of knowledge in the late twentieth century.

These three explanations roughly parallel the three combined demands that challenge the dominant "unidisciplinary political culture" of universities. Conservative elites, Mark Kann explains in his "The Political Culture of Interdisciplinary Explanation," want a specific kind of interdisciplinary explanation that enables them to solve problems related to political legitimacy and private accumulation, divorcing politics from science and culture from explanation. They frequently construct cross-disciplinarity on the basis of economics rather than philosophical justification (Brian Turner, "Interdisciplinary Curriculum"), justifying intellectual hierarchy and leaving the "first principle" of disciplinary organization intact. Radical dissidents demand an interdisciplinary explanation useful to oppressed groups seeking greater sociopolitical equality, justifying explanation from a multiplicity of perspectives and transforming the disciplinary structure of knowledge. Liberal intellectuals, caught between the older positivism and newer perspectives, seek a more harmonious middle ground that will enable peaceful interaction through self-reflectiveness and reason, accommodating the exceptional while leaving the "first principle" intact. The American academy, Kann himself concludes, is "increasingly contradictory today," and virtually no one is immune to the different cross-disciplinary pressures exerted by these three groups. The pressures, moreover, are not strictly academic. They indicate that larger cultural forces are mapping out possibilities open to social groups while reflecting and informing the larger political culture. Thus, the possibilities and limits of cross-disciplinary exchanges are embedded within American society as a whole.

Works Cited

Abbott, Andrew. *The System of Professions: An Essay on the Division of Expert Labor.* Chicago: Univ. of Chicago Press, 1988.

Alexander, E. R. "After Rationality, What? A Review of Responses to Paradigm Breakdown." *Journal of the American Planning Association* 50 (1984): 62–69.

Allan, George. "The Canon in Crisis." *Liberal Education* 72 (1986): 89–100.

Art Journal. 42 (1982). Special Issue, "The Crisis in the Discipline."

Bal, Mieke. "De-Disciplining the Eye." *Critical Inquiry* 16 (1990): 506–31.

Barricelli, Jean Pierre, and Joseph Gibaldi, eds. *Interrelations of Literature.* New York MLA, 1982.

Becher, Tony. *Academic Tribes and Territories: Intellectual Enquiry and the Cultures of Disciplines.* Milton Keynes: Society for Research into Higher Education and Open Univ. Press, 1989.

———. "The Counter-Culture of Specialization." *European Journal of Education* 25 (1990): 333–46.

Bergonzi, Bernard. *Exploding English: Criticism, Theory, Culture.* Oxford: Clarendon, 1990.

Bligh, P. H. "Territorial Physics." *Physics Bulletin* 28 (1977): 73.

Bucher, R., and A. Strauss. "Professions in Process." *American Journal of Sociology* 66 (1961): 325–34.

Burchell, R., and J. Hughes. "Planning Theory in the 1980s—A Search for Future Directions." *Planning Theory in the 1980s.* Ed. R. Burchell & G. Sternlieb. New Brunswick, N.J.: Center for Urban Policy Research, 1979.

Caldwell, Lynton K. "Environmental Studies: Discipline or Metadiscipline?" *Environmental Professional* 5 (1983): 328–48.

Campbell, Donald. "Ethnocentrism of Disciplines and the Fish-Scale Model of Omniscience." In *Interdisciplinary Relationships in the Social Sciences.* Ed. Muzafer and Carolyn Sherif. Chicago: Aldine, 1969.

Chubin, Daryl. *Sociology of Sciences: An Annotated Bibliography on Invisible Colleges, 1972–1981.* New York: Garland, 1983.

Clark, Burton R. *The Higher Education System: Academic Organization in Cross-National Perspective.* Berkeley and Los Angeles: Univ. of California Press, 1983.

Clough, Stanley B. "A Half-Century in Economic History: Autobiographical Reflections." *Journal of Economic History* 30 (1970): 4–17.

Cohn, Bernard. "Anthropology and History in the 1980s." *Journal of Interdisciplinary History* 12 (1981): 227–52.

Crow, Thomas. "Codes of Silence: Historical Representation and the Art of Watteau." *Representations* 12 (1985): 2–14.

de Bie, Pierre. Introduction to Special Section on "Multidisciplinary Problem-Focused Research." *International Social Science Journal* 20 (1968): 192–210.

Dogan, Mattie, and Robert Pahre. *Creative Marginality: Innovation at the Intersections of Social Sciences.* Boulder, Col.: Westview, 1990.

Easton, David. "The Division, Integration, and Transfer of Knowledge." In Easton and Schelling.

———. "Political Science in the United States: Past and Present." In Easton and Schelling.

Easton, David, and Corinne Schelling, eds. *Divided Knowledge: Across Disciplines, across Cultures.* Newbury Park, Calif.: Sage, 1991.

Fuller, Steve. *Social Epistemology.* Bloomington: Indiana Univ. Press, 1988.

Geertz, Clifford. "Blurred Genres: The Refiguration of Social Thought." *American Scholar* 49 (1980): 165–79.

Gieryn, Thomas F. "Boundary-Work and the Demarcation of Science from Non-Science: Strains and Interests in Professional Ideologies of Scientists." *American Sociological Review* 48 (1983): 781–95.

Habib, Hedi B. *Towards a Paradigmatic Approach to Interdisciplinarity in the Behavioral and Medical Sciences.* Karlstad, Sweden: Center for Research in the Humanities, Univ. of Karlstad, 1990.

Himmelfarb, Gertrude. *The New History and the Old.* Cambridge: Harvard Univ. Press, 1987.

"History and Anthropology: A Dialogue." *Historical Methods* 19 (1986): 119–28.

Hoch, Paul. "Migration and the Generation of New Scientific Ideas." *Minerva* 25 (1987): 209–37.

Hoddeson, L. "The Discovery of the Point-Contact Transistor." *Historical Studies in the Physics Sciences* 12 (1981): 41–76.

Horn, Thomas C. R., and Harry Ritter. "Interdisciplinary History: A Historiographical Review." *History Teacher* 19 (1986): 427–48.

House, James. "The Faces of Social Psychology." *Sociometry* 40 (1977): 161–77.

Jantsch, Erich. "Interdisciplinarity: Dreams and Reality." *Prospects* 10 (1980): 304–12.

Kann, Mark. "The Political Culture of Interdisciplinary Explanation." *Humanities in Society* 2 (1979): 185–200.

Kertzer, David. "Anthropology and History." In "History and Anthropology: A Dialogue." *Historical Methods* 19 (1986): 119–20.

Landau, Martin, Harold Proshansky, and William Ittelson. "The Interdisciplinary Approach and the Concept of Behavioral Sciences." In *Decisions, Values and Groups.* Ed. Norman Washburne. Oxford: Pergamon, 1962.

Mason, R. O., and I. Mitroff. *Challenging Strategic Planning Assumptions.* New York: John Wiley, 1981.

Messer-Davidow, Ellen. "Know-How." In *(En)Gendering Knowledge: Feminists in Academe.* Ed. Joan E. Hartman and Ellen Messer-Davidow. Knoxville: Univ. of Tennessee Press, 1991.

Miller, J. Hillis. "The Function of Rhetorical Study at the Present Time." In *Teaching Literature: What Is Needed Now.* Ed. James Engell and David Perkins. Cambridge: Harvard Univ. Press, 1988.

Minnich, Elizabeth. *Transforming Knowledge.* Philadelphia: Temple Univ. Press, 1990.

Physics in Perspective. Vol. 1. Washington, D.C.: National Academy of Sciences, 1972.

Pinch, Trevor. "The Culture of Scientists and Disciplinary Rhetoric." *European Journal of Education* 25 (1990): 295–304. Special issue, "Disciplinary Cultures."

Plakans, Andrejs. "History and Anthropology: Trends in Interaction." In "History and Anthropology: A Dialogue." *Historical Methods* 19 (1986): 126–28.

Preziosi, Donald. *Rethinking Art History: Meditations on a Coy Science.* New Haven: Yale Univ. Press, 1989.

Rabb, Theodore K. "Toward the Future: Coherence, Synthesis, and Quality in History." In *The New History: The 1980s and Beyond: Studies in Interdisciplinary History.* Ed. Theodore K. Rabb, Robert I. Rotberg, and Thomas Glick. Princeton: Princeton Univ. Press, 1983.

Rich, Daniel, and Robert Warren. "The Intellectual Future of Urban Affairs: Theoretical, Normative, and Organizational Options." *Social Science Journal* 17 (1980): 53–66.

Rittle, H. W. J., and M. M. Webber. "Dilemmas in a General Theory of Planning." *Policy Sciences* 4 (1973): 167–69.

Roederer, Juan G. "Tearing Down Disciplinary Barriers." *Astrophysics and Space Science* 144 (1988): 659–67.

Ruscio, Kenneth P. "Specialization in Academic Disciplines: 'Spokes on a Wheel.'" Paper presented at the Annual Meeting of the Association for the Study of Higher Education, 15–17 March 1985. ERIC fiche ED 259 643.

Rutman, Darrett. "History and Anthropology: Clio's Dalliances." In "History and Anthropology: A Dialogue." *Historical Methods* 19 (1986): 120–23.

Said, Edward. "Reflections on Recent American 'Left' Literary Criticism." *Boundary* 28 (1979): 11–30.

Schön, Donald A. *Educating the Reflective Practitioner: Toward a New Design for Teaching and Learning in the Professions.* San Francisco: Jossey Bass, 1987.

———. *The Reflective Practitioner: How Professionals Think in Action.* New York: Basic Books, 1983.

Scientific Interfaces and Technological Applications. Washington, D.C.: National Academy Press, 1986.

Scott, Peter. *The Crisis of the University.* London: Croom Helm, 1984.

Sewell, William. "Some Reflections on the Golden Age of Interdisciplinary Social Psychology." *Social Psychology Quarterly* 52 (1989): 88–97.

Silverman, Sydel. "Anthropology and History: Understanding the Boundaries." In "History and Anthropology: A Dialogue." *Historical Methods* 19 (1986): 123–26.

Stocking, G. W., and D. E. Leary. "History of Social Scientific Inquiry." *Items* 40 (1986): 53–57.

Swoboda, Wolfram. "Disciplines and Interdisciplinarity: A Historical Perspective." In *Interdisciplinarity and Higher Education.* Ed. Joseph J. Kockelmans. University Park: Pennsylvania State Univ. Press, 1979.

Thorpe, James, ed. *Relations of Literary Study: Essays on Interdisciplinary Contributions.* New York: MLA, 1967.

Tilly, Charles. "How (and What) Are Historians Doing." In Easton and Schelling.

Turner, Brian. "The Interdisciplinary Curriculum: From Social Medicine to Postmodernism." *Sociology of Health and Illness* 12 (1990): 1–23.

Turner, Ralph H. "The Many Faces of American Sociology: A Discipline in Search of Identity." In Easton and Schelling.

Verhagen, C. J. D. M. "Some Characteristics of Multi- and Interdisciplinary Activities." *Problems in Interdisciplinary Studies: Issues in Interdisciplinary Studies,* 2. Ed. R. Jurkovich and J. H. P. Paelinck. Aldershot, Hampshire: Gower, 1984.

Vlachy, Jan. "Interdisciplinary Approaches in Physics: The Concepts." *Czechoslovak Journal of Physics* B3 (1982): 1311–18.

Whitley, R. "The Rise and Decline of University Disciplines in the Sciences." In *Problems in Interdisciplinary Studies: Issues in Interdisciplinary Studies,* 2. Ed. R. Jurkovich and J. H. P. Paelinck. Aldershot, Hampshire: Gower, 1984.

Wolfle, Dael L. "Interdisciplinary Research as a Form of Research." *SRA: Journal of the Society of Research Administrators* 13 (1981): 374–83.

Social Sciences

Interdisciplinary Research for Integrated Rural Development in Developing Countries

The Role of Social Sciences

Dirk van Dusseldorp and Seerp Wigboldus

Abstract

This article is based on the experiences of various interdisciplinary research and planning teams at Wageningen Agricultural University. After giving a typology of interdisciplinary research, the authors examine the role of social sciences in interdisciplinary research in various fields of importance for rural development in developing countries. The type of interdisciplinary research discussed is the so-called "broad" interdisciplinary research in which participating disciplines have very different paradigms. The article closes with an overview of the potentials and constraints in broad interdisciplinary research and some general observations. Finally, systematic evaluations of interdisciplinary research programs will contribute to its progress.

The problems policy makers and planners are facing are becoming more and more complicated. Seldom is there a course of action that does not require the input of various ministries or departments. This also means, automatically, that the knowledge of several disciplines is needed to lay the foundation for sound policies and their implementation. As a result, interest in interdisciplinary research has increased in the last decades.

Hereafter the concept of interdisciplinary research pertains to the so-called "broad" interdisciplinary research. This means among others that a wide range of disciplines is involved, from technical to social disciplines.

A note of caution is in order right at the beginning. However important interdisciplinary research may be, there are many situations in which sound monodisciplinary research is not only effective but also more efficient. As will be shown hereafter, interdisciplinary research is a difficult type of research, with many pitfalls and possibilities for breakdowns. Consequently, there must be very compelling reasons before cumbersome interdisciplinary research is selected as the best approach for obtaining insight into the processes to be influenced in order to solve problems of a society or community.

van Dusseldorp, Dirk and Seerp Wigboldus. "Interdisciplinary Research for Integrated Rural Development in Developing Countries: The Role of Social Sciences." Issues in Integrative Studies 12 (1994), 93–138. Reprinted with permission.

The problems in interdisciplinary research are partly due to misunderstandings surrounding it. Therefore, there must be a clear understanding of what policy or action-oriented interdisciplinary research means, how it should be conducted, and what its potential and limitations are.

From recent literature (Wigboldus, 1991), it is clear that even though the discussion of interdisciplinary research is on-going, there is a certain stagnation in development of new theoretical concepts. Since the overview articles of Lekanne (1976) and Kockelmans (1987), few new ideas have come forward. Russell's edited publication (1982) contributed some interesting practical ideas. Chubin, *et al.*'s book (1986) consists, for the major part, of reprints of articles and chapters of books, but gives scarcely any new insights. For those interested in the present state of the art Klein's (1990) *Interdisciplinarity: History, Theory & Practice* can be useful.

Despite the avalanche of literature on this subject, the outcome of "broad" interdisciplinary research is still not very impressive. Partly due to ignorance of what interdisciplinary research should comprise, research proposals are often poorly designed. Furthermore, the outcomes of policy/action-oriented interdisciplinary research are in most cases not very highly appreciated by the scientific community. Outstanding scientists are often more interested in monodisciplinary research. This tendency occurs in many universities, and it affects the quality of interdisciplinary research. So a vicious circle is entered.

In the following, a typology of interdisciplinary research is drawn first, followed by a description of various approaches, that can be used in interdisciplinary research for rural development in the fields of regional (integrated) rural development, farming systems research, and in agricultural research using plant growth models. Finally, we can conclude with an overview of the potential and constraints of interdisciplinary research, ending with some general observations.

Types of Interdisciplinary Research

It is possible to distinguish between several types of interdisciplinary research. This distinction is useful because there are considerable differences in the constraints one encounters during the preparation and implementation of the different types of interdisciplinary research. Figure 1 gives an overview of "Types of Interdisciplinarity."

Interdisciplinary research projects differ for the following reasons:

1. The interdisciplinary team has representatives of disciplines using more or less the same paradigms and methods: for instance agronomists, soil scientists and climatologists; or biologists, chemists and physicists. In such situations communication is relatively easy—illustrating an example of narrow interdisciplinarity. However, when an interdisciplinary team consists of agronomists, soil scientists, economists and social scientists who have different paradigms and use different methods—illustrating an example of broad interdisciplinarity—the chances that there will be problems in the communication between the team members increase considerably.

A) Narrow Interdisciplinarity	B) Broad Interdisciplinarity
1) Interaction Between Disciplines with: —Same Paradigms —Same Methods *Disciplinary outputs can be easily integrated*	Interaction Between Disciplines with: —Different Paradigms —Different Methods *Disciplinary outputs are difficult to integrate*
2) Few Disciplines Involved *Simplifies communication*	Many Disciplines Involved *Complicates communication*
3) Representatives of Disciplines Located in Same Organization *Simplifies communication and organization*	Representatives of Disciplines Located in Different Organizations *Complicates communication and organization*
4) Representatives of Disciplines from the Same Culture *Simplifies communication*	Representatives of Disciplines from Different Cultures *Complicates communication*

FIGURE 1. Types of interdisciplinarity.

2. In small interdisciplinary teams the communication problem will be less than in large teams where, naturally, in most cases, a larger number of disciplines will be represented.
3. When the members of an interdisciplinary team are coming from different institutes, communication and organizational problems will be bigger than when they come from the same institute. Different organizations often have developed different organizational cultures which determine how to cooperate and communicate with each other.
4. Finally, members of an interdisciplinary team can come from different national cultures. This gives an additional complication in the communication between members of a team.

To summarize, starting from a team consisting of a small number of members with closely related disciplines of the same organization and the same culture, problems of communication and organization will continuously increase and will culminate in large interdisciplinary teams with representatives of disciplines which have little in common and with a different organizational and cultural background. In interdisciplinary research for integrated rural development, in which external donors are involved, the most complicated mode of interdisciplinary research always applies. Because in this case broad interdisciplinarity is required, a rather large team is needed, and researchers and their counterparts come from different organizations and cultures. This means that preparation of this type of interdisciplinary research requires more attention than simpler forms of interdisciplinary research.

Interdisciplinary Research for Regional Planning and Integrated Rural Development

Historical Background

Several decades ago it became clear that the project approach often failed because it was planned and implemented in isolation. Irrigation schemes were not used or not used optimally, because school and health facilities were not available. The successful introduction of new production technologies bogged down because neither the market system, nor the physical infrastructure (roads, storage facilities) could cope with the increasing volume of produce. During this period, the concept of regional planning, at least in developing countries, became popular. But most of the regional plans presented, often in several volumes, were seldom implemented, because they were too complex for the administrations of most developing countries. The fashion of regional planning was soon followed by the concept of integrated rural development projects (IRDP's). In this concept the ideas of bottom-up participation and programmatic approach were combined in one way or another. Taking into account the manpower and funding absorbed by this type of project, most of them cannot boast good track records for efficiency, effectiveness, or impact.

Interestingly, integrated analyses of regional plans, are still being used. However, in most IRDP's a sound general analysis of the area in which they are operating is missing. Sound analysis based on interdisciplinary research should not only be the basis of but is even crucial for the success of any regional plan or integrated rural development project.

The research process described hereafter is based on experiences of interdisciplinary teams commissioned with the formulation of regional plans. Before going into the process of interdisciplinary research, it is important to emphasize that the final outcome of interdisciplinary research is integration of outcomes of monodisciplinary research. A common misconception is that interdisciplinary research means all disciplines are merged: agronomists must involve themselves with economists, and sociologists should have as much to say about soil classification as soil scientists. Yet, this effort to arrive at a unified science is doomed to fail in broad policy/action-oriented interdisciplinary research, and will lead to shallow, if any, results. The integration of the disciplines themselves should not take place in interdisciplinary research. Rather, interdisciplinary research is characterized by:

1. An integrated research design, made and agreed upon by all disciplines involved.
2. A period during which monodisciplinary field research takes place, with an intensive exchange of information that can influence the direction of monodisciplinary research.
3. An integrated analysis of the problem under study.

Figure 2 illustrates the stages through which a policy/action-oriented interdisciplinary research project can and should go. Hereafter the interdisciplinary

Preparation	[1]	Problem Formulation by Policy Makers
	[2]	Translation of Policy Problem into Research Problems(s)
	[3]	Operationalization of Research Problems and Preparation of Work Program per Discipline
	[4]	Integration of Disciplinary Research Program into an Interdisciplinary Research Project
Field Work	[5]	General Orientation in the Field (Rapid Rural Appraisal [SONDEO])
	[6]	Adjustment of Research Problems and Work Program
	[7]	Monodisciplinary Research, with Regular Consultations and Exchange of Tentative Findings and, When Necessary, Adjustments of Disciplinary Research Problems and Work Programs
Synthesis	[8]	Presentation of Disciplinary Findings
	[9]	Integration of Findings via Regular Meetings
	[10]	Team Members' Following of the Way Their Inputs Are Used During the Integration Process
	[11]	Final Synthesis
Reporting		

FIGURE 2. Stages in policy-oriented interdisciplinary research.

research process for integrated rural development will be described. The numbers between square brackets ([]) of the various stages correspond with the numbers indicated in Figure 2. Note that it is not a linear but an iterative process.

Preparation of the Research Proposal

[1] The important difference between action-oriented research and scientific research is that the problem, for which the research project should provide information and lead to tentative solutions, is formulated by policy makers and not by researchers.

[2] This difference does not mean that the scientists do not have an important task in the stage of problem formulation. Often problems formulated by the policymakers have to be redefined for the following reasons:

a) The policy problem has to be translated into a research problem.
b) The policy problem identified is not the real cause of the undesirable situation the policy maker wants to solve. For instance, lack of acceptance of a new production technology is seen as the result of poor functioning of the extension service. However, in reality it is caused by poor performance of the market system. In such a situation hierarchies of explanatory variables that could have created the problem must be constructed (Bir-

gegard, 1980). As mentioned earlier, translation of the policy problem into a researchable problem (or problems) is a rather crucial stage in policy-oriented research process for the following reason. At this stage the views of scientists and policy makers may already diverge. Therefore, during this stage there must be regular consultation between researchers and the commissioner of the research (Lohuizen, 1983; Majchrzak, 1984).

[2] + [3] + [4]   There are also reasons, internal to the research process, that make these stages crucial. Firstly, representatives of the various disciplines have to reach agreement on the general research problems.

Often the policy problem is caused by several processes that have to be looked into by different disciplines. As a result the general research problems have to be dissected in several research problems. The singling out of particular processes for further research because they are deemed the most important (the principia media of Mannheim, 1960), is a crucial and at the same time very difficult decision. This is often an arbitrary decision strongly influenced by the world view of participating scientists. The disaggregation of general research problems into research problems for the various disciplines has to be done in a way that enables integration of the outcome of various monodisciplinary research sub-projects in the final synthesis. At this moment the framework for integration of monodisciplinary research results should be created. If this is not done at this stage, considerable problems can be expected in the synthesizing stage. There are also other important aspects that have to be taken into account in the preparation of the research proposal:

a) The results of the various disciplines must be comparable. In a regional analysis, for instance, the data can be compared on a geographical basis.

b) The outcomes of monodisciplinary research and analysis must be made available in such a way that they can be understood and used by other disciplines.

c) The level of information should be more or less the same. The integrated analysis will be biased when one discipline has far more information than the others.

d) Collecting too much data is a problem to avoid. In the final analysis often only a fraction of collected data are usually used. Sometimes abundance of data actually creates more confusion, instead of enabling transparent analysis of the potentials and constraints for development of an area or region. This very problem occurred in a research project in Benin (Daane, 1990). Granted, in the beginning it is not always easy to know exactly which data or information are needed. Careful advance consideration of the reasons data have to be collected, how they are processed, and who on the interdisciplinary team is going to use them, and for what purpose lengthens the preparation period. At the same time, this kind of attention to process shortens the overall period needed for data collection, and consequently diminishes the costs of data collection, the most expensive part of the research process.

e) The area or region under study is always a part of a larger entity, be it a river basin, a higher administrative unit, or a market system (Weintraub and Marguiles, 1986). For that reason some disciplines have to collect information outside the area or region. This step must also be discussed and coordinated in preparation of fieldwork. If this step is not taken misunderstanding may occur, especially when scarce resources such as transport facilities are required.

All these aspects have to be discussed in detail among the various disciplines involved. If this discussion is not handled properly big problems can be expected during implementation of fieldwork and certainly during the synthesis of the outcomes of various monodisciplinary research efforts.

On the basis of the framework of problems indicated above, the disciplines have to operationalize their research problem(s) and make a tentative work program. On most occasions there is only a limited amount of time or resources available. Consequently there are limitations to the depth of research, a situation that will have consequences for choice of methods. Limited time and resources necessitate careful coordination. On the basis of the work programs presented by the disciplines, a general work program for the team is prepared, designating what time each discipline is collecting what kind of data and, if possible, where collection will occur. Furthermore, the time when a discipline will deliver specific data to another discipline should be mentioned. If agronomists do not receive timely information from climatologists and soil scientists, they are not in a position to indicate the physical agricultural production potential of a region. Figure 3 is a model for visualizing the working program. It gives an overview of data collecting activities and exchange of information, thereby picturing the communication process that should take place within the team. More detailed charts for work programs for interdisciplinary research in regional planning appear in van Staveren and van Dusseldorp (1980).

Finally, a budget has to be made. For sizable teams that have to operate in large regions, special attention must be given to logistical aspects, such as transport, lodging, etc.

The work program has to be discussed and accepted by both the interdisciplinary team and its director or principal. Though every team member retains responsibility for the quality of outcomes of monodisciplinary research, the other members must still be able to ask critical questions that can influence operationalization of the research problem and final work program. At the same time, team members must respect each others' expertise. From the very beginning, there should be intensive communication among all disciplines. When the final research proposal is accepted by all team members, and the principal has agreed to fund the research proposal, fieldwork can begin.

Fieldwork

[5] After collecting and analyzing the available secondary data upon which already tentative hypotheses can be formulated, general orientation in the field

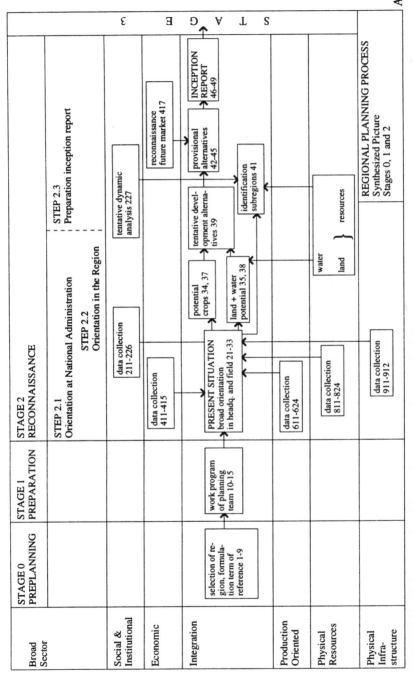

FIGURE 3A–C. An example of the work program of an interdisciplinary team.

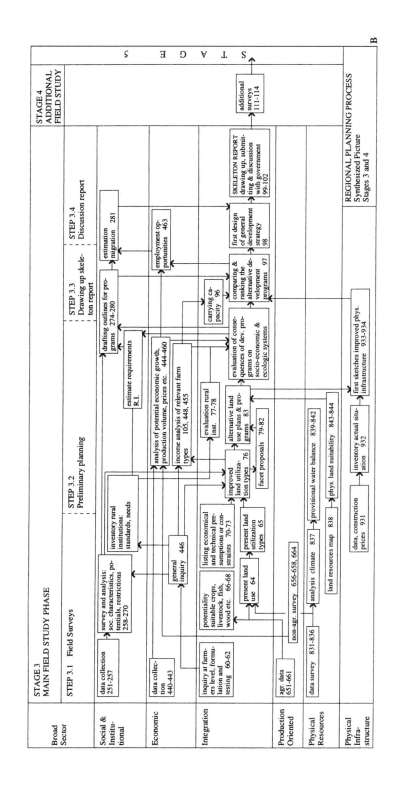

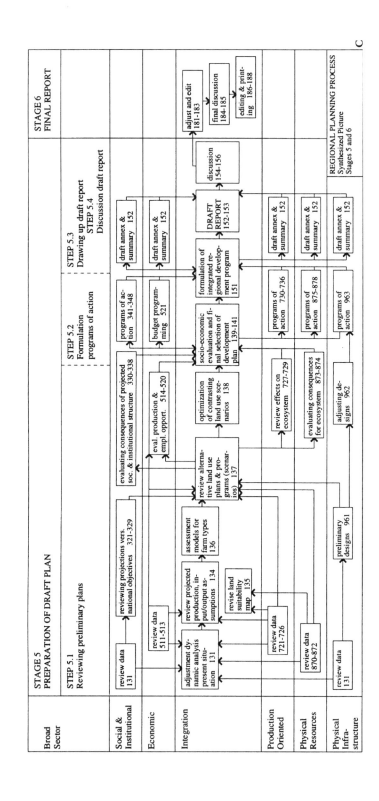

C

STAGE 5 — PREPARATION OF DRAFT PLAN
STAGE 6 — FINAL REPORT

STEP 5.1 Reviewing preliminary plans
STEP 5.2 Formulation programs of action
STEP 5.3 Drawing up draft report
STEP 5.4 Discussion draft report

REGIONAL PLANNING PROCESS
Synthesized Picture Stages 5 and 6

follows. This orientation can be accomplished via the Sondeo method (Hildebrandt, 1981), which can be a part of rapid rural appraisal approach (Beebe, 1985). Sondeo method is a simple procedure whereby team members go two by two into the field to observe and discuss potentials and constraints for development of an area, with the people in the field and among each other. Every day the couples are changed, so that all members of participating disciplines have had an opportunity to observe in combination the same area, albeit but from their different scientific angles. This arrangement facilitates an important basis for future communication during the period, in which each discipline goes, at least for sometime, its own way.

[6]   On the basis of the reconnaissance survey, an adjustment of research problems and work programs may possibly be necessary.

[7]   In the next step representatives of the various disciplines start their own research. During this period of monodisciplinary research, there should be regular consultations between team members. Exchange of tentative data and information makes it possible that mutual influence of the actual problem formulation as well as work program of participating disciplines occurs. The views and information presented by one team member can influence the perception of other team members. In response, they can focus on other issues or areas than those originally mentioned in their work program.

The type of data that has to be collected by various disciplines depends on the nature of the region. For the social disciplines, van Staveren and van Dusseldorp (1980) provide checklists for disciplines frequently involved in research for regional planning.

In research projects that are part of a regional planning exercise for predominantly rural areas, some disciplines have to contribute their information at an early stage: for instance with climatology, hydrology, geology, and soil science. On the basis of their input other disciplines then focus their own research and planning activities, such as agronomy and animal husbandry, that in turn provide the information for sociology and economy (see Figure 3). Some of the team members will have left the field already, because their research activities have finished by that stage. When they are stationed nearby, it is still possible to have them at team meetings, but often they have taken up other duties and their involvement would be expensive. In such a situation the disciplines leaving the team should have presented their reports in time, so these can be discussed in detail with other team members.

Synthesis

[8]   In this stage the findings of various monodisciplinary research efforts have to be made available to all team members.

[9]   When larger teams are involved, sometimes a nucleus team is given the first responsibility to combine information provided by participating disciplines into an integrated and dynamic analysis. However, all team members should

have opportunities to make suggestions about how integration should take place.

[10]   More important, team members follow closely how the results of their disciplines are being used in the integration process. This means that all team members should be available if possible. In addition, part of the integration can, and sometimes should, take place during fieldwork.

[11]   To reiterate, the outcome of interdisciplinary research, as presented in the final synthesis, is based on contributions of the separate disciplines, even when these contributions cannot be recognized. But the quality of such an integrated analysis is determined by the contributions of the disciplines. The building stones, which are the basis for analysis, have to be mentioned in the final report in appendices. If the building stones are not clear it will be difficult, if not impossible, to judge the quality of the integrated analysis, and to falsify it. From a scientific point of view this would be a poor performance.

An excellent integration of disciplinary contributions of poor or heterogeneous quality delivers a poor product and can create havoc during the preparation and implementation of action programs, especially in policy and action-oriented research. In such cases multidisciplinary study of good quality is preferable.

Reporting

In policy-oriented research it is important to pay special attention to presentation of the report. It should be understandable for policymakers and laypeople alike.

The Role of Social Scientists in Interdisciplinary Cooperation in Farming System Research (FSR)

Historical Background and Main Characteristics of FSR

Agricultural research has provided important inputs for rapid increase of agricultural production in Western as well as in developing countries. However, the farmers have been the primary beneficiaries, or those living in areas favored with good soils, climate, or infrastructure (e.g. irrigation systems). The development of innovations, such as high yielding varieties was mainly done in isolation from research stations. Little attention was paid to available indigenous knowledge (Brokensha *et al.*, 1980), or to the farmers' positions and their environments. Farmers were supposed to adapt themselves to the innovations developed by researchers. As a result, many of the innovations were not accepted, or only partly introduced. It may also take a long time before small farmers, by far the majority in developing countries, can profit from the outcomes of agricultural research.

In the last decades, appreciation of the knowledge of farmers, especially in less favored areas, has increased considerably. Obviously the detailed knowledge farmers have of their own environments is considerably larger than the knowledge of agricultural researchers. Box (1988) found in the Dominican Republic that farmers were aware of far more varieties of cassava than researchers. Many of these varieties, previously unknown to the research station, were crucial for their survival. This realization has led to a new approach towards agricultural research in the sense that more attention is paid to farmers' knowledge; moreover, a part of the experimentation takes place at the farm, in so-called farming systems research.

The main characteristics of farming systems research (FSR), according to Shaner *et al.* (1981:19–20), are the following:

1. *Farmer based.* It starts with farmers and their households, their knowledge of their farms and the (physical, biological economic, and social) environments in which they have to operate.
2. *Problem solving.* FSR tends to focus on short-term objectives. The approach identifies farmers' constraints and distinguishes between constraints that are within and constraints that are beyond their control. From this starting point, an assessment is made of whether actual cultivation practices can be improved or whether innovations still unknown to farmers can be fitted into their farming systems.
3. *Comprehensive.* FSR studies the whole farm setting in order to identify problems and opportunities, notes their interrelationships, sets research priorities responsive to farmers' and society's goals, carries out experiments, proposes changes in the light of these comprehensive perspectives, measures results in terms of their impact on farmers and society, observes farmer acceptance of change, and transfers acceptable results to implementing organizations. This means that not only farming practices are of importance. Attention must also be paid to non- and off-farm activities, because in many developing countries an important part of the income of households comes from outside the farm. This outside income is often on a working-hour basis and is higher than the farm income.
4. *Interdisciplinary.* The comprehensive approach requires an interdisciplinary effort. That is, different disciplines have to work in close contact with each other. Because women perform many, if not most, of the activities on the farm (in Africa), female researchers should be included on the FSR team.
5. *Complementary.* FSR replaces neither commodity nor disciplinary research nor extension. However important farmers' knowledge may be, there is still a considerable amount of knowledge beyond their horizon. But there should not be a one-way flow of information. Farmers' practices can open new avenues for agricultural research in the sense that specific problems are identified for research. Additionally, the ways farmers cope with their environment can create new insights for agricultural researchers. FSR can build bridges between the farmers, agricultural researchers, and extension workers. For improving cooperation with agricultural research stations, it is particularly important that the social sciences are included. The various roles they can fulfil there—go between and translator, monitor, assessor of social im-

pact, analyzer of indigenous knowledge, accommodator, or scout—have been elaborated by van Dusseldorp and Box (1990).
6. *Iterative and dynamic.* It is iterative because in a process that starts with partial information, insight is gained through studies and experimentation, leading in turn to modifications of actions. FSR is dynamic in the sense that objectives and approaches for future work can be adjusted in the light of the accomplishments.
7. *Responsible to society.* FSR operates from the farmers' and society's viewpoint. For instance, it is not sufficient to look only at maximal income of farmers in the short run. Sustainability also has to be taken into account. Farmers' practices that lead to accelerated erosion should be modified.

Recently, there have been indications that the heyday of FSR is over. Some of the criticism heard in developing countries indicates FSR is a very expensive research approach that can only be used if there are rich donors willing to fund it for a considerable time. Furthermore, some of the disciplines required are scarce, not employed in agricultural research stations, or not available at all, as is the case with social scientists. Finally replicability is not always easy. The recommendation domains (the areas in which the farmers can use the outcome of FSR) are often limited.

Sociological Theories That Can Be Used

In research that leads to recommendations for development and improvement of farming systems and rural development, adaptation of farmers' behavior is necessary. In other words, the farmers and members of their households have to decide to perform certain activities in a different way, to introduce new activities, or to eliminate activities performed in the past. In such cases, the sociologist has to indicate what these changes are and whether the farmers and their families are willing and able to adjust their behavior, taking into account their environment. The same holds true for farming systems research, in which knowledge of the farmer plays a central role.

It is crucial that sociologists make the theories they use explicit. In FSR research descriptive theories are first formulated and tested. On the basis of these descriptive theories, prescriptive theories can be developed, forming the intellectual basis for any action program that is to be designed. The action program, in turn, will indicate how to change or adapt the existing farming systems to new situations or innovations developed by participating disciplines on the FSR team.

In order to provide the information mentioned above, the sociologist has to focus attention on two main concepts: behavior and determinants that can influence behavior. The decision pattern of members of farmers' households is closely related to behavior.

Human behavior is "The acquired manner in which a human being acts in a given situation as a result of his previous human association" (Fairchild,

1955:21). Kunkel (1970) offers a behavioral model (theory) for explaining how human behavior is created and how it can be changed. This model has limitations, because it is a considerable reduction of reality. However, its simplicity and practical application possibilities are fruitful. It is also possible to use other theories, including existing decision theories. However, if other theories are selected, other data and information have to be collected.

In Kunkel's vision (1970:26–61) human behavior is shaped by stimuli. He distinguishes **reinforcing stimuli** (rewards) and **aversive stimuli** (punishments). On the basis of previous experiences, human actors know which type of activity was rewarded, or looked upon less favorably by the social environment. When activities are rewarded in a constant and consistent way, this activity will most likely be repeated in the future. When an activity will constantly be condemned (punished), very likely it will not be repeated. The main question is: what is an actor seeing as reinforcing stimuli and as aversive stimuli? This judgment depends on **state variables.** The state variables of actors are determined by the ideal values of their societies and their translation of these values into operating norms. These norms are changing over time, because actors are in constant dialogue with the value pattern of their society (Giddens, 1979). What is seen as immoral behavior in the immediate moment may be seen as acceptable behavior in the near future.

State variables present conditions of deprivation or satisfaction. For example, after a couple of hours working in the field, actors will be very thirsty. Their level of deprivation will be high. They will experience a glass of water as a great reward. However, after three glasses of water their level of deprivation will go down, a state of satisfaction (saturation) having been reached. At that moment water is no longer a reward. It can even become an aversive stimulus, if they are forced to drink more water. This holds true for all types of reward. The more specific a reward is the bigger the chance that a state of satisfaction will be reached quickly. When an effort is made to influence the behavior of actors via rewards one has to know what their level of deprivation is and for what specifically. Reinforcing stimuli must be found that can satisfy many demands. Obviously, money is such a **generalized reinforcing stimulus.**

Many activities are "rewarded" and "punished" at the same time. Earning a lot of money at the costs of others can be rewarding, but it can at the same time lead to a loss of social status, because the actors will be seen by their social environments as greedy and unkind people. This means that the actors have to make a cost/benefit assessment. Clearly, the human being is a cost benefit optimizer (van Dusseldorp, 1992).

In addition, the schedule of reinforcement must be considered. "Whether reinforcers are presented continuously or intermittently, on a ratio or interval schedule, on a fixed or variable basis, is largely a function of the social context, such as customary payment for work or periodic festivals" (Kunkel, 1970:43). For instance, when work is necessary to prevent erosion that in the long run can affect the very existence of a farm, it is questionable whether a farmer is willing to bear the punishment of this moment (costs in labor or other scarce resources needed for implementation of anti-erosion works), because the rewards in most cases can be expected only after many years. It is easy to point out to farmers in India that by continuing the present type of farming, they will destroy their farms, and they will be of no use for their children. Most likely, their answer will be that if they are not producing as they are now, there is little chance their children will survive. So, what will be the benefits?

The sociologist has to find out what actors are experiencing as rewards and punishments of their activities. The most simple way is to investigate why farmers have decided to start an activity in the past and what kind of cost/benefit assessments they have made. When these decisions were made long ago, this is not a simple affair. Some kind of rationalization will automatically take place. But there is another reason actors will have difficulty explaining why they have decided to start a specific activity, especially when it comes to activities that take place regularly and do not require a substantive amount of scarce resources. In such a situation the decision process often is made in a **pre-attentive way**. A ". . . pre-attentive process refers to any information processing, that is outside of a decision maker's ordinary attention and awareness" (Gladwin and Murtaugh in Barlett, 1980:117).

As mentioned earlier, the behavioral theory has limitations. It is a rather mechanistic view of human actors. In reality things are far more complicated. Due to changes in operating norms, it is difficult to predict, at least for a long period, the reinforcing stimuli by which behavior can be influenced. Even so, human behavior is shaped to a considerable extent by rewards and punishment. Unless there are suddenly considerable changes in the environment, operating norms will change only gradually. Therefore, for the short term some prediction is possible, albeit with prudence.

Position of the Social Scientist in the FSR Team

Before discussing the research activities of the sociologist, two positions the social scientist can have in an interdisciplinary FSR team, and in agricultural research in general, have to be mentioned.

a) In the **steering approach** (Van Dusseldorp, 1977; Van Dusseldorp and Box, 1990) sociologists, on the basis of their knowledge of the farmers' actual behavior, indicate what technical innovations can and should be introduced in order to improve the farming system. For instance, on the basis of the existing labor film the sociologists can indicate that the farmers' position could be improved if crops or animals are introduced. (The labor film is a graphic presentation of the hour of labor used for various activities over time.) They would require time and attention in periods when farmers have a surplus of labor, time and attention that cannot be used for other activities and are not needed for religious or other ceremonial obligations. With them, the farmer can obtain a higher income with available resources.

Dewalt calls this the "social science of agriculture." He explains: "the study of the interaction of the natural environment, socio-cultural patterns, market conditions, government policy, and technological systems in order to identify agricultural research and/or extension priorities, to determine appropriate institutional structures and responsibilities for research and extension, to predict the consequences of agricultural change, and to identify government, agency, and institutional policies that will facilitate the development of more just and equitable social systems" (Dewalt in McCorkle, 1989:43).

There are several reasons why sociologists should be careful not to overstress their steering function. Firstly, the predictive power of sociology is rather limited, especially when it comes to predictions that cover five or more years. This is typically the period required to develop, via breeding, new varieties with required characteristics. Secondly, in most cases people and their society adapt more easily to new circumstances than to their physical and biological environment. Thirdly, technical scientists do not appreciate having social scientists, including economists, tell them what direction their research should take. This was clearly demonstrated in the Centro Internacional de Agricultura (CIAT) in Columbia, where economists tried to determine policy over technical scientists and came, at least for some time, into great difficulties.

b) The **accommodation approach.** Here the first move is made by the technical disciplines, which indicate what kind of technical innovations are possible in the given physical environment. On the basis of their information the economist can make an assessment of expected benefits. The sociologist is then able to make an assessment of the social acceptability by comparing the present and desired future behavioral pattern, taking into account reinforcing and aversive stimuli that are available. The advantage for sociologists in this approach is knowing on which type of activities in the farming system research efforts should concentrate.

Categories of Information That Have to Be Provided by Technical Disciplines, When the Accommodation Approach is Followed

In actual practice the FSR team follows a mixture of the steering and accommodation approaches. Thus, whenever sociologists have, in the beginning of the research process, important information that can influence the direction of research of other disciplines they will make this information available. Hereafter special attention will be paid to the accommodation approach and the type of information that has to be exchanged between technical and social disciplines.

The sociologists have to find out what kind of behavior is required before the new innovation, or mix of innovations in the case of the so-called package approach, can yield expected benefits. Through intensive discussions, the technical disciplines have to indicate what farmers must do exactly, in order to obtain maximum results of the new (available or potential) innovation(s), and what the consequences are if the pattern of activities is not or only partly followed. When a new crop or a new variety of an existing crop is introduced with different properties then the following items have to be discussed:

a) *The time factor* is often of great importance. Therefore the agronomist must indicate in great detail what has to be done at which particular moment: for instance, when the land preparation must be ready and how much time is involved; when seed beds have to be prepared, at what time this has to be done, and how much time is required. In the case of transplanting or sowing, the period when it has to be done and the time required for these activities must be indicated. In addition, farmers must know what to do once the crop is established: for instance, weeding or the observance and combating of diseases; knowing when the harvest should take place and what kind of activities have to be performed, as well as the duration and which kind of activities are needed in storage and processing, when they have to take place, and their duration. In this way it is possible to make the labor film, which indicates what had to be done, when, and the number of human labor hours needed. By comparing this labor film with the existing labor film, a first assessment of the acceptability of the innovation for farmers and their households can be made. One question to consider is whether women have extra time available if household tasks remain the same.

b) *Time consciousness.* There is another aspect of time. Some crops or animals are very susceptible to certain diseases. When the occurrence of a disease is not recognized in time, this can have considerable consequences for production, or even lead to the death of crops and animals. In irrigation projects, farmers have to prepare their land at specific moments. Often great accuracy in timing is required during irrigation activities when water is scarce. Members of the farmer's household must have the ability to take the issue of timely action seriously. This circumstance can create problems in the first period of introduction, because many traditional crops do not require such a time-specific approach in observing diseases or infections and application of insecticides or medicines.

c) *Ergonometric and cultural aspects of labor.* Attention must also be paid to ergonometric aspects of the various activities. Does the activity require the power of a full grown man or can it also be performed by women and children? Here only physical aspects of the required labor are considered. But sociologists also have to determine whether labor that physically can be performed by women is also acceptable in a certain socio-cultural environment. Attention must also be paid to what kind of position in which activities have to be performed. Do they require bowing, kneeling or can they be done standing, etc.? Certain positions are sometimes perceived as socially demeaning. This cultural dimension requires special attention when new equipment is introduced. For instance, the Amhara farmers in the Awash valley in Ethiopia refused, at least in the beginning, to bow, a position required in the harvesting of cotton.

d) *Knowledge and skills.* What kind of knowledge and skills are required to perform the various activities needed for a successful introduction of an innovation. In the case of diseases farmers must be able to identify the symptoms of a certain disease and distinguish it from other diseases with more or less the same symptoms. Sometimes this requires that farmers be able to recognize new causalities. If they believe that certain diseases are caused by supernatural powers, they will either feel themselves in no position to do something or refer to magic. These responses do not mean that their behavior before was irrational. Within their worldview, taking belief in supernatural powers as an example, it was logical and rational to perform activities they did before (e.g. to sacrifice an animal to appease the spirits). When animals are new in the farming system, farmers have to know how to handle them and the same holds true for tractors or pumps, etc.

e) *Inputs.* What kind of inputs are required? Are these inputs available? Is the farmer familiar with these inputs? The use of insecticides or new mechanical equipment is not always easy and without danger.

f) *Benefits.* What are the extra benefits (reinforcing stimuli) for the farmers' household when the proposed innovation (or mix of innovations) is correctly introduced? It is important to know not only that production will increase, but also the economic benefits. Here the economist has a major role in providing the information.

g) *Risk.* Another aspect that needs attention is the risk factor. New varieties or a new breed of animals are often more susceptible to the vagaries of the environment. They may not be able to withstand drought or flooding very well, or are not immune against certain diseases. In other words, is it possible for technical disciplines to indicate clearly, and in a quantified way, the extra risks involved when an innovation is introduced and accepted. Especially for small farmers, even "small" risks should be avoided whenever possible, because these farmers have little or no risk absorption capacity. Researchers must be sensitive to this issue, because in most cases they have a wealth bias. As a result they are inclined to think (very) small risks are acceptable.

h) *Consequences of partial change in behavior.* Finally, technical disciplines must indicate what the consequences are if a certain activity is not performed in the proper way, or at exactly the right time. For instance, what will be the loss in production, in percentages or quantities, when the farmers are two days late in observing a disease or in applying an insecticide?

When this information is made available by soil scientists, agronomists, irrigation specialists and economists, sociologists have clearer insight into the behavior pattern required, as well as the benefits (incentives, reinforcing stimuli) and the costs and risks (aversive stimuli) that can be expected. This information is essential for discussions with farmers that must occur in order to find out what their opinion is regarding the new crops, animals, or production techniques which are already available or could be developed via research at agricultural research stations.

A Relational Model of the Farming System

In the foregoing section attention was focused on the behavior required from farmers in order to ensure the success of a specific innovation. Whether the farmer will accept an innovation is determined not only by the benefits of that specific innovation, but even more important, how the innovation fits into the farming system as a whole. Necessarily, then, the FSR team needs clear insight in all components of the farming system under investigation, and the interrelationships among these components. This insight can be achieved by making a model.

There are three types of models. In the **conceptual model** all components of a system are indicated, but no attention is given to relations among these components. The **relational model** indicates not only the components of a system but also their interrelationships. Finally, there is the **mathematical model,** in which relationships can be expressed in mathematical formulae. This type of model will be discussed later on.

A relational model is depicted in Figure 4. The lines indicate relations that exist between components. An essential part of the farming system is the work necessary for maintaining farm buildings, the repair or construction of farm equipment, and the time women need for looking after small children, cleaning the house, collecting water and/or firewood, cooking, and washing, repairing and making clothes for members of the household, etc. These activities are mentioned under the heading "reproduction activities." Another important component consists of activities outside the farming system, the so-called **off-farm** and **non-farm activities.** In many households in developing countries, these activities can provide 50% or more of total household income. It is necessary therefore to investigate the household as a whole, of which the farm is a sub-system.

As soon as possible the FSR team should make a relational model of the farming systems they are investigating. After making a conceptual model, construction of the relational model follows. It is not enough to indicate relationships by lines only, as indicated in Figure 4. When considering labor, it is necessary to find out how much labor is involved for the activities mentioned, both in the components and their interrelationships. For instance, it is not enough to know that firewood is collected from the forest. The amount of time this takes and who is involved in this activity should be indicated. Similarly, the volume of crops used as food for the household, fed to the animals, or sold at market should be known.

A relational model of the farming system can be an important tool for coordination of the activities of members of a FSR team. Such a model provides insight into the relative position of components, the various disciplines involved and the potential relationship they might have with other disciplines.

Three Periods in the History of the Household and the Farm

In the accommodation approach, sociologists try to determine, in cooperation with their colleagues, what the future behavior pattern should be. This determi-

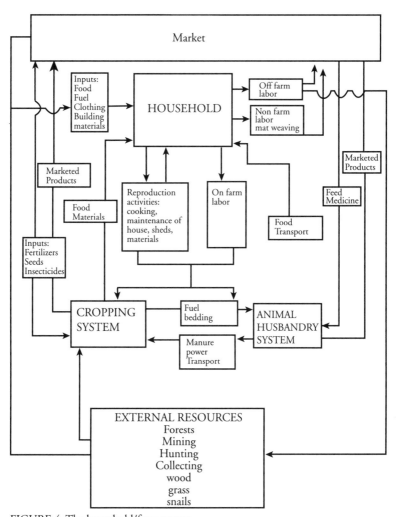

FIGURE 4. The household/farm system.

nation must occur before the introduction of certain innovations can be successful. The next step is to analyze the actual behavior pattern of members of farmers' households. In addition sociologists must obtain insights into reinforcing and aversive stimuli that have determined behavior. Present behavior is a result of events that have taken place in the past. It is necessary therefore to construct a history of the household and its farm. Dividing this history into three periods can be helpful:

a) *The formative years of the farmer and his wife.* This should include the background of their parents, composition of the families they came from, their education, and their activities before they started their own household and farm.

b) *The period from the start of the farm until the start of the FSR.* In this period an overview of important events that took place should be made, plus the various decisions that were made. The information obtained from this period has some weaknesses. Firstly, respondents may not remember exactly what took place in the past, because most of the events took place long ago. Secondly, members of farmers' households very likely will rationalize their reasons and arguments on the basis of which decisions were made. Hence, this information cannot be accepted at face value. It requires regular checking.

c) *The period of implementation of the FSR.* In most FSR a considerable amount of information is collected by technical and economic disciplines, indicating exactly what farmers did and what decisions they made. This information must be made available to sociologists, as soon as possible and be included in the schedule of the history of the farm (see Figure 5).

Past Events and Decisions to Investigate

Some events and decisions worthy of investigation follow. They can provide insight into the functioning of the household, and the reasons decisions were made, thereby helping to explain the present situation of the farm. In order to have a complete history of the household and farm, investigation should begin when the household and farm were founded. Because a long time may have passed, problems with memory of the respondents can be expected. For that reason, special attention should be given to major decisions made in the last five years.

A very detailed analysis must be made of decisions that have been registered during the FSR period. Because these decisions will have been made only a couple of weeks ago, the reasons will very likely be easily remembered. The main focus should be on the types of assessments actors have made of costs and benefits related to the decision under scrutiny, in addition to finding out whether other alternatives have been taken into consideration, and for what reasons they were discarded. Preferably attention should be paid to decisions which do not take place regularly and in which a considerable amount of scarce resources were involved. Otherwise the problem of pre-attentive decision making may occur. The respondent may not always be willing to provide this information. Informants have to be all the relevant household members, not only the head of household.

a) *Development of the household* is determined by the birth, death, adoption, and marriage of children, plus the moment that they leave the family. This information, combined with information obtained from their formative years, can be graphically presented in a family tree. Such a tool provides insight into that part of the farmers' networks, as far as they are based on kinship. This kinship network, though, can be quite large and may not be the source of the most useful members of a network. When

TIME	THE HOUSE-HOLDS	THE FARM					BUILDINGS		OFF/NON-FARM ACTIVI-TIES	CREDIT	MARKET-ING
		LAND	CROPS	LIVE-STOCK	EQUIP-MENT	INPUTS	HOUSE	STABLE, ETC.			
PERIOD 1 THE FOR-MATIVE YEARS			RICE/MAIZE/CASSAVA								RICE ONLY
PERIOD 2 START OF THE FARM UNTIL FSR											
YEAR 1		7 ACRES INHERITED	START PEPPER	+1 COW							RICE
2		+2 ACRES	STOP MAIZE	+3 GOATS						+10,000 RS.	RICE AND PEPPER
3		-1 ACRE	STOP PEPPER	-2 COWS			BUILT A NEW HOUSE	BUILT A STABLE FOR GOATS		-7,000 RS.	RICE
N											
PERIOD 3 PERIOD OF FSR	M	O	R	E		D	E	T	A	I	L
WEEK 1											
2											
3											
N											

FIGURE 5

+ = BOUGHT OR DEBIT
− = SOLD OR CREDIT

it comes to adoption of children into or departure of children out of the household it is important to find out the reasons.

b) *History of the land.* What was the size of the farm at the start? Was it inherited, bought, rented, share-cropped, etc.? Was new land bought, rented, share-cropped, or was land sold, rented, or shared with other persons? What was the price of purchased land, and what were the conditions when land was rented or shared? What were the locations of plots? Also to whom was land given, or sold, from whom was it obtained and for what reasons?

c) *Crops.* What crops were grown when the farm was started? Were new crops introduced and when? For what reasons and from where was information about these crops obtained and from where did seeds or seedlings come? Were crops eliminated from the farming system and for what reasons? Have farmers observed changes in yields or in disease occurrence? What kind of explanation do they give for these changes?

   From the crops presently grown the sociologist, together with agronomist, has to find out, in great detail, how these are cultivated and for what reasons the various cultivation practices are performed and by whom.

d) *Livestock.* When the farm was started were there livestock and of what type? Were new types of livestock introduced into the farm system and for what reasons? From whom was information obtained about new types of livestock? Was livestock sold, bought, or rented? Under what conditions, from whom and for what reasons? What was the purchase price of cattle? Did farmers or their families observe changes in productivity of animals or disease occurrence? What kind of explanation do they have for these changes?

e) *Inputs.* What kind of inputs did the farm household use—e.g. manure, fertilizer, or insecticides—when it started the farm? Were new inputs introduced, when and for what reasons? From whom was information about these inputs obtained? How did farmers get access to these inputs and under what conditions?

f) *Equipment.* What type of equipment did farmers have when they started their farms? Was new equipment introduced, when and for what reasons? From where did they obtain information about new equipment, such as a new type of plough, a small tractor, or spraying equipment? How did they obtain this equipment and under what conditions: for instance buying with or without credit, renting, borrowing or shared use? Did they make their own equipment?

g) *Buildings.* First the history of household dwellings should be pursued. In what kind of house did the household first dwell? Was it owned, rented or provided free? Were any improvements made? A new house built at the same location or at another plot? What materials were used in building and/or for improvement of the house? How and from whom were these obtained and under what conditions? What were the costs involved? The same questions mentioned above can also be asked for stables, sheds, or storage facilities on the farm.

h) *Off- and non-farm activities.* What kind of off- and non-farm activities were performed by various members of the household? When was the first time these types of activities were initiated? What were the reasons these activities were performed, and what was the renumeration per invested hour of labor? According to the opinion of the various respondents, what was the social status of this type of work? Were opportunities to do off- or non-farm activities not taken into consideration and for what reasons?

i) *Credit.* It is important to find out whether farmers and their households have taken credit (lending of money on whatever conditions), and at what moments in the history of the farm, for what reasons, from whom, and under what conditions? Did the farmers observe changes in the credit system or conditions under which credit is provided? What explanation do they give for these changes?

j) *Marketing.* What kind of products did the farmers' households sell? When, where, to and by whom were these products sold? When did the marketing of various products take place for the first time and for what reasons? What were the prices for various products? Have the farmers and their household members observed any changes in the marketing system and prices? What explanation do they have for these changes?

All of the important events and the related decisions made by farmers and their households can be brought together in a schedule of the history of the farm, as indicated in Figure 5.

The Social and Economic Environment

The members of a farm household are not operating in a vacuum. They are embedded in the cultural, social, and economic environment of their villages and regions. It is necessary therefore to gain insight into the value patterns and social structure of the society in which they are living, as well as the relations they have with various individuals, groups, and institutions.

On the basis of information farmers have been given—e.g., with whom they had contracts, whether in obtaining information or credit, or selling products, renting or selling of land—a **social network** diagram can be made. Such diagrams are useful, because they give insight into the systematic interaction of people engaged in activities that can alter institutions in which they are participating. They also have a definitive structure that influences the behavior and attitudes of the respondent in the center of the network (ego). This information can be of importance in a later stage of the FSR, when recommendations have to be made regarding how and via whom farmers can best be approached when introducing proposed innovations. Figure 6 is an example of such a network diagram.

It must be realized that the social network of farmers is larger, in the sense that they may also have relations not directly concerning the farm or household. They can be involved in other organizations such as religious groups,

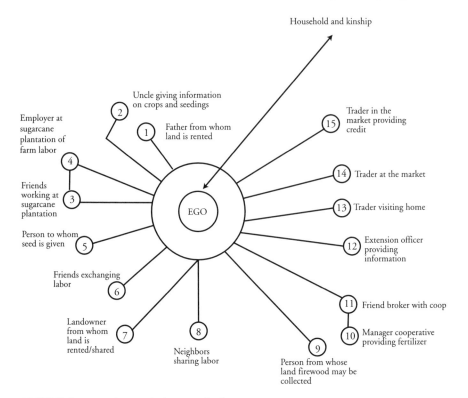

FIGURE 6.   A social network diagram of a farmer.

village councils, cooperatives, etc., from which they obtain assistance and many kinds of information. Moreover, insight into the networks of farmers' wives and the older children is significant.

Research Techniques to Be Used

Obviously the information sociologists want to obtain from their respondents may be sensitive. Not everybody is willing to give in great detail the reasons for specific decisions. Researchers have to be aware that if respondents are willing to answer questions, the answers are not always correct. They can have implicit objectives they do not like to reveal, because they are at the margin of the norm and value pattern of their societies. For instance, the main reason they bought a piece of land might not be that they wanted, in the first place, to extend their farms, but they tried to prevent their neighbors, with whom they had quarreled, from getting a bigger farm. In order to obtain this type of information, researchers have to put considerable efforts into building up good relationships with their respondents.

    In obtaining the data and information indicated above, researchers can use the diagnostic case study approach (Doorman, 1991). This approach relies on techniques of observation, as well as open and structured interviews. Once obtained, information must be put into field notes which can be analyzed at a later stage.

Researchers must realize that this type of intensive discussion with farmers can influence their future behavior. For example, it is possible that during a discussion with farmers on the various types of credit that are available, farmers start to realize that they can substitute the credit they take from middlemen by credit from other sources like NGO's. This will affect their future decision making. The researcher, however, will only have information on decision making in the past.

Presentation of Data and Information

Data and information can be presented as follows:

a) *The report.* Sociologists can write a report on the basis of their field notes. When it comes to the rather voluminous description of case studies, this must be done as detailed as possible in the draft report. In the final report only those events relevant for the line of argument have to be included. However, there is some danger that only that information will be used which supports the line of argument. Obviously this must be avoided.

b) *Schedule of the farm history and social network diagram.* The draft report, and even the final case study, may be too bulky and too technical for team members to read. Yet the findings of the diagnostic case studies must be discussed intensively with technical disciplines. Therefore, the findings of each farm in schedules should be presented as indicated in Figures 5 and 6.

How to Arrive at Recommendations

On the basis of the schedule of decision making in the past and present (Figure 5) it is possible to initiate a discussion with the other team members. The following issues are important.

a) Are there any activities or events that the sociologist has not observed or was not informed of, but other team members are aware of and consider important? If so, this information should be brought into the schedule.

b) Are there crucial decisions, according to the technical and economic disciplines, that require more in-depth information?

On the basis of these discussions, sociologists can revisit farmers in order to complete their information.

Now the sociologists have a clear insight into:

a) The past and actual behavior pattern of informants in a household, and the way they make cost/benefit assessments before arriving at specific decisions, and;
b) The desired behavior pattern needed for successful introduction of a specific innovation.

By comparing the two sets of behavioral patterns the sociologist can make an assessment of the changes that have to be made in the behavior and decision patterns of household.

On the basis of what the farmer and his household members experience as reinforcing and aversive stimuli, and expected reinforcing and aversive stimuli connected with the proposed innovation or mix of innovations, sociologists can:

a) Make an assessment of the likeliness that the innovation will be accepted;
b) Indicate, in case the chances of acceptance are low, how innovations should be adjusted, as far as technically and economically feasible, in order to obtain a higher rate of acceptance;
c) Mention what kind of other innovations would be acceptable to farmers' households;
d) Outline the kind of measures advisable, necessary, or recommendable to speed up the acceptance;
e) Indicate on the basis of the social network diagrams by which channels members of the household can best be approached.

Understandably these kinds of observations and recommendations can only be made **after intensive discussions with farmers** and their household members. Group discussions are preferable, though women and children may not participate in the discussion. The other disciplines in the FSR team should also participate in these intensive discussions. The opinions of farmers are crucial. They are the ones who must make the final decisions and have to take the risks.

The Interface Between Simulation Models and the Social Sciences

The use of mathematical models is penetrating agricultural research stations where crop simulation models have become popular. The interesting aspect of crop simulating models is that they are giving a specific framework for interdisciplinary cooperation between physiologists, agronomists, social scientists and entymologists.

Recently, efforts have begun to interface these models with linear programming models of economists and with mathematical models for land evaluation models. There are indications that, via interfacing of various mathematical models, a framework for policy-oriented interdisciplinary research can be developed. This interesting development has to be followed closely by social scientists, not so much because they have to try to obtain their place in these models, but to see at what moments and in what ways they can contribute to the agricultural research process as it is developing presently. If this interfacing does not occur the social sciences will become isolated in the field of interdisciplinary research for agricultural and regional development. In a recent (March 1992) workshop in Wageningen of modellers of agricultural development, sociologists were absent. The main comment of the other disciplines was: we continue with our work and the sociologists can write the instruction leaflet once we have decided what has to be done.

It is important to emphasize that experienced modellers are well aware that simulation models are tools and instruments which can facilitate agricultural research, nothing more nor less than that. They are a type of metamethod, indicated by Heckhausen (1972), and do not lead to transdisciplinarity. Nor can the output of these models be accepted at face value. Experiments in the field are necessary to test these outputs.

Penning de Vries, *et al.* (1989) explain these models as follows:

> A crop model is a simple representation of a crop. It is used to study crop growth and to compute growth responses to the environment. Crop models in common use can be distinguished as descriptive and explanatory model[s].

Descriptive Models

A **descriptive model** defines the behavior of a system in a simple manner. The model reflects little or none of the mechanisms that cause the behavior. Creating and using this type of model is relatively straightforward. Descriptive models often consist of one or more mathematical equations.

Explanatory Models

An **explanatory model** consists of a quantitative description of the mechanisms and processes that cause the behavior of a system. These descriptions are explicit statements of scientific theory and hypotheses. To create an explanatory model, the system is analyzed and its processes and mechanisms quantified separately. The model is built by integrating these descriptions for the entire system. An explanatory crop growth model contains descriptions of distinct processes such as photosynthesis, leaf area expansion, and tiller induction.

In such a model:

Each process must be quantified in relation to environmental factors, such as radiation and temperature; and in relation to the crop status, including leaf area, development stage and nitrogen content. Growth rates can then be computed for any stage of the growing season, depending on the actual crop status, the soil and the weather. All important factors can be accounted for in this way, provided there is sufficient theory and data to quantify them.

It is possible, with these explanatory models, to perform simulations, which lead to explanatory simulation models, in order to be able to perform simulations on effects of alternative developments.

Simulation models are relatively simple representations of the systems in the world around us. A system is defined here as well as delineated parts of the real world. The user identifies a system on the basis of objectives and on the intrinsic structure of the world as measured and observed. For an agronomist, a system may be a rice crop; its elements, plant organs (such as leaf stem and root), and processes (such as growth and transpiration) interact strongly. Weather is a driving variable because it exerts an important driving, or regulating effect on the crop. The crop, on the other hand, has virtually no impact on the weather. In general, driving variables influence the system and its behavior, but the reverse is not true.

The essence of the foregoing citations is that theoretical agronomists are able, via reduction, to create a crop growth simulation model through which it becomes possible to experiment by computer with a specific crop. This prospect does not automatically mean that results of such simulation exercises reflect what will happen in reality. Not all processes are taken into account in the model. Therefore field trials are necessary to test the results. Figure 7 shows how explanatory models can be constructed. Figure 8 is a simplified overview of the work program for an interdisciplinary research team.

The foregoing also indicates that such simulation models are of little value for the social sciences. First of all, their research objects (farmers) are reactive in the sense that they can and will change their behavior, either when there are changes or when they expect changes in the environment. This condition will have its effects on the environment. It is also close to impossible to test the outcome of simulation models introduced in social sciences.

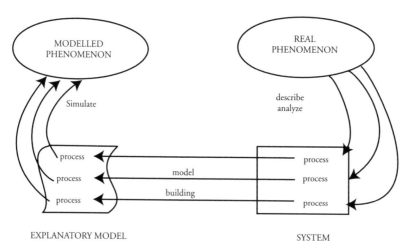

FIGURE 7. A scheme to indicate how real world observations are analyzed and integrated into an explanatory model to simulate behavior of the system.
Source: *Penning de Vries et al.* (1989). Simulation of ecophysiological processes in several annual crops.

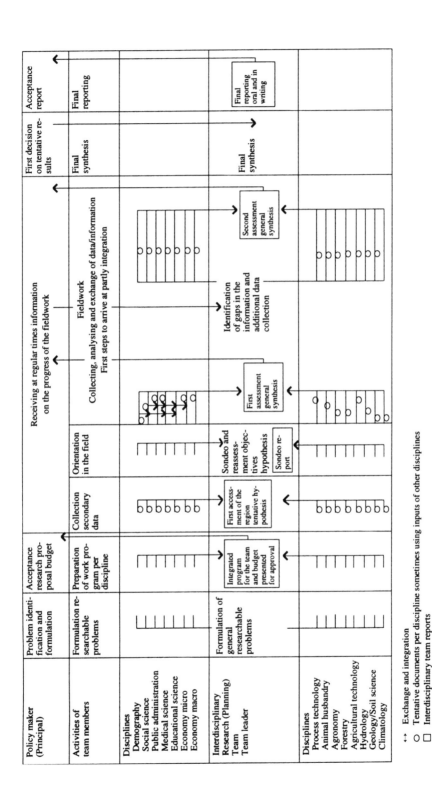

FIGURE 8. Simplified bar chart visualizing the work program for an interdisciplinary research team.

↔ Exchange and integration
○ Tentative documents per discipline sometimes using inputs of other disciplines
☐ Interdisciplinary team reports

To sum up, the advantages of crop growth simulation models in agricultural research are as follows:

a) The simulation model claims to give a framework that facilitates interdisciplinary research. It facilitates indication of precisely what is expected of each discipline in a specific research project.
b) The model makes it easier to indicate relations between applied and fundamental research. For instance, a rice crop does not absorb nitrogen from the soil after flowering. However, during the period of maturation a process takes place within the rice plants that leads to replacement of nitrogen. This process is far more important than was thought before. At present, insight into how this process works is missing, suggesting an important lead for further fundamental research.
c) The simulation model makes it possible to design more specific field experiments. A crop growth simulation model better facilitates knowledge of what exactly has to be tested.
d) Finally, the model enables obtaining the same results with fewer field experiments. By conducting experiments using the computer it is possible to find out which trials will give poor or no results. These trials can then be eliminated. Because field trials are a very expensive part of agricultural research, efficiency can be improved considerably.

Some of these advantages have been clearly observed in the field (McWilliam, Collison, van Dusseldorp, 1990). Simulation models can strengthen the interdisciplinary research efforts in agricultural research stations once they have been introduced. Whether use of simulation models will increase efficiency depends, however, on a sociological variable. A large area, covered by field trials, is an important status symbol from which directors of agricultural research stations are not always willing to part.

At the moment efforts are underway to interface results of simulation models of crops and animals with linear programming models of the economists. Most likely this interface can be achieved in a reasonably short period. This takes place in a research project in Indonesia. The first outlines are given in a paper by Stroosnijder and van Rheenen (1991). At the same time efforts are being made to combine results of farming system research with quantitative models for land evaluation (Fresco *et al.*, 1990). Such interfacing makes it possible to arrive at estimates of potentials and constraints for agricultural development on a regional basis.

The foregoing also indicates that simulation models are becoming powerful tools in agricultural research and can provide a sound basis for integrated rural development. De Wit *et al.* (1988), in "Application of Interactive Multiple Goal Programming Techniques for Analysis and Planning of Regional Agricultural Development," argue that with the help of simulation models, it is possible to assess the potential physical production of crops in a specific region on the basis of the physical characteristics of that area.

But this is not without danger, as mentioned by McWilliams, Collison, and van Dusseldorp when they say that,

> Interactive multiple goal linear programming (IMGLP) is an interesting technique when it addresses the complexities of the farm system. When it is used to arrive at policy options at the regional level on the basis of the outcomes of simulation models working at the crop level it bypasses the complex decision processes at the farm level. Introducing IMGLP without farm level analysis brings the danger of plans and projects of a top down nature. These are notoriously unsuccessful and wasteful of limited development resources because they are unattractive to farmers.

Modellers as well as policy makers are looking for possibilities for including socio-economic data in simulation models. But at the same time, some questions must be raised.

—First very complex models should be avoided. They may distract from what is happening in the model. Models should be kept small and clean, as are present crop growth models.
—Interfacing different types of models, in the sense that outputs of one model are used as inputs in other models, seems to be a better way, rather than combining the different levels of the real world. The process also becomes more transparent because it is easier to follow inputs of the various disciplines.
—One has to be careful not to force all disciplines to translate their information into a mathematical language that suits the computer. The social sciences are a case in point. There are no indications, at least at this moment and hopefully not in the future, that human beings and their society can be put effectively into simulation models. Sociological information can always be quantified, but the ranges will be enormous and will pollute simulation models.

The developments mentioned above have to be followed carefully by the social sciences. It is easy to stay at the sideline and to criticize the results post hoc. The green revolution and Feder's (1983) book *Perverse Development* provide good examples. It is crucial to determine at which moments in the agricultural research process, sociological information can be brought in using simulation models. There are possible moments when sociological information can be used:

a) The first moment occurs when the issues that have to be investigated must be selected. Socio-economic constraints at the farm level, identified by farm systems researchers or extension staff, provide ex-ante input to shape appropriate technical parameters in the crop simulation model. Labor availability, status of labor and remuneration of labor often have key influences on present and possible farm practices in the future. Farmers may only be able to weed their rice once, or an acute labor shortage at planting time may dictate the need for direct seeding as the only practical option. Such knowledge may be significant when using the model to identify rice varieties and management practices for a specific farming system. Demographic data and labor films are vital information that the social sciences can provide and that can be quantified. Certain values that can impede the introduction of new innovations can also be identified at this early stage (the steering approach).

b) The second moment occurs when, on the basis of the results of simulation, the selection of options to be tested in the field is made. At that moment the sociologist could already make a first assessment of the potential social impact the proposed variety or management practice could have at farm level, on rural communities and regional development. In case the knowledge required for such an assessment is not available yet, it gives the sociologists time to collect the necessary information.

c) Finally, when the testing has proved the technical soundness of the new variety or farm management practice, it is up to the sociologists to indicate what are the sociological prerequisites that have to be fulfilled for a successful introduction and what the potential social consequences are if the proposed innovations are accepted at farm and regional level (the accommodation approach).

The various issues the sociologist should take into account have been discussed above in the section on "The Role of the Social Scientists in the Interdisciplinary Cooperation in FSR." Without bringing the sociological information into the model the sociologists can still make an important contribution to agricultural research using simulation models, provided they are informed of the progress made by the technicians and willing to work at this level.

Potentials and Constraints of "Broad" Interdisciplinary Research

The **potentials** of interdisciplinary studies are obvious. In further analysis of complex phenomena, cooperation of disciplines is necessary in order to expand our present knowledge systems. Many problems that have to be solved are so complex that one discipline cannot provide a sound basis for action. It can be even dangerous when solutions for societal problems are based on the finding of one discipline, because, other disciplines are excluded. A clear example is in a IRD programme where agronomists are indicating that the main reason for poverty is that the poor do not have the opportunity to produce more, because they lack inputs like fertilizer. However, often the fact is overlooked that there are socio-political mechanisms like the market system that mean that, even when poor farmers or tenants receive the inputs, their increase in income will be siphoned off to the rich.

This does not mean that all research should be interdisciplinary. There are many problems that can be solved by monodisciplinary research. Because interdisciplinary research is a complex, time-consuming, and, therefore, a costly exercise, there have to be very good reasons for selecting the interdisciplinary approach.

The major **constraints** when it comes to interdisciplinary research are communication and organization.

The first constraint is that interdisciplinary research requires cooperation between individuals. Cooperation in general is not an easy affair, in whatever endeavor. However, this general problem is aggravated by the diverse educational backgrounds of members of interdisciplinary teams.

1. Due to the educational system, especially in universities during a considerable period of time, young people are specialized in one discipline and indoctrinated with its paradigms, levels of theoretical integration, methods and analytical tools, and last but not least its scientific jargon.
2. This education in disciplinary isolation often leads to the conviction among post graduates that their discipline is the most important one and most suited to solve specific societal problems.
3. University education is often oriented very much towards the individual's performance, thus stimulating orientation towards individual achievements.

Inevitably this type of educational background provides a poor basis for the kind of open and intensive discussion needed to arrive at compromises and does not increase willingness to respect the views of members from other disciplines and to change perspectives and ideas derived from one's own discipline. The solution is simple, at least on first sight. Change the university educational system. Give students more time to become acquainted with other disciplines so that they are able to understand other scientific languages and become aware of the relative importance of the discipline they study. Good interdisciplinary research is only possible when it is performed by scientists who are well qualified in their own disciplines. Universities must continue to produce individuals highly qualified in their specializations, but at the same time attention must be paid to their capabilities for communicating with other disciplines. Finding the optimal mix in educational programs is far from easy, taking into account the limited amount of time available. With this dilemma Wageningen Agricultural University has been wrestling for some time already—how to train students in a curriculum that was shortened from 5 to 4 years, in such a way that they have a good command of their own discipline, as well as being exposed enough to other disciplines so that they are able to understand and discuss objects of study that transcend their own discipline.

The second constraint is that of organization. Management of research is becoming increasingly an issue. In large research institutes or industrial enterprises, this problem has been solved more or less. However, in universities, with their fragmented structure in departments and faculties, this is certainly not the case. The problem is aggravated by the culture of individualism prevalent in universities. Taking the background of most team members into consideration, interdisciplinary research projects must be allowed a considerable period of time for team members to get to know each other as persons and to become acquainted with the way they handle their disciplines. Therefore joint formulation of a general research problem is an important first step.

Some General Observations

1. Interdisciplinary research is important and often necessary when it comes to expanding the boundaries of our knowledge of complex systems such as farming and household systems. It also plays an important role in policy/action-oriented research.
2. Integrated rural development needs as a basis interdisciplinary analysis of the area or region where development activities are taking place. Often such analysis is missing. Sometimes this is due to poor preparation, but the problematic around this, and costs of interdisciplinary research, could be reasons for such an omission.
3. The recent discussion of interdisciplinary research does not provide many new and applicable ideas. Moreover, performance of this type of research is not very impressive.
4. The complexity of interdisciplinary research is often underestimated, especially the time needed for preparation.
5. There are many problems that can be solved by interdisciplinary research. Yet, due to its costly aspects, sound arguments are necessary indicating its greater suitability over mono or multidisciplinary research.
6. Interdisciplinary research does not mean that disciplines are merged. The disciplines are influencing each other during the research process and, finally, the results of monodisciplinary research have to be integrated.
7. The quality of interdisciplinary research depends on:
   a. the attention given to the preparation stage,
   b. the quality of inputs given by the disciplines involved,
   c. the process of interaction during the research process, and
   d. the quality of the synthesis.
8. In the final synthesis input of the various disciplines cannot always be recognized. However, in order to facilitate appraisal of the quality of interdisciplinary research, and its accountability, the disciplinary building stones used in the final synthesis should be mentioned in appendices, or otherwise.
9. The introduction of simulation models and linear programming models could result in isolation of the social sciences. Researchers should clarify at what moments and in what ways social sciences can play a role in interdisciplinary research using simulation models.

Obviously, there is still much to be learned in the field of practical applications of interdisciplinary research. The best way to learn is via evaluation, be it internal-interim or external-ex post evaluation. Peston has defined some questions which should be taken into consideration when ex-post as well as ex-ante evaluation of inter-disciplinary research projects take place.

1. Does the project formulated in interdisciplinary terms show a recognition of the existing contribution made by the separate disciplines?
2. Is the interdisciplinarity genuine in the sense that the problems are formulated in terms which enable the different disciplines to get together rather than to compete with one another?
3. Is the method of data acquisition likely to be helpful to all relevant disciplines, or is it biased in a particular direction?
4. Does the interdisciplinarity enhance the possibility of hypothesis testing or does it obscure it?
5. What differences will the result of the research make to the policy decisions that will be taken eventually?
(Peston, 1979:59; in Wigboldus, 1991:25).

The first four questions can only be answered when the project design is written in such a way that it gives the internal as well as the external evaluator insight into the way the disciplines have agreed to cooperate and to exchange information. Furthermore, the communication processes taking place during field work and the final reporting should be well documented. When such evaluations are done regularly, more progress in the field of interdisciplinary research can be expected.

Literature

Beebe, J. (1985). Information collection: Rapid appraisal and related methodologies. Publication No. 4. *Socio-economic research on food legumes and coarse grains; Methodological issues.* Bogor, Indonesia: Center for Research and Development of Coarse Grains, Pulses, Roots and Tubers in the Humid Tropics of Asia and the Pacific.

Birgegard, L.E. (1980). *Manual for the analysis of rural underdevelopment.* Upsala: International Rural Development Center, Swedish University of Agricultural Sciences.

Box, L. (1989). Multidisciplinary research in development. How to get there? *IMWO Bulletin* 17, 4, 17–20.

Brokensha, D., Warren, D.M. & Werner, O. (1980). *Indigenous knowledge systems and development.* London: University Press of America.

Chubin, D.E. *et al*, eds. (1986). *Interdisciplinary analysis and research.* Mt. Airy, Maryland: Lomond Publications.

Daane, J. (1990). *Le diagnostique. Communication au seminar national sur le theme "recherche developpement au Benin": Acquis et perspective.* Coutonou: Université du Benin.

Dewalt, B.R. (1989). Halfway there: Social science in agricultural development. In C.M. McCorkle, *The social sciences in agricultural research.* London: Lynne Rienner. Pp. 39–61.

Doorman, F. (1989). Strengthening qualitative methodology in agricultural research: The social sciences contribution. *Sociologia Ruralis,* 29:250–264.

Dusseldorp, D.B.W.M. van (1977). Some thoughts on the role of social sciences in the agricultural research centers in developing countries. *Netherlands Journal of Agricultural Science,* 25:213–225.

Dusseldorp, D.B.W.M. van & Box, L. (1990). Role of sociologists and cultural anthropologists in the development, adaptation and transfer of new agricultural technologies. *Netherlands Journal of Agricultural Science,* 38:697–709.

Dusseldorp, D.B.W.M. (1992). *Development projects for rural development in the Third World: Preparation and implementation.* Wageningen: Agricultural University.

Fairchild, H.P. ed. (1955). *Dictionary of sociology.* Ames, Iowa: Littlefield, Adams and Co.

Feder, E. (1983). *Perverse development, Foundation for Nationalistic Studies.* Quezon City, Philippines.

Fresco, L., et al. (1989). *Land evaluation and farming systems analysis for land use planning.* Wageningen: FAO, ITC and the Department of Development Economics, Agricultural University.

Gladwin, H. & Murtaugh, M. (1984). The attentive-preattentive distinction in agricultural decision making. In P.F. Barlett, *Agricultural decision making: Anthropological contributions to rural development.* London: Academic Press. Pp. 115–136.

Giddens, A. (1979). *Central problems in social theory.* London: McMillan.

Heckhausen, H. (1972). Discipline and interdisciplinarity. In L. Apostel, ed., *Interdisciplinarity; Problems of teaching and research in universities.* Paris: Organization for Economic Cooperation and Development. Pp. 83–89.

Hildebrandt, P. (1981). Combining disciplines in Rapid Appraisal: The Sondeo Approach. *Agricultural Administration* 8, 6:423–432.

Klein, J.T. (1990). *Interdisciplinarity. History, theory and practice.* Detroit: Wayne State University Press.

Kockelmans, J.J. (1987). *Interdisciplinarity and higher education.* University Park: The Pennsylvania State University Press.

Kunkel, J.H. (1970). *Society and economic growth. A perspective of social change.* London: Oxford University Press.

Lekanne dit Deprez, B.E.J.C. (1976). Macht en onmacht van interdisciplinair samenwerken (Potential and impotence of interdisciplinary collaboration). *Intermediair* 12, 45: 1–7 and 46: 61–67.

Lohuizen, C.W.W. (1983). Enkele vraagstukken rond het planologisch onderzoek en beleid. In *Spanning in Onderzoek en Beleid.* Amsterdam: Cahiers beleidsonderzoek nr. 2 Stichting Interuniversitair Instituut voor Sociaal Wetenschappelijk Onderzoek. Pp. 8–57.

Majchrzak, A. (1984). *Methods for policy research.* London: Sage Publication.

Mannheim, K. (1960). *Man and society in an age of reconstruction.* London: Routledge and Kegan Paul.

McCorkle, C.M. (1989). *The social sciences in agricultural research.* London: Lynne Riener.

McWilliams, J.R., Collison, M.P. & Dusseldorp, D.B.W.M. van (1990). *Report on the evaluation of the SARP (Systems Analysis for Rice Production) Project.* Den Haag: Directoraat Generaal voor Internationale Samenwerking (DGIS).

Penning de Vries, F.W.T. *et al.* (1989). *Simulation of ecophysiological processes of growth in several annual crops.* Wageningen: Pudoc.

Peston, M. (1979). Some thoughts on evaluating interdisciplinary research. *Higher Education Review,* Spring 1979: 55–60.

Russell, M.G. (1982). *Enabling interdisciplinary research: Perspectives from agriculture, forestry and home economics.* Minnesota: Agricultural Experimenting Station.

Shaner, W.W.; P.F. Philipp & W.R. Schmehl (1981). *Farming system research and development: Guidelines for developing countries.* Boulder: Westview Press.

Staveren, J.M. & D.B.W.M. van Dusseldorp (1980). *Framework for regional planning in developing countries. Methodology for an inter-disciplinary approach to the planned development of predominantly rural areas.* Wageningen: International Institute for Land Reclamation and Improvement (ILRI).

Stroosnijder, L. & Rheenen, T. van (1991). Malang, Indonesia: Brawijaya University. *INRES farming systems analysis methodology.*

Weintraub, D.J. & Margulies, J. (1986). *Basic social diagnosis for IRDP planning.* Vermont: Gower Publishing Company.

Wigboldus, S. (1991). *An inquiry into the discussion on inter-disciplinarity.* Wageningen: Agricultural University, Department of Rural Sociology of the Tropics and the Subtropics.

Wit, C.T. de et al. (1988). Application of interactive multiple goal programming technique for analysing and planning of regional agricultural development. *Agricultural systems,* 26:211–230.

Advancing the Social Sciences Through the Interdisciplinary Enterprise

Marilyn Stember

Abstract

Although interdisciplinary work in universities has expanded in recent decades, the influence of academic disciplines is pervasive. The article makes explicit the opportunities and challenges of interdisciplinarity for the social sciences. The strategies offered for enhancing the interdisciplinary enterprise include selecting appropriate group members, establishing ground rules, explicating and bridging epistemological and methodological differences, and promoting infrastructural support.

The influence of academic disciplines in the university is dominant. Colleges are organized by departments of separate disciplines, faculty are hired and promoted by colleagues within their discipline, the identity and career development of faculty are enhanced by disciplinary guilds and professional associations, and students are expected to specialize in a discipline to meet graduation requirements.[1] While serving very useful purposes, academic disciplines create barriers that sometimes run counter to the very intellectual purposes of those who created the university.[2]

A quote from Margaret Mead's *Blackberry Winter* captures vividly the rationale for the interdisciplinary enterprise.

> Perhaps I can best illustrate the meaning of my thoughts by going back to Oppenheimer's felicitous metaphor of the house called "science." I would like to see us build a *new* room in that vast and rambling structure. This room, like the others, would have no door and over the entrance would be the words, *thought, reflection, contemplation.* It would have no tables with instruments, no whirring machinery. There would be no sound except the soft murmur of words carrying the thoughts of men [and women] in the room. It would be a Commons Room to which men [and women] would drift in from those rooms marked geology, anthropology, taxon-

Stember, Marilyn. "Advancing the Social Sciences Through the Interdisciplinary Enterprise." The Social Science Journal *28:1 (1991), 1–14. Reprinted with permission.*

I gratefully acknowledge Jean Watson who introduced me to the quote in Blackberry Winter *that became foundational for this paper. As Dean, she has been a significant intellectual and administrative mentor and has generously supported by commitments with the Western Social Science Association.*

omy, technology, biology, paleontology, logic, mathematics, psychology, linguistics, and many others. Indeed, from without the walls of the House would come poets and artists. All these would drop in and linger. This room would have great windows; the vistas our studies have opened. Men [and women] singly or together would from time to time walk to those windows to gaze out on the landscape beyond. This landscape in all its beauty, sometimes gentle, sometimes terrible, cannot be seen fully by any one of the occupants of the room. Indeed, it cannot be known fully by a whole generation of men [and women]. Explorers of each generation travel into its unknown recesses and, with luck, return to share their discoveries with us. So the life of the *new* room would go on—*thought, reflection, contemplation*—as the explorers bring back their discoveries to share with the room's occupants. This landscape that we gaze on and try to understand is an epic portion of the human experience.[3]

This metaphoric perspective calls attention to the need for interdisciplinary efforts to facilitate the integration and synthesis of knowledge toward a more complete understanding of the whole. The new room would be inviting to diverse scholars who bring their own methods and areas of expertise. But other than a prescription for thinking, reflecting, and contemplating, the metaphor stops short of informing scholars about how they might work together in that room. After affirmation of the opportunities and challenges of interdisciplinarity for the social sciences, several strategies for enhancing the interdisciplinary enterprise are suggested.

The **intellectual argument** for interdisciplinary work is that ideas in any field are enriched by theories, concepts, and methods from other fields.[4] Specialization in disciplines and subdisciplines has yielded tremendous gains in knowledge, but specialization is also the fragmentation of mind and subject matter. Specialties have become so defined and so isolated as to be quite distinct from each other. When a subject needs context, other disciplines are indispensable, forcing boundary changes. At their best, interdisciplinary programs go beyond intellectual integration to create a community of learning among faculty and students. This climate fosters group norms supportive of creative intellectual inquiry and facilitates approaching the same or related problems at different levels of analysis.

The **practical argument** for interdisciplinarity is that problems of the world are not organized according to academic disciplines.[5] The social sciences are an important intellectual resource in addressing virtually every problem of the day. Within the social science disciplines, some overlap exists in the subject matter considered. Topics concerning human motives, family, groups, institutions, and political and economic life, for example, are the focus of many social science disciplines. Understanding and finding solutions to pressing problems such as health, pollution, communications, and defense require perspectives and knowledge across several disciplines. Many of the most exciting developments cross traditional disciplinary lines encouraging the developments of new fields such as neurosciences, genetic engineering, informatics, and urban studies.

The **pedagogical argument** for interdisciplinary studies (i.e., that learning is hindered by fragmentation in the curriculum) has received a resurgence of support.[6] Several national reports of the past decade have called for greater coherence and integration in undergraduate education. Given this driving force behind academic reform, interdisciplinary studies are now mainstream requirements and take many forms: topical freshman seminars; required core courses in the humanities, social sciences, and natural sciences; advanced courses centered on problem or intellectual themes; and senior projects involving research, seminars, or artistic productions.

The historical development of disciplines provides an important context for the concept of interdisciplinarity.[7] Long ago the grand coherence of the medieval summa gave way to the trend of specialized diversification among the branches of knowledge. For many centuries the sciences showed a monarchical organization, constituting a system of subordinated members under the direction of one leading science such as theology or philosophy. What are now called disciplines and specialties are products of the nineteenth and twentieth centuries when the empirical disciplines one by one exerted their independence. Increasing specialization and segregation of disciplines affected all intellectual life.

In recent decades, signs clearly indicate a move again toward unity, but not the medieval type where disciplines were related under a strict system of subordination. The contemporary view is that disciplines exist in an open-minded confederation and that knowledge can be understood and advanced through interdisciplinary work.[8] One tendency has been to regroup disciplines according to fields of study. Engineering, for instance, involves mathematics, physics, and business administration among others, while nursing requires a different but equally diverse configuration including biology, chemistry, sociology, and psychology. Another tendency has been to create new disciplines (e.g., biochemistry, psycholinguistics) that cross traditional disciplinary lines.

Although interdisciplinary research and educational programs were launched in limited ways after World War II, the interdisciplinary experience in universities is only a few decades old.[9] Universities devised mechanisms to offset the risk of narrow specialization: joint course listings, joint faculty appointments, interdisciplinary thesis committees, research centers, special committees, and interdisciplinary majors.[10] Today, agencies that award research and training grants expect that some provision for cross-fertilization will be included.[11] Departments appoint faculty with academic preparation outside the discipline. For example, a few sociologists, anthropologists, and philosophers are likely to hold faculty positions in medical and business schools.

Higher education continues to experience significant new growth in interdisciplinary scholarship and programs. Most colleges and universities have made, or are in the process of making, reforms in their general education curricula. Surveys also document the increase in research programs, special study centers, colloquia, conferences, journals, and undergraduate degree programs.[12]

Although the interdisciplinary trend has been described as irreversible to the point of no return,[13] it is not without difficulties. Many research projects cease to be interdisciplinary after the funding is received. Social scientists are merely tolerated in some professional schools because it is fashionable or necessary for accreditation. Many interdisciplinary conferences consist of elbow rubbing among colleagues from different disciplines who talk at each other—not with each other. And many journals purporting to be interdisciplinary merely publish manuscripts from different disciplines.

Definitions of Interdisciplinarity

Collaboration between disciplines is possible in many forms, ranging from the relatively intimate self-regulated cooperation between two specialists who proceed in a friendly spirit to elaborately organized specialists supervised by complex administrative structures. All these efforts have their origin in a dissatisfaction with the compartmentalization of the disciplines and the productive expectations from a collaborative model.

The term interdisciplinary has been confusing and something of a misnomer.[14] In the literature the term interdisciplinarity is used in both broad and narrow senses. In the broad sense interdisciplinarity literally means between disciplines suggesting the basic elements of at least two collaborators, at least two disciplines, and a commitment to work together in some fashion in some domain. In the narrow sense, interdisciplinarity describes a specific type of nondisciplinary effort that is distinguishable from other nondisciplinary approaches to research and education such as crossdisciplinary or multidisciplinary. To confuse matters further, multidisciplinary and interdisciplinary are often used interchangeably, usually in the broad sense.

In an early attempt to clarify interdisciplinary research, Gordon W. Blackwell[15] characterized a continuum of types of research undertakings using the dimensions of number of people doing the research, kinds of actions involved in the research process, and the number of disciplines involved. On one end of the six-point continuum is the lone researcher working in one discipline and the last point is multidisciplinary team research where researchers from more than one discipline work collectively on a problem. Others[16] have followed attempting to develop descriptive terminology or clarify meanings. Despite these discussions, not withstanding their positive contributions, no consistent usage appears to be accepted by the scientific community.

The following uniform terminology is suggested for clarifying definitional concerns and underscoring the thrust of this article. As shown in Figure 1, at the base of the typology is *intradisciplinary,* within disciplinary work, followed by *crossdisciplinary,* a viewing of one discipline from the perspective of another. Examples of crossdisciplinary activity are a physics professor describing the physics of music or the art department offering a course in art history. *Multidisciplinary* is a level higher and involves several disciplines who each provide a

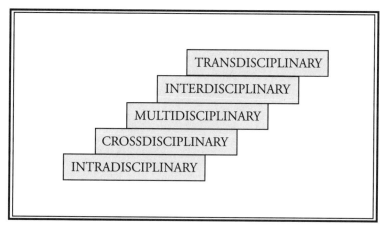

FIGURE 1. Typology for enterprises within and across disciplines.

different perspective on a problem or issue. A multidisciplinary example is faculty members from history, literature, and sociology who teach in a women's studies program or study women's position in society. Other examples include most general education courses and most social sciences conferences. In each of these cases the student or conference participant is required to integrate the often diverse ideas. Higher in the typology is *interdisciplinary* where integration of the contributions of several disciplines to a problem or issue is required. Interdisciplinary integration brings interdependent parts of knowledge into harmonious relationships through strategies such as relating part and whole or the particular and the general. A higher level of integrated study is *transdisciplinary,* concerned with the unity of intellectual frameworks beyond the disciplinary perspectives.[17]

The emphasis of this article is interdisciplinary in the narrow sense, although some of the issues and strategies for interdisciplinarity apply in a limited sense to other nondisciplinary activities. Although interdisciplinary is more productive than multidisciplinary, most activities in the social sciences are multidisciplinary rather than interdisciplinary. A genuine interdisciplinary enterprise is one that requires more or less integration and even modification of the disciplinary contributions while the inquiry or teaching is proceeding. In interdisciplinary efforts, participants must have an eye toward the holistic complex of interrelationships and take into account the contributions of others in making their own contributions.

Interdisciplinarity, then, is a complex endeavor that seeks to explicate relationships, processes, values, and context using the diversity and unity possible only through collaborative approaches. To do so successfully, Stephen H. Cutcliffe suggested that it:

> means developing an understanding, both generally and in specific
> instances, about what values are, how people come to hold them,

and how values evolve. It means understanding the genesis and function of societal institutions in the political, economic, and cultural realms. It means understanding in some general sense the internal essence and operation . . . with major current concepts and methodologies, with design and modeling strategies in the disciplines being studied. It also requires a holistic understanding of the complex interactions among these diverse components. And as if this were not enough, it also implies the study of these complexities as reflected in art, literature, philosophy, and history as well as through contemporary political, economic, and sociological analyses.[18]

Interdisciplinarity holds great promise for understanding the holistic complex of interrelationships. The challenge is to increase our capacity for truly interdisciplinary work.

Strategies for Interdisciplinary Work

Interdisciplinary research and education are difficult endeavors imbued with both pleasures and problems. While nothing may be more positive than imagining a dedicated group of clear minds working as one toward a common goal, the real process is often difficult at best. Crossing disciplinary lines that involve such diversity as the humanities and the sciences poses even greater problems than crossing lines that represent merely historical and probably necessary divisions of labor.[19] In recognition of these problems, strategies for the conduct of interdisciplinary work are suggested including selecting appropriate group members and leaders, establishing ground rules, explicating and resolving epistemological and methodological differences, and gaining infrastructural support.

Selecting Appropriate Members and Leaders

Commitment to a common interest is a paramount criterion for group membership. Successful interdisciplinary teams require a common focus for their work.[20] This clear, recognizable idea may be advanced by a single individual who is able to generate sufficient enthusiasm in others or it may be imposed by some external demand. Blackwell[21] suggested that a problem is more suitable for interdisciplinary study when a single discipline appears inadequate, the problem is on the fringe of two disciplines, conceptual integration of previous work is needed, and relevant disciplines appear ready and able to collaborate. Even though the problem may be initially broad and vaguely articulated, a strong commitment to the common interest from each member will facilitate and sustain cooperation throughout a project.

Successful interdisciplinary individuals are much like successful people in any endeavor, but several characteristics are notable. First, each person must be secure and have recognized competence in at least one discipline. Interdisciplinary efforts seldom work when members are not fully competent in their own field. Second, they must be broad in their perspective, have a taste for adventure into the unknown and unfamiliar, and have flexibility and versatility in semantics, theoretical orientation, and modes of inquiry.

Personal competencies, those qualities, skills, and abilities that allow people to function as a team, are also required. The most important include the ability to work toward outcomes; the ability to relate to feelings and needs of others, conveying interest and respect; the ability to schedule time and prioritize, handling multiple activities and meeting deadlines; the ability to be oriented to the team; the ability to act mature, being willing to be open and act responsibly when dealing with people and situations; and the ability to secure information, compare data, identify issues, and be creative in a group setting. In effective teams, the delicate balance of differentiation and integration is achieved.[22]

The right combination of commitment to the common interest, disciplinary competence, broad interests, and personal attributes may be difficult to determine, but no one of these is sufficient. Without a sufficient inclination for adventure, a competent disciplinarian may retreat from the group project. Similarly, someone with insufficient expertise in one discipline is likely to struggle even more in an interdisciplinary environment, treating important matters superficially at best. Difficult personalities are likely to jeopardize the fragile nature of interdisciplinary groups.

Individuals enter interdisciplinary activities with varied motives.[23] Some participants are drawn to the project by the strength of their interest in the problem. The time might be right for others who are sufficiently free of other obligations to have time to participate. Others are opportunists for whom collaboration is a chance to enhance personal prestige by working with someone of higher prestige or to establish a reputation in an important new substantive area. While the latter motives may be viewed as less worthy, they frequently operate in building an interdisciplinary group. Understanding motives may be helpful when critical problems occur.

Interdisciplinary efforts are easier when the participants and their respective disciplines enjoy a parity of prestige and standing within the scholarly community. However, great disparities are likely to exist. Teams often are composed of disciplines of unequal status and a mixture of senior and junior faculty members. Faculty in more prestigious departments have higher salaries, more eminent colleagues, lower teaching loads, more able students, better facilities, and better libraries.[24] They often glory in the rigor of their discipline and the contributions they have made.

Unfortunately, most social scientists are not among the more prestigious disciplines. Using their collaborative experience with physicians, Elina Hemminiki and Hellevi Kojo-Austin[25] noted that as long as social scientists work in a subordinate position performing tasks given to them, they are accepted by the medical profession. However, when they introduce paradigms from their own scientific area or suggest foci for study, conflicts arise. Conflicts were proposed to stem from professional imperialism, myths, and the unequal power. Imperialism is the tendency of a discipline to monopolize and control certain phenomena and to expand the empire by redefining others' problems in its own terms. Myths include the myth of experience (e.g., physician experience with patients is more valid than systematically gathered data) and the myth of simplicity (e.g., with just a little learning, anyone can conduct a sociological study). Power imbalance was consistent with occupational prestige. Recognition of the traits of professional imperialism and its myths may help to understand the underlying assumptions and dynamics of the interaction. Strategies for reducing power struggles should be employed including initial sets of meetings suggested for maintaining intellectual integrity and for explicating epistemological and methodological differences.

Leadership in research projects or educational programs is needed to synchronize the efforts of the individual members or teams. Such a director or coordinator must have the responsibility and authority to oversee the activities. Essential qualities for this individual include the ability to establish ground rules, develop a process-oriented activity, maintain professional and intellectual integrity, identify and resolve epistemological and methodological differences, and facilitate integration.

The time commitments for the administrator is often underestimated. James McEvoy, III[26] suggested applicants for interdisciplinary grants consider budgeting full support for their administrator. Similarly, administrators of programs must be relieved of teaching and other administrative duties in order to provide adequate supervision, monitoring, and integration.

Establishing Ground Rules

While a permissive attitude must generally pervade the workings, establishing a few operating guidelines is fundamental. One relating to process is a commitment that the group chooses to work in a congenial and rewarding atmosphere versus one of mutual bickering. To do so, some procedural rules should be applied. R. Richard Wohl[27] suggested initially establishing time for relatively free exploration of the problem from each participant's point of view. In turn, each specialist should have the opportunity to inform and educate the other colleagues presenting both theoretical and methodological views.

As the team works together in regular staff meetings, the responsibilities and timetables for completion must be made explicit. Generally, periodic presentations of progress are more helpful than finished reports. Such updates involve the work of all members and the thinking of each member or subgroup, yet maintains sufficient autonomy for each person to proceed to partial conclusions.

Other ground rules that provide some guidance are general decisions about approach. For example, does the group wish to formulate some prior conceptualization versus letting the theory emerge from the data. Agreement about multiple data sources versus a single data source is an example of a general methodological decision. Documenting all decisions in some manner provides an audit trail that is likely to reduce confusion and avoid redundant discussions.

Publication arrangements require early discussion and agreement. Multiple authorships are often difficult. Collaborators should have opportunities to play leading roles in different publications. Individuals and subgroups should be encouraged to explore their own disciplinary issues as well and to publish articles in their own fields. Because publications are such an important measure of personal achievement, they should reflect both individual and joint contributions.

Explicating and Resolving Epistemological and Methodological Differences

Observers of interdisciplinary group process[28] note that discussions often are reduced to the lowest common denominator. Failing to understand, appreciate, or agree with another perspective results in participants retreating to a common level shared by all. But such a level cannot make use of the disciplinary insights and it compromises the professional integrity of the members.

One of the most important investments of time and effort in commencing an interdisciplinary enterprise is the preliminary exploration by all members of what the discipline can offer to the problem of interest. Each exploration of the problem through the eyes of the various specialists should stress the positive contributions made by a particular discipline. To maintain professional integrity, participants must initially avoid confronting fundamental differences and requiring premature closure on important issues. In these meetings, fundamental questions concerning perspective and method should be reserved for later discussion and debate. Similarly, the temptation to establish consensus should be resisted. While a rough synthesis is sometimes useful, discontinuities of method and perspectives are to be tolerated and even celebrated as indicators of pluralism and diversity, hallmarks of interdisciplinary efforts. This intellectual hospitality[29] creates a canon of decorum and polite behavior, creating a constructive and comprehensive atmosphere. Few specialists can resist the opportunity of educating colleagues about their own disciplines.

In addition to seeking out potential contributions of each discipline and communicating basic elements, Blackwell[30] suggested that the team should explore whether the separate and additive use of concepts is needed to accomplish the research or whether new concepts are needed to develop integrative theories. Further, he encouraged an early interplay of empirical and theoretical work rather than potentially sterile theoretical discussions.

Participants need to recognize that different disciplines have different cognitive maps and that learning at least part of these maps is essential for turning multidisciplinary work into interdisciplinary work.[31] Hugh G. Petrie's[32] definition of cognitive maps includes basic concepts, modes of inquiry, what counts as a problem, representation techniques, standards of proof, types of explanation, and general ideals of what constitutes the discipline. Unless maps are shared, information will be misunderstood in terms of one's own map or participants may be unable to see the relevance of their colleagues' points of view. The overlap of cognitive maps may be great or small. Failure to learn concepts and other parts of another's disciplinary map results in communication at the lowest common denominator.

Further, members bring their own personal biography to the enterprise. To function together well, there must be an awareness of how persons locate themselves in the world. Particular life situations influence experiences and expectations. Every individual interprets from diverse angles and particular vantage points because of both professional and personal backgrounds.

Team members must work at cultivating diversity, respect for each other in their pluralistic views, as well as promoting meaningful exchange. Socrates and Plato offered some direction for meaningful exchange when they distinguished kinds of interaction between thinkers. "Dialectic" occurs when the participants have subordinated the demands of their egos and have a paramount desire for discerning what is meaningful and true in what the other says, if meaning and truth exists there and can be coaxed out. On the other hand, the "eristic" type of exchange includes the consuming desire to be persuasive to one's own view, philosophy, theory, or method—to overwhelm the other and to secure what must appear at the time to be a victory of wits and argumentative skill. Brilliance and wit are not enough for interdisciplinary progress. This work requires respect for the others' capabilities and intentions; commitment to common interests or problems; exceptional patience; the ability to hold in abeyance one's own position, theory, idea, or method; and a willingness to struggle to get inside the issues as presented.[33] As Horace Freeland Judson stated, "Science is enormously disparate . . . Nobody has succeeded in catching all this in one net. . . . behind the diversity lies a unity."[34]

Recognizing and explicating epistemological differences is one challenge, but reconciling or resolving those differences is another concern. Several strategies may be employed. Parallel coexistence of different paradigms (like parallel play during early childhood) is one way to solve the problem. A combinationist approach is another. While either may be more productive than choosing only one paradigm, the separatists will continue their advocation of uncontaminated methods while combinationists will continue to select, sometimes indefensibly, methods from any or all coexisting paradigms.

The preferred solution may be the use of the Transcendent Paradigm.[35] Redefining diverse paradigms as complementary rather than contradictory and viewing methods as logically independent fostered the evolution of this paradigm that not only permits but empowers investigators to examine the fullest context of phenomena by using multiple philosophies and methods. The Transcendent Paradigm was named because its intent is to go beyond the limits or the boundaries of the prevailing paradigms or disciplines; it seeks to transcend the limits of philosophical stances, research methods, data collection, and analytic procedures. For example, the nature of reality is singular and multiple, objective and subjective, as well as particularistic and holistic. Similarly, the paradigmatic assumption regarding the nature of truth is that the world is stable and dynamic. Both individual uniqueness and commonalities across individuals are highly valued. Investigators have the freedom to choose a mix of methodological attributes from currently prevailing paradigms that best fit the demands of the phenomena under study.

New or revised modes of inquiry that advance interdisciplinarity are needed.

Another challenge is to expand approaches that assist in integrating and interpreting the knowledge generated through various research strategies. Various forms of triangulation have been suggested.[36] The dialectic approach[37] has been proposed in which different paradigms are given equal status and dialectical reasoning assists in reconciling two seemingly contradictory responses. Others[38] suggested using structural and theoretical integration, metaphors, or models. These and other modes of integration need further articulation such that knowledge derived through interdisciplinary work can be synthesized.

Infrastructural Support

Infrastructures must be created to sustain and promote interdisciplinary efforts. Institutions often view interdisciplinary programs as low cost because relatively few new faculty resources are required.[39] But if the program is designed to be more than multidisciplinary, more faculty time is required for team-taught courses, development of new courses, and interdisciplinary research. Interdisciplinary programs may also require an administrator, space, support staff, and research support.

The debate continues about where to locate interdisciplinary programs.[40] Some advocate housing them in cluster colleges while others argue they must have a departmental base. If the programs are structured so they rely on faculty from other departments, sustained departmental support would be evidenced by continued faculty assignment, faculty reward decisions, and support for courses offered. To support interdisciplinary programs, departments may have to violate their own self interests because of the increased demands on existing faculty.

Margaret A. Miller and Anne-Marie McCartan[41] argued that interdisciplinary program heads need some degree of fiscal autonomy including an independent operating budget. They also noted that resources are required for faculty development toward inspired programs and for faculty support including graduate teaching and research assistantships.

Colleges and universities also need to address the effect of the disciplinary structure on faculty rewards. Promotion and tenure are pervasively awarded within disciplines. The exceptional letters from a psychology colleague for a chemist seeking tenure may be perceived with little relevance. Similarly, publications in interdisciplinary journals may not be evaluated as those in prestigious disciplinary journals. McEvoy[42] noted that interdisciplinary research is utterly without a professional reward system to sustain it. Interdisciplinary programs with some autonomy (e.g., department or division status) have the potential for rewarding individuals for their interdisciplinary roles and productivity.

While institutional support and the creation of supportive formal structures are likely to enhance the success of interdisciplinary programs, they cannot produce it. Wohl cautioned that "disciplines do not, like so many flowers, 'cross-fertilize' each other, but that clusters of scholars must be united in self-sustaining and satisfying social ties before creative collaborative work becomes possible."[43] Institutions must create conditions that foster continued interaction between specialists of different training and different outlooks to submerge those differences, temporarily and for particular purposes, to work on problems of common interest.

Interdisciplinary efforts do not suggest abolishing the distinction between the existing disciplines nor is a total reorganization of the university advocated. What is needed in most cases is a careful selection of a small number of people of different backgrounds who are concerned with related problems and are willing to engage in interdisciplinary effort, and arrangements that permit and reward joint efforts. Joseph J. Kockelmans[44] noted that the greatest problem in interdisciplinary ventures is still the development of coordination and cooperation among people who can pull together, instead of being pulled asunder, by disciplines, schools, and organizational pressures.

A Challenge to the Association

It has been my pleasure to serve as the President of the Western Social Science Association and for this opportunity I am grateful. An old proverb states, "Where there is no vision, the people perish." In my view, to thrive, and maybe even to survive, the Association needed to systematically reflect on its past and anticipate its future, creating the preferred future through deliberate planned action. The blueprint for the next decade was established in the **Ten Year Plan: 1990–1999**. If I leave any legacy, I believe it is portended in this article. While WSSA has been in the forefront of advancing study, research, and teaching in the social sciences, the annual conferences and the Association's publications reflect primarily disciplinary, crossdisciplinary, and multidisciplinary activities. Included in the vision I have brought into focus for WSSA is interdisciplinarity. WSSA should continue to maintain and appreciate the contributions of all social science disciplines, but it should enthusiastically nourish and cherish the interdisciplinary richness within its reach.

Interdisciplinary professional associations such as the Western Social Science Association help to construct and maintain the "new room" needed in the metaphorical house of science. As educators and scholars, we need to collaborate with other disciplines in our attempts to understanding our expansive world. As Maxine Greene in *Landscapes of Learning*[45] suggested, we need to seek paradigm shattering, emancipatory processes to engage in futuring, a going beyond, to what is not yet, but might be. The spirit of interdisciplinary work acknowledges a critical consciousness of the voids and liberates the mind.

Notes

1. Jerry G. Gaff, "Interdisciplinary Studies in Higher Education," *The Education Digest,* 55(2) (October, 1989): 57–60; Claude T. Bissell, *The Strength of the University* (Toronto: University of Toronto Press, 1968); Bruce Wilshire, *The Moral Collapse of the University: Professionalism, Purity, and Alienation* (Albany: State University of New York, 1990), pp. ix–xxv; Tony Becher, "The Cultural View," in *Perspectives on Higher Education,* edited by Burton R. Clark (Los Angeles: University of California Press, 1984), pp. 165–198; Donald T. Campbell, "Ethnocentrism of Disciplines and the Fish-Scale Model of Omniscience," in *Interdisciplinary Relationships in the Social Sciences,* edited by Muzafer Sherif and Carolyn W. Sherif (Chicago: Aldine Publishing, 1969), pp. 328–348; Carl R. Hausman,

"Introduction: Disciplinarity or Interdisciplinarity," in *Interdisciplinarity and Higher Education,* edited by Joseph J. Kockelmans (University Park: Pennsylvania State University Press, 1979), pp. 1–10.

2. See, e.g., Timothy Fuller (Ed.), *The Voice of Liberal Learning: Michael Oakeshott on Education* (New Haven: Yale University Press, 1989); Alfred North Whitehead, *The Aims of Education and Other Essays* (New York: The Free Press, 1929); Harry S. Broudy, *Enlightened Cherishing: An Essay On Aesthetic Education* (Urbana: University of Illinois Press, 1972), pp. 3–20; John S. Brubacher, *On the Philosophy of Higher Education* (San Francisco: Jossey-Bass Publishers, 1977); W. Werner Prange, David Jowett, and Barbara Fogel, *Tomorrow's Universities: A Worldwide Look at Educational Change* (Boulder, CO: Westview Press, 1982), pp. 103–125; George B. Jeffery, *The Unity of Knowledge* (Cambridge: The University Press, 1950).

3. An isolated quote attributed to her husband, Luther, Margaret Mead, *Blackberry Winter: My Earlier Years* (New York: Simon and Schuster, 1972), pp. 289–290.

4. Gaff, "Interdisciplinary Studies," p. 57; Ralph Ross, "The Nature of the Transdisciplinary: An Elementary Statement," in *New Directions for Teaching and Learning: Interdisciplinary Teaching,* no. 8, edited by Alvin M. White (San Francisco: Jossey-Bass, 1981), pp. 19–25.

5. Muzafer Sherif and Carolyn W. Sherif, "Interdisciplinary Coordination as a Validity Check: Retrospect and Prospects," in *Interdisciplinary Relationships,* edited by Sherif and Sherif, pp. 3–20; F. A. Long, "Interdisciplinary Problem Oriented Research in the University," *Science,* 171(3975) (March, 1971): 961; Kenneth D. Roose, "Observations on Interdisciplinary Work in the Social Sciences," in *Interdisciplinary Relationships,* edited by Sherif and Sherif, pp. 323–327.

6. Harry S. Broudy, B. Othanel Smith, and Joe R. Burnett, *Democracy and Excellence in American Secondary Education* (Chicago-Rand McNally and Company, 1964); Fuller, *Liberal Learning;* Gaff, "Interdisciplinary Studies," p. 57; Earl J. McGrath, "Interdisciplinary Studies: An Integration of Knowledge and Experience," *Change,* 7 (1978): 6–9; Heidi Hayes Jacobs, "The Growing Need for Interdisciplinary Curriculum Content," in *Interdisciplinary Curriculum: Design and Implementation,* edited by Heidi Hayes Jacobs (Alexandria, VA: Association for Supervision and Curriculum Development, 1989), pp. 1–12.

7. Wolfram W. Swoboda, "Disciplines and Interdisciplinarity: A Historical Perspective," in *Interdisciplinarity,* edited by Kockelmans, pp. 49–92; Hans Flexner and Gerard A. Hauser, "Interdisciplinary Programs in the United States: Some Paradigms," in *Interdisciplinarity,* edited by Kockelmans, pp. 328–350; Joseph J. Kockelmans, "Science and Discipline: Some Historical and Critical Reflections," in *Interdisciplinarity,* edited by Kockelmans, pp. 11–48.

8. Charles B. Fethe, "A Philosophical Model for Interdisciplinarity Programs," *Liberal Education,* 59 (1973): 490–497.

9. Sherif and Sherif, "Interdisciplinary Coordination," p. 3.

10. R. Richard Wohl, "Some Observations on the Social Organization of Interdisciplinary Social Science Research," *Social Forces,* 33 (1955): 374–383.

11. Sherif and Sherif, "Interdisciplinary Coordination," p. 3.

12. Margaret A. Miller and Anne-Marie McCartan, "Making the Case for New Interdisciplinary Programs," *Change,* 22(33) (May, 1990): 28–35; Jerry G. Gaff and Robert C. Wilson, "Faculty Cultures and Interdisciplinary Studies," *Journal of Higher Education,* 42 (1971): 186–201; Gaff, "Interdisciplinary Studies," p. 58.

13. Sherif and Sherif, "Interdisciplinary Coordination," p. 5.

14. William Caudill and Bertram H. Roberts, "Pitfalls in the Organization of Interdisciplinary Research," *Human Organization,* 10(14) (1951): 12–15; Joseph J. Kockelmans, "Why Interdisciplinarily?", in *Interdisciplinarity,* edited by Kockelmans, pp. 123–160; McGrath, "Integration of Knowledge," p. 6.

15. Gordon W. Blackwell, "Multidisciplinary Team Research," *Social Forces,* 33 (1955): 367–374.

16. Kockelmans, "Why Interdisciplinarily," pp. 127–129; L. Richard Meeth, "Interdisciplinary Studies: A Matter of Definition," *Change,* 7 (August, 1978), p. 10; Hugh G. Petrie, "Do You See What I See? The Epistemology of Interdisciplinary Inquiry," *Educational Researcher* (July, 1976): 29–43; Miller and McCartan, "Interdisciplinary Programs," pp. 28–30; Heidi Hayes Jacobs, "Interdisciplinary Curriculum Options: A Case for Multiple Configurations," *Educational Horizons,* 69(1) (Fall, 1989): 25–27, 35.

17. This typology is similar to Meeth except for the definition of transdisciplinarity; it differs from Kockelmans' who permits one scientist in an interdisciplinary project and uses terms such as "pluridisciplinary," which are not used here.

18. Stephen H. Cutcliffe, "Science, Technology, and Society Studies as an Interdisciplinary Academic Field," *Technology in Society,* 11 (1989): 424.

19. This argument was made by C.P. Snow, *The Two Cultures and the Scientific Revolution* (Cambridge,

England: Cambridge University Press, 1959), p. 2; and supported empirically by Gaff and Wilson, "Faculty Cultures," p. 200.

20. Petrie, "Interdisciplinary Inquiry," p. 32; Wohl, "Some Observations," pp. 377–379.
21. Blackwell, "Multidisciplinary Team," p. 370.
22. Carl E. Larson and Frank M. J. LaFasto, *Team Work. What Must Go Right/ What Can Go Wrong* (Newbury Park, CA: Sage Publications, 1989); Wohl, "Some Observations," p. 376.
23. Wohl, "Some Observations," p. 378.
24. Paul D. Allison and J. Scott Long, "Interuniversity Mobility of Academic Scientists," *American Sociological Review,* 52 (1987): 643–652.
25. Elina Hemminki and Hellevi Kojo-Austin, "Problems of Multidisciplinary Research in Health Care—The Case of Birth Services," *Acta Sociologica,* 32(3) (1989): 253–260.
26. James McEvoy, III, "Multi- and Interdisciplinary Research—Problems of Initiation, Control, Integration, and Reward," *Policy Sciences,* 3 (1972): 201–208.
27. Wohl, "Some Observations," p. 381.
28. Blackwell, "Multidisciplinary Team," p. 370; Caudill and Roberts, "Pitfalls," p. 13; Petrie, "Interdisciplinary Inquiry," p. 36; Wohl, "Some Observations," p. 379.
29. Wohl, "Some Observations," p. 381.
30. Blackwell, "Multidisciplinary Team," p. 371.
31. Becher, "Cultural View," pp. 165–198; Petrie, "Interdisciplinary Inquiry," p. 35–36; McEvoy, "Multi- and Interdisciplinary," pp. 204–205.
32. Petrie, "Interdisciplinary Inquiry," p. 35.
33. Wilshire, *Moral Collapse,* pp. 129–158.
34. Horace Freeland Judson, "The Rage to Know," *The Atlantic Monthly,* 245 (1980): 112–117.
35. Marilyn L. Stember and Nancy O. Hester, "Research Strategies for Developing Nursing as the Science of Human Care," in *The Nursing Profession: Turning Points,* edited by Norma L. Chaska (St. Louis: C. V. Mosby, 1990), pp. 165–172.
36. Mary E. Duffy, "Methodological Triangulation: A Vehicle for Merging Quantitative and Qualitative Research Methods," *Image: Journal of Nursing Scholarship,* 19(3) (1987): 130–133; Pamela S. Hinds and Katherine J. Young, "A Triangulation of Methods and Paradigms to Study Nurse-Given Wellness Care," *Nursing Research,* 36(3) (1987): 195–198; Todd D. Jick, "Mixing Qualitative and Quantitative Methods: Triangulation in Action," *Administrative Science Quarterly,* 24 (1979): 602–611; Ellen Sullivan Mitchell, "Multiple Triangulation: A Methodology for Nursing Science," *Advances in Nursing Science,* 8(3) (1986): 18–26.
37. Phyllis R. Schultz, "Toward Holistic Inquiry in Nursing: A Proposal for Synthesis of Patterns and Methods," *Scholarly Inquiry for Nursing Practice: An International Journal,* 1(2) (1987): 135–145; Mindy B. Tinkle and Janet L. Beaton, "Toward a New View of Science: Implications for Nursing Research," *Advances in Nursing Science,* 5(2) (1983): 27–36.
38. Deborah Flournoy Bockmon and Doris Johnston Riemen, "Qualitative versus Quantitative Nursing Research," *Holistic Nursing Practice,* 2(1) (1987): 71–75; Petrie, "Interdisciplinary Inquiry," pp. 40–42; Jonathan Broido, "Interdisciplinary: Reflections on Methodology," in *Interdisciplinarity,* edited by Kockelmans, pp. 244–305.
39. Miller and McCartan, "Interdisciplinary Programs," p. 34.
40. William T. Hill, "Curriculum Integration and Interdisciplinary Teaching in a Business School Setting: Dilemmas for Faculty," *Education,* 110(3) (1990): 313–318; Miller and McCartan, "Interdisciplinary Programs," p. 34.
41. Miller and McCartan, "Interdisciplinary Programs," p. 34.
42. McEvoy, "Multi- and Interdisciplinary," p. 207.
43. Wohl, "Some Observations," p. 376.
44. Kockelmans, "Why Interdisciplinarity," p. 136.
45. Maxine Greene, *Landscapes of Learning* (New York: Teachers College Press, 1978), pp. 53–73.

Humanities and Fine Arts

Reflections on the Interdisciplinary Approaches to the Humanities

Nancy Anne Cluck

What Is Interdisciplinary Study?

The interdisciplinary study of the humanities typically evokes enthusiastic support from professional scholars and laymen alike. Although we obviously do not experience our humanity in terms of disciplines, these categories of knowledge have been defined and circumscribed for heuristic purposes; the classification of human experience into such species as history, philosophy, and art confers a semblance of order to the learning process. Because of the fragmentation which too often arises from a narrow disciplinary viewpoint, the prospect of joining disciplines for the purpose of discerning their interrelationships inspires hosts of advocates.

At least two major problems hinder productive interdisciplinary research, however: first, traditional disciplinary training does not necessarily prepare the questioner for inquiry into another discipline, much less into the subtle area of the interdisciplines; and two, the methods for systematically approaching the common matrices between the disciplines have not been well articulated. As a result, much of the discourse which purports to be interdisciplinary betrays a soft foundation which gives way under probing. Many articles in allegedly interdisciplinary journals reveal a more narrow focus than the strictly disciplinary articles in traditional journals, and the methodology is problematic at best. It is time now for a hard look at the interdisciplinary matter; it is time to define our terms, to discover and articulate the most effective methods of inquiry, and to determine the value of the interdisciplinary view. In the final analysis it is the issue of merit that is most important, for if interdisciplinary study does not significantly contribute to our understanding of humanity, then the entire area must be called into question.

A consideration of interdisciplinarity should first distinguish among the terms *disciplinary, multidisciplinary,* and *interdisciplinary.* A disciplinary approach to the humanities consists simply of contemplating human experience through one category of knowledge. Through the imaginative mode of literature, for example, we come to understand areas of humanity which would otherwise be closed to us through actual experience, if only because one lifetime does not permit the variety that the vicarious experience of literature does. On the other hand, we may consider the humanities through the discipline of psychology in order to understand the mental and emotional wellsprings of

Cluck, Nancy Anne. "Reflections on the Interdisciplinary Approaches to the Humanities." Liberal Education *66:1 (1980), 67–77. Reprinted with permission.*

human activity. We may choose to deliberate upon the human condition through the discipline of biology in order to discover the natural laws which govern our span. A purely disciplinary approach to the humanities applies only one of these orders and is necessarily restricted in breadth though amplified in depth. The narrow viewpoint of any one discipline is counteracted by the deeper perspective it affords: the specialists's bird's-eye view provides for new discoveries in the field which will eventually benefit the entire range of humanistic study.

Multidisciplinary study proceeds from combined disciplinary provinces, and its methods differ little from the traditional ones. Through a multidisciplinary framework, one may consider the humanities sequentially through literature, then psychology, then biology; but these separate disciplines never intersect upon a well-defined matrix. Multidisciplinary examinations may be characterized as a juxtapositioning of disciplines. The clearly distinguished and sequential studies simply provide consecutive disciplinary views of the world.

Unlike disciplinary and multidisciplinary procedures, interdisciplinary approaches originate from conjunctive interaction between two or more disciplines. While the multidisciplinary approach may be distinguished as the juxtapositioning of disciplines sequentially, the interdisciplinary view emanates from the superimposition of disciplines upon one central problem or subset of the "human condition." This nexus upon which the disciplines converge serves as the core of interdisciplinary studies. Through the common areas in which the disciplines intersect, one can contemplate the humanities, the excellencies of human endeavor, in a manner quite different from that of disciplinary or multidisciplinary standpoints. This point is crucial to interdisciplinary studies and must be clearly understood if the approach is to be productive.

Because interdisciplinary inquiry concentrates on the nexus between two or more disciplines, researchers must have competence in each area. They must consciously reflect upon the purview of each discipline, its questions, its methodology, and its unique potential for the humanities. Interdisciplinarians or bidisciplinarians at this stage should isolate the province of history, for example, and determine what history can tell us that philosophy cannot, or at least, what history teaches us better than philosophy, art, or any other traditionally humanistic discipline. If they intend to apply the disciplines of music, the visual arts, or the theater, they must pursue the singular ways of knowing offered by the arts. Far from threatening or minimizing disciplinary study, the identification and refinement of conventional boundaries and potentials necessarily sharpens and enhances disciplinary methodology. With studied simplicity, both disciplinarian and interdisciplinarian profit from the return to the obvious questions: what do history, philosophy, religion, art, drama, and music reveal about the humanities? How does each uniquely illuminate the subject?

Paradoxically, disciplinarians may neglect the real core of their areas. Their deep, specialized study, indispensable in itself to the furthering of human knowledge and wisdom, too often results in a fatal side effect evidenced in forests which become completely obscured by innumerable species of trees. They may forget the place their disciplines serve in the larger body of the humanities; they may, in fact, through the necessary processes of pruning and polishing, strip it of its very humanistic qualities. The return to the primary questions clarifies the area and calls humanists back to their original purpose. It also conveys the relevance of the humanities to laymen and helps to answer the ubiquitous question: what is the use of the humanities?

Relieved of its subtleties, the fundamental business of history is with events of the past. It consists of a narrative ordering of human events through a process of selection determined by the particular interests of the narrator. For example, the historian may wish to instill patriotism by selecting nationalistic material, or to examine and interpret documents dealing with economic issues. Regardless of the specialized questions and purposes, the primary contribution of history to the human experience is to provide a past; without this, we would be like amnesiacs, having no memory to aid us in understanding our present or predicting our future. In his definitive introduction to *The Idea of History,* R. G. Collingwood affirms history's particular value:

> It is generally thought to be of importance to man that he should know himself: where knowing himself means knowing not his merely personal peculiarities, the things that distinguish him from other men, but his nature as man. Knowing yourself means knowing, first, what it is to be a man; secondly, knowing what it is to be the kind of man you are; and thirdly, knowing what it is to be the man you are and nobody else is. Knowing yourself means knowing what you can do; and since, nobody knows what he can do until he tries, the only clue to what man can do is what man has done. The value of history, then, is that it teaches us what man has done and thus what man is.[1]

Without history and its concerns with what really transpired in the human events of the past, we would be imprisoned in the present.

Philosophy is less concerned than history with individual human events. Its objective is to decipher how we perceive these events and ascribe meaning to them. Often defined as the pursuit of wisdom, philosophy involves the quest for the human nature and the nature of truth. A speculative discipline, it is more concerned with universals than with particulars. Whether it stems from logic, aesthetics, ethics, metaphysics, epistemology, linguistics, or any other subcategory, the goal of philosophy is truth through the understanding of how we think. It is a reflective mode because it entails the self-conscious awareness of thought itself. Collingwood differentiates between the philosopher and the historian in explaining that:

> it is the historian's business, not the philosopher's, to apprehend the past as a thing in itself, to say for example that so many years ago such-and-such events actually happened. The philosopher is concerned with these events not as things in themselves but as things known to the historian, and to ask, not what kind of events

they were and when and where they took place, but what it is about them that makes it possible for historians to know them.[2]

Collingwood's remarks may be expanded to include the philosopher who specializes in language, religion, or the arts; the primary concern derives not from language, religion, or the arts themselves, which are subordinate, but from the way the linguist, the theologian, and the artist think about the arts, and what they reveal about human nature generally.

While history deals with the narration of particular human events of the past and philosophy with the universal quest for meaning and wisdom, the objective of religion in its unaffected simplicity is the relationship of the natural and the supernatural, of the self and the other, or of us and god. It aspires to relate the various means by which we attempt to transcend our own corporeal mortality; it documents our desire for eternal union with perfect beings. The unique scope of religion, then, includes the commitment, beliefs, and practices surrounding our conception of supernatural beings.

The techniques of history, philosophy, and religion are similar, though not identical, because these disciplines furnish the narrative, factual, and theoretical framework for the humanities. Literature, drama, art, and music, on the other hand, emphasize the experiential basis. History may disclose what happened in the past; philosophy may contemplate the meaning of existence; religion may detail our mystical nature; but literature and the other arts present the *experience* of humanity within the parameters of history, philosophy, and religion. Through the first three disciplines we learn discursively of the human condition; through the fictive presentations of the arts, we enliven not only our own humanity but also that of the people of the past, of others in the present, and of those to come in the future.

Identifying Interdisciplinary Approaches

This preliminary account of disciplinary areas acquires heightened significance for the interdisciplinarian with further analysis of their common methodological dimensions. In his book *The Idea of the Humanities,* R. S. Crane isolates the techniques for approaching the humanistic disciplines. He classifies four groups of skills as belonging to linguistics, to the analysis of ideas, to literary and artistic criticism, and to historiography.

> There are the arts, first of all, of language, comprising the many and varied techniques we have for dealing with the symbolic media in which the achievements of men are embodied or through which they reach us, from grammar in the ordinary sense, through prosody, rhetoric, the simpler parts of logic, and textual criticism, to the refinements of modern general linguistics. There are the arts, in the second place, of which the special province is the analysis and appreciation of ideas—of the conceptions and reasons, of all kinds, which men have expressed either in the elaborate forms of philo-

sophic, scientific, and religious systems or more formally in works of literature and fine art. In the third place, there are the arts of literary and artistic criticism—the numerous devices at our disposal for grasping and appreciating the aesthetic structures which men have made. And finally, there are arts that give us knowledge and understanding of the particular historical situations and causes in the midst of which the objects of humanistic study have emerged.[3]

Crane implies the interdisciplinary nature of these arts in explaining further that:

> The four arts are the arts of the humanities, in short, because they are pertinent in varying degrees to all subject matters with which humanists commonly deal; they thus cut across the boundaries dividing the subject matters from one another; and it is precisely the convergence of all of them upon any subject matter that makes it, in the completest degree, humanistic; just as in any scientific field we become scientific to the fullest extent in proportion as we have learned, not merely some, but all, of the various distinct skills that make up what we call, vaguely, scientific method.[4]

This revision of the traditional disciplines, such as history, literature, and philosophy, to the arts of linguistics, ideas, aesthetic structures, and historiography initiates systematic interdisciplinary approaches to the humanities, although it does not explicitly outline the procedures for doing so.

Systematic interdisciplinary approaches can be formulated from a union of conventional disciplinary designs with Crane's hypothesis of the humanistic arts or disciplines. Four areas or approaches to humanities may be identified as possibilities for productive interdisciplinary inquiry because they furnish the common ground between disciplines. Historical periods, ideas, aesthetic themes, and structures furnish junctures which serve both as means and as temporary ends. That is, an investigator may examine a historical period, an idea, a theme, or a structure from an interdisciplinary standpoint, and each of the subsets of the humanities thereby becomes an end in itself. However, because an interdisciplinary inquiry has been made into it, the juncture provides the interdisciplinary approach to the larger field of the humanities. Hence, the linking areas between the disciplines are amenable to interdisciplinary scrutiny, and because of this receptivity, they supply an interdisciplinary conduit to the humanities at large.

The interdisciplinary inspection of a historical period is deceptively simple. One studies the documents of each discipline; these documents, in turn, furnish the evidence of the period, and the investigator then abstracts the gestalt of the era. The historical nexus, however, quite often leads to multidisciplinary layers rather than to an integrated whole. By juxtapositioning the documents of various disciplines, the researcher can acquire much information about a culture but will often fail to perceive the interrelationships. For truly interdisciplinary value, the documents must be superimposed upon a central focus which frequently takes the form of the major ideas of a particular epoch. Briefly, the analysis of past events, ways of knowing, and vicarious experience through the arts must eventually lead to a synthesis rather than remaining isolated bits of knowledge from different disciplines. A fuller understanding of the nineteenth century, for example, should stem from a convergence of the disciplines on such prevailing ideas as individualism, revolution, and primitivism, which may be traced through the philosophy of Hegel, the essays of Rousseau, Jefferson, and Mill, the music of Beethoven, the dramas of Hugo and Schiller, the works of Goethe, and the painting of Degas.

In another kind of interdisciplinary study, such ideas are not restricted to a chronological period but are examined throughout history. Philosophy typically defines and articulates the concept, but other disciplines refine, explicate, and vary it through their differing emphases. For instance, the idea of progress provides an excellent focus for interdisciplinary inquiry. While the idea reaches discursive expression in philosophy, a fully humanistic grasp of it requires also the special contributions of history, religion, literature, and the other arts. The concept of progress has been traced by J. B. Bury in his book *The Idea of Progress*,[5] which shows that the idea is not static but changes with the world view of different historical and geographical contexts. That the idea cannot be entirely contained in the disciplines of history and philosophy, however, becomes clear when religion and the arts are brought to bear upon it. Progress has long been a major concern of religion whether it is the progress of the Jew to the promised land, the progress of the Christian toward sanctification and the New Jerusalem, or the Eastern idea of the progressive shedding of the soul's encumbrances in order to reach nirvana. Additionally, progress can be experienced religiously as the temporal movement through the stations of the cross; politically, as the progresses of monarchs, particularly during the English Renaissance, and geographically, as the immigration to America during the seventeenth, eighteenth, and nineteenth centuries or to outer space during the twentieth.

The idea enters literature and the other arts at many junctures. During the seventeenth century, two poems of John Donne offer opposing views of this idea. In his "Progresse of the Soule" or "Metempsychosis," dated 1601, the domination of satirical elements discloses the inverted progress of the soul which steadily degenerates with each new incarnation from the vegetable to the animal kingdom until it finally reaches the nadir of its decadence in the body of man. Donne's more familiar "The Second Anniversary" or "The Progresse of the Soule," written in 1612, illustrates the spiritual movement to the Christian soul from its mortal existence to its immortal state in union with God, as exemplified by Elizabeth Drury, the poem's unnamed subject. In prose fiction, John Bunyan's *The Pilgrim's Progress* details the inward journey of the soul toward perfection. Certainly, these examples from literature do not exhaust the idea, but they are sufficient to suggest strongly that the idea of progress should be examined not only in the discursive disciplines of philosophy and history but also in the experience of literature.

The visual arts add still another dimension to the concept of progress. Probably its most familiar visual expressions occur in the eighteenth-century engravings of William Hogarth. *The Rake's Progress* and *The Harlot's Progress* satirize the optimistic notion; the caricatures display man's progressive degeneration through civilization and materialism. Hogarth's *The Rake's Progress,* in turn, supplies the focal point for the twentieth-century opera *The Rake's Progress* by Igor Stravinsky.

The idea of progress, then, verbalized by philosophy, refined and transformed through history, attains a metaphorical existence in religion where it deals with the progress of the soul to salvation or damnation. Progress in its fullness cannot be apprehended without this convergence of the disciplines upon an idea which transcends history. Its meaning and significance depends upon the unique wisdom offered by many disciplines.

Interdisciplinary methodology may reverse the process of tracing and illuminating philosophical and historical ideas in literature and the other arts by centering on an aesthetic theme and moving toward an idea. Rather than investigating the matter through which an idea becomes an aesthetic theme, as in the idea of progress, this kind of inquiry examines the transformation of theme into historical, philosophical, or religious idea. Aesthetic themes are contiguous with historical and philosophical ideas but are not synonymous with them. For example, the Faust theme in literature, music, and art gravitates around a cluster of ideas, including the insatiable desire for experience, for knowledge, and for salvation which arise from uncontrollable ambition. Yet, the ideas in themselves do not assume equal importance with the *experience* of them through the arts. The questioner might ask: How does the Faust in music differ from the Faust of literature? What can music divulge about the active Don Quixote that art cannot? Finally, the ideas surrounding these themes should be explored in religion, history, and philosophy, but the manner through which they are presented in the arts provides the paramount focus, while history, philosophy, and religion furnish the context. Hence, while aesthetic theme and historical and philosophical idea are similar, they exhibit distinctions which supply different links among the disciplines. The operative point is the center of focus: in the idea, history and philosophy provide the text; in aesthetic theme, literature and the other arts establish the concentration.

Still another approach to the larger question of the humanities is through structure. Those forms generally considered aesthetic by literary critics, musicians, and artists, should be compared with historical, philosophical, and religious structures. It is not enough simply to compare genres within one discipline, such as the epic and drama in literature or song form and sonata form in music. Rather, the critic should observe the intrinsic behavior of each genre in order to compare the dynamics of a literary form with a musical form. For example, dialectical polarities furnish a central framework of Western thought. This model provides a paradigm for Hegelian philosophy in which the dialectical energies arising from the conflict of thesis and antithesis are subsumed in the final synthesis. Through a similar process in music the dialectical tensions achieve structure in the sonata form. The harmonic conflict between theme groups presented in the exposition provides a musical analogy to the dichotomy produced by the thesis and antithesis of philosophical thought. The development section of sonata form explores the ramifications of the musical polarities in a manner similar to that accomplished discursively by philosophy. Ultimately, *musical* synthesis results from harmonic resolution of the recapitulation where both theme groups appear in the same key. Philosophic and musical paradigms do not necessarily influence one another but seem to arise from a manner of thinking characteristic of Western culture. This same dialectical energy may be observed in the Pindaric ode which predates Hegelian philosophy and sonata form by centuries. Again, the dichotomy between thesis and antithesis appears as that between strophe and antistrophe which is finally resolved in the epode. Hence, the behavior of at least two art forms and one philosophic form are found to have basic similarities which arise from a manner of thinking. Questions of structures are not sufficiently answered until the manner by which these structures imitate, illuminate, or otherwise model the structures of human experience has been suggested if not conclusively demonstrated.

Benefit of Interdisciplinary Study

At least four areas, then, can be identified as proper avenues for interdisciplinary study in the humanities. These intersecting points serve both as ends of inquiry and as a means to the larger question of the humanities. After a historical period, an idea, a theme, or a structure has been examined from an interdisciplinary viewpoint, it leads them to a consideration of the overriding view of the humanities in general. In other words, the humanities must be divided into subsets such as historical period, idea, theme, or structure which exist between the traditional disciplines and are amenable to interdisciplinary study.

Obviously, these four areas are not exhaustive. Disciplines outside these conventionally considered to constitute the humanities frequently supplement interdisciplinary study in the humanities. Bronowski suggests the similarity between scientific concepts and ethical concepts, for example, when he explains:

> For science is not a book, either of facts or of rules; it is the creation of concepts which give unity and meaning to nature. Such concepts exist in our understanding of man and society: truth, loyalty, justice, freedom, respect, and human dignity are concepts of this kind.[6]

Regardless of the interface chosen, interdisciplinarians must be imminently aware of which disciplines they use and of which juncture they approach. Above all, they must be apprised self-consciously of their technique for inquiry. They must understand the questions and the purview of each discipline; they must understand the unique contributions each discipline can afford to their exploration, and they must understand that interdisciplinarity focuses on the common ground between two or more disciplines, not merely on the juxtaposing of disciplines.

The question remains: what is the benefit of the interdisciplinary study of the humanities? Is it merely a new game for bored scholars or a system for vague speculations which add little to our understanding of our humanity? Only one answer is acceptable: the interdisciplinary inquiry into the humanities is worthwhile only to the extent that it proffers a new way of seeing our existence and of understanding more fully what it means to be human. The goal is difficult and challenging; interdisciplinary studies must not degenerate into the constricted focus which has little bearing outside the boundaries of academe. Interdisciplinary studies at their finest are creative and humanistic by definition. Bronowski's comment is again appropriate.

> A man becomes creative, whether he is an artist or a scientist, when he finds a new unity in the variety of nature. He does so by finding a likeness between things which were not thought alike before, and this gives him a sense at the same time of richness and understanding.[7]

Interdisciplinarity must attend to the rigor of disciplinary studies, to the self-consciousness of the scientific method, if a truly humanistic method is to be achieved. If interdisciplinarians proceed from a strong sense of what that term means—the interrelationships evolving from the nexus between disciplines—if they can identify the questions of the disciplines and be aware of which discipline they are using at all times, their insights through the approaches of historical period, idea, theme, and structure will result in a deeper understanding of the whole of the humanities, and part of the fragmentation of human experience will be integrated through seeing the similarity of unlike phenomena.

Endnotes

1. R. G. Collingwood, *The Idea of History* (New York: Oxford University Press, 1956), p. 10.
2. Ibid., p. 3.
3. R. S. Crane, *The Idea of the Humanities and Other Essays Critical and Historical* (Chicago: University of Chicago Press, 1967), II, 9.
4. Ibid., p. 10.
5. J. B. Bury, *The Idea of Progress* (New York: Macmillan Co., 1932).
6. J. Bronowski, "The Fulfillment of Man," in *A Sense of the Future: Essays in Natural Philosophy,* ed., Peiro E. Ariotti (Cambridge: MIT Press, 1977), p. 261.
7. Ibid., p. 12.

Introduction

Mieke Bal

This is the dream's navel, the spot where it reaches down into the unknown.

— Sigmund Freud, *The Interpretation of Dreams*

Balancing Vision and Narrative

Vermeer's *Woman Holding a Balance,* housed in the National Gallery in Washington, represents a woman in a blue dress, holding a balance above a table; on the wall, in the background, is a painting of the *Last Judgment.* Light streams in from a stained-glass window at the upper left. It is a strikingly still painting. It avoids narrative—both the anecdotal and the dynamic. Instead, it presents an image in terms of visual rhythm, equilibrium, balanced contrasts, and subtle lighting (Figure 1). As Arthur Wheelock, Jr. (1981:106–7) remarks, the painting stands in marked contrast to other works on related themes. In those other works the woman tends to look greedily at the precious objects on the table, whereas here she is self-absorbed. In those others the pans of the balance, here empty, tend to be heaped with gold or pearls so that action is implied. In this work the parallel between the *Last Judgment,* hung on the wall behind her, and the woman's act of weighing/judging is elaborated on the basis of similarity, not of narrativized contrast.

Svetlana Alpers, I assume from her *Art of Describing* (1985), would call this a descriptive painting. It is a painting that appeals to visuality if ever there was one, a case for Alper's opposition to Italian infatuation with narrativity. Any attempt to read the painting as a narrative can only misread it. It is a surface carefully balanced for visual experience, where the appeal to visuality is worked out in the tiniest details. On the upper left part of the painting, in the white wall near the represented *Last Judgment,* is a nail, and near that nail, a hole in the wall. The minutely detailed work of painting is so highly emphasized in these tiny details that both inside the hole and next to the nail we can see a shadow. The soft, warm light streaming in from the window on the upper left touches these two irregularities in the wall, as if to demonstrate that realistic description of the world seen knows no limits.

This light also generates other details in the overall darkness of the painting. The woman's dress underneath the mantle is foregrounded by it; between the

Bal, Mieke. "Introduction." Reading Rembrandt: Beyond the Word-Image Opposition. *The Northrup Frye Lectures in Literary Theory. New York: Cambridge University Press, 1991, 1–24. Copyright © 1992 Cambridge University Press. Reprinted with the permission of Cambridge University Press.*

two fur rims a slice of orange tissue protrudes, showing the dress's color that is in shadow. The dress may be in keeping with the fashion of the times, but for some viewers, questions may keep nagging: Why this soft light, why this striking color and shape, why does it fall *here*? These questions may lead one to interpret this detail: Since the part of the dress that is illuminated is the one that covers her womb, it may, through metonymy, come to represent the slit that opens the womb—her navel. And if we focus particularly on this element, we may come to associate the woman in this painting with the pregnant madonna as represented in the Italian Renaissance.[1] The woman's hairdress and the blue color of her mantle then may be taken to underscore the visual similarity in the distribution of surface space between her and God in the represented *Last Judgment*. An ordinary Dutch woman for some, an allegorical figure representing *Vanitas* for others, she may become Mary for those who pursue the interpretive game further. To some viewers who notice this detail, such an association will appeal; to others it won't. The point is not to convince readers of its appropriateness, or its truth, but to offer the speculative possibility.

For me it was the nail and the hole that the light made visible, produced; that instigated a burst of speculative fertility. When I saw this nail, the hole,

FIGURE 1. Vermeer, Johannes, *Woman Holding a Balance,* Widener Collection, Photograph © Board of Trustees, National Gallery of Art, Washington.

and the shadows, I was fascinated: I could not keep my eyes off them. Why are they there? I asked myself, Are these merely meaningless details that Roland Barthes would chalk up to an "effect of the real"? Are these the signs that make a connotation of realism shift to the place of denotation because there is no denotative meaning available? Or do they point to a change in the significance of the *Last Judgment*? Do they suggest that the represented painting which, according to Wheelock, is there to balance the work, to foreground the similarity, the rhyme, between God and this woman, has been displaced from an earlier, "original" position to a better, visually more convincing balance, leaving only the telltale trace of a nail hole? As it is, the woman stands right below God, a position that emphasizes the similarity between judging and weighing. Also, the separation between the blessed and the doomed is obliterated by her position, suggesting, perhaps, that the line between good and evil is a fine one. But in the midst of this speculative flourish, I am caught up short by the remembrance that we are looking at a painting of this balance, not at a real room. The painter surely did not need to *paint* the nail and the hole, even if, in setting up his studio, he actually may have displaced the *Last Judgment*.

If the room were a real room, the hole and the nail would evince traces of the effort to hang the painting in the right place. As such, they demonstrate the materiality of the difficulty and delicacy of balancing. Hanging a painting in exactly the right place is a delicate business, and the result is of the utmost visual importance. For the representation of this statement on visual balance, the nail alone would not do the trick; the failure of the first attempt to balance the represented painting correctly must be shown through an attempt still prior to it. The hole is the record of this prior attempt. The suggestion that the *Last Judgment* was initially unbalanced, with balancing as its very subject matter, threatens to unbalance the painting as a whole. While the metaphoric connection between the idea of judgment and this woman's activity is tightened by the final result, the difficulty of balancing and of judging is thus foregrounded.

In the painting, narrativity so blatantly absent on first—and even second—glance is found to have been inserted by means of a sign that makes a statement on visuality. The visual experience that encodes the iconic association between woman and God is not displaced but, on the contrary, underscored by this narrative aspect. We imagine someone trying to hang the painting in exactly the right place. We are suddenly aware of the woman's artificial pose: Instead of changing the painting's position, the artist arranging his studio could simply have changed the woman's place, or his own angle of vision. All of a sudden something is happening, the still scene begins to move, and the spell of stillness is broken.

The nail and the hole, both visual elements to which no iconographic meaning is attached, unsettle the poetic description and the passively admiring gaze that it triggered, and dynamize the activity of the viewer. Whereas before the discovery of these details the viewer could gaze at the work in wonder, now he or she is aware of his or her imaginative addition in the very act of looking. The work no longer stands alone; now the viewer must acknowledge that he or she makes it work, and that the surface is no longer still but tells the story of its making. That is what narrativity does to a work of art, be it visual or literary. Attracting attention to the work of representation as well as to the work of reading or viewing, the nail and the hole are traces of the *work* of art, in all senses of that expression and in all its specificity.

This, then, raises questions about the place of narrative in visual art. Narrativity is generally considered an aspect of verbal art, which can be mobilized in visual art under great representational pressure only. Something comparable is alleged for visual imagery, which literature strives for but can never completely realize. I propose to shift the terms of these questions and reconsider the typically medium-bound terms of interpretive scholarship—like spectatorship, storytelling, rhetoric, reading, discursivity, and visuality—as aspects rather than essences, and each art's specific strategies to deal with these aspects, as modes rather than systems.

This study, then is concerned with theoretical and interpretive problems pertaining to relations between verbal and visual art. Shifting attention from the study of the medium-bound, allegedly intrinsic properties of each domain to the question of reception, allows a systematic scrutiny of the ways in which the arts function in a culture where the public is constantly surrounded by images, yet trained to privilege words over images. Dehierarchizing the arts, and dispossessing a mythified author of a work given over to public use, this study is situated within the rapidly growing field of critical studies of culture. My goal is to contribute to cultural theory, to a different understanding of the powerful effects of certain works of art, and to the teachability of the arts across departments.

The Subject of This Study

This study centers upon Rembrandt. Each chapter confronts one or more of his works with texts related to them in various ways: as "source" or pre-text, as response, as thematic companion or counterpart, as theoretical subtext, surrounding context, or as critical rewriting. As for the verbal works selected, the choice is purposefully eclectic, not only to balance the concentration on visual images all by one artist but also because the arguments I am developing are theoretical rather than corpus-bound. I wanted to confront the visual works with a variety of verbal works, from different genres and contexts, and with different types of relations to the visual works. It is those relations, rather than the particular texts and works, that I wish to discuss. I take Rembrandt to stand for an exemplary painter in "high culture" and not as a particularly discursive or narrative artist. This art lends itself, therefore, to the kind of questions I wish to ask, without "begging" them.

The juxtaposition, in an interpretive venture, of verbal and visual "texts" has among many other advantages that of making the student of visual art and literature aware, not so much of those aspects of the works that inhere in the medium but more importantly of those that do not. This kind of interpretive juxtaposition can generate insight into the strategies of representation and of interpretation, as distinct from medium-bound devices, and can help generate a broader perspective on other cultural issues. This book is designed to explore some of the possibilities of this field of study.

The primary assumption underlying the book is that the culture in which works of art and literature emerge and function does not impose a strict distinction between the verbal and the visual domain. In cultural life, the two domains are constantly intertwined. In order to assess what a work means for the culture in which it circulates, we therefore need to overcome the artificial boundaries that form the basis of academic disciplines.

A second assumption underlying this work is that art is both entirely artificial—that is, not "natural"—and entirely real—that is, not separated from the ideological constructions that determine the social decisions made by people every day. Hence, nothing about art is innocent: It is neither inevitable, nor without consequences. In order to drive this point home, for example, Chapter 2, entitled "Visual Rhetoric," discusses the issues of rhetoric and rape in the Western representational regime, the one through the other.

Two other, intertwined assumptions need some comment. The one holds that any analysis and interpretation of visual or verbal works of art, even historical interpretations, are necessarily and by virtue of the semiotic status of art informed by the views, standards, ideologies, and background—in other words, by the subjectivity—of the person doing the analysis. Not that attempts to recover the past are futile; rather they tend to displace the issue of the epistemological status of the knowledge they produce and thus undermine the status of their own results. Most historical interpretation aims at restoring the author's intentions. But by obliterating and repressing the subjectivity of the analyst, the author's alleged intentions are burdened with, and sometimes buried under, projections by the former passed off as intentions of the latter. Thus intention and meaning, and work and analyst, are conflated.[2]

The question is not just whether "pure" historical knowledge is possible—and the answer has to be negative, even to historians less skeptical than Hayden White.[3] We must also ask what is to be gained by making explicit what happens when one tries. This study attempts to explore some aspects of that question by focusing here and there on the gestures of critical readers, foregrounding this difficulty, by endorsing a radically reception-oriented approach.

One can argue that the historical endeavor is not exhausted by the surprisingly tenacious search for intentions. But today a more sophisticated historical inquiry into the work and workings of a body of visual material would define the underlying historical question in a more social sense, as a search for the social situation and context out of which the work emerged. This inquiry includes economical and political factors and their influence on the structure of public life as analyzed, for example, by T. J. Clark; as well as what Martin Jay would call the "scopic regime," or Svetlana Alpers the visual culture of the time.[4] All these elements together constitute the answer to the question "What made this possible?"[5] This question situates the work in a social situation rather than in an individual genius. I acknowledge the value of such inquiry, which, indeed, I find indispensable.

Yet social history does not escape the problem of the presence of the critic as inseparable from historical knowledge. In addition, the very concept of context is as problematic as that of text. Jonathan Culler formulates the problem acutely when he writes:

> But the notion of context frequently oversimplifies rather than enriches discussion, since the opposition between an act and its context seems to presume that the context is given and determines the meaning of the act. We know, of course, that things are not so simple: context is not fundamentally different from what it contextualizes; context is not given but produced; what belongs to a context is determined by interpretive strategies; contexts are just as much in need of elucidation as events; and the meaning of a context is determined by events. Yet when we use the term *context* we slip back into the simple model it proposes. (Culler, 1988:xiv)

Context, in other words, is a text and thus presents the same difficulty of interpretation as any other text. The context cannot define the work's meaning because context itself defies unambiguous interpretation as much as the work. Culler goes on to argue that an alternative to the notion of context is that of framing:

> Since the phenomena criticism deals with are signs, forms with socially-constituted meanings, one might try to think not of context but of the framing of signs: how are signs constituted (framed) by various discursive practices, institutional arrangements, systems of value, semiotic mechanisms? (Culler, 1988:xiv)

This is, de facto, what Pollock (1988) as well as Alpers, Clark, and many others are doing, at least on the sender's side. But this still does not solve the question of meaning.

I would like to explore what the question "What *made* this possible?" fails to address by changing it into "What *makes* this possible?"—referring not to the work as a given but to its existence as both affected and effect. The meaning of the work is now situated as an effect of meaning. This effect is complicated by the social construction of visuality, the modalities of looking that we are trained to adopt, and the variability of identifications.[6]

Another, related assumption that underlies this study concerns the status of the artist as genius and of art as "high art." The choice of works by Rembrandt as the central body of visual art for this study may seem provocative. But although his authorship is currently under pressure, the status of his art goes unquestioned. True, some Rembrandt critics (the members of the Rembrandt Research Project are among them; see Bruyn et al., 1982), voluntarily question the quality of some of the works, and even take pride in their demythologizing attitude. Yet the very fact that these aesthetic criticisms lead to rejection of the authenticity of the works as "Rembrandt" provides evidence of the basically unchallenged status of both author as genius and of aesthetic quality as determinable. Hence these acts of judgment rest on the possibility to delimit "high art" from other art. An ever "higher," purer Rembrandt is thus safeguarded.

In the wake of a growing awareness of the mechanisms of exclusion inherent in both these notions of authorship and of aesthetic quality, a number of attitudes have come to prevail instead. One very powerful attitude has been to reject the preoccupation with the works of geniuses altogether, turning toward the products of popular culture, formerly denigrated as "low art" and today valued as more representative evidence of the cultural life of the people. Examples among many are Keith Moxey's (1989) study of popular early German woodcuts and Nathalie Kampen's (1981) study of sculpture in the Roman provinces, and, in an altogether different domain, the current revaluation of the nineteenth-century "sentimental novel," on which more appears in Chapter 5. The successful work in film studies, a field that deservedly has a leading position in cultural studies, ignores the boundaries between artistic and popular film and analyzes both indiscriminately.[7] Another approach is to criticize "high art" as ideologically flawed, examining racism, sexism, classicism in canonical works, and, subsidiarily, in art history and literary criticism (e.g., Said, 1978; Gates, 1985; Trinh, 1989).

In spite of the obvious importance of those endeavors, there seems to be room for a third attitude, which I can formulate most briefly as a paradox: "High art" is part of popular culture. In other words, I am interested in why a culture, largely but not exclusively colonized by the cultural leaders who have the power to impose their taste and stakes, continues to respond to a set body of works of art; I am also interested in what kind of response that body of works elicits. These works may be part of the elitist culture, but the responses they elicit are not. Issues like the relationship between storytelling and voyeurism; the thematic centrality of the nude as an object of vision, as well as a source of blindness, of the impotence to see; transparent representation and its limits—all are pervasively present in contemporary Western culture. It is my claim that the works traditionally attributed to Rembrandt elicit a response to, and reflection on, issues like these.

The opposition high–low is intrinsic not to the object under scrutiny but to the assumptions we bring to these (or any) works. Thus bringing the concerns of popular culture to bear on works of "high" culture debunks the latter and undermines the opposition between them. A similar dichotomy exists in feminist criticism: Is it necessary to expend ever more attention on the works of the male canon instead of looking at works by women? There, too, I would argue that both endeavors need to be pursued in tandem.[8]

To a certain extent, a culture makes its art and its artists. It is to be expected, then, that the art also makes the culture, by initiating or addressing issues that pertain to the culture at large. Thus I will argue, in Chapter 4, that the relationship between looking and power, which pervades this culture where positions in visual art are quire strongly gendered, is both exemplified and addressed by the works attributed to Rembrandt. The sections "Viewer," "Voyeurism," and "Focalizer" address current theories of the gaze, of spectatorship, and confront these with literary theories of point of view and focalization. The story of Susanna and the Elders, which thematizes looking, makes a good case.

That many of these works are now in the process of being disavowed as part of the Rembrandt corpus does not bother me; it rather supports my argument that "Rembrandt" is a cultural text, rather than a historical reality. "Rembrandt" constitutes these works *and* the response to them, responses that range from their mistaken (?) attribution to attempts to challenge their authenticity on the basis of a holistic and elitist concept of authorship. In this study, the name of an author is meant as a shorthand for this complex of readings of certain works *as* works by a particular artist. In order to keep in mind this definition of the author, I shall put the name "Rembrandt" in quotation marks, as the title of a text, whenever I am using the name in my own argument. I shall avoid using quotation marks when I render the views of others, lest using them would distort these views.[9]

This book represents an attempt to reflect systematically on these and a number of other related issues, which today receive ever wider attention, yet have not been pulled together. I hope to knit these strands together into a reception-oriented perspective of cultural critique. This book is based, not on a denial of difference between verbal and visual art, but on a provisional bracketing of the question as to what that difference might possibly be. Shifting attention from the question of intrinsic properties to that of response, the focus will be on the interaction between the visual and verbal "behavior" of those who deal with, process, or consume the works of art. The book is reading-oriented; the transfer of approaches traditionally limited to analyzing works of visual or of verbal art to the other is primarily to enrich the methods of analysis and interpretation currently in use, as well as to promote the reader's self-awareness as a critic. Each chapter focuses on a theoretical problem. For example: What can we do with rhetoric for the interpretation of visual images? How can images narrate? What are the status and the effect of a represented viewer in visual and literary art? These will be discussed as an issue of cultural criticism.

In order to be teachable, the approach needs to be elaborated through detailed analyses of works of art whose artistic status in the culture in which they function is undeniable. Therefore, the book will also contain a number of interpretations as well as discussions of extant interpretations of works of art. In these interpretative analyses, the relationship between (i.e., the approaches to) verbal and visual arts, and between the work and the world, will be explored with the help of specific examples. No claim to exhaustiveness is intended, nor are my interpretations meant to suggest that alternative or conflicting interpretations are invalid. On the contrary, conflicting meanings are, in my view, what art is about.

The book is designed to pursue a number of intertwined goals. First, I shall practice "reading"—that is, describing and interpreting images and stories both verbal and visual. At the same time, I shall reflect on what "reading" means. I shall reflect on the relationship between literature and the visual arts, a relationship between different, but not opposed, ways of producing signs and meaning. Thus I shall pursue insight into the rhetorical and pictorial devices used in the two arts. At the same time, I shall explore the different ways in which works by "Rembrandt" and certain verbal texts are or can be related. These reflections will point toward unexpected but crucial relationships between technical and ideological issues. Although each of the chapters of this book deals with a particular theoretical point, three issues derived from the above assumptions recur and intersect with the main points to constitute a subtext, uniting the various reflections. These three issues are the choice of "Rembrandt" in an anti-individualist study; the status of interpretation in a reception-oriented study; and the choice of certain terms of analysis, some of which have been compromised by their use in misogynist analyses, in a feminist study. I shall begin by discussing the first two of these issues, and, after presenting the various chapters in light of these, conclude with a brief discussion of the third.

Why "Rembrandt"?

In our culture, painting is art *par excellence,* and in a capitalist society, that excellence is taken quite literally, not only in the form of prices reached at auction, but also in the central position painting retains institutionally and ideologically within Western culture. There is nothing in the literary institution, for example, that really compares with the *museum.*[10]

Within the institution of art "Rembrandt" is a most representative figure, fetching among the highest prices ever paid per canvas, with the authenticity of the works—their autographic reliability—fully determining their worth. "Rembrandt" scholarship has become a paradoxical power; without being invested with power itself, it makes or breaks fortunes. If only for these reasons, "Rembrandt" presents a challenge to the analyst. Forgetting "Rembrandt" in order to pay more attention to popular works would leave these institutional aspects unchallenged.

A second answer to the question Why "Rembrandt"? can be found in his period. This artist belongs to an era still innocent of Freudianism—an innocence that makes his work a proper object for a psychoanalytic criticism that wishes to avoid circularity. There may not be in "Rembrandt" 's painting such wonderful coincidence of discourse as was the case with Freud and Sophocles.[11] But equally prestigious, and in many ways equally tragic, complex, and riddled with riddles, "Rembrandt" 's visual art, nevertheless, constitutes a suitable challenge to psychoanalysis.

A third answer to Why "Rembrandt"? rests in the *kind* of art his corpus contains. "Rembrandt" 's art being figurative, it presents us with both a problem and an opportunity. Representational art is "about" something and thus is open to reductionism. The reductionism that threatens the analysis of art is threefold: the reductionism of geneticism, as in intentionalist art history and classical psychoanalysis; the reductionism of interpretation, as in the unificatory tendencies of positivistic analysis; the reductionism of logocentrism, of "reading" the image only for its (monolithic) meaning. On the other hand, these tendencies can and should be challenged in their turn, and thus we come to our opportunity. By retaining the kind of openness and vulnerability described above, we can escape reductionism and engage a liberating analysis. "Rembrandt" is appropriate for exploring the ways in which interdisciplinary analysis can counter the tendency to reductionism.

A fourth answer to our question can be elicited by remembering that "Rembrandt" belongs to a tradition that considers skill the primary asset for a painter, an asset far more crucial than the "touch of craziness" that classical psychoanalytic criticism, as heir to the Romantic tradition, so often presupposes. With so little known about his life, and with that "knowledge" so riddled with romantic presuppositions that wild speculations about his neuroses can only be ridiculous, we are left only with what remains on the canvas and what can be inferred from the texts that frame the canvases. This state of affairs protects the enterprise of criticism against another well-known trap, what we might call the pseudobiographical fallacy. On the other hand, at least Rembrandt scholarship has been enlivened by Schwartz's "nasty" account of Rembrandt's person (Schwartz, 1985) and more profoundly by Alpers's (1988) book. Therefore, this kind of scholarship at the very least escapes the problem lying in wait for the many respectful but not sufficiently distanced studies that get bogged down by the laudatory discourse of attention in which respect is not an issue, and in which, ultimately, craziness, incoherence, and contradiction are possibilities, if only because the critic and viewer are never exempted.

Finally, the number of works in which blindness is thematized makes "Rembrandt" doubly appropriate for a study like this one. First, there is the question of the insistent presence of a theme that postmodernism relates to self-reflexivity, feminism to voyeurism, and psychoanalysis to castration. Second, there is the metaquestion of the critical blindness brought forth by sheer thematic psychoanalysis which obscures the work of representation. Both these questions deserve exploration.

"Rembrandt," then, is here treated as a cultural text that transgresses the imaginary boundaries between "high" and popular culture, a boundary I locate between the work as thing and its reception as event. It is the center of a body of reflection on art, visuality, and discourse. "Rembrandt" inserted itself into the cultural discourses and visual practices in the seventeenth century in Holland, and has been in constant movement and transformation since. Whenever historical "facts"—speculations about the biography of the painter named Rembrandt—partake of the event of reception, these facts and speculations themselves become part of the text. Conceiving the historical dimension of analysis in this way, I do not ignore it, but I do keep in mind that no historical position is innocent of the contemporary perspective of the subject doing the historiography. In fact, it is that historical position in which I am primarily interested.

In his famous attack on the concept and authority of the author, Foucault (1979) banishes four different concepts of authorship. Not only does he dispose of the psychological idea of the author, of the authorial intention, and of the historical author as origin of the work, he also jettisons the last stronghold of the concept of the author—the author function as the centering of meaning—by demonstrating it to be a projection of a reader who needs semantic centrality to deal with the work. Foucault's alternative is a radical proliferation of meaning, where the author/work becomes a fluctuating function, always interacting with other functions in the larger discursive field.

So far so good; but is there a limit to these fluctuations? Or are we constrained by an anything-goes attitude that makes any future shift in power relations within the culture invisible from now on? My position here is that there *are* limits, but not limits that can be authenticated by appeal to the author, even when interpreting "author" in the widest sense of the historical context. Instead, those limits are strategic, but fundamental. They are fundamental, for any position that does not assess the political basis of the status quo cannot challenge the established cultural powers, because, simply, these powers were established on political grounds. But once shifting, strategic limits are accepted as replacement for both "natural" starting point from which to develop a politics of reading that draws its legitimacy from political positions, not from any fictitious "real" knowledge. And once we acknowledge both the necessity and the strategic nature of limits to interpretation, we move from the question of the author back to the question of interpretation.

Why Interpretation?

The need for interpretation requires some additional comments at this point as well. A study that focuses on reading cannot but question the location of meaning and the related concern regarding the subject of interpretation. Such a task inevitably leads to the further question: Why bother to interpret if interpretation is subjective anyway?[12]

Here, again, strategy prevails. Whenever a literary scholar, moved by the commendable intention of putting an end to the current proliferation of interpretation, stands up to claim that some details in realistic texts have no narrative function, that they merely serve to produce an "effect of the real" (Barthes, 1968) or an effect of verisimilitude (*vraisemblance;* Genette, 1969b), someone else responds that the examples given do have a narrative function after all, if only one looks hard enough. There seems to be a resistance to meaninglessness that invariably looks convincing. As a consequence, we continue to assume that everything in a work of art contributes to, and modifies, the meaning of the work.

But if everything in a work of art participates equally in the production of meaning, then how do we know what texts and images are "about" and why? In other words, which signs convey, or trigger, which meanings? One answer is that there is no answer because texts and images do nothing; the interpreter invents the meaning. Putting the question differently, we may ask, On what basis do we process verbal and visual signs? The debate is particularly troublesome in literary theory because the question interferes with the apparent obviousness of the answer. We assume we know what signs are and which signs we process because we know what a letter, a word, and a sentence are, and we assume that words are the units we call signs in verbal works.

Here, visual poetics reminds us of this assumption's untenability, by forcing us to ask what the visual counterpart of a word is: Is it an image, as the phrase "word and image" too easily suggests? Mulling over this difficult equation, we become less sure that words are, in fact, the "stuff" of verbal signification.

The problem of delimiting signs and delineating interpretation—of distinguishing interpretation from description—is related. Since readers and viewers bring to the texts and images their own cultural and personal baggage, there can be no such thing as a fixed, predetermined meaning, and the very attempt to summarize meanings, as we do in encyclopedias and textbooks, is by definition reductive. Yet as soon as we are forced to draw from these views the inevitable conclusion that "anything goes" and that interpretation is a futile scholarly activity since it all depends on the individual interpreter, we draw back. We then turn around, trying to locate, in the text or image, not a meaning, but the "occasion" of meaning, the thing that triggers meaning; not fixity, but a justification for our flexibility.

As Jonathan Culler has argued, when confronting the dilemma of interpretation we face two mutually exclusive positions which nevertheless are complementary, continuous—that is, mutually inclusive.[13] Ernst van Alphen has argued convincingly in response to Culler that the dilemma can be resolved only by our letting go of a unified concept of meaning and being ready to distinguish at least two different "moments of meaning production" occurring at the two loci of the debate, text and reader. Van Alphen's solution is not a harmonizing of the conflict demonstrated by Culler; it is not a dialectic resolution but rather a radicalization of the poles of the opposition. Moreover, van Alphen leaves room for more than two kinds of meaning, and stimulates thinking about other possibilities.[14]

As I hope to show in the third chapter of this study, I subscribe to the general skepticism concerning the possibility of circumscribing meaning, but as my second chapter will demonstrate, I do not find interpretation futile. On the contrary, the continuity and interdependence between producing and processing works of art makes interpretation as important, as valuable, as writing and painting. But my continued adherence to interpretation is more polemical than that. While I find much that is intellectually attractive in the currently widespread resistance to interpretation presented in response to the recognition of the free play of signs and meanings, I also see it in a renewed threat to the freedom of cultural participation, a new form of censorship.

Censorship of art, be it overly political or subliminally social, is confirmed, strengthened, and perpetuated by censoring forms of interpretation. In a world where access to writing and painting is made difficult—by the institutional censors of art—for all individuals deviating from a self-asserting mainstream, making interpretation a privileged form of art processing subjugates it to the same mechanisms of exclusion.

But there is more to it. True, the academic practice of interpretation, linked with journalism and other more popular forms of interpretation through a common ideology and often even through shared personnel, can be a form of censorship in itself. Even where the margins built within art and the reigning concepts of beauty leave some space for the production of works that cannot be exhausted by mainstream response, the exclusions operating within the very activity of interpretation as a practice taught and learned can easily take care of all interpretations that might enhance the unsettling aspects of these not-so-mainstream works; of interpretations that make the works threatening. This is precisely the motive for the resistance coming from progressive scholars. But for the same reason, censorship *of* interpretation can be used to conceal the censorship *by* interpretation. And that is why the resistance to interpretation can receive such wide acclaim, from progressive as well as from conservative ideologues.

A more open academic and educational policy can make room to include the views of those who respond to art from a less predominant social position. Such a broadening is an indispensable next step toward a better, more diverse and complex, understanding of culture. In spite of its challenging and persuasive logic, we must place the resistance to interpretation within this dynamic. I am afraid that it cannot be an accident that the increasing participation of women and minorities in the academy coincides with a growing resistance to the very practices from which they had formerly been excluded. To put it overly simply, as soon as women began to speak, the subject of speech was no longer relevant; as soon as women began to interpret, there was no more need for interpretation. In other words, the same threat is acutely present as the one that the "death of the author" poses: As women gained access to signs, the sign was put to death.[15] This demonstrates precisely how the problematic of interpretation and the challenge to the sign are related.

In the following chapters, I shall not make a regressive claim for the reinstatement of the Saussurian sign with its system-ontological status and its safely sutured signified. My endeavor will be much more down to earth; I shall explore modes and possibilities, analyzing what does or can happen in the encounter between text and reader—an encounter that is never a true encounter and that always leaves rests, gaps, and "meaninglessness" anyway. I shall try to show that the determination of signs and the attribution of meaning to signs—acknowledged as readerly activities—follow various paths whose diversification is precisely the point. We do many different things under the unifying heading of interpretation that we call the response to signs. This is how the problem of interpretation joins the problem of the sign.[16]

The view of signs to which I shall adhere in this study posits the basic density of both verbal and visual texts. I use the term "density" in Goodman's (1976) sense: as conveying the fundamental inseparability of individual signs, as the opposite of discreteness. This view eliminates at least one difference between discourse and image. Resisting the early Wittgenstein's anguish about, and sympathizing with his later happy endorsement of, the cloudiness of language, I shall contend that the same density that characterizes visual texts obstructs the propositional clarity of verbal texts.[17] Thus, separate words cannot be taken to rule interpretation, and the ideal of "pure" propositional content longed for in the *Tractatus* is untenable: The elements of a proposition cannot have independent meaning. This recognition means that the difference between verbal and visual texts is no longer one of the status and delimitation of the signs that constitute them. And the visual model, apparently predominant, overwhelms the concrete particularity of the signifier, giving rise to "cloudiness" in each medium. Hence, the Wittgenstein of the *Tractatus* mourns the fact that there is no nondense language, whereas later, in the *Investigations,* Wittgenstein denounces the positivistic illusion that makes visuality the basis of interpretation, sacrificing both the signifier and the activity of semiosis. In this later work he endorses the view he earlier regretted, that language is as dense as pictures. This may not make language visual, but it does displace the difference between the two media.

Yet the density of both visual and linguistic signs is not really the issue. Rather, it is the dynamism of signs that the recognition of their density makes possible that is at issue. The perception of signs as static can be traced to the atomistic view of verbal signs, itself a relic of early structuralism which, in its turn, had inherited it from more explicitly positivistic schools of cultural scholarship.[18] The problem and source of this atomistic view are the semiotic positivism that claims ontological status for the sign. If the sign is a "real thing," then signs must be numerable, hence discrete and intrinsically static. A radically dynamic view, however, would conceive the sign not as a thing but as an event, the issue being not to delimit and isolate the one sign from other signs, but to trace the possible emergence of the sign in a concrete situation of work—reader interaction. Wittgenstein's concept of language games posits a dynamic view of the sign, which makes signs as *active,* and requires them to be both deployed *according to rules* and *public. A sign, then, is not a thing but an event.* Hence the meaning of a sign is neither preestablished and fixed, nor purely subjective and idiosyncratic.

Although this view seems to open the discussion to a paralyzing infinitude of phenomena, this apparent problem disappears as soon as we acknowledge that sign events occur in specific circumstances and according to a finite number of culturally valid, conventional, yet not unalterable rules, which semioticians call "codes." The selection of those rules and their combination leads to specific interpretive behavior.

The Content of This Study

In light of the preceding considerations, this book progresses from more general to more specific explorations of problems pertaining to the interpretation of verbal and visual art. The opening chapter, "Beyond the Word–Image Opposition," provides an overview of issues included in the general theme of the book, and relates these issues to some major works of art analysis that are currently influential in both art history and literary studies.

Chapter 2 begins to explore the hermeneutic exchange between literary and visual studies by demonstrating the possible gain of this exchange in terms of social issues. The chapter addresses the question of the relationship between representation and reality head-on through the elaboration of a "rhetoric of violence." It explores the interpretive possibilities for painting offered by literary concepts like metaphor and metonymy, and then proposes to reverse the perspective and read literary texts with a bias for visuality as it is thematized in many a text. The works discussed in that chapter all thematize rape, and Lucretia is the central character.

The issue of reading as a socially framed effect of meaning will be recurrently discussed in the following chapters. In Chapter 2, it is related to the problem of meaning and experience. In Chapter 3, it focuses on the elusiveness of meaning. "Visual Storytelling" centers upon the story of Joseph and Potiphar's Wife, examining devices for storytelling in a still medium, and then questioning the notion that storytelling in literature proceeds sequentially. This questioning focuses on the concept of myth as a token of permanency, as the petrified, transhistorical "hard core" of a story. In Chapter 4, inversely, an issue traditionally limited to the visual domain is explored. Through the story of Susanna and the Elders the meaning of looking and *its* status as reading is examined.

After exploring the interface between visual and verbal art in these first four chapters, in Chapters 5 through 9 I shall discuss the specific gestures by the reader that in the search for meaning bring about sign events. First, in the search for theme (iconography) and narrative, I shall juxtapose iconography with narratology. Next, I shall bring two other conflicting modes of reading to bear upon each other: the search for the "text" (the effect of the representation as a whole) and for the real (away from the work of representation). Both of these modes of reading, or codes, focus on signs that help us understand the work in terms of representation.

"Recognition: Reading Icons, Seeing Stories" (Chapter 5) will continue to pursue the relationship between visual and narrative in images and texts in terms of the tension between modes of reading. In this chapter, I shall examine the art historical dogma of the iconographic mode of reading and shall argue for its possible critical use. Then, I shall explore a narrative mode of reading, and analyze the tension between iconography and narrative. My analysis will ultimately call for a juxtaposition, a nonresolved dialectic, of the two. Finally, I shall conclude the chapter with a discussion of the relations between visual and textual representations of a number of Biblical narratives, ending in an iconographic reading of the novel *Uncle Tom's Cabin* and of the painting *Samson's Wedding*.

In "Textuality and Realism" (Chapter 6), a similar tension is at stake, this time between reading for textuality—for a complex and structured representation—and reading for realistic understanding, in which the representation is taken for granted and the represented object foregrounded. Again, although these modes of reading yield different results, both are equally valid. The thematic center of this chapter is the story of David and Bathsheba, and the "Rembrandt" painting *The Toilet of Bathshebah*.

The codes discussed in Chapters 5 and 6 open up the work to reflection on various aspects of meaning "external" to the work itself; in a meaning that is culturally validated; in a story that we know and may want to know better; in an idea of coherence; in the reality in which we stand and to which we want to suture the meaning of the work. In addition, many works of art also trigger reflection on the work itself. I shall therefore complement the outward-oriented modes of reading with a discussion of the search for the work and for the sign themselves. Signs "for the work" take various shapes, and it is rewarding to disentangle these, as the tendency today for interpreting every work ultimately as self-referential does not seem to foster understanding of specific works. The examination of what happens when one adopts a certain reading strategy inevitably leads to a critical analysis of the texts of art criticism itself. "Self-Reflection" (Chapter 7) is an in-depth analysis of modern art-critical discourse, which I shall argue partakes of the self-reflection which it claims the work emphasizes.

In this chapter, I shall first argue that self-portraits are only deceptively self-reflexive. Then I shall conduct a polylogue between two self-reflexive paintings—Velázquez's *Las Meninas* and a modest panel by "Rembrandt"—and a set of interdisciplinary responses to the former work. The chapter concludes with the view that self-reflection has a quadruple status, and that the resistance to any of its "four fundamental concepts" leads to entanglement in narcissistic speculation and specularity. Ultimately, the very appeal of the self-portrait as the false locus of self-reflection supports this view.

Throughout these chapters I shall thus propose that we accept that the modes of interpretation we use when reading verbal or visual art are basically similar, even when academics have assigned different names to those practices. I shall, however, admit that the modes in question come from general semiotic practices firmly anchored in modern Western culture and have no universal status. Keeping their historical specificity in mind, a few words on the terms of such an analysis are due, which will follow shortly.

The last three chapters lean strongly on the discourse of psychoanalysis. "Blindness or Insight?" (Chapter 8) uses narcissism to examine critically psychoanalysis as a discourse that interacts with images. This examination is pursued further in Chapter 9, "Blindness as Insight," where the plea for a psychoanalytic criticism of visual art focuses paradoxically on works in which blindness is an insistent thematic center.

"Dead Flesh" (Chapter 10) concludes by relating the awareness of problems of representation to the question of the attitudes toward gender that are readable in "Rembrandt"'s works, through the challenge posed by death.

The Terms of Analysis

The status of my own interpretations is strongly bound up with the terms I use to elaborate them. Most of the terms of analysis used here are necessarily derived from theories pertaining to a single discipline; the disciplines from which these terms are derived include feminist theory, rhetoric, narratology, and psychoanalysis. I shall discuss their relevance and the conditions for bringing them to the other disciplines in due course. Neither restrictive disciplinarity nor free eclectic borrowing will be taken for granted, and I shall try to justify explicitly any modifications of concepts. Although most concepts are derived from visual analysis and literary theory, the use of psychoanalytic and feminist concepts is so current in contemporary critical cultural studies that it seems that they need not be problematic. Yet I find that the self-evidence of those concepts sometimes precludes their efficacy, as imprecise, casual use alternates with precise, technical deployment.

I shall try to argue deliberately for my uses and possibly misuses of theoretical terms, but the general question of the relation between visual response and psychoanalysis must be mentioned right away. As I have argued before, the object of a reader-oriented analysis of art is *our relation to the image.* The "our" in this statement needs further analysis. Although this phrase is meant to suggest how deeply entrenched we are in any act of interpretation of images stemming from other times and places, "we" is emphatically not a monolithic subject. Within a psychoanalytic framework, this collective subject can be further differentiated. By "us" I mean a subject traversed and fraught by the unconscious, including the superego and its social implications: narcissism and its defensiveness against affect, desire, and the fantasy character of response. The way we perceive and interpret images is based on fantasy, and fantasy is socially based. Thus there is dissymmetry between men and women before male and female figures. But this dissymmetry is also unstable, varying according to which aspects of the unconscious are more or less strongly implicated in the act of looking. As I will argue, the response to the *Danae* is more likely to differ according to gender, whereas the response of women and men to *The Blinding of Samson* might differ less strongly, because this painting appeals to a pre-Oedipal fantasy. The differentiation, here, occurs not so much directly according to gender lines but primarily according to other divisions, like narcissistic fulfillment and the relative solidity of the ego.

Thinking about the uneasy fit between psychoanalysis—a basically verbal discourse—and visual art, and the equally uneasy fit between psychoanalysis—an overwhelmingly masculine discourse—and feminism, the strategies and concepts of deconstruction have often been quite helpful. The continual suspicion of binary oppositions, which informs this study as a whole, is, of course, a major tenet of deconstructive criticism. And for a study that puts interpretation in the center and questions the status of meaning, no concept seems more attractive than that of dissemination.[19] For dissemination also takes place in the space between verbal and visual reading, and calls into question the tenability of those categories through an alternative concept of textuality.

Earlier in this Introduction I discussed Vermeer's *Woman Holding a Balance,* a painting that might be considered the "purest" of images. As we have seen, it was textualized by the workings of narrativity, imported into the work by an act of reading. That discussion exemplifies the way in which I shall generally handle standard concepts; such a method is called for by this book's interdisciplinary status, but it accommodates neither purism nor eclecticism without problems. For, in an important sense, an image is not a text; but while irreducibly different, the visual and the verbal domains interpenetrate, influence, and inform each other. Why, then, speak about "reading" images as "texts"? Without trying to assimilate images to verbal texts, I want to make a case for an idea of visual textuality without that visual text losing its visual specificity.

Later on in this study, I shall more fully interpret "Rembrandt"'s *Danae,* but here I would like briefly to analyze that work as a text, offering this analysis as a model in miniature of just how this method will let visual texts be read without sacrificing their visuality. First, I shall present the *Danae* in the more traditional sense: as a narrative. But this concept of textuality will prove to be slightly problematic. If the concept of text illuminates the painting, so the painting shows the defects of the concept of text, with its fixed relation between sign and meaning, its hierarchical structure, its suppression of details, of the marginal, of the "noise." It is to such an oppressive notion of text that Derrida opposed the concept of dissemination, which enhances the slippery, destabilizing mobility of signs in interaction with sign users: here, viewers. Derrida replaces the metaphor of the phallus as the ultimate meaning with that of the hymen as the sheet—or canvas—on which meaning circulates without fixity.

The *Danae* (Figure 2) is more than a narrative in the traditional sense of a re-production, an illustration of a preexisting, narrative text. Let me briefly compare the verbal and the visual approach. The pre-text has it that this woman, forever barred from love by her frightened father, is, at the very moment the picture presents, visited by Zeus who managed, thanks to his disguise as a shower of gold, to break the taboo the woman's father had imposed on his daughter. In this pre-text's context, Zeus, the ever-loving mastergod, is also the first Oedipus slaying his jealous father. But this is a verbal story, and we want to pursue a *visual* text.

Looking at the picture, we see a female body, nude, displayed for the lust of the viewer who is allowed to peep into the intimacy of the doubly closed bedroom. But this is a visual story, the story of vision in Western culture. It is the story of the male voyeur and the female object, of the eroticization of vision; it is the story of the central syntagm—subject–function–object—in which the positions are fixed along gender lines—through which, indeed, gender itself is constructed. It is the scheme that is invariably nearly dominating, nearly exclusive, but never absolutely so, because the dynamic of narrative precludes its foreclosure. If only in order to break the monopoly of this visual construction of gender, undermining this verbal/visual opposition is worthwhile.

Between the text (the story of the welcomed arrival of Zeus) and the image (the exhibition of a female body for voyeuristic consumption), the painting produces its own narrative, reducible to neither—the work's visual/narrative textuality. The pre-text is literally a pretext: Its anteriority allows the painting's appeal to the general understanding of the story as a frame for its reversal. The story's centrality, as the theme of the work, allows everything decentered to slip in; it allows, that is, for the dissemination of meaning.

There is another way to phrase this. The work's genesis in a preexistent narrative helps to sever the tie between the two and to produce another narrative, irreducibly alien to it, void of the deceptive meaning the pre-text brought along. With its genesis, the severing of the tie, a central void, and the dissemination of what *matters,* an alternative to the hymen as the central bodily metaphor is creeping in here—and that alternative is the navel.

Starting from the pre-text, the divine lover who is supposedly welcome is visible only as a sheen. But the sheen, the border of light, so crucially "Rembrandtish," dissolves into futility. For in spite of deceptive appearances, Zeus's

FIGURE 2. Rembrandt Harmensz. van Rijn. *Danae,* 1636–50. Hermitage, St. Petersburg, Russia. CREDIT: Art Resource, NY.

gold does not illuminate the woman. Rather, the sheen delimits the space in which the woman is enclosed; it demarcates her private space, emphasizing the form of the opening in which the woman's feet disappear—her opening. The sheen emphasizes the opening, but it does not produce it; so in this way the sheen does not *count,* and the pre-textual story is undermined.

Looking at the image from a different angle, we must take our own position into account. The viewer is *also* supposed to come in and be welcomed—as voyeur, allowed to see the female body on display. But, at the same time, this viewer is deprived of his identity, as his eyes come in contact with his mirror image in the two represented onlookers. These two, the putto and the servant, form, according to a formal analysis, an insistent triangle with the female body as its base, paralleling and reversing the triangle of the exit-curtain. The putto refers iconographically to the pre-text, his tied hands a "symbol" of forbidden sexuality. While also offering a way of viewing the woman, it is an immature, childish way. For though he wrings his hands in despair, he is not looking at the woman's body. Perhaps he despairs over this lack, a lack imposed by the bonds on his hands, which, in fact, prohibit both touching *and* looking. Exasperated by the interdiction, the putto is visually self-enclosed. The servant, of whom more needs to be said later on, does not look at the woman at all.

These two stories—the purely textual, verbal pre-text and the story of the purely visual present—collude and collide in the work's textuality. They are in tension, but not in contradiction. They produce a new story, the text of the *Danae* as an interaction between the canvas and the viewer who processes it. In this text, Zeus, invisible as he/it is, thus becomes the pre-text the woman uses to get rid of the indiscreet viewer. The woman who at first sight seemed to be on display—as spectacle, in a static, visual reading—takes over and dominates both viewer and lover. Her genitals, prefigured by the slippers and magnified by the opening of the curtain at the other end of the sight line, are central in the framed text. They are turned toward the viewer, but they can be seen by neither viewer nor lover, because the viewer is sent away while the lover comes to her from the other side/sight. In this way her sexuality, in spite of its centrality, is a trace of the pre-text, for the conflicting lines of sight cut it off; it is also the locus of the metaphor that kept creeping into the vocabulary of my analysis: It is the navel of the text. But between sex and navel lies a difference—the difference between voyeurism and its deconstruction.

The metaphor of the navel is more satisfying than that of the hymen for the deconstructed image; diluted into a multiple textuality, it is a false center attracting attention to its void of semes—to its dis-semination. The metaphor of the navel pushes Derrida's dissemination to its limits, and beyond. Although he undermined the phallic view of the sign and of meaning inscribed in Saussure's semiotics, Derrida still could not quite let go: For his dissemination, meant to dissolve the penetrating power of the dualistic sign, comes dangerously close to an overwhelming dispersion of semen; coming all over the text, it spreads out so pervasively, so Biblically, that it becomes like the stars in heaven or the sand at the seashore: a promise to fatherhood. Derrida clings to the concept of the hymen, the veil that protects from penetration as an alternative for the phallic privileging of the invisible signified; but by invoking Hymen, he also embraces the moment when the virgin bride is torn open and pervaded by semen. Invoking Hymen invokes marriage. And marriage imperialistically prevails, threatening to become the metaphor for semiosis.

Deconstructing this metaphor with the help of visual images read as texts, I propose to replace it with the navel—both a trace of the mother, and the token of autonomy of the subject, male and female alike; a center without meaning, it is yet a meaningful pointer that allows plurality and mobility, that allows the viewer to propose new readings to meet his or her needs, but without letting those readings fall into the arbitrariness that leads to isolation.

This concept of textuality leaves room for the specificity of the visual; indeed, it builds the reading it suggests upon the image's visuality. Yet it enhances the irreducible textuality—its play between story and static image, its visual mobility, and the indispensable collaboration between the work and its socially and historically positioned viewers. The navel, then, is a metaphor for an element, often a tiny detail, that hits the viewer, is processed by her or him, and textualizes the image on its own terms. In the *Danae*, it is not the woman's "real" navel but her genital area in *The Toilet of Bathshebah,* another nude with an ostentatiously represented navel, the navel of the text is the left-hand corner of the letter the naked woman is holding in the Vermeer, it is the nail-and-hole. Later on, I shall argue that the navel of the Berlin *Susanna* is the fist of one of the Elders. In many works that I shall analyze in this study, the textualizing navel is an emptiness, a little surface which the work leaves unfilled.

This play with metaphors should not be taken for a meaningless linguistic game. By choosing a bodily metaphor, I also wish to demonstrate both my allegiance and my polemic opposition to much of psychoanalytic theory. Here the navel is the symbolization of a body part, just as the phallus is, and it too is loaded with the connotations of gender. Yet these are radically different in status. The phallus refers to gender in terms of haves and have-nots, or "to have it" versus "to be it." The navel, in contrast, is fundamentally gender specific—the navel is the scar of dependence on the mother—but it is also democratic in that both men and women have it. And unlike the phallus and its iconic representations disseminated throughout post-Freudian culture, the navel is starkly indexical.

Thus, the metaphor of the navel, as the detail that triggers textual diffusion, variation, and mobility of reading, is therefore a tribute not only to an antiphallic semiotic but also to an antiphallic genderedness that does not assign to woman a second-rate position. My position toward gender, then, is comparable to my attitude toward "high art." In both cases, the hierarchy is not denied, which it cannot be because it is a cultural reality, but it is shifted and thereby undermined.

In her seminal article on Freud's *Beyond the Pleasure Principle* (1922), Elisabeth Bronfen (1989) suggests that we focus on the navel as an image of primary castration. In support of that suggestion, she argues for the psychoanalytic importance of the experience of primary narcissism. She makes her case through a close analysis of Freud's repression, in that essay, of the place of the woman—his daughter and the mother of the child out of whose game the theory emerges. Freud's identification with the child as between father and son is based on the conflation of mother and daughter, and demonstrates the genderedness of the very formation of this theory and, by analogy, of theory in general. But when Freud, the day after the death of his favorite daughter, shifts attention from her death to his woundedness, calling her death an incurable assault on his narcissism, another identification—that between father and daughter/mother—is at stake. When the father/son is wounded, only then are gender boundaries crossed.

What emerges from this study, finally, is a "Rembrandt" full of ambivalence. Both highly disturbing and highly gratifying, this body of work gains in depth by readings in the mode of the navel; the readings in each chapter acknowledge visuality and do not shy away from discursive elements; they recognize where cultural commonplaces are mobilized, yet leave room for the marginal other; they endorse the "density" of visual signs and let that density spill over into literature, while not fearing to point out specific, discrete signs in visual works and the loci of density in literature. Each chapter pursues simultaneously a theoretical question, the interpretation of at least one "Rembrandt" work and at least one verbal text with which the visual work entertains a relation. Together these chapters offer an overview of issues and concepts relevant for the study of the interaction between image and discourse.

The interpretations set forth in this study are not meant to be full, comprehensive descriptions of what we see in the paintings; nor are they narratives reconstructing the pre-texts that give the works meaning. Instead, my interpretations start at the navel, the little detail that doesn't fit the "official" interpretation: the view of the work put forward by the terms of agreement among readers before me. For invariably those official readings leave a rest, a lack. They have one thing that isn't there and should be, or that is there but shouldn't, and thus trigger the alternative reading. What the classical narrative readings cannot unproblematically accommodate sets in motion another narrative, via the suspenseful encounter between the narrative and the visual. In this way, the concept of the "navel of the text" is programmatic: It proclaims an interaction, not an opposition, between discourse and image.

Endnotes

1. See Salomon's interpretation of this painting. See also Mary Jacobus's fascinating discussion of Raphael's *Sistine Madonna,* with reference to the Arezzo *Pregnant Madonna* of Piero della Francesca. Jacobus discusses the Raphael as it is read by Freud's patient Dora. See *"Dora* and the Pregnant Madonna," in Jacobus's *Reading Woman* (1986).
2. When speaking of literary history, Culler (1988:xv) phrases the problem in the following way:
   > If history is the name of the discrepancy between intention and occurrence, then literary theory has a pertinent model to hand in its debates about the problematical relation between meaning as intentional act (of a writer or reader) and meaning as textual fact (the product of grammatical, rhetorical, textual, and contextual structures).
3. See especially White's essay "Interpretation in History" (1978). Emphasizing the impossibility of reaching "pure" historical knowledge is not the same thing as denying that historical events really occurred. The knowledge of the events, the possibility of describing them outside of the present and hence of ascertaining their significance, are what is questioned, not their having really occurred.
4. See Martin Jay (1988), Svetlana Alpers (1985), and T. J. Clark (1985).
5. The phrase is Griselda Pollock's. She used it to explain her view of the social history of art during the N. E. H. Summer Institute on "Theory and Interpretation in the Visual Arts" in 1989.
6. Among recent reader-oriented studies of visual art I mention here only two: Kemp, ed., *Betrachter* (1985), a collection of essays representing various approaches of the reader; and Freedberg, *Power* (1989), a sustained effort to analyze the effect of images from a number of different angles.
7. See Silverman (1988) and Penley (1989). Both of these authors juxtapose avant-garde and popular films. See also the work of Anneke Smelik (e.g., 1989), who analyzes popular feminist films. This is another way of undermining the opposition insofar as the opposition rests on the unwarranted and often implicit assumption that high art is subversive whereas popular art is ideologically damaging.
8. In my work on literature I have myself mainly, though not exclusively, contributed to a rereading and critique of the male canon. But what I then set out to do is not to critique those works and dismantle their inherent sexism, but to argue that although no less sexist than the culture they stem from, these works tend to be misread in a way that obscures even the symptomatic signs of struggle with the sexism they cannot but display. I will pursue a similar goal here: Although on many occasions I will situate "Rembrandt" as just another case in a broadly male-oriented culture, I will *at the same time* argue that we make it worse than it need be. Thereby, we miss the opportunity to use these prestigious works to make statements about gender relations—statements that can be more productive than constant denunciation.
9. In fact, the same strategy should be followed for other names of authors. I have refrained from doing so to avoid burdening the text with too many signs of self-consciousness, which might hamper a pleasant reading. Since "Rembrandt" is the main focus of this study, that name cannot possibly be written unproblematically.
10. The library comes closest. But although the purchase of books for a library surely partakes of the exclusions inherent in gathering, the distinction between the museum's display and storerooms is unparalleled. The National Gallery in Washington, D.C., went so far as to remove a challenged "Rembrandt" from the exhibition rooms, thus bowing to the authority of the scholars, rather than leaving it to the public to decide whether a disattributed "Rembrandt" is still worth seeing or not.
11. For a subtly dialectic view of the relation between Freudian theory and the Sophoclean model, see Verhoeff (1984).
12. An overview of this discussion is offered by Culler (1981).

13. Culler's argument can be found in "Stories of Reading," in *On Deconstruction* (1983).
14. See Ernst van Alphen (1988b), ch. 6, for a full account of the problem of reading. A shorter version in English appears in a special (1989) issue of *VS Versus* on reading. That issue also has other important contributions on the problem at issue here.
15. Rosi Braidotti (1991) makes this point when speaking of the problematic relationship between feminism and philosophy. Her argument does not compel us, of course, to return to the authoritarian practice that the poststructuralist argument rightly discarded. Instead, the challenge we are facing is to embrace the vulnerability of interpretation, arguing for a more democratic and critical practice of it, a practice in which its status is radically changed.
16. If we want to assess to what extent we can circumscribe the signifying units called signs and understand our dealings with them, we must delimit the field of signs and meanings in two directions. At one extreme there are the subsemiotic technical aspects of the works of art. Although they all contribute to the construction of signs, stylistic variation, light and dark, composition, or more technical aspects like brushstrokes, paint thickness, and lines are not, a priori, signs in themselves; not any more than in a literary text sheer ink on the page, mere punctuation marks, and syntactic structures are. Although they are part of what make us interpret the work, we do not give them meaning in themselves, except in some truly special cases (cf. Meyer Shapiro's attempt to theorize the sign status of these subsemiotic elements).

 At the other extreme, there are the suprasemiotic holistic aspects of the works. Although there has been a tendency to conflate the concepts of "text" and "sign," and, by extension, of "work" and "sign," I think such a conflation only displaces the problem of what kinds of encounters signs and meanings are. This conflation has an unexpected and unfortunate consequence.

 The consequence of such a position is that the compound sign will be subdivided into discrete units, and this division will become a gesture at best either of articulation or of slicing up, delimiting, what supposedly adds up in the whole. This subdivision is held more acceptable for verbal than for visual art; indeed, the distinction between the two is often based on the very assumption that verbal works are composed of discrete units whereas visual works are "dense." The distinction is deceptively self-evident and can be deconstructed only by reversing it and arguing that to some extent verbal texts are dense—the sign of the effect of the real cannot be distinguished from the work as a whole on which it sheds a specific meaning—and that visual texts are discrete, which sometimes, and in some respects, they are. The distinction is untenable, but it nevertheless reflects different attitudes of reading that operate conventionally for each art. Attempts to assign to verbal details whose point is not obvious the function of producing an effect of the real or an effect of versimilitude can be seen as efforts to promote a reading of verbal art that seems more appropriate for visual art.
17. In the *Tractatus Logico-Philosophicus* (1921), Wittgenstein gives a visual dimension to verbal propositions and regrets language's cloudiness, thus suggesting that density is by definition visual, which it is not. In the later *Philosophical Investigations* (1953), he rejects his nostalgia for purity in the early work and argues that language is no less dense than pictures are. Here, he endorses language's ambiguity as one of its most basic features. See Allen Thiher's *Words in Reflection* (1984) for an account of Wittgenstein's views of language for the transition and break between modernism and postmodernism in literature. The assumed visuality of language plays a key role in that change.
18. A clear example is the historical-critical school in Biblical scholarship, which holds an even more dogmatic position than iconography in art history. Historical-critical scholarship works from the premise that the texts that today form the canon of Biblical texts have been composed out of fragments of diverse "layers" of various origin. Convincing as the hypothesis is in itself, the following step—slicing up each text into "layers" that can each be assigned a place in the history of the text—does not make the least sense in terms of the hypothesis itself. "Separation of sources" may be the phrase preferred by the historical-critical school for this approach, but Edmund Leach's killing phrase "unscrambling the omelette," with its unwitting Lacanian overtones, is far more telling. See Richter (1963) for an example of the sterility of this approach which I critique extensively in my *Murder and Difference* (1988b). In more up-to-date semiotics, however, this accumulative concept of text is still vital. Among many examples, the meager results of Greimas's detailed analysis of a short story by Maupassant (Greimas, 1976), show the limits imposed by this fallacious approach.
19. *Dissemination* (1981) is not only one of Derrida's most intriguing and richest books, but it is also provided with a brilliantly clear introduction by Barbara Johnson.

References

Alpers, Svetlana. 1985. *The Art of Describing Dutch Art in the Seventeenth Century.* Chicago: The University of Chicago Press.

————. 1988. *Rembrandt's Enterprise: The Studio and Market.* Chicago: The University of Chicago Press.

Alphen, Ernst van. 1988. *Bij wijze van lezen: Verleiding en verzet van Willem Brakmans lezer.* Muiderberg: Coutinho.

————. 1989. "The Complicity of the Reader." *VS Versus* 52–3, 121–32.

Bal, Mieke. 1988. *Murder and Difference: Gender, Genre and Scholarship on Sisera's Death,* translated by Matthew Gumpert. Bloomington: Indiana University Press.

Barthes, Roland. 1968. "L'Effet de réel." *Communications* 4: 84–89. [English: "The Reality Effect." In Roland Barthes, *The Rustle of Language,* translated by Richard Howard, 141–54. New York: Hill and Wang.]

Braidotti, Rosi. 1991. *Patterns of Dissonance: Feminism and Philosophy.* Cambridge, U.K.: Polity Press.

Bronfen, Elisabeth. 1989. "The Lady Vanishes: Sophie Freud and 'Beyond the Pleasure Principle'." *South Atlantic Quarterly* 88, 4: 961–91.

Bruyn, J., B. Haak, S. H. Levie, et al. 1982– . *A Corpus of Rembrandt Paintings.* Stichting Rembrandt Research Project. The Hague, Boston, London: Martinus Nijhoff Publishers (Vol. I, 1982; Vol. II, 1986; Vol. III, 1989).

Clark, T. J. 1985. *The Painting of Modern Life: Paris in the Art of Manet and His Followers.* London: Thames and Hudson.

Culler, Jonathan. 1981. *The Pursuit of Signs, Semiotics, Literature, Deconstruction.* Ithaca: Cornell University Press.

————. 1983. *On Deconstruction: Theory and Criticism After Structuralism.* Ithaca: Cornell University Press.

————. 1988. *Framing the Sign: Criticism and Its Institutions.* Norman, Okla. and London: University of Oklahoma Press.

Derrida, Jacques. 1981. *Dissemination,* translated, and with an Introduction and Additional Notes by Barbara Johnson. Chicago: The University of Chicago Press.

Foucault, Michel. 1979. "What Is an Author?" in *Textual Strategies: Perspectives in Post-Structuralist Criticism,* edited by Josué V. Harari, and translated by Donald Bouchard and Sherry Simon, 141–60. Ithaca: Cornell University Press.

Freedberg, David. 1989. *The Power of Images: Studies in the History and Theory of Response.* Chicago: The University of Chicago Press.

Freud, Sigmund. *Standard Edition of the Complete Works of Sigmund Freud,* edited by James Strachey. London: The Hogarth Press. [Hereafter *SE;* unless otherwise indicated, references listed below are to *SE.*]

————. 1990. The Interpretation of Dreams. *SE* IV and V. New York: Avon Books.

————. 1922. *Beyond the Pleasure Principle.* New York: W. W. Norton. *SE* XVIII: 7–65.

Gates, Henry Louis, Jr. (ed.). 1985. *"Race," Writing, and Difference.* Chicago: The University of Chicago Press.

Gennette, Gérard. 1969b. "Vraisemblance et motivation." *Figures II,* 71–100. Paris: Editions du Seuil.

Goodman, Nelson. 1976. *Languages of Art: An Approach to a Theory of Symbols.* Indianapolis: Hackett.

Greimas, Algirdas Julien. 1976. *Maupassant: Exercises pratiques.* Paris: Editions du Seuil. [English: *Maupassant: The Semiotics of Text, Practical Lessons,* translated by Paul Perron. Amsterdam and Philadelphia: J. Benjamins, 1988.]

Jacobus, Mary. 1986. *Reading Woman: Essays in Feminist Criticism.* New York: Columbia University Press.

Jay, Martin. 1988. "Scopic Regimes of Modernity." In *Vision and Visuality,* edited by Hal Foster, 3–28. Seattle: Bay Press.

Kampen, Nathalie. 1981. *Image and Status: Roman Working Women in Ostia.* Berlin: Mann.

Kemp, Wolfgang. 1985. *Der Betrachter ist im Bild: Kunstwissenschaft und Rezeptionsathetik,* edited by Wolfgang Kemp. Koln: Dumont Buchverlag.

Leach, Edmund. 1983. "Anthropological Approaches to the Study of the Bible During the Twentieth Century." In *Structuralist Interpretations of Biblical Myth,* by Edmund Leach and D. Alan Aykock. Cambridge: Cambridge University Press.

Moxey, Keith. 1989. *Peasants, Warriors, and Wives: Popular Imagery in the Reformation.* Chicago: The University of Chicago Press.

Penley, Constance. 1989. *The Future of an Illusion: Film, Feminism, and Psychoanalysis.* Minneapolis: University of Minnesota Press.

Pollock, Griselda. 1988. *Vision and Difference: Femininity, Feminism, and the Histories of Art.* London and New York: Routledge.

Richter, Wolfgang. 1963. *Traditionsgeschichtliche Untersuchungen zum Richterbuch.* Bonn: Peter Hanstein Verlag GmbH, Bonner Biblische Beiträge 18.

Said, Edward. 1978. *Orientalism.* New York: Pantheon Books.

Schwartz, Gary. 1985. *Rembrandt: His Life, His Paintings.* Harmondsworth: Penguin.

Shapiro, Meyer. 1969. "On Some Problems in the Semiotics of Visual Art: Field and Vehicle in Image-Signs." *Semiotica* 1, 3: 223–42.

Silverman, Kaja. 1988. *The Acoustic Mirror: The Female Voice in Psychoanalysis and Cinema.* Bloomington: Indiana University Press.

Smelik, Anneke. 1989. "Het stille geweld." *Tijdschrift voor vrouwenstudies* 38: 235–52.

Thiher, Allen. 1984. *Words in Reflection: Modern Language Theory and Postmodern Fiction.* Chicago: The University of Chicago Press.

Trinh, T. Minh-ha. 1989. *Woman, Native, Other: Writing Postcoloniality and Feminism.* Bloomington: Indiana University Press.

Verhoeff, Han. 1984. "Does Oedipus Have His Complex?" *Style* 18, 3: 261–83.

Wheelock, Arthur K., Jr. 1981. *Jan Vermeer.* New York: Abrams.

White, Hayden. 1978. "Interpretation in History." In *Tropics of Discourse,* 51–80. Baltimore: The Johns Hopkins University Press.

Wittgenstein, Ludwig. 1958. (1953). *Philosophical Investigations,* translated by G. E. M. Anscombe. New York: Macmillan Press.

———. (1921). *Tractatus Logico-Philosophicus,* translated by B. F. McGuinness. New York: The Humanities Press.

Music and Life

Barbara Carlisle

Interdisciplinary, cross-disciplinary, integrated. These terms are in today's conversations about teaching all subjects—especially the arts. What do they mean, and do they have any real bearing on teaching and learning music?

For some time education has been organized in disciplines. I don't think the world is so organized; this is one of the differences between education and the rest of life. The world is essentially chaotic, and experience comes to us often randomly and without focus. But in the world of teaching and learning we have come to identify ourselves with disciplines, from the base term *disciple:* a follower of a way. The word is explicitly associated with schooling. When I imagine a discipline I think of these things:

- a body of knowledge and skills organized by the point of focus and the manner of looking
- a process of expression contained by a set of media, skills and tools
- a tradition of forms and structures
- a tradition of hypotheses and conclusions
- a tradition of instrumentation for the organization of knowledge and expression

Even while I am convinced of the disorderly nature of experience, I doubt if there is such a thing in the human mind as a neutral phenomenon—existence that is not structured in some way by a point of view. When we teach about phenomena, formulations of the mathematician, the literary writer, the visual artist, the philosopher, the historian or the musician are familiar paths to understanding. The fact that they are dealt with separately, as if the phenomena that provoke them exist separately in the world, is where the disjunction takes place. Thomas Jefferson was a philosopher, politician, farmer, landholder, architect, slave holder, writer, husband and father—and he was all of these at once. Scholarship, however, has needed to divide him into separate parts.

For me, one of the rewards of interdisciplinary thinking is discovering the nature of a discipline. If we learn through a single mode, we take that mode to be truthful. Interdisciplinary learning helps us know the limitations and prejudices of a discipline. It also helps us discover the benefits and insights of a discipline. It helps us understand how a discipline works, simply by forcing us to see one discipline in the light of another.

A city, to a sociologist, is a collection of group interactions, a set of class

Carlisle, Barbara. *"Music and Life."* American Music Teacher *44 (June/July 1995), 10–13. Reprinted with permission.*

structures or a set of human interactions. To a geologist, a city is defined by its soils, rock outcroppings, underground rivers and earthquakes. To a political scientist, it is a history of transfers of power; to an economist, the marketplace of goods and services; to a storyteller, the drama of hundreds of histories.

It is all these things. We begin to realize that it is important to know with what tools, through whose eyes we are looking. Minneapolis as seen by a student of migration patterns is different from Minneapolis as seen by a student of educational philosophy. The study of Minneapolis could be, in that way, the entire curriculum. As one sees the city each time through new eyes, one begins to learn how to look, change perspectives, validate perspectives and compare them with one another.

Unfortunately, a great deal of disciplinary teaching teaches the results of the discipline but not the nature of the discipline itself. The student learns the dates and names of history, but not how one discovers history or uses it. The student learns to add or subtract a column of figures, but never learns why figures are in columns, or when adding and subtracting are useful. The student learns the notes of the staff and the fingerings, but nothing about the way musical sound works or how the notation system translates ideas of a composer to written text.

Interdisciplinary teaching can force us to re-examine our own disciplines because we are looking at similar phenomena from several perspectives. Music notation, mathematical notation and language notation have things in common—and they have differences. Looking at them side by side helps us understand all of them.

Interdisciplinary work is not, however, simple or simply described. There are different paths, different processes in interdisciplinary teaching that accomplish different ends. I would like to distinguish among them.

Finding New Angles

Taking different approaches to a set of phenomena is one standard form of interdisciplinary teaching. Experts in disciplines look at something together and explain what they see. This is typical when people look at historical periods—the music, art, philosophy, politics and economics of the Renaissance, for example. The structure of a historical period can be represented as a grid of parallel lines—each discipline is one line.

The risk in this method: parallel lines do not meet. A network of cross lines has to be created. If we study only the history of painting style—Raphael influenced by Michelangelo in Rome—separately from the history of papal politics, we leave it up to the students to make connections between them. However, Raphael was superintendent of antiquities and architect of St. Peter's at the same time that he was decorating rooms at the Vatican. If we use Raphael as a cross line, we can learn about the relationships among archeology, papal politics, church economics, the organization of a master craftsman's studio and papal taste.

The hard work is creating the cross lines and helping students understand that the phenomenon they are studying is simultaneously a number of things. Independent disciplines help us see each different thing distinctly. It is interdisciplinary thinking that helps us see the simultaneity, the interactions and the influences—the way choices in one arena affect choices in another. The deliberate threading of the shuttle across the loom is the task of interdisciplinary work.

This means attending to the fact that where Handel lived and worked has a connection with the specific music he wrote, and that the positions of power of his patrons, the technical operations of organs in churches and the salaries of musicians all play a part in his aesthetic, even in the way we play the music today. Each of us does not have to know all of this in detail, but we can find the cross lines with other disciplines to help students connect with the world of an artist and his music.

Metaphoric Transfer

How do we learn something new in the first place? When a phenomenon presents itself to us, our best way of understanding it is to compare it to something we already know. We probably use metaphoric transfer often without exploiting its power.

Did you know, for example, that a llama is considered a type of camel? When I thought about it before—if I ever did—I thought the llama was a type of goat. I have seen both goats and camels up close. So now that I know that a llama is a camel, I understand it in a framework that lets me predict its behavior and its character quite differently from when I treated it in my mind as a goat.

This is not an earth-shattering discovery, but it illustrates the power of metaphor. We say someone bubbled over with enthusiasm, fumed with fury or exploded into laughter when no bubbles, fumes or explosions occurred. Metaphor is so basic to our process of communication, we often forget how central it is in teaching and learning. It is my hope that interdisciplinary teaching and learning in the arts will go beyond the threading of tapestries or the overlays of grids to illumination through metaphor.

We can study music in a city—the discipline of musicology—and we can also study the city as music. The city can also be a metaphor for understanding a piece of music. We hear the music and are told that this is Minneapolis. We know something about Minneapolis that we did not know before. Likewise we know something about the music because we know Minneapolis.

A fugue can be a metaphor for conversation—conversation can be a metaphor for a fugue. We can teach ideas about conflict, anticipation and resolution through musical dissonance and cadences. The ideas of solitude, comfort, discomfort or community—there is no end to the concepts that can be expressed through a range of nonverbal metaphors. Thinking about them expands our vocabulary for working with students. It demonstrates the connections among things and forces imaginative thinking.

We can use concepts in the same way. If we propose to dancers the idea of unity and they create forms and images that express it, we discover more things about the nature of unity through the dance that is created. If, at the same time, we put a camera and the idea of unity in the hands of a visual artist, the images become metaphors and through them we know something about unity we did not know before.

The real richness comes when the teacher and student find metaphors in several forms—for example, when the student discovers that musical harmonies can nest as spoons can nest, as birds can nest. We encourage lateral leaps of the imagination and make the understanding of music deeper and broader at the same time.

The Language of Form

One avenue for understanding the arts is the language of form. I speak here not so much of the symphonic form or the concerto form, but rather of critical language that attempts to describe the structure of experience. Concepts exist in the language of form to help students understand both music and other arts. If we explore symmetry, for example, in planar, melodic, architectural, volumetric, rhythmic or kinetic terms, we can see the formal concept of symmetry working in every art form. We recognize, understand and, eventually, use it.

Can you hear symmetry? Can you see it in space? In solids? Can you see it in movement? How is it that the left and right hands playing scales that start simultaneously at the top and bottom of the keyboard have symmetry? How is ABA form like a farmhouse with a porch in the middle and two pairs of windows on each side? These formal constructs can also be applied metaphorically to other human functions. Can there be symmetry in male and female relationships? Can there be symmetry in historical developments? We make metaphoric transfers from these formal concepts to human and societal behavior.

Other terms to explore in various media: asymmetry, contrast, parallelism, theme, variation, linearity, counterpoint, harmony, dissonance, balance and accent. When we look at ideas in visual, aural, kinesthetic, mathematical, musical, architectural, even sociological and political terms, we test our understanding of them. These formal constructs transcend time, locale and ethnicity. They help us identify characteristics of the arts and open doors to traveling across disciplines, styles and modalities.

None of these interdisciplinary strategies is unfamiliar to the music teacher, but perhaps we have not noticed that they *are* interdisciplinary modes of instruction. In our enthusiasm to teach music, we sometimes may be unaware of how important it is to include other disciplines in our teaching. When we become a little more conscious, a little more explicit about that intent, we help the student make useful, meaningful connections with both the music and the rest of the world.

Engaging Many Disciplines

There are also some enterprises that by their natures engage many disciplines. Space travel is one. Physicists, mathematicians, astronomers, engineers, aviators, metallurgists and plastics chemists—many people contribute elements to the whole process. Opera is such an enterprise. So is musical theater. These enterprises are disciplines in themselves. People are doing jobs within them are also working within their disciplines.

It is valuable to participate in collaborative work where each discipline functions at its highest level of excellence to create something that can exist only if all do their parts effectively. When there is interaction about the needs of each partner, then the work can illuminate the operating principles of each and become truly interdisciplinary. If each partner works in isolation, little is learned and the venture is less likely to succeed. Musicians have a great deal to contribute and a great deal to learn from projects in which they are an integral part of the creation of the work. If they are just bodies with instruments, brought in to accompany and follow a leader, the activity is less likely to be useful to them, and less likely to open up the world of music to other participants. In designing and participating in musical theater and opera, it is critical to keep the dialogue open, the creative energies focused and each element a full partner.

Responding to Each Other

Artists working in response to each other or to similar stimuli is another form of interdisciplinary work. I have seen drawing classes brought into the dance room to draw while dancers dance. I would say that there is only a superficial interdisciplinary activity going on. The painters are painting using the dancers as stimuli. Only when the painter and dancer talk, or decide to encounter something together—to make connections through something—are they really testing the natures of their disciplines and making new discoveries. Architects and dancers exchanging projects—dancers building structures and architects making human body forms in the presence of each other—begins to get more at the core of new understandings. Musicians and mathematicians together creating visual images of rhythms, or dancers and painters alternating roles as movers and drawers, helps both see and respond with new comprehension. These are the cross lines, the connective tissue that matters.

One Discipline Examines Another

Each of the arts has the possibility of being a field of study for other disciplines. We can study the sociology of visual artists, or the economics of performing arts organizations, or the psychology of acting, or the politics of unionism in the arts. The sociologists are still acting like sociologists; the psychologists are still doing psychology. But by looking at an artistic discipline, the observers bring their analysis to it and reveal it in new lights. If the artists look back, they too will understand their work better.

What Real Interdisciplinary Work Is Not

We must not confuse breaking down departmental or social barriers with interdisciplinary teaching and learning. One is bureaucratic and organizational and has to do with human dynamics and power manipulation. The other has to do with learning new ways of thinking and imagining. It certainly may be necessary to break down departmental barriers or to get out of the studio and meet other artists in order to begin to think across disciplines, but it is the thinking and working that counts. Neither is it sufficient to do simple side-by-side teaching or merely illustrate concurrent events without illuminating the connections.

I believe that each of the processes I have described can be stated in terms of goals for interdisciplinary work:

- to make meaningful and regular connections among different observers and observations when looking at the same phenomenon
- to make leaps of learning by using the power of metaphor to transfer what is known in one area to what is unknown in another, and thus to throw new light on both
- to comprehend, identify and use formal relationships and concepts across art forms and across all kinds of experience
- to engage several disciplines in making work that requires the expertise of all of them, and to learn from each other in doing so
- to explore one discipline through applying the knowledge and strategies of another to its issues or problems
- to exchange ways of working between disciplines in order to see relationships and to advance both

Why Bother?

One of the reasons interdisciplinary teaching is effective with students is the fact that it not only teaches information and skills, but it also helps students understand the kinds of inquiry that lead to the information. Consequently students find they are more connected to what is being learned. They get a lot that they can use. They begin to see the connection between schooling, lessons and life.

Interdisciplinary teaching helps students understand their own ways of thinking, learning and imagining. They discover their enthusiasms and their own connections. They find how their minds work, how their bodies learn and how they engage with phenomena. Such knowledge can enable them to be directors of their own learning and, ultimately, independent learners.

When students work with metaphor, concepts or alternative applications of analysis to the same issues, they are constantly challenged to make new connections, to *rethink* what they know and do. In a world whose technology and information systems are expanding daily, it is critical that students have lively imaginations and make connections between what they know and the new world presenting itself. I hope they also might make more informed judgments about their discoveries.

If students are not taught processes—various ways to encounter phenomena—the distance grows wider and wider between schooling and life, between the studio and the creation of music, and the experience of music in the life of the student. Students feel it. They turn away. Some never come back.

Finally, if teachers draw from two or more disciplines, they have to look at the real subject. That direct encounter with life has vitality itself. Students see that lessons are not alienated from the world. There is engagement—and perhaps even a desire to learn something. That is where education begins.

Natural Sciences

The Nature of Scientific Integration

William Bechtel

The Ethnocentrism of Disciplines

The frequent calls for greater interdisciplinarity is, to a great degree, the result of a perceived isolation of disciplines or what Campbell (1969) called the "ethnocentrism of disciplines." Campbell characterizes this ethnocentrism as "the symptoms of tribalism or nationalism or ingroup partisanship in the internal and external relationships of university departments, national scientific organizations, and academic disciplines" (p. 328). This gives rise, according to Campbell, is "a redundant piling up of highly similar specialties, leaving interdisciplinary gaps." Since such ethnocentrism, to the degree that it exists, constitutes a serious obstacle for successful cross-disciplinary work, it is worth considering how such ethnocentrism results from various of the characteristics of disciplines that I discussed in the previous section.

Let us begin with some of the factors driving ethnocentrism that Campbell identified in his analysis: institutional factors like departmental structures and professional organizations. Taking departments first, Campbell argues that departments do not simply divide up the conceptual territory benignly but alter the terrain to make certain parts of it more important. He hypothesizes that those topics which fall within the central area of the department's domain generally attain greater value as their practitioners control such matters as departmental chairpersonships, core curriculum and degree requirements, promotions and tenure. (For Campbell, "central" is identified topologically in his multi-dimension topology of disciplines. One can equally interpret these points by identifying centrality in terms of other factors like historical precedence.) For example, Campbell suggests that unless there is an unresolvable conflict between two figures in central areas in a department, the chairpersonship will rarely go to someone working in a peripheral specialty. Campbell also considers mechanisms which force peripheral specialties to become more directed toward the central focus of the department and not allied with related specialties in other departments. For example, to insure that their students survive, faculty at the periphery must require that their students become well prepared in the

Bechtel, William. Excerpt from "The Nature of Scientific Integration." Integrating Scientific Disciplines, W. Bechtel (ed.). Dordrecht: Martinus Nijhoff, 1986, 21–52. Reprinted with kind permission from Kluwer Academic Publishers.

I am most grateful to Adele Abrahamsen, who has given me extensive help. Rita Anderson, Lindley Darden, and Steve Fuller have also made many very helpful comments on earlier drafts of this paper, of which I am most appreciative. Some of the ideas presented here were developed during a Fellowship for Independent Study and Research, awarded by the National Endowment for the Humanities, which I held during 1983.

central specialties and encourage pursuit of these over cross-disciplinary work. This turn away from cross-disciplinary work with other departments is further exacerbated by competition between departments for resources, which may encourage the deprecation of other disciplines.

Saxberg and Newell (1983) interviewed a large number of individuals involved in or responsible for administrating interdisciplinary work and compiled a catalogue of objections that departmental members are prone to raise to interdisciplinary endeavors, of which the following were the most prominent:

> "(1) interdisciplinary research by its very nature is shallow, (2) the researcher's skills and competence are underutilized and so lose their edge, (3) joining an interdisciplinary programme is an escape from the rigor of the discipline and thus an indication of failure, (4) the quality of interdisciplinary research is suspect because of the absence of applicable standards of evaluation" (p. 208).

Without at this point evaluating the legitimacy of these complaints, we can treat them as evidence that across disciplines there is a significant amount of prejudice against department members crossing beyond the domains of their particular department. Saxberg and Newell also recorded complaints about how interdisciplinary endeavors harmed individuals' careers because senior faculty within a department would be less familiar with the cross-disciplinary projects and would tend to discredit publications co-authored with members of other disciplines. As a result, they came to the conclusion "that a non-tenured faculty member should not become involved in interdisciplinary research" (208).

Training within a department can be a factor in developing ethnocentric attitudes in students, since such training serves not only to inculcate into students the skills and values of a particular discipline, but also a sense of group loyalty and distrust of other disciplines. Gold and Gold (1983) describe the extent of this experience of being socialized into a discipline:

> "The training and socialization that the student in a discipline undergoes lead to an identification with the disciplinary community that comes prior to, and is generally regarded as more persistent than, identification with a specific employer or particular task. In combination with normative differences these feelings of identification and loyalty to the disciplinary community can, and often do, develop to the point of professional chauvinism, providing barriers severe enough to defeat interdisciplinary collaboration at the earliest phases. A milder manifestation of community identification is that individuals from different disciplines tend at first to regard each other as exchangeable representative specimens of their respective disciplines" (94).

Campbell also explores the ethnocentric aspects of professional organizations and journals. He argues that the way professional organizations and journals are organized provides additional pressures to keep researchers' attention directed inwards to the core of their discipline rather than to related specialties in other disciplines. For example, referees for journals require one to cite appropriate work in the discipline represented by the journal and to use the research tools approved by it, giving less credence to citations and research tools of other disciplines. To gain a hearing by the discipline with which one wants to collaborate one must become almost as competent in that discipline as (or perhaps more competent than) its own members, clearly a foreboding task.

Campbell focused predominantly on the organizational and institutional factors contributing to the ethnocentrism of disciplines. He does indicate, as well, factors impinging on the cognitive activities of individual researchers. One of the most significant is the constraint of time which limits not only one's ability to keep up with journal literature, but also one's ability to maintain contacts with others in professions of interest. These are important in terms of learning of recent findings that may affect one's work as well as learning newly developed techniques for research. Pursuing each of these requires a commitment and investment, an investment that may be taken away from one's core area.

Other cognitive aspects of disciplines also help enforce ethnocentrism. Not only can the research techniques, theories, and background knowledge of a discipline be a barrier against those from other disciplines, they also represent an investment made by members of the discipline itself. Like all investments, researchers may not want to relinquish them. Shapin (1982) comments:

> "The analysis in terms of socially acquired technical competences may even be extended to encompass scientists' investments in the practical or interpretive line of their previous work. If a group of scientists have accomplished a body of publicly available research in which they argue for a given point of view, theory or interpretation, they may well wish to defend that position from attack and display its value and scope over other positions—even if they are technically able to work from another cognitive or practical orientation. What is involved is a strategy for defending and furthering interests, based on complex calculations about the consequences of various courses of action." (165).

Shapin analyses a number of historical conflicts, including the conflict over taxonomical approaches between morphologically trained botanists and those trained in cytology or genetics, in these terms.

These differences can arise even when one is not trying to push one's investment in a particular methodology but is trying to cooperate on an interdisciplinary team. Thus, Barmark and Wallen (1980) in describing an interdisciplinary forest ecology project, note intense conflict between those who were conversant and comfortable with the mathematics and systems models being used in the project, and those more comfortable with traditional biological techniques. The results were the development of incommensurable pieces of data that could not be readily assimilated to the theoretical model being developed.[1] Gold and Gold (1983) present these differences in conceptual frameworks as more general problems for bridging disciplinary boundaries, making it difficult for researchers from different disciplines to agree on a common project.

> "As a result of cognitive, subject matter, and normative differences, scientists of different disciplines may have difficulty agreeing upon appropriate sets of goals, an appropriate framework for pursuing those goals, and an appropriate evaluative framework" (93).

Disciplines are also divided by standards for reviewing research. As I noted above, such standards are critical both to maintaining quality within the discipline and to giving direction to individual researchers. But this can often be an obstacle to developing cross-disciplinary connections and so foster ethnocentrism (Russell, 1983). An example will dramatize this effect. In American experimental psychology experimenters tend to utilize a particular conception of data, experimental design, and statistical analysis that emphasizes control over some factors and systematic manipulation of others, rendering all subjects as comparable "units." Piaget and Inhelder's seminal work in developmental psychology generally did not fit this conception; much of their data was generated using the "revised clinical method," by which different children are presented with somewhat different questions or situations depending on the responses they are giving. For Piaget and Inhelder's contributions to become more widely accepted, it was necessary for their major findings to be replicated by others in the American manner—that is, presenting children in rigidly-defined age ranges with standardized questions in standardized or counterbalanced order, and submitting the results to inferential statistical analysis using conventional levels of significance.[2]

So far I have approached ethnocentrism as largely a secondary consequence of the social and institutional aspects of disciplines. But at the stage of discipline founding, there may often be a deliberate attempt to foster an ethnocentric perspective and to set one's own discipline off from any others. Gaining the recognition and status of a discipline can often be very important, for it is as a discipline that one can have academic appointments, award degrees, gain grant support, and the like. Several sociologists have thus characterized the process of discipline creation in conflict terms. Bourdieu, for example, introduces the concept of a "field" (using the term in a very different way than Darden and Maull) in which disciplines struggle to establish their stake:

> "As a system of objective relations between positions already won (in previous struggles), the scientific field is the locus of a competitive struggle, in which the *specific* issue at stake is the monopoly of *scientific authority,* defined inseparably as technical capacity and social power, or, to put it another way, the monopoly of *scientific competence,* in the sense of a particular agent's socially recognized

capacity to speak and act legitimately (i.e., in an authorised and authoritative way in scientific matters" (Bourdieu, 1975, p. 19).

When one focuses on the activities of creating disciplines, one can see at the outset a powerful force for making disciplines ethnocentric. Setting up such a structure is not a neutral activity, for the way it is done and who does it may determine what status particular individuals will hold in the science. Creating a discipline is a means of gaining credibility for oneself as a scientist. Thus, Cambrosio and Keating (1983), in chronicling the development of chronobiology as a separate discipline, offer a reason why it was so important for some practitioners to gain disciplinary status:

> "To constitute oneself in a disciplinary form, which defines the rules of the rules of the game, is to release oneself from the domination of one's competitors and to dictate, in relative autonomy, one's own rules of the game: the disciplinary form thus functions as a machine which (re)-produces its own rules of legitimation" (328).

This characterization of the scientific activities in economic terms may seem to constitute a denial of the cognitive pursuits of disciplines. However, it need not. A significant part of carving out a disciplinary stake (Cambrosio and Keating's term) is to establish a distinctive intellectual context of research. Thus, in describing the endeavors of Franz Halberg in establishing chronobiology, Cambrosio and Keating describe how Halberg developed the notion of rhythms in direct contrast with the notion of homeostasis, which he viewed as the central notion in the competing discipline of physiology. Coleman (1985), who does not work within this conception of science as economic conflict, nonetheless, in discussing Bernard, describes how he was developing a cognitive framework to distinguish experimental physiology for both vitalism and experimental chemistry. Thus, even the cognitive endeavor of creating a new discipline often involves drawing boundaries between oneself and others which can be the fuel for ethnocentrism within the discipline.

In this section I have discussed a number of factors that contribute to the differentiation of disciplines and their ethnocentrism. Recognizing why disciplines have an ethnocentric character is important as we now turn to considering the process of crossing disciplinary lines to integrate various endeavors in science.

Reasons for Crossing Disciplinary Boundaries

It may seem almost sacrilegious to some people to seek reasons for crossing disciplinary lines and becoming interdisciplinary. Many have operated as if being interdisciplinary or participating in interdisciplinary endeavors is a good in itself that does not require a justification. However, there may be something pathological, as Gusdorf (1977) suggests, in many calls for interdisciplinarity. They may simply represent an inability to accept the complexity and accompanying fractionation of modern science and a desire for "a reaffirmation of a lost wholeness" (p. 581). There are, however, somewhat better reasons that can be adduced for participating in cross-disciplinary endeavors in science. Campbell's discussion of ethnocentrism in science which I discussed in the preceding section was part of a call for a more interdisciplinary approach to science. While he would disown the "Leonardesque aspiration" of individual omniscience, he endorses interdisciplinarity as a vehicle for omniscience within the species. Adopting for a moment this *a priori* perspective on human knowledge, I can suggest two additional benefits which are complementary to the one noted by Campbell. First, problems that receive insufficient attention primarily because of disciplinary ethnocentrism could get the attention due them in a fully interdisciplinary environment. Second, if ethnocentrism were to wane, scholars would find it easier to locate other scholars who could aid their particular inquiry.

Although it sounds like a worthy goal, one may question how important the kind of omniscience Campbell advocates really is. One may also question my extension of his view by asking whether there really are significant problem areas untouched by current disciplines. As it stands, scientists and their disciplines tend to be politically opportunistic, looking for problem areas into which they can expand. As a result, most problems ripe for solution are likely to be attacked by disciplines capable of solving them. Moreover, interdisciplinarity is not without costs.[3] One is that the heritage of what a science has accomplished is only preserved through the disciplinary structure. If there were no disciplinary cohesion, the result might not be greater progress, but a loss of past wisdom (necessitating retreading old ground and re-committing old mistakes). Second, if there were not a cohesive discipline, there would not be the kind of peer review process that, as discussed above, has been instrumental in guiding research and ensuring that mistaken ideas are rejected. Third, disciplines tend to develop specialized discourse in order to develop their insights into a particular domain. While these specialized modes of discourse sometimes constitute an obstacle to interdisciplinary discourse, sacrificing them might also prove counterproductive.

Rather than continuing in this *a priori* vein, it will be more productive to look at the actual motivations scientists have for crossing disciplinary boundaries. (Scientists do not always reveal their motives for pursuing a particular line of inquiry; hence, some of what follows will involve attempts to interpolate the motivation from the inquiry pursued.) The kinds of factors that motivate crossing disciplinary boundaries can be both sociological and cognitive. Since most of the emphasis in this volume will be on cognitive motivations for cross-disciplinary boundaries, let me briefly mention some of the more social factors that sociologists and social historians have identified as motivations for engaging in cross-disciplinary work. This list of motivating factors is not intended to be exhaustive, but rather to provide a starting perspective that can be extended through further investigations.

An important consideration suggested by social studies of scientific communities is that while there is often a strong bias towards ethnocentrism of disciplines, there is also a significant amount of openness in the scientific community. While the notion of an "invisible college" suggests a closed unit, and much of the analysis has focused on the importance of the central figures in such "invisible colleges," Crane (1969) herself has also noted the importance of openness in such units:

> "Most problem areas are open to influences from other fields. The desire for originality motivates scientists to maintain contacts with scientists and scientific work in areas different from their own in order to enhance their ability to develop new ideas in their own areas" (p. 349).

Hagstrom (1970) claims that many researchers end up working in more than one specialty at a time and do change specialties over time, albeit the changes may be between closely related specialties. While recognizing that for most individual scientists, the discipline in which one is trained constrains the potential for later changes, Chubin (1976) proposes that the boundaries of scientific specialties are often fluid intellectually and socially. This fluidity may involve members actually working in multiple specialties or switching between them as well as the inclusion of outliers in the specialty who serve as conduits between specialty groups.

Sociologists have given the label "migration" to the phenomenon of scientists changing from one area of science to another. The most commonly adduced reason for such migration is opportunity for advancement. For example, Ben-David and Collins (1966) trace Wundt's move into psychology to the lack of opportunities for career development in physiology. According to their analysis, Wundt left a high prestige field where opportunities for advancement were very limited, physiology, for a less prestigious discipline, philosophy, where he nonetheless recognized an opportunity to develop a new research domain. In Mullins' (1972) characterization of Delbruck's migration into biology, the factors were not so much personal ambition as a sense that major new developments were not in the offing in physics, the recognition of problems that could be addressed using the methods of physics on biological problems, and finally the hope that these biological pursuits might end up forcing a revision in the understanding of basic principles in physics. Lemain, MacLeod, Mulkay, and Wingart (1976), in introducing a collection of papers on the emergence of new scientific disciplines, identify migration as a factor in developing new disciplines and indicate a variety of social factors that can lead to migration:

> "Scientific migration is not a random process, for the scientists moving into a new field tend to come from other areas with specifiable characteristics. In particular, they come from research areas which have experienced a pronounced decline in the significance of current results; from areas where there are few or no avenues or research easily available; from areas whose members have special

competence in or knowledge of techniques which appear to have wider application; and from areas which have been disrupted, often by events originating outside the research community, and whose members have consequently no firm commitment to an established field. They tend to move into areas which appear to offer special opportunity for productive research, for the utilization of their particular skills, and, consequently, for career development" (5).[4]

While migration may be a particularly startling way of crossing disciplinary boundaries, the notion of interdisciplinary research is more commonly applied to researchers who fundamentally retain their disciplinary identity but pursue work that involves utilizing and interacting with another discipline. Here too there can be social factors motivating the activities. From the same interviews where they derived a number of reasons for not engaging in cross-disciplinary endeavors, especially if one lacks tenure, Saxberg and Newell (1983) also elicited a number of positive benefits that were found in cross-disciplinary activities:

> "(1) funding . . . may be available for time released for research, (2) an approved budget may include allowance for travel to professional meetings, printing costs of journal articles, supplies, computer time, etc., hard to come by within a university's regular operating budget, (3) the opportunity exists to generate papers and articles for publication, (4) tenure, promotion, and merit may be favourably effected by extensive and successful research, (5) new avenues of teaching and research may open up as a result of interdisciplinary involvement, (6) interactions and collaboration with colleagues may prove stimulating and ensure research productivity, and (7) interested graduate students with a commitment may be available and supported to assist in the research project" (209).

While the negative aspects they identified raised the prospect that cross-disciplinary endeavors will not be valued, these positive features all point to the fact that opportunities may be found in cross-disciplinary endeavors where there may be limited prospects in the heartland of the discipline. In choosing to work intra- or interdisciplinarily, then, one may be making a calculated gamble as to whether to pursue low probability but highly valued activities within the mainstream of the discipline or higher probability but low valued activities at the fringes where contact with other disciplines is possible.[5]

Besides the social factor of perceived opportunity in cross-disciplinary work, there is almost always also a strong cognitive factor, at least amongst those designing the project. One very common cognitive factor influencing a decision to cross disciplinary lines is a recognition that the problem one is encountering cannot be adequately dealt with within one's own discipline. Darden and Maull (1977) raise this as a common reason for developing what they call interfield theories (see section 5 below). One of the things investigators might seek in another discipline is a mechanism that can explain the phenomenon which has been identified within one discipline but cannot be explained within it. Both biochemistry and the synthetic theory of evolution can be seen as stemming from the inability to explain phenomena within one discipline alone. In both these cases, the mechanism behind the phenomena resided at different levels. Thus, the mechanism responsible for physiological processes like oxidation and fermentation required appeal to the chemical level while, according to Darden's analysis (this volume) the problem of speciation could not be addressed at either the level of natural selection or genetic replication and required appeal to a new level at which isolating mechanisms could divide populations.

A second reason is found in cases where the problem was not one of finding a mechanism, but rather of acquiring guidance in developing a theoretical explanation. The exchanges between psychology and linguistics both in the late 19th century (Blumenthal, forthcoming) and in the 1960s (Reber, forthcoming) are partly due to the fact that first linguists and later psychologists saw in the other discipline models that might be fruitfully used to solve problems within their own discipline. These were not merely analogies in the sense in which nuclear physicists drew upon analogies from astronomy. The relationship was thought to be much more integrative, since the generative models for one phenomenon (e.g., language) were thought to be readily extended to provide models for the other (cognitive activity). Several of the papers below show a similar reason for crossing disciplinary boundaries. For example, Mason and Anderson are crossing the disciplinary lines between animal ethnology and human cognitive psychology in the hope of gaining a theoretical perspective for guiding their inquiry in their own discipline: Mason appeals to cognitive frameworks that have been established first to understand human behavior so as to understand animals, while Anderson is turning to animal ethnology for help in finding ways to incorporate ecological perspectives into human cognitive psychology. Kauffman presents a slightly more complex case of the same thing. While trying to bridge the gaps between evolutionary and developmental biology, he appeals to yet a third area, mathematical thermodynamics. Using models drawn from that field, he hopes to represent the regulatory system in the genome. This provides a basis for discovering implications for evolutionary theory.

A third reason for working across disciplinary lines is the awareness of incommensurabilities in the approaches to the same domain by different disciplines. One response to such incommensurabilities would be to simply affirm the rightness of one of the approaches. Another would be to press each against the other, in the hope that the dialectical interaction might advance the understanding in both enterprises. This is exemplified in recent work on language aphasias discussed by Richardson in this volume. This work began with the recognition that the kinds of functions aphasia researchers considered important in accounting for language disruption (comprehension and production) were orthogonal to the set of distinctions which linguists take as central (phonology, syntax, semantics, pragmatics, and lexical structure). Initially, the endeavor was to recast the aphasia research in terms of the linguistics distinctions (so as to treat Broca's aphasia as involving a syntactic deficit—see Bradley, Garrett, and Zurif, 1980). Now the aphasia work is suggesting that a further modification may be required in the linguistics categories so as to focus on a distinction between automated and non-automated functions (Grodzinsky, Swinney, and Zurif, 1983). Thus, a dialectic is occurring between different approaches to distinguishing cognitive function, with ideas from each discipline being modified to fit the other.

A fourth cognitive motivation for crossing disciplinary boundaries is found in the paper of Rumbaugh and Sterritt in this volume. In their work they are not seeking a mechanism at another level to explain a phenomenon observed first at one level. Rather, they are trying to explain the origin of a phenomenon that has traditionally fallen within the domain of one discipline, but where the origin requires entering the domain of another discipline. Thus, intelligence is an attribute much discussed in human psychology. To explain its origin, however, requires a phylogentic inquiry. An attempt to trace its origins, however, requires one to enter the domains of disciplines where the concept of intelligence has not played a central role. As in the interchange between aphasia work and linguistics, a dialectical process results from this inquiry. In turning to the study of other animals to try to explain the origin of intelligence, Rumbaugh and Sterritt discover the need to develop a new conception of intelligence, since its expression in other animals cannot be detected by the same measures as are employed in linguistic species.

Sometimes the basis for building a bridge to another discipline may not originate with any special interest in building such a bridge. This is found in the case of Savage-Rumbaugh and Hopkins. While the proposal they have developed is here considered from the perspective of how it might enhance cognitive science, which has already developed as an interdisciplinary endeavor focused on human cognition, that is not the motivation for developing their proposal. Rather, they recognized that the set of research techniques they were using in teaching forms of language to primates yielded results that did not fit either the models of animal learning or animal ethology. To handle these results, Savage-Rumbaugh and Hopkins propose a theoretical framework with a central emphasis on intentional communication. This framework then offers a suggestive basis for extending the cross-disciplinary work already occurring in cognitive science.

The reasons noted here are ones that have provided motivations for scientists to cross-disciplinary boundaries; they do not depend on any idealized conception of knowledge but on problems that arise in the actual conduct of research. Drawing attention to these motivations is important for two reasons: (1) as these factors are ones that have drawn scientists to cross-disciplinary endeavors in the past, they are ones likely to do so again; and (2) the motivations scientists have for pursuing cross-disciplinary work may well affect the kinds of products that result from that work. As the early parts of this section acknowledge, these motivations may be both social and cognitive. We must bear these different motivations for crossing disciplinary boundaries in mind as we turn now to the institutional and cognitive products of interdisciplinary work.

The Institutional Products of Cross-Disciplinary Research

Just as I have adopted the term "discipline" to refer to the units of science in as theoretically neutral a manner as possible, I intend for the term "integrating" to be understood in a neutral manner, covering various possible modes of relationship that can be developed between disciplines. When attempts to cross-disciplinary boundaries are at least partly successful, both social and theoretical arrangements tend to emerge. In this section I will focus on the social and institutional structures that result from cross-disciplinary endeavors and reserve discussion of their theoretical and empirical products to the next section.

In the first section I noted some of the organizational and institutional characteristics of disciplines, such as having academic departments, professional organizations, and journals. I also explored some of the reasons why they are important to the survival of the discipline. Similar organizational and institutional structures must be developed by cross-disciplinary researchers if they are to flourish and maintain themselves. For example, researchers must find ways of training new researchers if the cross-disciplinary project is to continue. As I indicated earlier, one vital function of academic departments is to educate new students to accept the goals and employ the techniques and theories produced by the research endeavor. Journals and professional organizations provide channels for the communication and transmission of ideas and for establishing reputations. Hence, it is unsurprising that interdisciplinary endeavors often seek to establish comparable structures.

The importance of such institutional and organization mechanisms can be recognized by considering the numerous handicaps their absence places on researchers. Building a community of co-workers can be very difficult without such mechanisms. When Delbruck made his first forays into biology, he was still in a department of physics, where few graduate students were interested in joining his endeavor. Many of the early converts to the phage program came through Delbruck finding an alternative institutional arrangement—running a summer phage course at Cold Springs Harbor. Through this course other researchers were educated and recruited into the program (see Mullins, 1972). Job opportunities in the academic world follow departmental structure, making it difficult for those working outside of established departmental units to find employment. Professional organizations are often the ones responsible for putting on conferences and publishing journals, so without such organizations, scholars encounter difficulties in getting their ideas and results published. Finally, the structure of grant-giving agencies often mirrors the organizational structure of academia, so that those whose work falls outside of the established boundaries often have difficulty getting financial support.

A factor that needs to be considered is whether establishing such social and institutional arrangements has the effect of creating new disciplines out of cross-disciplinary endeavors. This seems to be what happened in the case of biochemistry, which began with researchers drawn from a number of different research areas with focuses on different levels of organization, but resulted in a new discipline with not only its own conceptual unity (which is discussed in

Holmes' and Bechtel's papers) but also its own social and institutional unity (see Kohler, 1982). But this is not the only possible outcome. One can maintain a much looser organizational and institutional structure for the cross-disciplinary endeavor. Its institutions can coexist with the basic departmental institutions and not replace them.

There have been a number of experiments in recent decades whereby institutions have tried to alter departmental structures to combat their role in furthering ethnocentrism (some of these are discussed in Campbell, 1969; see also Malchup, 1982). The simplest approach has been to develop inter-departmental programs or committees in which faculty may hold secondary appointments and in which students can receive degrees. (The University of Chicago is well known for such committees as the Committee on Evolutionary Biology.) In many universities, such committees are authorized degree-granting units, whereas in others the degrees are still governed by one of the participating departments. To be sure, there are a variety of tensions in such arrangements, both for students and faculty. If faculty hold their primary appointment within a disciplinary department, evaluations of them for tenure and salary will likely follow the policies of the discipline, which may or may not be compatible with significant investment in cross-disciplinary activities. For students, a major challenge is often finding employment. Since the structure of cross-disciplinary units varies quite widely between institutions, students may find difficulty matching their training to the requirements for departmental appointments. For example, they may not be judged qualified to teach the core courses of the home disciplines. A further problem with such structures is that they are viewed as a threat to existing departments, especially when there is a limit to resources. (See Campbell, 1969, for a discussion of the dissolution of Yale University's Institute for Human Relations as a result of pressure from other departments. See also Saxberg and Newell, 1983, for accounts of the difficulties such arrangements face.)

Another approach is to employ an administrative division orthogonal to that which differentiates departments. Such an approach might divide faculty into colleges independently of their department affiliation. I am aware of one case in which college membership rather than departmental membership determined one's office location (University of California, Santa Cruz) and one in which each college had its own departments, resulting in considerable duplication of courses (Rutgers University). In both of these cases, changes since the mid-70s have brought these schools to structures more like that of the University of California, San Diego, in which college affiliations exist but not usually determine faculty location or result in duplication of departments. Another approach, which seems fairly stable where it has been tried, is to do away with departmental divisions and simply have very broadly defined units, such as the School of Social Sciences at the University of California, Irvine. These have been meccas for those academics with a strong interdisciplinary bent but may be viewed less favorably by those with more traditional disciplinary interests.

Another vehicle for institutionalizing cross-disciplinary endeavors within academia is through research institutes. (In discussing research institutes, one should bear in mind that probably the majority of such institutes are undisciplinary structures, not vehicles of interdisciplinary activities.) Insofar as these institutes are organized primarily for research, they avoid some of the conflicts that are encountered by developing educational programs orthogonal to the departmental structure of the university. (An educational function can still occur in such institutes, but it usually involves students working on specific projects with faculty from their own departments. Thus, their status is that of a research assistant within the institute; they fulfill their degree requirements in a standard department.) However, there are still a host of difficulties facing such institutes. Externally, they are in competition with other components of the university for resources. Internally, there is often competition between researchers from different disciplinary orientations as to how to define the research objectives of the institute. One might expect that once established, such institutes would further cross-disciplinary endeavors, since many of the difficulties that might impede individual projects could be worked out at the initial establishment of the institute. A study by Birnbaum (1978) covering several interdisciplinary projects in the United States, however, does not support that assumption:

> "Permanent institutes with full managerial hierarchies, permanent staffs, expensive equipment and permanent space were found to provide significantly more integrating devices but were not found associated with higher performing projects, to provide significantly greater interdisciplinary activity, or to reduce the time spent by principal investigators in planning and assembling resources when compared to projects operating independently of institutes" (95).

(For further evaluation of cross-disciplinary research in specially designated institutes and a discussion of the problems encountered by such institutes see Saxberg, Newell, and Mar, 1979; Teich, 1979; and Cutler, 1979.)

It seems clear that there are significant problems in arriving at a suitable organizational relationship for cross-disciplinary research in academic institutions. Some of these difficulties are overcome when the place of employment is outside the university and part of the corporate world. Here, project goals can provide focus for research endeavors. However, what is often lost in the corporate world is the commitment to pursuing basic science. One of the rare exceptions where a corporation pursued basic research was Bell Laboratories. Here researchers from a number of disciplines were able to carry out basic research either within a disciplinary orientation or by integrating into interdisciplinary teams. However, this opportunity may have largely been an artifact of the peculiar legal status of American Telephone and Telegraph Company; its recent court-ordered reorganization has removed much of this support and what remains of the research efforts seem to be directed in a more applied vein. Thus, basic research seems still to be the most common in the university setting, and here the institutional obstacles to cross-disciplinary endeavors do not seem to have any totally satisfactory answer.

At the level of professional societies and journals, on the other hand, there are far fewer obstacles to developing feasible cross-disciplinary arrangements. There are numerous examples of professional societies which deliberately try to draw members from several disciplines whose interests connect (sometimes as a result of sharing a common domain). These societies often put on their own conferences and publish journals that cross disciplinary lines. A clear example is the Cognitive Science Society, which puts on an annual conference and publishes the journal *Cognitive Science.* The society and journal are explicitly committed to fostering interdisciplinary communication between cognitive psychology, artificial intelligence, linguistics, neurobiology, and philosophy. The existence of such organizations is not to suggest that they are a panacea for those interested in cross-disciplinary endeavors in the area of focus. Even when practitioners from a variety of disciplines all espouse an interest in a common phenomenon like cognition, they need not understand it in the same way. Moreover, they may carry over their standards for doing research to the interdisciplinary arena, and so be hypercritical of those from other disciplines who do not adhere to the same standards of research. This makes the task of organizing conferences and editing interdisciplinary journals a particularly risky endeavor, for one can easily offend and alienate those disciplines with whom one is trying to interact.

Despite the difficulties confronting these various organizational and institutional structures for cross-disciplinary research, it is clear that there is an alternative to the institutional and organizational model of traditional disciplines. We can speak of these arrangements of cross-disciplinary committees and institutes in universities, interdisciplinary professional organizations and interdisciplinary journals as characterizing "interdisciplinary research clusters". While these clusters may not provide all the support that are provided by more traditional disciplinary units, they nonetheless do allow for research collaboration and cross-disciplinary communication. As well, they can also provide a focal point for funding. To return to the example of cognitive science, there has been a rapid development of cross-disciplinary academic programs in this area, especially in the United States, which have been fostered in part by the targeting of funds for this purpose by the Department of Defense and by private institutions like the Sloan Foundation.

To illustrate further the idea of an interdisciplinary research cluster, we can consider one of the historical examples of a cross-disciplinary project discussed in this volume, the evolutionary synthesis. The evolutionary synthesis contrasts with that of the other historical case considered, that of biochemistry, in that in this case no new unified discipline was established to which practitioners transferred their disciplinary identity. The disciplines incorporated into the synthesis, primarily transmission genetics, population genetics, systematics, and paleontology, and secondarily, cytology, embryology, and morphology,[6] remain distinct, having their own departments in some larger institutions and, in any case, having their own identities as specialties as a result of having professional organizations and journals. What happened is that, alongside the established departments and professional organizations, new ones emerged that served the interdisciplinary function. Thus one finds interdepartmental committees (The Committee on Evolutionary Biology at the University of Chicago), interdisciplinary societies like the Evolution Society, and multi-disciplinary journals like *Evolution.*

One final question that needs to be addressed is whether one can identify factors that determine whether the social and institutional arrangements in any particular interdisciplinary endeavor will take the form of a new discipline or of an interdisciplinary research cluster. Several factors affect this decision. One is whether there is sufficiently unified domain that could provide the focus for a discipline. This may have been one of the factors that led to the formation of a new discipline in biochemistry. While evolutionary phenomena do constitute a domain, it is both an extremely broad domain and one that includes almost all of the domains of the disciplines constitutive of that interdisciplinary research cluster. This made it impractical for evolutionary science to constitute itself as a single discipline. A second factor is the degree to which those interested in the cross-disciplinary area can maintain their status within their host disciplines. In the case of biochemistry, the case has been made that those researchers interested in questions at the border of chemistry and physiology could not acquire significant status and appointments in either discipline, motivating the development of autonomous departments and disciplinary organizations (see Kohler, 1982). Cambrosio and Keating present a similar view of Halberg's drive to create a separate discipline of chronobiology as a result of the inability to gain status within established disciplines. When, on the other hand, researchers can achieve status within their own discipline, the alternative organizational and institutional arrangements provided by interdisciplinary research clusters may suffice and the demand to form separate disciplines may be less urgent.

There are also significant reasons for practitioners in interdisciplinary areas to maintain allegiances to their initial discipline. Often the particular problems and modes of approach to problems, even in the interdisciplinary area, are brought from one's original discipline and so one continues to have strong ties to other members of one's discipline not involved in the interdisciplinary activity. Then researchers may have no incentive to break free from their own disciplines, but only to enrich their endeavors by contact with those working on related problems who happen to come from other disciplinary backgrounds.

While it may be too early to make reliable prognoses about the contemporary cases of cross-disciplinary endeavors discussed in this volume, we can make tentative projections about whether they are likely to follow the tradition of forming interdisciplinary research clusters or of forming separate disciplines. In none of the cases do the ingredients appear to be present that would dictate the formation of new disciplines. For one, the domains involved are not tightly unified. The domain of cognitive and animal ethology, for example, would have to include much of the domain of cognitive science (minus, for the most part, those components primarily directed at language activity of the kind found in humans) and animal ethology. The other cases involve possible extensions to two already functioning interdisciplinary research clusters, one in evolutionary biology and one in cognitive science. Adding to an existing cluster is unlikely to produce a more consolidated disciplinary structure. What may be more likely is that the proposed expansions would make the clusters so large that they will have to divide. However, it seems most likely that the products of such divisions would still remain interdisciplinary clusters, not structured disciplines. Thus, one should not expect the formation of a new discipline for any of the contemporary cases examined in this volume.

Conceptual Products of Cross-Disciplinary Endeavors

By far the topic that is of most concern in the papers that follow concerns the kind of conceptual connections that are involved in or result from attempts to link research in different disciplines. The historical sessions have focused on the kinds of cognitive structures that developed in the case of biochemistry and the evolutionary synthesis while the authors of the papers focusing on current cross-disciplinary endeavors try to lay out conceptual frameworks through which cross-disciplinary research might proceed. The reason for this focus is obvious. One of the chief problems those engaged in interdisciplinary research readily recognize is that researchers from different fields approach problems with different conceptual tools and conceptual orientations. Kuhn (1970) spoke of these as "paradigms" and "disciplinary matrices" and, while there is room for plenty of disagreement as to the precise character of these conceptual frameworks, there is no doubt that investigators from different disciplines do construe their problems differently, use different theories to characterize the problem domain and possible solutions, and use different research techniques to deal with the problems. Given these differences, researchers coming from different disciplines may find serious problems in communicating and working together.[7] As a result, most meta-scientists who have examined interdisciplinary projects stress the need to develop integrating conceptual frameworks in which cross-disciplinary research can proceed.

Often appeals for scientific integration have been accompanied by elaborate schemes in terms of which all the disciplines of knowledge could be brought together. Two of the best known of these in the 20th century are the program of unified science proposed by the Logical Positivists and general systems theory of Von Bertalanffy. Common to both programs is the idea of a general integrating framework in which all human knowledge can be linked. A principal endeavor of the Unity of Science Project was to produce an "International Encyclopedia of Unified Science" which, according to Neurath (1938), was

> "to integrate the scientific disciplines, so to unify them, so to dovetail them together, that advances in one will bring about advances in the others" (p. 24).

The program was never carried out, but the strategy that was to be used to accomplish this integration is clear, especially from the contribution of Carnap (1938) to the original project. The tool for unification was theory reduction.

As celebrated as that model of unification is, it is interesting that not a single paper in this volume employs the theory reduction model, or any of the subsequent modifications that have been proposed. One might well be puzzled by this inasmuch as a number of the writers are philosophers of science. To try to resolve that puzzle and to show that kind of connections actually are salient in these cases, I will begin by considering the deficiencies of the formal theory reduction model as a basis for cross-disciplinary research and then turn to alternative models of cognitive integration.

The model of theory reduction portrays the theories of different disciplines as being related deductively. (See Nagel, 1961, for the classical presentation of theory reduction, Schaffner, 1967, for some important modifications, and Ruse, 1973, for an attempt to use theory reduction as a unifying scheme for biology). Causey (1977) provides a recent account of what unity of science via theory reduction would involve, which I will employ as the basis for this discussion.[8] Causey views nature as consisting of levels, where entities at higher levels are structured wholes comprised of entities at lower levels. At the higher level one has a theory that characterizes the behavior of the structured wholes. The first task in performing a reduction is to provide a specification of these structured wholes in terms of their composition from lower level entities. Then one can identify the terms referring to objects at the higher level with lower level terms specifying their composition. One must similarly identify predicates in the upper level theory with those whose extension includes the structured wholes specified in lower-level terms. As long as one is willing to allow that entities apparently similar at the upper level may have diverse composition, and that similar lower level units may be components of different higher level units, the ability to carry out this much of the program is unproblematic. But it is a project that is, in itself, uninteresting. All it shows is that we can characterize the entities of the higher level in terms of their constitution of lower level entities.

The interest in the reductionist program comes with the requirement that the law statements about structured wholes (as stated in the lower-level theory) be derivable from law statements about their components and statements of prevailing environmental conditions. It is with the last condition that the program of unification of science through microreduction becomes problematic, for it is far from obvious that the necessary derivation will always be possible. Without offering a detailed response to Causey (see McCauley, 1981, for such a response), I will simply note a couple of the factors that make the ability to develop the necessary derivation of properties of structured wholes from properties of components problematic.

Although Causey's formal treatment does not require this, in his discussion he proposes that those engaged in a microreduction research program would identify the properties of the components of structured wholes by studying them when they are not incorporated into the structured wholes (Causey's non-bound condition), and then derive their behavior in the structured whole from this plus statements describing the organized structure in which they are bound and prevailing environmental conditions. It seems by no means obvious that one will learn all the properties of the parts when one studies them in the non-bound condition; in particular, one may question whether one will learn how they function when bound into structured wholes. If the non-bound and the bound properties of components are different, then we will have to incorporate knowledge of their behavior in bound conditions into the lower level account. This raises the question as to how much one is permitted, in the course of carrying out a microreduction, to modify the account of the components so as to support a derivation of the behavior of structured wholes from it. Causey is concerned about this problem, since unlimited revisibility can lead to trivializing the problem of reduction by simply allowing us to incorporate all the laws of higher level science as additional laws at the lower level. However, he has no specific proposals as to limit the acceptable modifications.

Hooker (1981) is much more open to fundamental revisions in the lower level theory in the course of developing a reduction. Once one has modified the lower level theory sufficiently to allow for the derivation, the issue becomes whether one has a truly unified theory at the lower level, or just a variety of theories stated in one vocabulary. In particular, the issue is whether the theoretical statements accounting for the behavior of parts in the non-bound condition are integrated with those introduced to explain their behavior in bound conditions. Causey sets forth elaborate conditions for theories being unified, but these conditions do not seem to exclude the possibility of there being two sets of statements in the theory that do not interact with each other. If that occurred, we would not really have a unified theory at the lower level, but merely a unified vocabulary. In this event, reduction has not really advanced the cause of unifying science.

There is yet a further problem with treating the reductionist program as a unification program. Throughout his book, Causey defers questions about the origin of particular structures to an analysis of evolutionary theories, which he promises to sketch at the end. When he gets to that sketch, Causey proposes to explain how structures come into existence by applying basic or derived dynamic laws (to which the reductionistic account had been directed) to specific environmental conditions (laws specifying selection might be of such a kind). This makes the question of whether the causal interaction between objects and their environment is correctly characterized at the lower level critical. It seems plausible that these causal relations will be between the structured wholes. Causey will find this requirement unproblematic as long as the laws governing structured wholes can be derived from laws governing their components. Numerous people have argued, however, that structured wholes which behave identically at the upper level may in fact have widely different internal composition (see Fodor, 1974). Causey's response (and Hooker's) is to bifurcate the upper level kinds in such cases, treating structured wholes as different if they have different compositional characteristics, even if their interactive behavior is identical. The result of this, however, may not be to unify science, but splinter it, for we will end up with different accounts of cases that initially appeared to be the same. (Pylyshyn, 1984, has used the argument that one can state generalizations in the language of folk psychology that cannot be captured in the language of neuroscience or behaviorism to argue for the legitimacy of that level of discourse despite that fact it cannot be reduced in a simple fashion to lower level laws. His argument that these generalizations capture real features of nature despite the differences that may exist between different instances that fulfill the generalization seems a good reason to treat the higher level account as the more unified for that domain.)

The point of the previous two paragraphs is to question whether the program of reduction really would produce a unified science. Even if it did provide for a unified science, however, there are additional reasons why such a program may not serve the interests of scientists actually engaged in integrative research. Causey presents himself as describing a research program of scientists, but it is unclear to what extent scientists are engaged in such a program or what they could hope to gain from it. Causey presents such a program as providing explanation as well as ontological simplification and unification. Considering first the ontological simplification and unification, there are times when recognizing ontological connections can help the endeavor of a scientist. For example, recognizing that genes were units on chromosomes advanced research insofar as it revealed additional facts about the entities in question. But the kind of simplification and unification envisaged in the reductionists' program does not seem to offer any explanatory advantages to scientists. They do not expand their scope of explanation by showing that the theories they have developed can be derived from other theories at more basic levels. Moreover, the objective of most scientists working across disciplinary boundaries has not been to achieve ontological simplification and unification. The reasons are fairly obvious. Nickles comments:

> " 'Reduction' *means* 'elimination,' 'trimming down,' 'consolidation' " (1973, p. 183).

Few scientists want to consolidate with others in a way that "eliminates" or "trims down" their own theories, since, as I noted above, having specialized theories is one of the defining characteristics of a discipline. Reducing one's theories to those of another discipline reduces oneself to an applied practitioner of that other discipline.

The other goal of reductionistic research programmes is potentially more significant, that of gaining explanatory power. This, however, depends on accepting a particular conception of scientific explanation, one according to which explanation involves deriving a statement describing what is to be explained from other statements. This conception has been seriously questioned in the literature (see Salmon, 1972 and 1984, Scriven, 1962, and Bromberger, 1965). This is not the place to continue that debate, but it should be noted that it is not obvious that a scientist in one discipline extends his or her explanatory power by deriving the set of laws used in that discipline from those of another. This is not to say that there are not sometimes very good reasons to go to another level in nature for explanation. Richardson (1980), argues that one of Donnett's major insights is to show that scientists frequently turn to other levels when a system they are studying does not behave in the way the principles thought to explain that system predict. It is deviations from expectations that need explaining, and going to another level may sometimes provide the needed explanation. However, such explanations do not require a deductive argument from lower level facts to the higher level generalization; they only require a demonstration of how the parts of the system equip the whole to behave in a certain manner.

Perhaps the most general difficulty with the formal model of theory reduction as a basis for interdisciplinary work is that it works with completed, formally presented theories, not with theories still under development. But researchers engaged in interdisciplinary work are generally engaged in the ongoing process for discovery, not with the attempt to systematize what is known. In rejecting such various formal models, including the model of theory reduction, as bases for interdisciplinary research, Gusdorf (1977) makes an important comment:

> "Interdisciplinary learning should be a logic of discovery, a reciprocal opening up of barriers, a communication between the different realms of knowledge, a mutual fertilization—not a formalism that cancels out all meaning and bars all outlets. . . . This grand design [of a formally unified science] presupposes the possibility of reducing all kinds of knowledge to unity and projecting them on to the same epistemological dimension, without denying the specificity of each. But the realm of knowledge has many dimensions. . . . The fact that there are many different disciplines of knowledge entails a diversity of approaches, none of which can claim to incorporate all the others. The idea of interdisciplinarity does not mean a search for a lower common multiple or a highest common factor; it is concerned with the entire epistemological space within which the separate kinds of knowledge are deployed like so many paths through the unknown" (595–597).

So, while granting the need for integrating frameworks in order to integrate the resources of different disciplines, we must also disown the kind of formalism as that represented by theory reduction and seek a model of integration more compatible with an ongoing process of discovery.

In giving up the search for a formal integrating scheme for unifying all sciences, we need to find some other means of bringing together the conceptual frameworks of different disciplines so as to provide a basis for integrating their research. A number of years ago, Darden and Maull (1977; see also Maull, 1977) argued, using historical studies, for a quite different conception of how to unify science without reduction. They argued for what they termed "interfield theories." (Although, as I noted in section 1, Darden and Maull's conception of a field was more limited than the broad notion of a discipline being employed here, the same kinds of cross-disciplinary relations may be found between disciplinary units that do not fit their specific definition of a field.)

One of the important features of interfield theories is that such theories have evolved to serve actual explanatory ends of scientists; in particular, to solve problems that could not be solved in one field of inquiry alone. Another feature, and one that distinguishes an account of integrating science in terms of interfield theories from a reductionist account, is that the end product is typically just one theory that spans fields, not two theories related by a derivation relation.[9]

Interfield theories characterize the relations between the entities or phenomena studies in different fields. Darden and Maull introduce several kinds of relations that may be considered in interfield theories: identifying in one field the physical location of an entity or process discussed in another, frequently showing a part-whole relation between the two; finding in one field a description of the physical nature of an entity or process characterized in the other theory; discovering in one field the structure underlying a function described in the other theory; and finding in one field the cause of an effect noticed in another field. Darden and Maull analyze a number of examples of interfield theories: the chromosomal theory of Mendelian heredity, which linked cytology and genetics; the operon theory, which related genetics and biochemistry, and the theory of allosteric regulation, which connected biochemistry and physical chemistry.

To show some of the character of an interfield theory as Darden and Maull conceived it (none of the cases considered in this volume show exactly this pattern), I will briefly summarize their discussion of the chromosomal theory. By 1903, geneticists had recognized Mendelian factors as the unit of heredity, but had not identified their physical location. Independently, cytologists had discovered chromosomes and had determined that they were involved in hereditary functions, but could not explain their role in producing individual hereditary characteristics. In this context, Boveri and Sutton developed an interfield theory by postulating that Mendelian factors are located on or in chromosomes. Although Darden and Maull point to ways in which the chromosomal theory modified ideas in both disciplines, it was genetics that primarily benefitted. The chromosomal theory provided the foundation for the classical genetics program of the Morgan school, which worked out a detailed account of the location of genes on chromosomes. The other cases considered by Darden and Maull differ from this in the kinds of relations they posit between the entities or processes in different fields. Through the operon theory, biochemistry provided a mechanism for regulation of gene expression, a phenomenon already identified by geneticists. In the theory of allosteric regulation, a physical-chemical cause is provided for the biochemically observed alteration in the level of protein activity. Common to all their examples, though, is one field filling in missing information about a phenomenon that was already partially understood in the other field.

In concluding their paper, Darden and Maull call on others to investigate additional cases of interfield theorizing in science so as to provide a better basis for understanding the ways in which scientists cross between fields of research. I have recently discussed a case (Bechtel, 1984) that differs from those studied by Darden and Maull in a couple of respects. The cases considered by Darden and Maull all involved one field posing a problem to another field. In the case I analyzed, in contrast, the interfield connection linking vitamin research with metabolism research (B vitamins being constitutent parts of respiratory coenzymes) was discovered fortuitously. Once discovered, it helped to illuminate further research in the fields where each entity had first been discovered. The case is also distinguished from Darden and Maull's cases in that the linkage between the fields was discovered only after a critical reconceptualization occurred in each field separately. Nonetheless, this case is like the cases discussed by Darden and Maull in that the researchers did not endeavor to reduce one theory (the theory of coenzymes) to the other (the theory of vitamins). The integration of research that was important for the scientists was accomplished without reduction. It involved identifying relationships between entities that had been studied independently that allowed researchers in each field to learn new information about the entities that were of primary interest to them.

Many cases of interfield theories involve relations between levels and illustrate an alternative to reductionism as a way of relating levels. These interfield theories make appeals to lower level entities to explain features of higher level entities without necessary providing a full account of the upper level entity. However, in some cases there will be reason to go the other direction and appeal to higher level entities to account for lower level behavior (Campbell, 1974). In particular, there will be reason to go up when selection forces are operating on higher level entities that determine the continued existence or replication of lower level entities. In this case, one can take a teleological perspective and view lower level entities as serving functions defined by higher level selection forces (Wimsatt, 1972). Machamer (1977) proposes that this kind of relation between different levels provides another important alternative to reduction. What is involved is an interfield connection which involves the interaction between the processes described in two theories, one of which explains how a system operates and the other tries to account for its existence. (I have discussed this model for interlevel theorizing further in Bechtel, 1985.)

Several of the case studies presented in this volume further take up the call of Darden and Maull and explore other kinds of theoretical connections between disciplines. Because any analysis of these cases must draw heavily on the specifics of the cases, I will postpone detailed comments until the Editor's Commentary following each set of papers. At this point I will merely note some of the patterns of cross-disciplinary connections that were revealed. The first such pattern involves developing sufficient conceptual links between disciplines so as to use perspectives developed in one discipline to modify the perspective adopted in another related disciplines, without developing major theoretical structures that subsume the disciplines in question. This mode of cross-disciplinary theorizing applies to Richardson's discussion of the use of linguistic frameworks to re-analyze neurological deficits in aphasics and to Kauffman's and Wimsatt's proposals of how to use developmental considerations to reconceptualize some aspects of evolutionary theorizing. A second pattern involves the recognition of a new level of organization with its own set of processes to solve problems unsolved within existing fields. This pattern is illustrated in two cases, the development of biochemistry and the development of the synthetic theory of evolution. The new theories developed at the new levels were designed to interact with the perspective previously adopted at other levels, but it was the framework developed at the new level that was decisive in solving previously unsolved problems. Beatty's analysis of the evolutionary synthesis shows a third pattern of interfield theorizing, wherein one uses research techniques developed in one discipline to help elaborate a theoretical model in another. A fourth pattern involves taking a theoretical framework from one domain and modifying and extending it in order to apply it in another domain where independently researchers think such extension is plausible (Mason's and Anderson's proposals for taking cognitive perspectives adopted in human psychology to understand animal behavior). A final pattern involves developing a new theoretical framework that will reconceptualize research in now separate domains as it tries to integrate them. Rumbaugh and Sterritt exemplify this when they introduce their control theory as a vehicle for integrating the study of intelligence amongst humans and other animals. Savage-Rumbaugh and Hopkins' focus on the idea of communicative intention in order to overcome inadequacies of both the ethological and learning perspectives for dealing with animal communication further illustrate this pattern. This last case offers the prospect of further modifying another discipline, human cognitive psychology, insofar as the framework of communicative intention is found to be useful in dealing with human linguistic behavior.

All of the cases have in common that disciplines are being brought together and integrated so as to help solve identifiable problems. To this extent, Darden and Maull's concept of interfield theory is applicable. However, there is variation in the degree to which one well-developed theory is being proposed to bridge the disciplines. In the historical cases, such theories are more apparent, but one should not expect such well-worked out theories at the initiation of a cross-disciplinary research endeavor. Rather, one should expect suggestive frameworks that will need to be elaborated and tested. Some of the proposals in the three contemporary cases are more developed than others, but all are still at the stage of working proposals for developing interfield theoretical connections.

Conclusion

Within this introduction I have sketched a framework in which to examine interdisciplinary research. I have considered first various ways we might understand the units of science that can be labelled disciplines and then considered how these units have become isolated from each other so as to make interdisciplinary endeavors problematic. I have also tried to indicate some of the factors that actually motivate scientists to engage in cross-disciplinary research so that our focus is on the real activities of science, not those of the *a priori* theorist of knowledge. Finally, I have explored some of the social and institutional as well as cognitive arrangements that are employed in cross-disciplinary endeavors.

The analysis offered here is not intended as a definitive statement about what interdisciplinarity does or should involve, but only to provide a framework for further development. Some of that development is offered by the cases that follow, but they are only a small selection of possible cases for consideration in the life sciences. The topic of cross-disciplinary research is ripe for further inquiry both by scientists engaged in such efforts and by historians, philosophers, sociologists and others interested in meta-science. With such detailed studies we can hope to get past the idealizations that have frequented discussions of interdisciplinarity in science and come to a sound understand of what cross-disciplinary research entails, what it can accomplish, and how we can improve the potential for its success.

Endnotes

1. Barmark and Wallen analyze this inability and reluctance to work within new conceptual frameworks in terms of costs to the researchers: "The cost of learning a new competence was too high and was worthless as a skill when they had to return to their original disciplines after the project" (226).
2. During the conference at which the papers in this volume were originally presented, Mason noted how a number of these factors impeded his attempt to pursue cross-disciplinary work. In his work as a comparative psychologist he arrived at a physiological proposal to account for the differences between two species of monkeys. However, he faced a number of difficulties in getting a physiologist to work with him. First, he had to deal with significant methodological differences. For example, whereas psychologists view a single organism as representative of a species. Moreover, the particular physiological idea he wished to pursue was now considered passe by most physiologists. Finally, neither journals in physiology nor psychology were interested in the particular problem.
3. Some of these costs were pointed out by Donald Campbell himself in his introductory remarks to the conference from which this volume is drawn.
4. Lemain, MacLeod, Mulkay, and Wingart see in these factors a possible explanation for the phenomenon of multiple discoveries in science. They propose that due to the kind of factors they itemize, numerous researchers may migrate at the same time without communication. Coming from similar backgrounds, they will then direct themselves at the same obvious and general problems, resulting in similar simultaneous solutions.
5. Barmark and Wallen (1980), in discussing why some researchers joined an interdisciplinary forest project, noted that for some it was the only available opportunity to find work related to their field, supporting the idea that engaging in interdisciplinary work may appeal most strongly to those without opportunity within the mainstream of their discipline.
6. See Mayr and Provine (1980) for a discussion of how these various fields fit into the synthesis.
7. In their long-term study of a forest ecology project, Barmark and Wallen (1978 and 1980) noted that even those who shared an ecological perspective had trouble integrating their work because of the differences in their research orientations. Wallen (1981) provides examples of the problems: "In addition to the self-evident differences in background knowledge, some concepts had different meanings in different disciplines. This is not a linguistic problem; rather they had different explanations of phenomena in reality. For instance "mineralization" could be regarded as a mainly chemical phenomenon or as a biological one. It is a basic characteristic of science to simplify and isolate certain objects for study. But every level in the ecosystem is studied on its own premises and it is difficult to overcome these borders. The plant physiologists for instance work with small parts and their models are fast (one day), their methods have been laboratory oriented and exact. Studies of plant growth and plant ecology used models encompassing 1–100 years and they are more field-oriented and have other standards for their data." See Gold and Gold, 1983, for further discussion of these problems.
8. There is an alternative sense of reduction, that between predecessor and successor theories, that does not require a deductive relationship between theories at different levels. The whole idea of deductive relationships is inappropriate in this context since the replacement theory is presumably changing and improving on the old theory. Rather, the endeavor is to show the similarities and differences between the theories which is of particular use in evaluating the improvements brought by the new theory. See Nickles, 1973, Wimsatt, 1976, and McCauley, in press, for further discussion of the differences between these modes of reduction, which have often been confused in the literature.

9. As Steve Fuller has pointed out (personal communication), there remains a danger, once interfield theories have been developed, of one field (e.g., genetics) seeking to dominate another (e.g., cytology). The notion of an interfield theory does not bar the kind eliminative reduction proposed by Churchland (1979) and Rosenberg (19XX), wherein one science (neuroscience or evolutionary biology) comes to supplant another (cognitive psychology or sociology). However, such a result would not be a necessary product of an interfield theory and would be due more to the social character of the interacting disciplines than to the creation of an interfield theory.

References

Barmark, Jan and Wallen, Goran (1978). Knowledge production in interdisciplinary groups. Report number 37, second series, Department for Theory of Science, University of Gothenburg.

Barmark, Jan and Wallen, Goran (1980). The development of an interdisciplinary project. In Karin Knorr, Roger Krohn, and Richard Whitley (Eds.), *The social process of scientific investigation. Sociology of the sciences, Volume IV.* Dordrecht: Reidel.

Barnes, Barry (1977). *Interests and the growth of knowledge.* London: Routledge and Kegan Paul.

Barth, Richard T. and Steck, Rudy (1979). *Interdisciplinary research groups: Their management and organization.* Vancouver: International Research Group on Interdisciplinary Programs.

Bechtel, William (1984). Reconceptualizations and interfield connections: The discovery of the link between vitamins and coenzymes. *Philosophy of Science,* 51, 265–292.

Bechtel, William (1985). Teleological functional analyses and the hierarchical organization of nature. In N. Rescher, ed., *Teleology and natural science.* Landham, MD: University Press of America.

Ben-David, Joseph and Collins, Randall (1966). Social factors in the origins of a new science: The case of psychology. *American Sociological Review,* 31, 451–465.

Birnbaum, Philip H. (1978). Academic context of interdisciplinary research. *Educational Administration Quarterly, 14,* 80–97.

Birnbaum, P. H. (1983). "Predictors of long-term research performance. In S. R. Epton, R. L. Payne, and A. W. Pearson, eds., *Managing interdisciplinary research.* New York: John Wiley and Sons.

Bloor, David (1976). *Knowledge and social imagery.* London: Routledge and Kegan Paul.

Blumenthal, Arthur L. (forthcoming). The emergence of psycholinguistics.

Bourdieu, P. (1975). The specificity of the scientific field and the social conditions of the progress of reason. *Social Science Information 14:* 19–47.

Bradley, D.; Garrett, M.; and Zurif, E. (1980). Syntactic deficits in Broca's aphasia. In D. Caplan (ed.), *Biological studies of mental processes.* Cambridge: MIT Press.

Brandon, Robert (1982). The levels of selection. In P. Asquith and T. Nickles (Eds.), *PSA 1982.* Volume 1. East Lansing: Philosophy of Science Association.

Bromberger, S. (1965). An approach to explanation. In R. J. Butler, ed., *Studies in Analytical Philosophy.* Second Series. Oxford: Blackwell.

Cambrosio, Alberto and Keating, Paul (1983). *The disciplinary stake: The case of chronobiology. Social Studies of Science,* 13, 323–353.

Campbell, Donald T. (1969). Ethnocentrism of disciplines and the fish-scale model of omniscience. In M. Sherif and C. W. Sherif, eds., *Interdisciplinary relationships in the social sciences.* Chicago: Aldine Publishing Company.

Campbell, Donald T. (1974). 'Downward causation' in hierarchically organized biological systems. In F. Ayala and T. Dobzhansky, eds., *Studies in the philosophy of biology.* Berkeley: University of California Press.

Carnap, Rudolf (1938). Logical foundations of the unity of science. In O. Neurath, R. Carnap, and C. Morris (Eds.), *International encyclopedia of unified science.* Volume I. Chicago, The University of Chicago Press.

Causey, Robert L. (1977). *Unity of science.* Dordrecht: Reidel.

Chubin, Daryl E. (1976). The conception of scientific specialties. *The Sociological Quarterly, 17,* 448–476.

Chubin, D. E. (1982). *Sociology of sciences: An annotated bibliography on invisible colleges, 1972–1981.* New York: Garland.

Churchland, Paul M. (1979). Scientific realism and the plasticity of mind. Cambridge: Cambridge University Press.

Coleman, William (1985). The cognitive basis of the discipline: Claude Bernard on physiology. *Isis,* 76, 49–70.

Crane, Diana (1969). Social structure in a group of scientists: A test of the invisible college hypothesis. *American Sociological Review,* 34, 335–352.

Crane, Diana (1972). *Invisible colleges.* Chicago: University of Chicago Press.

Cutler, Robert S. (1979). A policy perspective on interdisciplinary research in U.S. universities. In Richard T. Barth and Rudy Steck (Eds.), *Interdisciplinary research groups: Their management and organization.* Vancouver: International Research Group on Interdisciplinary Programs.

Darden, Lindley, and Maull, Nancy (1977). Interfield theories. *Philosophy of Science,* **44,** 43–64.

Edge, D. (1979). Quantitative measures of communication in science: A critical review. *History of Science,* **17,** 102–134.

Epton, S. R.; Payne, R. L.; and Pearson, A. W. (1983). *Managing interdisciplinary research.* New York: John Wiley and Sons.

Fodor, Jerry (1974). Special sciences (Or: Disunity of science as a working hypothesis. *Synthese,* 28, 97–115.

Garfield, E. (1979). *Citation indexing.* New York: Wiley.

Gold, S. E. and Gold, H. J. (1983). Some elements of a model to improve productivity of interdisciplinary groups. In S. R. Epton, R. L. Payne, and A. W. Pearson (Eds.), *Managing interdisciplinary research.* New York: John Wiley and Sons.

Grodzinsky, Y.; Swinney, D.; and Zurif, E. (1983). Agrammatism: Structural deficits and antecedent processing disruptions. In M. L. Keane, ed., *Agrammatism.* New York: Academic Press.

Gusdorf, Georges (1977). Past, present, and future in interdisciplinary research. *International Social Science Journal,* **29,** 580–600.

Hagstrom, W. O. (1965). *The scientific community.* New York: Basic Books.

Hooker, C. A. (1981). Towards a general theory of reduction. *Dialogue,* **20,** 38–59; 201–236; 496–529.

Hull, David (1978). A matter of individuality. *Philosophy of Science,* **45,** 335–360.

Hull, David (1982). Exemplars and essences. Unpublished manuscript.

Knorr, Karin D. (1981). *The manufacture of knowledge. Toward a constructivist and contextual theory of science.* Oxford: Pergamon.

Knorr-Cetina, Karin D. and Mulkay, Michael (1983). Introduction: Emerging principles in social studies of science. In K. D. Knorr-Cetina and M. Mulkay, eds., *Science observed.* London: Sage.

Kohler, Robert E. (1977). Rudolf Schoenheimer, isotopic tracers, and biochemistry in the 1930's. *Historical Studies in the Physical Sciences,* **8,** 257–297.

Kohler, Robert E. (1982). *From medical chemistry to biochemistry.* Cambridge: Cambridge University Press.

Krantz, David and Wiggins, L. (1973). Personal and impersonal channels of recruitment in the growth of knowledge. *Human Development,* **16,** 133–156.

Krohn, Roger (1980). Introduction: Toward an empirical study of scientific practice. In K. D. Knorr, R. Krohn, and R. Whitley, eds., *The social process of scientific investigation. Sociology of the sciences, Volume IV.* Dordrecht: Reidel.

Kuhn, Thomas (1970). *The structure of scientific revolutions.* Second Edition. Chicago: University of Chicago Press.

Lakatos, Imre (1970). Falsification and the methodology of scientific research programmes. In I. Lakatos and A. Musgrave, eds., *Criticisms and the growth of knowledge.* Cambridge: Cambridge University Press.

Latour, Bruno and Woolgar, Steve. (1979). *Laboratory life. The social construction of scientific facts.* Beverly Hills: Sage Publications.

Laudan, Larry (1977). *Progress and its problems.* Berkeley: University of California Press.

Law, John (1973). The development of specialties in science: The case of X-ray protein crystallography. *Science Studies,* **3,** 275–303.

Lemaine, Gerald; MacLeod, Roy; Mulkay, Michael; and Weingart, Peter (1976). Introduction: Problems in the emergence of new disciplines. In *Perspectives on the emergence of scientific disciplines.* The Hague: Mouton.

Machamer, Peter (1977). Teleology and selection processes. In Robert G. Colodny, ed., *Logic, laws and life: Some philosophical complications.* Pittsburgh: University of Pittsburgh Press.

Machlup, Fritz (1982). *Knowledge: Its creation, distribution, and economic significance. Volume II. The branches of learning.* Princeton: Princeton University Press.

Maull, Nancy (1977). Unifying science without reduction. *Studies in the History and Philosophy of Science,* **8,** 143–162.

Mayr, Ernst and Provine, William B. (1980). *The evolutionary synthesis. Perspectives on the unification of biology.* Cambridge: Harvard University Press.

McCauley, Robert (1981). Hypothetical identities and ontological economizing: Comments on Causey's program for the unity of science. *Philosophy of Science,* **48,** 218–227.

McCauley, Robert (in press). Intertheoretic relations and the future of psychology. *Philosophy of Science.*

Merton, Robert K. (1973). *The sociology of science.* Chicago, The University of Chicago Press.

Mullins, Nicholas C. (1972). The development of a scientific specialty: The phage group and the origins of molecular biology. *Minerva,* **10**, 51–82.

Nagel, Ernst (1961). *The structure of science.* New York: Harcourt, Brace and World.

Neurath, Otto (1938). Unified science as encyclopedic integration. In O. Neurath, R. Carnap, and C. Morris (Eds.), *International encyclopedia of unified science.* Volume I. Chicago, The University of Chicago Press.

Nickles, Thomas (1973). Two concepts of intertheoretic reduction. *The Journal of Philosophy,* **70**, 181–201.

Polanyi, Michael (1966). *The tacit dimension.* New York: Doubleday, 1966.

Popper, Karl (1972). *Objective knowledge.* Oxford: Oxford University Press.

Price, Derek J. de Solla (1961). *Science since Babylon.* New Haven: Yale University Press.

Pylyshyn, Zenon (1984). *Computation and cognition.* Cambridge: MIT Press/Bradford Books.

Reber, Arthur S. (forthcoming). The rise and (surprisingly rapid) fall of psycholinguistics.

Richardson, Robert C. (1980). Intentional realism or intentional instrumentalism. *Cognition and Brain Theory,* **3**, 125–135.

Rosenberg, Alexander (1980). *Sociobiology and the preemption of social science.* Baltimore: Johns Hopkins University Press.

Rosenberg, Charles (1979). Toward an ecology of knowledge: On discipline, context, and history. In A. Oleson and J. Voss, *The organization of knowledge in modern America: 1860–1920.* Baltimore: Johns Hopkins University Press.

Rossini, F.; Porter, A. L.; Chubin, D. E.; and Connolloy, T. (1983). Cross-disciplinarity in the biomedical sciences: A preliminary analysis of anatomy. In S. R. Epton, R. L. Payne, and A. W. Pearson (Eds.), *Managing interdisciplinary research.* New York: John Wiley and Sons.

Ruse, Michael (1973). *The philosophy of biology.* London: Hutchinson.

Russell, M. G. (1983). Peer review in interdisciplinary research: Flexibility and responsiveness. In S. R. Epton, R. L. Payne, and A. W. Pearson (Eds.), *Managing interdisciplinary research.* New York: John Wiley and Sons.

Salmon, Wesley (1971). *Statistical explanations and statistical relevance.* Pittsburgh: University of Pittsburgh Press.

Salmon, Wesley (1984). *Scientific explanation and the causal structure of the world.* Princeton: Princeton University Press.

Saxberg, Borje O., Newell, William T., and Mar, Brian W. (1979). The integration of interdisciplinary research with the Organization of the University. In Richard T. Barth and Rudy Steck (Eds.), *Interdisciplinary research groups: Their management and organization.* Vancouver: International Research Group on Interdisciplinary Programs.

Saxberg, B. O. and Newell, W. T. (1983). Interdisciplinary research in the university: Need for managerial leadership. In S. R. Epton, R. L. Payne, and A. W. Pearson (Eds.), *Managing interdisciplinary research.* New York: John Wiley and Sons.

Schaffner, Kenneth (1967). Approaches to reduction. *Philosophy of Science,* 34, 137–147.

Scriven, Michael (1962). Explanations, predictions, and laws. In H. Feigl and G. Maxwell (Eds.), *Minnesota studies in the philosophy of science.* Minneapolis: University of Minnesota Press.

Shapere, Dudley (1974). Scientific theories and their domains. In F. Suppe (Ed.), *The structure of scientific theories.* Urbana: University of Illinois Press, pp. 518–565.

Shapere, Dudley (1984a). Remarks on the concepts of domain and field. In D. Shapere (Ed.), *Reason and the search for knowledge.* Dordrecht: Reidel.

Shapere, Dudley (1984b). Alteration of goals and language in the development of science. In D. Shapere (Ed.), *Reason and the search for knowledge.* Dordrecht: Reidel.

Shapin, Steven (1982). History of science and its sociological reconstructions. *History of Science,* **20**, 157–211.

Teich, Albert H. (1979). Research centers and non-faculty researchers: Implications of a growing role in American universities. In Richard T. Barth and Rudy Steck (Eds.), *Interdisciplinary research groups: Their management and organization.* Vancouver: International Research Group on Interdisciplinary Programs.

Toulmin, Steven (1972). *Human understanding.* Princeton: Princeton University Press.

Wallen, Goran (1981). The interaction between the development of knowledge and organization in the Swecon project. Unpublished internal report.

Whitley, Richard (1976). Umbrella and polytheistic scientific disciplines and their elites. *Social Studies of Science,* **6**, 471–497.

Whitley, Richard (1980). The context of scientific investigation. In K. D. Knorr, R. Krohn, and R. Whitley (Eds.), *The social process of scientific investigation.* Dordrecht: Reidel.

Whitley, Richard (1982). The establishment and structure of the sciences as reputational organizations.

In N. Elias, H. Martins, and R. Whitley (Eds.), *Scientific establishments and hierarchies. Sociology of the sciences, Volume VI.* Dordrecht: Reidel.

Whitley, Richard (1984). The rise and decline of university disciplines in the sciences. In R. Jurkowich and J. H. P. Paelinck (Eds.), *Problems in interdisciplinary studies.* Hampshire: Gower Publishing Company.

Wimsatt, William C. (1972). Teleology and the logical structure of function statements. *Studies in the History and Philosophy of Science, 3,* 1–80.

Wimsatt, William C. (1976). Reductionism, levels of organization, and the mind-body problem. In G. Globus, G. Maxwell, and I. Savodnik (Eds.), *Consciousness and the brain: A scientific and philosophical inquiry.* New York: Plenum Press.

Interdisciplinary Thought

Ursula Hübenthal

Abstract

This essay examines types of overlapping thought between subjects. The definition of "interdisciplinarity" that is proposed is a
thought process that overlaps subjects. It is oriented toward a
topic as a whole, leading to standardization of the comprehension
of phenomena by connecting partial explanations of different sciences with one another. The task of interdisciplinary research is
not to be solved with a global interdisciplinary theory. It must be
pursued within individual sciences in daily usage, and must entail
attention to problems of language and clarifying the core questions. Theory should nurture practice, effecting a gradual change
that promotes attention to questions that border on individuals'
areas of specialization.

This essay is a synopsis of my dissertation which I completed at the end of
1989 in the subject of Philosophy at the University of Cologne. The idea for
the thesis grew out of my studies in the subjects of biology and philosophy,
and was ultimately germinated by the need to answer pressing (in the broadest
sense anthropological) questions, which have emerged and remained unanswered both in the natural sciences as well as in the humanities.

Given this background a paper developed, which deals with different examples of overlapping thought between subjects. The goal was to discover as many
forms of cooperation as possible and to systemize them. The primary focus was
directed at the relation between the humanities and natural sciences, because it
is here where the most interesting problems as well as the greatest difficulties
lie for creating a bridge. Because I was concerned with generally promoting the
exchange between different disciplines, I use the term "interdisciplinarity" as
broadly as possible, and I will propose a definition that includes all possible
forms of collaboration between the sciences.

The ever-increasing criticism against specialization is mainly attributed to
the fear that we cannot, through specialization alone, master the pressing problems of modern mankind, such as the scarcity of nourishment or the destruc-
tion of the environment. These problems are much too complex to be judged
appropriately, let alone be solved merely with the subject-knowledge of a single
discipline or through a simple comparison of the details of knowledge from
many disciplines. What is missing is an examination of the larger contexts,
which are not apparent by stringing together our knowledge of individual de-

Hübenthal, Ursula. "Interdisciplinary Thought." Issues in Integrative Studies *12 (1994),
55–75. Translated by Denise M. Doyle, Wayne State University. Reprinted with permission.*

tails because this approach fails to comprehend the interactions between different factors. These interactions, however, often have an impact on the total behavior of a system and are usually subject to their own laws. A more comprehensive understanding of the phenomenon than currently exists will therefore have to be acquired if we hope to influence complex systems.

On the other hand, the necessity of a highly detailed analysis is undisputed if a topic is to be understood. Due to time limitations, it is already hardly possible given the extent of existing knowledge to be competent in even a single specialized discipline, let alone to be able to keep up with the developments in the neighboring sciences.

How is this dilemma to be solved?

In recent years the catchword "interdisciplinarity" has been set forth as an answer to this question. Interdisciplinarity is used as a collective term for subject-overlapping thought, i.e. for the characterization of every collaboration which bridges disciplines. One usually finds the term "interdisciplinarity" employed without specification as to what it is that is to be understood about it and an exact clarification of its meaning is seldom furnished with its utilization. It often appears that the term is used without awareness of the complexity of its meaning or the difficulties which are linked with the realization of the challenges of subject-overlapping research. Talk of "interdisciplinarity" occurs so often and in the most varied contexts that one can gain the impression that we are not dealing with a concrete concept, but rather with a catchword, which is connected with rather diffuse hopes for modification of the situation. Ultimately, it remains an open question as to if, and to what extent, a unity of science can be achieved within this essay.

It is therefore my opinion that it is necessary to undertake an exact systemization of interdisciplinary procedures. The potential and limitations of the various alternatives which should be known before beginning an interdisciplinary project will only become visible through the differentiation of application possibilities of this approach, which has until now remained very general. Only in this manner can the prospects of success be appraised realistically and the greatest possible benefit be gained.

This latter point is especially important, because many of these projects yield only marginally unsatisfactory results, or at best less than the desired success. One learns almost exclusively about successful teamwork in the technical-scientific sphere. If no reasons for an unsuccessful coordination are identified and thus no fruitful exchange has been achieved, the danger exists that no further attempts will be undertaken. In part, this type of resignation has already been noted in reports about attempts at interdisciplinary problem solving. If this increase in "disillusionment" should prove to be premature, there might be reason for hope.

With the demand for interdisciplinarity, the question of overlapping unity among sciences is implicitly raised. This unity could provide a basis for all of the overlapping attempts to provide answers. The opinion which I advocate in this regard is the following:

Hopes should not be pinned to an approach which attempts with a *single* blow to establish unity among scientists on a meta-theoretical level, for example, the thesis that there is a method monism among all sciences or an ultimate unity of all scientific topics. Apart from the fact that meanwhile the sciences are too diverse and complex, such a theory would inevitably be much too general to provide concrete directives for the procedure of subject-overlapping research on a specific topic. But this is obviously what is missing. In addition, (and this is aimed at method monism) there is a firmly established tradition of separation between the so-called humanities and natural sciences. In these sciences it appears that totally different topics are being pursued, i.e. different subjects are dealt with which do not always lend themselves to the formation of any type of unifying scheme of scientific procedures. To my knowledge, these methods are not followed by scientists who occupy themselves with interdisciplinarity, just as little as other historic proposals for the creation of a unity amongst the scientists, such as those of Wilhelm von Humboldt, have been.

I am equally doubtful that subject-overlapping research can be facilitated through the development of a meta-language. Meta-language would be totally abstract, and it is unlikely that the aspects which a speciality science examines on a specific topic could be considered differentially enough and still maintain their specificity. This level of specificity is what is at stake however in the completion of any complex research inquiry into which the different scientific approaches shall be integrated. Besides, it is hardly conceivable that the scientists of all disciplines would be prepared to learn this meta-language, and if only for the previously mentioned reason of time constraints.

Rather, I would like to more precisely define "interdisciplinarity" or "interdisciplinary thought" as the attempt to connect the explanatory approaches of the different sciences with one another, with the goal of *explaining a specific phenomenon in its totality,* in other words with all the attributes that are ascribed to it. Under the word "phenomenon," I include all the conceivable research topics of the sciences, be they atoms, complete species in a biological sense, a philosophical theory, a historical epoch, or whatever else is viewed as deserving of research. As the leading thought for the pursuit of science, the goal of explaining phenomena, no matter the type, is presupposed. These should now be explained *in totality* during interdisciplinary research, and that means that the dividing line between them must be overcome, in as far as their different attributes fall under the "explanatory responsibilities" of different speciality disciplines. In other words, the chasms between the different lines of inquiry and their accompanying answers, should be overcome. One can describe this as an endeavor to establish unity of thought through the intermeshing of the questions of various lines of inquiry. Smooth transitions must be established between the subject-specific answers to these questions in such a manner that no gaps remain between them, which leave further questions concerning the relationships, i.e. the interactions between the different partial phenomena. In as far as a term does exist that expresses the supposition that something represents a unity in and of itself, the issue should be understood as a complex totality, whose individual aspects are analyzed by the respective disciplines which specialize in them. It is *the method of interaction of the individual pieces* which must be clarified in interdisciplinary questions; this method will not be analyzed by any discipline if the interacting components of a system do not fall into the responsibility sphere of that same discipline. The chasm existing here between the different levels of explanation is obviously that which is worth bridging in interdisciplinary research. The problem to be solved by a theory of interdisciplinarity is, in other words, that of how knowledge can be combined into a uniform picture.

The newness of this approach, in contrast to historic attempts, is that despite the uniformity of thought, variability in the scientific approach to problems remains perceived. In other words, the possibility of a flexible approach is associated with the idea of uniformity. In my opinion herein lies the importance of this paper: perhaps there is a new opportunity to create unity if one looks for smooth transitions between explanations by different areas of specialization. It must presently remain open whether the boundaries between sciences are completely dissolved through this transition. The unity would then lie not in a common foundation for all sciences, but in the subsequent overcoming of boundaries between individual sciences which aim at the research topic presenting the most diverse set of questions. This partial unity starting from the topic, from the bottom so to speak, consequently constitutes the difference from the previous attempts to create uniformity. Hope exists that the sciences can grow together into a whole through the production of vertical cross connections *by means of the topics,* and that the diversity of the research subjects will do justice despite the established relationships between them.

From this perspective of creating uniformity, the only aim in an interdisciplinary approach can be to point out the different possibilities of subject-overlapping thought, instead of looking for a directive to a fundamentally uniform means of approaching interdisciplinary research. The purpose of interdisciplinarity cannot be to overcome the abundance of specialization, specifically because the great variety of the research possibilities should be kept. No alternative to specialization is currently being explored; however a counterpole is, because the overview of the total object is in jeopardy of being lost with the advancing knowledge of details. It consequently does not make sense to overcome specialization, but rather to overcome a pursuit of science that stops at the fractionary method of looking at things necessary to specialized research.

Depending on the individual explanations to be connected, this requires very different cooperative attempts between the involved scientists, i.e. differing degrees of willingness to discuss the respective approaches foreign to the subject. For this reason alone it is my opinion that the task of interdisciplinary research is not to be solved with a global interdisciplinary theory.

Interdisciplinarity should also not be pursued primarily by theoreticians; rather it should find increasing acceptance within the individual sciences in daily usage. In other words, it should lead to a gradual change in position vis-a-vis the pursuit of science, to the extent that more attention is afforded the questions bordering one's own area of specialization. Only then can the accomplishments of "science as a whole" be integrated so that one's own individual position can be determined within it.

What is important at this point is the diversely expressed idea that the classification of phenomena, as perceived by humans and reflected in sciences, corresponds less to their nature, but instead is a more artificial classification (see for example Dirtfurth and Weizsäcker). These boundaries were possibly drawn only because our intellect cannot process the things any differently than as they are categorized in this artificial form. It is only due to this classification of cultivated specific conceptualization (i.e. developed different technical terminologies are responsible) that we now experience a problem relative to uniformity of the sciences. Perhaps this classification over time has let us forget that a complex topic is essentially constituted of the interaction between its individual pieces. For the most part, the present individual sciences perform research on specific aspects of phenomena and can therefore always only illustrate and comprehend partial processes. The existing interactions, however, refer to other partial aspects not taken into account. The problem of explanation in this interpretation therefore exists in understanding the respective dependencies between the partial aspects.

Consequently the individual sciences are to be understood as *purveyors of partial explanations in the need of complement*. To pursue interdisciplinary research, the method of interaction of the parts must be clarified. In this manner the dividing lines between the areas of specialty can be overcome, whereby the variability of the analytical approaches remains perceived.

In order to retain this perspective, the comprehension of phenomenon must be placed in the foreground, in other words, not the ability to formulate the research results into specific technical terminology, but to make rational comprehension accessible. By this, it is presupposed that it is possible to make one's own respective approaches intelligible to a scientist independent of his subject area, in so far as he is interested and is willing to enter in the explanation. Therefore, the "meta" language of interdisciplinarity would not be a formalizable language; rather it would "supersede" the technical terminology only in as far as it is not tied to a specific technical language and is comprehensible to every logically thinking person. So subject terms can be used without further problems, they must only be defined in an understandable language for all the scientists involved, and the same term cannot be given varying meanings, as is so often the case with different technical terminologies.

Hence, in interdisciplinary research, the connection of knowledge *elements* predominates, not the connection of whole sciences. Interdisciplinary research is therefore independent of the respective valid classification of the given sciences.

The interdisciplinary position described is in a certain sense comparable to that of a person trying to solve a puzzle; it is of no use to have only the individual pieces in your hand. If one wants to see the entire picture, one must put the pieces together, and for this purpose we must look at every single piece exactly, in terms of what is represented on it as well as its perimeters. The whole puzzle is only comprehensible after assembly when one views the picture from the overall perspective rather than examining the individual pieces, because as long as one perceives the boundaries clearly, they impede the viewer's ability to grasp the whole and thus the purpose of the enterprise is not achieved.

Because an interdisciplinary research effort as described orients itself on the respective individually important questions which transgress the boundaries of the speciality science, it has a predominantly pragmatic character. Also, because the cooperation between the sciences must therefore make use of different means as to the problem at hand, the development of a unified interdisciplinary theory cannot be stated as the desired goal. The prospect of being able to provide a valid general interdisciplinary methodology, which goes beyond very general recommendations, appears negligible to me. Therefore, I have attempted to undertake the classification of the numerous examples for clarification of the different possibilities of subject-overlapping collaboration, which can be viewed as approaches to interdisciplinary exchange which are already being practiced.

Before proceeding, let it be said that I do not want to emphasize that sciences be tied to another as a whole, thereby creating new "interdisciplines," as it is often stated (examples for such interdisciplines are biochemistry, paralegal sociology, psychoneuroimmunology, etc.). These are, of course, in each case proof for a successful and already established exchange, but they are only examples of extensive cooperation, and I would like to include every possibility for the direct reciprocal stimulation between the sciences even if no concrete results yet exist. The creation of a discipline is not really necessary if the priority in interdisciplinarity is a complete explanation of a phenomenon. It can be totally sufficient for the solution of a subject-overlapping problem only if the individual results or methods of one discipline are utilized by the other for its own research. In such a case, only partial spheres of different sciences would be integrated with one another, as it happens so often in interdisciplinary practice.

For the classification itself, I would like to differentiate between the already mentioned *total phenomenon, the research topic* and the *research, i.e. partial aspects,* independent of the type of interdisciplinary cooperation. Relative to one of these aspects, a common interest must exist in different sciences if there is to be a reason for interdisciplinary research. The individual object with all of its constituted characteristics, which appears to us as a uniform whole in the pre-scientific experience, is to be understood by the term *total phenomenon.* The term *research topic* refers to all partial phenomena which a specific science can analyze on this total phenomenon; and a single *aspect* on one such topic corresponds to a possible research perspective of the partial phenomena. In this manner, for example, one can analyze a specific behavior on the total phenomenon "human" (and thereby a partial phenomenon of this whole object) through neurophysiological, hormonal, psychological and sociological aspects, and although very different disciplines are involved in this case, come to the conclusion that it is a question of a specific unequivocally defined sickness, such as, for example, manic depressive behavior. Yet the individual "thrusts" can be triggered through specific outer influence and the course of the sickness can be dependant on numerous factors.

The term "research topic," therefore, usually coincides with the "total phenomenon" only from an interdisciplinary viewpoint; in individual sciences it may only rarely be the case. This differentiation between total phenomenon, research topic and aspect seems to be very important for an evaluation of the interdisciplinary cooperative possibilities, because these various possibilities should relate to the individual knowledge *elements* of the different sciences and not to the whole of science. The individual findings which are to be linked to one another, namely, have a more or less extensive claim to clarification in reference to the total phenomenon. Their need for complement is thereby connected to other sciences, as well as the decision as to what extent a certain question deals with an interdisciplinary problem.

With regard to the individual distinctions of the various forms of teamwork, I agree with Vosskamp that there are different possibilities of classification and not only a succession of increasing degrees of interaction. In my opinion at least two dimensions must be taken into consideration for this classification, which I have termed as "levels" on the one hand and "criteria" on the other based on the pattern of Vosskamp.

Relative to the *criteria* noted above, I would first like to differentiate whether two (or more) disciplines which are involved in an interdisciplinary research project can only contribute their internally gained facts for the resolution of a problem separately because they analyze different partial phenomena, i.e. aspects of an object, or if they are able to recognize commonalities in the topics they analyzed by themselves. In the latter case, their *analysis topics* (and that which is characterized by the terms utilized in sciences) must be at least partially identical (see examples below). This means that the involved scientists must acquaint themselves with the mode of thinking of each of the different disciplines to a considerable degree. It is only when they really understand which questions this methodology is trying to answer that both (or more) of the research approaches can formulate a common concept for addressing overlapping questions. What is to be analyzed is to what extent the terms used in the different sciences, be they identical or not, represent the same thing. If the results of many sciences are integrated in this manner, I will use the term *"intermeshing"* to express the close interwovenness of the analyzed topics. Eventually, it is even possible that the disciplines will exchange their foundations and use them for continued research. If the analyzed topics, as well as the corresponding terms, can still be unequivocally kept apart even after the joint work, I will term this *"complementing"* to emphasize the possibility of a sharp demarcation. The term "intermeshing" should thus only be used when sciences intersect relative to the topics they analyze, whether inclusive of the analyzed partial aspect (= *analytic viewpoint*) or not. Therefore, I characterize the two criteria as follows:

1. *Intermeshing:* Agreement in respect to the analyzed topic.

   a) The closest relationship probably exists between sciences in which the analysis *aspect* is in agreement, because they regard the same partial phenomenon from different viewpoints (from differing starting points). This conceptualization is also used when the same partial phenomenon is to be observed on different individual objects (total phenomenon), in other words, the same analysis topic exists in the different analysis objects, for example, the same chemical reaction in plants, animals and non-living systems. The clearest examples of this are probably provided by the interdisciplinary connections ("interdisciplines") of the natural sciences (including the technical sciences). In this way, biochemistry expresses the close bond between biology and chemistry. Biology focuses on the organism as a whole and in the analysis of the phenomena which constitute life, delves deeper into the detail of the structure, i.e. the meaning of the parts of the whole take precedence (the function of the elements for the whole system). Chemistry, on the other hand, focuses on the individual elements (which are the fundamental building blocks of all matter) and analyzes only their immediate interactions. As such, the analysis aspect for both is the same however, in as far as biology proceeds until it reaches these elements. Graphically it can be visualized in this manner:

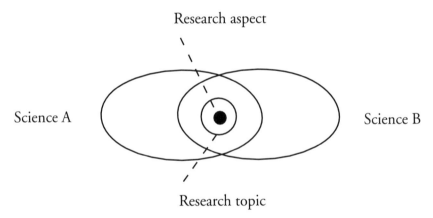

Research aspect

Science A   Science B

Research topic

   b) In the second place the connection between the sciences can be found because characteristics, which one assumes are in close correlation with one another, are being analyzed on the same total phenomenon. There exists here a conformity in respect to the analyzed *topic,* but not in respect to the analyzed *aspect.* The different aspects could be interpreted in such a manner that together they make up a partial phenomenon which is to be explained. An example of this is psychosomatic medicine. With such assumptions of immediate connections, it is frequently not exactly clear if the characteristics of the phenomenon in question have the same causes more or less independent of one another, making up one observable characteristic through interaction, or if the causes are themselves dependent on one another. It can also turn out that different effects are traceable to the same cause for which one previously postulated separate causes. In each case it should be clarified as to what one assumes based on the achieved level of analyses. Thus, it is possible that the analysis topics are identical, even if it was not previously assumed and one used different terms to describe them. What is decisive is that *no definite separation* can be undertaken between the observed aspects from the point of view of the phenomenon. The graphic illustration of this could look like this:

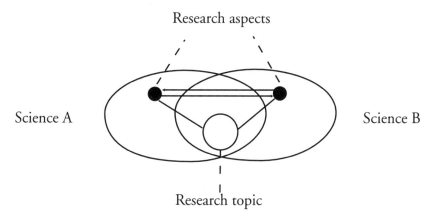

2. *Complementing:* Agreement in respect to the researched total phenomenon.

I have termed the less tightly connected form of interaction as complementary. I will use the term complementary when there is agreement that the analysis topics of different sciences belong to the *same total phenomenon,* but *largely continue to function independent of one another.* In other words, while the analyzed partial phenomena constitute a whole, one cannot assume that they are in close correlation to one another. Graphically this can be illustrated as follows:

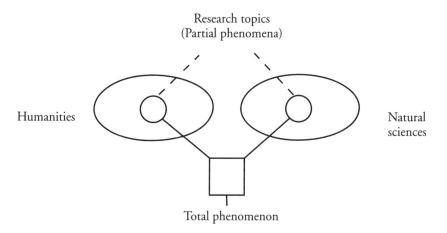

Other *criteria* of interdisciplinary research which I have adopted from Vosskamp are problem-, concept- and method-interdisciplinarity.

In *problem-interdisciplinarity* one question predominates, of which from the beginning, it is unclear which sciences will be affected by it. Examples for problem-interdisciplinarity are communication and environmental research, as well as the utopian research undertaken by Vosskamp. In the course of the analysis, it is usually unclear at the onset which results will become of interest from which discipline, and thus remain open until the conclusion of the project. From this explanation it is probably clear as to what is meant and no further description is necessary for problem-interdisciplinarity.

The term *concept-interdisciplinarity* refers to a collaboration in which one science adopts a model from another, the latter of which has developed as a subject-specific problem, that is, it turns out that this model is applicable to a larger sphere than one had originally anticipated. Examples of concept-interdisciplinarity are provided by the so called structure sciences. In my dissertation, I have dealt with system theory, cybernetics, information theory, synergetics, game theory, semiotics, as well as structuralism in their own chapters respectively. The reason for this detailed representation is that what these sciences can achieve for an interdisciplinary approach can only be made clear through concrete examples. The agreement found here between research objects from the different disciplines has fascinated me. This agreement provides a reason for high expectations because it doesn't only analyze formal analogies like the purely mathematical sciences do, but also uncovers further commonalities through the targeted search for additional contextual parallels stemming from these sciences. If one must be satisfied by the "purely" formal sciences of logic and mathematics relative to striving for standardization with the discovery of laws which can only be formally described, then in a narrow sense common methods of function are found in the structural sciences and through this, structural affinities are indicated. Since the reference to the concrete individual topics is immediate (even if the methods are formal), an opportunity is provided for the discovery of direct relationships between different objects which are able to utilize the same model. On the round about way of formal comparability, identical underlying (physical-chemical) mechanisms have been discovered by the structural sciences in several cases, and this means that substantially closer relations exist here than one first assumes. In order to substantiate this premise, I would also like to examine it in more detail.

What is at stake in the sciences is the manner of connection between the elements of dynamic systems in the broadest sense. The viable models presented here have proven themselves as decisive for their methodology. Their type of interconnectivity will, therefore, be analyzed independent of the type of elements themselves, even on a formal level. What is important is their functional coherence, which one mainly tries to grasp through mathematical means. The goal is the systemization of functional principles which might account for different systems. The term "functional equivalence" as used here means that certain parts of an intermeshing pattern can play *identical roles for the total system,* despite the difference in the elements that form them. If there are more direct relationships existing between the systems which can utilize the same model (for example, based on the agreement of the underlying chemical reaction, the similarity in the types of system building blocks or even their identity), then in a further step, additional analysis can occur in each case.

Since the structural sciences analyze which characteristics systems have based on the intermeshing design of their elements (i.e. due to the special type of interaction they produce) and not because of their existence as such, one can say that they attempt to grasp the phenomenon of "complexity." Because interdisciplinary research is often necessary due to the complexity of an analysis topic which cannot be mastered by one discipline, the structural sciences have special significance for subject-overlapping research.

If these sciences can work out the meaning of the connection between types of elements, a potential influence exists on the individual sciences in the following respect: in the explanation of phenomenon, these sciences are made aware of the fact that *the type of relationship between the individual pieces* should also to be taken into consideration. Some attributes develop only through their combination and therefore, they escape a purely analytical examination. In light of interdisciplinarity, the following notion can be derived: if new attributes *automatically* develop through the combination of certain already well-known and well-understood elements without some third item having to be added as a causal element, as representatives of these sciences would contend, then one should not demand that an additional theory is necessary beyond the present scientific explanation in order to further illustrate the correlation of the phenomenon in question, so that the existence of close interdisciplinary relationships between the relevant sciences is guaranteed. What is missing then, is the necessity to overcome a chasm or barrier between the different terms which we are forced to use to describe different levels of complexity. The bridge would already exist with proof of the immediate development of new attributes on an object through the combination of those already known, and there would be nothing additional to explain. The seamless bridging from one description to another, as demanded for interdisciplinary research, would thus already be achieved.

To begin with, *method-interdisciplinarity* is present between all disciplines which make use of the formal model of logic and mathematics. The commonalities however, do not exceed the purely abstract analogies as described for the structural sciences, so that the connecting effect usually remains very low. On the other hand, within a subject area like the natural sciences, the often observed commonalities of a large part of the methods express a high level of similarity between their work technique, i.e. the close relationship in how they approach a problem. The fact that many methods are simultaneously utilized is, at the same time, an indication that the analysis topics being dealt with are closely related to one another. In this way, for example, chemical-physical methods are often used in biology because their objects can be, to a large degree, described by them.

It must immediately be added, however, that although the assumption of methods between sciences is an indication that comparability of objects exists, it does not follow that one can therefore be reduced to the other. In this way, for example, biology cannot be reduced to physics and/or chemistry just because a large part of its analysis utilizes the methods of these sciences. Physical and chemical processes make up only partial aspects of living organisms; in other words, no total identifiability is provided. There are different levels of description for attributes of total phenomena. On every level there are different demands for explanation; i.e. different types of explanations are expected. On one hand, there are different degrees of integration which might explain the attributes of a system from the combination of its elements and on the other hand, there are different degrees of capabilities (at least with living organisms). This is what makes the utilization of a different vocabulary necessary; the problem, therefore, exists in creating bridges between the different terminological systems without succumbing to the danger of reductionism. At the beginning of such an "explanation hierarchy," a physical-chemical descriptive level can exist, as in the case of the explanation of a living organism's functioning. The language utilized here describes the behavior of the smallest building blocks of matter (i.e. a partial aspect of living organisms), and does not contain the terms which are utilized in the description of "behavior" in an ethological sense or offer recourse by explaining the motives of behavior. A physical description of process occurrences can, therefore, provide no satisfactory explanation for this "behavior"; very different *explicanda* exist here. Additional explanations for the correlations become necessary for each higher level of description, and on each level there can be an individual special discipline with its own particular terminology. This is why 'explanation' means something different on every level and why each level has its own catalog of questions! It is precisely these questions, which belong to the individual levels of description that are at stake, and it is important to keep them apart.

Naturally, several of the criteria mentioned can be applied to a certain research project, that is to say, no classification exists which allows for the strict segregation in light of individual interdisciplinary research plans. Moreover, what is at stake in the differentiation of criteria is reaching clarity in each case as to the extent of exchange between the sciences during a concrete project, and in which regard the exchange exists.

Beside these criteria, there are also different *degrees* of interdisciplinary cooperation, of which I differentiate the following:

1. The lowest level in regard to the attributes which connect subjects are constituted by logic and mathematics because they offer the most general forms of subject-bridging models at our disposal, namely those on a purely abstractual level (see above). The commonalities uncovered by them are described with abstract measures, which means that the comparable aspects are so restricted that one can only speak of an indirect connection. It is a question of synthesis

on a purely theoretical level, i.e. on the level of the form and not of the topics themselves.

2. It is difficult to decide the placement of the aforementioned structural sciences in the succession of levels as their results feature very different and far-reaching connections between the individual disciplines. I would like to place them in between the purely formal sciences and subsequent levels because of their high participation in formal usage of scientific mechanisms, although in part they uncover intermeshing between disciplines which are distantly related.

3. The next highest form of cooperation which I call *transdisciplinarity* denotes the connection between the humanities and natural sciences. What is at stake here, is the connection between disciplines which are classified into different spheres in the conventional scientific system; one which has been viewed for a long time neither as neighboring nor being in close relationship due to their topics. In the meantime, a rapprochement can be observed and the boundaries between these two spheres seem to have been partially overcome, although one cannot always speak of a fusion of the spheres. The fact that questions are even posed, which allow for the overstepping of these conventional boundaries between the spheres, can be expressed by the term "transdisciplinary thought."

As an example for transdisciplinary *complementing*, I have dealt with the epistemological problems of modern physics (theory of relativity, quantum theory and complementarity) in detail in my work, as well as the epistemological and anthropological problems of modern biology ("evolutionary epistemology" and ethology). Developmental psychology, gestalt psychology and the medical sciences are examples of transdisciplinary *intermeshing* between the humanities and the natural sciences, as is the much discussed (and very graphic) example of psychosomatic medicine in transdisciplinary research. "Both sides," i.e. most psychologists as well as most doctors, are in agreement that a close dependency exists between the phenomena they analyze, but the correlations are clarified only in a few cases.

What takes place with such connections is less often a direct exchange of facts but more a reciprocal sensitization to the problem at hand. The manysidedness of the problems at hand comes to light whenever a question, whose answer would overtax one or the other sphere, is approached from different starting points. This may cause the individual sciences to more strongly differentiate their explanation than they had previously done. It is also possible that the participating individual sciences become aware that their explanation does not cover the entire phenomenon through this process, but rather provides only a partial explanation. To fully understand a phenomenon, a reciprocal crossover of either purely natural scientific methods of observation or those of humanities is often necessary. The ability to change perspectives can therefore be stated as characteristic of transdisciplinary thought.

This is not to imply, however (as could possibly be concluded), that a connection between humanities and natural science approaches would have to lead to a uniform method of thought which might supersede the old. If, for example, as in the case of physics, the natural scientists recognize that their difficulties in the development of theories are of epistemological nature, one would hardly want to term physics as a hybrid form of humanities and the natural sciences. Rather, the development within a natural science has led to questioning in humanities, i.e. philosophical questioning, because the queries could no longer be answered purely by means of the natural sciences. If the physicists seek a new epistemological foundation for their discipline due to this, they do it explicitly in the consciousness of continuing to think philosophically; this, in turn, has influenced philosophy, which has received new input and has had to develop new procedures for the specification of its querying.

If such a close dependency exists without being able to call it intermeshing (because the querying from different disciplines refers directly to one another, but different terminology systems have to be used when dealing with them, as in the case of epistemological problems of modern physics), I will term the phenomenon as *connection points*. This term will denote that a direct relationship is nevertheless at hand. In the pattern of the previously shown graphics, such "connection points" can be illustrated in this way:

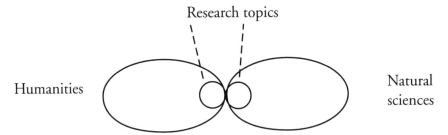

Transdisciplinarity places the highest demands on collaboration because one is dealing with widely disparate terminology systems and the communications are thus very difficult. One can therefore also characterize transdisciplinarity as "interdisciplinarity in the broadest sense."

4. Transdisciplinarity is followed by *interdisciplinarity in the narrowest sense,* which I interpret as the collaboration between disciplines within the same scientific sphere, in other words, either as natural sciences or humanities. Biotechnology, biomedical engineering or administrative sciences are examples of *complementing* here; examples of *intermeshing* are ecology, social biology, linguistics or neuroinformatics.

5. Aside from these "true" types of subject-overlapping cooperation, the problem of having to relate the individually acquired knowledge of the different parts of a very comprehensive discipline to one another can also arise. It can obviously not be taken for granted that all specialty areas of one discipline are in close relationship to one another. For examples in my work, I have again selected physics and biology, whose historical development I have more closely analyzed.

From the beginning, it is in no way clear *how* hormonal conditions influence the behavior of a living organism, even if no doubt exists as to the close connection between these living phenomena. The degree of difficulty in comprehending the reciprocal interactions between the different parts of a whole is especially apparent in such complex "whole phenomena" as living organisms. Evolutionary theory can be viewed as a thought which uniformly establishes biology as a discipline. Physics, on the other hand, primarily strives to find a uniform theoretical foundation for all of the individual forces analyzed in it; it is sometimes called the "world formula." Its history can also be illustrated as an increasing standardization through the development of overlapping theories, i.e. theories that encompass more and more phenomena.

In both cases, a striving for a uniform method of viewing underlies the scientific efforts which can be seen as comparable to striving for unity within different sciences. I will, therefore, term the connection between individual sub-disciplines of a subject as *"interdisciplinarity in the smallest sense."* It represents the closest form of collaboration in which possible contradictions can eventually and rather quickly come to light between two research approaches.

A scientific theoretical requirement of fundamental significance for interdisciplinary research is the following:

Because the exchange of results between sciences is what is at stake in interdisciplinarity, every interdisciplinary project should begin with a clarification of the questions for which a science is solely responsible, as well as a clarification of how the same analysis topics are approached by different sciences. In the first case there would then be no intersection, rather the participating sciences would complement each other; whereas in the agreement of the analysis topics it is a matter of interweaving between sciences (see above). The spheres for which only one science poses its special type of inquiry and has the appropriate method of response can thus be termed as purely subject-specific. Intersections do exist however, if the same questions (see above: analysis aspects) can be approached with differing methods.

Depending on the expanse of the analysis perspective, the different inquiries (approaches) of a discipline can encompass an individual topic as a whole (the *whole phenomenon*) or only a part of it. Since interdisciplinary considerations push the whole phenomenon into the foreground, in contrast to the far-reaching isolated analyzed aspects in the individual sciences, the term "analysis topic" can usually be utilized synonymously with the term "whole phenomenon."

If one works with interdisciplinarity, several problems soon emerge which are related to this type of scientific pursuit. A few have already been mentioned. One of the main problems is unquestionably that of language. The development of technical terminology is undoubtedly unavoidable if the objects and methods of a science are to be exactly defined. The question which arises stems from how various languages differ from one another. Two cycles of questions exist here: on one hand, there are different types of languages and, on the other, different terms are used. In other words, the utilization of the same term does not guarantee equivalent meaning.

If different disciplines utilize the same terms but define them differently, it can be assumed that they also have different objectives in mind. If indeed this is the case, it may not be beneficial for the comprehension of a phenomenon if one would disregard these different emphases for the purpose of uniform definition.

If two sciences discover that they are describing the same phenomena with different terms, the problem is minimized, but we must still come to an agreement as to which aspects of this phenomenon will be emphasized. Different points of emphasis can be ascribed in almost all cases since the disciplines clearly analyze the phenomenon within the context of different systems. This means that one must mutually strive to understand the other respective approaches as a whole.

In relation to this, there is often talk of a "translation problem" which must be solved; however, this constitutes only one element of the language problem. If different sciences analyze not only *different topics* but *different types of topics* as well, and because of this utilize different languages, then it is questionable whether it is even possible to translate from one to the other. The already mentioned definitions which are generally understood must, therefore, be formulated in order to make the individual terms clear for colleges from other disciplines.

It nearly always becomes problematic when a science has a problem sphere for a topic which it analyzes exclusively, because there is often no translation for some of the subject-specific terms. One must consequently explain the whole relationship in which these terms are used in order to make their meaning comprehensible.

Several possible psychological barriers constitute additional problems, for example, the problem of ingrained thought habits, of which we are usually unaware. The self-evidence with which one approaches problems as an experienced scientist, using a certain technique to arrive at a solution, is surely a factor that is not to be underestimated. Because lengthy explanations are often necessary, the patience of the scientists participating in an interdisciplinary dialog is often tested. An additional problem is the amount of time expended. Often there is also a close personal bond with one's chosen subject, which can become a problem if interdisciplinary collaboration deems that a correction is necessary in the results that were previously viewed as correct. In most cases however, any claim to control would probably be unjustified due to the fact that interdisciplinary problems are by definition subject-overlapping and, therefore, cannot be solved by one science alone. This makes it clear that in the final analysis it is the willingness for discussion which is decisive for the success of a subject-overlapping research project.

Of the items noted, one might conclude that it is especially important for interdisciplinary thought to analyze the terms which are utilized in the description and explanation of phenomena. These terms must be exactly analyzed for content in order to decide whether intersections exist between the analysis topics of the different sciences. Even if it would only be agreed to determine which terms can solely be defined by one special discipline, and which can be clarified interdisciplinarity, progress is already in motion because one can conduct more effective discussions. On one hand, for the same reason, it should be noted which problems each individual scientist deems solvable by one specific theory (and not by another) and on the other, from the onset, it should be clear as to which problems are viewed as solvable only through interdisciplinary solutions. In both cases the opinions may vary because diverse problems exist, or do not exist, for different approaches to solutions. Only then can we further contemplate how the results of scientific inquiry are connected to one another, i.e. how closely the sciences in question are related.

In summary, "the partial scientific unity of the empirical subject" can be formulated as the leading theme for interdisciplinary cooperation, as Helmut Schelsky, the founder of the Center for Interdisciplinary Research in Bielefeld (ZiF) noted in 1966. This means that interdisciplinary methodology takes a different path than the foundation of unity through a single moment, namely that of uniformity in the comprehension of concrete topics (in the broadest sense) *as totalities.* The leading question for interdisciplinary projects should therefore be: "Which questions make up the catalogue for a specific problem and which questions must be answered so that this problem can be viewed as fully solved?" The dissolution of discipline boundaries can also be achieved if the need for a reciprocal complement is recognized.

In order to once again emphasize it, I demand neither a uniform language nor a uniformly theoretical concept for interdisciplinary cooperation, rather merely the conviction that a formulated problem cannot be solved by one science alone. The willingness of scientists to discuss subject-foreign topics and methodologies is the deciding factor. The uniformity, therefore, lies more in the mentality rather than in the method.

In light of these thoughts, I would like to define the term "interdisciplinarity" as *a thought process which overlaps subjects that is oriented on a topic as a whole, leading to standardization of the comprehension of phenomena in that it connects the partial explanations of different sciences with one another.* The result can either be a partial merging of these individual disciplines into an "interdiscipline," or its direct reciprocal complement, or the cognizance that one is dealing with a transdisciplinary problem which surmounts the framework of the humanities as well as that of the natural sciences. For all of these interdisciplinary exchange possibilities, in an individual case it does not have to be clear how the connections between the respective analysis aspects of different sciences occur; rather it must be unanimously presumed that relationships *do* exist, so that the parties may continue to search for them together.

If interdisciplinary research is to be effective, it is paramount that one first agrees on a generally recognized definition for it, which in my opinion has not occurred until now. Interdisciplinary theory should facilitate concrete interdisciplinary research by clarifying what will be attempted on the whole through a clear classification of different types of subject-overlapping collaboration. One should know exactly what one is doing, i.e. is entering into, if one is to do it well; in other words, one must also realize where the respective difficulties and boundaries lie.

In conclusion, I would like to reemphasize that interdisciplinarity should not become a predominate scientifically theoretical problem, but rather a connection of knowledge elements should take place in the minds of scientists. The result should be that scientists will understand more of a phenomenon and its complexity than they had previously understood, so that in their future research they do not forget that the partial aspect just being analyzed is in interaction with other partial aspects in an intact total phenomenon.

General Lessons From Specific Interdisciplinary Fields

Environment

Julie Thompson Klein

Environmental studies promised to do for the environment what urban programs promised to do for the city. Before the 1960s and 1970s environmental consciousness and concern were not prominent in the university or in government. During the late 1960s the advent of ecology and the rapid rise of environmental awareness generated popular support for the cause of saving the earth. Spurred by media coverage, a flurry of conferences, and some corrective legislation, the mounting of environmental programs followed. Like its urban counterpart, environmental studies entered universities on waves of social capital and interdisciplinary rhetoric.

A similar diversity of programs and courses emerged. Although they were significant in number, their structural identity was not always clear. Many existing programs simply added "environmental" to their titles. "Sanitary engineering," for example, became "environmental engineering," and "environment" replaced "conservation" in many course descriptions. Some departments contributed entire courses to an environmental studies program, such as environmental geology, environmental psychology, and environmental law. But this "syncretic assemblage" rarely resulted in synthesis. Instead of coalescing into a discrete field, Lynton Caldwell recalled in a genealogy of the field, environment-related aspects of the disciplines and professions were brought together into a curriculum that was and still is, "essentially eclectic" (1983, 249–51).

Like urban studies, environmental studies also suffered disengagements of economic and social capital during the late 1970s and early 1980s. Opinion polls documented continuing public support for environmental quality and protective measures, but moderate arguments for "balance," "common sense," and "reason" gained favor over radical action. This stance was reinforced in formulations of public policy. Except where mandated by statute, federal assistance ended for the most part with the Reagan administration. The Office of Environmental Education was discontinued, and many political supporters either left Congress or shifted their attention to other priorities. Environmental protection measures remain in place, but policy reversals in the form of budget cuts and eased regulatory measures have continued to undermine the environmental movement. In addition, several large private foundations dropped or significantly reduced their interests in environmental research and education (Caldwell 1983, 251–53).

Political shifts had analogues in academic structure and values. During the

Klein, Julie Thompson. "Environment" from Ch. 4 "Interdisciplinary Studies." Crossing Boundaries: Knowledge, Disciplinarities, and Interdisciplinarities. Charlottesville: University Press of Virginia, 1996, 96–101. Reprinted with permission of the University Press of Virginia.

late 1960s new titles, courses, and programs conveyed the hope that academic institutions would cultivate good environmental citizenship and respect for nature. Prospects for achieving critical mass dimmed with economic cutbacks and competition from social programs focused on people-oriented issues such as poverty, racism, and war. By the early 1980s several universities were reviewing their environmental and natural resource-related programs, considering elimination. At roughly the same time, a shift in professional values occurred. Confidence in specialization, reductionist methods, statistical rationalization, and the primacy of economic considerations was reasserted (Caldwell 1983, 252). The parallel to urban studies is not a mere coincidence. The limits of traditional academic values were widely conceded, but these values were heavily relied on in formulating public policy. In a meeting with one hundred leaders of environmental studies programs in fifty-six universities, Russell Peterson found most of them felt they were treated as second-class citizens on their campuses. They have lost ground in budgets, degree approval, and faculty tenure cases (1990, 221).

The question of identity also yields parallel answers. Environmental studies encompasses the subject matter of many fields of knowledge, thereby straining the disciplinary concept. Like "urban," certain aspects of the "environment" have also become objects of professional and technical training and practice. This means relations need to be clarified with pertinent fields of practice, such as architecture, agriculture, engineering, law, and medicine, and the practical concerns of human society, such as pollution control, urban design, resource management, public health, and economic growth (Caldwell 1983, 248). In practical settings or in professional schools, one set of academic disciplines relates broadly to natural resources. This commitment is evident in schools of agriculture and natural resources. Another set, evident in schools of engineering and technology, relates to industry. Other areas, which may be classed as service sectors, relate to medicine, law, business, and finance. These multiple affiliations reflect divisions of rural/agricultural and urban-industrial sectors (Dahlberg 1986, 13). A secondary set of interests creates added conflict across divisions of the environmental issue. They take the form of segmented social and political commitments to air and water pollution, eutrophication of lakes and streams, degradation of landscapes, and decimation of wildlife (Caldwell 1983, 248).

In the related field of natural resources, two patterns of specialization have emerged. One is based in intellectual separation of natural resource systems from urban/industrial areas and problems. The other is based in disciplinary specialization. These patterns generate a number of intellectual and practical problems in universities. Tensions arise between practically oriented and theoretically oriented approaches and departments. Often couched in terms of "applied" versus "basic" research, these tensions reflect differences in approach and underlying rationale. Academic work on natural resources has tended to be strongly based on the natural sciences, although organizational separations are made between aspects related to resource exploitation and aspects related to conservation. These divisions manifest themselves organizationally in separate departments of soil science, plant physiology, forest management, and so on. Within the social sciences, separate subdisciplines or departments have tended to develop in agricultural economics, rural sociology, and economic geography. Until recently, little attempt was made to involve the humanities (Dahlberg 1986, 13).

The most common educational format has been a topical focus on "environment" in a coordinated multidisciplinary program. This is the least disruptive arrangement, but it still depends on cooperation from disciplines. It does not readily lead to new insights into environmental relationships or reveal gaps in scientific knowledge that handicap formulation of sound environmental policies. An applied problem focus may be adopted, but it will not automatically integrate disciplinary inputs unless a concerted effort is made to establish a hybrid interlanguage. The problem of synthesis is further implicated in the differing status accorded to holism, reductivism, and pluralism. Ecology emerged early as a lead framework, yet the idea of a holistic strategy for ecosystem development has been controversial. Theorists have erected complex systems, but general statements are criticized because they are not based on observation and testing. Pressure continues to jettison "multidisciplinary mishmash" in favor of "real" science, defined in terms of reductionist approaches, observation, and testing (Caldwell 1983, 254).

Despite these difficulties, ecology remains an important locus for integration. A broad discipline, ecology is composed of linked subdisciplines that Likens (1992) depicts along a gradient extending from strictly biological concerns to strictly physical phenomena. Meteorology, geology, and hydrology exhibit an abiotic focus. Systematics, genetics, and physiology exhibit a biotic focus. In most subdisciplines, though, a mix of abiotic and biotic focus is necessary. Hence subdisciplines such as biogeochemistry, chemical ecology, and population ecology appear at points between abiotic and biotic ends of the gradient.

The number and diversity of journals, publications, and scientific societies that address ecological topics have also increased. New data, creative tests, and novel generalizations have been produced. New or neglected questions are being addressed, and use of ecological information has increased in such key areas as environmental policy and management, conservation biology, restoration ecology, watershed management, and global environmental change. This growth makes the hybridity of the underlying category of knowledge, but it also exacerbates fragmentation. As subdisciplines become more dense, they develop their own viewpoints and assumptions, definitions, lexicons, and methods. This divergence is apparent in the different meanings given to the same terms. "Regulation," "development," and "evolution" have different meanings in studies of population, community, and ecosystem ecology. Over time, as the conceptual frameworks of areas continue to diverge, interrelating subdisciplinary viewpoints becomes more difficult. Physiological ecology and biogeography, for instance, have common roots, but at present they barely intersect (Pickett, Kolasa, and Jones 1994, 3–5).

What might constitute a workable synthesis? Several answers have emerged all across interdisciplinary fields: a multidisciplinary matrix of disciplinary parts, a broad field with a particular disciplinary dominance, a metadiscipline that overrides special interests at a global level, or an open critique that permanently resists fixing identity. The parallel field of science, technology, and society (STS) offers an illuminating analogy. Like urban and environmental studies, STS arose from social upheavals of the 1960s and 1970s. Alongside emerging critiques of the idea of progress, cognate changes in a number of disciplines beckoned a shift away from internalist-oriented subdisciplines interested in history and philosophy of science and technology to more externalist and sociologically oriented interpretations of academic disciplines. STS programs now number approximately a hundred. Hundreds more courses, groups of courses, professional organizations, and assessment groups are concerned with STS issues. In an account of the field, Stephen Cutcliffe suggested that interdisciplinarity can be achieved from more than one perspective. Relations among multiple commitments and constituencies must be clarified, though, in a general way, at the level of theory (Cutcliffe 1989). This task is complicated by conflicting constructions of the field, ranging from business as usual and a strong science program to differing degrees of contingency (Fuller 1993, 11).

Ecology again provides a parallel, with generic points of importance to interdisciplinary fields highlighted. Whether *combining separate areas* into a new composite understanding or *extracting components of different areas* in order to produce a new understanding, the mechanics of integration and synthesis require a strong community. Strengthening the community may entail *progressive sharing of empirical and theoretical contents* or *focusing on a specific linking relationship.* Integration can occur at *any scale or breadth of scope,* from a finer scale that combines models relatively close in focus and approach to a grander scale that links disparate approaches to ecology. Components of prior theories may be excluded, but *contradictions between theories* may require developing deeper theories that expose unity among phenomena. This step has occurred in current theories of the four fundamental forces in modern physics. Perhaps the important general lesson is that integration is not necessarily a matter of reductionism or grand unity. It may involve *nested hierarchies* of several broad theories that might yield a novel integration (Pickett, Kolasa, and Jones 1994, 129–34).

The category "urban" provides a parallel on another count. Realistically, Rich and Warren concluded, synthesis is more likely to emerge from "a tentative and shifting coalescence of concepts" (1980, 60, 65). After three decades, there is no precise or commonly used definition of "urban," though most definitions include the interrelation between people and space. The literature reflects the continuing diversity of topics, backgrounds, and methodologies. Multiple paradigms mark conflicts over basic assumptions, choice of methods, and the relation between basic research and application. Some convergence has occurred in shared theories and methodologies. Convergence is also suggested by the general agreement that urban research should include the characteristics of urban space, the organization of institutions and processes underlying urban political, social, and economic relations, and links between urban centers and their relations with the larger political system, society, and the economy. Often a single topic functions as a matrix of underlying processes and outcomes. Research on urban economic development, for instance, involves examining issues such as local political institutions and processes, intergovernmental policies and policymaking, regional labor markets and transportation systems, and educational and cultural institutions. Each component, in turn, may fuel further research projects. The curriculum echoes this diversity, encompassing courses such as anthropology, architecture, economics, geography, history, political science, planning, and sociology in addition to explicitly interdisciplinary programs (Andranovich and Riposa 1993, 3–5).

The shared conceptual problem at stake in all interdisciplinary studies is how best to move beyond narrow sectoral interests that make environment, urban, and other hybrid categories one more competing special interest, not a representation of general interests. Interdisciplinary categories are organizational and intellectual principles that focus attention on the importance of clarifying and bridging the ways that different approaches and overlapping fields of interest order knowledge (after Caldwell 1983, 254). Evaluation is complicated by their relative youth. Questions of scope and content are still unanswered, and for most fields academic status remains unsettled. The lessons of critical mass underscore the importance of a collective commitment to generation and synthesis of new knowledge, an adequate number of advanced research and graduate programs, and a stable infrastructure of communication networks, meetings publications, and flow of students into programs. The key element in stimulating an infrastructure of community is dialogue. Dialogue opens up lines of communication within which there may be—indeed should be—competing answers (Rich and Warren 1980, 65).

Ultimately the problem of interdisciplinary studies is the problem of fit. The metaphor of fit, Caldwell concluded from the experience of environmental studies, prejudges the epistemological problem at stake. Interdisciplinary categories arise because of a perceived misfit among need, experience, information, and the prevailing structure of knowledge embodied in disciplinary organization. If the structure must be changed to accommodate the new field, perhaps the structure itself is part of the problem. Environmental and urban studies, like all studies of the second kind, represent "a latent and fundamental structuring of knowledge and formal education" (Caldwell 1983, 247–49). They mark the broader move into complex structure, and they operate as boundary concepts. The boundary work of advancing interdisciplinary claims pulls them centripetally toward specific investments. At the same time, they respond to and stimulate centrifugal movement toward hybrid constructs. As a result they wind up caught between their shadow location and pressure to fit into the surface structure by establishing legitimacy in a political economy that forces them into competition for resources with more strongly positioned disciplines. Legitimacy, though, may come at a high price—the loss of openness that gave rise to interdisciplinary claims in the first place.

References

Andranovich, Gregory, and Gerry Riposa. 1993. *Doing Urban Research.* Applied Social Research Methods Series 33. Newbury Park, Calif.: Sage.

Caldwell, Lynton K. 1983. "Environmental Studies: Discipline or Metadiscipline?" *Environmental Professional* 5:247–59.

Cutcliffe, Stephen. 1989. "Science, Technology, and Society: An Interdisciplinary Academic Field." *National Forum* 69, 2:22–25.

Dahlberg, Kenneth. 1986. "The Changing Nature of Natural Resources." In Dahlberg and Bennett 1986, 11–35.

Fuller, Steve. 1993. *Philosophy, Rhetoric, and the End of Knowledge,* Madison: Univ. of Wisconsin Press.

Likens, G. E. 1992. *Excellence in Ecology* Vol. 3, *The Ecosystem Approach: Its Use and Abuse.* Oldendorf/Luhe, Germany, Ecology Institute.

Peterson, Russell. 1990. "Why Not a Separate College of Integrated Studies." In *Rethinking the Curriculum: Toward an Integrated, Interdisciplinary College Education,* ed. Mary E. Clark and Sandra A. Wawrytko, 215–26. Contributions to the Study of Education 40. New York: Greenwood.

Pickett, Steward T. A., Jurek Kolasa, and Clive G. Jones. 1994. *Ecological Understanding: The Nature of Theory and the Theory of Nature.* San Diego: Academic Press.

Rich, Daniel, and Robert Warren. 1980. "The Intellectual Future of Urban Affairs: Theoretical, Normative, and Organizational Options." *Social Science Research* 17, 2:53–66.

Women

Julie Thompson Klein

Once again, the underlying category is not new. Historically, knowledge about women was largely a by-product of work done in disciplinary contexts. In coeducational and all-female institutions, some women offered courses and conducted research pertaining to women, especially sex and gender issues. Until the women's studies movement of the late 1960s and 1970s, though, their experiments were largely ignored or even abandoned. Over the course of two decades, the growth of a feminist presence on campus resulted in women's studies becoming, for many, an exemplary model of a successful interdisciplinary field. Women's studies was enabled by a combination of historical events and social capital. They included a new push for general education reform, demands for social justice and racial equality, concerns about dissipation of the talents of educated women, the entrance of women of all races and classes into the public labor force, and new technologies of reproduction that helped to redefine women's sexuality (Stimpson 1992, 254–56).

Like urban and environmental studies, women's studies is "the academic arm" of a larger social and political movement (Coyner 1991, 349). The first program in the United States was formally approved in 1970 at San Diego State University, though the first "political" women's studies course was reportedly taught at the Free University of Seattle in 1965 (Boxer 1982, 663 n. 6). In 1969 roughly 16 courses in the country were devoted to the subject of women and gender (Stimpson 1992, 257). By 1973, approximately 5,000 courses on women were being offered in American institutions of higher education (DuBois et al. 1987, 4 n. 4). In 1977, when the National Women's Studies Association (NWSA) was founded, 276 programs were in place nationwide. By 1982 there were more than 300 programs and more than 30,000 courses in colleges and universities (Boxer 1982, 662). By 1990 there were 520 programs, 235 of them undergraduate majors and 404 minors. A recent survey by the American Council on Education found courses at 68 percent of all United States universities, 48.9 percent of all four-year colleges, and 26.5 percent of two-year colleges. Across this curricular array, more students take courses in women's studies than major in it, and double majors are the norm ("Women's Studies" 1990, 214).

The intellectual history of the field is as revealing as its institutional history. What began as "compensatory education" became nothing less than "a comprehensive intellectual and social critique" that addressed hegemonic issues

Klein, Julie Thompson. "Women" from Ch. 4 "Interdisciplinary Studies." Crossing Boundaries: Knowledge, Disciplinarities, and Interdisciplinarities. *Charlottesville: University Press of Virginia, 1996, 115–123. Reprinted with permission of the University Press of Virginia.*

("Women's Studies" 1990, 209). Reflecting the field's origin in a larger social movement, the syllabi of early courses were dominated by popular writings, such as Simone de Beauvoir's *The Second Sex,* Caroline Bird's *Born Female,* Betty Friedan's *The Feminine Mystique,* and Kate Miller's *Sexual Politics.* These courses aimed to promote greater reflection on female experience and feminist goals. Usually taken as electives, they were not firmly anchored in their host institutions (Boxer 1982, 663 n. 7, 681). They were taught mostly by women, many of them political activists. Few had status as resident faculty in women's studies programs.

The field grew rapidly for two reasons. It met urgent political and intellectual needs. Its founders also took advantage of existing frameworks and structures employed by other interdisciplinary fields, especially Black, ethnic, and American studies ("Women's Studies" 1990, 210; Gerstenberger and Allen 1977). In the early 1970s, Sandra Coyner recalls, "women's studies" was a restricted choice from limited alternatives that were not of women's own design. A pattern for name and structure already existed, permitting women's studies to become established relatively quickly and obviating the need to fight more general battles about innovation and crossing disciplinary boundaries. Seldom, though, was there debate on whether that structure was the most appropriate one, let alone what the ideal structure might be (1991, 350).

By the late 1980s a formidable scholarly apparatus was in place in the form of specialist journals, newsletters, professional networks, and a viable presence in universities and on some commercial press lists. Production of knowledge about women followed a common pattern in interdisciplinary fields. Initial gains are greater in the accumulation of data and information. Early feminist criticism appeared to be "an empirical orphan in the theoretical storm" (Showalter 1981, 180). The data/theory split, though, is not a strict dichotomy or a simple diptych, an observation Chalmers Johnson made in area studies. Data gatherers are not arrayed on one panel, with theory builders on the opposite panel (1975, 81). New empirical work challenged and reinvigorated existing theory, exposing the partiality of conventional axioms, received truths, and the premise that facts were neutral. The archaeological mission of ciphering and translating silent sediments of the historical past (Kroker 1980, 9) raised substantive questions: Why did gaps and voids exist in the first place? Why were they treated as "in-between" spaces, not as primary spaces?

Mere accretion of woman-centered topics—the augmenting strategy Charlotte Bunch dubbed "Add women and stir" (Shumway and Messer-Davidow 1991, 215)—would not be adequate. Only radical reconstruction of knowledge and consciousness would effect genuine change, moving the field beyond "mainstreaming" knowledge about women as a subset or component of knowledge about men to a genuine "transformation" capable of "breaking the disciplines" (Minnich 1990, 12; Howe 1978). The goal of challenging dominant intellectual traditions and institutional structures, enshrined in the founding rhetoric of the NWSA, has been accomplished in a number of ways. The scholarly practices that define and advance the field span older and newer traditions of liberal humanism, challenges to established disciplinary canons, strategies of reading that emphasize differences within language, and specific methods and theories linked with structuralism and poststructuralism, cultural studies, neo-Marxist theory of ideology, and women's perspectives on African American and postcolonial experience and identity (Stimpson 1992).

No single description adequately accounts for this diversity, though several stages of feminist scholarship have been identified. Early deconstructions of error and bias led to reconstruction of philosophical and scientific reality and, in turn, to the construction of general theories (Stimpson 1978, 14–26). The first generation of scholars addressed primarily omissions and distortions in the form and content of traditional disciplines (Hoagland 1978, 17). This initial phase was characterized by identification of male bias and discovery of how it led to omission or distortion of the study of women. The second phase was characterized by development of original feminist perspectives on the methods and assumptions of disciplines (DuBois et al. 1987, 15–18, 40). Stages of development have not been neat or consecutive. Three major activities have supplemented, corrected, and sometimes overlapped one another: defiance of difference; celebration of difference; and recognition of differences among women (Stimpson 1992, 259–67). The recent turn into gender studies encompasses interests that were formerly identified as feminist along with studies of masculinity, sexuality, and lesbian and gay studies (Schor 1992, 262, 275).

Inevitably, as feminist scholarship developed within and across disciplines, the question arose whether women's studies was a discipline. The emergence of specialized terminology suggested the possibility. In distinguishing two modes of feminist literary criticism, for example, Elaine Showalter (1981) coined the terms "gynocritics" and "gynocriticism" to distinguish intellectual work that focused on the woman writer and a genuinely women-centered ground of inquiry. Later Alice Jardine (1985) used the term "gynesis" to label expansion into cultural representations of gender and patterns of masculinity and femininity. Taking women's writing as the primary subject forced the leap to a new conceptual vantage point, away from the ideological dilemma of reconciling revisionary pluralism into an epistemology grounded in difference. Research, teaching, and service premised on difference often begin by redressing grievances and building on existing models.

Diane Elam (1990) defines the space of women's studies as a "discipline of difference," a construction that calls into question the autonomy of discipline by appealing to disciplinarity as "cross-disciplinarity." Disciplinary borders are crossed through continuous inter- and intradisciplinary cross-fertilization. Reconstituting disciplinarity as cross-disciplinarity does not elevate feminism to the status of theoretical metalanguage or a totalizing master narrative. Like argument 3, embodied in Jeffrey Peck's vision of a critical interdisciplinarity in German studies, this move asserts that borders are neither stable nor impenetrable. The premise of difference is comprehensive. Older critiques of disciplinary structure are joined by new demands for self-definition, reflexivity, and alternative forms of knowledge production (Boxer 1982, 686). Epistemological concerns are also realigned with their political implications.

Despite their differences, ethnic, minority, and women's studies exhibit an implicitly shared epistemology that dismantles the boundary separating knowledge from action, discipline from politics. In a notable parallel, Russell Thornton (1977) argued that Native American studies should be allowed to define and build its own intellectual traditions, based not on the differentiated social and political systems of Anglo culture but on the holistic "undifferentiated systems" of Native American cultures. That means focusing on oral traditions, treatises and treaty rights, tribal government, forms of organization, group persistence, Native American epistemology, and the practical needs of community. Similarly, Ronald Walters argued that African American studies is "disciplined" by the centrality of racism in American life. Curriculum and research are based on the "unity and the order of Blackness." They are defined by praxis, not grand theory (1970, 144). Analysis is not objective in the traditional sense but is interested work—corrective, descriptive, and prescriptive work. Theory building and problem solving have an integral relation grounded in the needs of community (Semmes 1981, 15).

The fusion of critique and problem solving theoretically places political and intellectual work on the same level. Yet they are not valued that way in the academic reward structures, or among members of the same field. In women's studies, some of the most extensive debates have focused on the relation between activist and academic goals. This tension requires a balancing act in the NWSA among individuals who came to women's studies at different periods, through different routes, with differing conceptualizations of the field (Boxer 1982, 674–75). Furthermore, despite a handful of feminist public policy centers and organizations composed of friends of women's studies, few structures span academic and other communities. Despite courses that treat social change historically, theoretically, or practically, knowledge of discourse has not been of significant use to child incest victims whose stories are discredited in court because they are inconsistent with standard judicial criteria for valid discourse. Models exist, among them a Mankato State University course called "Collective Action/Analysis" and an internship in feminist organizations at the University of Massachusetts, Boston. They are still few in number, however (Messer-Davidow 1991, 301). Moreover, despite other manifestations of feminism on campus—centers that address sexual assault and harassment, advocacy and action groups, affirmative action offices, activities by and for minority women, and special programs for women in math, engineering, and the sciences—women's studies scholarship has rarely acted directly to produce change (Coyner 1991, 351).

Women's studies has also had to confront its own exclusions and distortions. "Women" is not a category unto itself. It is part of a matrix of interrelations with gender, race, class, and national culture. The founding generation of academic feminists found themselves charged with being an elite corps holding good jobs and privileged positions but removed from the social circumstances of many of the women they purported to represent. In the past, heterosexual, white, and even upper-class female perspectives dominated feminist inquiry, fostering what Micaela di Leonardo called the "feminist metonymic fallacy" of universalizing women's experiences without regard for power differentials

(Addelson and Potter 1991, 260). Mainstream feminist scholarship has been critiqued in the work of African American, Chicana, Native American, and lesbian scholars who are engaged in their own projects of rediscovery and re-evaluation (DuBois et al. 1987, 63). The emergence of Black women's studies during the 1980s and a clearly defined community of African American women writers created new institutional locations where Black women intellectuals are producing new specialized knowledge. Black women's history and feminist literary criticism have been important sites in this renaissance (Collins 1991).

Women's studies also confronts the dilemma of professionalism. The notion of a "both-and" strategy emerged early, in the vision of a core of faculty trained in more than one discipline to become "interdisciplinary women" capable of working with interested teachers in their diverse locations. This strategy, on the surface, implies a professional paradox of being "both in the disciplines and in opposition to them" (Messer-Davidow 1991, 281–82). Progress in all of the studies, though, has been bidirectional. Scholars and teachers work across the grain and against it, operating both inside and outside discipline. One coordinator of a women's studies program argued early on that "in order to change or add to the traditional perspectives of disciplines, women's studies has to be of them, in them, and about them" (Boxer 1982, 671 n. 34, 693). Being located within institutions while wielding their forms of power and authority for interested purposes amounts to a dismantling from within a professional class position (Addelson and Potter 1991, 271).

The question of interdisciplinarity is complicated by the plurality of disciplinary and ideological perspectives. From the beginning, women's studies was conceived as interdisciplinary in the sense of providing programs where disciplinary boundaries could be broken down and a broader, more complete approach to understanding women developed. This conception often embodies implicit criticism of the entire structure of higher education. Gloria Bowles speculated early on that one day the Renaissance man might be replaced by "the interdisciplinary woman" (cited in Boxer 1982, 687). Her exact identity has been debated ever since. In the 1975 inaugural issue of *Signs,* the founding editors suggested several patterns of work. They ranged from one person skilled in several disciplines but focused on one subject *to* several persons skilled in single disciplines yet focused collaboratively on a subject together *to* a group of disciplinarians who publish in random conjunction within the same journal. Two years later, Catherine Stimpson acknowledged that the interdisciplinary promise had proved more difficult than envisioned. Resistance to moving outside one's field of expertise was as strong in women's studies as in other interdisciplinary fields. Stimpson called for translators able to "interpret the languages of one discipline to persons in another" (Boxer 1982, 685–87).

In the ensuing years the term "interdisciplinary" appeared in conjunction with a number of strategies: developing alternative curricular structures and pedagogies, borrowing disciplinary methodologies, engaging in community service and political work through activism, and forging a new body of knowledge through self-defined epistemology. Reflecting a widely shared belief that women's studies is a prototype of academic organization in the twenty-first century, the metaphors of a matrix, a network, connection, and dialogue have been prominent in descriptions of the field ("Women's Studies" 1990, 212). In the curriculum, the familiar umbrella structure loosely relates a variety of practices that are mostly multidisciplinary and interdepartmental (Boxer 1982, 683). Programs typically mix courses from single disciplines and courses with a topical approach. Women's studies journals typically publish research from both disciplinary and interdisciplinary perspectives (DuBois et al. 1987, 1, 4).

Over the past decade a number of collections have weighed the impact of feminist scholarship on the disciplines, foremost among them *A Feminist Perspective in the Academy: The Difference It Makes* (1983), *Feminist Scholarship: Kindling in the Groves of Academe* (1987), and *(En)Gendering Knowledge: Feminists in Academe* (1991). The journal *Signs* also continues to provide reports on the latest research emerging from the disciplines. The collaborative team that wrote *Feminist Scholarship* found that feminist scholarship simultaneously challenges and is shaped by disciplinary inquiry. Patterns of journal publication from 1966 through 1980 in five disciplines (history, literature, education, anthropology, and philosophy) revealed uneven influence. Measuring impact is complicated by the multiple ways feminist scholarship develops at different sites. The general trend has been toward increasing receptivity. Distribution, however, varies. The diversity of topics that may be counted as "on women" complicates measurement. A significant portion of scholarship appears in interdisciplinary journals devoted to women's studies. Special issues echo the problem of fit. They heighten awareness, but they have an ambiguous status. They raise awareness, but they do not substitute for sustained consideration in the mainstream. Building distinct subfields and assigning special rubrics are effective ways of mounting a feminist presence, but this strategy may ultimately reinforce marginalization (DuBois et al. 1987, 155–202).

The authors of *Feminist Scholarship* concluded that research frameworks and standard analytic concepts such as family, class, race, community, socialization, social control, and social conflict must be reformulated in order to take into account relations between men and women and to encompass research on women (DuBois et al. 1987). Sociology is an example. Citation analysis shows that feminist work has been slow to enter mainstream journals of the discipline. The journal *Signs,* edited in part by sociologists, was cited only a handful of times in a sampling conducted by Craig Calhoun, and interdisciplinary periodicals on women's and gender studies accounted for an almost "negligible" part of overall citation patterns. Feminist work in sociology has centered on studies of the social circumstances and problems of women in a fairly conventional sociological manner. It has not been a sustained occasion for more fundamental reconsideration or reconstruction of mainstream disciplinary orientation (1992, 163 n. 35).

The early assumption that research on women would coalesce into a single interdisciplinary field has been limited by the complexities of doing interdisciplinary work and differences of disciplinary location. Analytic concepts such as gender, oppression, and agency have been powerful unifying themes. In addition, most of the women interviewed in Aisenberg and Harrington's *Women of*

Academe reported preferring "cross-disciplinary" to discipline-bound inquiry. They have been more likely to study unformulated subjects at the edges of disciplines rather than sharply defined subjects at their centers (Hartman 1991, 18, 30). Nevertheless, some boundaries have been more permeable than others. Citation data indicate that much of feminist scholarship retains a strongly disciplinary character. The deepest differences are methodological. Even when focused on the same topic, research results may be disparate and incommensurable. This tendency underscores another duality of interdisciplinary scholarship. An overall commonality exists, but the work produced just as often bears the stamp of a particular field (DuBois et al. 1987, 38–39, 198–202).

From their locations within the disciplines feminists have dispersed centripetally into specializations. Within the shared space of women's studies, they have moved centrifugally to "cross-disciplinary" research and teaching (Hartman and Messer-Davidow 1991, 5). The broader field offers intellectual community and an institutional site for feminists who are still doing most of their work within disciplines, further legitimating courses, journals, conferences, research, and projects that use gender as a category of analysis (Addelson and Potter 1991, 271). In developing gender as a category of analysis, they have used the practices of disciplines to change focus and even the practices themselves. Feminist scholarship, as a result, is less a single map than "a portfolio of maps." In establishing the unreliability of other knowledge maps, scholars and teachers have charted new knowledge territory and heightened reflexivity on all map-making (after Stimpson 1992, 251).

Defining women's studies by patrolling its borders or specifying its center is less reliable a descriptive strategy than reading efforts to understand the relation of disciplinary parts to an interdisciplinary whole, including links with the feminist movement that fostered a new academic field (DuBois et al. 1987, 196). The whole in question is not a totalizing unity. It is a complex critical holism anchored by a hybrid category of knowledge—gender. The term "feminist" has many meanings: political, professional, theoretical, and practical (Addelson and Potter 1991, 259). Correspondingly, the label "women's studies" rarely specifies a single identity. Most people working in the field also identify with another academic community, as feminist historian, literary critic, psychologist, or social worker. Naming tends to designate a position in a program—as women's studies faculty, student, or director—rather than the work performed. Women's studies is a location—institutional, political, and sometimes physical. The kinds of work done in these locations can be inferred from practice more than name. They span teaching and curriculum, miscellaneous advocacy, organizing speeches and events, research, publishing, and scholarship. More than anything else women's studies attempts to identify and actualize a space shared by two important institutions and establish a place within each of them. These moves brought feminism into the academy while adding applied teaching and scholarship to the goals of the women's movement. Depending on which home is most salient, definition shifts (Coyner 1991, 349–51).

Echoing the ambivalence in other interdisciplinary studies, feminists sometimes proclaim that new scholarship has changed the very nature of academic work. At other times they despair that research on women is ignored and shunted to the margins of disciplines (DuBois et al. 1987, 158). Feminism, like Marxism, contains political dimensions that threaten the very foundations of disciplines. Yet individual disciplines, Ben Agger (1989) found in a parallel examination of textbooks for introductory sociology courses, flatten their critical nature and agenda. Descriptions of the field vary according to perceived containment. By and large, feminist scholarship has not transformed the academy. Assessing the current state of the field, authors of the report on the field for the Association of American Colleges and Universities' study-in-depth project, concluded that women's studies remains in the shadow structure. Yet conditions of marginality are at the same time conditions of strength: "By insisting on interdisciplinary flexibility and reflexivity, by refusing conventional categories and labels, and by asserting obligations to a self-conscious critique of the politics of knowledge, we resist absorption into an 'acceptable' (and safe) liberal pluralism at the expense of our radical critique." The epistemological power of women's studies depends on its location in spaces where conventional intellectual boundaries are blurred ("Women Studies" 1990, 210–11).

The categories of knowledge at stake in all interdisciplinary studies are caught in a seized conjunction, in the hedged grammar of "Yes . . . but." Gerda Lerner (1979) framed the issue for women's studies in terms of "contribution history." The danger is being reduced to a contributing role in a framework whose analytic categories are not of one's own making. Carol Berkin (1991) framed the issue in terms of "dangerous courtesies" that plague women's history and other disciplines of the humanities. Three of the seven courtesies plague other interdisciplinary fields as well. The "roll call" adds women to lists but does not change underlying categories or measures of achievement. The "intermezzo" includes vignettes, biographical sketches, or dramatic moments of history but treats them as self-contained, not part of the central text. "Waiting in the wings" charts progress but still consigns women to backstage as understudies.

Most of the dangerous courtesies are common to interdisciplinary categories. They take the generic form of inclusion in texts but exclusion from interpretation and additive stances that hold interdisciplinary studies in abeyance. The newest and final example, cultural studies, is the ultimate testing ground for a critical interdisciplinarity that moves beyond accommodation to reconceptualization.

References

Addelson, Kathryn Pyne, and Elizabeth Potter. 1991. "Making Knowledge." In Hartman and Messer-Davidow 1991, 259–77.

Agger, Ben. 1989. *Socio(onto)logy: A Disciplinary Reading.* Urbana: Univ. of Illinois Press.

Berkin, Carol. 1991. " 'Dangerous Courtesies': Assault Women's History." *Chronicle of Higher Education,* 11 December, A44.

Boxer, Marilyn J. 1982. "For and about Women: The Theory and Practice of Women's Studies in the United States." *Signs* 7, 3:661–95.

Calhoun, Craig. 1992. "Sociology, Other Disciplines, and the Project of a General Understanding of Social Life." In Halliday and Janowitz 1992, 137–95.

Collins, Patricia Hill. 1991. "Learning from the Outsider Within: The Sociological Significance of Black Feminist Thought." In Hartman and Messer-Davidow, 1991, 40:65.

Coyner, Sandra. 1991. "Women's Studies." *NWSA Journal* [National Women's Studies Association] 3, 3:349–54.

Dubois, Carol Ellen, et al. 1987. *Feminist Scholarship: Kindling in the Groves of Academe.* Urbana: Univ. of Illinois Press.

Elam, Diane. 1990. "Ms. en Abyme: Deconstruction and Feminism." *Social Epistemology* 4, 3:293–308.

Gerstenberger, Donna, and Carolyn Allen. 1977. "Women's Studies/American Studies, 1970–1975." *American Quarterly* 29 (bibliography issue) 262–79.

Hartman, Joan E. 1991. "Telling Stories: The Construction of Women's Agency." In Hartman and Messer-Davidow 1991, 11–39.

Hartman, Joan E., and Ellen Messer-Davidow, eds. 1991. *(En)Gendering Knowledge: Feminists in Academe.* Knoxville: Univ. of Tennessee Press.

Hoagland, Sarah. 1978. "On the Reeducation of Sophie." In *Women's Studies: An Interdisciplinary Collection,* ed. Kathleen O'Connor Blumhagen and Walter Johnson, 13–20. Westport, Conn.: Greenwood.

Howe, Florence. 1978. "Breaking the Disciplines." In *The Structure of Knowledge: A Feminist Perspective,* ed. Beth Reed, 1–10. Ann Arbor, Mich.: Great Lakes Colleges Association Women's Studies Program.

Jardine, Alice A. 1985. *Gynesis: Configurations of Woman and Modernity.* Ithaca: Cornell Univ. Press.

Johnson, Chalmers. 1975. "Political Science and East Asian Studies." In *Political Science and Area Studies: Rivals or Partners?* ed. Lucien Pye, 78–97. Bloomington: Indiana Univ. Press.

Kroker, Arthur. 1980. "Migration across the Disciplines." *Journal of Canadian Studies* 15 (fall): 3–10.

Lerner, Gerda. 1979. *The Majority Finds Its Past: Placing Women in History.* New York: Oxford Univ. Press.

Langland, Elizabeth and Walter Gove, editors. (1983). *A Feminist Perspective in the Academy: The Difference it Makes.* Chicago: University of Chicago Press.

Messer-Davidow, Ellen. 1991. "Know-how." In Hartman and Messer-Davidow 1991, 281–309.

Minnich, Barbara. 1990. *Transforming Knowledge.* Philadelphia: Temple Univ. Press.

Peck, Jeffrey M. 1989. Introduction and "There's No Place Like Home? Remapping the Topography of German Studies." *German Quarterly* 62, 2:141–42, 178–87.

Schor, Naomi. 1992. "Feminist and Gender Studies." In Gibaldi 1992, 262–87.

Semmes, Clovis E. 1981. "Foundations of an Afrocentric Social Science: Implications for Curriculum-Building, Theory, and Research in Black Studies." *Journal of Black Studies* 12, 1:3–17.

Showalter, Elaine. 1981. "Feminist Criticism in the Wilderness." *Critical Inquiry* 8,2:179–205.

Shumway, David. 1988. "The Interdisciplinarity of American Studies." Unpublished manuscript. Available from the author.

Shumway, David, and Ellen Messer-Davidow. 1991. "Disciplinarity: An Introduction." *Poetics Today* 12,2:201–25.

Stimpson, Catherine R. 1992. "Feminist Criticism." In Greenblatt and Gunn 1992b, 251–70.

Thornton, Russell. 1977. "American Indian Studies as an Academic Discipline." *Journal of Ethnic Studies* 5 (fall): 1–15.

Walters, Ronald. 1970. "The Discipline of Black Studies." *Negro Educational Review* 21,4:138–44.

"Women's Studies." 1990. In *Liberal Learning and the Arts and Sciences Major. V. II. Reports from the Fields,* 207–24.

Interdisciplinary Research and the Future of Peace and Security Studies

Richard Ned Lebow

Abstract

This essay describes different kinds of interdisciplinary research and the contribution they can make to peace and security studies. It discusses the institutional and professional impediments to interdisciplinary research and indicates what foundations already supporting research in this field could do to encourage such research. Finally, it outlines a substantive agenda for future research, urging scholars to devote less attention to analyzing the causes of international conflict and rather more to discovering what can be done to encourage governments to behave in more responsible and sensible ways. KEY WORDS: conflict; interdisciplinary; peace studies; foundations.

Introduction

In the course of the last few years there has been a growing interest in interdisciplinary research in peace and security studies. The MacArthur Foundation, Ford Foundation, and Carnegie Corporation have allocated substantial funds toward this end. The first two have made interdisciplinary research or training the fundamental goal of some of their more important grant programs. How valid and helpful is this emphasis? Will new faces, new disciplines, and new collaborations result in important new ideas? Or, as critics might contend, is it a misdirected effort to cope with the difficult intellectual and political problems of peace and security studies whose solution has so far eluded researchers and activists?

I believe that multi- and interdisciplinary research is not only valuable but critical to peace and security studies. I will attempt to demonstrate this in two ways: first, by exploring the kinds of contributions this kind of research can make; and, second, by developing a research agenda for the field that highlights the necessity for interdisciplinary insights and collaboration. My judgments and recommendations are bound to be controversial. But this is all to the good because dissent can only stimulate thought and debate about some of the broader intellectual issues raised by peace and security studies. Until now, these

Lebow, Richard Ned. "Interdisciplinary Research and the Future of Peace and Security Studies." Political Psychology 9:3 (1988), 507–525.

This article was originally a memorandum prepared for the Social Science Research Council. One section, "A Research Agenda," has appeared in Political Psychology.

have largely been ignored by scholars, intent instead on directing their attention toward more specific, substantive problems.

Any analysis of the utility of interdisciplinary research presupposes a working definition of the field of peace and security studies. The very notion of a "field," implies the existence of a recognized intellectual domain, something clearly absent in this case. For this reason, it seems best to think about peace and security studies as a "subject" that resides somewhere in the interstices of several traditional disciplines and area studies whose own boundaries are fuzzy and often controversial. If there is confusion and uncertainty about our subject's intellectual domain, there is outright conflict about its political mission. For some scholars it is the prevention of superpower nuclear war. Others criticize this objective as too narrow and define peace as the attainment of social and economic justice on a worldwide scale. Needless to say, there is even more disagreement about the means by which either goal is to be accomplished.

The lack of any methodological and substantive consensus, while at times frustrating, is nevertheless a healthy phenomenon. As the subject of peace and security studies is still in a state of relative intellectual infancy, any narrowing of its horizons would be premature and probably destructive to its subsequent maturation. It seems advisable instead to encourage the application of diverse methods and approaches to a broad range of problems. Even if many of these ventures ultimately prove disappointing, as assuredly they will, the subject as a whole will profit from such experimentation. Trial and error is the best way for researchers to develop a good sense of what is appropriate, possible, and advisable.

The Need for Interdisciplinary Research

For practical reasons, I will adopt a restrictive definition of peace and security studies. I will consider it to be anything that concerns the prevention of superpower nuclear war. If interdisciplinary research is necessary within this narrow domain, it is certainly pertinent to any broader definition of the subject. The case for interdisciplinary research is in any event a relatively simple one to make because important problems are almost always interdisciplinary.

Scholarly inquiry can best be conceptualized as a matrix, with problems representing the horizontal dimension and disciplines the vertical one. Most problems, whether they be in the sciences, humanities, or social sciences, cut across the domains of two or more disciplines; their treatment requires the cooperation of researchers from these different disciplines or the utilization of their respective methods and findings.

Population studies offers a typical example. For years, one of the most important questions in this field was why industrialization in Western Europe, North America, and Japan, was associated with a sharp drop in the death rate followed by an approximately equivalent decline in birth rates about 50 years later. Demographers sought economic, medical, and social explanations. They involved economic, medical, and social historians in the problem which led to the now widely accepted notion that public health measures were primarily responsible for the drop in the death rate. At the same time, economists, political scientists, and sociologists expressed an interest in this research because of its obvious relevance to contemporary development problems and strategies in many Third World countries.

Demographers at least recognized that they had to turn to other disciplines for answers to their problem. This does not always happen; scholarly imagination can be so circumscribed by disciplinary boundaries that researchers remain ignorant of the contributions other disciplines can make or that they can make to other disciplines.

My favorite illustration of this concerns the unexpected way in which paleontology came to the rescue of geophysics. Astronomers knew that the rotation of the earth was slowing down due to the tidal friction caused by the moon. However, they had no way of determining the rate of deceleration because this depends on the ever-changing configuration of continents, oceans, and seas. For more than a century, paleontologists had been aware of growth lines on some fossils but had largely ignored them until the 1960s when John Wells speculated that the very fine striations within the coarse bands might record daily growth rates. In a now famous paper, Wells reported that a group of corals about 370 million years old had something fewer than 400 lines per band. They had lived in an era of 400-day years. Subsequent research has extended our understanding of this phenomenon and of lunar periodicities as well.

There is an additional interdisciplinary dimension to peace and security studies. Researchers must consider not only problems but also mechanisms for coping with them. The physicist who one day succeeds in proving or disproving the hypothesis of proton decay has solved a problem, even though his success will undoubtedly give rise to new and thornier ones. The social scientist who discovers the processes responsible for certain kinds of conflict must then direct his attention to the strategies and mechanisms that might succeed in preventing or controlling it. Success here would still be insufficient; policy-makers would then have to be persuaded to adopt those strategies or mechanisms. The discovery of remedies and the translation of recommendations into policy are also interdisciplinary tasks.

The Nature of Interdisciplinary Research

It is unnecessary to belabor the point that many different disciplines can make significant contributions to peace and security studies. The important and more interesting question is just how those contributions can best be made. Should researchers continue to work, as most do, in their largely separate disciplinary worlds? Should they seek greater cooperation with researchers in other disciplines and fields? Ought they to familiarize themselves with the research methods, concepts, and findings of those fields with a view toward incorporating them in their own work? I believe that all of these approaches are necessary; each has a distinctive and critical contribution to make.

Traditional Disciplinary Research

Individuals in different disciplines working independently of each other on different or sometimes similar problems constitutes far and away the most common kind of research. There are obvious advantages to this approach: it requires training in only one discipline, encourages researchers to develop idiosyncratic, and often productive, approaches to problems, and is career-enhancing, given the disciplinary organizational structure of most academic institutions.

There are also drawbacks. The most obvious are the lack of coordination in research effort and general unfamiliarity with the results of related or useful research conducted in other disciplines. Researchers may be unaware that their findings have implications for peace and security studies; they may have been motivated to carry out their work because of purely theoretical concerns or interest in other substantive issues. Another common problem is naive or superficial treatment of questions within the domain of other disciplines that are nevertheless relevant to the researcher's problem.

Multidisciplinary Research

This consists of cooperative research by scholars from different disciplines. It is much less common than individual research or cooperative efforts among scholars in the same fields but has resulted in some important work. Multidisciplinary collaboration is best suited to problems that can be factored into distinct disciplinary components. The Strategic Defense Initiative (SDI) is a case in point. As the Union of Concerned Scientists and Stanford University studies attest, physicists and engineers, working within the confines of their own discipline, can assess the feasibility and likely operational characteristics of various kinds of defensive systems (Union of Concerned Scientists, 1983; Drell *et al.,* 1984). Political scientists and Soviet scholars can then use these findings to evaluate their strategic and political consequences.

Multidisciplinary research is also relevant to problems that require a more integrated cross-disciplinary perspective. An example is the study of the command and control of nuclear forces conducted by the Cornell Peace Studies Program. Kurt Gottfried, a physicist, brought together scientists, engineers, organizational sociologists, political scientists, retired military officers, and former political leaders, to study ways of reducing crisis instability. The products of this research, a report, several books and articles, represent perspectives that rise above traditional disciplinary vantage points (Gottfried *et al.,* 1988; Lebow, 1987a,b; Blair, 1987; Bracken, 1987a,b).

The same is true of some of the more recent studies of the nuclear winter hypothesis, based as they are on efforts to model the interaction of effects normally studied in isolation from one another by researchers in different disciplines (Turco, 1983; Ehrlich *et al.,* 1983, 1984; National Research Council, 1985).

Despite its promise, multidisciplinary research also confronts problems. Researchers sometimes talk past each other; each approaches a problem from his own disciplinary perspective with the result that there are no or few points of contact. The distinctive "mindsets" associated with different disciplines can even render dialogue fruitless.

I have witnessed discussions of this kind between sociologists and historians with the former rooted in a world view based on structural determinism and the latter emphasizing free will. I have also co-taught a course with a physicist whose billiard ball view of the arms race explained everything neatly in terms of technological imperatives. He in turn felt frustrated and even scornful of my proclivity for "overdetermination," an appropriate response, I believed, to the complexity, unpredictability, and messiness of real-life politics. We also differed in terms of our respective concerns for establishing proof for explanatory hypotheses versus finding policy remedies and the means of implementing them.

Despite these problems, multidisciplinary research should be encouraged for several important reasons. It is simply essential when addressing problems that cut across disciplinary lines; scholars from any one discipline could not possibly have made a comprehensive evaluation of the merits and dangers of SDI and C³I modernization.

Multidisciplinary research also functions as a kind of permeable membrane surrounding individual disciplines. It is a point of contact with the outside world, allowing new concepts, methods, and findings into disciplines and permitting its own contributions to go forth and penetrate other disciplines. In the absence of collaborative research efforts of this kind, much less interdisciplinary exchange would take place.

Finally, multidisciplinary research efforts frequently encourage the scholars involved to learn more about another discipline or, at least, to remain alert to the possible contributions it can make to problems of interest to them. As the striated fossils demonstrate, help can come from unexpected quarters.

Interdisciplinary Research

True interdisciplinary research represents the work of scholars cross-trained in two or more disciplines, or at least *au courant* with their literature. Interdisciplinary research infuses disciplines with new concepts, methods, and research tools. At its best it promotes new syntheses or paradigms that represent broader, more comprehensive, and more thorough treatments of problems. These can result from scholars making use of insights from other disciplines or using the methods of their discipline to analyze a problem usually considered in the domain of another. Peace and security studies have already profited from both kinds of contributions.

We need more research of this kind because of the nature of the problems we face. Take the question of crisis instability, recognized for many years by international relations scholars as a serious threat to peace. For two decades, however, crisis instability was thought to be more or less synonymous with the danger of preemption. Political scientists devoted their attention to studying technical considerations that might encourage one side or the other to strike first in a crisis in which war appeared likely.

Only recently, have we come to recognize the equally grave, if not greater, danger of loss of control arising from the complexity and vulnerability of nuclear command and control. This awareness is the result of work by organizational theorists who became interested in strategy and by political scientists, already in the field, who borrowed insights from organizational theory (Steinbruner, 1981–1982; Ball, 1981; Bracken, 1983).

The story does not end here. Psychologists and political scientists, drawing on the psychological literature, have now begun to emphasize the ways in which stress, motivated bias, and cognitive bias and heuristics, could seriously impair crisis decision-making. They have identified a third sequence to war, miscalculated escalation, which may represent an even more serious cause of crisis instability (Stein, 1985a,b; Lebow, 1987b, Chapter 4).

The study of crisis instability has benefitted enormously from concepts and researchers from diverse fields. Engineers and scientists (to determine the effects of nuclear attack on communications and command and control facilities), political scientists, historians (to shed light on the causes of crisis instability in previous confrontations that have led to war), sociologists, and psychologists have all facilitated and greatly expanded our understanding of the problem (Carter *et al.,* 1985).

It has also been necessary for some scholars at least to familiarize themselves with the methods and findings of these several disparate disciplines in order to develop an integrated analysis of the causes of crisis instability. This is the only way the full implications of the phenomenon can be grasped. Such an overview is also essential to policy because measures designed to ease one contributing cause of crisis instability may greatly aggravate another. Steps taken, for example, to facilitate retaliation, and thereby reduce the pressure to preempt, can heighten the risks of loss of control. Intelligent tradeoffs between these and other competing requirements of greater stability can only be made in reference to a comprehensive understanding of the problem.

There is nothing unique or unusual about crisis instability; almost all important questions in peace and security studies are similarly complex. Their diagnosis and remedy both require interdisciplinary research and, ultimately, interdisciplinary synthesis.

We might even be said to stand at an important threshold in this regard. Considerable research has been done on a whole range of important issues and problems in peace and security studies. New disciplinary perspectives would be helpful—in some cases they are essential—to further progress. Progress would also be facilitated by an overall view of the subject, or at least of some of its more important substantive problems. Such views from the mountain top are something that only interdisciplinary integration can provide. There is a pressing need to discover the ways by which this can be encouraged.

Before discussing ways of encouraging interdisciplinary research a word is in order about the kind of training this requires. Some familiarity with the methods, problems, and findings of another discipline is of course essential. However, I do not believe that scholars need to be fully conversant with two or more disciplines before attempting interdisciplinary research. Selective knowledge may be quite sufficient depending on the purposes in mind. As training in second and third disciplines is expensive and time-consuming, we must be careful not to impose too great a burden on institutions and researchers. Overly rigorous requirements will only inhibit interdisciplinary training by raising its cost in money and time, thereby discouraging at least some of those who would otherwise commit themselves to it.

There are also good reasons for scholars to maintain at least some distance from a second discipline. Let me illustrate this from my own experience with psychology. I developed an interest in psychological approaches because they seemed particularly germane to the kinds of problems I was interested in. Initially, this had to do with the origin and effects of social stereotypes in colonial policy and, subsequently, with the range of biases and heuristics that affects crisis decision-making. I found that psychology had much to teach me in both areas but that the core interests and concerns of the discipline were to a great extent irrelevant to me. Moreover, I had no interest whatsoever in the kinds of interdisciplinary disputes, common to all disciplines, that appeared to motivate so much of the research effort. I did not want to participate in the development of the discipline but rather wanted to be a consumer of psychological knowledge, taking way with me insights and approaches that were relevant to my own intellectual concerns.

This, too, required some distance from the discipline. Most psychologists generate data through experiments and surveys: my data were historical and not subject to the kinds of controls that characterize good experiments. Psychologists are primarily interested in the behavior of individuals and groups; I was concerned with nations and their policymaking elites. I was also studying one-time events, not large runs of events on which so much psychological knowledge is based. Real policymakers grappling with problems of war and peace also seemed far removed from students pondering questionnaires in a college laboratory. To make psychology useful to my work I not only had to modify or reformulate the approaches I borrowed but also had to apply them with an unusual degree of caution. I had to learn about psychology without adopting its perspective on the world.

I suspect that my experience can probably be generalized. It would be interesting to know if this is so. What strategies do other interdisciplinary researchers adopt? Do they maintain the perspective of their own disciplines, become "converts" to the outlook of the new one, or develop some kind of uneasy interdisciplinary synthesis? To what extent are these choices a function of the researcher's personality, choice of fields, or extent of immersion in a new field? Which orientation, if any, leads to the most fruitful kind of interdisciplinary research? Answers to these and other largely unexplored questions are vital to the development of effective interdisciplinary training programs.

Approaches to Interdisciplinary Training

Attempts to improve the quality of training *within* disciplines and fields must be part and parcel of any effort to foster interdisciplinary training. This is especially true of area studies. Soviet and Chinese specialists, probably the worst offenders in this regard, emphasize the language, history, and culture of their respective areas at the expense of methodological sophistication and comparative knowledge. Their research often lacks rigor and fails to benefit from awareness of how other political systems have dealt with similar problems or developments.

Traditional disciplines suffer from a different kind of intellectual limitation. Departments frequently succumb to trends within their disciplines and discourage students from adopting methods or tackling problems that are out of vogue or, worse still, out of discipline. Even more pluralist departments usually look askance at students wanting to do a substantial amount of their training in another department. Course and examination requirements, the thesis proposal process, and the structure of the job market, all tend to discourage interdisciplinary adventures. Younger faculty members suffer from similar constraints. Promotion and tenure are usually based on publications in one's own discipline; the more "mainstream" the publications, the better they will be received.

The intellectual and institutional impediments to interdisciplinary training and research are imposing but should not be a cause for despair. There are things that can be done to encourage multi- and interdisciplinary research. The following proposals should be considered in this regard:

1. Continuation of the MacArthur-Social Science Research Council training programs in a second discipline, area, or field, for scholars with a commitment to peace and security studies. Funding levels might be increased to permit the possibility in some cases of a second year of guided research. As presently administered, these programs place a high priority on attracting new people to peace and security studies. The two foundations should place even more emphasis on cross-training researchers who have already made significant contributions to this subject. Such individuals are not only deserving of support but they are better "horses" to bet on, by virtue of their established track record, than freshly minted Ph.D.'s.

2. Set up summer symposia in different disciplines and fields (e.g., psychology, economics, anthropology, communications technology, international relations, Soviet studies, nuclear strategy) to which a wide variety of interested scholars could be invited. These could range from 3-week to 2-month courses. Taught by recognized authorities, their objective would be to expose researchers to the concepts, methods, findings, and literature of an unfamiliar discipline or field. Symposia of this kind would give researchers the necessary foundation for independent study and, ultimately, research in the new discipline or field.

3. Preparation of continually updated reading lists and abstracts in peace and security studies, broken down by discipline and problem area. These should be supplemented by a "resource list" of scholars and other authorities who would be willing to offer guidance or even supervision to researchers unfamiliar with their particular discipline or subject area. Contacts could be arranged directly by the interested parties. Perhaps some funding could also be made available to facilitate personal contact and other forms of professional exchange. A network of this kind would serve as a nice complement to the

symposia described above. It would facilitate more limited or specialized inter-disciplinary training but do so on a much larger scale. It would also be relatively inexpensive to fund.

The following measures would facilitate multi- and interdisciplinary cooperation:

4. Support of existing and new multidisciplinary peace and security programs at universities and research institutions. This should be a major funding priority because programs of this kind are the principal forums for bringing together experts from different fields to discuss and work on problems of common interests.

The Cornell Peace Studies Program, the one with which I am most familiar, facilitates interdisciplinary knowledge and cooperation in several different ways. It acts as magnet for members of the university community interested in East-West and nuclear issues, drawing large numbers of people to weekly seminars and lectures on these topics. In doing so, it exposes them to a variety of disci-plinary and political perspectives. Peace Studies also serves as a catalyst for multi- and interdisciplinary research. Every year, the program's "technical arms control seminar" brings together scientists, engineers, and a few social scientists with a science background, to work on a technical problem with important implications for arms control or nuclear strategy.

The program has also facilitated collaborative research between political sci-entists and psychologists, classicists and political scientists, and physicists, histo-rians, and political scientists. In addition, it has helped a small number of scholars, some of them visitors to the Program, to cross-train themselves in a second discipline. Similar programs at other universities accomplish the same ends.

5. Periodic conferences on specific security topics designed to bring together people from different disciplines and fields in order to expose them to research, with which they may be unfamiliar, that is nevertheless germane to their sub-ject. Conferences of this kind would encourage participants to take a broader perspective of the field and the particular problems of interest to them. If held on a regular basis, they would probably also succeed in building bridges across disciplines, something that could serve as an important catalyst of multi- and interdisciplinary research.

While all of the steps outlined above would be extremely useful, it is also necessary to address the in-bred resistance, even opposition, to interdisciplinary training and research that exists in so many academic departments. Here, a cue might be taken from Peter the Great, as interpreted by Montesquieu. In his *Spirit of the Laws,* the great French philosopher, when tackling the problem of directed change, makes a distinction among laws, customs, and manners. He argues that laws are the least effective way of bringing about such change. He tells the story, perhaps apocryphal, of Peter's efforts to compel his *boyars* to shave their beards and adopt Western dress. *Ukase* after *ukase* failed to have its effect, in part because judges in beards and caftans refused to impose heavy fines on offenders. In desperation, the czar hit upon the idea of bribing the half dozen or so most popular courtesans in Petersburg to bestow their favors only upon cleanly shaven men who wore western-style clothes. Within a few months, hirsute men in caftans were relative rarities in the salons of the capital.

Rewards, not punishments, and manners, not laws, are the mechanisms best suited to promoting change. Foundations could emulate Peter the Great, albeit with a different end in mind to be obtained by somewhat different means. The several major foundations in the field could agree among themselves to place greater emphasis on multi- and interdisciplinary training and research as an important criterion, even a requirement in some cases, for graduate and faculty fellowships. They should also create a prestigious prize and fellowships at the senior level for interdisciplinary research.

Both programs would help to legitimate this enterprise in the broader scholarly community. They would also significantly influence the choice of research projects because scholars, and even more so, as yet uncommitted graduate students, are "lucretropic"; their instincts move them toward a source of funds. Many graduate departments might even consider incorporating some kind of interdisciplinary training in their programs in order to make their students more competitive for these fellowships.

A Research Agenda

Peace and security researchers confront three big questions: (1) identifying the causes of international tension and wars; (2) devising strategies, mechanisms, and policies that could reduce those tensions and lower the risk of war; and (3) persuading American, Soviet, and other leaders to embrace their policy recommendations. Needless to say, researchers disagree among themselves about the substantive aspects of all three questions. How should a foundation begin to thread its way through this morass?

A useful starting point would be recognition of what I consider to be three verities about our subject. The first of these is that peace and security research must be policy-oriented. Unlike many other kinds of scholarly endeavors where intellectual discovery is an end in itself, our goal is to devise better means of reducing the risk of war without sacrificing important national interests. Our research effort must accordingly be directed toward policy as well as theoretical questions.

Ideally, foundations should encourage research that attempts to link the two together. Policy recommendations, regardless of the political perspective they represent, can and should be theoretically informed. Research should also respond to policy needs in the broadest sense. Unfortunately, theoretical and policy-oriented researchers tend to live in largely separate worlds. With a few notable exceptions in both camps, they are interested in different questions, use a different vocabulary, and read and publish in different journals. Much needs to be done to stimulate greater interaction between them, interaction from which both could only benefit.

Second, is the realization that research will never result in any consensus about the nature of the problem or the remedies best suited to it. Scholars starting from fundamentally opposed premises are almost certain to arrive at contradictory diagnoses and prescriptions. The most we can hope for is that research will promote more sophisticated and cautious arguments on all sides by testing, as far as possible, the axioms and propositions of competing security perspectives.

Research of this kind is absolutely essential because so many strategic and foreign policy controversies turn on the untested assumptions of the respective protagonists. The putative political utility (or lack of utility) of nuclear weapons, the relevance (or irrelevance) of the nuclear balance for the behavior of third parties, the importance (or lack of importance) of a country's bargaining reputation for other state's assessments of its resolve, are questions that have critical policy significance and are amenable to some kind of empirical validation. Even when research cannot prove or disprove a claim, it is likely to generate insights that could raise the overall level of the policy debate. Simply making people aware of the nature of the assumptions on which their arguments rest would probably be a real contribution in this regard.

Third, not enough effort has been made to develop and perfect alternative approaches to conflict management and resolution. In this connection I find it useful to think about adversarial relationships as a triangle with each vertex representing a different possible cause of conflict (see example below).

One vertex would represent pure hostility and characterize conflicts in which one or both parties were, for ideological, ethnic, or other reasons, motivated by outright opposition to the other's political existence. Conflicts between Protestant and Catholic states in 17th-century Europe, and more recently, between India and Pakistan, North and South Korea, China and Taiwan, and many Arab states and Israel, have been motivated to a large degree by such hostility.

Deterrence may be appropriate to such conflicts because, more than in any other kind of conflict, fear of the consequences of war is the principal restraint to the use of force. Even so, deterrence will not always succeed in forestalling a military challenge. As the 1973 Middle East War attests, the domestic costs of inaction may outweigh the expected military costs of going to war against a superior adversary (Stein, 1985a,b). Such a dynamic has also characterized Iraqi-Iranian relations since the onset of their costly and indecisive war (Cottam, 1986; Tripp, 1986).

THE CONFLICT TRIANGLE

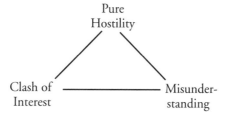

A second vertex of the triangle represents clashes of interest. These run the gamut from pinprick irritations to war-threatening disputes. They can be very specific, as in the case of Argentina and Britain's conflicting claims to sovereignty over the Falklands-Malvinas, or more amorphous, as in the case of the conflict between the superpowers about the post-war future of central Europe.

To the extent that a dispute is the cause and not the symptom of conflict, adversarial relations should improve in the aftermath of its settlement. Toward this end diplomats have over the centuries developed an elaborate repertoire of strategies and techniques. These include negotiated compromises and trade-offs, mediation, arbitration, the delineation of spheres of influence or buffer zones, and the canalization of competition into less threatening arenas.

The third vertex of the triangle represents conflicts caused by mutual fears and suspicion. These can arise from systemic- and actor-related causes. The former, generally described under the rubric of the "security dilemma," are attributable to the anarchy of the international system which can compel states to take defensive precautions, political and military in nature, that are perceived as offensive in intent by other actors. Some scholars explain the Cold War in terms of the pernicious influence of the security dilemma. Actor-related conflicts arise when leaders mistakenly conclude, for whatever reason, that another state's leaders are implacably hostile toward their state, its foreign policies, or its political system. Conflicts based on misunderstanding can also lead to crises and unnecessary wars.

There is probably no better example of this latter dynamic than Chinese-American relations. The key to rapprochement was reassurance; gestures and policies designed to overcome the mutual fear and hostility that had characterized Sino-American relations for so many years. This was accomplished primarily by means of personal contacts among leaders and public and private assurances on symbolic issues of importance to one or both sides.

Reassurance, was also the critical pre-condition for an improvement in Egyptian-Israeli relations. It overcame what had been a principal stumbling block toward peace: Egypt's insistence on return of the Sinai as the *minimum* condition for diplomatic recognition coupled with Israel's unwillingness to make any territorial concession that would jeopardize its military security (Stein, 1983; Quandt, 1986).

Each vertex of the conflict triangle is associated with a different generic cause of international conflict. Each of these causes in turn has a strategy or set of strategies that are appropriate to it. Deterrence is most suited to conflicts motivated by hostility, traditional diplomacy to conflicts brought about by clashes of interest, and reassurance to those caused by misunderstanding.

The mechanisms associated with two of these three strategies are well-known. There is a substantial literature on deterrence, most of it devoted to technical questions concerning its implementation. The same is true for diplomacy. Historians, political scientists, psychologists, and practitioners of the art, have written widely about negotiation, arbitration, mediation, and related techniques of conflict management or resolution. However, much useful research could be done to establish the domestic and international conditions essential for the success of any of these techniques.

Reassurance, by contrast, is still largely *terra incognita*. To be sure, much thought has been devoted to arms control and various other kinds of confidence-building measures, but very little effort has been made to develop a theoretical understanding of just how such measures can or could alter adversarial perceptions. This remains a critical task.

Knowledge of this kind would be helpful but still an insufficient guide for policymakers. International conflicts are rarely unidimensional. They are much more likely to incorporate elements of all three causes of conflict. The Cold War is a case in point. The superpowers are certainly motivated by some degree of hostility toward each other. Moscow and Washington would both like to remake the world in its own image—although, since 1945, neither has seemed willing to risk war with the other in pursuit of this goal. The conflict is also based on a clash of interests. It arose as a competition for influence in central Europe, a region both superpowers deemed vital to their security. For more than two decades, this struggle for ascendancy generated acute tensions. Soviet-American tensions are also fanned by an undeniable component of fear, misunderstanding, and misperception.

Policymakers and scholars alike often succumb to the fallacy of single causes. Interpretations of Soviet-American relations are clustered at each apex of the conflict triangle. Hard-line, anti-communist, Cold Warriors are convinced that the Soviet Union is unalterably expansionist and motivated by unremitting hostility to the West and its way of life. For them, deterrence based on military strength and backed up by an unquestioned will to use that strength, is the only effective means of coping with this threat.

Self-styled "realists" attribute the conflict to a clash of political, economic, and security interests. Proponents of this view generally stress the role of diplomacy in regulating the manifestations of conflict and perhaps in mitigating some of its causes.

Finally, there are those who believe the Cold War to be a tragic misunderstanding. Partisans of this interpretation emphasize the pernicious role of the security dilemma as an engine of arms racing and false perceptions of threat or, alternatively, the distorting role of competing ideologies and divergent national traditions. They advocate arms control, confidence building measures, and cultural contact as the most important means of easing tensions.

In my judgment, the Cold War cannot be neatly placed at any vertex of the conflict triangle. Rather it resides somewhere in the middle as all three generic causes of conflict contribute to it. Efforts to regulate superpower relations and reduce tensions must accordingly take them all into account. An attempt to address any one cause in isolation is almost certain to fail and may aggravate one or both of the other causes.

Instead, policymakers must employ a careful blend of strategies appropriate to the diverse causes of conflict. Such an approach should be predicated on a carefully thought out conception of the sequence and manner in which these causes ought to be addressed. Foreign and security policies of this kind presuppose greater knowledge of the causes of conflict, mechanisms for coping with them, and the conditions associated with their successful implementation. Development of this knowledge and, with it, integrated approaches to conflict management, should be given a high priority on our research agenda.

Peace and security research is, I have argued, by definition a multi- and interdisciplinary exercise. It should be apparent that this holds true for all of the important research areas within the subject as well, especially the three problem areas I have identified. First, however, we need in some cases to involve individual disciplines in one or more of the problem areas that they have neglected until now. Beyond this, we must find ways of encouraging interdisciplinary approaches, for all three problem areas have political, psychological, technical, economic, and ethical dimensions. For this reason, the full range of multi- and interdisciplinary research strategies that I have described is relevant to them.

How Do We Get There From Here?

There is a famous Irish story about a visitor to Dublin who asks a resident for directions to Trinity College. "Ah," he replies, "if I were you I wouldn' be startin' from here." In the context of a foreigner's search for a well-known Dublin landmark the proffered advice is refreshingly naive. If the objective is to find a way out of the arms race, the Dubliner's observation may be profound. For the difficulty for doing this lies not so much in the complexity of the route ahead but in the nature of the path already trod.

In the course of the last four decades the superpowers have put themselves into a position from which peaceful relations seem a remote, perhaps even unattainable destination. Part of the reason is internal. Superpower foreign policy elites have become entrapped in Cold War mindsets, abetted by large military establishments and a defense industry anxious to keep them supplied with the latest in weapons.

Strategies for coping with this problem range from far-reaching pleas à la Jonathan Schell for doing away with national sovereignty to mass mobilization of public opinion to force governments to modify their security policies, to the "fine tuning" of those security policies, advocated by many of those who have chosen to work within the establishment. Very little serious effort has been made by scholars in the security field to study the prospects, feasibility, and limitations of these and other approaches to change. We need to know a lot more about the whole range of possible strategies for influencing security policy, the tactics associated with them, their feasibility in democratic and authoritarian systems, and their requirements for success.

Let me venture the proposition that research needs and funding are inversely related. We know a great deal, although certainly not enough, about the causes of conflicts and wars. We also have a number of good ideas about what could be done to ameliorate those tensions and reduce the prospect of superpower war. We know very little about how to translate any of these recommendations into policy or how to improve the quality of national security decisionmaking. Ways of overcoming any of the obstacles that stand in the way of good policymaking and good policy are unquestionably the most difficult and least understood aspect of the problem. It also receives the least funding. The big bucks go to diagnosis instead of therapy. There are several reasons why this is so.

Most scholars feel at home analyzing causes but out of their element proposing remedies. Research into causes, by virtue of its theoretical objectives or implications, is also more in line with traditional disciplinary interests. It has the additional virtue of being political *and* apolitical at the same time. By addressing questions related to war and peace, researchers can convince themselves, with reason, that they are doing something about a serious global problem. For those of us who feel uncomfortable collecting signatures or waving a banner at a protest rally, our intellectual commitment frees us from any guilt we might otherwise feel about not taking more direct kinds of political action.

Scholarly preference is reinforced by foundation restraint. Foundation executive themselves often have university backgrounds and reflect the academic view of the world. Beyond this, institutional values also dictate caution. Most foundations in the peace and security field feel more comfortable supporting research than they do political action. The former is scholarly, non-partisan, or at least several steps removed from the political arena. It probably elicits few, if any, complaints from trustees, corporations, or the government. Policy activism, by contrast, raises the specter of undesired controversy and perhaps even legal challenges from disgruntled trustees or family members of the foundation's benefactors. These are reasonable concerns.

Foundations have nevertheless become increasingly involved with the question of war and peace because they are responding to widespread elite and popular fears of nuclear holocaust. At the same time, foundation executives are understandably reluctant to take sides, roll up their sleeves, and get involved in the political process. Remedies, however, will have no effect in the absence of some notion of how they can be implemented. And foundations can help in this regard without opening the Pandora's box of partisan political participation.

Foundations ought to encourage a shift in the focus of research away from the causes of conflict toward the measures for controlling it and the means of gaining acceptance for those measures. Foundations can comfortably support research of this kind because it can and should be as scholarly as research into the causes of war. No doubt, it will also lead to a more sophisticated understanding of the political process, something that is in itself a worthwhile intellectual objective. Pressure groups, lobbies, and politically motivated individuals of all kinds could, of course, make use of the findings as they see fit.

Needless to say, research about the mechanism for influencing security policy needs to be interdisciplinary given the scope of the problem. Several disciplines already have sub-fields concerned with relevant components. These include attitude formation and change at the individual, group, institutional, or national level; the development, appeal, and functioning of mass protest movements; bureaucratic and organizational behavior, especially receptivity and resistance to change; and the role of public opinion, Congress, and the executive branch in the formation of security policy.

At least some of the researchers in these fields should be urged to direct their attention to the peace and security implications of their work. In doing so, they should also be coaxed to climb out of their disciplinary trenches in order to survey the entire battlefield. Some of the measures I have proposed to foster multi-disciplinary cooperation and interdisciplinary research could be directed at this professional audience.

Case studies of past efforts to influence security policy in the United States and abroad should also be encouraged; they constitute an important data base that can be used to develop and test hypotheses about all aspects of non-government efforts to reorient security policy. Unfortunately, much of the case study literature tends to be descriptive and insufficiently analytical. It is also sometimes disturbingly polemical, a failing apparent in so many of the recent American writings about European peace movements. We need more dispassionate, theoretically informed studies that offer us something in the way of general knowledge about the interaction between governments, parties, and pressure groups in democratic societies. Such knowledge would help us to formulate better and more effective strategies aimed at influencing security policy.

In the way of a conclusion let me make explicit the assumption that has guided this article. This is my belief that means cannot be considered divorced from the ends they are meant to achieve. Interdisciplinary research is challenging, exciting to those of us who engage in it, and, in the last resort, necessary to provide a comprehensive analysis of any important problem. It is not, however, a goal in itself. Rather, it should be seen as instrumental in promoting a better understanding of the causes of conflict, the mechanisms that can regulate it, and the process by which governments can be brought around to adopt them.

Foundations interested in supporting interdisciplinary research ought to recognize this and draw up an overall strategy for approaching the subject of peace and security. This should determine the nature and focus of the multi- and interdisciplinary training and research they support. I have offered my own agenda in this regard in the hope that it might serve as a starting point for reflections of this kind.

References

Ball, D. (1981). *Can Nuclear War Be Controlled?* Adelphi Paper No. 169, International Institute of Strategic Studies, London.

Blair, B. G. (1987). Alerting in crisis and conventional war. In Carter, A. B., Steinbruner, J. D., and Zraket, C. A. (eds.), *Managing Nuclear Operations*, Brookings, Washington, D.C., pp. 75–120.

Bracken, P. (1983). *The Command and Control of Nuclear Forces*, Yale University Press, New Haven, Conn.

Bracken, P. (1987a). War termination. In Carter, A. B., Steinbruner, J. D., and Zraket, C. A. (eds.), *Managing Nuclear Operations*, Brookings, Washington, D.C., pp. 197–216.

Bracken, P. (1987b). Delegation of nuclear command authority. In Carter, A. B., Steinbruner, J. D., and Zraket, C. A. (eds.), *Managing Nuclear Operations*, Brookings, Washington, D.C., pp. 352–372.

Carter, A. B., Steinbruner, J. D., and Zraket, C. A. (1985). *Managing Nuclear Operations*, Brookings, Washington, D.C.

Cottam, R. (1986). Iran—Motives behind its foreign policy. *Survival* (November–December) 28: 483-494.

Drell, S. D., Farley, P. J., and Holloway, D. (1984). *The Reagan Strategic Defense Initiative: A Technical, Political, and Arms Control Assessment,* Center for International Security and Arms Control, Stanford.

Ehrlich, P. R., *et al.,* (1983). Long-term biological consequences of nuclear war. *Science* (December) 23: 1293–1300.

Ehrlich, P. R., *et al.,* (1984). *The Cold and the Dark: The World After Nuclear War,* Norton, New York.

Gottfried, K., *et al.,* (1988) *Crisis Stability,* Oxford University Press, New York.

Lebow, R. N. (1987a). Clausewitz and crisis stability. *Polit. Sci. Quart.* 103: 81–110.

Lebow, R. N. (1987b). *Nuclear Crisis Management: A Dangerous Illusion,* Cornell University Press, Ithaca.

National Research Council, Committee on the Atmospheric Effects of Nuclear Weapons (1985). *The Effects on the Atmosphere of a Major Nuclear Exchange,* National Academy Press, Washington, D.C.

Quandt, W. B. (1986). *Camp David: Peacemaking and Politics,* Brookings, Washington, D.C.

Stein, J. G. (1983). The alchemy of peacemaking: The prerequisites and corequisites of progress in the Arab-Israel conflict. *Int. J.* 38: 531–555.

Stein, J. G. (1985a). Calculation, miscalculation, and conventional deterrence I: The view from Cairo. In Jervis, R., Lebow, R. N., and Stein, J. G. (eds.), *Psychology and Deterrence,* Johns Hopkins University Press, Baltimore.

Stein, J. G. (1985b). Calculation, miscalculation, and conventional deterrence II: The view from Jerusalem. In Jervis, R., Lebow, R. N., and Stein, J. G. (eds.), *Psychology and Deterrence,* Johns Hopkins University Press, Baltimore.

Steinbruner, J. (1981–1982). Nuclear decapitation. *Foreign Policy* 45: 16–28.

Tripp, C. (1986). Iraq—Ambitions checked. *Survival* (November–December) 28: 495–508.

Turco, R. P. (1983). Nuclear winter: Global consequences of multiple nuclear explosions. *Science* (December) 23: 1283–1292.

Union of Concerned Scientists. (1983). *The Fallacy of Star Wars,* Random House, New York.

There's No Place Like Home?

Remapping the Topography of German Studies

Jeffrey M. Peck

> Once knowledge can be analyzed in terms of region, domain, im-
> plantation, displacement, transposition, one is able to capture the
> process by which knowledge functions as a form of power and dis-
> seminates the effects of power.
>
> —Michael Foucault, *Questions on Geography*[1]

I

In 1914 Bronislaw Malinowski, a Polish anthropologist living in England with
an Austrian passport, became technically a British enemy and was unable to
leave Australia. A little over two decades later, preceding another Great War
more central to our concerns, Erich Auerbach, a German-Jewish philologist,
fled Nazi Germany for Istanbul.[2] These two men were exiled victims of nation-
alistically motivated power struggles and ironically, because of their unwilling
sojourns in foreign "homes," were to write books of major significance. Clearly,
such events alone are not compelling enough to draw our attention. In fact,
until recently these personal events would have remained mere anecdotes and
would not have had any more influence than enlivening the biographies of two
men who became central figures in their respective disciplines. However, post-
structuralist thinking about the discursive constitution of (multiple) subjectivities and in particular Foucault's work on institutional and disciplinary formation have changed all that. We now are more attentive to how such spatial
configurations organize and shape knowledge.[3] We philologists—to cite Nietzsche, who lurks behind my ruminations—are beginning to see that our scholarly apparatus and the academic environment where we work are as significant
as the (literary) texts to which we had traditionally devoted ourselves.

"Place" or "location" or "site" (in Foucault's terms) expand and enrich the
spatial field by acknowledging the potential for meaning in an environment
that itself can be *text*ured, that is, read like a text. The metaphor of the text
and the significance of cultural (con)texts taken from reading and interpreting
traditional literary works are now being applied to any situation, phenomenon,
or event. For our analysis here, it means that the Trobriand Islands or Istanbul
are more than just a mere backdrop to the production of monumental works

Peck, Jeffrey M. "There's No Place Like Home?: Remapping the Topography of German Studies." Special issue "Interdisciplinary Theory and Methods." German Quarterly 62:2 (Spring
1989), 178–187. Reprinted with permission.

like *Argonauts of the Western Pacific* (1922) and *Mimesis* (1946). These places, in fact, constitute networks of institutional and discursive relations that themselves deserve the critical gaze of the modern-day philologist/literary critic as well as the ethnographer.[4] Malinowski and Auerbach are quite different in the way that they and their disciplines were reshaped by their individual forms of displacement. However, their experience in two closely related fields mutually preoccupied with culture draws our attention today to the way in which place—nationally, culturally, academically—determines how we "read" various meaning systems, especially when they conflict or clash.

The renewed enthusiasm for culture is, however, more than just "seeing" it as a positivistic panorama or "feeling" it as some spiritually-historical super-*Geist.* Committed to redefining such a limited notion, the historian/anthropologist Bernard Cohn argues for a refashioning of history and anthropology that benefits these two fields as well as joins their interests to literary study in the pursuit of culture. He points out "a common subject matter," "otherness," "concern with text and context," "explicating the meaning of actions of people rooted in one time and place, to persons in another," and therefore "[b]oth . . . entail[ing] the act of translation," and "develop[ing] . . . understanding and explanation." He concludes with the most obvious connection when he acknowledges that "[b]oth are dependent upon reporting their results in a literary form."[5] He alerts us to how culture is always being constituted and constructed for all three of these disciplines. By this he "mean[s] systems of concepts, meanings and beliefs which are incorporated in and made manifest by symbols."[6] Such disciplinary comparisons based on deciphering cultural meaning of a variety of "texts" or textualized situations show why many of those practicing history, anthropology, or literary study are drawn to redefined intellectual configurations such as "Cultural Studies" or "German (Culture) Studies."

The preoccupation with "cultural construction" leads us in the national philologies to survey two central constitutive locations—the national and the academic—that are (con)texts demanding the kind of anthropological thinking and textual analysis (philology) that Cohn calls for in his project of "anthropological history." If one shifts the disciplinary constellations a bit further, to anthropology and to geography, there emerges between these two what I call "topographical discourse." It complements more obvious temporal or chronological schemes conceived in specified periods, such as literary history. Further, it draws our attention to intellectual *surfaces* and academic *contours,* critical *boundaries* and scholarly *fields* of demarcated interests, as well as the cultures that inhabit those territories[7]—in short, *Germanistik* as well as Germany.

Topographical discourse, as I see it, accentuates the discursive similarity between national/ethnic and academic cultures, while at the same time affirming definitions of culture that focus on multiplicity, divergence, and incompleteness. Culture is meaningful, that is, "full of meaning" because of (rather than in spite of) its partiality. This step toward expanding the theoretical dimension of the culture concept is defined by the historian of anthropology, James Clifford. He introduces one of the few studies, not coincidentally entitled "Writing Culture," that link anthropology to literary study:

Cultures are not scientific "objects" (assuming such things exist, even in the natural sciences). Culture, and our views of "it," are produced historically, and are actively contested. There is no whole picture that can be "filled in," since the perception and filling of a gap leads to the awareness of other gaps. . . . If "culture" is not an object to be described, neither is it a unified corpus of symbols and meanings that can be definitely interpreted. Culture is contested, temporal, and emergent. Representation and explanation—both by insiders and outsiders—is implicated in this emergence. . . . It is thoroughly historicist and self-reflexive.[8]

This expanded yet differentiated notion of culture frees *Germanisten* from the burden of a culture concept with a capital "K" that unfortunately represents a particularly German form of intellectual domination. This redefinition allows us to undertake cultural analysis of Germany as well as of the Trobriand Islands, of advanced industrialized societies as well as of the so-called primitive lands. The implications are far-ranging for analyzing academic institutions and disciplines. There too we can uncover and "make visible"—in Foucault's archaeological sense—patterns of domination and oppression constituted in discourse, that is, statements made, views authorized, the ways any discipline has been taught, settled, or ruled over.[9] If we compare topographically a German *Germanistik* to its offspring, American German Studies, we highlight the "spaces" where they were formed and the newly emerging places where our profession can be practiced. What James Clifford has elsewhere called "spatial circulation"[10] points to the displacement in our profession that has taken place in the literal as well as the intellectual migration of *Germanistik* and *Germanisten* to America.

The history of *Germanistik* provides convincing evidence for the way a sphere of knowledge has been territorialized intellectually and geographically, since these histories have attempted to construct a certain coherent notion of "German" grounded in a specific place. Topographical discourse begins to unravel the meaning of categorizing a person or thing in such a totalizing or uniform fashion. It shows how the close alliance between the struggle for political unification represented in the nation "Germany" and the function and practices of an academic discipline committed to aid that cause were joined precisely where discourse constituted this new field of study. For example, Jacob and Wilhelm Grimm's grand project, *Das Deutsche Wörterbuch,* along with their other philological enterprises, aimed to promote a national consciousness through the exploitation of the romantically-charged, magical power of the word to create new worlds—in this case, a newly unified Germany.[11]

The discipline *Germanistik,* along with other fields such as history, sociology, economics, geography, and even anthropology "occupies" Germany, or at least the knowledge produced about it. In fact, all these academic and scholarly territories are dominated by a repertoire of spatial metaphors such as boundaries, borders, territory, domain, region, and field that are not only politically charged, but also open to imperialistic readings. Foucault himself notes their "juridico-political," "economico-juridicial," "military," "fiscal," and "administrative" derivations and connotations.[12] For those who study "Germany," a number of rich and powerful images stand out: the Nazi ideology of *Lebensraum,* the crossing of the Polish "border" marking the beginning of World War II, or more recently, the obvious division of East and West Berlin by the ultimate icon of spatial arrangements, the Wall. Each discipline uses this topographical language not only to inquire into, but also to create an object specific to its own field of interest. The Wall, for example, a metaphor for division and unity in the work of Peter Schneider, appeals to literary critics; the partition of the city and country into two separate political, economic, and urban entities would demand the attention of political scientists, economists, geographers and urban planners, respectively. Obviously the list could go on to include even architects and building engineers who might study how the Wall was constructed or what materials were used to fortify it against the impact of escaping cars.

The nation and the disciplines that strive to describe, explain, analyze, interpret, and legitimate such an entity are constituted by categories, taxonomies, and statements governed by rules of organization and formation that divide intellectual and national territory, both literally and figuratively. These organizational structures shape meaning and offer themselves especially to the cultural/symbolic anthropologist, as well as to the literary critic. Such structures are also always sites of political contestation.[13] Thus topographical discourse based on such spatial delineations of nation and discipline, especially in "border" regions, is always implicated in conflicts over power and authority. This is particularly true in the case of Germany, divided between East and West. The struggles that take place on the national as well as the academic battlefield are often altercations over territories and contests for the control of their representations. In the case of the two Germanies, postwar tensions over the control of Berlin marked the city as a potent signifier. First, it had symbolized the centrality and unity of the Third Reich; now it literally continues to (re)present a divided Germany. The disciplinary battles, although less material, are nonetheless compelling. They take place in a highly political tug-of-war between two *Germanistiks.* Both claim alternative configurations of knowledge that are represented in their clashing appropriations of the German literary heritage.

In his disciplinary study *Orientalism,* Edward Said, indebted to Foucault, elaborates on the distinctions that emerge when one operates spatially:

> It is perfectly possible to argue that some distinctive objects are made by the mind, and that these objects, while appearing to exist objectively, have only a fictional reality. A group of people living on a few acres of land will set up boundaries between their land and its immediate surroundings and the territory beyond, which they call "the land of the barbarians." In other words, this universal practice of designating in one's mind a familiar space which is "ours" and an unfamiliar space beyond "ours" which is "theirs"

is a way of making geographical distinctions that *can be* entirely arbitrary.[14]

The arbitrary nature of such "imaginative geography," as Said calls it, should not be seen as in any way undermining the juxtaposition of national and academic culture. On the contrary, recognizing how "man-made" these two spheres are only demands further reflection on ways that they are constructed, linked together, and then defined. The urge for self-definition or structuring identity delineated by boundaries for Germanists as well as the Germans preoccupies a number of the disciplines responsible for studying Germany. In history or political science, for example, there are works such as Gordon Craig's *The Germans,* or the volumes of collected essays searching for coherence and identity themselves, such as Werner Weidenfeld's *Die Identität der Deutschen,* or *Die deutsche Neurose. Über die beschädigte Identität der Deutschen.* In *Germanistik,* the many studies written in the 1970s in Germany, or more recently, articles on the pages of *Monatschefte* attest to how chronic this situation has become.[15]

One of the problems for the discussion of identity is particularly evident in its relation to nation, one of its most obsessive forms. This may be the case because "nation" is the "readiest account of place," according to Said.[16] National identity has often been based on a binary opposition, neither part of which satisfactorily accounts for the problem. Such an opposition has been characterized in general terms by the intellectual historian Dominick LaCapra as either a "fixated reversal" or an "undifferentiated equivocality."[17] Neither overcomes the polarities of idealism and materialism, which themselves are embedded in thinking about what it means "to be German." The former—defined by blood or physiognomy—and the latter—defined by the possession of a passport—do not adequately explain national identity, since they are based on essentialist, "common sense," and "objectivist" notions. More appropriate would be an expansion of the space created figuratively between these two polarities, better described by the notion of symbolic materiality. This category highlights the representational rather than the literal quality of objects that acquire meaning in any cultural system. This orientation would be closer to what some cultural anthropologists and literary critics are pursuing in contemporary cultural studies when they analyze nonprimitive cultures or academic culture itself. The anthropologist Paul Rabinow's call for the study of "micropractices of the academy"[18] moves toward contextualizing all the "places" that shape interpretation, ours as well as those at the point of origin. National identity can then be acknowledged as a discursive formation, much like a discipline or text that is constituted in the statements about it as an object of analysis represented in symbolic forms. Recognized as variable, inconsistent, arbitrary, and heterogeneous, national identity in this form would undermine any "fixation" on the absolute validity of any one position or identity emanating from national consciousness or any "undifferentiated" internationalism created by a flattening of all categories.

To bring the theoretical discussion of space "closer to home," let me draw on a recent Gallup survey that attracted a great deal of attention.[19] Inspired by the pronouncements of the triumvirate of Allan Bloom, William Bennett, and E. D. Hirsch, a newspaper article dramatically announced, "Americans fail geography test. Most can't even find Britain or Pacific Ocean on a map." The deplorable state of American students' geographical knowledge is "most alarming," in the words of the president of the National Geographic Society. What is more alarming to me, however, are the assumptions behind this kind of "literacy" poll. Any educated person would agree that students should be able to locate the Pacific Ocean. Missing, however, is any discussion of why such information should be considered worth learning. To be polemical, one might ask why one should be able "to find" Great Britain or the Pacific Ocean "on a map." Isn't it more important to know what these geographical sites mean in relationship to other countries, bodies of water, or mountain chains? What geo-political significance do these relationships have? What kinds of power are revealed when these configurations are studied? Moreover, the author of the article and, obviously, even the president of the National Geographic Society have failed to make one important semiological distinction that concerns us here: they have mistakenly granted the country on the map reality value; in short, they have mistaken the sign for what it represents.

This trivial example points to the seriousness of a situation I want to address regarding Germany and *Germanistik.* By recognizing the representational quality of disciplines as cultures that organize our thinking and form statements that have meaning, we open the way to acknowledge, as part of interpretation, our own implication in any "ethnography" that we may write or interpretation that we may make. Like the "pregnant hyphen" in Kleist's "Die Marquise von O . . . ," behind which the rape takes place, this mere orthographic sign between the prefix "re" and the stem "present" veils as well our interpretive position in the making of meaning. It is precisely in that space where we insert ourselves and declare our hermeneutic participation.

This involvement, as we know from the ideological excess of Nazi *Germanistik,* for example, is not innocent; we are implicated in our re-presentations, far less blatant and not any less dangerous than typical for such demagogery. Cohn characterizes the manifestation of asymmetrically representing other cultures in the metaphor of colonialism:

> This process of construction of cultures can be studied through representations. . . . I mean, among other things, etiquette, codes of conduct, large-scale political/religious rituals, and the various forms of mythics which underlie such representations. . . . The study of cultural constructions are more accessible than many anthropologists and historians [and, I would add, literary critics] like to think they are. Anthropological "others" are part of the colonial world. In the historical situation of colonialism, both white rulers and indigenous peoples were constantly involved in representing to each other what they were doing.[20]

In many recent studies anthropologists have acknowledged and exposed the colonialist underpinnings of their disciplinary activity.[21] Their reconstructions of cultures from the almost sacred field work experience to its representation in the ethnographic narrative are seen to be complicitous with repressive—or at least oppressive—regimes or power structures. In literary studies our work to uncover power, dominance, and oppression in cultural representations, as well as in our own academic and disciplinary environments, is not comparable with struggles of resistance in "real" colonial situations. But this comparison can alert us to academic or disciplinary imperialism, although of a less directly brutal sort. We can extrapolate from the metaphor to sharpen our awareness of struggles for power. The division, constitution, occupation and, some would say, colonialization of Germany after the war were based on the Allies' interpretation of how political power and spheres of influence should be marked territorially. Similarly, we can see how the realignments in our own discipline—between *Germanistik* and German Studies—set up new arrangements of power. In short, we are in the process of remapping our discipline—with the emendation, however, that in these disciplinary realignments we will take into account from the beginning the meaning of our collaboration and coexistence with those who administrate power, such as tenure committees and editorial boards.

This kind of approach arises particularly in *Auslandsgermanistik,* whose position "outside the center" compels its practitioners to be conscious of their difference, foreignness, or otherness when they are practicing in a foreign country a national philology that does not really belong to them. Rather than trying to become German and to identify with either the native Germans or the native *Germanisten*—to relive ("einleben") in Dilthey's sense, their experience—the *Auslandsgermanist/in* should preserve that distinction characterized as alienation or strangeness, both from Germany and from his/her own national identity.

Critical reflection emerges, in fact, just at this "place" where being outside or on the margins is thematized as part of the *Germanistik* project. The outsider becomes insider, but only in so far as she/he can remain "in-between," in that mediating reflective space between Germany and America, majority and minority, strong and weak, or any two poles of an exaggerated or reified binary opposition that represent relations of power. This "in-between" the borders of national or disciplinary territories or fields expands as those who were once excluded inhabit, rather than occupy, this once narrow territory, without the urge to remain in or to reify any one fixed position.

Here we can learn a great deal from feminism. The feminist subject is no longer being defined as "unified or simply divided between positions of masculinity and femininity" but rather as "multiply organized across positionalities along several axes and across mutually contradictory discourses and practices."[22] Like these feminists, we can resist the urge to choose one or the other, to think in such binary alternatives and reside only in one home. As Biddy Martin and Chandra Talpade Mohanty have pointed out in an appropriately entitled essay, "Feminist Politics: What's Home Got to Do With It?":

> "Being home" refers to the place where one lives within familiar,
> safe, protected boundaries; not "being home" is a matter of realiz-

ing that home was an illusion of coherence and safety based on the exclusion of specific histories of oppression and resistance, the repression of differences even within oneself.[23]

Predicated on the productive vacillation of anyone's position—nationally, academically, sexually—between boundaries and across divergent spaces, always away from "home," a notion of Germany (or any subject) as sovereign and secure that determines the course of all *Germanistik* is decentered and destabilized. Clearly the subject, individual human agency, or authorial personality (whatever we call it) does exist in the formation of a discipline and its scholarly and critical apparatus. Feminist thinking, in particular, reminds us of the constant struggle between individual subjectivities on the one hand, and institutions within social/cultural contexts on the other. Therefore, I would not assert or even imply here that reality, or what we perceive as reality, is only constituted in language or by impersonal institutions. The suffering inflicted by the materiality of bombs or disease cannot be explained away for their victims by a discursive slight of hand. However, as the situations of Malinowski and Auerbach show, institutional contingencies determined to a large extent what and how they would write their individual masterworks. Without overplaying the Nietzschean connection, institutions have a will of their own to create knowledge, as Foucault has shown in his analysis of the hospital, the prison, the bedroom, and the educational institution. His perspective on disciplines and their formation highlights the constraints and limitations that dominate our thinking (and our actions), for example, in medicine, criminology/law, sexology/psychology, and pedagogy. The physician, the warden, the man, and the teacher are inscribed by the institution and the discipline with power and authority that legitimize their discourse. At the same time the institution constitutes, objectifies, and strategically normalizes their subjects—the patient, the criminal, the woman, and the student—by instituting certain prohibitions inculcated in rules of behavior and speech. Here the double meaning of "discipline" emerges: as an organizing taxonomy and as a structure for constraint and control.

II

Once "discipline" is differentiated to maximize its epistemological and political potential, the notion of "interdisciplinarity" becomes more than a simplistic description of movement across disciplinary boundaries. As a theoretical concept with a practice that emerges out of spatial relations, it should be the place where scholarly and academic thinking could best become critical and reflective. Unfortunately the term is often invoked merely because it can grant power and authority in the university: it often improves one's chances of getting research grants; it marks innovative teaching and curriculum development; at the least, it makes one sound as if one were at the forefront of scholarly reform. As "one of the most familiar features of the academic landscape [sic]," to cite a recent article in "The Chronicle of Higher Education,"[24] the term "interdisciplinary" itself is being exploited for its own representational value. Any performative power it might have is undermined when it is reified rather than reflected upon, that is, when the meaning and function of its practice are ignored. Over a decade ago, Roland Barthes declared that:

> Interdisciplinary work, so much discussed these days, is not about confronting already constituted disciplines (none of which, in fact, is willing to let itself go). To do something interdisciplinary it's not enough to choose a "subject" (a theme) and gather around it two or three sciences. Interdisciplinarity consists in creating a new object that belongs to no one.[25]

I do not imply here that any object is constituted "free" from historical specificity or completely indeterminate, as Barthes' declaration might suggest. German Studies could be seen, however, as this new object that "belongs to no one" and, I would add, to everyone who constitutes it; that is, it is both institutionally and individually determined. German Studies, then, is neither like the territory—Germany—divided up by the Allies, which can simply be put back together again to form a unity, nor the intellectual field territorialized by the historians, sociologists, and political scientists, whose interest in "things German" simply adds up to the traditional German Studies program.

In a reconstituted field this new object cannot be taken apart or disengaged from its subject. As a model for interdisciplinary study, German Studies, as a discursive formation, becomes that site or strategic location where the discipline reflects on itself and its practices, both critical and academic, where the variety of discourses about Germany—the literary, political, sociological—converge or diverse. As the in-between space where the clash of multiple subjectivities can foreground difference, it stimulates reflection on how such a new object is constituted. It is at this in-between level where Germany is constructed, talked about, and represented by the practitioners of the fields that make up the more differentiated practice of German Studies.

I must emphasize here that my notion of the "in-between" is not a middle-of-the-road, harmonious resolution or transcendence. In fact, I would hope that this less political, more hermeneutic version could be transformed by poststructuralist, feminist, and recent anthropological thinking to account for, explain, and give meaning to such discourse that is "culturally determined" and institutionally defined. Focusing on this spatial dimension can uncover the oppositional potential in the friction between borders, when they clash and mark out the space in-between for multivocal, multinational, and multidisciplinary positions. There we can expose the competing vocabularies struggling for power, and we can make a place for counter-hegemonic discourse to emerge.

This kind of analysis has great potential for German Studies or any so-called interdisciplinary academic "unity," such as International or Area Studies Programs. It exposes how institutions and disciplines shape subjectivities, how each discipline's own paradigmatic discourse constitutes and controls the object for its own interests, and how each disciplinary practitioner's assumptions, expectations, and goals define their object differently and potentially work at cross-purposes. Interdisciplinary study therefore always totters on the brink of fragmenting into a collection of pieces. Not surprisingly, however, there emerges at the interdisciplinary level a global replay of the colonialist paradigm where different disciplines now compete on an epic scale to oversee a sphere of knowledge. Only now the prize, if one disciplinary paradigm can "win out," is the domination of an entire intellectual terrain tenuously held together by an overarching internationalist, mythically objective and totalized "form" supposedly "full" of continuity and coherence. I would claim that this metaphorical ill(all)usion of an enclosed or circumscribed object, containing a definitive or cumulative content on an international or regional level, represents the problem of "Area Studies Programs" merely defining themselves around a country. The disciplinary parts are simply larger than the national whole.

This place or space for German Studies rather than *Germanistik* defines "replacement" as literally situating a new object of study in an alternative place, rather than substituting one for the other. It means a remapping of boundaries for the Germanist as well as for the German, both of whom are searching for an identity appropriate to a contemporary understanding of the world, which makes division and displacement a productive and positive element in its self-definition. Our distance from a supposed site of origins in Germany can work to our advantage, if we problematize this displacement, our positioning between Germany and America, between literary, political, or sociological texts. Let us not dissolve the boundaries, but keep crossing over them, reconfiguring our disciplinary and academic territories so that different forms of knowledge can emerge, while always foregrounding the difference that emerges when disciplines as well as nations clash.

With Germany displaced as a center of operations, German Studies, especially as it is practiced abroad, is opened up to different kinds of texts and practitioners who were excluded or at least disadvantaged under a narrower, exclusively (literary) text-centered scholarship. It is not surprising that many of the participants in this symposium would emphatically define their academic/ scholarly interests in forms that are not homologous with traditional disciplinary definitions; in the past, topics such as film, feminism, and ethnic identity/ minority discourse would have been more comfortably lodged and categorized in Departments of Communication, Sociology or Anthropology, or even, more recently, in Ethnic Studies.

The transformation from *Germanistik* to German Studies is from the literary text to reflection on how the discipline and the institution inform the way a variety of texts are placed in specific contexts—national, critical, academic, or pedagogic, inside and outside the classroom, in teaching as well as in research. In these contexts the emergence of new voices, previously submerged, ignored, or trivialized, signals the shifting of power relations as well by relativizing any one discourse, especially the dominant one. Here German Studies can become oppositional and counter-hegemonic[26] in a way that traditional *Germanistik* could only achieve through the content or structure of a literary text. Here the national and academic "divisions" in German territory promote the new interdisciplinary paradigm, German Studies, for other less fragmented nations and disciplines that are recharting their boundaries. At this "external" rather than purely "internal" level, German Studies, as disciplinary and discourse analysis, can offer alternatives and questions, can make us think in terms of problems rather than absolute answers or solutions. By promoting tentativeness and relativity, it enhances the modesty and tolerance that counteract ethnocentrism on the disciplinary as well as on the national level.

If *Germanistik* in America is to have a future that we can bequeath to our students, then they have to be empowered to participate in the constitution of the discipline as well as in the interpretation of texts. Under these conditions, German Studies becomes a practice that stimulates critical thinking for all their studies by teaching them to recognize that they are multipositional subjects and that they are implicated in constituting their objects, whether Germany or *Germanistik.* By thinking spatially as well as temporally, they will understand the meaning of those geographical relations on the map, rather than just knowing where they are to be found; they will realize that the process of establishing such value can mobilize its disestablishing potential. They will learn that cultures, whether disciplinary or national, are not bounded objects, complete and finished, to be observed with detachment; they will see that recognizing the representational quality of the human sciences includes, rather than excludes, their participation.

Even with the map of *Germanistik* being redrawn to make a place for German Studies, this new field may be marking its own limitations and demise, since there is always the danger that even a field that promotes variability, multiple positionality, and difference will become either dispersed or itself univocal. Its practitioners need to insure that a critical stance is maintained by always drawing attention to movement, to deflection rather than simple reflection, by interference as resistance to the urge to own any one position. Whatever its institutional fate, it does provide a place where future Malinowskis and Auerbachs can reside. They can practice their philological tasks without apologies for their geographic predicaments and with the recommendation for making anthropological reflection—as it has been proposed here—the foundation of their project.

Notes

1. Michel Foucault, "Questions on Geography," *Power/Knowledge: Selected Interviews & Other Writings 1972–1977,* ed. Colin Gordon (New York: Pantheon Books, 1980) 69. In this essay Foucault also defines "discursive formation" specifically as it contributes to thinking about "geographical discourse": "[it] is defined neither in terms of a particular object, nor a style, nor a play of permanent concepts, nor by the persistence of a thematic, but must be grasped in the form of a system of regular dispersion of statements" (62).

2. On Malinowski I follow the discussion of Dan Sperber, "Introduction," *On Anthropological Knowledge. Three Essays* (Cambridge, Paris: Cambridge UP, Maison des Sciences de l'Homme, 1985) 4–5. He devotes a number of pages to the scandal that erupted after the publication of Malinowski's field diaries, which revealed a less than "objective" side to the master in his personal confessions about fieldwork. For an important analysis of the role of "place" for Auerbach see Edward Said's chapter "Secular Criticism" in *The World, the Text, the Critic* (Cambridge, MA: Harvard UP, 1983) 1–30

and more recently, the study by Paul Bové, *Intellectuals in Power. A Genealogy of Critical Humanism* (New York: Columbia UP, 1986).

3. Foucault's two most important works for the foundations of his theory are *The Archaeology of Knowledge,* trans. A. M. Sheridan Smith (New York: Harper & Row, 1972) and *Discipline and Punish. The Birth of the Prison,* trans. Alan Sheridan (New York: Vintage, 1979).

4. See my articles on the application of "anthropological" approaches to redefining literary study. Peck, "The Institution of *Germanistik* and the Transmission of Culture: The Time and Place for an Anthropological Approach," *Monatshefte* 79 (Fall 1987): 308–19 and "Advanced Literary Study as Cultural Study: A Redefinition of the Discipline," *Profession 85* (New York: MLA, 1985) 49–54.

5. Bernard S. Cohn, "History and Anthropology: The State of Play," *Comparative Studies in Society and History* 22 (April 1980): 188–89.

6. Cohn 215.

7. Literary critics influenced by Foucault are increasingly exploiting spatial metaphors to talk about theory today. See Joseph A. Buttigieg's "Introduction: Criticism Without Boundaries," in *Criticism Without Boundaries. Directions and Crosscurrents in Postmodern Critical Theory,* ed. Joseph A. Buttigieg (Notre Dame: U of Notre Dame P, 1987) 1–22.

8. James Clifford, "Introduction: Partial Truths," *Writing Culture. The Poetics and Politics of Ethnography,* ed. James Clifford and George E. Marcus (Berkeley, Los Angeles: U of California P, 1986) 18–19.

9. I follow here and throughout Edward Said in his introduction to *Orientalism* (New York: Vintage, 1978) 3.

10. James Clifford, "Panel Discussion 3," *Inscriptions,* "Feminism and the Critique of Colonial Discourse," nos. 3/4 (1988): 145.

11. This relationship between the origins of *Germanistik* and discourse are worked out in my article " 'In the Beginning Was the Word': Germany and the Origins of German Studies." Manuscript under consideration.

12. Foucault, "Questions on Geography" 68.

13. See the study of John Borneman, "Patterns of Belonging in Berlin/Berlin: Transformations in Kinship and Nation-Building 1945–1988," diss., Harvard U, 1989.

14. Said 54.

15. Gordon Craig, *The Germans* (New York: Meridien, 1982); Werner Weidenfeld, ed., *Die Identität der Deutschen. Fragen, Positionen, Perspektiven* (Munich: Carl Hanser, 1983); Anton Peisl and Arnim Mohler, eds., *Die Deutsche Neurose. Über die beschädigte Identität der Deutschen* (Frankfurt a.M., Berlin, Vienna: Ullstein, 1980). In *Germanistik* see, for example, Jürgen Kolbe, ed., *Ansichten einer künftigen Germanistik* (Munich: Carl Hanser, 1969) and Jürgen Kolbe, ed., *Neue Ansichten einer künftigen Germanistik* (Munich: Carl Hanser, 1973). The journal *Monatshefte* has published two occasional volumes devoted to reevaluating American *Germanistik,* the first was *German Studies in the United States. Assessment and Outlook* (Madison: U of Wisconsin P, 1976) and more recently, *Teaching German in America. Prologomena to a History* (Madison: U of Wisconsin P, 1988). The journal often publishes articles on the topic, for example, *Monatshefte* 71 (1979) and *Monatshefte* 79 (1987).

16. Said, "Secular Criticism" 8.

17. LaCapra pointed this out in a lecture given at the University of Washington.

18. Paul Rabinow, "Representations are Social Facts: Modernity and Post-Modernity in Anthropology," in Clifford and Marcus 253; see note 8.

19. The article appeared in *The Seattle Post-Intelligencer* 28 July 1988: A3, as well as with a less dramatic title in *The New York Times* on the same day (p. 8).

20. Cohn 217.

21. See for example Tal Asad, *Anthropology and the Colonial Encounter* (London: Ithaca Press, 1973); Johannes Fabian, *Time and the Other. How Anthropology Makes Its Object* (New York: Columbia UP, 1983); and the essays in the aforementioned *Writing Culture. The Poetics and Politics of Ethnography;* see note 8.

22. Teresa de Lauretis, "Displacing Hegemonic Discourse: Reflections on Feminist Theory in the 1980s," *Inscriptions,* nos. 3/4 (1988): 136. Also see other important essays in this volume that deal with the problem of difference in-between: Deborah Gordon, "Writing Culture, Writing Feminism: The Poetics and Politics of Experimental Ethnography" 7–24. Trin T. Minh-ha, "Not You/Like You: Post-Colonial Women and the Interlocking Questions of Identity and Difference" 71–93.

23. Biddy Martin and Chandra Talpade Mohanty, "Feminist Politics: What's Home Got to Do with It?" *Feminist Studies/Critical Studies,* ed. Teresa de Lauretis (Bloomington: Indiana UP, 1986) 196.

24. See "Interdisciplinary Research: How Big a Challenge to Traditional Fields?" *The Chronicle of Higher Education* 7 October 1987: A1.

25. Barthes in "Jeunes Chercheurs," cited by Clifford in his "Introduction" 1; see note 8.

26. See Henry Schmidt, "What is Oppositional Criticism? Politics and German Literary Criticism from Fascism to the Cold War," *Monatshefte* 79 (Fall 1987): 292–307.

The Interdisciplinary Curriculum

From Social Medicine to Postmodernism

Bryan S. Turner

Abstract

Academic specialisation has often been criticised, because it brings about a narrow and partial orientation to research and teaching. Hence interdisciplinarity often appears to be a positive and alternative framework for the progressive reorganisation of higher education curricula. This paper examines various aspects of the development of interdisciplinarity in relation to the medical curriculum, locating these changes in the social context of the development of scientific medicine. These interdisciplinary perspectives are illustrated by an examination of four cases (social medicine, sociology of health and illness, the interdisciplinary research centre, and the postmodern melange) which necessarily imply some critical appraisal of the medical profession and its status in society, because they implicitly or explicitly suggest new approaches to the medical curriculum. However, these four examples indicate that the notion of 'interdisciplinarity' covers a variety of very different perspectives on curriculum reform in higher education. Social medicine and the sociology of health and illness have been typically critical evaluations of monodisciplinary assumptions about medical intervention and medical training. By contrast, the research centre orientation, which followed the Rothschild Report, has been primarily a response to financial constraints. The development of postmodernism in social theory has also involved a challenge to the unitary assumptions of monodisciplinarity, but there may be a convergence between the commercialisation of medicine and the emergence of postmodernistic criticism of the conventional medical curriculum, in which case interdisciplinarity will produce a fragmentary pastiche of disciplines rather than intellectual integration.

Introduction: Definitions

Although experiments in the reorganisation of the medical curriculum have been a constant feature of higher education systems in the post-war period (Bloom 1988; Light 1988), universities currently face acute financial and organisational problems, which in turn have major implications for professional education and professional autonomy (Abbott 1988). The reorganisation of higher education systems is significant not only for separate disciplines, but for

Turner, Bryan S. "The Interdisciplinary Curriculum From Social Medicine to Postmodernism." Sociology of Health and Illness *12:1 (1990), 1–23. Reprinted with permission.*

the relationships between disciplines. Indeed one major component of contemporary curriculum development is the plea for greater interdisciplinarity, which is typically combined with the demand on the part of governments for greater social relevance and problem orientation. Interdisciplinarity has emerged in a context where it is claimed that contemporary health (or more generally social) problems cannot be tackled on a monodisciplinary basis; the interdisciplinarity debate is tied therefore to the quest for effective 'problem-solving'. Although the notion of interdisciplinarity as a general objective of education reform is contentious (Kocka 1987, Piaget 1970), there is some agreement (however minimal) that the scientific study of health and illness is an area which is peculiarly suited to an interdisciplinary approach. For example, the British Open University course on health and illness is based upon the assumption that "Neither health nor disease are straightforward matters, and that they can only be fully understood by adopting an interdisciplinary stance' (Black *et al*, eds, 1984: xi). Similarly, it can be argued that 'health and illness is an area which, theoretically, is ripe for fruitful interdisciplinary efforts' (Charmaz 1986: 279). While these claims have a *prima facie* validity, we need a more elaborated notion of interdisciplinarity in order to understand why it may be more theoretically fruitful than conventional monodisciplinary approaches. What is interdisciplinarity?

For heuristic purposes, let us argue that the social organisation of the sciences can be conceptualised in terms of a hierarchy of growing complexity: disciplinarity, multidisciplinarity and interdisciplinarity. Although I shall subsequently challenge this view, we may define a discipline as a more or less coherent study of a topic or field from a more or less unitary perspective. This definition is deliberately minimalist, because the outcome of this paper is to suggest that what look like coherent disciplines turn out to be typically loose affiliations or federations of theories, perspectives, topics and methods which could be easily redistributed within the university system. Multidisciplinarity is simply a collection of such disciplines which are assembled for the study of a topic or range of topics. There is no necessary attempt to produce a coherent assembly or a theoretically systematic re-grouping of existing disciplines. Whereas monodisciplinarity is an *ad hoc* assemblage, interdisciplinarity aims in principle at academic fusion. Interdisciplinarity, because it seeks a reorganisation and integration of disciplines, involves a critique of disciplinary practices. Because interdisciplinarity challenges the organisation of the conventional curriculum, it ultimately raises questions about the professional division of labour in health-care systems. This account of the nature of interdisciplinarity is not merely descriptive; it contains implicit normative views about academic change. Given the complexity of health issues, the approach of medical and social sciences *ought* to be interdisciplinary. However, in this paper I attempt to contrast (what we may call) positive and negative forms of interdisciplinarity. The positive case (for example, social medicine) is based on some theoretical principles, which stipulate interdisciplinarity as a necessary basis of the curriculum for reasons which are broadly scientific. The negative example (which is referred to in this paper as the McDonaldisation of the curriculum) is the unintended consequences of changes in the organisation of research and teaching, which are brought about for reasons which are broadly economic.

In order to go beyond a merely monodisciplinary approach to create a genuinely integrated interdisciplinary field, it is necessary for interdisciplinarity to adopt an epistemologically creative and critical stance towards existing disciplinarity. For example, one justification for an interdisciplinary reorganisation of both medical and social science faculties would be that an adequate scientific approach to health and illness requires an understanding of the complex causality of illness and disease, and that a valid therapeutics must be grounded in a holistic view of the patient. Thus, the claim that an interdisciplinary approach is essential for the development of medical science will come to depend eventually on what we mean by 'complexity'. An interdisciplinary approach will have to develop a fairly sophisticated epistemology of disease which would entail at least the following. Interdisciplinarity requires reflexivity, that is an awareness of the historical and social setting of scientific concepts. A sociology of knowledge of health and disease entities is a necessary feature of such an epistemology (Turner 1987). This reflexivity would lead either to a relativistic view of disease entities or to some notion of social constructionism (Bury 1986). A constructionist epistemology throws doubt upon the idea of theory-neutral medical facts and more importantly casts doubt upon the idea of unambiguous medical progress. For example, Michel Foucault, following Gaston Bachelard's concept of the 'epistemological rupture' (Bachelard 1934), has made us familiar with the idea of major discontinuities in the development of scientific knowledge. The recent revival of interest in the work of Ludwik Fleck (Cohen and Schnelle 1986) has drawn sociological attention to the notion that the emergence of a scientific fact is the effect of various thought-styles (*Denkstil*) which in turn are supported and maintained by a thought collective (*Denkkollektiv*). The epistemology of an interdisciplinary approach is sceptical with respect to professional and other claims to truth. Interdisciplinarity, for example, tends to be sceptical as to the claims of scientific medicine and the medical model, and it is based upon the notion of the essential multicausality of social, individual, biological, and cultural phenomena. This critical epistemology implies reorganisation of the medical curriculum, the transformation of the relationship between medicine and the academy, and a different relationship between doctors and patients. Interdisciplinarity will inevitably involve conflictual professional relationships. These occupational conflicts are in part a function of the tension between the aspiration for interdisciplinarity and the 'solidarity of the medical profession' (Strong 1984: 346). In the final analysis, interdisciplinarity throws doubt, not only on the professional claims of medical science, but on the character of the disciplinary division of the social sciences.

The final component of interdisciplinarity which we need to consider is the question of the problem-focused character of such research. This orientation to problem-solving is the most uncertain component of the interdisciplinary complex. By way of oversimplification, we can note that historically clinical medicine was focused on the discomfort (that is the disease) of the individual patient. Empirical medicine has taken a specifically hostile stance towards the theoretical justification of adequate clinical practices, and there has been characteristically a division between experimentally based medicine, medicine within the university and the clinical practice of the general practitioner. For example, Sydenham and Locke were critical of experimental pathological anatomy on the grounds that it was dominated by an abstract theoretical enquiry which was irrelevant to the day-to-day practice of medicine and the management of patients. The empiricist revolution of the seventeenth century against the theoretical orientation of Galenic medicine left a legacy in which there is a divorce between theoretical enquiry in the natural sciences and a clinically based medical practice (King 1982). The development of this positivisitic problem-oriented medicine resulted in a specialisation of medical disciplines around various parts of the human body, thereby excluding on professional and scientific grounds the claims of a holistic approach to medical practice, at least until the 1960s when there was a revival of so-called bio-psychosocial medicine in the United States (Gordon 1984). We may assert at this stage that a radical interdisciplinary approach is related to the notion of holistic medicine, and both regard the idea of a medical problem as itself problematic. The creation of a comprehensive interdisciplinarity within the social sciences, and between medicine and social science requires some reconciliation between an a-theoretical clinical practice, the theoretical development of the fundamental sciences which underlie medical knowledge, and the applied social sciences. In the historical development of modern medicine, various attempts have been made, either explicitly or implicitly, to achieve some or all of the goals of interdisciplinarity within and between the medical and social sciences. In this overview of some aspects of the development of interdisciplinarity, the problems and prospects of change in the medical curriculum will be reviewed through four examples starting with the most general, namely the idea of a social medicine.

Social Medicine

The concept of 'social medicine' has had a complex and changing history, referring at different times to very different practices (Porter and Porter 1988). However, despite these various definitions and meanings, the idea of social medicine provides us with an important historical precursor for the development of interdisciplinary social medical sciences. Social medicine had its origins in the eighteenth century and was associated with the development of greater state intervention under the doctrine of mercantilism. George Rosen (1979) in an important article on 'the evolution of social medicine' notes that the idea of public intervention in health matters arose in the context of the development of police science (*Polizeiwissenschaft*) within which health administration was seen to be an important part of the general policing of society, giving rise to the idea of a medical police (*Medizinalpolizei*). For example, between 1779 and 1817 Johan Peter Frank produced his six volume analysis of the government interventions which would be necessary for the protection of individual health within a social context (*System einer vollständigen medizinischen Polizei*).

Frank advocated a public-health policy which, in its surveillance of the population, was paternalistic and authoritarian. However, it did pioneer the development of a thorough and systematic approach to the health-problems of social life, but it was in France in the nineteenth century that a more theoretically sophisticated advance in social medicine was finally established. In the urban crises following the industrialisation of France in the late nineteenth century, and as a long-term consequence of the political disturbances of the French Revolution, the influence of St. Simonian social reformism was fully experienced. It was Jules Guèrin (1801–1886) the editor of the *Gazette Medicale de Paris* who developed the term 'social medicine' as a consequence of the innovative public surveys of Nantes in 1835, which employed new statistical methods of survey analysis to understand the extent of public illness. Guèrin in *Medicine sociale au corps médicale de France* (1848) divided social medicine into social physiology, social pathology, social hygiene and social therapy. Guèrin gave particular emphasis to the social and political functions of the physician's role in a revolutionary context where he called for an organised medical intervention into all social spheres. It is not surprising therefore that Foucault saw in these medical surveys and medical programs the true origins of modern sociology, and he dismissed Montesquieu and Comte as the founders of a scientific science of society (Foucault 1980: 151). It was this 'accumulation of men' which produced 'population' as the great 'object of surveillance, analysis, intervention, modification' (Foucault 1980: 171; Turner 1985). My proposal is that this conception of social medicine implied an interdisciplinary approach to the political management of populations in terms of their health and general social requirements, but it was also part of a systematic critique of the conventional role of the medical man in society.

In Germany these revolutionary French ideas were converted to a self-conscious critical social sciences of human medical problems, and in particular it was Rudolf Virchow who harnessed medical science to the political transformation of European societies (Ackerknecht 1953). In his famous report on the typhus epidemic in Upper Silesia in 1847–1848, Virchow developed the argument that the causes of this epidemic were as much social, political and economic as biological and physical in character; the health of communities could ultimately only be firmly improved as a consequence of major political, social and environmental reform, including the democratisation of the political system. In short, the health-problems of society could only be resolved as a consequence of radical intervention based on an interdisciplinary approach, and he developed the radical slogan that 'medicine is a social science, and politics nothing but medicine on a grand scale' (Virchow 1848: 2). Virchow understood that health could only be improved by socio-economic as well as medical interventions, but he equally recognised that the impediments to such intervention were also political in their essence, and therefore he has to some extent anticipated the radical political economy of health represented in the work of writers like Vincente Navaro (Taylor and Reiger 1984). However, the defeat of radical politics in 1848 in both Germany and France brought about a temporary halt to the movement for a radical interdisciplinary health program in social medicine, but many of Virchow's ideas were either implicitly or explicitly reproduced elsewhere in Europe. For example in England Edward Edwin Chadwick's *Enquiry into the Sanitary Conditions of the Labouring Population in 1842* and Friedrich Engels's *Condition of the Working Classes in England in 1845* came to rather similar conclusions as to the importance of social medicine.

From this brief sketch of the early history of social medicine, we may derive three characteristics of this movement. First, there was, particularly in the work of Virchow, the recognition that illness has to be understood in multicausal terms. Secondly, to understand and therefore to change the nature of the health-status of a population, it is essential to undertake social and political intervention and reform. Thirdly, and as a consequence to the first two, social medicine emerged as a radical political movement which was critical, not only of the intervention of traditional medicine, but of the entire society. It is not an accident that social medicine emerged in response to and as a consequence of the French Revolution and later the revolutionary conflicts of 1848. René Sand in his *Vers la Medicine* sought the origins of social medicine in broader social changes (such as the emergence of social insurance, the institutional development of the general hospital and the expansion of social sciences), but it is interesting that social medicine has often been referred to, or been confused with, the idea of socialised medicine. Henry Sigerist (1937) in particular treated social medicine as socialised Campbell and developed a clear political conception of the operation of a free public-health system based upon general taxation which he thought would emancipate medicine from the economic constraints of a competitive capitalist economy. In a similar fashion, George Rosen in his study on public health also suggested that the medical man was the natural ally of the poor and that medicine had, as it were, a natural function in social amelioration.

Of course, there is no *necessary* connection between social, preventive or socialist medicine, and indeed in the English context, when interventionist medicine was combined with eugenics, then a reactionary doctrine emerged in which the state was involved in the biological planning of the community through the development of a mechanism for selective breeding. The eugenic ideology provided a new basis for the state to institute a total government of the body (Turner 1982). However, both left-wing and right-wing versions of social medicine had one thing in common, a particular view of the state:

> Social medicine depended on scientifically informed, technocratically determined actions by the state. This technocratic vision differentiates the ideas of social medicine from theories of socialist medicine in which the vision of the state is political, not technical. The latter looks for the causes of health and sickness in the economic relations of production and social relations of class and seeks preventions through changing the political relations of power (Porter and Porter 1988: 102).

Given this promising start for a social medicine, based upon the idea of a multicausal model of disease, which in turn implied an interdisciplinary approach to medical intervention and medical training, how might we explain the growing dominance of a specialised medicine in the late nineteenth century, based upon fee-for-service, and the rise of a professional medical group with a monopoly over allopathic medicine?

In the mid nineteenth century, the medical profession was demoralised and lacked effective professional regulation, organisation and status. It could not demonstrate any significant therapeutic efficacy and it did not possess a monopoly over the delivery of medical services to any specific clientele. Because the whole system of the metropolitan general hospital had not been developed, the majority of patients received medical care in their homes on a private basis. Between 1875 and 1920, however, the status of general primary care was greatly transformed and the social standing of the general practitioner was significally enhanced (Rosen 1983; Starr 1982; Starr and Immergut 1987). The growth in the demand for medical services was an effect of economic development, significant urbanisation and the evolution of an urban system of mass transport. The dominance and the autonomy of the medical profession was reinforced in this period by the growth of licensing laws which had the support of the state. A middle-class clientele developed a specific demand for privatised scientific medicine, and furthermore the growth of an ideology of science greatly contributed to the receptivity of the population to technological medicine. In North America the combination of liberalism and individualism fostered the professional individualism of the doctor-client relationship which in turn was opposed to the social interventionism required by social medicine. Alongside these cultural and social conditions, there were a number of major advances in medical technology and scientific knowledge which made surgery, treatment and hospitalisation increasingly safe and effective. There were improvements in anaesthesia, there was the important development of germ theory through the research of Semmelweiss, Lister and Pasteur, and there were major advances in antiseptic procedures following Lister's use of antiseptic precautions for surgery which were widely accepted by the 1870s. Similar developments took place in the evolution of scientific medicine in Victorian Britain (Youngson 1979).

There is a tension between scientific and social medicine, because the former developed on the basis of a privatised relation between doctor and patient to the exclusion of other professional intervention, and was based upon a monocausal view of disease grounded in the germ theory as the foundation of a medical model. By contrast, social medicine implied the development of an interdisciplinary approach to public illness based upon state intervention in the management and regulation of the environment rather than the medical management of the patient. The symbolic arrival of scientific medicine to social dominance was signalled by the publication of the Flexner Report in 1910 by Abraham Flexner, who proclaimed the importance of scientific medicine and provided a model for future medical development and medical training, not only in North America, but in Europe in his *Report on Medical Education in the United States and Canada*.

According to the Flexner Report, scientific medicine would require an extensive and protracted university-based training in scientific medicine and the implication of this requirement was that medical practitioners would only come from the middle and upper classes, because the cost of medical training would be, over a long period of time, quite prohibitive. Following the Flexner Report, 'the necessity for a college degree and the four year curriculum allowed only upper class students to continue to study medicine' (Berliner 1984: 35). The report also had the effect of reducing the admission of blacks and women into the medical profession; for example, all of the five existing medical schools which provided a medical education for women to become physicians were closed. The recruitment of blacks and women into professional medical education did not show any signs of revival until after 1970 (Mumford 1983: 322). The Flexner Report also both recognised and legitimated the dominance of a research-oriented scientific medicine, in which the biological sciences and laboratory training were to provide the foundation of medical education as a whole. While the dominance of a research-oriented scientific medicine looks like the dominance of allopathy over homeopathy, Berliner (1984: 35–36) makes the important point that in its early period 'scientific medicine was a unique way of organising the clinical experience, but it was not, at that time, a clinical medicine. . . . Since the research program of scientific medicine had not yet produced a significant number of clinically effective outcomes, public support for scientific medicine was based on the success of science in endeavours other than medicine'. Scientific medicine also involved an increasing specialisation of knowledge and a division of labour often organised around separate organs of the body rather than around an understanding of the whole person. There was also further sub-discipline specialisation, for example molecular biology from biology. For Flexner, the good physician was someone with a specialised knowledge of the medical sciences and those disciplines which were relevant to the theoretical basis of medicine, and secondly, the good physician was highly critical in the treatment of the evidence of experience; the production of these scientific doctors required a special type of medical training and specialisation which were in practice to be modelled upon the curriculum of the Johns Hopkins Medical School (King 1982: 299).

This specialisation of medical knowledge also ultimately resulted in the spacial and functional separation of the medical faculty from other faculties of the university which had the effect of further reinforcing the professional isolation of scientific medicine from other disciplines. The geographical isolation of the medical school, while contributing to the social solidarity of medical students, clearly makes interdisciplinary scholarly work extremely difficult to achieve. Even within the medical faculties, basic science facilities are often removed from the clinical disciplines which tend often to be centered in hospitals and their clinics. This sub-specialisation and its geographical isolation are further intensified by the technical character of medical scientific language and the rapid expansion of knowledge in physiology and pharmacology (Perrin and Perrin 1984).

It is common in the history of medicine to argue that the Golden Age of scientific medicine was located in the period 1910 to 1950 in which Flexnerian medicine was never significantly challenged; this period was also one in which the general metropolitan hospital came to dominate the health-care system, as that location within which scientific medical practice had its primary focus. The growing importance of the general hospital was clearly associated with the growing status and prestige of the scientifically-trained professional general practitioner within the community. There were in addition significant developments in the training of nurses for a specific place within the medical division of labour. Improvements in hygiene and sanitation within hospitals also had the consequence of significantly reducing high morbidity rates, thereby making hospitals safe for a middle-class clientele who became the main audience for the new medical technology (Larson 1977). It was the great era of the medical-industrial complex (Ehrenreich and Ehrenreich 1970). A number of writers, especially through the influence of Paul Starr (1982) have suggested that the Golden Age of scientific medicine may have either terminated or been transformed by changes in the economic basis of health-care systems and more generally by the changing character of the corporation within the capitalist economy (Cockerham 1986; Navarro 1986; Starr and Immergut 1987).

It is possible to present a fairly broad context within which we can understand the erosion of research-centered, specialised scientific medicine. First, there has been an important change in the disease structure of contemporary society. There has been a shift from acute to chronic disease and illness. For example, the leading causes of death in the United States at the turn of the century were influenza, pneumonia, tuberculosis and gastro-enteritis; in the 1980s the leading causes of death by contrast were diseases of the heart, malignant neoplasms, vascular lesions of the central nervous system and accidents (Turner 1987: 8). These changes in the character of disease are related to the ageing of the population and the success of scientific medicine in providing solutions to the acute illnesses of the nineteenth century, especially for contagious disease. In the United States the population over the age of 65 in 1900 was 4 per cent, which had increased to over 11 per cent by 1980, but the projection for the year 2050 is for almost 22 per cent of the population to be over the age of 65 (Cockerham 1986: 33). The elderly are more likely than any other age-group in society to require hospitalisation and medication, partly because minor diseases become more rapidly transformed into life-threatening conditions which can no longer be treated in the home; in short, the elderly make far greater demands on the health-care system than other age-groups (Russell 1981). In summary there has been a transition in mortality towards diseases which do not have a specific or exclusive biological origin, to mortality rates which are explicable in terms of degenerative diseases, accidents and suicides. Thus there has been a change towards diseases which have 'a strong social component and a multifactorial etiology e.g. cancer, heart-disease, cerosis and arteriosclerosis' (Berliner 1984: 40).

The consequences of these changes for conventional medical training are dramatic. The changing character of disease and the growth of the dependent population require a change in the medical curriculum towards interdisciplinarity, because the scientific medical curriculum, with its emphasis on acute illness and heroic medicine, can no longer provide appropriate medical solutions to the changing character of mortality and morbidity. Of course, there has been little evidence so far of any dramatic change in the scientific medical curriculum, which has retained an emphasis on the dominance of the fundamental components of the natural science disciplines, to the exclusion of a systematic study of the psychological, sociological, economic, political and environmental causes of human illness (Berliner and Salmon 1980). In addition to this hiatus between scientific medicine and the actual requirements of contemporary health-care systems, there has been a growing social critique of scientific medicine, specifically with reference to iatrogenic disease and to so-called 'unnecessary surgery' (Inglis 1981; Illich 1976; Navarro 1976).

Alongside the growing critical awareness of the social limitations of scientific medicine, there has been a mounting critique (from both the left and the right) of hospital management, hospital costs and the alienating consequences of hospitalisation. Mental hospitals in particular came under criticism as primary illustrations of total institutions (Goffman 1961). In more recent years in Britain, there have been extensive enquiries into the mismanagement of hospitals and the neglect, or indeed abuse, of patients especially the elderly (Martin 1984).

These changes have, so to speak, brought the question of interdisciplinarity and social medicine back on the agenda for the reform and training of medical practice in the late twentieth-century. Part of my argument has been therefore that there is typically a tension between social medicine and scientific medicine, and between medical dominance and interdisciplinarity in the academic curriculum. I now wish to consider two responses to the perceived need for a change in the medical curriculum, namely the notion of a sociology health and illness and the idea of interdisciplinary research centres as models for university curriculum development.

The Sociology of Health and Illness

The story of the transition from medical sociology to a critical sociology of health and illness is well known. Medical sociology is seen to have had a late and uncertain start moving from an applied sociology in medicine to a more critical sociology of medicine (Cockerham 1986). A major turning point in the history of medical sociology was the development of the notion of a sick role by Talcott Parsons in *The Social System* (1951). Although the sick role concept has been much criticised, it did indicate the theoretical grounds for an interdisciplinary approach to the nature of illness by combining elements of Freudian psychoanalysis with the sociological analysis of roles and a comparative cultural understanding of the importance of values in structuring the nature and distribution of illness in industrial societies (Holton and Turner 1986). However, while Parsons made the sociological analysis of illness central to sociological theory in the 1950s, medical sociology developed in two directions, one an applied sociology (sociology in medicine) and a more critical sociology of medicine (Strauss 1957). Criticism of traditional approaches led eventually to the notion of a sociology of health and illness as a more independent, relevant and theoretically informed perspective in the 1970s.

Although the advent of sociology of health and illness was often seen to be an optimistic and possibly imperialistic phase in the development of medical sociology (Strong 1979) over a longer historical period we can see that the relationship between sociology and medicine has been ambiguous and conflictual. Within the hierarchy of the sciences, the scientific credentials of both medicine and sociology are relatively low, both lacking the precision and mathematisation characteristic of sciences like physics. Furthermore, to some extent sociology and medicine compete for the same audience, and sociology has often sought clinical status as an applied science alongside medicine. It was Lewis Wirth (1931) who recognised the development of clinical sociology as an important addition to the management and understanding of behavioural problems (especially in children). Wirth noticed that the sociologist, who had been previously neglected by psychiatry, could be an important addition to the therapeutic team, by developing a 'cultural approach' to behavioural problems. However, clinical sociology has never been fully established at a professional level (Glassner and Freedman 1979). It is the case however that medical sociologists have been able to penetrate the medical establishment, but the relationship between sociology and scientific medicine remains ambiguous. For example, while medical sociology often adopted a defensive position in response to critical commentary from either the medical profession or the basic sciences in the biochemical field (Jeffreys 1978), the intrusion of sociology into the medical curriculum can also be seen as an aggressive intervention in the medical academy. Of course, when the implicit or explicit critique of the sociology of health and illness was combined with a feminist analysis of the function of medical dominance in the lives of women (Oakley 1980) or with a political economy critique of the place of medicine in contemporary capitalism especially in a period of economic recession (Doyal 1979), then the prospect for a successful or fruitful interdisciplinary program between the social and the medical sciences has been remote and untenable.

Although the sociology of health and illness often adopts a radical stance with respect to the medical profession, it is not clear that sociology by itself could effect significant changes in the medical curriculum and that in the past the radical transformation of medical practices and academic medicine have been the consequence of political disturbance, a crisis of legitimacy and a consequent change in the relationship between the state and the professions (Foucault 1973). For example, significant changes in the French medical curriculum appear to be more the consequence of political change such as the Napoleonic revolution, the Gaulist regime and the student revolution of the late 1960s (Herzlich 1982; Jamous and Peloille 1970; Weisz 1980). The prospects of an interdisciplinary approach to medical analysis and health-care may be paradoxically enhanced by the current erosion of the professional dominance of the physician as a consequence of greater government involvement in the health-care system, as a consequence of a stronger consumer lobby among the wealthy and the middle class, and finally as a consequence of the growing dominance of corporate power in the health-delivery system, especially in the private market (Starr 1982). One immediate result of corporate control of the private sector is the fact that the professional doctor in fact becomes merely an employee:

> The great irony is that the opposition of the doctors and hospitals to public control of public programs set in motion entrepreneurial forces that may end up depriving both private doctors and local voluntary hospitals of their traditional autonomy (Starr 1982: 445a).

The professional autonomy which characterised doctors in the great era of scientific medicine has been gradually replaced by subordination to corporate power or to the mediation of the state (Johnson 1972). Starr has argued that as health-centres are translated into profit-centres, there will be a new requirement in the training of the physician by various forms of corporate socialisation into business practice and commercial arrangements. Commercialisation also 'constitutes a threat to the idea that professional physicians possess their own distinct body of general systematic knowledge' (Ritzer and Walczak 1988: 13). The full implication of these changes for interdisciplinarity are clearly matters of speculation. However, other changes following from government intervention in the higher education curriculum are topics which have already drawn the attention of educational theorists. In the next section therefore I examine the implications of a research centre model of interdisciplinarity in a period of monetaristic control following current attempts to reduce the welfare budget.

The Research Centre Model: The McDonaldisation of Medicine (Ritzer and Walczak 1988)

Both the sociology of health and illness and social medicine implicitly required the development of an interdisciplinary approach to health issues; this commitment to interdisciplinarity was ultimately based upon a philosophical view of 'the whole person' as the focus of health care. Scientific medicine is limited because it is based upon a narrow, specialised and technical view of the human body as a machine which responds in a determinate way to the therapies derived from clinical experience and basic research. By contrast, proposals for interdisciplinarity were therefore based primarily upon a philosophical view of the body, the person and social relationships. There is however a very different set of pressures bringing about a reduction of specialisation and an increase in interdisciplinarity which is essentially economic, and which is based upon a criticism of fundamental science which is often seen to be remote from real social problems and issues, and which is furthermore too costly in terms of real outcomes. A number of universities in the United Kingdom (such as Bradford and Sussex) have created interdisciplinary undergraduate programs, while during the period of Thatcherite deregulation various attempts have been made to create research centres which are problem-oriented, programs which break down disciplinary specialisation and arrangements which give financial incentives to universities competing for research funding. In the Netherlands, government pressure for higher educational reform resulted in the creation of an interdisciplinary social science program at the Rijksuniversiteit of Utrecht in the 1980s. In Germany more theoretically guided schemes, influenced by the work of Helmut Schelsky, have attempted to establish centers of interdisciplinary research, for example the Zentrum für Interdisziplinaire Forschung at the University of Bielefeld (Kocka 1987). Other prestigious illustrations would include the institutes for advanced studies at Princeton and Stanford.

In the United Kingdom, the reform of natural science research has been heavily influenced by the Rothschild Report, which has done much to break down disciplinary isolation, to focus natural sciences on specific problems relevant to the national interest and to academic arrangements which maximise funding and profitability. These macro-changes in the organisation of science have brought about important transformations of careers in natural sciences, involving a transition from reputational to organisational career models (Ziman 1987). Before the Rothschild reorganisation, the ideal or the characteristic scientific career was reputational, based upon specialisation in one clearly defined subfield of a discipline, followed by promotion on the basis of a public reputation demonstrated by papers presented at scientific meetings, membership of professional organisations and specialist publications. By contrast, the economic climate of Reagonomics and Thatcherism, which have involved continuous underfunding and cuts in the educational program, require constant changes of academic fields, research topics and research technology, because scientists with organisational careers will be forced constantly to change their jobs, their research locations and as a result their domestic arrangements. The absence of long-term contracts in research institutes or the absence of tenured positions within the academy force highly trained scientists within the monodisciplines to change career paths in order to compete within the new research centres and the R and D institutions, where academic promotion and credibility will probably depend less on the quality and length of publications and more on the flexibility of research approaches and the ability to raise funding on a competitive market place. In the new competitive deregulated academic market place, those scientists who are unable or unwilling to adopt the new institutional career patterns will be faced by the threat of retrenchment or redundancy, as more traditional scientific fields are destroyed either as a consequence of government policy or by the sheer speed of change within the natural science field. These career patterns contrast sharply with the more traditional structure of the career of the established scientist. Within a non-competitive academic market characterised by tenure, there is the Matthew Effect (in which success breeds success) and the notion of 'undue persistence' in research or academic fields where individuals continue to draw upon their existing academic investment (or intellectual capital) long after the period in which such knowledge had relevance to a given field. Under these reputational conditions, scientists will be rewarded for their persistence in a given topic. Within this traditional structure therefore, the normal scientist rarely migrates between academic fields but at the very most drifts between adjacent problems. There is therefore much about the conventional academic market place which precludes Kuhnian revolutions in knowledge, because the entire structure of reputation contributes to inertia. Of course, to argue that the reward system of science tends to produce specialisation and concentration on the solution of specific issues within subfields is to take a particular view of the character of scientific innovation. By contrast, some sociologists of science have emphasised the importance of scientific migration between various branches of a discipline or subdiscipline (Mulkay 1975). However, while the creation of a new discipline or subdiscipline produces career opportunities and new outlets for publication, there is, as it were, an ageing process in science where fields become established and stabilised as the original innovations become consolidated and recognised. In normal science therefore persistence and concentration are rewarded by power and resources which tend to reinforce this pattern of specialisation (Zuckerman 1988).

In Britain, while research is undertaken with a variety of institutional settings (universities, research councils, public-sector research institutions and private-sector research groups), in the deregulation of scientific activity in the 1970s and 1980s a common set of assumptions has come to dominate much of scientific research, with a special emphasis on relevance and urgency in which funding is more and more based upon a customer-contractor principle. One consequence of this post-Rothschild reform era is the growing importance of interdisciplinarity in research and development groups, which has challenged the traditional isolation and specialisation of a monodisciplinary training. Because R and D organisations are typically funded to solve specific problems, they will recruit graduates with a broad-based training which emphasises flexibility and versatility. If this type of research becomes increasingly predominant, then it will begin to have important implications for university training and for the maintenance of monodisciplinarity. This type of interdisciplinarity, which I have suggested is brought about by strong economic pressure on the university system from the state, is not based upon a coherent philosophical position (or indeed on any strong educational philosophy at all) recommending interdisciplinarity as a norm. In this institutional context interdisciplinarity is more an unintended consequence of economic necessities rather than a consciously selected epistemological goal. This form of development produces ad hoc and short-term alliances and coalitions between scientific sectors, rather than an elegant and coherent map of the sciences. It results in a fragmented and decentralised scientific landscape. In this respect a Thatcherite model of science may, again for unanticipated reasons, ironically come to resemble the type of scientific world implied by postmodernism.

A Postmodern Model of Science

It is neither possible nor necessary to enter into the complicated debate as to the origins, character and significance of postmodernism (Hassan 1985). For the sake of argument I shall take postmodernism to include at least the following: (1) the argument that the great rational project of the seventeenth century has come to an end, creating a situation in which there is no longer a single coherent rationality, but rather a field of conflicting and competing notions of the rational: thus we live in a fragmented, diversified and decentralised discursive framework; (2) because we can no longer appeal to the court of a single rationality and a single morality, the 'grand narratives' of previous epochs (Science, Reason, Enlightenment, Humanity) have collapsed into a pile of conflicting myths and stories; (3) the hierarchies within science, morality and aesthetics have simultaneously broken down, thereby obscuring the relationship between elite culture and mass culture; (4) because of the impact of consumerism on all aspects of intellectual life, the institutional division between the university intellectual and the leader of pop culture has also become blurred and ambiguous, with the result that intellectuals may just as well seek an audience within the global television circuit as much as within the global academic market place; (5) there is therefore an associated transition in which the aesthetic and the moral are combined, just as there is a transition from the discursive to the figural. At various levels of modern society, these changes have given rise in architecture, in literary criticism, in design and more recently in the social sciences to the notion that we live in a constructed metaphorical reality in which, in the absence of a unifying or authoritative metaphor, culture is merely a melange. Although postmodernism itself is clearly a fashion, it does point to significant and enduring changes in the social status and function of the intellectual and therefore to the social function and character of the university (Bauman 1987).

It is not therefore surprising that one of the great points in the debate over postmodernism, namely Jean-François Lyotard's *La condition postmoderne* (1979), was specifically a discussion of knowledge and of the possible function of the university in a postmodern period. The relevance of this discussion to university life is also underlined by the fact that the study *La condition postmoderne* was originally commissioned at the request of the Conseil des Universités of the government of Quebec and was dedicated by Lyotard to the Institute Polytechnique de Philosophie of the Université de Paris VIII (Vincennes). Lyotard starts by embracing the conclusions of sociological research on the notions of post-industrial society (with its emphasis on the communications revolution, cybernetics, the spread of computerisation, the growth of knowledge banks, and the associated dominance of the service sector and the university within the information society) which he combines with contemporary trends in epistemology (associated with the work of Paul Feyerabend) to produce a critique of Habermas's view of consensual legitimacy; the result is that post modernism involves what Lyotard calls an incredulity towards the meta-narratives of conventional science.

In *La condition postmoderne,* Lyotard recognised two narratives for the legitimation of knowledge in two separate and distinct models of the university. The first was derived from the reforms adopted by Napoleon for higher education in which the main function of the university is to produce the administrative and professional personnel and skills which are essential for the stability of the state. In the second model, which was taken from the idea of Wilhelm von Humboldt and the founding principles of the university of Berlin, the university exists to provide a moral training for the nation, namely to bring about a Bildung-effect. The meta-narrative was behind this model of the university involved notions about the emancipation of the people and the legitimation of the state through some general conception about idealism (Habermas 1987). With the technological and computer revolutions of the post-war period, Lyotard argues that the meta-narratives of legitimacy have broken down and the traditional divisions of labour and hierarchies within the university have equally disappeared. He thus argues:

> The classical dividing lines between the various fields of science are thus called into question—disciplines disappear, overlappings occur at the borders between sciences, and from these new territories are born. The speculative hierarchy of learning gives way to an immanent and, as it were 'flat' network of areas of inquiry, the respective frontiers of which are in constant flux. The old 'faculties' splinter into institutes and foundations of all kinds, and the universities lose their function of speculative legitimation. Stripped of the responsibility for research (which was stifled by the speculative narrative), they limit themselves to the transmission of what is judged to be established knowledge, and through didactics they guarantee the replication of teachers rather than the production of researchers (Lyotard 1986: 39).

Because the universities are no longer committed to the production of ideals, they become merely instruments for the production of skills. At the level of epistemology and philosophy, the traditional questions about truth are similarly replaced by questions about pragmatics (that is reliability, efficiency and commercial value). Because monodisciplinarity is no longer necessarily the most efficient means of research or training in skills (and especially in fixed or permanent abilities), interdisciplinarity arises as the organisation of knowledge relevant to the postmodern condition:

> The idea of an interdisciplinary approach is specific to the age of delegitimation and its hurried empiricism. The relation to knowledge is not articulated in terms of the realization of the life of the spirit or the emancipation of humanity, but in term of the users of a complex conceptual and material machinery and those who benefit from its performers' capabilities (Lyotard 1986: 52).

Alongside these changes in the organisation of knowledge, there is a greater emphasis on team-work and disciplinary collaboration such that the traditional role of the single individual professor is destroyed, because the old individualism legitimised the idea of the professor or the autonomous intellectual has given way to the ethos of the interdisciplinary team (with its problem orientation) and its computer-banks and knowledge storage capacities.

The commercialisation of medicine and the translation of health into a calculation of profitability has been outlined by Paul Starr in his influential *The Social Transformation of American Medicine* (1982). For Starr, the medical idealism of the Hippocratic tradition has been translated into a marketable skill, but this particular case may in fact describe a very general commercialisation of knowledge which will, along with the end of philosophy, announce the end of the university. The independent and autonomous general practitioner will become as archaic as the individual professor of a monodiscipline. The paradox is that the very success of the information revolution may have undermined the traditional status and function of the intellectual as 'a man of ideas'. For example:

> It was the intellectuals who impressed upon the once incredulous population the need for education and the value of information. Here as well their success turns into their downfall. The market is only too eager to satisfy the need and supply the value. With the DIY (Electronic) technology to offer, the market will recap the rich crop of the popular belief that education is human duty and (any) information is useful (Bauman 1988: 225).

The commercialisation of intellectual life, alongside the commercialisation of medicine as a specific instance, raises questions about the traditional institutions of professional knowledge, namely the license and mandate to practice (Hughes 1958). Of course, the principle ideologue of free market competition has argued that 'licensure should be eliminated as a requirement for the practice of medicine' (Friedman 1962: 158). If deregulation and postmodern epistemologies are both effects of changes in consumption, economic production and advanced technology, then we may expect the hierarchical division between scientific medicine and alternative medicine (like the distinction between high culture and mass culture) to collapse as the traditional autonomy of the medical profession is eroded through the invasion of corporations into the health market. Interdisciplinarity would then become, not only a feature of the research institute and the training of medical personnel, but also a feature of consumption and production. The medical market would become a deregulated supermarket of health products just as the cultural world is, according to postmodern theory, itself a deregulated arena of hyper-consumption. There is therefore a peculiar (and to my knowledge unanalysed) relationship between the McDonaldisation of culture, postmodernism and the dominance of Thatcherism as an economic and political principle.

Conclusion

I have considered four examples in medical history which have promoted some form of interdisciplinarity as either the ideal of medical training and intervention, or have implied interdisciplinarity as a desirable aspect of the medical curriculum. The first two (social medicine and the sociology of health and illness) were premised upon some notion of 'the whole person' set within a complex social environment where illness was the consequence of multiple causality (involving social, cultural and biological factors). Social medicine typically adopted a comprehensive and critical approach to the medical profession in which the physician would become merely one figure within a team of health police, whose aim was the complete regulation of society in the interests of a global condition of health. By contrast, the ambitions of sociology have been typically more modest; sociologists-in-medicine would be part of an interdisciplinary approach to health-care where sociology would be generally in a subordinate relationship to medicine and the natural sciences. Although social medicine and sociology were the product of rather different social and historical circumstances, they have tended to adopt a holistic perspective on medicine and have therefore at least implied a critique of the more specialised and narrow conception of the human being as a machine-like creature. The limited success of social medicine and sociology are at least partly an effect of the superior professional organisation of medicine, which has until recently enjoyed the support of the state in protecting its licensed practice, and secondly the limitations of social medicine were partly the consequence of the success of scientific medicine in dealing with acute illness. The prospects for sociology may have been enhanced by the growing chronicity of illness and the more popular critique of scientific medicine.

By contrast, I have examined two other examples exerting pressures towards interdisciplinarity which probably share a similar cause, namely the commercialisation of knowledge and professional practice. One type of interdisciplinarity (the creation of research centres based upon teamwork with private and/or public funding) was the consequence of a political critique of the costs of modern technological medicine based upon monodisciplinary specialisation. This type of interdisciplinarity will further lead to a fragmentation of professional autonomy and transfer the traditional career path of the scientist from a reputational to an organisational career model. Secondly, the growth of the interdisciplinary research unit may be simply a small feature of a much larger historical and social transformation of modern societies by a process of postmodernisation. If scientific medicine was simply the modern expression of the medical revolution of the seventeenth century based upon a Cartesian model of experimental science, then the challenge of postmodernism would deconstruct the meta-narratives of medicine into fragmented and disorganised claims to power. Postmodernism exposes the fact that monodisciplines are federations of thematic components which are held together by the pressure of professional authority and the vested interests of their practitioners.

References

Ackerknecht, E. (1953) *Rudolf Virchow, Doctor, Statesman, Anthropologist.* Wisconsin: University of Wisconsin Press.

Abbott, A. (1988) *The System of Professions, an essay on the division of expert labour.* Chicago, University of Chicago Press.

Bachelard, G. (1934) *Le nouvel esprit scientifique.* Paris: Alean.

Bauman, Z. (1987) *Legislators and interpretors: on modernity, postmodernity and the intellectuals.* Cambridge, Polity Press.

Bauman, Z. (1988) 'Is there a postmodern sociology?' *Theory Culture & Society* 5, 217–237.

Berliner, H.S. (1984) 'Scientific medicine since Flexner', in: J.W. Salmon (ed) *Alternative Medicines, Popular and Policy Perspectives,* London, Tavistock, 30–56.

Berliner, H.S. and Salmon, J.W. (1980) 'The holistic alternative to scientific medicine: history and analysis' *International Journal of Health Services,* 10, 133–147.

Black, N., Boswell, D., Gray, A., Murphy, S. and Popay, J. (1984) *Health and Disease, a reader.* Milton Keynes, Open University Press.

Bloom, S.W. (1988) 'Structure and ideology in medical education: an analysis of resistance to change' *Journal of Health and Social Behavior* vol. 29, 294–306.

Bury, M.R. (1986) 'Social constructionism and the development of medical sociology', *Sociology of Health and Illness,* 8, 137–169.

Charmaz, K. (1986) 'Social Sciences in health studies: an interdisciplinary approach'. *Sociology of Health and Illness,* 8, 278–290.

Cockerham, W.C. (1986) *Medical Sociology,* Englewood Cliffs, New Jersey, Prentice-Hall.

Cohen, R.S. and Schnelle, T. (eds) (1986) *Cognition and Fact, materials on Ludwik Fleck,* Dordrecht, D. Reidel Publishers.

Doyal, L. (1979) *The Political Economy of Health,* London, Pluto Press.

Ehrenreich, B. and Ehrenreich, J. (1970) *The American Health Empire, power, profits and politics.* New York, Random House.

Featherstone, M. (1988) 'In pursuit of the postmodern, an introduction', *Theory Culture & Society,* 5, 195–215.

Foucault, M. (1973) *The Birth of the Clinic, an archaeology of medical perception,* London, Tavistock.

Foucault, M. (1980) *Power/Knowledge, selected interviews and other writings 1972–1977* (edited by Colin Gordon), Brighton, Harvester Press.

Friedman, M. (1962) *Capitalism and Freedom,* Chicago, University of Chicago Press.

Glassner, B. and Freedman, J.A. (1979) *Clinical Sociology,* New York, Longman.

Goffman, E. (1961), *Asylums,* Harmondsworth, Penguin Books.

Gordon, J.S. (1984) 'Holistic health centres in the United States' in J.W. Salmon (ed), *Alternative Medicines, popular and policy perspectives.* New York, Tavistock, 229–251.

Habermas, J. (1987) *Eine Art Schadensabwicklung,* Frankfurt, Suhrkamp.

Hassan, I. (1985) 'The culture of postmodernism', *Theory Culture & Society,* 2, 119–132.

Herzlich, C. (1982) 'The evolution of relations between French physicians and the state from 1880–1980', *Sociology of Health and Illness,* 4, 241–253.

Holton, R.J. and Turner, B.S. (1986) *Talcott Parsons on Economy and Society,* London, Routledge and Kegan Paul.

Hughes, E. C. (1958) *Men and their Work,* Glencoe, Ill., Free Press.

Illich, I. (1976) *Medical Nemesis.* New York, Pantheon.

Inglis, B. (1982) *The Diseases of Civilisation,* London, Hodder and Stoughton.

Jamous, H. and Peloille, B. (1970) 'Changes in the French University-Hospital System', in J.A. Jackson (ed), *Professions and Professionalization,* Cambridge, Cambridge University Press, 11–152.

Jeffreys, M. (1978) 'Does medicine need sociology?' in D. Tuckett and J.M. Kaufert (eds), *Basic Readings in Medical Sociology,* London, Tavistock, 39–44.

Johnson, T. (1972) *Professions and Power,* London, Macmillan.

King, L.S. (1982) *Medical Thinking, a historical preface,* Princeton, New Jersey, Princeton University Press.

Kocka, J. (ed) (1987) *Interdiziplinaritat, praxis, herausforderung und ideologie,* Frankfurt, Suhrkamp.

Larson, M.S. (1977) *The Rise of Professionalism, a sociological analysis,* Berkeley, University of California Press.

Light, D.W. (1988) 'Toward a new sociology of medical education', *Journal of Health and Social Behavior,* 29, 307–322.

Lyotard, J.F. (1979) *La Condition postmoderne: rapport sur le savoir,* Paris, Les Editions de Minuit; English translation 1986, Manchester, University of Manchester Press.

Martin, J.P. (1984) *Hospitals in Trouble,* Oxford Basil Blackwell.

Mulkay, M.J. (1975) 'Three models of scientific development', *Sociological Review,* 23, 509–526.

Mumford, E. (1983) *Medical Sociology, patients, providers and policies,* New York, Random House.

Navarro, V. (1976) *Medicine under Capitalism,* New York, Prodist.

Navarro, V. (1986) *Crisis Health and Medicine, a social critique,* New York, Tavistock.

Oakely, A. (1980) *Women Confined,* Oxford, Martin Robertson.

Parsons, T. (1951) *The Social System,* London, Routledge and Kegan Paul.

Perrin, E.C. and Perrin J.M. (1984) 'Anti-intellectual trends and traditions in academic medicine' in W.A. Powell and R. Robbins (eds), *Conflict and Consensus, a festschrift in honor of Lewis A. Coser,* London, Collier Macmillan, 313–326.

Piaget, J. (1970) *Main Trends in Interdisciplinary Research,* London, George Allen and Unwin.

Porter, D. and Porter, R. (1988) 'What was social medicine? an historiographical essay' *Journal of Historical Sociology,* 1, 90–106.

Ritzer, G. and Walczak, D. (1988) 'Rationalization and the Deprofessionalization of Physicians' *Social Forces,* 67, 1–22.

Rosen, G. (1979) 'The evolution of scientific medicine' in H.E. Freeman, S. Levine and L.G. Reeder (eds), *Handbook of Medical Sociology,* Englewood Cliffs, N.J. Prentice-Hall, 23–50.

Rosen, G. (1983) *The Structure of American Medical Practice 1875–1941,* Philadelphia, University of Philadelphia Press.

Russell, C. (1981) *The Aging Experience,* Sydney, Allen and Unwin.

Sigerist, H.E. (1937) *Socialised Medicine in the Soviet Union,* London, Gollancz.

Starr, P. (1982) *The Social Transformation of American Medicine,* New York, Basic Books.

Starr, P. and Immergut, E. (1987) 'Health care and the boundaries of politics', in Charles S. Maier (ed), *Changing Boundaries of the Political,* Cambridge, Cambridge University Press, 221–254.

Strauss, R.R. (1957) 'The Nature and Status of Medical Sociology', *The American Sociological Review,* 22, 200–204.

Strong, P.M. (1979) 'Sociological imperialism and the profession of medicine', *Social Science and Medicine,* 13(A), 199–215.

Strong, P.M. (1984) 'Viewpoint: the academic encirclement of medicine?' *Sociology of Health & Illness,* 6, 339–358.

Taylor, R. and Rieger, A. (1984) 'Rudolf Virchow on the typhus epidemic in Upper Silesia: an introduction and translation', *Sociology of Health & Illness,* 6, 201–217.

Turner, B.S. (1982) 'The government of the body: medical regimens and the rationalization of diet', *British Journal of Sociology,* 33, 254–269.

Turner, B.S. (1985) 'The practices of rationality: Michel Foucault, medical history and sociological theory in R. Fardon (ed), *Power and Knowledge, Anthropological and Sociological Approaches,* Edinburgh, Scottish Academic Press, 193–213.

Turner, B.S. (1987) *Medical Power and Social Knowledge,* London, Sage.

Virchow, R. (1848) *Die Mediszinische Reform, Eine Wochenschrift,* Berlin, Duck und verlag von G. Reimer.

Weisz, G. (1980) 'Reform and conflict in French Medical education 1870–1914' in R. Fox and G. Weisz (eds), *The organization of Science and Technology in France 1808–1914,* Cambridge, Cambridge University Press, 61–94.

Wirth, L. (1931) 'Clinical Sociology', *American Journal of Sociology,* 37, 49–66.

Youngson, A.J. (1979) *The Scientific Revolution in Victorian Medicine,* Canberra, Australian National University Press.

Ziman, J. (1987) *Knowing Everything about Nothing.* Cambridge, Cambridge University Press.

Zuckerman, H. (1988) 'The sociology of science' in Neil J. Smelser, (ed), *Handbook of Sociology,* Newbury Park, Sage, 511–574.

Things Fall Together

A Critique of Multicultural Curricular Reform

Grant H. Cornwell and Eve W. Stoddard

Identity should be understood dialectically through analysis of historical and contemporary cultural encounters. Framed this way, the cultural politics being played out within the United States will be seen as one instance of a dynamic that has global-historical roots and analogues. General education curricula should foreground issues of culture and identity; this is done best via interdisciplinary and intercultural curricula.

How Should We Agree to Talk?

Multiculturalism. All the labels used to encompass curricular development beyond what has traditionally been understood as "Western culture" carry with them implicit political, metaphysical, and epistemological assumptions and commitments. Of these labels, multiculturalism is the most popular, and perhaps for this reason the most politicized. It has served well to bring to national attention that American culture is comprised of numerous ethnic traditions, and this recognition is empowering these traditions by creating public space for them. As Houston Baker puts it:

> It is precisely a sense of a full, diversifying, and ever-proliferating household on earth that has brought us to the sign "multiculturalism." The sign has unfolded in the same critical and intellectual space that has witnessed the coming to fullness of such denominations as black studies, women's studies, Chicano and Chicana studies, gay and lesbian studies, Native American studies, and Asian American studies. Here, we might say—in these denominations—is the earth's plenty.

Yet despite, or perhaps because of, its celebratory signification of cultural traditions, "multiculturalism" has serious limitations as a paradigm for the study of cultures and their interactions.[1]

Cornwell, Grant H. and Eve W. Stoddard. "Things Fall Together: A Critique of Multicultural Curricular Reform." Liberal Education (Fall 1994), 40–51. Reprinted with permission of the Association of American Colleges and Universities.

An earlier version of this article was first presented at AAC&U's Cultural Legacies Institute; this revised version benefited from critical responses of colleagues. The ideas grew out of the three-year Cultural Encounters Curriculum Development project at St. Lawrence University, supported by grants from FIPSE and the Mellon Foundation.

Multiculturalism suggests a cafeteria-style array of different cultural traditions, conceived of and studied in separation from each other. Often, though
not always, the term is understood to refer more to ethnic traditions within the
United States than to those of other countries, suggesting that cultural diversity
is a peculiarly American phenomenon, related to the older metaphor of the
melting pot. Yet the fact that people use the term vaguely and also to encompass
global traditions has led to muddled discussions of the issues.

The work done under the banner of multiculturalism sometimes treats cultures as if they have essential, traditional natures that are unified and unchanging. By characterizing cultures as multiply discrete entities, the focus shifts away
from the dynamics of cultural encounters.[2] Failing to foreground cultural interaction makes invisible the power relations which are at work interculturally. In
contrast, courses that focus on the interactions between and within cultures
are more likely to confront the political implications of difference itself, of
asymmetrical valuations of cultural beliefs and practices, and of the systematic
depreciation of them. As Hazel Carby points out:

> The paradigm of multiculturalism actually excludes the concept of
> dominant and subordinate cultures—either indigenous or mi-
> grant—and fails to recognize that the existence of racism relates to
> the possession and exercise of politico-economic control and au-
> thority and also to forms of resistance to the power of dominant
> social groups.

Yet taking account of oppression should not result in presenting subordinate
groups solely as victims; as Carby suggests, we must also attend to the ways
that less powerful groups resist the authority of the dominant culture.

Diversity. In debates over curriculum reform, the rhetoric of "diversity"
serves many of the same ends as that of multiculturalism. Many colleges and
universities have adopted diversity requirements, have deans of diversity, and
the like. The advantage of "diversity" over "multiculturalism" is that it readily
extends to categories like gender and sexual orientation that are often not understood as cultural. But the agenda for diversity, like that of multiculturalism,
is often limited to an uncritical recognition or celebration of difference, as if all
cultural practices were morally neutral or legitimate. We give attention to the
vexing problems of relativism this raises later.

There is a troubling implication latent in the terms "difference" and "diversity," suggesting that diversity exists through opposition to some unified norm
or standard; thus emphasis on difference *per se* reinforces the notion of a norm.
Not too long ago, gay and lesbian issues were taught in sociology courses on
social deviance. Even if we assume the best intentions—helping students overcome prejudices and stereotypes—the curricular frame of these issues types
them in ways which mitigate against the very goals they seek to achieve. What
message does it send to require a course in diversity, especially when such
courses typically examine texts, traditions, and cultures of people of color? Such
a requirement seems guilty of both tokenism and exoticism. While the intent

is, presumably, to begin to challenge the hegemony of white, male, heterosexual, Euro-American perspectives in the curriculum, in times of budgetary restraint it seems probable that deans distributing scarce resources will consider the diversity agenda to be completed by such a requirement. And what is worse, so might the students. In addition to this tokenism, the single course requirement seems too much like the Grand Tour of older notions of bourgeois liberal education, where to be educated, to be cultured, was to have experienced exotic cultures and far away places.

Also, neither multiculturalism nor diversity encourages consideration of common human needs across cultures or interdependence among groups who identify themselves as different. In the current global and national condition, it seems important to educate students in ways which encourage mutual tolerance and respect, and this is done by asking students to discover and create commonalities across differences. College campuses are balkanized residentially and socially, and courses predicated on ethnic or cultural separatism mirror, rationalize, and reproduce divisions rather than providing sites where divisions might be bridged.

International/Global Studies. There is a *de facto* division of labor in the academy between those working on issues of American cultural pluralism and those working on issues of global cultural encounter. The dominant use of the term multiculturalism limits the domain of discourse to cultural diversity within the United States, often assuming that the United States is uniquely multicultural.

However, efforts to internationalize the curriculum go to the opposite extreme, focusing attention on cultural diversity outside America and avoiding the thorny political issues raised by multi-ethnic and racial realities within the United States. We believe that the curriculum must be international in scope, but not at the expense of neglecting issues raised by American pluralism. Thus the paradigm of international studies is problematic, not only because it directs attention outside the United States, but also because it privileges the nation as the object of knowledge, often without reflection on its status as an ideological construct of Western political thought and history. But more importantly, internationalism, by focusing on the nation, tends to obscure the cultural multiplicity within the boundaries of contemporary countries, a multiplicity which lends itself to comparison with that of the United States.

Yet to point out the conceptual limitations of internationalism is not to dismiss the importance of nationhood for many peoples who are struggling to emerge from colonialism. For them, positing and identifying with a nation-state is critically important. Thus, for example, young persons in Kenya have to develop a complex and critical understanding of the balance between ethnic and national identities. They affirm Kenya as an act of will, and understand the necessity of national identity for recognition in world markets and politics. Yet this is balanced against a primary ethnic identity born of early language development and local cultural traditions. Therefore, while it is important to design curricula which help students understand the role of national identity in contemporary world politics, we should also help them see that national and cultural identities often exist in tension.

The term that is replacing "international education" in many contexts is "global studies." Whereas international suggests a colloquy of separate, coherent nation states, the term global tends to connote the interconnectedness of lives, belief systems, economic relations, and histories of peoples around the world. "Global" encourages us to study cultures relationally, in process, and not as static, reified entities. It also suggests a way of locating ourselves and our students as agents who have responsibilities as local, national, and global citizens. And it de-centers the United States and the West by placing them in a web with other geographical and cultural entities. While this epistemological and ethical decentering is valuable, it should not obliterate the very real power and resource imbalances that affect the lives of everyone in the world.

Interculturalism

If today's students are to be prepared for citizenship and careers, they need to learn both about the complexity of their own society and about global interconnections. They can best understand the cultural pluralism within the United States by seeing it as one instance of the cultural changes, interactions, and multiplicities that make up human history. In order to comprehend the cultural diversities within and outside the United States under one rubric, we prefer the term "intercultural studies" over "multicultural," "diversity," "international," or "global." A relatively new term, it synthesizes the cross-cultural work of anthropology with the international studies of political science, area studies, and study abroad programs.

Whereas anthropological work has tended to be comparative of cultures that are apprehended as self-contained entities, the prefix "inter-" suggests studying the interrelations of cultures as they evolve through time and as they interact geographically at any given point in time. While it shares with global studies a paradigm of cultures as constantly changing and interrelating, intercultural studies seems to claim a less holistic domain; it does not proclaim that it will cover all areas of the world. Rather, it implies that the object of study will be relationships between cultures, whether they are embodied in separate nation-states or found within the borders of a single state. It is a less polemicized and politicized term than multiculturalism because it has not been bandied about the media as a buzzword for the breakdown of Western civilization on our campuses. But more significantly, "inter-" demands that we examine cultures interacting, calling attention to cultures as dynamic processes and to the inevitable power relations that inform cultural interchange, however complexly.

Academic Disciplines and the Study of Culture

Intercultural inquiry and teaching must be interdisciplinary just as each discipline, using the tools at its disposal, isolates a spectrum of reality as its object, so each culture lives its reality through its history, language, and material conditions. Just as some disciplines overlap in the objects they study, so some cultures share common realities. One needs knowledge from multiple disciplines and multiple cultures to begin to understand the dynamics of cultural identity, cultural interaction, cultural critique. No single disciplinary perspective is going to comprehend any given culture or cultural form. Neither is it adequate to string a series of distinct disciplinary courses together, without sites of synthesis and integration.

Cultures, in their ever-shifting interactions and complexities, need to be both researched and taught from interdisciplinary perspectives. Thus in *Culture and Imperialism* Edward Said insists that "cultural forms are hybrid, mixed, impure, and the time has come in cultural analysis to reconnect their analysis with their reality." This reconnection is inhibited by the fact that "most scholars are specialists; most of the attention that is endowed with the status of expertise is given to fairly autonomous subjects, e.g., the Victorian industrial novel, French colonial policy in North Africa, and so forth. The tendency for fields and specializations to subdivide and proliferate . . . is contrary to an understanding of the whole, when the character, interpretation, and direction or tendency of cultural experience are at issue." Whereas Said is especially attentive to the interrelations between literary/artistic cultural production and the arena of international politics, Eric Wolf has called for a return to political economy from the separate disciplines of sociology, economics, political science, history, and anthropology. The organization of knowledge took a wrong turn, Wolf argues, when inquiry into the nature and varieties of humankind split into separate (and unequal) specialties and disciplines. This split was fateful, leading not only forward into the intensive and specialized study of particular aspects of human existence, but turning the ideological reasons for that split into an intellectual justification for the specialties themselves. Wolf's point is that the separation of disciplines not only distorts and impedes our ability to grasp the dynamics of cultural encounters, power relations, and change, but also that the disciplines themselves have become reified political entities with aggressive territorial claims.

These territorial claims stand in the way of new developments in cultural and intercultural studies on many campuses. Some of our colleagues think faculty have no business teaching in any area other than that in which they were professionally trained. Who, then, has the authority to teach about cultures and cultural diversity? This question can be taken in two senses. Taken one way it is a question about academic training; traditionally the academy has seen authority as vested in disciplinary expertise. When it comes to speaking about cultures, anthropology is the acknowledged pioneer.

Anthropologists, of course, have an important role in cultural studies, but not an exclusive one. The current theoretical controversies internal to anthropology are particularly interesting and useful for the kind of intercultural work we envision. In *Anthropology as Cultural Critique: An Experimental Moment in the Human Sciences,* George Marcus and Michael Fischer criticize the ahistorical and apolitical nature of traditional cultural anthropology, which they characterize as "a research process in which the anthropologist closely observes, records, and engages in the daily life of another culture—an experience labeled as the field work method—and then writes accounts of this culture, emphasizing descriptive detail." Indeed, some anthropologists, such as Geertz, Clifford, Marcus, and Fischer, themselves argue that, unless problematized, ethnography will masquerade as something which it cannot be—fact, objective description based on detached, disinterested observation. The paradigm of being a fly on the wall—present but not present—has always been a fiction, and we would do well to treat ethnographies as the complex texts they are. The study of cultures, then, should take account of their interactions over time, tracing cultural appropriations and borrowings. Ethnographies have a great deal to contribute to new forms of inquiry and teaching about cultures, but they can be read more critically and more richly with the addition of tools from other disciplines.

Other disciplines, such as history, literary criticism, and political economy, have challenged and enriched anthropology's understanding of itself and its work. Cultures are too complex to be comprehended by any single discipline or methodology. Disciplines are lenses which bring into focus different dimensions of culture. No single perspective is authoritative; in fact, we see the paucity or inappropriateness of the very notion of authority or expertise when disciplines engage in conversation with one another about culture. This is an argument for syncretism, not relativism; the understanding obtained through the contest and conversation of multiple disciplines is more complete and complex than that available through any single discipline.

Who Ought to Speak

Taken in another sense, the question of who has authority to teach about cultures is not about academic credentials, but rather about the politics of identity. The foregrounding of cultural diversity in the academy has challenged the authority of disciplinary expertise with the authority of identity and experience. These are epistemological questions: Who has knowledge and on what basis do they know? But they are also political questions: Who should be allowed to speak about specific cultures? Who is to be trusted and who is not? These are critical questions in any forum where intercultural issues are discussed. While our epistemological position mistrusts and critiques the essential certainties of identity politics, our political position recognizes the practical imperative certain identities exert in the real world of unequal power relations and unequal access to public speech and writing.

The strongest epistemological claim of identity politics is that only those persons who belong to a particular group, whether it is biologically or culturally or sociologically defined, have the ability to know and understand the perspective, needs, cultural productions, desires, etc., of that group. The most essentialist position is the allegedly biologically-based one which locates personal identity in skin color or reproductive organs. Most defenders of identity politics, however, would view race or gender as socially constructed identities that are signified by certain physical markers, even though the identity itself is not produced by those physical characteristics. In fact the identity which locates a person in a particular group such as black American or woman has been historically imposed by the dominant group which has constructed those outside it as "others."

The main point is that authority to speak about and interpret cultures is grounded in identity and experience. Presumably, then, we can only know, with authority to write and teach, matters pertaining to our own particular cultural legacies. In *Loose Canons,* Henry Louis Gates asks:

> What would we say to a person who said that we couldn't teach Milton because we are not Anglo-Saxon, or male, or heterosexual—or blind! We do nothing to help our discipline [African-American Studies] by attempting to make of it the equivalent of a closed shop, where only blacks need apply. On the other hand, to say that ethnic identity is socially constructed is not to say that it is somehow unreal, to deny the complexities of our own positionality, to claim that these are not differences that make a difference.

But even here, ethnic identity is presented as something clearly identifiable, readable, even, off of one's phenotype. This is a kind of essentialism, a reification of fluid, ephemeral particulars that denies the complex multiplicity of every individual. It assumes a unitary self that is both fictional and limiting, and it assumes that we all have a clear sense of that self.[3] As Gayatry Spivak writes in "A Literary Representation of the Subaltern": "The position that only the subaltern can know the subaltern, only women can know women, and so on, cannot be held as a theoretical presupposition . . . for it predicates the possibility of knowledge on identity . . . [and] knowledge is made possible and is sustained by irreducible difference, not identity."

The position that we somehow have more accurate, less clouded, access to our own history and experience, or that of our particular cultural legacies, than those of others, and that we and only we can speak with authority about our own case, without a dialectical interaction with those whose histories and experiences are different, is a kind of intellectual separatism that approaches solipsism. With Karl Jaspers we might say that the truth begins with two; it is in the dialectic between the insider and the outsider, in the negotiation of perspectives, that the complexity of identity is brought out. We need to talk across differences in a way that both recognizes and tries to subvert existing power dynamics.

The political argument of identity politics is compelling, though problematic. Put simply, those groups, whether within the United States or in former colonies around the world, who have not had a voice in the histories told about them and who have access to a disproportionately small share of world resources, fear and resent the appropriation of their stories by the same white Euro-American elites who only recently dominated them through physical force. With much historical validity, they suspect the motives of white middle-class intellectuals who suddenly want to jump on the bandwagon of multiculturalism or third world studies. Even when scholars and teachers operate with the best intentions, we run the risk, with the blindnesses produced by affluence and power, of misunderstanding and worse, of appropriating the voices of those we seek to learn about.

Does this mean we should back off and return to our nationalistic, ethnocentric disciplinary domains? It seems clear to us that the answer to this is no, that it would be intellectually, ethically, and politically irresponsible to perpetuate the fiction of a white male Eurocentric intellectual tradition. But how then do we avoid behaving as neo-colonialists? Spivak has an interesting take on this. In response to the questions of whether men should theorize feminism, whether whites should theorize racism, whether Westerners should theorize post-colonialism, she writes: "It is when *only* the former groups theorize that the situation is politically intolerable. Therefore it is crucial that members of these groups are kept vigilant about their assigned subject-positions." bell hooks makes a similar point when she writes:

> Even if perceived "authorities" writing about a group to which they do not belong and/or over which they wield power, are progressive, caring, and right on in every way, as long as their authority is constituted by either the absence of the voices of the individuals whose experiences they seek to address, or the dismissal of those voices as unimportant, the subject-object dichotomy is maintained and domination is reinforced.

Thus it is important that we all do this work, especially since any alternative seems to perpetuate, implicitly or explicitly, historical patterns of power distribution. But it is also important that we do this work aware of our particular cultural legacies and listening closely to the insights of those whose cultural legacies differ. To quote hooks, "Learning about other groups and writing about what we learn can be a way to unlearn racism, to challenge structures of domination."

Interdisciplinary, Intercultural General Education

We believe that the study of various cultures within general education courses should have two major goals, one epistemological or cognitive and the other ethical or political. The first goal is to help students understand that their own identities are embedded in a complex network of cultural histories and interactions as are the identities of others. We would like to extend the ability to think critically to include thinking critically about cultures and the claims made on their behalf, both inside and outside the academy. The second goal is preparation for global citizenship in a shrinking and diverse world.

Understanding Culture and Identity

In many of the new curricula and in much of the literature, the educational agenda of multiculturalism seems limited to literacy: that students acquire knowledge of various cultural practices and traditions. This is a starting point, but not an adequate educational goal. An approach which simply surveys multiple cultures tends to misrepresent the nature of cultures by reifying them into discrete, immutable entities, unchanged over time, and formed in isolation. Many new core curricula require courses on various areas of the globe; such courses are characterized by "the wholesale lumping together of all Native American, African, and Asian cultures or, a move that raises the stakes of generality, the imagining of Third World culture as a concrete entity apart from the naively fixed viewpoint of an imaginary monocultural West. . . . The claim for diversity at the center of multiculturalism is thereby undermined by these practices demanding unity in cultures and subjects and necessarily finding it" (Stewart 1993, 13–14). Such curricula tend to have several shortcomings: they fail to emphasize multiplicity within cultures, they de-emphasize changes in cultures over time, and they downplay interactions between cultures. A curriculum should not reproduce by its structure monolithic views of the cultures being studied.

The point of having students learn about how other cultures see and arrange things, is, in the case of general education, *not* primarily in the service of multicultural literacy. It is not about developing expertise in the ways of another nor only about acquiring or imparting some kind of synoptic, multidisciplinary understanding of another world view. Although it is important within programs of general education to acquire some knowledge of other cultures, their histories, their beliefs, their practices, their contacts and complexities, that knowledge is not an end in itself. Our work is to create a critical and theoretical context for more specialized courses of study, such as anthropology, international politics, history, or literature. It is to form, float, examine, and criticize theories about the dynamics of culture and identity, to speculate about how persons become who they are, how persons construct meaning, how persons see and talk about themselves as being related to and/or distinct from others. As we have said, it is also to recognize the forms of power within and between cultures, and how these forms influence human possibilities. We want to enable our students to interrogate the very idea of culture, to understand that, while useful and meaningful to both academic inquiry and lived experience, a culture is a reification that overlooks multiplicity, difference and particularity.

Thus, one goal of intercultural general education is to enable students to begin to understand how a person's particular identity evolves in dialogue— sometimes harmonious, sometimes conflictual—with various cultural histories and affiliations. That is, as individuals we are all, whether Kikuyu or Anglo-American, man or woman, Jewish or Buddhist, sites of complex cultural encounter. It is a mistake to think that any person's identity is comprehended by any single allegiance, category, or belonging. This is not to say that people don't identify with one another on the basis of common histories, beliefs, values, and practices, nor to deny that these identifications are some of the most important bearers of meaning. The goal is to help students recognize their own individual particularity and cultural influences as they learn about how others identify themselves. The work of general education, as we see it, is to disturb ourselves and our students, to defamiliarize our own world view in all of its categories and details, to confront, as Martha Nussbaum says, difference in areas we tend to see as neutral, necessary, and natural: "Exploring the way in which another society has organized matters of human well-being, or gender, or sexuality, or ethnicity and religion (or politics, or property, or family, or views of other animals . . .)—this will make the pupil see that her own ways are not the only ones, that other people in viable societies have done things very differently." Detailed information about the history and structure of other cultures allows one to see in a more detailed way what is common, what is different. Encountering and exploring particular differences, understood in cultural history and context, brings us closer to the sites of identity construction.

Preparation for Global Citizenship

Thus far our analysis has assumed a certain poststructuralist stance in its critique of unified cultures and univocal identities. For our purposes, we adopt the position that ethics and politics persist as legitimate domains of discourse, occupying an epistemological space outside of objectivism.

Against this backdrop we wish to offer what we see as the ethical goals of intercultural curricular reform. One of the goals of intercultural general education is to prepare students for responsible global citizenship. What does this mean? What are the issues that lie beneath this cliché of institutional rhetoric? Research and teaching about cultures takes place in the academy, a privileged domain within a world where real people suffer under various forms of oppression, physical hardship, and deprivation. There is something grotesque about constructing education as the pursuit of knowledge for its own sake, especially when that knowledge has as its subject people who are oppressors and oppressed, people whose lives are shaped by complex economic and political relationships. Thus programs of intercultural general education should help students understand that their choices, how they live, how they vote, where they work and travel, take place in a global network of complex interrelations, and in this sense are political. We must attend, then, to helping students become not only responsible, critical, sophisticated consumers of information about world events, but also political actors.

To say that one of the educational goals of intercultural studies is ethical or political is immediately to distinguish intercultural studies from certain disciplinary approaches to knowledge, especially those aspiring to scientific objectivity, whose creed is to look, not judge. This method implicitly dehumanizes the people being studied. To be able to see differences as interesting, in a cool, dispassionate way, is to see them as something other than live options for oneself, as legitimate human possibilities; that is, the distancing encouraged by this method is tantamount to objectification. When practiced well, students can observe others without emotional involvement or empathy; that is, they can look at others as objects of knowledge. In the classroom, as opposed to the field, students should encounter people from other cultures as much as possible in their own voices, and they should reflect on their own cultural identities and practices in relation to those of the people they study.

The "objective" study of cultures and their practices is intentionally apolitical and nonjudgmental, and implicitly leaves students with dispositions toward either ethnocentrism or relativism, and sometimes both in unrecognized contradiction with each other. As the discipline which pioneered in cross-cultural study and teaching, anthropology is the *locus classicus* of a pervasive relativist ethos in the academy, developed in the service of tolerance and respect, out of a commitment that students should seek to understand, not evaluate. Anthropologists, in their teaching, and after them, many of us in ours, want to disabuse students of their tendency to apply their own cultural norms in evaluating the practices of others. This is an important first step. But if we stop there, we are contributing to political passivity. And herein lies the central difference between the social scientific approach to culture and the one we are advocating for the purposes of general education. Criticism, judgment, and political action are essential to any kind of citizenry. The task of intercultural education is *not* to undermine these capacities, but to ensure that they are exercised carefully, critically, and with a complex mixture of caution and resolve.

We do not mean to suggest that we should indoctrinate students into any particular political position, or even into a rejection of cultural relativism as a committed stance. We are saying, rather, that these very issues, cultural relativism versus critical evaluation—the grounds for human rights, the possibility of universal human experiences across different cultures, the validity of identity politics—these issues should be central topics for reflection and debate. Students need to be informed about the complexities and political implications of these issues. And perhaps more critically, they need to question certain U.S. legal practices and policies, which they tend to take as paradigmatic of justice. Ultimately, general education is that part of the curriculum dedicated to liberal rather than specialized education, to preparing students to be generous and open-minded, yet skeptical and critical, especially toward their own most cherished beliefs, as they assume their adult responsibilities in a world that is both highly interdependent and deeply fissured.

In summary, our argument is that general education at this moment in the academy needs to be intercultural, and that to be so adequately means to be interdisciplinary. We need to study American pluralism in conjunction with global cultural diversity, and intercultural studies comprehends both. In general education courses, we need to teach students to problematize the concept of culture as a unified field of meaning, to understand that all cultures have always been in flux, interacting and mingling, that change and multiplicity are their defining attributes. This can only be done through interdisciplinary approaches that bring multiple perspectives and modes of expression to bear on the complex topics of human culture and personal identity. This theoretical questioning of the nature of culture and identity does not preclude the political reality that celebration of diverse cultures is needed in order to recognize and affirm traditions that have been devalued or neglected in American higher education, but we need to see such celebration as a politically necessary fiction. Otherwise we risk recreating the stereotypes and objectifications that have fostered white, male Euro-American hegemony for so long.

Endnotes

1. For recent discussions of multiculturalism, see Carby, Gates, Giroux, Nnaemeka, Raz, Scott.
2. Eric Wolf argues that "Even anthropology, once greatly concerned with how culture traits diffused around the world, divides its subject matter into distinctive cases: each society with its characteristic culture, conceived as an integrated and bounded system, set off against other equally bounded systems" (1982, 4).
3. Renato Rosaldo points out that "Creative processes of transculturation center themselves along literal and figurative borders where the 'person' is criss crossed by multiple identities" (1989, 216).

References

Baker, H. 1993. Introduction. *MLA Profession* 93: 5.
Carby, H. 1980. Multi-culture. *Screen* 34: 62–7.
Clifford, J., and G. E. Marcus. 1986. *Writing culture: The poetics and politics of ethnography.* Berkeley: University of California Press.
Gates, H. L., Jr. 1992. *Loose canons.* New York and Oxford: Oxford University Press. 127.
———. 1993. Beyond the culture wars: Identities in dialogue. *MLA Profession* 93: 6–11.
Geertz, C. 1973. Thick description: Toward an interpretive theory of culture. In *The Interpretation of Cultures.* New York: Basic Books.
Giroux, H. 1992. *Border crossings: Cultural workers and the politics of education.* New York and London: Routledge.
hooks, b. 1989. *talking back: thinking feminist, thinking black.* Boston: Beacon Press, 43, 46.
Jaspers, K. 1954. *Way to wisdom.* New Haven: Yale University Press.
Marcus, G. E., ed. 1992. *Rereading cultural anthropology.* Durham and London: Duke University.
Marcus, G. E., and M. M. J. Fischer. 1986. *Anthropology as cultural critique: An experimental moment in the human sciences.* Chicago: University of Chicago Press, 18.
Mouffe, C. 1988. Radical democracy: Modern or postmodern? In *Universal abandon? The politics of postmodernism,* edited by A. Ross. Minneapolis: University of Minnesota Press.
Nnaemeka, O. Forthcoming. Bringing African women into the classroom: Rethinking pedagogy and epistemology. In *Borderwork: Feminist engagements with comparative literature,* edited by M. Higgonet. Ithaca: Cornell University Press.
Nussbaum, M. 1994. Citizens of the world: Core values in liberal education. Lecture given at Saint Lawrence University, 17–18 January.
Pratt, M. L. 1991. Arts of the contact zone. *MLA Profession* 91: 33–40.
Raz, J. 1994. Multiculturalism: A liberal perspective. *Dissent* (winter): 67–79.
Rosaldo, R. 1989. Border Crossings. *Culture and truth.* Boston: Beacon Press.
Said, E. 1993. *Culture and imperialism.* New York: Alfred A. Knopf. 13–14.
Scott, J. 1992. Multiculturalism and the politics of identity. *October* 61:12–19.
Spivak, G. C. 1988. A literary representation of the subaltern. In *Other worlds: Essays in cultural politics.* New York and London: Routledge. 244, 253.
Stewart, S. 1993. The state of cultural theory and the future of literary form. *MLA Profession* 93: 12–15.
Suleri, S. 1993. Multiculturalism and its discontents. *MLA Profession* 93: 16–17.
Wolf, E. 1982. *Europe and the people without history.* Berkeley and Los Angeles: University of California Press.

Putting It All Together

Professionalizing Interdisciplinarity

Literature Review and Research Agenda

William H. Newell

Are you a veteran interdisciplinarian, or participating in an interdisciplinary course or research project for the first time? An administrator of an interdisciplinary program, chair of the curriculum committee, or head of an interdisciplinary research institute or center? Are your degrees in an interdisciplinary field or in a discipline? Do you think of yourself as an interdisciplinarian, or simply as someone with interests that extend beyond your discipline? Whatever your responses, you have probably confronted fundamental questions about the nature of your interdisciplinary activity for which no satisfactory answers were available:

- Is what I am doing really interdisciplinary (and does it make any difference)?
- How can I make my focus more interdisciplinary?
- How should I present my focus to colleagues with more narrowly disciplinary interests?
- How can I make my interdisciplinary activity more coherent and integrated?
- Ultimately, am I doing good interdisciplinary work (and how could I do it better)?

The literature on interdisciplinary studies selected for this volume contains a wealth of information on such questions, whether your interest in interdisciplinary study relates to teaching, curriculum and program development, or research. Teachers and researchers can find help in the purely practical task of identifying and incorporating more effective techniques into their existing interdisciplinary course or project. Those interested in rethinking how they do interdisciplinary work can use this literature to raise their level of interdisciplinary sophistication. Scholars and researchers can use it to probe the nature of interdisciplinarity itself.

This literature can be difficult, even frustrating, to break into without some assistance, however. Most of its articles and books were written by practitioners unaware of much of the rest of the literature. The result is a fragmented and sometimes contradictory array characterized by inconsistent terminology.

Moreover, most people have come to interdisciplinary studies after completing their formal education and have not had an opportunity to explore the interdisciplinary studies literature as a whole in graduate school. Even those who received degrees in an interdisciplinary field such as environmental studies were expected to master the professional literature on that subject and often remained unaware of a literature on interdisciplinary study per se.

We can even question whether there is a single interdisciplinary studies profession, because many people engaged in interdisciplinary study do not think of themselves as interdisciplinarians and many of those who do identify primarily with their substantive field of study. Nonetheless, at the general education level alone, college and university faculty teach thousands of interdisciplinary courses each year in the United States and face thorny curricular and pedagogical issues that are addressed in a growing though hitherto widely scattered literature. Membership in the Association for Integrative Studies, the professional association for people interested in interdisciplinary study per se, has grown to over 1,000 members. It is fair to say that an interdisciplinary studies profession is now taking shape. This volume will contribute significantly to its development by making key writings readily available and by starting the process of integrating them into a coherent professional literature.

This chapter will assist you in using the interdisciplinary studies literature by reviewing the works included in this volume. The goal is to identify those areas in which there is something approaching consensus in the profession and, where there is not, to set out the nature of the disagreement and the range of positions. To this end, seven major categories of questions are identified on which the literature focuses and around which this essay is organized:

1. What is interdisciplinary study?
2. Why engage in interdisciplinary study?
3. What should be the relation between the disciplines and interdisciplinary studies?
4. What is integration or synthesis?
5. What are the prerequisites for integration or synthesis?
6. How is integration or synthesis achieved?
7. What assumptions underlie interdisciplinary study?

This chapter aims at promoting greater clarity and precision of thought about interdisciplinary studies by both its adherents and its detractors. A clearer sense of the key concepts and primary distinctions should raise the general level of discourse about interdisciplinarity. Finally, I hope to provide direction to scholars and practitioners working on interdisciplinary projects. Indeed, at the end of each section is a list of questions requiring further research that should reduce the number of people reinventing wheels and increase the number designing better ones. More interdisciplinary scholars will now be able to build directly and explicitly on the work of those who have gone before them. Out of this professionalization of the field should emerge new professional identities as more people engaged in interdisciplinary studies come to think of themselves as interdisciplinarians. Thus, as intimated earlier, this chapter is as much about developing a field as surveying it.

Note: Numbers in parentheses after quotations refer to page numbers in this text.

What Is Interdisciplinary Study?

An emerging consensus on the definition of interdisciplinary study is identified by Julie Thompson Klein and William Newell in "Advancing Interdisciplinary

Studies," in Jerry Gaff and James Ratcliff (eds.), *Handbook of the Undergraduate Curriculum* (San Francisco: Jossey-Bass, 1997), and reprinted in this volume. They write:

> [I]nterdisciplinary studies may be defined as a process of answering a question, solving a problem, or addressing a topic too broad or complex to be dealt with adequately by a single discipline or profession. . . . IDS draws on disciplinary perspectives and integrates their insights through construction of a more comprehensive perspective. (See page 3.)

This mainstream definition reflects a degree of agreement about some essential features of interdisciplinarity that seemed unattainable 15 years ago, before interdisciplinary studies began to be widely accepted in higher education. While discussions of definitions can become quite tedious, it will soon become apparent that such consensus is important, because seemingly small differences in definition can lead to large differences in practice and resulting outcomes.

With some notable exceptions, this emerging consensus extends as well to the now-standard distinctions among multidisciplinarity, interdisciplinarity, and transdisciplinarity that the Organization for Economic Cooperation and Development (OECD) first set out in their seminal volume, *Interdisciplinarity: Problems of Teaching and Research in Universities* (1972).[1] Multidisciplinarity is distinguished from interdisciplinarity primarily by the absence of any deliberate attempt at integration; e.g., a course in which faculty from different disciplines take turns lecturing on the same topic. (See the "Guide to Interdisciplinary Syllabus Preparation" on p. 97 for a review of the pragmatic as well as theoretical differences.) Transdisciplinarity, at the other extreme, differs from interdisciplinarity in that it seeks an integration so comprehensive and fundamental that the contributing disciplines are subsumed under or replaced by a kind of superdiscipline, such as general systems theory, Marxism, or structural functionalism.

The exceptions to the above terminological consensus tend to assign to interdisciplinarity some of the characteristics of transdisciplinarity. Joseph Kockelmans, editor of a parallel to the OECD volume in this country, *Interdisciplinarity and Higher Education*, argued in 1979 that what we might call hyphenated disciplines (e.g., psycholinguistics, biophysics) are the natural product of interdisciplinary integration. [His term "cross-disciplinary" is closer to what is called interdisciplinary today, though he limits its application to large research projects. William Bechtel, writing in 1986, also used cross-disciplinarity for interdisciplinarity.] Steve Fuller and Bryan Turner present conceptions of interdisciplinarity even closer to transdisciplinarity, though they see themselves more in the vein of offering critique. Fuller takes a radically critical stance toward disciplinarity:

> I want to move away from the common idea that interdisciplinary pursuits draw their strength from building on the methods and

findings of established fields. Instead, my goal is to present models of interdisciplinary research that call into question the differences between the disciplines involved, and thereby serve as forums for the renegotiation of disciplinary boundaries. (123)

Similarly, Turner takes the position that "interdisciplinarity aims in principle at academic fusion . . . it seeks a reorganization and integration of disciplines." For a contentious critique of this radical perspective, which he incorrectly attributes to all interdisciplinarians, see Stanley Fish's attack on interdisciplinarity.

In recent years, scholars have proposed several *additional categories* of interdisciplinary work, though none have had time to achieve much currency. Most promising is the distinction by Dirk van Dusseldorp and Seerp Wigboldus between broad and narrow interdisciplinarity. Broad interdisciplinarity involves interactions among many disciplines with different paradigms and methods, where the researchers are from different institutions, even different cultures. Narrow interdisciplinarity involves interactions among a small number of disciplines with the same paradigms and methods, where the researchers are from the same culture, even the same institution. In his "Wide and Narrow Interdisciplinarity," *Journal of General Education* 45:2 (1996), James Kelly makes a simpler distinction based solely on what he calls the "epistemological distance" between disciplines.[2] Ursula Hübenthal prefers to talk about "degrees of interdisciplinary cooperation." Each of these authors is proposing language to get at the frequent but casual observation of interdisciplinary practitioners that it is much more difficult to pull together an interdisciplinary course or research project that crosses the humanities, social sciences, and natural sciences than an effort limited to any one of these areas.

Whichever precise definition is eventually selected, the terms broad and narrow should be taken as purely descriptive. Broad interdisciplinarity is not necessarily better than narrow interdisciplinarity. While a broadly interdisciplinary course may be more comprehensive than one that is narrowly interdisciplinary, each must be judged according to its appropriateness for the particular context. A course designed to meet a physical science general education requirement, for instance, ought to be narrowly interdisciplinary. A course that tries to cover too many disciplinary perspectives or ones too far beyond the competence of the faculty would be overly ambitious as well as broadly interdisciplinary.

A separate distinction comes out of Marilyn Stember's recognition that "interdisciplinarity" is sometimes used loosely to refer to any nondisciplinary effort as well as in the more rigorous sense. However, her suggested use of the same terms—broad and narrow—leads to confusion with the distinction above. Kockelmans employs the terms broad and narrow in the same way as Stember. Instead, it is helpful to think of interdisciplinary process as situated somewhere along a spectrum between pure disciplinarity and full interdisciplinarity. That process (in the words of Klein and Newell) "draws on disciplinary perspectives and integrates their insights through construction of a more comprehensive perspective." Because any steps away from pure disciplinarity are to be encouraged on the grounds that they move the scholar that much closer to full interdisciplinarity, the inclusive thinking of many interdisciplinarians makes them loathe to use language that excludes from interdisciplinarity any intermediate positions on the spectrum.

I suggest using instead the terms full and partial interdisciplinarity, because those intermediate positions typically include at least some element of full interdisciplinarity. Thus a multidisciplinary project would be partially interdisciplinary in that it includes one element of interdisciplinarity, namely the perspectives of more than one discipline, while it excludes another element of interdisciplinarity, namely the integration of these perspectives. Even more partial would be various forms of disciplinary borrowing, which draw insights from other disciplines while viewing those insights through the lens or perspective of the borrowing discipline.

What constitutes full interdisciplinarity depends on the context of the activity. Klein and Newell assert that "diverse motivations and purposes" have led to the current ascendancy of interdisciplinary education. They cite quite disparate concerns—general and liberal education; professional training; social, economic, and technological problem solving; social, political, and epistemological critique; faculty development; financial exigency (downsizing); and the production of new knowledge—that have come together to form what we label interdisciplinarity. Fifteen years ago, Kockelmans was careful to distinguish between interdisciplinary education and interdisciplinary research, but most authors since then have chosen to discuss interdisciplinarity generically. Now that more than half a dozen distinct motivations and purposes can be differentiated within the interdisciplinary rubric, perhaps it is time to assess the ways in which they lead to different as well as similar understandings of interdisciplinarity.

Giles Gunn states that interdisciplinary study goes "all the way back in the West to classical antiquity, when Greek historians and dramatists drew on medical and philosophical knowledge, respectively, for clues to the reconception of their own material." His claim raises the question of whether we need to make an additional distinction between interdisciplinarity and pre-disciplinarity. In what sense is it meaningful to talk about interdisciplinarity prior to the advent of disciplines? Clearly, scholars have long borrowed ideas and information from other fields, but the interdisciplinary practice of adopting the perspective of another field is less common and much more recent. Indeed, the interdisciplinary motivation to seek a more comprehensive perspective would have had little urgency prior to the development of the distinctive worldviews of reductionist disciplines. Thus interdisciplinarity is appropriately seen as a response to the development of academic disciplines and the intensification of specialization that dates back to the late nineteenth century.

It is also instructive to examine what leading scholars insist interdisciplinary study is not. Kockelmans asserts that the interdisciplinarian is not a generalist; otherwise, the alternative to disciplinarians who know everything about nothing would be interdisciplinarians who know nothing about everything. Indeed, Newell (1983) believes specialization should be seen as essential, not antithetical, to interdisciplinarity. On the other hand, interdisciplinarians need not have expertise in each discipline that they use. Richard Lebow points out that in peace studies "scholars need [not] be fully conversant with two or more disciplines before attempting interdisciplinary research. Selective knowledge may be quite sufficient," though they should be "cross-trained" in the relevant portions of the disciplines and "au courant with their literature." Finally, Bechtel argues that in the sciences, interdisciplinarity is not limited to the interstices between disciplines because "scientists and their disciplines tend to be politically opportunistic, looking for problem areas in which they can expand. As a result, most problems ripe for solution are likely to be attacked by disciplines capable of solving them." While these arguments may be persuasive, the issues they address have not yet been fully explored.

Where do interdisciplinary questions come from? In the consensus definition, the interdisciplinary process is a response to a question (which may grow out of a problem or topic). How is the question generated? Because most interdisciplinary studies address real-world problems that do not respect disciplinary bounds, we might infer that interdisciplinary questions emanate from society, not from the academy, and certainly not from the disciplines. Yet interdisciplinary study is usually initiated by academicians, most of whom have predominantly disciplinary training. Moreover, Armstrong, Hershberg, Kockelmans, Stember, and van Dusseldorp and Wigboldus all conceive of interdisciplinary study as a team activity, in which most (or all) members of the team are included because of their disciplinary expertise. For this reason, van Dusseldorp and Wigboldus believe research questions should be formulated by policymakers rather than disciplinary researchers. Yet scholarship not directed by major funding agencies is likely to be defined by the researchers themselves. The problem is that disciplinarians tend to ask questions they can answer, not the more comprehensive questions that call for interdisciplinary treatment. Thus the challenge is to develop procedures to ensure that interdisciplinary questions emerge from the complexity of the problem or issue studied, not from narrower disciplinary interests.

In light of the problematic nature of how questions are initiated, we must start paying more attention as well to how questions change during interdisciplinary study. Van Dusseldorp and Wigboldus observe that questions change during a team research project. Newell and William Green give the example of an interdisciplinary course on U.S. energy policy in which "[a]s more disciplines were brought to bear and new sets of questions were answered, the nature of the energy problem shifted." They also point out that one result of an interdisciplinary course may be that the nature of the initial question is re-evaluated. In their model of the interdisciplinary process, Barbara Hursh, Paul Haas, and Michael Moore come close to addressing this issue: they see a feedback loop from evaluating the conclusion back to operationalizing the problem and identifying salient disciplinary concepts and perspectives. These authors however accept the initial question or statement of the problem as given. In *Interdisciplinarity: History, Theory, and Practice* (Detroit, Michigan: Wayne State University Press, 1990), Klein presents a model of interdisciplinarity drawn from work on bioethics by Maurice de Wachter that incorporates feedback to the initial question.[3] Still, interdisciplinarians need to examine more thoroughly how the initiating question changes during the interdisciplinary process and what the implications are of that change.

Klein places interdisciplinary study within a larger process of knowledge generation that evolves from specialization to fragmentation to hybridization, the last of which she sees as including interdisciplinary study. In fact, her most recent book, *Crossing Boundaries: Knowledge, Disciplinarities, and Interdisciplinarities* (Charlottesville: University Press of Virginia, 1996), is devoted to exploring the implications of disciplinary "boundary-work" for interdisciplinarity by embedding both in this larger process.[4] Drawing on Mattei Dogan and Robert Pahre, *Creative Marginality* (Boulder, Colorado: Westview Press, 1990), Klein identifies the distinctive conceptual processes of boundary-work—trading, pidgin, and Creole zones; hybrid roles and communities; boundary-blurring, contextualizing, and genre mixing; and cross-fertilization—and explores their implications for interdisciplinarians.[5]

Various authors have pointed out that the nature of the disciplines themselves is ambiguous or evolving, raising (usually implicit) questions about the nature of interdisciplinarity, defined as it is in terms of disciplines. Newell and Green claimed in 1982 that "[m]uch of the confusion over the definition of interdisciplinary studies can be traced to the ill-defined nature of the disciplines themselves"; they then attempted to revisit their own definition with that problem in mind. Two years earlier, Clifford Geertz published his classic essay on "Blurred Genres," in which he argued that the effect of large-scale borrowing by disciplinary scholars has led to the blurring of disciplinary boundaries and the mixing of genres. He concluded that the consequence for disciplinarity was "not the redrawing of the cultural map—the moving of a few disputed borders . . . but an alteration of the principles of mapping. Something is happening to the way we think about the way we think." Geertz was talking about the disciplinary terrain that interdisciplinarians must negotiate rather than about interdisciplinarity itself; indeed, he asserted that "[i]t is not interdisciplinary brotherhood that is needed, nor even less highbrow eclecticism." In spite of frequent references to Geertz's article and the growing popularity of his theme, interdisciplinarians have yet to come to grips with the full implications of the resultant blurring of the distinctions between disciplinarity and interdisciplinarity.

Several authors place interdisciplinarity within the context of power relations. Fuller, characterized above as radical, asserts that "[i]nterdisciplinarity can be understood as either a fact or an ideology" and presents himself as an "ideologue of interdisciplinarity." His rhetoric is replete with terms such as "pressure points," "natural enemy," and "throw down the gauntlet." He asks us to think of interdisciplinarity not as a purely disinterested intellectual task but as a commitment to a value-laden political agenda. Feminist scholars also focus on power relations and make similar demands for social and political engagement (though they would be unlikely to title a chapter, as Fuller does, "The Position: Interdisciplinarity as Interpenetration"). While the politicization of interdisciplinary (and disciplinary) studies has been explored by radical scholars, their perspective has not yet been applied to the other issues raised in this chapter.

Power relations can enter into not only the research agenda of interdisciplinarians but the very process of carrying out interdisciplinary studies. While Armstrong presents them as opportunities, the differences between faculty that he points out—between scientists with and without high-powered mathematical skills, or between those in more- and less-prestigious departments—can affect their interactions on an interdisciplinary team. Combined with personal differences such as who yells loudest or is the best debater, power differences can color logic and data and thus influence which arguments prevail on an interdisciplinary team. The "open and intense discussions needed to arrive at compromises" among team members and the importance of "willingness to respect the views of members" to which van Dusseldorp and Wigboldus refer become even more problematic when power differentials are factored in. Instead of ignoring such interpersonal dynamics within the interdisciplinary process, we need to examine them as potential inherent limitations on interdisciplinarity. In general, interdisciplinarity must be seen as a fully human activity, not merely an abstract intellectual exercise.

To the extent that interdisciplinary study is about providing context, the ultimate limitation to interdisciplinarity may have been identified by Mieke Bal when she observed that "the very concept of context is as problematic as that of text." Indeed, she points out that "[c]ontext . . . is a text and thus presents the same difficulties of interpretation as any other text." Thus, the critical gaze of postmodernism must be turned on interdisciplinarity. Instead of accepting context at face value, interdisciplinarians must ask who decided which contexts to include and probe what values, biases, and objectives lay behind the decision. The challenge, for interdisciplinarian and postmodernist alike, is to avoid being trapped in an infinite regress of theoretical caution, a kind of modern-day Zeno's Paradox: the questions about context must themselves be contextualized and questioned, and so on. The danger is that we might never get on with whatever interdisciplinary task is at hand.

At a more pragmatic level, interdisciplinarians face the problem of deciding how much context is enough. Van Dusseldorp and Wigboldus point to major constraints such as limited training in other disciplines and the departmental organization of universities as well as limited time and resources. If we were to accept uncritically the facile claim that "everything is connected to everything else," however, no amount of context would suffice. Even when we recognize that some phenomena are more closely linked than others so that contextualizing can legitimately be finite, the question of how much context is required or even desirable remains.

In summary, our thinking about the nature of interdisciplinary study needs to be more nuanced. While the emerging consensus is gratifying after the wild variations in definitions of decades past, our understanding of interdisciplinarity needs to be more complex and clarifying and should confront a number of important issues:

- What are the relative advantages and disadvantages of the mainstream and radical perspectives? How can mainstream conceptions benefit from radical critiques?
- What is the essential difference between broad and narrow interdisciplinarity?
- What do partial and full interdisciplinarity have in common that justifies placing them on a single spectrum?
- What are the essential characteristics of disciplines that distinguish pre-disciplinary from interdisciplinary study? Can interdisciplinarity accommodate non-disciplinary perspectives (for example, those grounded in religious belief or political ideology)?
- What is the difference between a generalist and an interdisciplinarian?
- How much and what kinds of expertise in disciplines are required for interdisciplinary study?
- What are the defining characteristics of an interdisciplinary problem or question?
- How do interdisciplinary problems or questions arise?
- What are the potential effects of the interdisciplinary process on the initiating question or problem?
- How does the nature of interdisciplinary study vary with the motivation for it?
- What are the implications for interdisciplinarity in the blurring of disciplines?
- How do power differentials affect the interdisciplinary process? How can those effects be mitigated?
- How can postmodern sensitivities about the bias of contextualization best be incorporated into the interdisciplinary process?
- What are the appropriate criteria for deciding how much context is enough?

Why Engage in Interdisciplinary Study?

Because the motivations for interdisciplinary study are largely pragmatic, the appropriate test for alternative conceptions of interdisciplinarity is what outcomes they produce when they are put into practice. More generally, the relative merits of disciplines and interdisciplinarity should be judged by what kinds of students are graduated, what kinds of problems get solved, and what kinds of new insights are generated. This section sets out what is known about the consequences of interdisciplinary study.

Claims by practitioners and scholars concerning the outcomes of interdisciplinary study are numerous and diverse. They are organized here by proximity to the actual process of study, starting with the individual student or researcher/scholar and moving outward to the institution, the entire academy, and finally society as a whole. The evidence in support of these claims, however, is often anecdotal or inferential rather than quantitative or experimental; it will be evaluated briefly at the end of this section.

It is claimed that students taking interdisciplinary courses improve their intellectual insight, taken broadly to mean cognitive, affective, and developmental growth. The lengthy list of cognitive skills attributed to interdisciplinary education includes critical thinking, problem solving, synthesis or integration, contextual understanding, coping with complexity, making connections, reflexive thinking, unconventional or original or creative thinking, facility with analogy and metaphor, sensitivity to bias and ethical issues, awareness of embedded values, receptivity to new ideas, broadened horizons, tolerance of ambiguity (embracing irony or tolerating paradox), recognizing commonalties and differences, ability to identify and willingness to challenge assumptions, ability to see different sides of an issue, ability to shift perspective, evaluation of expert testimony, openness of mind, and a wide range of more traditional academic skills. (See Cornwell and Stoddard, Cluck, and Hursh, Haas, and Moore, as well as Klein and Newell, Newell (1983), Newell (1990), and Newell and Green.)

Affective outcomes attributed to interdisciplinary education include self-confidence and empowerment, empathy and compassion, respect for difference, ability to work on a team, and investment in a political and ethical agenda, according to Cornwell and Stoddard, Klein and Newell, and Newell (1990). Developmental growth such as movement through stages of moral and cognitive development to "commitment with relativism" are identified by Cornwell and Stoddard as well as Hursh, Haas and Moore. The latter also claim that students come away from interdisciplinary courses with a better understanding of the academy and its disciplines.

The longer-term career impacts of interdisciplinary education on students include higher academic achievement, higher rates of admission to graduate and professional schools, and more successful employment. Higher academic achievement means everything from enhanced general knowledge to higher grade-point averages, higher degree aspirations, revising papers more frequently, reading more books, engaging more often in intellectual discussions, and participating in research with faculty, according to Klein and Newell and Newell (1992). Klein and Newell also report more success in admission to graduate and professional schools. Newell (1983) also finds employer satisfaction with the results of interdisciplinary education, especially graduates' ability "to think conceptually, to identify and solve problems, to understand other value systems, to evaluate alternatives and decide on a course of action, and to change one's opinion in the light of facts."

The most engaging rationale, however, comes from Martin Trow, who speaks of the joy of participating in interdisciplinary courses. He points to the "sheer pleasure in the intellectual play that they afford to students and teachers alike, the pleasures of roaming across disciplinary boundaries, and of finding connections and links, illuminations and insights in the ideas and discoveries of disparate disciplines." This theme is echoed by several authors in Gaff and Ratcliff (1997), *Handbook of the Undergraduate Curriculum*.[6]

Because individual teachers or researcher/scholars find themselves to some extent in the role of co-learners in interdisciplinary courses and research projects, many of the above advantages accrue to them as well. In addition, participation in interdisciplinary studies offers freedom: Klein and Newell talk about "enabling faculty to escape from departmental confines"; Kockelmans speaks of "follow[ing] a research project wherever it may lead"; and Newell and Green refer to "the opportunity to follow an issue without regard to artificial disciplinary barriers." Bechtel observes that "[t]he desire for originality motivates scientists to maintain contacts with other disciplines and scientific work in areas different from their own in order to enhance their ability to develop new ideas in their own areas." In the humanities and fine arts, Bal emphasizes coping with complexity, which yields a study "full of ambivalence [that is] both highly disturbing and highly gratifying." Most important, perhaps, interdisciplinarity offers perspective: Cluck calls it seeing "forests which [otherwise] become obscured by numerous species of trees"; for Hursh, Haas, and Moore, it is a "metaperspective"; while Kockelmans refers to "a broader framework in which social phenomena can be more adequately described and explained."

This desire for perspective plays out a little differently in the various areas of knowledge. Kockelmans says that interdisciplinary social science "attempts to examine man and society from a perspective that transcends disciplinary interests and institutional loyalties . . . and remains much closer to the social phenomena as they are experienced by living human beings in actual societies." Cluck asserts that "interdisciplinary inquiry into the humanities is worthwhile only to the extent that it proffers a new way of seeing our existence and of understanding more fully what it means to be human." Regarding the natural sciences, Bechtel focuses on "inter-field theories."

The advantages of interdisciplinary activity to individual academic institutions are evidenced in the areas of curriculum, faculty development, administrative flexibility, and academic community. Klein and Newell point to greater "curricular coherence." Likewise, Stember emphasizes "greater coherence and integration in undergraduate education." Newell (1990) discusses student motivation, claiming that "[t]he topical or issue-oriented approach of most interdisciplinary courses is inherently more interesting." For Kockelmans, interdisciplinary courses "avoid exposing students to a one-dimensional contact with Western civilization."

Armstrong makes a pragmatic case for interdisciplinary education as a source of faculty development in that it offers "close peer support" and "a context in which all participants are simultaneously expected to be teachers and learners," though he cautions that it works best with faculty who are "broadly educated individuals with a high degree of ego strength, a tolerance for ambiguity, above-average initiative and assertiveness, and a fairly well-developed understanding of what is involved in interdisciplinary work." Newell (1990) points out that interdisciplinary programs "can provide an opportunity for administrators faced with tenured faculty in underutilized departments to reallocate faculty resources to where there is more student demand." Stember claims that interdisciplinary education at its best produces "a community of learning among faculty and students."

There is much less agreement about the advantages of interdisciplinarity for the academy as a whole, reflecting fundamental differences over its goals as well as clashing conceptions of interdisciplinarity. The extent of agreement is that interdisciplinary studies can result in new disciplines, though authors differ about whether that is just one option (Hübenthal), a necessary outcome that nonetheless is compatible with the disciplines (Kockelmans), or a deliberate strategy for "academic fusion"—whether that be what Turner calls in medicine "a reorganization and integration of disciplines," or the "critiquing and reconstructing [of] the knowledge system" that Fuller seeks for studies in science, technology, and society.

The disagreement is between academic liberals, who seek a place for interdisciplinarity alongside the disciplines, and academic radicals, who seek the overthrow of disciplines. Gunn sees this as a division between "those who see the study of cultural representation as a political struggle over the sources and symptomatics of power and those who view that study, instead, as a hermeneutic struggle over the hierarchies and heuristics of value." He wants to redraw not the map of disciplines but the cartography of critical inquiry, believing that interdisciplinarity results in "dialogue, contestation, and diversity of opinion" that includes the voices of women and minorities historically excluded by the disciplines. Thus questions of outcomes link back to questions of definition.

Almost every author views interdisciplinarity at the level of society as a whole as contributing to the solution of real-world problems. The exceptions are postmodern interdisciplinarians, whose focus is a meta-level removed. Jeffrey Peck sees interdisciplinary German studies as "the in-between space where the clash of multiple subjectivities can foreground difference" with the result that it "always totters at the brink of fragmenting into a collection of pieces." Hardly a prescription for problem solving. Turner goes even further, asserting that "a radical interdisciplinary approach [to medicine] is related to the notion of holistic medicine, and both regard the idea of a medical problem as itself problematic." Cornwell and Stoddard define the contribution to society of an interdisciplinary approach to multiculturalism, what they term interculturalism, as the development of mutual tolerance and respect combined with ethical and political commitment. They argue against uncritical acceptance of difference, seeking instead a kind of societal-level relativism with commitment.

These, then, are the claims for interdisciplinarity. If they are all correct, then interdisciplinary study is indeed an educational panacea. But the evidence supporting these claims is often anecdotal and inferential. Except for studies by Aston and by Pascarella and Terenzini, reported in Klein and Newell, a few surveys of employers reported in Newell (1983), data from one interdisciplinary program reported in Newell (1992), and some longitudinal studies of learning communities reported in Tinto, Love, and Russo's *Building Learning Communities for New College Students* (University Park, Pennsylvania: The Pennsylvania State University NTLA, 1994), there is little by way of hard evidence.[7] Clearly, if we as interdisciplinarians are to build a convincing case for skeptics, we need to get down to the business of operationalizing and testing these claims. The picture for interdisciplinary research is not much better. Van Dusseldorp and Wigboldus observe that with respect to social science contributions to agricultural research, "the outcome . . . is still not very impressive," citing "ignorance of what interdisciplinary research should comprise" as well as lack of interest on the part of outstanding scientists.

We need to ground our claims for interdisciplinarity in the best available research in cognitive and developmental psychology and in educational research focusing on learning and on cognitive and moral development. Hursh, Haas, and Moore build their model explicitly on the work of John Dewey, Jean Piaget, and William Perry, and while there are scattered references to these scholars elsewhere in the literature on interdisciplinary studies, there is scant use of the research done in the last quarter century. Our assessment of interdisciplinary outcomes needs to be informed by sophisticated insight into how people learn and grow intellectually as well as by the nature and practice of interdisciplinary study.

We also need to engage in some hard thinking about which outcomes can be expected from which kinds of interdisciplinarity. Building on issues summarized at the end of the previous section, how should we expect outcomes to differ between

- broad and narrow interdisciplinarity?
- full and partial interdisciplinarity?
- mainstream and radical interdisciplinarity?
- individual and team interdisciplinarity?
- interdisciplinary teams that are democratic and those with power differentials?
- interdisciplinarity motivated by liberal education and that motivated by professional training, problem solving, radical critique, faculty development, downsizing, or knowledge production?
- interdisciplinary study based on traditional disciplines and that based on interdisciplinary fields or on disciplines with blurred boundaries?

In short, as we hone our thinking about the nature of interdisciplinarity, we need to assess the implications of our clearer and more complex understanding for the outcomes we claim on behalf of interdisciplinary studies. Then we need to test those claims.

What Should Be the Relation Between the Disciplines and Interdisciplinary Studies?

Because interdisciplinarity is defined in terms of disciplines, and the emerging consensus according to Klein and Newell is that interdisciplinary study "draws on the disciplines," understanding the role of disciplines in interdisciplinary studies should be central to a full understanding of interdisciplinarity. In fact, their precise role ought to be pivotal in distinguishing among alternative conceptions of interdisciplinarity. And because the conception of interdisciplinarity underlying a course or research project may have important consequences for its educational or knowledge outcomes, the role of disciplines has major implications for why we should engage in interdisciplinary studies.

There is an emerging agreement among mainstream interdisciplinarians that interdisciplinary study should build explicitly and directly upon the work of the disciplines. Interdisciplinary courses are paying increasing attention to the disciplines themselves as well as to the insights drawn from them, while interdisciplinary researchers have long confronted the disciplinary bases underlying the conflicting contributions of team members. Interdisciplinarians are becoming interested not only in what the disciplines have to say but why they say it. Even radical scholars who advocate using interdisciplinary study to alter or replace the disciplines still end up paying close attention to the assumptions and practices of the disciplines.

Beneath this agreement, however, lie unresolved questions and significant differences in how interdisciplinarians think about disciplines (their characteristics, internal structure, relationships to other disciplines, and evolving nature), in the precise nature of the relationship they advocate between the disciplines and interdisciplinarity (its nature and consequences and its impact on the disciplines themselves), and in precisely what they use from the disciplines and how they use it (in courses, programs, and research).

Those who take exception to this agreement, as Klein (1996) points out, include not only radical interdisciplinarians but what might be called antidisciplinarians, scholars who have been so marginalized by society and the academy that they reject the disciplines altogether. Klein observes, for instance, that Russell Thornton has argued that "Native American studies should be allowed to define and build its own intellectual traditions" and that Ronald Walters insists that "African American studies is 'disciplined' by the centrality of racism in American life."

Not surprisingly, interdisciplinarians of every stripe tend to characterize the disciplines in rather critical terms. Perhaps the most neutral language comes from Barbara Carlisle, who reminds us that disciplines come from "the base term *disciple*—a follower of a way." Newell and Green place "way" in an institutional context, as "a socio-political organization which concentrates on a historically linked set of problems." They go on to distinguish among disciplines "by the questions they ask about the world, by their perspective or worldview, by the set of assumptions they employ, and by the methods which they use to build up a body of knowledge (facts, concepts, theories) around a certain subject matter." Others point to the incompleteness of disciplinary insight into that set of problems: Hübenthal speaks of disciplines as "purveyors of partial explanations"; Lebow points to their "naive or superficial treatment of questions within the domain of other disciplines"; and Newell (1983) refers to a discipline as a "challenging intellectual game at best, and a sterile and meaningless exercise at worst, when it is taken out of the context of human experience, which is always too broad and complex to be captured fully by any one discipline."

But the criticism is usually tempered with respect. Responding to the oft-asserted "arbitrariness" of the disciplines, Tom Benson observes that, "although the arbitrary hands of chance and politics have played important roles in the definition of disciplines, their latter-day contours and boundaries turn out, on the whole, to make surprisingly good sense." Hursh, Haas, and Moore point out that disciplines provide "indispensable tools with which to assess relationships among . . . variables," thus "deciphering . . . causal links," while Cornwell and Stoddard value their "lenses which bring into focus different dimensions of culture." Generally speaking, disciplines combine those tools and lenses to provide the depth of insight or "requisite knowledge and information" for what Klein and Newell call the "working balance among breadth, depth, and synthesis" that characterizes interdisciplinarity.

Within her study of disciplinary boundaries, Klein (1993) examines the internal structure of disciplines. Following Donald Campbell, she sees "unidisciplinarity as a myth" because "most modern disciplines embrace a wide range of subspecialties with different features." Thus disciplines are best understood as "congeries of specialties." Still, a discipline has at least some internal structure. It features a "center or core of propositions, procedures, and conclusions, or at least a shared historical object of theory and practice" and an "innovative frontier" where researchers are incessantly borrowing from adjacent disciplines, causing a "blurring of disciplinary boundaries." These arguments, and their implications for interdisciplinarity, are developed at length in Klein's *Crossing Boundaries*.

Klein's focus on borrowing between disciplines contrasts with how Hursh, Haas, and Moore look at relationships between disciplines. They emphasize the "specialized nomenclature" of disciplinary specialists that "threatens to erect a new Tower of Babel," which is dysfunctional for communicating with others in the same discipline, much less for the "comprehension of interrelationships among disciplines." Fuller concurs that, "left to their own devices, academic disciplines follow trajectories that isolate them increasingly from one another and from the most interesting intellectual and social issues of our time." Cornwell and Stoddard see disciplines as "reified political entities with aggressive territorial claims." At the other extreme, Stember argues that "[t]he contemporary view is that the disciplines exist in an open-minded confederation." (See also the discussion of the nature of the disciplines in the section on What Is Interdisciplinary Studies?, on page 530.) One wonders if these authors are even looking at the same universe of disciplines. Presumably a closer examination of how disciplines in fact interrelate would clarify the intellectual milieu to which interdisciplinary study must relate, perhaps narrowing differences of opinion about the role of interdisciplinary study vis à vis the disciplines.

Klein and Newell attempt to strike a balance regarding the appropriate relationship between disciplinarity and interdisciplinarity: "interdisciplinary study is not a simple supplement but is complementary to and even corrective of the disciplines." At one end of the spectrum, Newell (1983), Hübenthal, and Lebow all use the term "complementary," and Kockelmans and Stember speak of "balance." Van Dusseldorp and Wigboldus call it a "common misconception" that "all disciplines are merged" in interdisciplinary research; in fact, they insist that "[t]he integration of the disciplines themselves should not take place." Carlisle points out that interdisciplinary thinking "helps us understand how a discipline works, simply by forcing us to see one discipline in the light of another." Trow even suggests that "the blurring of distinctions between what is done in interdisciplinary programs and in departments may be the kind of imitation that is the sincerest form of flattery."

At the other end, Fuller wants interdisciplinary study to "call into question the differences between the disciplines involved," and Turner argues that "it is necessary for interdisciplinarity to adopt an epistemologically creative and critical stance towards existing disciplinarity," one that is "skeptical with respect to professional and other claims to truth." Gunn also emphasizes that interdisciplinary inquiry "reconfigures the constituent disciplines that compose it." In her review of women's studies programs, Klein (1996) reports that practitioners came to feel that "[o]nly radical reconstruction of knowledge and consciousness would effect genuine change, moving the field beyond 'mainstreaming' knowledge about women . . . to a genuine 'transformation' capable of 'breaking the disciplines.'" (See also the section on Why Engage in Interdisciplinary Study?, on page 537.)

Considering the general agreement that interdisciplinarity builds on disciplines, there is quite a diversity of opinion over what exactly disciplines contribute to interdisciplinary study. Newell and Green say that disciplines provide insights. Newell (1992) focuses on perspectives:

> While interdisciplinary courses indeed make use of concepts, theories, methods, and factual knowledge from various disciplines, the interdisciplinary understanding they develop is grounded primarily in the perspectives from which those concepts, theories, methods, and facts emerge. (216)

Van Dusseldorp and Wigboldus refer primarily to the use made of data and variables from each discipline. Likewise, Hershberg points to the "concerns and variables of different disciplines [that] were integrated." Hübenthal speaks of disciplines yielding partial explanations, while Bechtel points out that disciplines contribute "past wisdom" and "the kind of peer review process that . . . has been instrumental in guiding research and ensuring that mistaken ideas are rejected."

In spite of the lack of agreement on what the disciplines contribute to the interdisciplinary enterprise, we can piece together a remarkably coherent picture of how those contributions should be utilized. The focus here is on criteria for how contributions should be drawn from the disciplines, to the extent that authors make it possible to distinguish between that process and how disciplinary contributions are synthesized or integrated. An appropriate starting point is Kockelmans's generalization that interdisciplinarians "try to solve a problem or set of problems . . . by employing insights and methods or techniques of some related disciplines."

The most important criterion is the accuracy with which those insights and methods or techniques are employed. In general, Benson insists that interdisciplinarians need "a firm hold on . . . the arguments, methods, and insights from the diverse contributing disciplines." Newell (1992) narrows Benson's requirement to the topic at hand, arguing that a firm hold on those disciplines does not require "expertise in their full range of concepts, theories, and methods." Instead, Newell emphasizes "an informed appreciation of the perspectives of other disciplines." In the context of general education, he argues that "[i]f students are to develop a feel for a discipline's perspective, they must learn to think like a practitioner of that discipline . . . [in] the way they approach the topic—the questions they ask, the concepts that come to mind, and the theories behind them." When the interdisciplinary activity centers on research rather than education, a narrow command of disciplinary tools and a broad feel for disciplinary perspectives must extend to practice as well as theory. The interdisciplinary researcher must understand how the relevant concepts, theories, and methods underlying each discipline's perspective are operationalized.

Pointing to another criterion, Peck suggests interdisciplinarians temper their "feel" for a discipline's perspective by maintaining some distance from it: the interdisciplinary "position 'outside the center' compels its practitioners to be conscious of their difference, foreignness, or otherness when they are practicing in a foreign [discipline] that does not really belong to them." Rather than trying to become a member of that discipline by reliving their experience, the interdisciplinarian should "preserve that distinction characterized as alienation or strangeness," from both the foreign discipline and the home discipline. That distance aids in keeping the discipline's contribution in context. As Turner points out, "Interdisciplinarity requires reflexivity, that is, an awareness of the historical and social settings of scientific concepts."

Distance from the discipline also helps in carrying out Klein and Newell's injunction to probe the implicit dimensions of each discipline: "The worldview and underlying assumptions of each discipline must be made explicit." Placing the discipline in context and making its implicit dimensions explicit assist in carrying out Lebow's request for modification and caution: "I not only had to modify or reformulate the approaches I borrowed but also had to apply them with an unusual degree of caution."

Even so, Hursh, Haas, and Moore point out that the interdisciplinary question must be modified before each discipline can make its contribution. For example, a question on income distribution might be broadened to a consideration of poverty as a whole. Newell and Green expand on this line of thought:

> To such a[n interdisciplinary] question, it is necessary to bring a variety of narrowly disciplinary insights, each of which grows out of a more specific question, appropriate to, and approachable by, a single discipline. It is the set of answers to these latter questions— questions which can be addressed by disciplines using disciplinary methods—which is then reconciled and integrated. (26)

To continue the example, political scientists might focus on the powerlessness of the poor, anthropologists on the culture of poverty, etc.

Having identified the separate disciplinary contributions, we must still address how they interact, since the totality of disciplinary contributions is greater than the sum of its parts. Some authors stress simultaneity: Cluck proposes "the superimposition of disciplines upon one central problem"; Trow suggests we "use perspectives of seemingly disparate disciplines simultaneously and interactively to define common problems, issues and ideas, and to pose solutions based on genuine dialogue." Similarly inclined authors may place more stress on the complementary interaction of disciplines: Gunn asks us to "explore analogies" from other disciplines, while Carlisle suggests "finding new angles" and seeking "metaphor transfer."

Cornwell and Stoddard, on the other hand, see disciplines as in conflict; they prescribe "contest and conversation of multiple disciplines." Fuller goes even further, proposing a procedure to promote that contest: "'the interpenetration of opposites,' also known as 'the unity and conflict of opposites,' is one of the three laws of dialectics identified by Friedrich Engels . . . a thing's identity inheres in parts whose tendencies to move in opposite directions have been temporarily suppressed." Fuller continues, "one discipline already takes for granted a position that contradicts, challenges, or in some way overlaps a position taken by another discipline." Broad interdisciplinarity, of course, would be more likely to produce conflict than would narrow interdisciplinarity.

Because most interdisciplinarians would probably agree that both complementarity and conflict characterize the range of possible interactions between disciplinary contributions, they should be able to make use of the full range of suggestions above. More qualitatively oriented interdisciplinarians might think of disciplinary contributions as producing a fruitful tension, while those who are more quantitatively oriented might think of variables from different disciplines as having powerful interaction effects.

While it is clearly possible to link together these separate insights into how interdisciplinarians should draw upon disciplinary contributions, no one has yet taken on the challenge of examining as a whole the process referred to in the consensus definition of interdisciplinary studies. Before that is possible, a number of questions need to be explored more fully:

- What does interdisciplinary study draw from the disciplines?
- How does interdisciplinary study draw from the disciplines?
- How can the need for accuracy in the use of the disciplines be reconciled with the need to maintain a distance from them?
- How do disciplinary contributions to interdisciplinary study interact?
- What are the salient characteristics of disciplines for interdisciplinarians?
- How do differences in those characteristics between disciplines affect their use by interdisciplinarians?
- How does variation within disciplines affect their use by interdisciplinarians?
- How do blurring of disciplinary boundaries and borrowing among disciplines affect interdisciplinary studies?
- What relationship between disciplinarity and interdisciplinarity best serves the interests of the academy or the larger society?

Even then, the process needs to be reexamined in the light of a more nuanced understanding of the nature of interdisciplinarity. How does the process differ between full or partial interdisciplinarity, broad or narrow interdisciplinarity, etc.? And which outcomes (for students, researchers/scholars, the academy, and society) can reasonably be expected to accrue in each case?

What Is Integration or Synthesis?

Central to understanding the nature of interdisciplinarity is understanding integration or synthesis, which is its distinguishing feature. In fact, it is helpful to think of the nature of interdisciplinarity, its outcomes, the role of disciplines, and the nature of synthesis or integration as a package of four interrelated issues, or perhaps a system of four simultaneous equations. The resolution of each issue is dependent on decisions about the other three, much as the solution to any one equation depends on the other three. The outcomes of interdisciplinary study, for example, are critically dependent on what is meant by interdisciplinarity and integration and on how the disciplines are used.

While all the conceptions of integration or synthesis in this volume are vague, it is still possible to discern three distinct visions: a conceptual framework, a comprehensive perspective, and a locus of activity. Within the first vision, Kockelmans speaks of an "overarching conceptual framework," such as "a broader framework in which social phenomena can be more adequately described and explained." Focusing on theory, Bechtel (using *cross-disciplinary* for *interdisciplinary*) also mentions "the need to develop integrating conceptual frameworks in which cross-disciplinary research can proceed." Focusing on practice, van Dusseldorp and Wigboldus refer to a "framework for integration of monodisciplinary research results" that produces "an integrated and dynamic analysis." Significantly, all of these authors are focused more on scientific research than on education.

Within the second vision, Klein and Newell suggest that the goal of interdisciplinary education is "a more comprehensive perspective"; i.e., "a larger, more holistic understanding of the question, problem, or issue at hand." Hursh, Haas, and Moore illustrate their concept of "metaperspective" with the example of a fruit basket that creates a new entity out of four distinct entities—an apple, an orange, a peach, and a pear—and thus unity or order. Newell (1990) believes we should seek a "new whole that is larger than its constituent parts, that cannot be reduced to the separate disciplinary insights from which it emerged." He rejects the notion of "integration as analogous to completing a jigsaw puzzle," at least for the social sciences and humanities, on the grounds that "human beings . . . are rife with internal contradictions." Drawing on the work of R.S. Crane, Cluck enumerates "[h]istorical periods, ideas, aesthetic themes, and structures" as evidence that "[s]ystematic interdisciplinary approaches can be formulated from a union of conventional disciplinary designs." For her, these are "linking areas between the disciplines [that] are amenable to interdisciplinary scrutiny, and because of this receptivity, they provide an interdisciplinary conduit to the humanities at large." Thus each becomes a fruit basket or metaperspective.

The third vision of interdisciplinary integration as locus of activity is described by Peck as a "mediating reflective space" where "the outsider becomes insider, but only insofar as she/he can remain 'in-between.'" He goes on to observe that "This 'in-between' the borders of . . . disciplinary territories or fields expands as those who were once excluded inhabit, rather than occupy, this once narrow territory, without the urge to remain in or reify any one fixed position." Fuller's "interpenetration" is a process that transforms the disciplines in ways that help them "to see each other as engaged in a common enterprise." Thus interdisciplinary research serves as "forums for the renegotiation of disciplinary boundaries." Fuller goes on to construct a typology of modes of interpenetration, depending on whether the rhetorical aim is to seek common ground or oppose spurious consensus, and whether the trade strategy of the discipline involves importing or exporting ideas from other disciplines. Again, authors holding this vision are more likely to have research than education in mind, and they come to this view from a postmodern, humanities-oriented angle.

All three visions seem to agree that integration should be limited in time and space. Kockelmans argues that "It is obviously mandatory to integrate the scientific knowledge that immediately pertains to the problems at hand; however, it is not assumed that the integration achieved in this way and the experience so gained can be used as a paradigm for the solution of other analogous problems, without major modification." Similarly, Hübenthal believes that "Hopes should not be pinned to an approach which attempts with a *single* blow to establish unity among scientists on a meta-theoretical level." She says, "I am equally doubtful that subject-overlapping research can be facilitated through the development of a meta-language." Instead Hübenthal insists that interdisciplinary study have "the goal of *explaining a specific phenomenon in its totality*" (emphasis in original).

These discussions of the nature of interdisciplinary integration raise two important questions. First, what is changed? Does integration change only the contributions of the disciplines or the disciplines themselves? All the authors in this volume concur that disciplinary contributions must change for interdisciplinary integration to proceed—the days of the jigsaw puzzle metaphor are gone. But the same debate that rages over the appropriate relationship between disciplinarity and interdisciplinarity plays itself out in the context of integration as well. Thus we find Kockelmans, Bechtel, van Dusseldorp and Wigboldus, Hübenthal, etc., arguing that while change may take place in the contributing disciplines, this is not required. Fuller, Gunn, and Turner in contrast see disciplinary transformation as an essential feature (if not the raison d'être) of interdisciplinary integration. This debate is more likely to become an issue in the context of broad rather than narrow interdisciplinary activity.

Second, must integration succeed to be interdisciplinary? In other words, must interdisciplinary integration lead to a solution, or merely an appreciation of the complexity of the problem? Most authors talk about solving complex problems as though they have clear-cut solutions. But what if they do not? Is a study that fails to arrive at a solution ipso facto not interdisciplinary? Partially but not fully interdisciplinary? Is a course that explores a complex issue but fails to achieve its full resolution thereby not interdisciplinary? Yet, if interdisciplinarity does not solve these complex problems, what claim does it have to superiority over a disciplinary approach? This conundrum does not appear all that difficult to resolve, but it does demand our explicit attention.

Finally, three authors in this volume propose conceptual schemes for integration that address degrees of integration—levels, ways, and kinds of integration, respectively. Armstrong, coming out of educational administration, identifies four levels of integration that might be reflected in courses. At the lowest level (closest to multidisciplinarity), integration is left entirely up to the students. At the second level, the institution provides the opportunity for students to work together toward integration, say, through a capstone seminar. At the third level, faculty join in the integration effort, at least to the extent that one faculty member has to decide which colleagues to bring in as guests, what they should lecture on, and how the course fits together. The fourth (fully interdisciplinary) level "is marked by the attempt fully to integrate material from various fields of knowledge into a new, single, intellectually coherent entity."

Bal, coming out of the humanities and fine arts, proposes a variety of ways of integrating that reflect how texts of one discipline can be related to those of another: "as 'source' or pre-text, as response, as thematic companion or counterpart, as theoretical subtext, surrounding context, or a critical rewriting." (*Text* should be taken broadly here to refer to the contributions of a discipline to a question or problem.)

Hershberg, coming out of public administration as well as the social sciences, focuses on different kinds of integration. He contrasts "analytical integration" with "operational integration." The former, he finds, is difficult to achieve because it is "too difficult, too abstract, and too boring." The latter, on the other hand, can be achieved in the context of specific project proposals when focused directly on goals, actors, and actions.

To resolve the nature of synthesis or integration, several issues must be settled:

- How can the visions of conceptual framework, comprehensive perspective, and locus of activity be interrelated?
- Are these visions grounded in different assumptions about the world? Different ideologies or theoretical frameworks?
- With which conception of the nature of interdisciplinarity does each of these visions fit best?
- Do these visions suggest different roles for the disciplines in interdisciplinarity?
- What are the differences in outcomes that seem likely from the various combinations or visions of integration or synthesis, conception of interdisciplinarity, and role of the disciplines?

In short, the available thought on synthesis or integration takes the form of alternative visions, each compelling in its own way. Until these visions are reconciled, their differences are negotiated, or one achieves ascendancy, so that something approaching agreement on the nature of synthesis or integration is achieved, fundamental questions about the nature of interdisciplinarity, the role of disciplines in interdisciplinary study, and the outcomes of interdisciplinarity must remain unanswered as well.

What Are the Prerequisites for Integration or Synthesis?

The pragmatic and epistemological value of interdisciplinary study is ultimately determined by the success of interdisciplinarians in carrying out synthesis or integration, because all save the antidisciplinarians identify that as its distinguishing feature. Theoretical clarity and agreement concerning the nature of interdisciplinarity, its outcomes, the role of disciplines, and the nature of synthesis or integration would be of no avail if interdisciplinarians were unable to accomplish integration. The respect of disciplinarians in the academy, the demand for interdisciplinarians to assist in solving complex societal problems, the success of radical critiques, and the long-term prospects for interdisciplinary education are all dependent on the proven success of integration.

Before examining what the literature has to say about the process of integration, this section looks at its prerequisites. First, in what kind of environment does integration thrive, i.e., what characteristics of individuals, courses and programs, and institutions are most conducive to integration? Second, what are the tools of integration—the initiating questions and conceptual frameworks required to carry it out? Third, what are the goals of integration? Finally, what team procedures promote integration?

The environment for integration is influenced most powerfully by the individual characteristics of interdisciplinarians. Take as a starting point their receptivity to other disciplines and to the perspectives of those disciplines. Armstrong calls it being "prepared to learn new concepts, new vocabulary, and new uses of the concepts he [sic] may once have seen as the province of his discipline alone," perhaps because interdisciplinarians are "feeling constrained from some intellectual pursuit by the confines of their discipline." Newell (1992) refers to receptivity as "willingness, and preferably an eagerness, to learn other perspectives." Stember speaks of having "a taste for adventure into the unknown and unfamiliar." Bal thinks of it as "openness and vulnerability."

But receptivity must lead to command of the relevant portions of those disciplines and of the worldview and assumptions of each discipline as a whole. Newell and Green speak of "an appreciation of the full complexity of the disciplines involved, especially an awareness of their often-unconscious assumptions," such that the interdisciplinarian is "well-versed in how each discipline looks at the world, what questions it has asked or would ask in a given situation." Armstrong says we must "meet various fields of knowledge on their own terms, especially by understanding and respecting the epistemologies and methodologies which underlie those fields." Gunn refers to "considerable mastery of the subtleties and peculiarities of each [discipline]." Hübenthal concludes that "the involved scientists must acquaint themselves with the mode of thinking of each of the different disciplines to a considerable degree." Cluck says simply, "researchers must have competence in each area."

Beyond receptivity and command, perspectives on personal characteristics vary, depending on whether the author thinks of integration as an individual or a team effort. With respect to the individual integrator, Klein and Newell emphasize basic cognitive skills such as "differentiating, comparing, and contrasting different disciplinary and professional perspectives." Newell and Green add "creativity." Gunn goes on to mention "sufficient imagination and tact, ingenuity and persuasion, to convince others of the utility of their linkage." The fact remains, however, that the literature has paid little attention to the kind of individual needed to carry out the actual integration of disciplinary insights.

In contrast, Stember and Armstrong speak at some length about the requisite characteristics of members of an interdisciplinary team (some of which apply to individual integrators as well). In the context of research, Stember says they should "have recognized competence in at least one discipline . . . be broad in their perspective . . . and have flexibility and versatility in semantics, theoretical orientation, and modes of inquiry," as well as the personal competencies normally valued in team members. Armstrong points out that in an educational setting, an interdisciplinary team member must be prepared to "step out from under that comfortable, protective blanket of theory and say 'I do not know all the answers or all that I need to know in this area'" so that "'together we may begin to discover things that each of us separately could never know.'"

It should be pointed out here that effective participation in an interdisciplinary team effort is not solely a matter of individual characteristics. To a considerable extent, it is learned behavior. People who participate repeatedly in interdisciplinary team activities can eventually become good at it. They develop intellectual skills such as both/and, metaphorical thinking, and dialectical thinking, which are discussed in the section on How is Integration or Synthesis Achieved?, as well as patterns of interaction that permit them to learn from as well as to teach the other members of the team. The characteristics identified by Stember and Armstrong operate in part by predisposing individuals to develop those skills and interaction patterns.

The literature has little to say about the characteristics of courses and programs that promote integration. Gaff affirms Jonathan Smith's "iron law" that "Students should not be expected to integrate anything that faculty can't or won't." Instead, Gaff believes that "faculty members from different academic disciplines must engage in dialogue over substantive issues and build an academic community." The "Guide to Interdisciplinary Syllabus Preparation" also makes a number of implicit recommendations regarding course level, how faculty work together, and so forth.

Institutional characteristics remain nearly as unexplored. Klein and Newell identify "non-hierarchical structures that foster dialogue, self-criticism and risk-taking, trust and mutual respect, and a sense of mutual ownership" as institutional characteristics that promote integration. They also recommend that the institution "promote a general climate of innovation in which a variety of activities can co-exist." Klein (1996) observes that integration requires a "strong community. Strengthening the community may entail progressive sharing of empirical and theoretical contents or focusing on a specific linking relationship."

Turning to the tools of integration, a few authors offer insights into the initiating questions that set up the process of integration. Newell and Green are most explicit about the role of initiating questions: "What we envision is a process that starts with a question of such scope that it lies outside the purview of a single area of knowledge (e.g., 'What form should U.S. energy policy take in the 1980s?')." This involves "finding the right question and couching it in such terms that the disciplines can complement, not talk past, one another." Hübenthal concurs that, "[i]n problem-interdisciplinarity one question predominates."

Newell and Green believe that "many if not most questions phrased in everyday language are properly interdisciplinary, while questions phrased in the technical language of a discipline are typically limited to treatment by a single discipline." Van Dusseldorp and Wigboldus make a similar point when they identify the first stage in policy-oriented interdisciplinary research as "problem formulation by policy-makers." In contrast, Bechtel refers to "one field posing a question to another field," though he is writing about the sciences, where research questions are often quite technical. Bal, taking a radical/critical approach to the humanities and fine arts, states: "My interpretations start at . . . the little detail that doesn't fit the 'official' interpretation."

More attention has been given to the conceptual frameworks supporting integration. Kockelmans emphasizes their central role but cautions that approaches such as general systems theory, structuralism, or cybernetics "provide us with only the formal skeleton of a conceptual framework; to the question of how in each case this formal framework is to be concretized, no universally valid answer is to be expected." Using the example of a general education course on health care delivery, Hursh, Haas, and Moore focus on "organizing constructs, or metaperspectives," which, they say, "include conceptions of relationships; frameworks that allow for categorizing on qualitative as well as quantitative dimensions."

In the humanities, Cluck suggests "[h]istorical periods, ideas, aesthetic themes, and structures" as conceptual foci, or what she calls "junctures." In the natural and social sciences, van Dusseldorp and Wigboldus value simulation models for "giving a specific framework for interdisciplinary cooperation"; they suggest interfacing various mathematical models (e.g., linear programming) to create "a framework for policy-oriented interdisciplinary research." In the natural sciences, Bechtel stresses "the need to develop integrating conceptual frameworks in which [interdisciplinary] research can proceed." Klein (1996) points out, however, that "integration is not necessarily a matter of reductionist or grand unity. It may involve nested hierarchies of several broad theories."

When the goals of integration are discussed, the divergence of perspectives becomes most evident. Authors who focus on liberal education tend to look for an impact on the individuals involved. Hursh, Haas, and Moore state that the goal of their general education model is "to aid the student's cognitive development toward reasoned action grounded in relativistic thought," though they allow that "movement from any stage to the next is certainly acceptable progress." Cornwell and Stoddard agree that "[t]he work of general education, as we see it, is to disturb ourselves and our students, to confront, as Martha Nusbaum says, differences in areas we tend to see as neutral, necessary, and normal." Similarly, Carlisle wants interdisciplinary integration to help her music students "see the connection between schooling, lessons, and life" and "to rethink what they know and do."

Researchers whose vision of integration is a conceptual framework tend to look for complementary interactions. Bechtel, after Georges Gusdorf, seeks "interdisciplinary learning," which is characterized as "a logic of discovery, a mutual opening up of barriers, a communication between the different realms of knowledge, a mutual fertilization." The implicit goal of integration for Hübenthal seems to be to address the interaction effects of variables studied by different disciplines (see her Venn diagrams on pages 64–65 of what she calls intermeshing and complementing interactions of disciplines).

Scholars whose vision of integration is a locus of activity look for conflictual interactions. Bal wants a "nonresolved dialectic" between competing approaches to interpretation. Peck similarly seeks "not middle-of-the-road, harmonious resolution or transcendence" but the uncovering of "the oppositional potential in the friction between borders, when they clash and mark out the space in between for multivocal, multinational, and multidisciplinary positions."

Finally, authors most concerned with interdisciplinary research, especially in the sciences, are concerned with team procedures that promote integration. Several address the team process apart from the intellectual process of integration discussed earlier. Stember identifies key procedural rules, such as "establishing time for relatively free exploration of the problem" so that each specialist has a chance to "inform and educate the other colleagues presenting both theoretical and methodological views." She recommends that participants "initially avoid confronting fundamental differences and requiring premature closure on important issues." Stember encourages "an early interplay of empirical and theoretical work." Participants, she says, need to "recognize that different disciplines have different cognitive maps and that learning at least part of these maps is essential." By following these procedures, team members gain the requisite knowledge of other disciplines emphasized previously.

Van Dusseldorp and Wigboldus echo Stember in advocating "a considerable period of time for team members to get to know each other as persons and to become acquainted with the way they handle their discipline." Armstrong adds that a team member must exhibit "openness and particularly well-developed interpersonal skills" and become "an active contributor of what he [sic] knows, as well as a processor of what others know"—"both teacher and learner simultaneously."

Eventually, however, Kockelmans believes "the members of a given team must in each case discover or develop their own [interdisciplinary] frame of reference with its typical theoretical framework and its characteristic methodology." Indeed, excessive focus on the team process may divert attention from the intellectual process of integration lying behind it.

To sum up, even though underlying visions of synthesis or integration differ dramatically, there seems to be remarkable agreement on the characteristics of successful integrators but too little attention paid to the characteristics of courses, programs, and institutions forming the environment within which those individuals must carry out integration. A few valuable insights are available concerning the tools of integration, both the questions that initiate the process of integration and the conceptual frameworks employed, but no attention has been paid as yet to how those questions and frameworks must differ to accommodate the three visions of integration. Although it is clear that those visions have a major influence on the specific outcomes sought through integration, these connections remain unexamined. Finally, authors concerned with interdisciplinary teams need to disentangle the roles of group procedure, individual characteristics, and intellectual process in achieving integration.

To complete our understanding of the prerequisites for integration, then, the following questions must be answered:

- What are the differences in the types of individual characteristics demanded by each of the three visions of integration?
- Just how much mastery of other disciplines is required?
- What characteristics of courses, programs, and institutions establish an environment most conducive to interdisciplinary integration?
- How should initiating questions and conceptual frameworks differ for each of the three visions of integration?
- How should the different visions of integration or different motivations for interdisciplinarity influence the specific outcomes sought for integration?
- What are the distinctive contributions of group procedure, individual characteristics, and intellectual process in establishing an environment for integration? How do these influences interact?

How Is Integration or Synthesis Achieved?

Having completed an examination of the interrelated issues regarding the nature of interdisciplinarity, the resulting outcomes, the role of disciplines in interdisciplinary studies, and the prerequisites for and nature of integration, this editorial introduction turns at last to the process of integration. What it reveals are important differences, even some fundamental confusion, but also a number of fascinating insights. The first task is to identify precisely what it is that disciplines contribute to integration. The next is to split the approaches to integration into those who see the process as essentially one of combining disciplinary contributions and those who see it as confronting contradictions between those contributions. Finally, approaches that utilize dialectic, metaphor, metalanguage, and common ground are treated separately because they are equally amenable to both the combining-contributions and confronting-contradictions approaches.

Just what do disciplines contribute to integration? The answers vary widely, even wildly, suggesting not only differences but also some confusion. Stember focuses on epistemologies and paradigms; Newell and Green on insights; Hursh, Haas, and Moore on definitions of salient concepts; Newell (1990) on perspectives; Kockelmans on findings; Fuller on concerns; van Dusseldorp and Wigboldus on inputs, perspectives, and ideas; Cluck on unique potentials; Bal on strategies and interpretations; and Bechtel on knowledge, theory, epistemo-logical dimension, entity, and process (if that can be considered focusing). In short, an author can have just about anything related to a discipline in mind when thinking about integration. Because interdisciplinary integration is so dependent on what is being integrated, interdisciplinarians as a profession need to pay much closer attention to this issue.

The majority of interdisciplinarians thinks of integration as combining disci-plinary contributions. In some cases, this approach involves the modification of those contributions. Van Dusseldorp and Wigboldus contrast the steering and accommodation approaches to integrating inputs from the various disci-plines represented on an interdisciplinary research team. The discipline that presents first tends to steer the others by setting the terms or constraints within which the others must operate and to which they must accommodate. When utilizing a "historical nexus," Cluck recommends documents be superimposed; otherwise the analysis often leads to "multidisciplinary layers rather than to an integrated whole." In discussing the integration of the examination of ideas throughout history, she observes that "Philosophy typically defines and articu-lates the concept, but other disciplines refine, explicate, and vary it through their different emphases." Hübenthal suggests a process of "reciprocal sensitiza-tion to the problem at hand" that leads each discipline's contribution to be reexamined in the light of the others. She sees this process as especially impor-tant when the humanities and sciences are both involved.

In interdisciplinary studies focusing exclusively on the sciences, modification is often seen as unnecessary. Bechtel favors the interfield theories proposed by Darden and Maull, which involve:

> identifying in one field the physical location of an entity or process discussed in another, frequently showing part-whole relation be-tween the two; finding in one field a description of the physical nature of an entity or process characterized in the other theory; discovering in one field the structure underlying a function de-scribed in the other theory; and finding in one field the cause of an effect noticed in another field. (419)

"Common to all [interfield theory] examples, though, is one field filling in missing information about a phenomenon that was already partially understood in the other field, [and] all involved one field posing a problem to another field." Van Dusseldorp and Wigboldus advocate the "interfacing of different types of models, in the sense that the outputs of one model are used as inputs in other models."

Summarizing the position of those who see integration as combining disciplinary insights, Newell and Green say that "If the interdisciplinary insights are in fact interdependent and mutually enriching, they may be integrated by reconciling them if they are inconsistent, or combining them into a larger whole if they are consistent." For instance, some concepts may "merely need extending to a more comprehensive domain." This generalization seems to hold across interdisciplinary research and teaching alike.

Especially when modification is required, the key to combining disciplinary contributions is to engage in both/and thinking. Stember characterizes this way of thinking as "redefining diverse paradigms as complementary rather than contradictory and viewing methods as logically independent." The goal of both/and thinking is "to go beyond the limits or boundaries of the prevailing paradigms or disciplines . . . to transcend the limits of philosophical stances, research methods, data collection, and analytical procedures." Thus, for example,

> the nature of reality is singular and multiple, objective and subjective, as well as particularistic and holistic. Similarly, the paradigmatic assumption regarding the nature of truth is that the world is stable and dynamic. Both individual uniqueness and commonalties across individuals are highly valued. (346)

Stember observes that "various forms of triangulation have been suggested" in the social sciences as a way to combine disciplinary contributions. This strategy of seeking convergent validity through eclecticism has considerable appeal. Why not let the strengths of one method compensate for the weaknesses of another?

Fuller provides a thought-provoking critique of triangulation, however. He argues that triangulation reveals the "fallacy of eclecticism" in that it cannot, as claimed, "ensure that the inherently partial and reductive nature of a given research tool does not obscure the underlying complex reality the researcher is trying to capture." Instead, Fuller explains, "triangulation often is around the researcher's preferred account of the phenomenon." Because triangulation may not reveal "the nature and potential scope of the inadequacies" of the methods triangulated, it "simply defers an airing of differences to another day."

Fuller's caveat about triangulation should stand as a caution to all attempts to modify disciplinary contributions. The presumptions of the modifier can influence how the contributions from other disciplines are modified. Concern about this bias leads to the next category of integration.

While Fuller represents the concerns of many humanists and some social scientists, he is in the minority of interdisciplinarians as a whole when he presents integration as confronting contradiction between disciplinary contributions. In general, this approach involves the transformation of those contributions. Fuller characterizes his method of interpenetration as "the incorporation and elimination of opposites in a more inclusive formulation." His argument is that "when disciplines (or their proper parts, such as theories or methods) interpenetrate, the 'test' is a mutual one that transforms all parties concerned." He explains that

> It is not simply a matter of one discipline being tested against the standards of its epistemic superior, or even of both disciplines being evaluated in terms of some neutral repository of cognitive criteria (as might be provided by a philosopher of science). Rather, the two disciplines are evaluated by criteria that are themselves brought into being only in the act of interpenetration. (126)

Fuller sees this process as involving translation, "in which the concerns of different disciplines are first brought to bear on a particular case . . . and then bootstrapped up to higher levels of conceptual synthesis." He likens this to the linguistic model where a trade language evolves into "a community's first language, or creole, which over time may become a full-fledged, grammatically independent language." The trade language Fuller has in mind is different from the trading zone of economics "in which goods do not change their identity" as they are traded—they are redistributed, not transformed—and of "Big-Science-style physics," because "Monte Carlo simulation did not evolve at the expense of one of the disciplinary languages which spawned it."

Similarly, Bal proposes to "shift the terms of these questions" to "the place of narrative in visual art." Her approach is to "reconsider the typically medium-bound terms of interpretive scholarship . . . as aspects rather than essences, and each [discipline's] specific strategies to deal with these aspects, as modes rather than systems." Thus Bal is "[s]hifting attention away from the study of the medium-bound, allegedly intrinsic properties of each domain." This involves a "provisional bracketing of the question as to what that difference [between verbal and visual art] might possibly be."

Gunn believes integration involves not only the active use of "a disciplinary poaching license" but a "redescriptive impulse" that

> almost of necessity places one discipline in a position of subordination to another. As a result, the subordinated discipline is not only destabilized but threatened with subsumption in an anomalous, substitutionary structure that on the pretext of situating itself, as the prefix *inter* implies, between the two more traditionally constituted matrices, actually manages to incorporate them both in some larger hegemonic framework. (256)

Finally, turning to general techniques of integration that are appropriate to both the combining insights and confronting contradictions approaches, Stember observes that "[t]he dialectical approach has been proposed in which different paradigms are given equal status and dialectical reasoning assists in reconciling two seemingly contradictory responses." Bal, citing Jonathan

Culler, argues on the other hand that "when . . . we face two mutually exclusive positions . . . the dilemma can only be resolved by our letting go of a
unified concept of meaning," yielding "not a harmonization of the conflict [or]
a dialectical resolution but rather a radicalization of the poles of the opposition
[which] leaves room for more than two kinds of meaning, and stimulates thinking about other possibilities." Similarly, Peck advocates a "clash of multiple
subjectivities [that] can foreground difference" that emerges when disciplines
clash. The treatment of the dialectical approach by Bal and Peck should be
understood as the foregrounding of process and of the partial, tentative, and
contextualized nature of the integrative insights that emerge from the process,
not as a rejection of integration.

Stember also identifies metaphor as a possible technique of integration. Bal
makes extensive use of metaphor, deconstructing through one discipline the
metaphor proposed by another, thus arriving at a new metaphor that "allows
plurality and mobility, that allows the viewer to propose new readings to meet
her or his needs." She warns that "[t]his play with metaphors should not be
taken for a meaningless linguistic game. By choosing a bodily metaphor [for a
painting she is analyzing], I also wish to demonstrate both my allegiance and
my polemical opposition to much of psychoanalytic theory." Thus Bal sees her
metaphor as "the detail that triggers textual diffusion, variation, and mobility
of readings." While such use of metaphor is common in the humanities, Bal's
methodological self-reflection could be particularly useful to interdisciplinarians outside the humanities.

Kockelmans advocates the development of a metalanguage in interdisciplinary research. In fact, he says:

> I cannot envision a meaningful dialogue or discourse between the
> representatives of different disciplines except on the basis of a (per-
> haps limited) realm of meaning that they share or at least are willing
> to agree upon, and which they do not wish to question, at least for
> as long as they engage in this kind of dialogue. (80)

Kockelmans goes on to caution that "[i]t will simply not do to refer to the
lifeworld they all share or appeal to our ordinary language." Likewise, Armstrong emphasizes the importance for interdisciplinary education of "developing a language through which to communicate clearly," at least building "a
vocabulary that can be precisely understood across the fields of knowledge"
because "the communication barrier is the first that the would-be interdisciplinarian must clear."

Hübenthal, on the other hand, is "doubtful that subject-overlapping research can be facilitated through the development of a meta-language. Meta-
language would be too abstract, and it is unlikely that the aspects which a
specialty science examines on a specific topic could be considered differentially
enough and still maintain their specificity." Instead, she argues that "the 'meta'
language of interdisciplinarity would not be a formalizable language; rather it
would 'supersede' the technical terminology only in so far as it is not tied to a

specific technical language and is comprehensible to every logically thinking person." Underlying Hübenthal's argument is an awareness of the complexity of the phenomena studied through interdisciplinary research and a sense of the futility of capturing such complexity in one formalized system. Fuller makes a similar argument, insisting that the route to integration is not through creation of a " 'metalanguage' that enables the revolutionary theory to subsume disparate data domains," though he advocates the "bottom up" development of a "trade-language." Thus, both authors see any interdisciplinary metalanguage as partial and as growing out of interactions among more specialized disciplines.

Kockelmans's analysis is sprinkled with references to common ground, for which a metalanguage is a precondition. He points out that "economists, social scientists, physicians, and architects trying to find a better solution for the housing problem in a large city . . . must have some common ground; the work proceeds from such a common ground but does not aim at developing this ground":

> Without such a common ground there would be no overarching conceptual framework, and thus genuine communication between those who participate in the discussion would be impossible. It is very difficult to discover or establish such a common ground, in that everyone who participates in the discussion brings with him [sic] his own discipline's conceptual framework and sensitivity for methods and techniques. Furthermore, when at first agreement sometimes seems to exist . . . , often it later becomes clear that the agreement was merely verbal. (82)

Taken together, the literature on interdisciplinarity is weakest when dealing with the process of integration itself. There are numerous pragmatic suggestions and a majority position, but conceptual confusion leaves the process itself unclear. Foremost among the problems is the variety of presumptions about what it is that disciplines contribute to integration. While most interdisciplinarians concur that integration involves the combination of disciplinary contributions, it is still unclear what circumstances determine how much those contributions must be modified, even though a number of valuable suggestions on strategies and techniques for integrating them have been proposed. Nor have most interdisciplinarians adequately addressed the concerns raised by the minority who see integration as confronting contradictions between disciplinary contributions.

Thus a number of fundamental issues remain to be resolved:

- What can a clarified understanding of the role of disciplines in interdisciplinarity contribute to agreement on the contributions of disciplines to integration?
- Under what circumstances do disciplinary contributions to integration need to be modified?

- What circumstances determine the amount of modification required in disciplinary contributions to integration?
- How can the understanding of integration as combining contributions and as confronting contradictions be reconciled?
- What can the majority combining-contradictions view learn from the minority confronting-contradictions view?
- How must answers to the questions above be modified as the vision of integration evolves?
- What is it about techniques of integration such as both/and thinking, dialectical thinking, metaphor construction, and metalanguage development that make them effective? How can they be used more effectively? How can they be taught?

What Assumptions Underlie Interdisciplinary Study?

This chapter would not be complete without an examination, however brief, of the assumptions of interdisciplinarity. Every field has its assumptions, which shape its activities to a considerable extent. As with most fields, the assumptions of interdisciplinary study are largely implicit and unexamined. However, a close reading of the articles in this volume reveals a number of assumptions made explicit by individual authors. Whether those assumptions are shared by other authors is uncertain. Still, directing attention to those assumptions that are revealed is the first step toward uncovering the full range of the assumptions of each author. With fuller understanding of the ground on which authors build their interpretations should come insight into the sources of agreement and disagreement over the various issues surrounding interdisciplinarity. Ultimately, it will only be through assessing these assumptions that areas of disagreement among interdisciplinarians can be narrowed. Because so little has been done to probe the assumptions of interdisciplinarity, the brief discussion that follows can merely point out the direction for future research. The assumptions identified here relate to the nature of reality, human beings, culture, and knowledge.

Stember believes "the nature of reality is singular and multiple, objective and subjective, as well as particularistic and holistic." Newell (1990) seems to concur when he says that "the external reality scholars confront is complex, variegated, and contradictory, so that mutually incompatible assumptions can all be 'correct.'" In a consistent vein, Hübenthal refers to the "many-sidedness of the problems at hand." Carlisle thinks "[t]he world is essentially chaotic, and experience comes to us often randomly and unfocused." Turner sees human behavior taking place within "a complex social environment" and responding to the "essential multicausality of social, individual, biological, and cultural phenomena." In contrast, whether because of the nature of reality or of human beings, Peck believes (citing James Clifford) that "[t]here is no whole picture that can be 'filled in,' since the perception and filling of a gap leads to the awareness of other gaps."

If there is a reality and it is as complex as these authors indicate, then it should come as no surprise that reality looks different to interdisciplinarians viewing it from different vantage points or to those focusing on its different aspects. Assumptions may vary from the humanities to the social and natural sciences, from those focused on "texts" to those seeking explanations for patterns of behavior or natural phenomena, and from those focused on more micro to more macro levels of reality. Assumptions may also vary with the nature of the interdisciplinary task. Interdisciplinarians seeking solutions to real-world problems may make different assumptions about reality than those developing critiques of disciplines or those concerned with liberal education. The "reality" on which they are focused may be different. Thus context, in various guises, becomes a central concern once again for interdisciplinarians.

Newell (1990) finds that "human beings are rife with internal contradictions." Peck understands culture as "contested, temporal, and emergent." Klein and Newell report that "knowledge has become increasingly interdisciplinary." Newell and Green question the notion that "knowledge is somehow all of a piece and deserves to be treated as such," and Bechtel, as discussed earlier, is likewise skeptical of attempts to demonstrate the "unity of science." Again, the object of inquiry may influence the nature of the interdisciplinarity employed in that inquiry.

As long as major disagreement remains within the interdisciplinary studies profession over the nature of interdisciplinarity and the assumptions on which it rests, authors such as Fish will continue with impunity to ascribe to all interdisciplinarians the assumptions and worldview of a minority within the profession. By (supposedly) discrediting those minority views, hostile critics can cast doubt on the validity of interdisciplinary studies as a whole. It becomes important, then, to disentangle the characteristics of interdisciplinarity per se from the characteristics of valuable complementary perspectives such as feminism, postmodernism, antilogical positivism, and left-wing politics. (Preferably, this analysis should be carried out by scholars sympathetic both to those perspectives and to interdisciplinarity.) Otherwise, as such complementary perspectives divide the academy or are even eventually replaced by new perspectives, interdisciplinarity may be relegated to one portion of the academy or swept out entirely.

Conclusion

This chapter invites reflective interdisciplinarians to think in a more complex, nuanced way about some basic concepts such as integration and interdisciplinarity itself. It also asks them to think in an integrated way about four interrelated issues—the nature of interdisciplinarity, the outcomes of interdisciplinarity, the role of disciplines, and the nature of integration. To make matters even more difficult, it also identifies some principled alternative conceptions (labeled in this essay as mainstream or majority and radical or minority) of these basic issues, as well as more than a little confusion. In short, the challenge is to engage in thinking about interdisciplinary studies that is at once complex, integrated, and open to conflicting perspectives. Put differently, the challenge is to step back a meta-level and direct the kind of thinking required in doing interdisciplinary work toward thinking about how interdisciplinary work should be done.

Those willing to accept the challenge are faced with the question of where to begin. While the profession will surely benefit from a diversity of approaches, some suggestions are in order for those seeking guidance. Regarding the need for thinking that is open to conflicting perspectives, a useful starting point would be to think comparatively about the contrasting majority and minority perspectives. Use each to probe the other, exposing its implicit assumptions and biases. This strategy may not yield a synthesis of those perspectives, but it should at least clarify the alternatives and explore the ways each can learn from the other.

Regarding the need for integrated thinking about the four interrelated issues—the nature of interdisciplinarity, the outcomes of interdisciplinarity, the role of disciplines, and the nature of integration—a useful approach is to compare predicted outcomes. After all, the motivations for interdisciplinary study are pragmatic. Identify pairs of complementary perspectives on the nature of interdisciplinarity and the nature of integration, then ask what role for disciplines is most compatible with each pair and, finally, identify the outcomes that can be predicted for each pair. At some point, researchers will need to test these predictions empirically, and that will prove no easy task, because outcomes will be dependent not only on the pair selected but on how well the perspectives are implemented and on which nuanced conception of interdisciplinarity is at work.

This brings us to the need for nuanced thinking about interdisciplinarity that reflects its complexity. Interdisciplinarity has long been distinguished from related concepts such as multidisciplinarity and transdisciplinarity, and it needs to be distinguished as well from predisciplinarity and the activity of generalists and disciplinary borrowers. What this chapter brings out in addition is that interdisciplinarity is not simply a distinct process, it is a multidimensional one, represented by the distinctions between broad and narrow interdisciplinarity and between full and partial interdisciplinarity. It is no longer sufficient to speak globally about interdisciplinarity. Careful thinking requires that we specify the range of interdisciplinarity we have in mind, how broad an interdisciplinarity, and how full.

Once these conceptual issues have been addressed, interdisciplinarians can then turn to the challenge of implementation; specifically, how integration is best carried out. The stakes are high. The future of interdisciplinary studies hinges on our effectiveness in delivering desirable educational outcomes, in contributing to the solution of complex societal problems, in constructing useful new knowledge, and, perhaps, in assisting the disciplines in their own reconceptualization. The acid test of all the theorizing is how good interdisciplinarians can get at drawing on disciplinary perspectives and integrating them into a more comprehensive, useful perspective.

References

1. Organization for Economic Cooperation and Development, 1972, *Interdisciplinarity: Problems of Teaching and Research in Universities*, Paris, France: OECD.
2. Kelly, James, 1996, "Wide and Narrow Interdisciplinarity," *Journal of General Education* 45:2.
3. Klein, Julie Thompson, 1990, *Interdisciplinarity: History, Theory, and Practice*, Detroit, MI: Wayne State University Press.
4. Klein, Julie Thompson, 1996, *Crossing Boundaries: Knowledge, Disciplinarities, and Interdisciplinarities*, Charlottesville, VA: University Press of Virginia.
5. Dogan, Mattei and Pahre, Robert, 1990, *Creative Marginality*, Boulder, CO: Westview Press.
6. Gaff, Jerry and James Ratcliff, 1997, *Handbook of the Undergraduate Curriculum*, San Francisco, CA: Jossey-Bass.
7. Tinto, Vincent, Anne Goodsell-Love, and Pat Russo, 1994, *Building Learning Communities for New College Students*, University Park, PA: The Pennsylvania State University NTLA.